In *Sword, Miter, and Cloister*, historian Constance Bouchard provides a fresh perspective on social and ecclesiastical life in the High Middle Ages. Drawing on a vast range of primary sources including ecclesiastical cartularies, chronicles, papal bulls, necrologies, and letters, she reveals the surprisingly close relationship between the nobility and reformed monasteries in Burgundy. By focusing on a region considered to be the heart of aristocratic and monastic Europe during this era, Bouchard is able to develop themes and reach conclusions that can be applied to much of Europe.

Bouchard divides her narrative into three sections in which she explores different aspects of the interaction between the church and the nobility. In Part I she analyzes the familial and social ties between the leaders of the church and of secular society. She reevaluates the reactions of noble men and women to monastic reform in Part II and offers a new interpretation of their role in reforming the religious houses. In Part III she looks at the changing nature of the property that the nobility presented to monasteries and investigates the motives behind these gifts. Bouchard also supplies three richly detailed appendixes that will prove exceptionally useful to researchers: Appendix A presents the family trees of twenty-eight of the most important Burgundian noble families; B offers a complete list of the bishops in the six Burgundian sees; and C lists the abbots in the twenty-three most prominent abbeys of the eleventh and twelfth centuries.

Sword, Miter, and Cloister convincingly demonstrates how changes in the composition and character of the nobility directly influenced and were influenced by changes in the forms of monasticism. A major contribution to the history of the High Middle Ages, the book will be valuable reading for medieval historians and for scholars interested in the history of women and the family, spirituality, and France during these centuries.

Sword, Miter, and Cloister

Frontispiece. A noble lord gives a church to a saint

In this sculpture from the altar at Avenas (late eleventh or early twelfth century), King Lou the Pious is depicted giving the church at Avenas (which still looks almost exactly the sam today) to Saint Vincent, the patron saint of the cathedral of Mâcon. (This transaction recorded in the cathedral cartulary, M 61, p. 49.)

Sword, Miter, and Cloister

NOBILITY AND THE CHURCH
IN BURGUNDY, 980–1198

Constance Brittain Bouchard

CORNELL UNIVERSITY PRESS

Ithaca and London

First published 1987 by Cornell University Press.

International Standard Book Number 0-8014-1974-3
Library of Congress Catalog Card Number 86-29158
Printed in the United States of America
Librarians: Library of Congress cataloging information
appears on the last page of the book.

The paper in this book is acid-free and meets the guidelines for
permanence and durability of the Committee on Production Guidelines
for Book Longevity of the Council on Library Resources.

To my father, W. Lambert Brittain

Contents

Preface   11
Abbreviations   13
Introduction   23

Part One: Leaders of the Church and Leaders of Society   45

  1. Noble Entry into the Church   46
  2. The Social Origins of Ecclesiastical Leaders   65

Part Two: Monastic Reform and the Nobility   87

  3. The Tenth-Century Background of Reform   90
  4. Monastic Foundations and Reform in Burgundy   102
  5. The Patrons of Monastic Reform   125
  6. Monastic Patronage over the Generations   150

Part Three: Noble Generosity to Reformed Monasteries   171

  7. Types of Noble Gifts to Reformed Monasteries   173
  8. The Timing and Location of Gifts   190
  9. Gifts, Claims, and Other Transactions   209
10. Motivations for Noble Generosity to Reformed Monasteries   225

Conclusions   247

Appendix A: Family Trees   255
    The Dukes of Burgundy (257); The Counts of Burgundy and
    Mâcon (261); The Lords of Aigremont and Bourbonne
    (279); The Counts of Auxois (284); The Lords of Bâgé
    (287); The Lords of Beaujeu (289); The Lords of Brancion
    and Uxelles (295); The Counts of Chalon (307); The Lords
    of Choiseul (314); The Lords of Clefmont (317); The
    Counts of Dijon and the Lords of Beaumont (319); The

Viscounts of Dijon (324); The Lords of Donzy (327); The
Lords of Fontaines-lès-Dijon (329); The Lords of Grancey
(332); The Lords of Montbard (334); The Lords of Montréal
(338); The Counts of Nevers, Auxerre, and Tonnerre (340);
The Lords of Saulx (351); The Lords of Seignelay (355);
The Lords of Semur (357); The Lords of Sexfontaines
(361); The Lords of Sombernon (363); The Lords of
Tilchâtel (366); The Counts of Tonnerre (369); The Lords
of Toucy (372); The Lords of Vergy (375); The Lords of
Vignory (379)

Appendix B: The Burgundian Bishops   385
The Bishops of Autun (386); The Bishops of Auxerre (387);
The Bishops of Chalon (391); The Bishops of Langres (393);
The Bishops of Mâcon (398); The Bishops of Nevers (400)

Appendix C: The Burgundian Abbots   402
The Abbots of Auberive (402); The Abbots of Beaulieu
(403); The Abbots of Bèze (403); The Abbots of La
Bussière (405); The Abbots of Cîteaux (405); The Abbots of
Clairvaux (408); The Abbots of Cluny (410); The Abbots of
La Crête (413); The Abbots of La Ferté-sur-Grosne (414);
The Abbots of Flavigny (414); The Abbots of Fontenay
(416); The Abbots of Longué (417); The Abbots of
Maizières (418); The Abbots of Molesme (419); The Abbots
of Morimond (421); The Abbots of Pontigny (422); The
Abbots of Quincy (423); The Abbots of Reigny (424); The
Abbots of St.-Bénigne of Dijon (424); The Abbots of St.-
Germain of Auxerre (426); The Abbots of St.-Seine (428);
The Abbots of Tournus (429); The Abbots of Vézelay (430)

Printed Sources   433
Selected Bibliography   440
Index   451

Illustrations, Maps, and Figures

Plates

	A noble lord gives a church to a saint	frontispiece
1.	Romanesque church of Blanot	36
2.	Twelfth-century church at Bâgé	82
3.	Tower of St.-Germain of Auxerre	105
4.	South transept of Cluny	108
5.	Old front doors of the abbey church of Cluny	109
6.	Village and twelfth-century church of Brancion	165
7.	A noble gives a church to a bishop	178
8.	The weighing of souls	242
9.	Two knights fighting	245

Maps

1.	Medieval Burgundy	30
2.	Fontenay, its neighbors, and its possessions	135
3.	Morimond, La Crête, and their neighbors	140
4.	The possessions of the Grossi of Brancion and Uxelles	162
5.	The early acquisitions of Cîteaux	203
6.	The early acquisitions of Clairvaux	205

Figures

1.	Social and ecclesiastical origins of the Burgundian bishops in the eleventh and twelfth centuries	68
2.	Family ties between the principal patrons of Cluny	144

Preface

This account of the relationships, mental, social, and familial, between the nobles, church leaders, and monasteries of the eleventh and twelfth centuries is intended as a work of both social and ecclesiastical history. The church deeply influenced the nobility's views of itself and its purposes, and the nobility made a fundamental impact on the reform of the high medieval church. In discussing these interactions, I have focused on the duchy of Burgundy, which if not the political heart of medieval France was certainly the spiritual heart. There were six bishoprics and, by the end of the twelfth century, over seventy-five monasteries, nunneries, and houses of canons regular in the duchy, most of which left cartularies and collections of archival documents. The Burgundian churches and the roughly thirty most powerful noble families of the region are therefore among the best documented in France.

I have incurred many debts of gratitude in writing this work. The French archivists and librarians were uniformly helpful in making the medieval documents available and preparing microfilms; I warmly thank the staffs of the Bibliothèque nationale, the Archives nationales, the Bibliothèque municipale of Dijon, and the Archives départementales of Allier, Aube, Côte-d'Or, Haute-Marne, Haute-Saône, Nièvre, Saône-et-Loire, and Yonne. I also thank members of the Institut für Frühmittelalterforschung in Münster for their cordial welcome. Professor John Benton of the California Institute of Technology generously shared his knowledge of medieval French cartularies. Research in France in 1982 was funded by a Fellowship for Independent Study and Research from the National Endowment for the Humanities, FA—21752—82.

Professors Barbara Rosenwein of Loyola University of Chicago, Stanley Chodorow of the University of California, San Diego, and Karl Morrison of the University of Kansas read and commented on early drafts of this book. It would have been poorer without their suggestions. Professor Rosenwein especially offered encouragement, criticism, moral support, and her own knowledge of the modern Cluniac literature and of tenth-century Cluny. Professor Chodorow provided a congenial working place where the final version of this book was completed.

Above all, I thank my husband, Robert Bouchard. He has been supportive in innumerable ways throughout the long growth of this book, listening to my ideas, reading and making cogent comments on several drafts, driving with me through Burgundy, and ripping the perforated edges off computer printouts. I could not have written the book without him.

This book is dedicated to my father, W. Lambert Brittain, to whom I owe both my respect for intellectual rigor and my sense of humor. He has enough confidence in my professional abilities (more than I sometimes have myself) that he has never deliberately set out to instruct me in being a scholar, especially since he is a developmental psychologist and I am a medieval historian. But I have learned a vital lesson from his example, that it is much less important to have grand theories than it is to try to understand the people one is studying and the reasons *they* have for doing what they are doing, whether they are nursery-school children or monks and nobles of the twelfth century.

CONSTANCE BRITTAIN BOUCHARD

La Jolla, California

Abbreviations

The following list of abbreviations also serves as a list of the principal chronicles and cartularies consulted for this book. Cartularies are normally cited by the name of the monastery. If a monastery left more than one cartulary, I have numbered them I, II, etc., according to the order in which they are bound or cataloged, not necessarily the order in which they were composed. For the cartularies, I have cited volumes by Roman numerals, and sections, pages, folia, and document numbers by Arabic numerals. A period has been used to separate section and document numbers, a colon to separate volume and page numbers: hence, 1.37 is document number 37 within Part 1, and I:37 is Volume I, page 37. If possible, I have cited by document number first, followed by page numbers within parentheses. This was not practical however for some unedited cartularies, which I have cited first by folio number and then by document number (if the documents are numbered). For the monumental editions, I have cited by volume, followed by page or column.

Arch. Allier	Moulins, Archives départementales de l'Allier.
Arch. Aube	Troyes, Archives départementales de l'Aube.
Arch. Côte-d'Or	Dijon, Archives départementales de la Côte-d'Or.
Arch. Haute-Marne	Chaumont, Archives départementales de la Haute-Marne.
Arch. Haute-Saône	Vesoul, Archives départementales de la Haute-Saône.
Arch. nat.	Paris, Archives nationales.
Arch. Nièvre	Nevers, Archives départementales du Nièvre.
Arch. Saône-et-Loire	Mâcon, Archives départementales de Saône-et-Loire.
Arch. Yonne	Auxerre, Archives départementales de l'Yonne.
Auberive I	Arch. Haute-Marne, 1 H 3.
	Late thirteenth-century cartulary of Auberive.
Auberive II	Arch. Haute-Marne, 1 H 4.
	Early thirteenth-century cartulary of Auberive.

Autun/Église	Anatole de Charmasse, ed., *Cartulaire de l'église d'Autun*, 2 vols. (Paris, 1865–1900).
Autun/Évêché	Anatole de Charmasse, ed., *Cartulaire de l'évêché d'Autun* (Autun, 1880).
Autun/St.-Martin	J.-Gabriel Bulliot, ed., *Essai historique sur l'abbaye de Saint-Martin d'Autun*, II, *Chartes et pièces justificatives* (Autun, 1849).
Autun/St.-Symphorien	André Déléage, ed., *Recueil des actes du prieuré de Saint-Symphorien d'Autun de 696 à 1300* (Autun, 1936).
Beatrix	Pierre-François Chifflet, ed., *Lettre touchant Beatrix, comtesse de Chalon* (Dijon, 1656).
Beaujeu	M.-C. Guigue, ed., *Cartulaire de l'église collégiale Notre-Dame de Beaujeu, suivi d'un appendice et d'un tableau généalogique de la maison de Beaujeu* (Lyon, 1864).
	Documents in the appendix are prefixed by the letter "a," for example, a4.
Bernard of Clairvaux, *Opera*	Bernard of Clairvaux, *Opera*, ed. Jean Leclercq and H. Rochais (Rome, 1957–).
BN	Paris, Bibliothèque nationale.
	Manuscripts in the Latin series are cited as MS lat., and those in the "nouvelles acquisitions" Latin series as MS nouv. acq. lat. Manuscripts in the Baluze, Bourgogne, Champagne, and Moreau collections are cited respectively as Coll. Baluze, Coll. Bourgogne, Coll. Champagne, and Coll. Moreau.
Bouton and Van Damme, *Textes*	Jean de la Croix Bouton and Jean Baptiste Van Damme, eds., *Les plus anciens textes de Cîteaux*, Commentarii Cistercienses, Studia et documenta 2 (Achel, 1974).
La Bussière	BN, MS lat. 5463.
	Early fourteenth-century cartulary of La Bussière.
C	Auguste Bernard and Alexandre Bruel, eds., *Recueil des chartes de l'abbaye de Cluny*, 6 vols. (Paris, 1876–1903).
Canivez, *Statuta*	Josephus-Maria Canivez, ed., *Statuta capitulorum generalium ordinis Cisterciensis*, I, *Ab anno 1116 ad annum 1220*, Bibliothèque de la Revue d'histoire ecclésiastique 9 (Louvain, 1933).
Chalon	BN, MS lat. 17090.
	Early fourteenth-century cartulary of the chapter of Chalon, copy made by Jean Bouhier in 1721.
La Charité	René de Lespinasse, ed., *Cartulaire du prieuré de La Charité-sur-Loire* (Nevers, 1887).
Châtillon	Arch. Côte-d'Or, 18 H cart. 205.
	Fourteenth-century cartulary of the Augustinian canons of Notre-Dame of Châtillon.

Chron. St.-B.	E. Bougaud and Joseph Garnier, eds., *Chronique de l'abbaye de Saint-Bénigne de Dijon, suivie de la Chronique de Saint-Pierre de Bèze*, Analecta Divionensia 9 (Dijon, 1875). Also printed in PL CLXII:753—1006, from d'Achery's edition.
Cîteaux I	Arch. Côte-d'Or, 11 H 63. "Cartularium vetus" of Cîteaux, composed in the late thirteenth century.
Cîteaux II	Arch. Côte-d'Or, 11 H 64. "Cartulare antiquum" of Cîteaux, composed in the late twelfth or very early thirteenth century.
Cîteaux/Marilier	J. Marilier, ed., *Chartes et documents concernant l'abbaye de Cîteaux, 1098—1182* (Rome, 1961).
Clairvaux I	Arch. Aube, 3 H 9. This and the following are Volumes I and II of a thirteenth-century cartulary of Clairvaux. Cited by page number.
Clairvaux II	Arch. Aube, 3 H 10.
Clairvaux/Waquet	Jean Waquet, ed., *Recueil des chartes de l'abbaye de Clairvaux, XIIe siècle* (Troyes, 1950—1982). Two fascicles, containing documents from between 1121 and 1173, have appeared so far. The second, which is paginated consecutively with the first, was completed by Jean-Marc Roger and Philippe Grand. The second fascicle begins with document number 74.
Corbigny	Anatole de Charmasse, ed., "Chartes de l'abbaye de Corbigny," *Mémoires de la Société Eduenne*, n.s. 17, (1889), 1—39.
Cowdrey, "Studies"	H. E. J. Cowdrey, "Two Studies in Cluniac History, 1049—1126," *Studi Gregoriani*, 11 (1978), 1—297. This includes an edition of the *vitae* of Abbot Hugh of Cluny.
Crisenon	BN, MS lat. 9885. Late thirteenth-century cartulary of Crisenon.
DHGE	*Dictionnaire d'histoire et de géographie ecclésiastiques* (Paris, 1912—). To date, volumes in this series have appeared through the letter G.
La Ferté	Georges Duby, ed., *Recueil des pancartes de l'abbaye de La Ferté-sur-Grosne, 1113—1178* (Paris, 1953). Documents from La Ferté after 1178 may be consulted in the Arch. Saône-et-Loire, H 24—25, and the Arch. Côte-d'Or, series 14 H.
Flavigny	BN, MS lat. 17720. Early twelfth-century cartulary of Flavigny, copy made by Jean Bouhier in 1721. Also analyzed by M. Collenot, "Cartulaire du monastère de Flavigny," *Bulletin*

	de la Société des sciences historiques et naturelles de Semur, ser. 2, 3 (1886), 40–101.
Fleury	Maurice Prou and Alexandre Vidier, eds., *Recueil des chartes de l'abbaye de Saint-Benoît-sur-Loire*, 2 vols. (Paris, 1900–1937).
Fontenay I, II	Arch. Côte d'Or, 15 H 9. Two cartularies of Fontenay bound together. The first one in the volume (called I here) is late thirteenth-century, the second early thirteenth.
GC	*Gallia Christiana in provincias ecclesiasticas distribuata.* Cited by volume number, followed by the column of the *instrumenta* section.
Genus illustre	Pierre-François Chifflet, ed., *S. Bernardi Clarevallensis abbatis genus illustre assertum* (Dijon, 1660). Selections from this were reprinted in PL CLXXXV:1383–1544.
Gesta pontificum	*Gesta pontificum Autissiodorensium*, ed. L.-M. Duru, *Bibliothèque historique de l'Yonne*, I (Auxerre, 1850), pp. 309–509. Cited by page number. A reprint of Labbe's seventeenth-century edition is in PL CXXXVIII:219–394.
Hefele-Leclercq	Charles-Joseph Hefele, *Histoire des conciles*, trans. and aug. H. Leclercq, 10 vols. (Paris, 1907–1938).
Jobin, *St. Bernard*	Abbé Jobin, *Saint Bernard et sa famille* (Paris, 1891). Citations are to the "Pièces justificatives."
Jully	Ernest Petit, ed., "Cartulaire du prieuré de Jully-les-Nonnains," *Bulletin de la Société des sciences historiques et naturelles de l'Yonne*, 34 (1880), 249–302. Cited by page number.
Langres	Hubert Flammarion, ed., *Le grand cartulaire du chapitre cathédral de Langres* (diss., Université de Nancy II, 1980).
Layettes	Alexandre Teulet, ed., *Layettes du trésor des chartes*, I–II (Paris, 1863–1866).
Lebeuf IV	Abbé Lebeuf, *Mémoires concernant l'histoire civile et ecclésiastique d'Auxerre et de son ancien diocèse*, new ed. by M. Challe and Maximilien Quantin, IV, *Recueil de monuments, chartes, titres et autres pièces inédites* (Auxerre, 1855).
Longué	Arch. Haute-Marne, 6 H 2. Two thirteenth-century cartularies of Longué, bound together and foliated consecutively. The first is somewhat later. There is a large amount of overlap between them.
Lugny	BN, MS lat. 10948. Thirteenth-century cartulary of the Carthusian house of Lugny.

M	M.-C. Ragut, ed., *Cartulaire de Saint-Vincent de Mâcon* (Mâcon, 1864).
Marcigny	Jean Richard, ed., *Le cartulaire de Marcigny-sur-Loire (1045–1144). Essai de reconstitution d'un manuscrit disparu* (Dijon, 1957).
MGH	*Monumenta Germaniae Historica*
Capitularia	*Legum sectio II, Capitularia regum Francorum*
DD	*Diplomata*
Epp.	*Epistolae selectae*
Libelli de lite	*Libelli de lite imperatorum et pontificum*
LL	*Leges*
SS	*Scriptores*
Molesme	Jacques Laurent, ed., *Cartulaires de l'abbaye de Molesme*, 2 vols. (Paris, 1907–1911). Most of the documents from the second (thirteenth-century) cartulary of Molesme are only summarized by the editor.
Mores	Charles Lalore, ed., "Chartes de l'abbaye de Mores," *Mémoires de la Société académique d'agriculture, des sciences, arts et belles-lettres du département de l'Aube*, 37 (1873), 5–107.
Morment	Odile Grandmottet, ed., "Catalogue des actes de l'hôpital de Morment (1121–1302)," *Cahiers haut-marnais*, 62/63 (1960), 99–175. About half the twelfth-century documents of the Hospitallers of Morment are edited; the rest are given in summary.
Nevers/St.-Cyr	René de Lespinasse, ed., *Cartulaire de Saint-Cyr de Nevers* (Nevers, 1916).
Nevers/St.-Étienne	René de Lespinasse, ed., "Les chartes de Saint-Étienne de Nevers," *Bulletin de la Société nivernaise des lettres, sciences et arts*, ser. 3, 12 (1908), 76–130.
Obit. Lyon I	*Obituaires de la province de Lyon*, I, *Diocèse de Lyon, première partie*, ed. Georges Guigue and Jacques Laurent (Paris, 1933).
Obit. Lyon II	*Obituaires de la province de Lyon*, II, *Diocèse de Lyon, deuxième partie, diocèses de Mâcon et de Chalon-sur-Saône*, ed. Jacques Laurent and Pierre Gras (Paris, 1965).
Obit. Sens I	*Obituaires de la province de Sens*, I, *Diocèses de Sens et de Paris*, ed. Auguste Molinier (Paris, 1902).
Obit. Sens III	*Obituaires de la province de Sens*, III, *Diocèses d'Orléans, d'Auxerre, et de Nevers*, ed. Alexandre Vidier and Léon Mirot (Paris, 1909).
Obit. Sens IV	*Obituaires de la province de Sens*, IV, *Diocèses de Meaux et de Troyes*, ed. M. Boutillier du Retail and M. Piétresson de Saint-Aubin (Paris, 1923).

Paray   Ulysse Chevalier, ed., *Cartulaire du prieuré de Paray-
                           le-monial* (Paris, 1890).
Pérard   Estienne Pérard, ed., *Recueil de plusieurs pièces
                           curieuses servant à l'histoire de Bourgogne* (Paris, 1664).
                           Cited by page number.
Peter the Vener-   *The Letters of Peter the Venerable*, ed. Giles Constable,
able, *Letters*   2 vols., Harvard Historical Studies 78 (Cambridge,
                           Mass., 1967).
Petit I, II, III, IV, V   Ernest Petit, ed., *Histoire des ducs de Bourgogne de la
                           race capétienne*, I–V (Paris and Dijon, 1885–1894).
Pflugk-Harttung   J. v. Pflugk-Harttung, ed., *Acta pontificum Romanorum
                           inedita*, 3 vols. (Stuttgart, 1881–1886; rpt. Graz,
                           1958).
PL   J.-P. Migne, ed., *Patrologiae cursus completus, Series
                           Latina*.
                           Cited by volume and column number.
Plancher   Urbain Plancher, ed., *Histoire générale et particulière de
                           Bourgogne*, 4 vols. (Dijon, 1739–1781).
                           Cited by volume number and document number.
Pontigny   Martine Garrigues, ed., *Le premier cartulaire de
                           l'abbaye cistercienne de Pontigny (XIIe–XIIIe siècles)*,
                           Collection de documents inédits sur l'histoire de
                           France 14 (Paris, 1981).
PU Berry   Wilhelm Wiederhold, ed., *Papsturkunden in Frank-
                           reich. V. Berry, Bourbonnais, Nivernais und Auxerrois*,
                           Nachrichten von der Königlichen Gesellschaft der
                           Wissenschaften zu Göttingen, Philologisch-historische
                           Klasse (Berlin, 1910).
PU Burgund   Wilhelm Wiederhold, ed., *Papsturkunden in Frank-
                           reich. II. Burgund mit Bresse und Bugey*, Nachrichten
                           von der Königlichen Gesellschaft der Wissenschaften
                           zu Göttingen, Philologisch-historische Klasse (Göt-
                           tingen, 1906; rpt. 1967).
PU Champagne   Hermann Meinert, ed., *Papsturkunden in Frankreich,
                           neue Folge. I. Champagne und Lothringen*, 2 vols.,
                           Abhandlungen der Akademie der Wissenschaften in
                           Göttingen, Philologisch-historische Klasse, ser. 3, 3–
                           4 (Göttingen, 1932–1933; rpt. 1972).
PU Franche-Comté   Wilhelm Wiederhold, ed., *Papsturkunden in Frank-
                           reich. I. Franche-Comté*, Nachrichten von der König-
                           lichen Gesellschaft der Wissenschaften zu Göttingen,
                           Philologisch-historische Klasse (Göttingen, 1906; rpt.
                           1967).
Quantin I, II   Maximilien Quantin, ed., *Cartulaire général de l'Yonne*,
                           2 vols. (Auxerre, 1854–1860).
                           Cited by volume number and document number.
Quantin III   Maximilien Quantin, ed., *Recueil de pièces pour faire
                           suite au Cartulaire général de l'Yonne* (Auxerre, 1873).

Raoul Glaber, *Historia*	Raoul Glaber, *Historia*, ed. Maurice Prou (Paris, 1886).
Reomaus	Petrus Roverius, ed., *Reomaus, seu Historia Monasterii S. Joannis Reomaensis* (Paris, 1637). With a handful of exceptions, all the documents from Moûtier-St.-Jean from before the thirteenth century are known only from this edition. Cited by page number.
RHGF	*Recueil des historiens des Gaules et de la France.*
St.-B. I	Joseph Garnier, ed., "Chartes bourguignonnes inédits des IXe, X^e et XIe siècles," *Mémoires présentés par divers savants à l'Académie des inscriptions et belles-lettres de l'Institut national de France*, ser. 2, 2 (1849), 1−168.
St.-B. II	Georges Chevrier and Maurice Chaume, eds., *Chartes et documents de Saint−Bénigne de Dijon (990-1124)* (Dijon, 1943). Documents after 1124 may be consulted in the Arch. Côte-d'Or, series 1 H. An additional volume is promised soon.
St.-Étienne I	J. Courtois, ed., *Chartes de l'abbaye de Saint-Étienne de Dijon (VIIIe, IXe, X^e et XIe siècles)* (Paris and Dijon, 1908).
St.-Étienne II	Adrien Bièvre Poulalier, ed., *Chartes de l'abbaye de Saint-Étienne de Dijon de 1098 à 1140* (Dijon, 1912).
St.-Étienne III	M. Bourrier, ed., *Chartes de l'abbaye de Saint-Étienne de Dijon de 1140 à 1155* (Paris and Dijon, 1912).
St.-Étienne IV	Georges Valat, ed., *Chartes de l'abbaye de Saint-Étienne de Dijon de 1155 à 1200* (Paris and Dijon, 1907).
St.-Marcel	Marcel and Paul Canat de Chizy, eds., *Cartulaire du prieuré de Saint-Marcel-lès-Chalon* (Chalon, 1894).
St.-Seine	Arch. Côte-d'Or, 10 H 6, pp. 245−76. Thirteenth-century cartulary of St.-Seine. Cited by page number.
Savigny	Auguste Bernard, ed., *Cartulaire de l'abbaye de Savigny* (Paris, 1853).
Theuley	Arch. Haute-Saône, 1 Mi−3 (R1). Late twelfth-century cartulary of Theuley, on microfilm; the cartulary itself is in a private collection. An eighteenth-century copy of the cartulary is in the BN, Coll. Moreau 873, fols. 106r−164v.
Tournus	Pierre Juénin, *Nouvelle histoire de l'abbaïe de Saint-Filibert et de la ville de Tournus*, II, *Preuves* (Dijon, 1733). Cited by page number.
Vergy	BN, MS lat. 5529A. Thirteenth-century cartulary of St.-Denis of Vergy. Cited by page number.

Vézelay	R. B. C. Huygens, ed., *Monumenta Vizeliacensia. Textes relatifs à l'histoire de l'abbaye de Vézelay*, Corpus Christianorum continuatio mediaevalis 42 (Turnhout, 1976).
Vézelay suppl.	R. B. C. Huygens, ed., *Vizeliacensia II. Textes relatifs à l'histoire de l'abbaye de Vézelay*, Corpus Christianorum continuatio mediaevalis 42, supplementum (Turnhout, 1980).
Vignory	J. d'Arbaumont, ed., *Cartulaire du prieuré de Vignory* (Langres, 1882).

The citation of charters of Vignory is somewhat complex, because of the way in which the editor compiled his volume. There are three series of charters edited here. The charters of the first, the cartulary of St.-Étienne of Vignory, are cited by Roman numerals. The charters of the second and third, which are found in appendixes 1 and 2, are a collection of documents concerning the priory of Vignory and the lords of Vignory; they are cited by Arabic numerals, preceded by a section indication (1 or 2). The page numbers refer to the *instrumenta* section of the volume.

Vita Willelmi   Raoul Glaber, *Vita Willelmi*, ed. Niethard Bulst, "Rodulphus Glabers Vita domni Willelmi abbatis. Neue Edition," *Deutsches Archiv für Erforschung des Mittelalters*, 30 (1974), 462–87.

Sword, Miter, and Cloister

Introduction

The classic distinction between those who pray, those who fight, and those who work, a distinction stated most unequivocally by Bishop Adalbero of Laon in the early eleventh century, has influenced the picture of medieval society for nine centuries.[1] Yet, like all neat classifications, Adalbero's was oversimplified. Many people fell between categories, and in practice the distinction between "those who pray" and "those who fight" was especially unclear. Adalbero himself was not presenting a picture of society as it existed but rather as he thought it ought to be.[2] In eleventh- and twelfth-century France, the leaders of the church and the leaders of secular society, far from being separated into Adalbero's tidy compartments, were interrelated and interdependent to the point that they were virtually one.

This book discusses the intimacy of the ties between the first two "orders" of society and argues that the spread of reformed monasticism, one of the most significant aspects of the religious life of the eleventh and twelfth centuries, was dependent on the goodwill and active assistance of the local nobility. It treats three broad and interrelated topics in separate sections. The first is a discussion of noble entry into the church and of the familial and social ties between members of the nobility and ecclesiastical leaders. In this section the

[1] Adalbero of Laon, "Carmen ad Rotbertum regem," ll. 295–96, ed. Claude Carozzi, *Poème au roi Robert*, Classiques de l'histoire de France au moyen âge 32 (Paris, 1979), p. 22. The same distinction was drawn by Girard of Cambrai, at about the same time or perhaps a few years earlier. See Georges Duby, *The Three Orders: Feudal Society Imagined*, trans. Arthur Goldhammer (Chicago, 1980), pp. 5–9; and Robert T. Coolidge, "Adalbero, Bishop of Laon," *Studies in Medieval and Renaissance History*, 2 (1965), 66–93.
[2] Claude Carozzi, "Les fondements de la tripartition sociale chez Adalbéron de Laon," *Annales: Économies, Sociétés, Civilisations*, 33 (1978), 689–92. Coolidge, "Adalbero," pp. 72–75.

term "the church" is used primarily to indicate monasteries and cathedral chapters, the religious corporations in which the influence of the nobility was the greatest. The second part examines the role of the nobility in the spread of monastic reform: reforming old houses or founding new ones and, acting as monastic advocates, protecting the monks from their enemies. The third part is a discussion of the gifts that members of the nobility made to reformed monasteries: the type of gift, the timing and location of such gifts, and the possible motives behind them. Throughout, I concentrate on one geographic area, the French duchy of Burgundy, the heart both of so-called feudal Europe and of the monastic life of the High Middle Ages.

My theme is that monasteries required the friendship of the secular nobility for their maintenance and growth, and that monasteries in turn fulfilled a noble's need to find salvation through adopting a way of life—either vicariously or in person—uniquely differentiated from his own. By concentrating on one geographic area, I am able to trace the relations between monasteries and noble families over the generations, as new monasteries were founded and new noble lineages rose to power. This book examines the interactions of the aristocracy with monasticism in order to illuminate certain aspects both of the high medieval church and of the ruling sector of medieval society.

Nobility and the Church

Most of the documents that survive from the eleventh and twelfth centuries are a record of the interactions of churches with the local nobility. And yet, somewhat surprisingly, the relation of nobles with the church is a relatively neglected scholarly topic, especially for the twelfth century. The documents have been used primarily to give either a history of the church or a history of the nobility, as though the two were separate entities. Such works can of course have tremendous value; our understanding of the relations between man and man in secular society and of the inner spiritual life of the cloister would be much poorer had scholars not been able to extract information on these topics from documents originally intended for other purposes.[3] But modern scholarly literature has developed an imbalance that should be corrected; more attention should be given to the fact

[3]For example, Louis J. Lekai's monumental study of the Cistercian order leaves a discussion of the monks' relations with secular society to a short section at the very end; *The Cistercians: Ideals and Reality* (Kent, Ohio, 1977). Georges Duby's classic work on secular society in the Mâconnais scarcely mentions the church, even though his major sources are the archives of Cluny and of the cathedral of Mâcon; Duby, *La société aux XIᵉ et XIIᵉ siècles dans la région mâconnaise*, 2nd ed. (Paris, 1971).

that in the sources of the eleventh and twelfth centuries churchmen and nobles almost always appear side by side.

Both Alexander Murray and Georges Duby have recently argued the artificiality of the division of society into "orders," indicating that church and nobility could be closely tied. Penelope Johnson has used the example of one French monastery, la Trinité of Vendôme, to discuss the relations between monks and their noble neighbors.[4] However, most of the studies on the relations between medieval churches and their noble neighbors have been the work of German scholars. Aloys Schulte first demonstrated the interdependence of church and nobility in his classic work on the Rhineland, in which he indicated the family ties between the leaders of the church and the leaders of secular society. More recent work has focused especially on Cluny in the eleventh century. Johannes Fechter and Gerd Tellenbach with his students have argued convincingly that Cluny, where most of the abbots and monks were of noble blood, was dependent for its expansion on the goodwill of the Burgundian nobility. A number of workers, especially in the Institut für Frühmittelalterforschung at Münster, are presently using both Cluny's charters and Cluniac *libri memoriales* to discuss the relations between church and society, especially as seen in Cluny's care and prayers for the dead. Barbara Rosenwein, whose work has been strongly influenced by that of German scholars, has even suggested psychological explanations—"ritual aggression" and anomie—as to why warlike nobles were willing to support and protect monks or leave the world for the monastic life at Cluny.[5]

Regrettably, much recent scholarship on Cluny's relations with the leaders of lay society has tended to become bogged down in a rather sterile debate over whether Cluny was "feudal" or "anti-feudal." The debate will never be satisfactorily resolved until there is consensus on what is meant by "feudal." Bede K. Lackner has called Cluny feudal because of the monks' close relations with their secular neighbors; but Kassius Hallinger argued that Cluny's freedom from the direct control of these neighbors distinguished anti-feudal Cluny

---

[4]Alexander Murray, *Reason and Society in the Middle Ages* (Oxford, 1978), pp. 319, 350–82. Duby, *The Three Orders*, pp. 141–44, 156. Penelope D. Johnson, *Prayer, Patronage, and Power: The Abbey of la Trinité, Vendôme, 1032–1187* (New York, 1981).

[5]Aloys Schulte, *Der Adel und die deutsche Kirche im Mittelalter* (Stuttgart, 1910), pp. 61–73. Johannes Fechter, *Cluny, Adel und Volk* (diss., University of Tübingen, 1966). Gerd Tellenbach, "Il monachesimo riformato ed i laici nei secoli XI e XII," in *I laici nella "Societas christiana" dei secoli XI e XII*, Miscellanea del Centro di studi medioevali 5 (Milan, 1968), pp. 118–51. Gerd Tellenbach, ed., *Neue Forschungen über Cluny und die Cluniacenser* (Freiburg, 1959). Dietrich Poeck, "Laienbegräbnisse in Cluny," *Frühmittelalterliche Studien*, 15 (1981), 68–179. Barbara H. Rosenwein, "Feudal War and Monastic Peace: Cluniac Liturgy as Ritual Aggression," *Viator*, 2 (1971), 145–57; and Rosenwein, *Rhinoceros Bound: Cluny in the Tenth Century* (Philadelphia, 1982), pp. 101–12.

from feudal Gorze. Cluny could be considered feudal if this means being a manorial landlord controlling a large number of peasant tenants; but Jean-François Lemarignier has called Cluny anti-feudal because it represented stability rather than "feudal anarchy." Cluny is feudal if by this is meant being the center of a network of dependent monasteries, free from the authority of bishop or king, as Georges Duby has used the term, but anti-feudal if by this is meant being governed by a strict rule rather than by disorderly and haphazard arrangements.[6] One can hope that this feudal/anti-feudal dichotomy will be put aside for a more productive examination of Cluny's relations to secular society. I myself attempt to avoid using the term "feudal" at all, restricting its meaning, in the instances where its use is unavoidable, to the narrow, technical sense of fief-holding.

The nobility appear in this work primarily at the most pious moments in their lives. If I do not in general portray them as a warlike crew, it is not entirely because I think this view is mistaken, but rather because this view has already been widely presented. Individual nobles may well have been rough and vicious, but others—or even the same ones at different periods of their lives—provided the support that made the reformed religious life possible. Certainly the High Middle Ages was no Age of Faith, if that is understood to be an age of blind belief in a single-minded and monolithic church, but it was a period in which religious concerns at least occasionally influenced all members of the aristocracy.

The High Medieval Nobility

A brief discussion is necessary on the composition of the nobility and of noble families in the High Middle Ages. The nobility of western Europe did not begin to constitute a juridic class, clearly separated from the rest of society by firm criteria, until the end of the twelfth century or later. And yet it was usually quite obvious to

[6]A survey of the feudal/anti-feudal arguments—of which the above are only a few examples—appears in Fechter, *Cluny*, pp. 19—22; and in Rosenwein, *Rhinoceros Bound*, pp. 16—17, 20—22. Bede K. Lackner, *The Eleventh-Century Background of Cîteaux*, Cistercian Studies Series 8 (Washington, D.C., 1972), pp. 75—77, 90. Kassius Hallinger, *Gorze—Kluny: Studien zu den monastischen Lebensformen und Gegensätzen im Hochmittelalter* (Rome, 1950), pp. 41—42, 742. Jean-François Lemarignier, "Structures monastiques et structures politiques dans la France de la fin du Xe et les débuts du XIe siècle," in *Il monachesimo nell'alto medioevo e la formazione della civiltà occidentale*, Settimane di studio del Centro di studi sull'alto medioevo 4 (Spoleto, 1957), pp. 358—60, 369—73. Duby, *The Three Orders*, pp. 140—42. The difficulties of all historians in trying to reach a consensus on the term "feudal" are detailed by Elizabeth A. R. Brown, "The Tyranny of a Construct: Feudalism and Historians of Medieval Europe," *American Historical Review*, 79 (1974), 1070—77.

contemporaries whether a man was a member of the nobility. Dukes and counts, castellans and knights were a clearly distinguished minority within society. Documents and chronicles speak of a noble as *dominus, vir illuster, vir nobilis*, or (if appropriate) by his ducal or comital title. A noble could be recognized by his superior wealth, his position of power, and his nobility of birth, although there was no consensus on the precise amount of wealth or power required, and one could often be assigned "noble birth" with only one incontestably noble man or woman in one's immediate ancestry. Social position was naturally the clearest for those families who had held positions of high rank for the longest time. In practice, in the eleventh and twelfth centuries there was no doubt that dukes, counts, and viscounts, with their immediate families, were all nobles.[7]

Their status was solidified not only by their long establishment but by comparison with newer lineages, lineages that were also recognized as noble in this period in spite of their more recent appearance. Though most comital families go back to the tenth century—and indeed often constructed genealogies themselves in the twelfth century to record this ancestry—the castellans of the twelfth century recalled no ancestors earlier than the eleventh century.[8] As I have argued in more detail elsewhere, many Burgundian counts were originally viscounts or other lesser officials, serving the Carolingian aristocracy. These men were able to seize the power they had originally been delegated in trust during the tenth century, then consolidate their position, and, through advantageous marriages, give their children ancestors among the better-established nobility. In the eleventh century, many castellans followed the same pattern, making their own the castles that the counts had delegated them and taking their places in the ranks of the nobility as they imitated the manners of the older nobility and sought to marry women of a higher social position than their own. The castellans seem to have been the descendants of ambitious dependents of the older nobility, who were given castles to hold when permanent castles began to replace the old rough fortifications on the strategic hilltops of Burgundy at the beginning of the eleventh century.[9]

In France in the twelfth century there was still a distinction between men at the lower fringes of the nobility and the knights (*milites*), but

---

[7]On the medieval concept of nobility, see especially Jane Martindale, "The French Aristocracy in the Early Middle Ages: A Reappraisal," *Past and Present*, 75 (1977), 5–45.

[8]Léopold Genicot, *Les généalogies*, Typologie des sources du moyen âge 15 (Turnhout, 1975).

[9]Constance B. Bouchard, "The Origins of the French Nobility: A Reassessment," *American Historical Review*, 86 (1981), 501–32; and Bouchard, "Consanguinity and Noble Marriages in the Tenth and Eleventh Centuries," *Speculum*, 56 (1981), 268–87.

that distinction was disappearing. Knights, originally only retainers on horseback (though France did not have the *ministeriales* or serf-knights of the Empire),[10] had gradually come to be considered part of the nobility by the beginning of the thirteenth century. Before that, nobles could be knighted, but knights were not necessarily nobles. The confusion between the two meanings of "knight" in English—an armed retainer and a young noble who had received his dubbing or initiation ceremony—is also found in the Latin of the period, where both are called *miles*, although the vernacular languages made a clear distinction.[11]

The French nobility of the eleventh and twelfth centuries was a group in the process of change, not yet firmly defined, with new members constantly joining it. In addition, members of this group, especially the newer members, always faced the possibility of sliding out of the nobility. Even if they kept the status that came with noble birth, their exercise of power was precarious. Individuals were in constant danger of losing their hard-won authority and wealth—through accidents of heredity or war—to their neighbors, to the dukes and counts whose power was greater than their own, to the increasingly prosperous townsmen, or to the king. The high medieval nobility, which rose to power with the decay of centralized authority and kept its power through its military activity, somewhat ironically attained a defined legal status only in the early thirteenth century, just when effective royal power was reestablished and mercenaries were replacing feudal levies of the nobility for most military purposes. The nobility that the castellans of the eleventh century and the knights of the twelfth were eager to join, far from being a static class, was a collection of families whose position and purpose had high potential but were highly unstable.

---

[10]In Burgundy, the term *ministeriales* was used to designate the lords' chief domestic servitors and those who acted as their provosts and agents on outlying estates; Duby, *La société mâconnaise*, pp. 297—307. For the German *ministeriales*, see John B. Freed, "The Formation of the Salzburg Ministerialage in the Tenth and Eleventh Centuries: An Example of Upward Social Mobility in the Central Middle Ages," *Viator*, 9 (1978), 93—98. In the Empire those called "knights" were usually warriors, but they were not even necessarily on horseback before the thirteenth century; Joachim Bumke, *The Concept of Knighthood in the Middle Ages*, trans. W. T. H. and Erika Jackson (New York, 1982), pp. 22—45.

[11]For the distinction between knights and the nobility, see the discussions by Theodore Evergates, *Feudal Society in the Bailliage of Troyes under the Counts of Champagne, 1152—1284* (Baltimore, 1975), pp. 145—51; by Jean-Pierre Poly and Éric Bournazel, *La mutation féodale, X^e—XIIe siècles* (Paris, 1980), pp. 171—83; and especially by Bumke, *The Concept of Knighthood*, chap. 5, "The Noble Knights," pp. 72—106. Duby, who originally argued that knights and nobles were identical from the end of the tenth century, has recently accepted the evidence that these two groups did not fully fuse until the thirteenth century; *The Three Orders*, pp. 154—57, 293—301.

When speaking of noble "families," one must keep in mind that the modern meaning of the word does not correspond to any word in medieval Latin. In modern usage the term "family" generally denotes either the nuclear family of father, mother, and children, or else a broad and ill-defined group of cousins and in-laws. The Middle Ages had neither a term nor probably a concept for either of these meanings. Our word "family" is derived from the Latin *familia*, meaning that group of persons—many of them unrelated—who lived under one roof and formed an economic unit. Though the household, rather than the family (in the biological sense), was the basic unit of economic activity, medieval nobles were acutely aware of who were their blood relatives, their *consanguinei* in Latin. These *consanguinei* helped make many of the decisions that modern society considers a matter for the individual, such as choice of marriage partner and disposition of personal effects by testament, and, as seen below, the decision to enter the church. Where the word "family" appears in the following pages it will designate a group of blood relatives, aware of themselves as a unit (occasionally called a *stirps* or *gens* in the aggregate by chroniclers), and descended from a common ancestor.[12]

In the eleventh and twelfth centuries, such families were most conscious of the male line of descent; the common ancestor with whom family members identified was generally also the original holder of the castle or office now inherited by the living members of the family. If the castle or county had at some point passed through female hands—for example, if a young man had inherited it from his maternal grandfather—family identification tended to follow the castle or office rather than, strictly speaking, the male line. Ecclesiastical members of the family might provide a link between two patrilineally defined lineages: ecclesiastics often helped their nephews on either the maternal or paternal side to advance within the church. The fortunes of many families can be traced through the course of the eleventh and twelfth centuries by the record of their generosity to one or two monasteries. A family that never made gifts to the local monasteries (or, in any event, never appeared in monastic cartularies either as a donor, a confirmer, or an antagonist) is today generally untraceable.

[12]For a fuller discussion of this point, see Constance B. Bouchard, "The Structure of a Twelfth-Century French Family: The Lords of Seignelay," *Viator*, 10 (1979), 41−44; and Anita Guerreau-Jalabert, "Sur les structures de parenté dans l'Europe médiévale," *Annales: Économies, Sociétés, Civilisations*, 36 (1981), 1030−31.

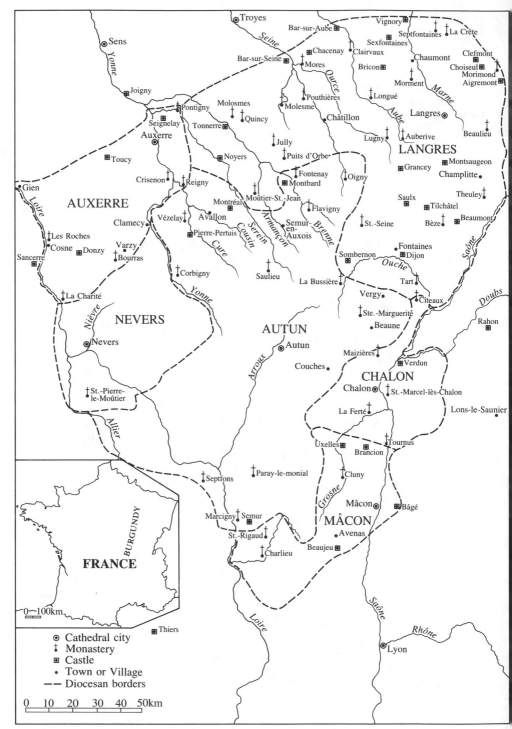

Map 1. Medieval Burgundy

Burgundy in the High Middle Ages

Located between the German empire on the east and the area of the French king's greatest influence to the northwest, halfway between Paris and Provence, Burgundy was the heart of western Europe in the Middle Ages. The Cluniacs and the Cistercians, the two most influential monastic orders of the High Middle Ages, were both centered in Burgundy, where they were founded and where the greatest number of their houses were concentrated. In the eleventh and twelfth centuries, the dukes of Burgundy controlled a compact area shaped roughly like an inverted triangle with its bottom corner knocked off. Bounded on the west by the Loire and on the east by the Saône and the Marne, it stretched from just south of Sens and Troyes to the northern edge of the Lyonnais. This triangle measured roughly two hundred kilometers from north to south, about two hundred kilometers across at the widest, northern edge, and sixty kilometers across at the narrow, southern end. The exact borders of the dukes' power were not however particularly stable.[13] Indeed, the boundaries of the political area called *Burgundia* shifted quite substantially throughout the Middle Ages. Besides the eleventh- through fourteenth-century duchy of Burgundy, there was a kingdom of Burgundy in the fifth century which was absorbed by the Franks; a ninth- and early tenth-century kingdom that stretched from Vienne to Arles and was sometimes called Burgundy and sometimes Provence; and an independent kingdom of trans-Saône Burgundy, located north of the preceding, centered in the archdiocese of Besançon, which existed from 888 until 1032, when it was absorbed into the German empire (this area later became known as the Franche-Comté of Burgundy).[14]

In this book, I define Burgundy not by any political boundaries but rather by diocesan boundaries, which had remained essentially unchanged since Merovingian times. The dioceses of Autun, Auxerre, Chalon-sur-Saône, Langres, Mâcon, and Nevers were each considered by chroniclers of the central Middle Ages to constitute part of *Burgundia*.[15] Auxerre and Nevers were within the archdiocese of

[13]Jean Richard, "Les institutions ducales dans le duché de Bourgogne," in *Institutions seigneuriales*, ed. Ferdinand Lot and Robert Fawtier, Histoire des institutions françaises au moyen âge 1 (Paris, 1957), p. 209.

[14]Bernard Bligny, "Le royaume de Bourgogne," in *Karl der Grosse, Lebenswerk und Nachleben*, ed. Wolfgang Braunfels, I (Düsseldorf, 1965), 247—68. Bligny has studied church reform in the trans-Saône kingdom of Burgundy; *L'Église et les ordres religieux dans le royaume de Bourgogne aux XIᵉ et XIIᵉ siècles* (Paris, 1960).

[15]Eugène Jarry, *Formation territoriale de la Bourgogne*, Provinces et pays de France 3 (Paris, 1948), pp. 123—25. Sens and Troyes were also sometimes referred to as part of Burgundy, but by the twelfth century these two were generally considered part of the county of Champagne; therefore I have not included them.

Sens, and the other bishoprics were within the archdiocese of Lyon. The dioceses of Auxerre, Chalon, and Mâcon were suppressed at the time of the Revolution (the diocese of Auxerre was absorbed into that of Sens, and the other two were absorbed into the diocese of Autun), and Dijon, originally part of the diocese of Langres, has been a separate diocese since the early eighteenth century. The "Burgundy" defined by these dioceses corresponds roughly to the modern departments of Côte-d'Or, Nièvre, and Saône-et-Loire, the southern halves of Haute-Marne and Yonne, and small pieces of Ain, Allier, Aube, Haute-Saône, Loire, Loiret, and Rhône.

The bishops and the most important noble families of Burgundy appear frequently in this book, so a few words on them specifically is appropriate. The Burgundian bishops represented the oldest continuous form of government in the region but by no means the only one. Their chief competitors in the eleventh and twelfth centuries were the counts, who made their capitals in the same cities as the bishops and whose counties roughly corresponded to the bishops' dioceses, since both sets of boundaries were eventual descendants of those of the Roman *pagi*, or administrative units. Only at Autun were the bishops free of competition from the local counts, since the dukes of Burgundy—whose capital was relatively distant, at Dijon—held the office of count of Autun. At Autun, Auxerre, and Langres the bishops had taken over the old Roman *castrum* in the early Middle Ages and had their cathedral perched on a hill in the center of the city. At Chalon and Mâcon, however, the bishops stayed at the outskirts of the Roman city, where their church had originally been founded at the site of a Christian cemetery or perhaps a pagan temple, leaving the central hill and the old *castrum* to the counts. At Mâcon, the cathedral was built so far outside the *castrum* as to be on the actual floodplain of the Saône; the nave, built on foundations of sand, had to be taken down in the eighteenth century, though the twelfth-century towers and narthex still stand, just far enough from the river to be founded on bedrock. At Nevers, the arrangement was unusual: both count and bishop shared the *castrum* in the middle of the city. This juxtaposition of count's castle and cathedral may explain why for most of the eleventh century the viscounts of Nevers (who governed the city while the counts were at Auxerre) had brothers or uncles who were bishops of Nevers.[16]

___

[16]On the origins of the Burgundian episcopal cities and their relationships with the counts, see, most recently, Reinhold Kaiser, *Bischofsherrschaft zwischen Königtum und Fürstenmacht. Studien zur bischöflichen Stadtherrschaft im Westfränkisch-französischen Reich im frühen und hohen Mittelalter*, Pariser historische Studien 17 (Bonn, 1981), pp. 341–85, 612–23.

The most powerful secular figures in Burgundy in the eleventh and twelfth centuries were the dukes.[17] In the first half of the tenth century the title of duke of Burgundy had been held by Richard le Justicier and his descendants and by a certain Giselbert, who seems to have married a woman of Richard's family. But in 956 the duchy was taken by the Capetians, going in succession to two of Hugh Capet's brothers, Otto and Henry. Henry's death in 1002 however triggered a long war over the succession between the supporters of Duke Henry's stepson and King Robert II, Henry's nephew. Robert eventually prevailed and made his son Robert duke, an office his descendants held until the middle of the fourteenth century.

Second in power to the dukes were the counts of Burgundy and Mâcon. They were descended from Adalbert, last king of Italy, who fled to Burgundy when he was driven out of Italy by the emperor Otto I in 962. Adalbert's son, Otto-William, was adopted by Duke Henry of Burgundy—who married Otto-William's mother after Adalbert's death—and took the county of Mâcon by marrying the widow of the last of the tenth-century counts. Otto-William lost his claim to the duchy of Burgundy in the wars after 1002, but he and his descendants retained the county of Mâcon and called themselves counts of Burgundy, even though they could not call themselves dukes. They expanded their power east of the Saône, in the region around Salins and Besançon, especially after the death of the last king of trans-Saône Burgundy in 1032. Frederick Barbarossa reasserted the imperial claim to this region by marrying the heiress of Burgundy in 1156, but her cousins continued to control Mâcon and indeed called themselves counts of Burgundy well into the thirteenth century.

The two other chief comital lineages of the area were the counts of Chalon-sur-Saône and the counts of Nevers. The counts of Chalon started as viscounts serving the heirs of Richard le Justicier, but around 960 Lambert took the office of count of Chalon. His oldest daughter, Gerberge, married first Adalbert of Italy, bearing him Otto-William, and then, as mentioned above, Duke Henry of Burgundy. The counts of Burgundy and Mâcon did not claim Chalon, however; the county went first to Gerberge's brother, who was also bishop of Auxerre, and then to the descendants of her younger sister Mathilda. The counts of Nevers were descended from castellans of the Nivernais. Landric, the first to call himself count, had served Duke Henry and received the counties of Nevers and Auxerre as a reward for his service at the time Landric married Otto-William's daughter. He held Auxerre against King Robert II in the Burgundian wars after 1002, but he and the king were soon reconciled, and Landric married his son

---

[17]For all these noble families, see Appendix A.

Raynald to King Robert's sister. Raynald married his own son to the heiress of Tonnerre, the descendant of counts who had held power since the tenth century, and henceforth the three counties of Nevers, Auxerre, and Tonnerre were held by the same family until the line ended with the death of Count Gui in 1176; his daughter and the three counties were taken in 1184 by Peter of Courtenay, the king's cousin.

Besides these families of counts, there were also a number of castellan lineages, of which the most powerful and the best documented in the eleventh and twelfth centuries were the lords of Bâgé, the lords of Beaujeu, the lords of Beaumont, the lords of Brancion, the lords of Donzy, the lords of Saulx (also counts of Langres until 1178, an office they held in fief from the dukes), the lords of Seignelay, the lords of Semur-en-Brionnais, the lords of Tilchâtel, and the lords of Vergy. Several important families of Champagne, especially the counts of Troyes and the counts of Bar-sur-Seine, also sometimes played a significant role in Burgundian ecclesiastical history.[18]

As there were a variety of nobles in Burgundy, so there were a variety of monasteries they patronized. Some houses in the duchy had their origins long before the ninth century, most notably St.-Bénigne of Dijon, St.-Germain of Auxerre, St.-Marcel-lès-Chalon, St.-Martin of Autun, and Flavigny, all of which suffered losses of property and regularity during the tenth century and were subsequently reformed. There were very few completely new foundations in the ninth through mid-eleventh centuries in Burgundy, but those which were founded in this period had a significant impact on the religious life of the region: Vézelay and Tournus, both founded in the mid-ninth century (Tournus by monks fleeing the Viking invasions and carrying the relics of St. Philibert with them), and Cluny, later the mother house of a very large and wealthy order, founded in 909. These three were all houses of Benedictine monks which were able to retain their regular life through the central Middle Ages and attracted the gifts of a number of noble patrons. Toward the end of the eleventh century new foundations became more common. The most notable of these foundations were Molesme, founded in 1075, Cîteaux, founded in 1098 by Molesme's abbot and several of its monks, and then, in the twelfth century, a great many Cistercian houses, beginning with Cîteaux's "four eldest daughters," La Ferté, Pontigny, Clairvaux, and Morimond. Thus Burgundy not only nurtured several of the most successful and influential of the older Benedictine houses but was also the cradle of the reforming Cistercian

---

[18]For the noble families of the region of Troyes, see Evergates, *Feudal Society in the Bailliage of Troyes*, pp. 155–211.

order, intended by its founders to provide a way of life more rigorous and closer to the Benedictine Rule than any other form of monasticism then practiced.

The medieval duchy of Burgundy, the geographical setting for this social and ecclesiastical diversity, was then, as now, a land of varied topography. In the center rises the Morvan, a wild area, even today, of old (500 million years) mountains, mostly granite, worn down in the passage of time to less than 1000 meters. Though not high by the standards of the Alps to the east (formed some fifty million years ago), the mountains of the Morvan are still a significant watershed and a barrier to communication across Burgundy. North of the Morvan, the rivers flow north into the Seine basin and eventually into the English Channel. To the west and south, the rivers flow west into the Loire—the western boundary of Burgundy—and then northwest toward the Atlantic. East of the Morvan, the rivers flow into the Saône, Burgundy's eastern border, and then south into the Rhône and the Mediterranean. The floodplain of the Saône has worn away the limestone deposited over the ancient granite to make an abrupt drop along much of the eastern side of the duchy. This is the Côte, a region where the good drainage and the morning sun falling on the grapes have produced superb wines, which have been traded throughout Europe since Gallo-Roman times. Taken together, these factors made Burgundy a nexus, receiving influences from and disseminating ideas to most of Europe, while still retaining its local identity.

The chronological limits for this book have been set, somewhat arbitrarily, at 980 and 1198. In 980, Bruno became bishop of Langres and began a long career of church reform, and in 1198 Innocent III became pope, beginning a pontificate that signaled the end of much local ecclesiastical autonomy. This book then treats the Burgundian church in a period when ecclesiastical reform was very important and carried out for the most part locally. The eleventh and twelfth centuries were a high point of religious activity in Burgundy which has not since been duplicated. Although many of the churches in the cities were rebuilt between the thirteenth and fifteenth centuries—including the cathedrals of Auxerre, Chalon, and Nevers, and the now-destroyed nave of the cathedral of Mâcon—the cities of Autun and Langres still keep their twelfth-century cathedrals (the one at Langres regrettably marred by a neo-classic facade). And the countryside and small towns are still dominated, as they have been since the twelfth century, by the square or octagonal towers of their Romanesque churches.

Plate 1. The Romanesque church in the village of Blanot,
north of Cluny

The Sources

The major sources for this book are the cartularies and archival documents from Burgundian monasteries and bishoprics, supplemented with contemporary chronicles. There is also much valuable evidence in letters and *vitae*, though these are much scarcer than the documents recording transactions and agreements which constitute the cartularies and archival collections. There are about forty major cartularies surviving from the Burgundian churches of the eleventh and twelfth centuries and many more small collections. (The composition of cartularies is discussed below.) The majority have been edited, and there are also editions of collected documents from a variety of other churches. Several important cartularies, however, still exist only in manuscript. It should be noted that most houses for which a cartulary exists also have some number of existing archival documents. Both the cartularies and chronicles upon which I have principally relied are enumerated in the Abbreviations. The most important unedited cartularies and archival collections are those from the houses of Auberive, Beaulieu, La Bussière, La Crête, Crisenon, Flavigny, Fontenay, Longué, Maizières, Morimond, Septfontaines, and Theuley, as well as the documents of Cîteaux and Clairvaux from the final decades of the twelfth century.

The archives of medieval monasteries were composed primarily of documents recording binding legal agreements with noble laymen: gifts, confirmations of gifts, sales and leases, and the arbitrated settling of quarrels. Cathedral archives contained the same type of documents, as well as a fairly high number recording disputes that involved other churches but were settled by the bishop. The archives of all churches generally also contained some confirmations of privileges by the pope—or less frequently by the king—and records of agreements with other churches.[19]

Pious gifts were first recorded in writing with any regularity in the seventh century. Indeed, the form donation charters should take was specified in the Germanic law codes of the period. The early eighth-century Alamannic Law, for example, began with a statement of how someone should transfer property to a church.

> If any freeman wishes to hand over his property or himself to a church, let no one, neither the duke, nor the count, nor any person, have permission to prohibit him . . . And whoever wishes to do this, let him

---

[19]See also David Walker, "The Organization of Material in Medieval Cartularies," in *The Study of Medieval Records: Essays in Honor of Kathleen Major*, ed. D. A. Bullough and R. L. Storey (Oxford, 1971), pp. 134–35. This article covers only English cartularies.

confirm it through a charter in which he expresses his wish to give his property to a church, and let him call six or seven witnesses; and let the charter contain their names, and let him place it on the altar in the presence of the priest who serves that church; and let the ownership of that property always remain with that church.[20]

Throughout the Middle Ages, donation charters kept the form specified in the eighth century: the charter expressed the donor's wish to give a particular piece of property, which would belong to the church perpetually, and it was witnessed by at least a few witnesses and occasionally dozens. For most important gifts, both the secular donor and the recipient monks provided their own witnesses.

These documents, it must be stressed, were *records* of agreements, not the agreements themselves; the legal transfer of property was contained in the sworn and witnessed statements of the principals, all of which were made orally. The charter might be drawn up several days or even several years after the fact.[21] The necessary formality was not the signing or sealing of a charter but rather the symbolic gesture by which the donor made his gift. Often he put a copy of the New Testament on the abbey's altar to symbolize his donation, though sometimes if the donor could not come to the abbey another symbol might be employed.[22] Such a gesture created a binding agreement by itself, and the charter was drawn up to guarantee that the agreement was remembered after the principals had died or forgotten what they had done.[23]

The charter attesting to a gift to a monastery—or a sale or the end of a quarrel—was a rather stylized record of what might have been a long and involved transaction or negotiation. The charter, which often began with an invocation such as "In nomine sancte et individue Trinitatis," was generally cast in the first person, with the "Ego" sometimes the donor and sometimes an important person, such as the bishop or the duke, who attested to the donation. After a description of the donation or other transaction, a description that

[20]*Lex Alamannorum* 1, MGH LL V:63—64. I am using the translation by Theodore John Rivers, *Laws of the Alamans and Bavarians* (Philadelphia, 1977), p. 66. The Bavarian laws, a slightly later compilation based largely on Alamannic law, begin with almost precisely the same ruling; *Lex Baiwariorum* 1, MGH LL V:268—69.

[21]For example, the foundation charter of the Premonstratensian house of St.-Marien of Auxerre says that it was drawn up "three years after the gifts were originally made"; Lebeuf IV.35 (p. 38).

[22]For example, when Lord Aimo Rufus of Tilchâtel was dying, around 1170, he asked the abbot of St.-Étienne of Dijon to come to his deathbed and gave him everything he had at Ahuy, and symbolized this gift by putting a stone in the abbot's hand; St.-Étienne IV.34 (pp. 50—51).

[23]Typical is a twelfth-century charter of the bishop of Chalon, which contains a short prologue, "Since, in this world, unless things are corroborated in writing, they are often lost to negligence or oblivion, therefore . . ."; Chalon, pp. 98—99.

might be short or quite detailed, came a list of the witnesses, "Huius rei testes sunt." The witnesses were vital; they validated the donation by their presence, and if a question later arose they could be called upon to affirm that they had seen the donation take place.

At the end of the charter came the date, if any, and the seals. The date might be recorded in full, "Done at" with the place, "in the year of the incarnation" (or, in Spanish documents, the Era, which dated from 38 B.C.), with the day of the month, the epact, and the indiction all specified.[24] There was often a reference to the current reign of the king, the duke, and the bishop. Some of this information might be eliminated; or there might only be a vague reference, "done when Louis was king and Odo duke." The bottom of the parchment on which the charter was written was folded over once, in a narrow strip, and holes were punched in this double thickness through which strings could be run for attaching seals to the charter. The donor usually did not seal the charter himself; before the second half of the twelfth century, few laymen other than the kings had their own seals, and then only the most powerful men. The charter was typically sealed by the bishop, if he drew up the charter, or sometimes by the ecclesiastical witnesses or the abbot of the recipient house. Though the charters thus tended to follow a stylized format, no two were identical. The general form was always modified, depending on the circumstances. The charter was a standardized tool for recording transactions, not an ironclad structure.

The documents of most houses were periodically copied, more or less verbatim, into large books called cartularies. A cartulary was drawn up for the same purpose as the original charters, to ensure that the transactions recorded in the documents were not forgotten. As the preface to the cartulary of Marcigny says, "We can oppose the audacity of false claimants with wise action, if we commit to writing those things we do in the present, so that an undisciplined posterity will not dare to violate those things done by their predecessors, when they see them confirmed by witnessed charters."[25] Although a book was the most common form of cartulary, another, somewhat more primitive, form may be seen at the abbey of St.-Rigaud, where a whole series of gifts to the house were copied, at different times and in different hands, onto three large sheets of parchment during the 1060s and 1070s.[26] The Cistercians originally kept records in the same way, inscribing brief notices of donations in one area onto separate sheets of parchment, one for each area or *villa*. These lists of

[24]The indiction was a cyclical calendar fifteen years long. The epact was a number based on the position of the moon in its cycle at the beginning of the year.

[25]Marcigny 4 (p. 6).

[26]Arch. Saône-et-Loire, H 142.

acquisitions were often all confirmed at once, by the bishop, in a pan-carte that enumerated them.[27]

The first known real cartularies were composed in the ninth century, notably the cartulary of Lorsch, in which hundreds of property transactions from the eighth and ninth centuries were copied in highly abbreviated form.[28] The first Burgundian cartulary was Cluny A, composed around the middle of the eleventh century, at the urging of Abbot Odilo.[29] It was drawn up, according to the preface, to "eliminate the malicious misrepresentation of those who would overthrow the sanctuary of God in their perversity and who foolishly dare to seize the alms piously given to the mother church." The monks' defense was found in "the perusal of many written records."[30] The majority of Burgundian cartularies seem to have been composed, to judge by the dates of the charters included in them, either in the first decades of the twelfth century or toward the end of the thirteenth century. They were generally drawn up only after the monks had acquired a large and unwieldy number of donation charters. The Cistercians of the thirteenth and fourteenth centuries were particularly assiduous at recording their acquisitions in cartularies; there is only one known original twelfth-century document for La Bussière, for example, which is not also in the cartulary.

In these cartularies gifts and agreements were generally grouped geographically rather than chronologically, so that gifts to a house in a particular locality, dating from an early gift by (say) Charles the Bald to a very recent one, were recorded in the same section. The medieval scribes also tended to group separately all confirmations of possessions given by pope, king, or bishop. The monks' archives themselves, from which a scribe would compose a cartulary, seem to have been grouped by locality; in the records of Fontenay, for example, in which there is some overlap between the cartulary and surviving twelfth-century documents, much of the cartulary follows the order of the grouping of the original charters.[31] Within each section, charters were commonly arranged chronologically, or at least approximately so.

[27]For the Cistercian practice of keeping brief notices of their acquisitions, see Cîteaux/Marilier, pp. 19–20.

[28]*Codex Laureshamensis*, ed. Karl Glöckner, 3 vols. (Darmstadt, 1919–36).

[29]BN, MS nouv. acq. lat. 1497.

[30]Edited by Ernst Sackur, *Die Cluniacenser in ihrer kirchlichen und allgemeingeschicht-lichen Wirksamkeit bis zur Mitte des elften Jahrhunderts*, I (Halle an der Saale, 1892; rpt. Darmstadt, 1965), p. 377. The compiler of Cluny A, who organized his work by abbacy, unfortunately placed among the early tenth-century documents some whose participants and witness lists definitely assign them to the eleventh century; see below, n. 33.

[31]Both cartulary and original documents are in the Arch. Côte-d'Or, in the series 15 H. For a similar pattern in England, see Walker, "Medieval Cartularies," p. 140.

But even the most meticulous compiler could not be chronologically exact when the charters he was copying were not dated. Until the middle of the twelfth century, even original charters were frequently not dated, or dated only by a vague phrase such as "Done when Hugh was bishop and Louis was king," that is, one of the several twelfth-century bishops named Hugh and either Louis VI or Louis VII. Even when the original charter was dated, the dating was sometimes eliminated when it was copied into a cartulary. Internal evidence, such as the names of witnesses (though witness lists were frequently abbreviated in cartulary copies), often make it possible to date a document to within twenty years or less, but it is impossible to date them all precisely, much less give exact birth and death dates for the men appearing in them.

Because of the ravages of time and the destruction brought about by the sixteenth-century Wars of Religion and the eighteenth-century Revolution, followed by the dissolution of most religious corporations, there is no church for which the records of the eleventh and twelfth centuries survive intact. For some monasteries, only the cartularies or fragmented remains of a cartulary survive.[32] Some Burgundian houses, like the Cistercian houses of Bourras, Les Roches, and Septfons (all located along the Loire, where the destruction of the Wars of Religion was especially intense), are known from only a few scattered twelfth-century charters. A surviving cartulary will however include, even if in abbreviated form, all the documents that the ecclesiastics of the time considered especially worth preserving. For many churches, a number of original documents survive as well as—or even instead of—the cartulary in which documents were later copied. The greatest number of documents, from both cartularies and collected original charters, come from the monastery of Cluny; the edition contains over six thousand charters from the ninth to the thirteenth century.[33]

---

[32]See for example the reconstruction of the cartulary of Marcigny, done by Jean Richard.

[33]The six large volumes of this edition still, infuriatingly, lack an index. There is however a partial index on cards at the Bibliothèque municipale of Dijon; see M. Oursel-Quarré, "À propos du chartier de Cluny," *Annales de Bourgogne*, 50 (1978), 103–7. A group of scholars at the Institut für Frühmittelalterforschung at Münster, under the direction of Joachim Wollasch, are preparing a computer index of personal names, which has been completed through the end of the eleventh century. The ninth-century documents among Cluny's charters are the records of property transfers by which a layman would acquire a piece of property; these records were given to Cluny with the property as proof of title. Many of the documents that the editors date to the reign of the first or second abbots of Cluny are in fact later; see the suggested changes in dating proposed by Maurice Chaume, "Observations sur la chronologie des chartes de l'abbaye de Cluny," *Revue Mabillon*, 16 (1926), 44–48; 29 (1939), 81–89, 133–42; 31 (1941), 14–29, 42–45, 69–82; 32 (1942), 15–20, 133–36; 38 (1948), 1–6; 39 (1949), 41–43; 42 (1952), 1–4; and D. van den Eynde, "Remarques chronologiques sur le cartulaire de Cluny," *Antonianum*, 43 (1968), 216–59.

Even with several thousand documents, as for Cluny, or with a relatively complete collection of both cartulary and original charters, as for twelfth-century Pontigny, one has details only on such affairs as were considered worth recording at the time. Some small Benedictine houses, such as Pouthières, St.-Pierre-le-Moûtier, and St.-Vivant of Vergy, seem to have attracted very few gifts in the High Middle Ages and thus never had more than a few charters from this period. Between the loss of many documents and the stylized and legal nature of those which survive, there is always some uncertainty about the details one might hope to obtain from such documents: exactly what property a monastery owned, all the ramifications of a family tree, or even the precise dates of the reigns of the Burgundian bishops and abbots. When taken together, however, the documents do present a clear picture of the relations between church and nobility in eleventh- and twelfth-century Burgundy, a picture unlikely to be altered in its broad outlines by the discovery of new charters. There are after all thousands upon thousands of documents surviving from the period which record the interactions between Burgundian nobles and churches. Though I cannot pretend to have pondered each fully, I have at least tried to look at them all. The general statements made in the following chapters are based on conclusions drawn from the perusal of a great many documents. I have not tried to do statistical analyses of the documents, to state, for example, that a certain percentage of the total deals with a certain topic, because that would only create a specious air of numerical certainty unjustified by the randomness with which documents have survived. But one can still draw qualitative conclusions, even without quantifying. I would suggest as an analogy that the documents function as a hologram, in which a projection of the whole may be found in each individual piece. After one has read a certain number of ecclesiastical documents from the eleventh and twelfth centuries, reading still another cartulary may provide welcome detail on some points but is unlikely to alter significantly the picture of secular-ecclesiastical relations in Burgundy which other documents have already provided.

An examination of the relations between monks and nobles of course touches on a number of other issues, most of which I have dealt with only in passing, including the growth of canon law, the development of scholastic learning, the multiplication of wandering preachers proclaiming the apostolic life, the rise of papal government, the increase in the number of hermits, canons regular, and heretics during the twelfth century, the interior spiritual life of the cloister, the growth of urban society, the economic changes that can be glimpsed through ecclesiastical documents, and the role of parish priests. All these phenomena of course affected the religious life of the High

Middle Ages; "the church" in its fullest sense can be considered to include all Christians, both lay and ecclesiastical.

This book concentrates instead on the interactions between the medieval church and one segment of society. As I shall demonstrate, the maintenance and spread of the spiritual life was dependent on worldly cooperation between nobles and ecclesiastical leaders. But theirs was always an ambivalent relationship, for while the leaders of the church and the leaders of society came from the same social background, they did not necessarily share a unity of purpose. Conscientious churchmen often had to put the interests of their churches above the interests of their families. Nobles did not support the local churches either uniformly or consistently; the gifts the churches needed from powerful laymen arrived at irregular intervals, were often disputed by the donor's relatives, and were prompted by sometimes mixed motives. The monastic reform of the High Middle Ages was not carried out in the face of a hostile nobility, nor was it the product of a happy and harmonious relationship between nobles and churchmen. Rather, it was the result of a series of complex interactions, between men of similar backgrounds but different goals, in which different purposes coincided at least some of the time in the spread of the religious life.

PART ONE

LEADERS OF THE CHURCH
AND LEADERS OF SOCIETY

This section examines the relationships between members of the aristocracy and members of the church hierarchy to demonstrate the familial unity of church and nobility. I argue that, while leaders of the church and leaders of society came from the same families, it was by no means automatic for nobles to put their children into the church; there were great variations depending on a family's position, the era, and the convert's age; and the goals of secular leaders were not the goals of their brothers in the church. Though the examples are Burgundian, they could as easily be drawn from other areas of France. The first chapter discusses the process by which nobles entered the church from the viewpoint of individual nobles and their families, the second from the viewpoint of the churches, whose leaders were overwhelmingly drawn from the noble class.

[1]

Noble Entry
into the Church

Both men and women could and did enter the religious life at virtually any stage in their lives. Although it was possible for someone
from any level of society to enter the medieval church, so long as he
or she was not bound by servitude, in the eleventh and twelfth centuries a much higher proportion of the aristocracy put their sons and
daughters into the church or made adult conversions themselves than
did members of any other social class. Though the scanty evidence on
the social backgrounds of many monks and priests makes it impossible
to cite any exact figures on what proportion of the noble class entered
the church,[1] it is clear that the vast majority of church leaders were
drawn from noble or knightly backgrounds in this period (as I demonstrate in the next chapter) and that the aristocracy, always a tiny
minority in the overall population, contributed such a high proportion
of its members to the church that half of all churchmen may well
have been noble.

A man or woman's decision to enter the cloister or a collegiate
chapter was always more than an individual decision: it affected or
was influenced by the convert's relatives. Noble families, the groups
of blood relatives who acted together, frequently put their sons and
daughters into the church at a relatively young age. The decision that
a child would enter the church involved not only the choice of a

---

[1]Among the families in Appendix A, roughly 15 percent of the men were ecclesiastics. This is an extremely approximate figure, since it does not include the churchmen
whose families are not known or the many Burgundian families not important enough
or well enough documented for me to include them in the appendix; nor does it take
into account the differences between cathedral canons and monks, between the upper
and lower nobility, and between the eleventh and twelfth centuries. Alexander Murray
estimates that as many as 25 percent of all nobles may have entered the church; *Reason
and Society in the Middle Ages* (Oxford, 1978), pp. 342—44. Michel Parisse estimates
that, in Lorraine, the figure may have been about 20 percent; "La noblesse Lorraine,
XIᵉ—XIIᵉ s." (diss., Université de Nancy II, 1975), pp. 339—40.

particular church but also a certain kind of church. In the eleventh and twelfth centuries in Burgundy, the chief choice for boys was between a cathedral chapter or house of secular canons, on the one hand, and a monastery or house of canons regular on the other. Virtually no one from the nobility seems to have become a chaplain or parish priest. Girls were restricted to entering a nunnery, the primary consideration being the relative strictness of life.

Each Burgundian cathedral had a chapter, composed of canons responsible for services in the cathedral church; they helped the bishop in the administration of the diocese and elected the new bishop when the old bishop died or otherwise left the see. Though during much of the eleventh century the local secular authorities had a major say in who was elected bishop, and by the end of the twelfth century the pope's influence was increasingly important, the cathedral canons were always responsible at least in theory for choosing the new bishop, and in the majority of cases he came from their ranks.[2] Burgundian cathedral chapters did not adopt a strict rule of common life, as did a few French chapters (primarily in the south) during the course of the twelfth century,[3] nor were were they composed of monks, as was the case at some English cathedrals.

They were governed by the 816 Rule of Aix, which had originally been intended to be less strict than the monastic rule, and its discipline was further loosened in the ninth and tenth centuries. Cathedral canons commanded their own property in the eleventh and twelfth centuries, rather than holding possessions in common. The cathedral patrimony was split between the bishop and the canons, and the canons' portion was divided into shares called prebends. Although canons were generally forbidden to sell or otherwise alienate the property that constituted their prebends, they could live off the income in relative independence. In most sees, they had individual houses, grouped near the cathedral. The canons were discouraged from spending protracted periods of time away from the cathedral, and the rule of chastity was enforced upon them, apparently quite effectively from the beginning of the eleventh century, but their way of life still differed markedly from that of monks. In the eleventh century there were a number of other Burgundian houses of canons who did not follow a strict rule. In these cases, a small body of priests served a

---

[2]Martine Chauney, "Le recrutement de l'épiscopat bourguignon aux XIe et XIIe siècles," *Annales de Bourgogne*, 47 (1975), 203. Constance B. Bouchard, "The Geographical, Social and Ecclesiastical Origins of the Bishops of Auxerre and Sens in the Central Middle Ages," *Church History*, 46 (1977), 285–87.

[3]Georges Duby, "Les chanoines réguliers et la vie économique des XIe et XIIe siècles," in *La vita comune del clero nei secoli XI e XII*, Miscellanea del Centro di studi medioevali 3 (Milan, 1962), pp. 72–89.

church together, but they enjoyed a fair amount of autonomy and did not share their personal property. By the middle of the twelfth century, however, almost all these houses had been reformed, either to a monastic rule or to the so-called Augustinian Rule (see below, Chapter 4), so that the cathedral chapters were virtually the only collegiate bodies of ecclesiastics left in Burgundy who did not live in common in strict obedience to a superior.[4]

In contrast to cathedral canons, monks and canons regular followed a tight regimen, based on the Benedictine or Augustinian Rule, observing individual poverty and collective property. They were expected to be entirely obedient to their abbot or prior, not leaving the abbey for any reason except at his direction. Much of the monastic day was spent in performing the liturgy within the privacy of the cloister; canons regular were in addition often responsible for carrying out divine services for members of secular society, since their church frequently functioned as a parish church. The church a noble might typically enter, whether a monastery or a cathedral chapter, depended to a large extent on the convert's age, and the pattern of the twelfth century was somewhat different from that of the eleventh. The following sections discuss in turn entry into the church in childhood or early adolescence, in young adulthood, and in old age, the three stages at which most noble conversions were made.

Oblates and Youthful Conversions

Throughout the eleventh and twelfth centuries, most members of most monasteries—and the majority of nuns—entered the church as child oblates, their parents' offering to the monasteries. The children were supposedly serving a noviciate, and it was still possible for them to leave the monastery before taking final orders, but such a departure was rare.[5] The usual pattern may be seen in Raoul Glaber's *Vita* of Abbot William of St.-Bénigne of Dijon, written around 1040. He said that William's parents, inspired by a vision, decided to "offer him to

---

[4]For the application of the Rule of Aix, see Jacques Hourlier, *L'âge classique, 1140–1378: Les religieux*, Histoire du droit et des institutions de l'Église en Occident 10 (Paris, 1971), p. 82. For the effectiveness of the enforcement of chastity, see C. N. L. Brooke, "Gregorian Reform in Action: Clerical Marriage in England, 1050–1200," *Cambridge Historical Journal*, 12 (1956), 1–21. See also Constance Brittain Bouchard, *Spirituality and Administration: The Role of the Bishop in Twelfth-Century Auxerre*, Speculum Anniversary Monographs 5 (Cambridge, Mass., 1979), pp. 23–24; and Julia Barrow, "Cathedrals, Provosts and Prebends: A Comparison of Twelfth-Century German and English Practice," *Journal of Ecclesiastical History*, 37 (1986), 536–64.

[5]Pierre Riché, "Les moines bénédictins, maîtres d'écoles, VIIIᵉ–XIᵉ siècles," in *Benedictine Culture, 750–1050*, ed. W. Lourdaux and D. Verhelst, Mediaevalia Lovaniensia, Studia 11 (Louvain, 1983), pp. 98–100.

Christ" shortly after his birth, and he went on to live his whole life in a monastery.[6] Regular canons and houses of nuns received oblates in the same way. In 1170 a woman widowed by her second knightly husband gave her *infans* son and all her late husband's property to the canons of Châtillon, specifying that her son should become a canon there.[7] Though in the twelfth century there was some attempt to reduce the incidence of oblates—the new Cistercian order banned their reception, and reforms within the Cluniac order set out to reduce their frequency—most new monks were still quite young. Even when an age limit was set, it was usually fairly low,[8] and the practice of child oblation continued even where forbidden, as witness the number of Cistercian abbots reprimanded by the chapter general in the later twelfth century for allowing the practice.[9]

Although cathedral chapters do not seem to have received young boys as canons, at least in the twelfth century, it seems to have been common for a boy destined for a life in the chapter to begin while young as a student in the cathedral school, being accepted into the chapter after a certain period of training there. For example, Hugh, later abbot of Cluny, entered the cathedral school at Auxerre around 1030 or 1035, though at age fifteen he decided, against his father's wishes, to enter the monastery rather than the cathedral chapter. William of Seignelay, bishop of Auxerre and Paris at the beginning of the thirteenth century, had been set while young into the cathedral school of Sens by his father and joined the chapter there after a few years.[10] In cathedral schools, as in monasteries, a young boy was not immediately a full member of the community, but he was generally training to become a canon or monk with the full expectation that he would do so after a suitable passage of time.

[6]*Vita Willelmi* 3–4, pp. 464–65. For oblates, see also Wolfgang Teske, "Laien, Laienmönche und Laienbrüder in der Abtei Cluny. Ein Beitrag zum 'Konversen-Problem,' I. Teil," *Frühmittelalterliche Studien*, 10 (1976), 278–79.

[7]Petit 505 (II:341).

[8]The Cistercian legislation of 1134 specified that no one could become a novice until age fifteen, further specifying that *pueri* could not be taught their letters within a Cistercian house. Later the age of entry was raised to eighteen years; Canivez, *Statuta*, I:31, no. 48; 62, no. 28. When Viscount John of Ligny decided to make his son a monk at the Cistercian house of Pontigny in 1150, he specified that the boy would not actually enter the house until "ad annos aptos ordini pervenit," even though John made his entry gift immediately; Pontigny 116 (pp. 182–83).

[9]The abbot of La Ferté was disciplined in 1195 for admitting novices under the age of fifteen; Canivez, *Statuta*, I:190, no. 55. For examples of Cistercian oblates, see Fontenay II, fols. 3r–v, no. 45; fol. 11r, no. 25; and Clairvaux I, p. 17, no. 5. See also Joseph H. Lynch, *Simoniacal Entry into Religious Life from 1000 to 1260* (Columbus, Ohio, 1976), pp. 36–40; and Jean Verdon, "Les moniales dans la France de l'Ouest aux XIe et XIIe siècles: Étude d'histoire sociale," *Cahiers de civilisation médiévale*, 19 (1976), 251.

[10]For Hugh, see Appendix C, p. 410. For William, see *Gesta pontificum*, p. 453; Bouchard, *Spirituality and Administration*, p. 122; and Appendix A, p. 356.

The church in which a family decided to set a boy was often determined by which houses already contained his relatives. In general, a family that sent some of its sons into the church (it should be kept in mind that some noble families produced no ecclesiastics) sent them, generation after generation, into the same one or two houses. In fact, a family that sent sons into the cathedral chapter almost never sent them into a monastery and vice versa. The type of religious life found appropriate for sons in the church seems to have varied from family to family. For example, the lords of Vignory put a son into the cathedral chapter of Langres in at least half of the generations between 1025 and 1260 (the number may well be higher). The viscounts of Nevers regularly sent a son into the cathedral chapter of Nevers in the eleventh century, men who usually became bishops. The dukes of Burgundy had brothers in the cathedral chapters of Autun and Langres for most of the time from the end of the eleventh century until the end of the twelfth—all of these canons became bishops. These families, important in the cathedral chapters, produced no monks or almost none: the only monks in the family of the eleventh- and twelfth-century dukes of Burgundy, for example, are Raynald, abbot of Flavigny (1084–1090), and his brother, Duke Hugh I, who retired to Cluny after having been seriously wounded in battle.

While some families consistently produced cathedral canons, others produced only monks. The evidence for the family attachments of monks is not as good as that of cathedral canons, but it does indicate that families that began sending their sons into a particular church continued to do so over the generations.[11] The lords of Semur-en-Brionnais for example produced an abbot of Savigny at the end of the tenth century and a number of monks of Cluny in the eleventh and twelfth centuries: Hugh, abbot of Cluny (1049–1109) (mentioned above), made his nephews Hugh and Gervais and his great-nephew Raynald all monks under him, and Hugh and Gervais became (in succession) abbots of St.-Germain of Auxerre. Hugh later became bishop of Auxerre (1115–1136), while Raynald became abbot of Vézelay in 1106 and archbishop of Lyon in 1125. In 1088, most of the secular members of the family of the lords of Semur followed their relatives into the cloister, the men, including two generations of

---

[11]William Mendel Newman has found a similar pattern in Picardy, where some families produced only cathedral canons, some only monks and canons regular, and some neither; *Les seigneurs de Nesle en Picardie (XIIᵉ–XIIIᵉ siècle)*, 2 vols. (Paris and Philadelphia, 1971), I:10–12. See also Constance B. Bouchard, "The Structure of a Twelfth-Century French Family: The Lords of Seignelay," *Viator*, 10 (1979), 52 and n. 41; and Joseph H. Lynch, "Monastic Recruitment in the Eleventh and Twelfth Centuries: Some Social and Economic Considerations," *American Benedictine Review*, 26 (1975), 430.

lords, entering Cluny, and the women entering Marcigny, a house the family had founded in 1054 for Cluniac nuns.[12] Here the family's decision to enter a church always involved Cluny and her daughters; the family members who became bishops were all promoted from the position of abbot of a Cluniac house, not from the cathedral chapter.

Of course a family's decision to send sons into a monastery or into a cathedral chapter was not fixed for all time. The lords of Bricon, for example, produced two Cistercian monks in the later twelfth century, Rudolph, abbot of Longué, and his brother Simon, who became a monk at Clairvaux in his later years. In the next generation, however, the family produced no known monks but rather two members of the cathedral chapter of Langres, one of whom became dean of the chapter around 1205.[13] But, at any one time, the sons of a particular family generally entered either a monastery or a cathedral chapter, and generally chose a house that probably already included family members as monks or canons.

The preceding discussion has focused especially on sons, for the evidence is better for monks and cathedral canons than for nuns. In the eleventh and twelfth centuries the number of religious houses for men greatly exceeded that for women; the modern pattern, where nuns far outnumber their brothers in the church, had not yet been established. But the evidence, as much as is available, suggests strongly that girls sent into the church when young were, like their male counterparts, most often sent to a house where older relatives were already established. For example, the nieces of Peter the Venerable, abbot of Cluny (1122–1156), became nuns at Marcigny when his mother, their grandmother, decided to join the house.[14] Even if one cannot be certain that a new nun had aunts or a grandmother in the church, her family's consent was usually specified in the entry charter.[15]

The choice whether to make a child an oblate or to send a boy into the cathedral school was generally made by the family as a whole. The child does not seem to have had much say in the matter, and indeed the family objected strenuously if he tried to make any changes

---

[12]For the lords of Semur, see Appendix A, pp. 360–61. See also Joachim Wollasch, "Parenté noble et monachisme réformateur. Observations sur les 'conversions' à la vie monastique aux XIᵉ et XIIᵉ siècles," *Revue historique*, 535 (1980), 10–14; and Teske, "Laien, Laienmönche, II. Teil," *Frühmittelalterliche Studien*, 11 (1977), 326.

[13]Longué, fol. 56r–v. Clairvaux II, p. 219, no. 19. These documents are both edited by Jean-Marc Roger, "Les Morhier Champenois," *Bulletin philologique et historique du Comité des travaux historiques et scientifiques*, 1978, pp. 118–20, nos. 20–21.

[14]Peter the Venerable, Letter 185, *Letters*, I:427–34. See also Verdon, "Les moniales," p. 254.

[15]See, for example, the viscount of Bassigny's donation of his daughter, together with three *mansi* of land, to the nuns of Poulangy in 1038, "with the assent of all my relatives"; Jobin, *St. Bernard*, pp. 555–56, no. 1.

in the life they had chosen for him. For example, the eleventh-century chronicle of St.-Bénigne of Dijon tells the story of Halinard, whose relatives placed him in the cathedral chapter of Langres when he was young. After a few years however he converted to the monastic life and joined the abbey of St.-Bénigne (he eventually became abbot in 1031), and, the chronicle relates, his relatives were furious.[16] This sort of family pressure was not restricted to the eleventh century. In the early twelfth century, Bernard of Clairvaux argued, without success, that his own nephew Robert should not be bound to Cluny by an oath his parents had taken for him when he became an oblate there. Bernard also stated that a young man who had left a house of Augustinian canons for the cathedral chapter of Langres at the prompting of his uncle, the dean, ought to ignore this uncle's advice. "What has tempted you to leave the path you began so well?" Bernard demanded of the young canon. "'Uncle,' you say, just as Adam said, 'My wife,' and Eve, 'The serpent,' when trying to excuse their sin."[17] It was generally only the holy and the saints who were able, as boys or youths, to make their own decisions, in spite of pressure from their relatives.

Once a family had decided to make a son or daughter an ecclesiastic and had determined which church he or she should enter, the next decision to be made was the size and type of gifts which would accompany the new ecclesiastic. As the work of Joseph Lynch has made clear, a church receiving a new member always expected a gift at the same time. This was true whether the convert was a child oblate, an adolescent, or a mature adult. Although the amount of the gift was not fixed, being quite variable even among people who entered at the same time, and although the changing concept of simony during the twelfth century changed the entrance gift theoretically from a required payment to a free-will offering, in practice some sort of gift to the church was always expected to accompany the new oblate. Monasteries, cathedral chapters, and nunneries all expected such gifts throughout the eleventh and twelfth centuries.[18]

---

[16]See Appendix C, p. 425.

[17]Bernard of Clairvaux, Letters 1–2, *Opera*, VII (Rome, 1974), 1–22. The dean of Langres who insisted that his nephew join him in the cathedral chapter was probably Willenc of Aigremont, later bishop (1125–1136). The nephew went on to become archdeacon of the chapter. See Appendix B, pp. 395–96.

[18]Lynch, *Simoniacal Entry into Religious Life*, pp. 17–18, 27–36, 49–50; and Lynch, "Monastic Recruitment," pp. 431–36. Lynch's work is primarily on monasteries, but cathedral chapters too regularly received entrance gifts. See for example M 386 (pp. 221, 254). For the entry gifts that accompanied nuns, see Crisenon 56 (fol. 22v); Marcigny 18, 21, 22, 25 (pp. 18–21, 23); Arch. Côte-d'Or, 7 H 1830, 1845 (entry gifts to La Chapelle d'Oze, a nunnery dependent on Molesme); and, more generally, Verdon, "Les moniales," p. 252. For English parallels, see J. C. Ward, "Fashions in Monastic Endowment: The Foundations of the Clare Family, 1066–1314," *Journal of Ecclesiastical History*, 32 (1981), 436.

Late in the eleventh century, two knights who entered the Cluniac priory of St.-Marcel-lès-Chalon gave the monks a great deal of property, both allods and fiefs, with the consent of the wife and son of one of the knights. When another knight entered St.-Marcel in 1091, he recorded his entry gift and stated that he was "leaving the world and desired to inherit in the world to come." When the knight Agano of Bar entered Clairvaux around 1140, he gave a large amount of land to the monks with the consent of some of his relatives; these relatives later helped Clairvaux recover this property from other relatives who had not originally consented to the gift and tried to reclaim it.[19] The entry gift was such an important part of a noble's entry into the church that it went with him when he changed churches, as was the case in the late twelfth century when Lord Josbert of Vosne decided to move from Cîteaux, where he originally made an adult conversion, to Cîteaux's daughter house of La Bussière.[20]

Nobles, knowing that monks required a substantial entry gift, sometimes tried to avoid paying it by making an earlier property transfer stand in the place of the entry gift. Josbert of Vosne's sizable entry gift for Cîteaux, which he later took to La Bussière, had actually been given to the monks several years before his original conversion. At the end of a donation charter might be the comment that the abbot had promised to receive the donor as a monk if he later decided to leave the world. This provision was especially common in eleventh- and early twelfth-century charters. Generally, however, the donor had to make an additional entry gift when he came to convert, even though his original gift had assured him that at least his petition would be acceptable to the monks. For example, when Hugh of Tory and his wife gave half a *mansus* to Marcigny in the 1130s, the donation charter specified that they would be received there if they decided to take the habit. However, when Hugh fell ill a short time later and did take the habit, he gave Marcigny some additional allodial land and also confirmed his initial gift.[21]

If the monks felt that someone's gift was too insubstantial to promise to receive him as a monk, they were alert to any later attempt to let this initial gift serve as an entry gift. For example, in the first half of the twelfth century, the knight William of Corabois gave the Cistercian monks of Fontenay a large amount of land, between Flacey and Seigny (some seven kilometers southeast of the abbey), in return for twenty-seven pounds Provins, forty solidi Dijon, and a palfrey. His father and his brother, his feudal lord, and the local viscount all

[19]St.-Marcel 67, 108–9, 114 (pp. 65, 91–92, 94). Clairvaux/Waquet 19 (pp. 45–46).
[20]La Bussière 2.1 (fol. 12r). Cîteaux and La Bussière are thirty kilometers apart, with Vosne halfway between.
[21]Marcigny 201, 202 (pp. 117–18).

approved. William stated in the attesting charter that, if one of his young sons (still too young to confirm his father's transaction) became a monk at Fontenay, he would not "duplo redderet" this land, because it was already the monks.'[22]

An entry gift might be a sum of money or the right to receive a certain revenue, or it might be a gift of servile dependents,[23] but usually the entry gift involved a piece of land. The agreement of the whole family was needed in order to alienate part of their inheritance, and in fact the monks of a house receiving a new oblate generally demanded the approval of all relatives, in the hope (not always fulfilled) that they would not later try to reappropriate a gift to which they had agreed (see below, Chapter 9).

Young Adult Conversions

All the elements of an oblate's entry into the church—the choice of a type of religious life, of a particular house, and the gift that should be made—required the decision and cooperation of his older relatives. When a man (or, more rarely, a woman) converted to the religious life in young adulthood, he had to make most of these decisions himself. Adult converts almost always chose a monastery or house of regular canons, very rarely a cathedral chapter or other body of secular canons. Although there were always some men who, on reaching adulthood, decided to leave the secular life their parents had chosen for them in favor of the cloister, they were rather uncommon in the eleventh century. In Cluniac constitutions, they were called *conversi*, converts who, not having learned Latin as boys, could not normally participate fully in the liturgy.[24]

In the early twelfth century, by contrast, the houses of the new orders, most notably the Cistercian order, were peopled largely by men who had decided to join the monastery as adults. The early explosive growth of the order was possible only because a considerable number of young nobles decided to leave the secular world for the rigorous life and sanctity of the order. Some of the new converts had already learned their Latin in secular schools (as had Bernard of Clairvaux), some learned it at the monastery, and some, the Cistercian *conversi*, were illiterates, often of peasant stock, who were not expected to sing in the choir with the monks but were counted on to provide much of

[22]Fontenay II, fols. 15r–16r, no. 41.
[23]The viscount of Avallon's daughter made two servile families her entry gift to St.-Julien of Auxerre in the 1130s; Quantin I.161, p. 277.
[24]Teske, "Laien, Laienmönche, I. Teil," pp. 255–57, 282–85. See also Peter the Venerable, Letter 112, *Letters,* I:299–301.

the agricultural labor. Nobles who decided to join the Cistercian order almost invariably became choir monks, a practice institutionalized by the Cistercian chapter general in 1188.[25]

The decision that these young adults had made to forsake the secular world might have taken them on Crusade instead of to the cloister. In the mid-twelfth century Peter the Venerable, abbot of Cluny, wrote to a young knight who was hesitating between Jerusalem and the monastery to argue that the humility and poverty of the monastic life served God better than the pride and luxury of a trip to Jerusalem, and that it was better to meet Christ face to face in heaven, after a life as a monk, than, as a Crusader, only to see the land His feet had trod.[26] In either event, crusading or a monastic conversion both required a denial of the normal comforts and expectations of a knight or noble. Orderic Vitalis, writing about forty years after Cîteaux's foundation, said that a great many young nobles (*multi nobiles athletae*) flocked to join the Cistercian order and "willingly embraced the unaccustomed rigor of its life."[27] Overall, most of the young men who joined the Cistercian order as choir monks were of the lower nobility or from the ranks of knights, men like the *armiger* of Lord Thomas of Marle, who persuaded Bernard of Clairvaux around 1117 to let him join Clairvaux, becoming a member of "Christ's militia" rather than a knight in the "secular militia," as Lord Thomas had wanted him to be.[28]

Though the decision to leave the world for the "apostolic life" was made by the young adult convert himself, his family usually had plenty to say on the matter. Some families supported their sons' conversions, but others tried actively to prevent it. Bernard of Clairvaux urged several young men to become Cistercian monks even against their parents' objections, quoting Jesus, "He that loveth father or mother more than me is not worthy of me" (Matt. 10:37), and Jerome, "If your father lies prostrate on the doorstep, if your mother shows you the breasts from which you sucked, if your little nephew hangs from your neck, tread over them, with dry eyes fixed on the Cross."[29] Bernard recognized that this attitude was harsh, but he nonetheless believed the individual's salvation lay in his breaking away from his family and their concern for things of the world.

But it was not always easy to break away from the world. If the

[25]Canivez, *Statuta*, I:108, no. 8.

[26]Peter the Venerable, Letter 51, *Letters*, I:151−52.

[27]Orderic Vitalis, *Historia ecclesiastica* 8.26, ed. Marjorie Chibnall, IV (Oxford, 1973), 326.

[28]Bernard of Clairvaux, Letter 441, *Opera*, VIII (Rome, 1977), 419.

[29]Bernard of Clairvaux, Letters 104, 110, 111, 322, *Opera*, VII:261−63, 282−85; VIII:256−58. Jerome, Letter 14, ed. Isidorus Hilberg, *Epistolae*, Corpus scriptorum ecclesiasticorum Latinorum 54 (Vienna and Leipzig, 1910), pp. 46−47.

man was the heir to his parents' castle, the inheritance had to be arranged otherwise.[30] If the man was already married, his wife would have to consent—and generally enter a convent herself—before any monastery would accept him.[31] Even when the family raised no objection to the young man's decision to become a monk, they had to agree to the gift that he made to the monastery upon entering. Family solidarity was so strong that a man who decided to enter the cloister as an adult often persuaded a number of his relatives to accompany him, as indicated below.

Conversions in Later Life

Even men who had determined to become monks tended to put off conversion as long as possible. The biographer of Herluin, the founder of the important Norman abbey of Bec in the 1030s, said that Herluin faced ridicule for leaving a knightly position for the monastery in the prime of his life. More typical was one of Bec's neighbors, who used to say he would become a monk "after he had grown weary of arms and satiated with worldly pleasure." In the 1130s Bernard of Clairvaux warmly commended a young Cistercian convert who had resisted the "advice" of his friends that he wait to take the habit until he had reached "maturiorem aetatem."[32] But mature converts were common even among the Cistercians. For example, the knight Salo of Bouilly, who served the lords of Seignelay in his youth and was given the fief of Bouilly by these lords in his middle years, married, raised a family, and entered the Cistercian house of Pontigny as a monk only when his son was old enough to inherit. Old-age or even deathbed conversions were always common among the Burgundian nobility, since they wished to continue enjoying the secular life as long as they were healthy, even though they wanted to die in the sanctity of the cloister.[33] Sometimes even men

[30]See also Wollasch, "Parenté noble et monachisme réformateur," p. 4; and Brenda M. Bolton, "Paupertas Christi: Old Wealth and New Poverty in the Twelfth Century," in *Renaissance and Renewal in Christian History*, ed. Derek Baker, Studies in Church History 14 (Oxford, 1977), p. 96.

[31]At a council at Rome around 1075, Pope Gregory VII ordered that, if a man or woman wished to enter the cloister, his or her spouse should ideally also become a nun or monk, or at a minimum agree to live chastely; Pflugk-Harttung, II:126, no. 20.

[32]Gilbert Crispin, "Vita Herluini," PL CL:699, 703. See also Sally N. Vaughn, *The Abbey of Bec and the Anglo-Norman State, 1034–1136* (Woodbridge, England, 1981), p. 6. Bernard of Clairvaux, Letter 322, *Opera*, VIII:256–58.

[33]Pontigny 129, 139 (pp. 190–91, 198–99). Quantin I.334 (pp. 487–89). Peter the Venerable tried to keep older men, who had no intention of learning the liturgy or doing manual labor, from becoming monks at Cluny, saying that their idleness led to devastation of a monastery; *Statuta* 48, PL CLXXXIX:1038.

who had spent much of their adult lives attacking the possessions of the local monks might try to buy their way to salvation by taking the habit at the end of their lives.

Bishops as well as powerful nobles often took the monastic habit. In the eleventh century, a bishop might retire to the monastery to live out his final years. Such was the case with Bishop Walter of Mâcon (1031–1061), who retired to Cluny. In the twelfth century, it was more common for a bishop to wait until he was dying to become a monk, as did Bishop Robert of Langres, who in 1111 took the habit at Molesme, located in his diocese, or Hugh III, bishop of Auxerre (1136–1151), who returned to Pontigny, where he had once been abbot, to die. Alain, bishop of Auxerre (1152–1167), who had been a monk at Clairvaux earlier in his career and retired there for the last fifteen years of his life, was quite unusual among bishops of the twelfth century in that he retired to the cloister while still healthy.[34] These bishops all chose houses familiar to them, often houses in their dioceses, perhaps houses where they had once been monks themselves or houses with which they were otherwise well acquainted.

Noble widows, like their male counterparts, frequently joined a religious house in their maturity, especially in the twelfth century. While men often waited until they were in their declining years to convert, however, women often entered a nunnery after their husbands' deaths and long before their own.[35] The best-known house for noble widows was Fontevraud, located between Anjou and Poitou. It had begun as a group of hermits and wandering disciples following Robert of Arbrissel, but Fontevraud early lost its itinerant nature. The influx of wealthy widows mitigated the harshness of its original life, but Fontevraud still represented a house where noble women could hope to find salvation as well as refuge.[36]

In Burgundy, the principal house for widows in the eleventh and twelfth centuries was Marcigny, a daughter of Cluny, as mentioned above. Even quite powerful women from other parts of Europe were attracted to Marcigny; Adela, countess of Blois and daughter of William the Conqueror, was a nun at Marcigny in the first part of the

---

[34]For these bishops, see Appendix B, pp. 398, 395, 389–90. For other examples of bishops becoming monks, see Joachim Mehne, "Cluniacenserbischöfe," *Frühmittelalterliche Studien*, 11 (1977), 267–69, 275–76.

[35]See also Verdon, "Les moniales," pp. 251–55.

[36]See, most recently, Jacques Dalarun, *L'impossible sainteté: La vie retrouvée de Robert d'Arbrissel (v. 1045–1116), fondateur de Fontevraud* (Paris, 1985), pp. 176–91. See also Jean-Marc Bienvenu, "Robert d'Arbrissel et la fondation de Fontevraud (1101)," *Cahiers d'histoire*, 20 (1975), 227–43; Jacqueline Smith, "Robert of Arbrissel: *Procurator mulierum*," in *Medieval Women*, ed. Derek Baker (Oxford, 1978), pp. 175–84; and Penny Schine Gold, *The Lady & the Virgin: Image, Attitude, and Experience in Twelfth-Century France* (Chicago, 1985), pp. 93–113.

twelfth century.[37] The other principal Burgundian nunneries were Larrey, dependent on St.-Bénigne, St.-Julien of Auxerre, and St.-Andoche and St.-Jean-le-Grand of Autun. In the twelfth century, newly formed nunneries included Tart, a house loosely affiliated with Cîteaux, and Jully, which was dependent on Molesme. These houses provided refuge for women who, having often married men much older than they, expected a long widowhood. When Bernard of Clairvaux's aunt Aanold was widowed for the second time, she became a nun at Jully and gave the house the ten pounds a year of income at Bar-sur-Aube which her husband had held in fief from the count of Troyes, with the consent of this count, her late husband's brother, her son, and her nephews, including Bernard of Clairvaux.[38]

As this example indicates, when men or women converted to the religious life in old age, they still had to deal with their relatives' opinions. The family had to confirm the entrance gift, and if the convert was married the family's approval was needed to allow him or her to leave the world. For example, when Hugh of Vaux and his wife Maria decided to take the monastic habit around 1105, they agreed that they would both serve God under Abbot Hugh of Cluny; he entered the priory of Paray-le-monial and she entered Marcigny. In the early twelfth century, when the knight Walter of Avalleur felt he was dying, he had his children carry him to Molesme, where he took the habit. After his death his children tried to reclaim the property he had given the monks but were persuaded to drop their claim to a gift they had earlier approved.[39]

Though the family of a convert was thus always influential at whatever age he entered the church, from the individual's point of view conversion was a somewhat different process if he joined the church in his later years. The decision of a mature convert was usually not the decision to spend his entire life struggling for holiness, but rather to spend the last years of his life in as holy an atmosphere as possible. To leave the world for a life of obedience and personal poverty was an act of penance, and participation in the community life was considered to ensure participation in the community's spiritual benefits. Older men generally entered the house of the region with the greatest reputation for holiness; Cluny in the eleventh century, Molesme at the end of the eleventh and beginning of the twelfth centuries, and Cistercian houses throughout the twelfth century were thronged with mature converts.

[37]Peter the Venerable, Letter 15, *Letters*, I:22.
[38]Jully, pp. 257–58; the editor incorrectly identifies Aanold as the mother of Bernard of Clairvaux. See Appendix A, p. 337.
[39]Marcigny 115 (pp. 84–85). Molesme 1.203, 209 (II:187, 192–93).

Motives for Noble Conversion

While it is fairly clear that a late religious impulse and a fear of imminent death impelled a number of mature converts, many modern scholars have been unwilling to accept religious conviction as the chief motivating force behind noble parents' decision to make their young children ecclesiastics. Often it is assumed that, if a family produced more children than could be conveniently set up in the world, the cathedral or the cloister provided a handy way to dispose of the excess.[40] Similarly, young adults who decided to enter the church are sometimes described as seeking an easier life or greater dignity of office by becoming ecclesiastics.[41] But an examination of the sources shows that the situation was in fact much more complicated.

First, it should be noted, placing children in the church was not a cheap way to assure them a living. The large entry gifts that monasteries, nunneries, and cathedral chapters expected to accompany new ecclesiastics often seems to have required an outlay comparable to what it would have cost the parents to give a son a share of the inheritance or a daughter a dowry and set them up in the world. In the late eleventh century, Anna, daughter of Richard of La Douze, was made a nun at St.-Jean-le-Grand of Autun by her parents when she was very young, and the nuns later noted explicitly that they had received her "for that land which her mother had received as her own marriage portion."[42] Since unmarried younger sons often remained in an older brother's castle with him or, if they left, did homage to him for their lands,[43] in many cases it seems in fact to have been economically sounder to keep younger sons in the secular world, where their share of the inheritance would remain attached to their older brother's patrimony, rather than to send them into the cloister, where the property they took with them would be permanently alienated from the family. And in the case of cathedral canons, since they (unlike

---

[40]Georges Duby, *The Knight, the Lady and the Priest: The Making of Modern Marriage in Medieval France*, trans. Barbara Bray (New York, 1983), p. 105.

[41]Jean-François Lemarignier, "Les institutions ecclésiastiques en France de la fin du Xe au milieu du XIIe siècle," in *Institutions ecclésiastiques*, ed. Ferdinand Lot and Robert Fawtier, Histoire des institutions françaises au moyen âge 3 (Paris, 1962), pp. 62–63. See also George T. Beech, *A Rural Society in Medieval France: The Gâtine of Poitou in the Eleventh and Twelfth Centuries* (Baltimore, 1964), p. 89.

[42]Marcigny 175 (p. 104). When Otbert, abbot of the Augustinian house of Ste.-Marguerite, agreed in 1140 to pay his niece's entry gift to St.-Andoche of Autun, after his sister (the girl's mother) had given his house a large amount of land, he said that raising the required amount was done "not without serious hardship"; Arch. Côte-d'Or, 20 H 674.

[43]Georges Duby, *La société aux XIe et XIIe siècles dans la région mâconnaise*, 2nd ed. (Paris, 1971), pp. 322–24. Bouchard, "The Structure of a Twelfth-Century Family," pp. 49–51.

monks) could continue to claim a share of the inheritance even after entering the church,[44] the family could scarcely hope to reduce the number of claims on the patrimony simply by sending sons into the cathedral. Of course ecclesiastics who took a vow of chastity would not produce additional children for their relatives to provide for, as might their secular brothers, but this future economic advantage alone scarcely counterbalanced the immediate and permanent loss of property. Clearly, economic gain to the family is not the only explanation for the placement of members in the church.

Similarly, entering the ecclesiastical life was not equivalent to entering a life of ease and dignity. Novices in the monastery or new members of the cathedral chapter indeed generally lost some of their dignity of position: from being noble sons with a flock of attendants to obey them, they became ecclesiastics whose first duty was obedience to their superiors. The rise to capitular or claustral office or other position of authority generally took years, especially in the twelfth century. And, indeed, the most austere religious movements of the twelfth century, the ones in which converts adopted a life of sharp humiliation and poverty and which enforced long noviciates, were those which attracted the greatest number of noble converts.

That noble families were not simply disposing of excess children in sending them into the church is further attested by the fact that a number of families produced no ecclesiastics at all for generations. And those families were not necessarily the ones with only a few children. The lords of Beaujeu, for example, who can be traced back to the mid-tenth century, are known to have produced two adult sons in the first generation after the castellany was founded, three sons in the second generation, three in the third, four in the fourth, and four in the fifth, but it was not until the fifth generation that any of these sons entered the church. The counts of Chalon are not known to have sent any sons into the church after Hugh, who was simultaneously count of Chalon and bishop of Auxerre (999—1039), even though they produced as many as five adult males in one generation at the end of the eleventh century.[45]

Similarly, many families with numerous female children sent no daughters into the cloister, which suggests that the nunnery was more than an escape valve for families with too many daughters. The lord

---

[44]When three knightly brothers of Toucy gave some servile peasants to St.-Germain of Auxerre in 1155, their two brothers in the cathedral chapter of Sens also had to confirm; Quantin I.373 (pp. 533—34). For other examples of cathedral canons inheriting, see Molesme 1.28, 217 (II:40—43, 198—200); and Crisenon 146 (fol. 74r).

[45]See Appendix A, pp. 289—95, 307—14. Though Parisse, in studying the nobility of Lorraine, called it a "classic rule" that at least one son per generation was sent into the church, his own evidence indicates that numerous Lotharingian families produced no ecclesiastics; "La noblesse Lorraine," pp. 340, 403.

of Ramerupt had seven daughters in the middle of the eleventh century, but, rather than sending any into the church, he married them all off, and married them well.[46] The dukes of Burgundy sent only one daughter into the church in the eleventh and twelfth centuries, even though they produced a large number of daughters in several generations, and several of the girls' brothers were cathedral canons. Clearly noble families were not helpless in finding appropriate positions for their children in the secular world.

In contrast, some families committed what Alexander Murray has called "dynastic suicide" by regularly sending into the church more sons than could conveniently be spared if the family were to ensure continued existence and reproduction. The family of Tescelin Sorus, lord of Fontaines-lès-Dijon, is strikingly illustrative. In 1113 Tescelin's son Bernard, the future abbot of Clairvaux, became a monk at Cîteaux (a monastery located twenty-five kilometers south of Fontaines) and persuaded all his large family (five brothers and a sister) to convert. None of them had previously shown any tendency toward the church or been encouraged to take up the ecclesiastical life by their parents, even though the lordship of Fontaines was scarcely a wealthy one. Bernard's biographer tells the charming story of Bernard's youngest brother, who had been designated as the one to remain in the world and continue the family after all his relatives became monks. He complained that he had been deprived of heaven by remaining in the world and shortly followed his brothers into the monastery. Bernard's neighbors, the *Vita* indicates, had a very real fear that he might similarly entice all *their* sons and brothers into the cloister, ending their lineages as he had ended his own.[47]

Examples of such dynastic suicide could certainly be multiplied. During the 1120s, Lord William of Tilchâtel made one of his sons a canon at the Augustinian church of St.-Étienne of Dijon, but, not satisfied with having thus disposed of an excess son, he stipulated that if this son died, a second would become a canon, and indeed that if the second died, a third should join the church.[48] Bochard of Seignelay, who lived toward the end of the twelfth century, originally intended his two sons who survived infancy for the knightly life, but

---

[46] Alberic de Trois-Fontaines, *Chronica* 1063, MGH SS XXIII:794.

[47] *Vita prima Sancti Bernardi* 1.3, PL CLXXXV:235−36. See also Appendix A, pp. 329−31; Murray, *Reason and Society*, pp. 346−47; and Wollasch, "Parenté noble et monachisme réformateur," pp. 20−21. For another example of dynastic suicide, the founder of the first Cistercian house in Languedoc, who persuaded his wife and children to leave the world with him, see Derek Baker, "Popular Piety in the Lodèvois in the Early Twelfth Century: The Case of Pons de Léras," in *Religious Motivation: Biographical and Sociological Problems for the Church Historian*, ed. Derek Baker, Studies in Church History 15 (Oxford, 1978), p. 41.

[48] St.-Étienne II.29 (pp. 38−39). See also Appendix A, p. 368.

he was instead persuaded by his brother, the archbishop of Sens, to send them *both* into the cathedral of Sens.[49] Indeed, Joseph Lynch's statistical study of the family size of those families which sent oblates into eight northern French monasteries suggests that in over 10 percent of the cases the oblate was the only son.[50] Certainly there were more considerations involved than economic expedience if some families functioned perfectly well without making any sons churchmen and others threw dynastic prudence to the winds in a rush to join the church.

For those families which did send children into the church, the evidence suggests that the decision was made when they were quite young; families did not simply wait, until ignorance of birth control and/or a decline in child mortality produced an uncomfortably large number of adolescents, to determine that some should be sent into the church. That a son was intended for the cloister or cathedral chapter from the time of his birth is often indicated by his parents' naming him after an older relative already in the church.[51] For example, Bishop Bruno of Langres was the great-nephew of Bishop Bruno of Cologne, and he himself had a nephew Bruno who was a canon at Langres under him. Gibuin, bishop of Châlons in the second half of the tenth century, had a nephew Gibuin, bishop of Châlons at the very end of the tenth century, who was the uncle of the secular canon Gibuin of Beaumont. Robert, bishop of Langres at the beginning of the twelfth century, was great-uncle of Robert, bishop of Autun later in the century.[52] In all these cases, these names were used exclusively in the particular family, or nearly so, for ecclesiastics. Since names were not given haphazardly in the eleventh and twelfth centuries, parents who gave their infant sons such names were clearly identifying them with older ecclesiastical relatives. In destining their sons from an early age to careers in the church, medieval families were establishing that someone would occupy a position they believed was very worthwhile.

Though the monks always felt a need to be vigilant against parents who might put unwanted or infirm children into the church, there is little evidence of this practice before the thirteenth century, and

---

[49]*Gesta pontificum*, pp. 451–53. See also Appendix A, p. 356.

[50]Lynch, *Simoniacal Entry into Religious Life*, p. 43.

[51]Although it could be argued that a boy's name might have been changed when he entered the church, such a practice was rare before the thirteenth century. Bochard of Seignelay's sons, mentioned above, appear in the charters with the same names before and after they left the knightly life for the cathedral school. When children (lay or ecclesiastical) took a new name, they generally took a *double* name rather than abandoning their old one (for example, Otto-William, count of Burgundy, or Hugh-Rainard, bishop of Langres).

[52]See Appendix A, pp. 269, 320, 258–60.

healthy children always predominated among oblates.[53] When in 1178 Geoffrey of Menou gave the Cistercian monks of Les Roches all the property he had at Chenet, it was on the condition that the monks clothe and feed his (apparently) retarded son, but there was no intention on either side that the boy become a monk. Indeed, Geoffrey specified that if the boy chose to leave the house, the monks need no longer care for him; had he been a monk, he would not have been able to leave the monastery.[54]

Rather than attempt to project modern notions of practical gain onto the actions of those medieval families which sent children into the church, it may be more profitable to consider the very real issue of spiritual return. The monk, whose way of life was considered to make him more holy than men in the world, would be more likely to have his prayers answered than other men. And a great many families felt the need of efficacious prayers, which a relative in the cloister would provide. But entry into the church could be prompted by motives and interests other than the family's concerns. Alexander Murray has advanced several possible explanations why individual members of the nobility would have been more likely than members of any other social class to be moved by religious considerations. Seeing nobles as characterized above all by their power, wealth, and military function, Murray suggests that each of these attributes made them particularly susceptible to thoughts of leaving the world for the church. Their power and the greatness of soul they attempted to display, he continues, led them to assaults on ever-higher rungs in the ladder of virtue and to such grand gestures as leaving behind a life of power for a life of humiliation. Similarly, their wealth often led to a "sickness of soul" when it became clear that things of the world could never completely satisfy, and their military function put them in positions where they had to face the likelihood of their own death or experienced revulsion at their own violence to others.[55] His suggestions are indeed stimulating and should encourage debate on their psychological validity, even though they are applicable only to young adult conversions, but their greatest contribution perhaps is in making it clear that many factors besides worldly prudence could move men to convert from the worldly life.

The medieval nobility must, like modern men, have acted for a variety of reasons, and economics or a realization that a particular

[53]Lynch, *Simoniacal Entry into Religious Life*, pp. 40–43; and Lynch, "Monastic Recruitment," p. 429.

[54]Arch. Nièvre, H 143, no. 7. The castle of Menou is southeast of Les Roches, eight kilometers west of Varzy. Chenet is located three kilometers to the north.

[55]Murray, *Reason and Society*, chap. 15, "Religious Effects of the Noble Condition," pp. 350–82.

child was not really fitted for the noble life may have often played a part in their decisions, but they must also have had a belief in the importance of salvation and a belief that salvation could be most easily obtained with relatives in the church. And this concern for salvation was always expressed, at whatever age a person entered the church, in terms of the family: the family's traditional ties with a particular church, or relatives within the cloister, the family's willingness to grant part of their patrimony to the church along with the new ecclesiastic, and their interest in obtaining the benefit of the prayers the convert would offer for them.

Nobles therefore followed several different patterns in entering the church, correlated in large part with the age of the convert. Those who had entered the church as children were found particularly in cathedral chapters, most of the eleventh-century monasteries, and the more traditional houses of the twelfth century. The parents of these oblates decided for them what sort of religious life they would pursue and in which particular house they would pursue it. They set these children in the church as their own offering of a precious possession to the church and to provide a worthwhile life for the child himself.[56] Those who entered the church in young adulthood (a pattern much more common in the twelfth century than in the eleventh) seem to have done so out of weariness for the world or a sudden strong religious conviction; they tended to enter the strictest houses, where the monks sought to seize salvation through humiliation and fervent prayer. Conversion in young adulthood was much more a personal decision, and the role of the convert's family seems often to have been to try to dissuade him. Those who entered the church toward the end of their lives entered a spectrum of monasteries, including both the newer, stricter houses and more traditional monasteries; there they pondered their sins and tried to prepare themselves for the salvation promised those participating in the house's spiritual benefits.

There are several common factors involving noble entry into the church at whatever age the conversion was made: oblates and converts almost always entered nearby houses, often ones their relatives were already in, and they entered because of their own or their relatives' belief in the value of at least some aspects of the religious life. Moreover, far from constituting merely a surplus component consigned to a sanctified and comfortable oblivion, the noble offspring who entered the church as child oblates and those who converted as young adults provided the pool from which most church leaders were drawn, as the following chapter shows.

[56]See the Cluniac formula by which a man gave his son as an oblate, promising not to take this offering back again; *Consuetudines Cluniacensium antiquiores cum redactionibus derivatis*, ed. Kassius Hallinger, Corpus consuetudinum monasticarum 7, 2 (Sieburg, 1983), pp. 378–79.

[2]

The Social Origins of
Ecclesiastical Leaders

Because nobles entered the church more frequently than did other members of society, there was a disproportionately large number of noble ecclesiastics in the pool from which new church leaders were chosen. There was however no consensus on whether it was to the church's advantage for its leaders to be the brothers of the leaders of secular society. This chapter briefly surveys the opinions expressed in the Middle Ages on giving high church office to those noble by birth, then discusses the social origins and the changes in the origins of the men who headed Burgundy's sees and major abbeys in the eleventh and twelfth centuries.

Medieval Attitudes toward Noble Churchmen

Ecclesiastical thinkers had a somewhat ambivalent attitude toward the nobility. On the one hand, the monks and cathedral canons who elected the sons and brothers of secular lords to church office had a great respect for family origins. Indeed, nobility was sometimes a contributing factor in determining someone's suitability for high ecclesiastical office. At the end of the eleventh century, for example, the canonist Ivo of Chartres emphasized not only the regularity of the election but also the noble blood of an archbishop of Sens whose ascension he supported, when the election was questioned by the papal legate.[1] On the other hand, some theoreticians argued

[1]Ivo of Chartres, Letter 59, PL CLXII:70. See also Constance B. Bouchard, "The Geographical, Social and Ecclesiastical Origins of the Bishops of Auxerre and Sens in the Central Middle Ages," *Church History*, 46 (1977), 283; and Georges Duby, *The Three Orders: Feudal Society Imagined*, trans. Arthur Goldhammer (Chicago, 1980), p. 225.

electing nobles to high church office, saying that their powerful relatives could disrupt church affairs or that rich trappings were inappropriate in a church of "Christ's poor."[2]

Ambivalent attitudes toward noble church leaders went back at least to Carolingian times. The election of a new abbot of Fulda in the early ninth century, for example, was the occasion for arguments on both sides. Those who wished a monk *de nobili genere* for their new abbot argued, "If we elect him, he will defend us against the counts and those more powerful than us, and indeed he will attract the emperor's favor because of his high position." Other monks, however, recalling 1 Cor. 1:26–28, said that God had preferred the "weak things of the world and things which are despised" and that the humility necessary in a follower of Christ precluded nobility. Paul's words in 1 Corinthians, "not many mighty, not many noble, are called," became a commonplace in arguments against making nobles abbots or bishops.[3]

But the Bible could also provide citations in favor of secular nobles as ecclesiastical leaders. In the early twelfth century, for example, Bernard of Segni began his commentary on Matthew by arguing that the genealogies of the first chapter were meant to show that Mary, Jesus's only human parent, was the heiress of a line of great nobles. This was a perfectly logical conclusion at the time, for genealogies composed in the twelfth century were routinely used to demonstrate noble lineage.[4]

Both the positive and negative attitudes toward noble leadership can be seen in Guigo of Chartreuse's *Vita* of Bishop Hugh of Grenoble, written shortly after Hugh's death in 1132. Instead of beginning his work with the standard account of the saint's parents and birth, Guigo opened with a lengthy argument that divine judgment is concerned not with one's ancestors but with one's way of life, that power does not increase merit, and that Christ himself was born of poor parents, and his chief apostles were fishermen. He added the standard reference to 1 Cor. 1:26–28 to these arguments. But then he continued, "Since those who treat of the virtues of the saints are not found to be silent on their carnal births, I shall mention briefly . . ." and went on to describe Hugh's noble ancestry and castellan father. Although Guigo himself believed that noble birth had no ultimate importance,

[2] Alexander Murray, *Reason and Society in the Middle Ages* (Oxford, 1978), pp. 319–30.

[3] Candidus, "Vita Eigilis abbatis Fuldensis" 5, MGH SS XV:224. Murray, *Reason and Society*, p. 328.

[4] Bernard of Segni, "Commentaria in Matthaeum" 1.1, PL CLXV:73. Georges Duby, "French Genealogical Literature: The Eleventh and Twelfth Centuries," in *The Chivalrous Society*, trans. Cynthia Postan (Berkeley and Los Angeles, 1977), pp. 149–57.

he felt he could not avoid mentioning Hugh's exalted parentage, influential in this world if not in the next.[5]

The discussion on whether it was good to have the church headed by men noble by secular criteria was carried on in a church in which bishops, abbots, and abbesses were in fact generally noble.[6] This discussion then was far from theoretical; it grew out of the question whether the church's hierarchy ought to continue to be drawn from the same social group, or whether there should be substantial changes. No drastic changes came about during the High Middle Ages; church leaders continued to be drawn from the nobility. Yet there *are* differences, subtle but real, between the origins of ecclesiastical leaders in the eleventh century and in the twelfth, as the following survey of Burgundian bishops and abbots indicates.

The Social Origins of Burgundian Bishops

During most of the eleventh century, Burgundian bishops were generally put into office because of the influence of their secular relatives. Less frequently a great lord made one of his non-noble servitors bishop as a reward for his loyalty, a practice that went back at least to the Carolingians.[7] Adalgar, bishop of Autun at the end of the ninth century, had been given his office by the king and used his position to help the advancement of his nephew, ancestor of the eleventh-century counts of Nevers.[8] The kings, dukes, and other great lords who chose many of the bishops of the eleventh century chose primarily men from the upper nobility.

At Auxerre the six bishops who held office between the end of the tenth century and the end of the eleventh included Heribert (971–

---

[5]Guigo of Chartreuse, "Vita S. Hugonis Gratianopolitani" 1, PL CLIII:763–74.

[6]Jean Gaudemet, "Recherches sur l'épiscopat médiévale en France," in *Proceedings of the Second International Congress of Medieval Canon Law*, ed. Stephan Kuttner and J. Joseph Ryan (Vatican City, 1965), pp. 139–54. Bernard Guillemain, "Les origines des évêques en France aux XIe et XIIe siècles," in *Le istituzione ecclesiastiche della "Societas Christiana" dei secoli XI–XII: Papato, cardinalato ed episcopato*, Miscellanea del Centro di studi medioevali 7 (Milan, 1974), pp. 384–85, 394. Joseph H. Lynch, "Monastic Recruitment in the Eleventh and Twelfth Centuries: Some Social and Economic Considerations," *American Benedictine Review*, 26 (1975), 425–26. Martine Chauney, "Le recrutement de l'épiscopat bourguignon aux XIe et XIIe siècles," *Annales de Bourgogne*, 47 (1975), 203–4. Bouchard, "Origins of Bishops," pp. 282–83.

[7]In the Rhineland in the same period the emperors appointed many of the bishops, most of them either royal relatives or priests of the royal chapel. Timothy Reuter, "The 'Imperial Church System' of the Ottonian and Salian Rulers: A Reconsideration," *Journal of Ecclesiastical History*, 33 (1982), 352–54. Michel Parisse, "L'évêque et l'Empire au XIe siècle. L'exemple lorrain," *Cahiers de civilisation médiévale*, 27 (1984), 96–98.

[8]See Appendix A, p. 341.

	Family				Ecclesiastical background		
	Upper nobility (dukes, counts, viscounts)	Lower nobility (castellans, knights)	Lowborn	Unknown	Secular clergy	Regular clergy	Unknown
Auxerre							
Heribert I, 971–996	x				x		
John, 996–999			x		x		
Hugh I, 999–1039	x				x		
Heribert II, 1039–1052		x			x		
Geoffrey, 1052–1076	x				x		
Robert, 1076–1092	x				x		
Humbald, 1092–1114		x			x		
Hugh II, 1115–1136		x				x	
Hugh III, 1136–1151		x				x	
Alain, 1152–1167				x		x	
William, 1167–1181		x			x		
Hugh IV, 1183–1206		x			x		
Langres							
Bruno, 980–1016	x				x		
Lambert I, 1016–1031	x				x		
Richard, 1031				x	x		
Hugh, 1031–1049	x				x		
Harduin, 1049–1065	x				x		
Hugh-Rainard, 1065–1084	x				x		
Robert, 1084–1111	x				x		
Lambert II, 1112		x			x		
Joceran, 1113–1125				x	x		
Willenc, 1125–1136		x			x		
William, 1138		x				x	
Geoffrey, 1139–1163		x				x	
Walter, 1163–1179	x				x		
Manasses, 1179–1193	x				x		
Warner, 1193–1200		x				x	
Mâcon							
Milo, 981–993			x		x		
Letbald, 993–1016		x			x		
Jocelin, 1016–1031			x				x
Walter, 1031–1061		x			x		
Drogo, 1061–1072		x			x		
Landric, 1074–1096		x			x		
Berard, 1096–1122		x			x		
Joceran, 1122–1143			x		x		
Ponce, 1144–1166			x				x
Stephen, 1167–1182		x			x		
Raynald, 1182–1198		x			x		

Fig. 1. Social and ecclesiastical origins of the Burgundian bishops in the eleventh and twelfth centuries

	Family				Ecclesiastical background		
	Upper nobility (dukes, counts, viscounts)	Lower nobility (castellans, knights)	Lowborn	Unknown	Secular clergy	Regular clergy	Unknown
Autun							
Walter I, 978–1018				x			x
Helmuin, 1018–1055				x			x
Agano, 1055–1098		x			x		
Narjod, 1098–1112				x	x		
Stephen I, 1112–1139		x			x		
Robert, 1140	x				x		
Humbert, 1140–1148		x			x		
Henry, 1148–1170	x				x		
Stephen II, 1170–1189				x	x		
Walter II, 1189–1223				x		x	
Chalon							
Rudolph, 977–994				x			x
Lambert, 994–1015				x	x		
Geoffrey, 1015–1039				x			x
Gui, 1044–1058				x			x
Achard, 1059–1070				x	x		
Roclenus, 1072–1079		x			x		
Walter I, 1080–1123		x			x		
Jotsald, 1123–1126				x	x		
Walter II, 1126–1158		x			x		
Peter, 1158–1178		x			x		
Engelbert, 1178–1180				x		x	
Robert, 1180–1215				x	x		
Nevers							
Roclenus, 978–1011				x			x
Girard, 1015				x			x
Hugh I, 1016–1069	x				x		
Malguin, 1069–1074				x	x		
Hugh II, 1074–1096	x				x		
Gui, 1097–1099				x			x
Hervé, 1099–1110				x	x		
Hugh III, 1110–1119				x			x
Fromond, 1119–1145				x	x		
Geoffrey, 1146–1159				x			x
Bernard, 1159–1176		x			x		
Theobold, 1176–1188				x	x		
John, 1190–1196				x	x		
Walter, 1196–1202		x			x		

996), illegitimate son of Hugh the Great; John (996–999), a man of undistinguished ancestry, made bishop in return for his service to Hugh Capet; Hugh of Chalon (999–1039), count of Chalon in his own right; Geoffrey (1052–1076), son of the viscount of Nevers; and Robert (1076–1092), son of the count of Nevers and count of Auxerre in his own right. Robert was investigated at the legatine council of Autun in 1077 to determine whether he had received investiture from the king, and though his investiture was declared canonical, he was censured for having taken the office when too young (under the age of thirty).[9] The seven eleventh-century bishops of Langres were Bruno (980–1016), nephew of the Carolingian king Lothair, who put him into office when he was only twenty-four; Lambert (1016–1031), whose sister seems to have been a countess; Richard (1031), imposed by the king on an unwilling chapter; Hugh (1031–1049), son of the count of Verdun, put into office by the king after his first candidate, Richard, had been driven out; Harduin (1049–1065) and Hugh-Rainard (1065–1084), who were first cousins from the family of the counts of Tonnerre; and Robert (1084–1111), brother of the duke of Burgundy. The five eleventh-century bishops of Mâcon included representatives of two of the most powerful families of the Mâconnais: Letbald (993–1016) and Walter (1031–1061), uncle and nephew, from the family of the lords of Brancion; and Landric (1074–1096), brother of the lord of Berzé.[10]

The three eleventh-century bishops of Autun included Agano (1055–1098), brother of the lord of Mt.-St.-Jean. At Chalon, among the six bishops who held office between the late tenth century and the end of the eleventh were Roclenus (1072–1079), of a noble family, and Walter of Couches (1080–1123), called *generosi stemmatis prosapia ortus* in the description of his election.[11] The six eleventh-century bishops of Nevers included two named Hugh (1016–1069 and 1074–1096), great-uncle and great-nephew, both brothers of the viscounts of Nevers, who between them served during most of the century.

Thus, of the bishops elected at the three Burgundian sees for which the documents are plentiful (Auxerre, Langres, and Mâcon), three-quarters can definitely be said to have come from the upper nobility. At the other three dioceses (Autun, Chalon, and Nevers), where documentation is less complete and many more episcopal origins are

---

[9]Chauney incorrectly calls Robert and his predecessor Geoffrey cousins; "Le recrutement de l'épiscopat," p. 198. For these and the following bishops, see the references in Appendix B.

[10]For the importance of these families, see Georges Duby, *La société aux XIe et XIIe siècles dans la région mâconnaise*, 2nd ed. (Paris, 1971), pp. 336–53.

[11]GC IV:231, no. 12.

unknown, about one-third are still known to be noble, and none are known to be of low social status. Overall, well over half the eleventh-century Burgundian bishops, even including those from the less well-documented sees, are definitely known to be of the nobility. Of the others, only John of Auxerre is definitely known to be non-noble—and even he had some family connection to the high aristocracy, for his mother seems to have been the concubine of Hugh the Great before she married his (lower class) father, and John was thus half-brother of Heribert, his predecessor in the see of Auxerre.

A number of those bishops of unknown social origins may have been from the nobility; it is difficult to determine the origins of many, especially those who held office for a very short time, such as Richard, bishop of Langres for five months in 1031, or Bishops Girard (1015) and Gui (1097—1099) of Nevers, who left little record other than their names. But if one postulates that such factors as a bishop's length of time in office, rather than the status of his relatives, determine whether his origins will be known to modern scholars, one can conclude that many of the bishops whose families are not known also came from the upper levels of the aristocracy. This pattern is not limited to Burgundy; studies of the bishops of Liège, Périgueux, Normandy, Brittany, Bordeaux, the Loire valley, the Rhineland, Lorraine, and Sens have shown that in the eleventh century almost all those whose origins are known came from the upper nobility.[12]

In the eleventh century, the selection of men from the upper nobility as bishop can be attributed primarily to the influence of the great lords of the region. Auxerre, closest of the Burgundian sees to Paris, had two bishops chosen by the Capetians. Langres, the largest diocese of the six, had bishops chosen by the next-to-last Carolingian king, by the Capetian king Robert II, and by the Capetian duke of Burgundy, whose capital was in the diocese, at Dijon. The sees of Mâcon, Autun, Chalon, and Nevers, more remote from the influence of the kings of France, were dominated by the relatives of the regional

---

[12]Léopold Genicot, "Haute clergé et noblesse dans le diocèse de Liège du XIe au XIVe siècle," in *Adel und Kirche*, ed. Josef Fleckenstein and Karl Schmid (Freiburg, 1968), p. 246. For a few corrections to Genicot's list of bishops, see Stefan Weinfurter and Odilo Engels, *Series episcoporum ecclesiae Catholicae occidentalis ab initio usque ad annum MCXCVIII*, ser. 5, vol. I (Stuttgart, 1982), pp. 43—83. Muriel Laharie, "Évêques et société en Périgord du Xe au milieu du XIIe siècle," *Annales du Midi*, 94 (1982), 349—50. Guy Devailly, "Les grandes familles et l'épiscopat dans l'ouest de la France et les Pays de la Loire," *Cahiers de civilisation médiévale*, 27 (1984), 49—55. Jacques Boussard, "Les évêques en Neustrie avant la réforme grégorienne (950—1050 environ)," *Journal des savants*, 1970, pp. 170—86. Aloys Schulte, *Der Adel und die deutsche Kirche im Mittelalter* (Stuttgart, 1910), p. 62. Michel Parisse, "La noblesse Lorraine, XIe—XIIIe s." (diss., Université de Nancy II, 1975), pp. 408—12; and Parisse, "L'évêque et l'Empire," pp. 99—101. Bouchard, "Origins of Bishops," pp. 282—83. See also Reuter, "'Imperial Church System,'" p. 355.

counts, viscounts, and powerful castellans. In many cases the great
lords merely imposed their relatives on a cathedral chapter. But the
influence of the great nobility could also be expressed more subtly.
The cathedral canons of the eleventh century, many of them noble
themselves, seem to have stood in awe of those ecclesiastics whose
relatives were more powerful than their own. After the bishop of
Langres was deposed for simony by Leo IX and the Council of Reims
in 1049, the canons of Langres proceeded to elect a successor in the
canonically approved fashion, but they still chose a son of the count of
Tonnerre.

It should also be noted that the noble bishops of the eleventh century were almost invariably from the secular clergy. The only bishop
in the group who might have been a monk was Milo, bishop of Mâcon
(981–993), who had controlled the revenues and called himself abbot
of Bèze before becoming bishop. However, since Bèze was essentially
deserted at the time, it seems most likely that, like the many counts
in the tenth century who called themselves abbots, Milo was not actually a monk himself.[13] Especially in the first half of the eleventh century, the bishops who were imposed by powerful laymen had sometimes come from outside the region; thus, at Langres, Bruno had been
a cleric at Reims and Hugh of Verdun a cleric at Chartres, and, at
Auxerre, John had been a cleric at the royal court. In the majority of
cases, however, the bishops had been canons at the cathedrals where
they eventually became bishops.

At the end of the eleventh century there was a change in the
episcopal origins. Burgundian bishops increasingly came from the
middle and lower levels of the nobility rather than the upper nobility,
as I indicate below. The turning point was the Gregorian reform, the
movement that had begun before Gregory VII and involved much
more than his quarrel with the emperor over investitures, though the
whole movement has been given his name. Gregory never argued
that the bishops whose allegiance he wanted to direct toward Rome
should not be selected from among the relatives of worldly princes.
The change in the social origins of bishops which took place at the
end of the eleventh century was not the result of a conscious decision
but rather the indirect result of changes in the way bishops were
elected.

A key element of the Gregorian reform was the regularization of
episcopal and abbatial elections. A free election by "clergy and people," which had long been a stereotyped phrase, became a realizable
goal. Popes and councils, beginning with Leo IX at the Council of
Reims in 1049, sought out and disciplined or deposed bishops who

[13]For lay abbots, see below, Chapter 4.

had bought their offices or otherwise obtained them through uncanonical influence (Reims deposed Bishop Hugh of Langres and reprimanded Bishop Hugh I of Nevers).[14] Thereafter, the chief responsibility for the election of a church leader was given to those who would be submitted to him, that is, the cathedral chapter or the abbey's monks. The role of "the people" was primarily acclamatory,[15] and the power of the local aristocracy to foist one of their own onto an unwilling church was radically reduced. There were of course some nobles who still tried to force cathedral chapters to accept their candidates, but they were largely unsuccessful. Count Theobold of Champagne, for example, decided to make his son William a bishop while he was still a boy (drawing a rebuke from Bernard of Clairvaux, whom the count had asked for help in his enterprise); but William eventually became archbishop of Sens only much later, in 1168, after a canonical election.[16]

When the canons of a cathedral chapter were left to elect their leader, they elected one of their own. Since in every region and in every cathedral chapter the scions of the few great houses were greatly outnumbered by the sons of the petty noblemen who constituted the majority of the region's aristocracy, the canons ceased choosing the sons of the greatest aristocracy in favor of the sons of castellans.[17] The body of canons was a fairly homogeneous group in the twelfth century. New canons generally had to be approved by the cathedral chapter—in one case, when the bishop of Chalon tried to make his candidate a canon in 1182 without the chapter's approval, that body was able to overthrow his appointment through appeal to the pope.[18]

[14]Anselm of St.-Remi, "Historia dedicationis ecclesiae Sancti Remigii," PL CXLII:421–40.

[15]Robert L. Benson, The Bishop-Elect (Princeton, 1968), pp. 28–30. Jean Gaudemet, Le gouvernement de l'Église à l'époque classique. IIe partie: Le gouvernement local, Histoire du droit et des institutions de l'Église en Occident 8 (Paris, 1979), pp. 57–60.

[16]Bernard of Clairvaux, Letter 271, Opera, VIII (Rome, 1977), 181–82. See also Bouchard, "Origins of Bishops," p. 268. The king tried to influence the elections at Auxerre in 1114 and 1152, and the count also tried to intervene in 1152, but their candidates were passed over; see Constance Brittain Bouchard, Spirituality and Administration: The Role of the Bishop in Twelfth-Century Auxerre, Speculum Anniversary Monographs 5 (Cambridge, Mass., 1979), pp. 37–38, 70–71; and Chauney, "Le recrutement de l'épiscopat," p. 196.

[17]For a similar pattern in Provence and Speyer, see Jean-Pierre Poly, La Provence et la société féodale, 879–1166 (Paris, 1976), pp. 258–66; and Lawrence G. Duggan, Bishop and Chapter: The Governance of the Bishopric of Speyer to 1552 (New Brunswick, N. J., 1978), pp. 46–56. See also Guillemain, "Les origines des évêques," pp. 379–80. Chauney, who did not note the change from the upper nobility to the lower nobility, concluded that the social origins of Burgundian bishops were the same before and after the Gregorian reform; "Le recrutement de l'épiscopat," p. 203.

[18]Chalon, pp. 68–69. See also Jean-Marc Boissard, "Structures et attributions du chapitre cathédral de Chalon-sur-Saône du milieu du XIIe au milieu du XIVe siècle," Mémoires de la Société d'histoire et d'archéologie de Chalon-sur-Saône, 42 (1970/71), 94–96.

This group of sons of the local petty nobility chose men like themselves to join their chapter and generally elected one of these chapter members as their new bishop. The best way for a young canon to advance to the bishopric was to gain capitular office; the dean, the head of the chapter, was elected by the rest of the canons, but the other major officers, the provost and the archdeacons, were generally appointed by the bishop.[19]

While it is not possible to do a complete social analysis of the cathedral chapters, since many members are known only by their Christian names if at all, the cathedral canons whose families are known were almost invariably from the ranks of local knights or castellans—and often had relatives within the church as well.[20] Girard, archdeacon of Langres in the 1130s and 1140s, was the son of the castellan of Montsaugeon and Mirebeau. Landric, a canon at Mâcon in the mid-twelfth century, was a brother of Lord Joceran IV Grossus of Uxelles and Brancion, and his nephew Humbert became archdeacon of the chapter in 1166.[21] Walter, son of the castellan Hugh of Berzé, was archdeacon of Mâcon in 1171. Bernard, archdeacon of Chalon in the 1170s, was the brother of Gui, lord of Verdun-sur-le-Doubs. Simon, canon at Langres in the 1180s, was brother of Lord Rayner of Nogent.[22] Everard, of the family of the lords of Bricon, a canon at Langres who was archdeacon for Dijon for the final decades of the twelfth century and became dean of the chapter by 1205, had a nephew or cousin (*consanguineus*), also named Everard, as a canon at Langres under him.[23] These chapter dignitaries from the ranks of the lesser Burgundian castellans—generally castellans who lived near the cathedral cities in question—are typical of the men who became cathedral canons in the twelfth century.

When the canons did not elect a member of the group as bishop, they generally elected the abbot of a local regular monastery instead (especially in the first half of the twelfth century), and the abbots of

---

[19]Bouchard, *Spirituality and Administration*, pp. 23–24. Jacques Laurent and Ferdinand Claudon, *Abbayes et prieurés de l'ancienne France*, XII, iii, *Diocèses de Langres et de Dijon*, Archives de la France monastique 45 (Paris, 1941), p. 162.

[20]One of the few well-documented French cathedral chapters of the twelfth century is that of Tournai. In studying this chapter, Jacques Pycke discovered that a good two-thirds of the canons whose origins are known were of the families of knights and nobles, most from the immediate region; Pycke, *Le chapitre cathédral Notre-Dame de Tournai de la fin du XIe à la fin du XIIIe siècle: Son organisation, sa vie, ses membres* (Louvain, 1986), pp. 84–92.

[21]GC IV:163, no. 40. Theuley, fol. 5r. For Landric, see Appendix A, p. 305.

[22]Molesme 2.371 (II:391). C 4240 (V:594). Arch. Saône-et-Loire, H 54, no. 5. Langres 30 (pp. 400–401).

[23]Longué, fols. 56r–v, ed. Jean-Marc Roger, "Les Morhier Champenois," *Bulletin philologique et historique du Comité des travaux historiques et scientifiques*, 1978, pp. 118–19, no. 20.

these houses, as indicated in the following section, were almost always of the petty nobility as well.[24] In Burgundy more Cistercian abbots became bishops than did abbots of any other single order, but Cluniac monks were also represented. The Cistercian bishops in Burgundy were Geoffrey of Langres (1139–1163), who before his election had been prior of Clairvaux and abbot of Fontenay; Warner of Langres (1193–1200), who had been abbot of Clairvaux; Hugh III of Auxerre (1136–1151), who had been abbot of the Cistercian house of Pontigny; and his immediate successor, Alain (1152–1167), who had been abbot of the Cistercian house of Larrivour. The Cluniac monks who became abbots of Burgundian dioceses were William of Sabran, elected to Langres but quickly deposed (1138); and Hugh II of Auxerre (1115–1136), who had been a monk at Cluny and abbot of St.-Germain of Auxerre. The only monastic bishop who was neither a Cistercian nor a Cluniac was Engelbert of Chalon (1178–1180), who had been abbot of Molesme.

By the end of the twelfth century there were scarcely any great nobles at the heads of Burgundian churches—or for that matter even among the members of these churches.[25] Their places had been taken by members of castellan or even knightly families. The only family of the upper nobility which consistently launched sons into ecclesiastical careers in the twelfth century was that of the dukes of Burgundy, and these sons all went into the cathedral chapter, not the cloister. In giving these sons high office, the dukes did not have to override the objections of the churches involved; the sons all acceded through perfectly canonical elections, though their family's prestige may well have helped influence the electors.

The seven bishops of Autun in the twelfth century included two brothers of the duke of Burgundy (Robert, 1140, and Henry, 1148–1170); the origins of the others are not altogether clear, but at least two seem to be the brothers of local castellans. At Auxerre at

[24]For abbots who became bishops, see Bouchard, "Origins of Bishops," pp. 287–90, and the references cited there. A similar pattern is found in Provence and León; see Poly, *La Provence*, p. 269; and R. A. Fletcher, *The Episcopate in the Kingdom of León in the Twelfth Century* (Oxford, 1978), pp. 79–80. Cistercians in general were usually from the ranks of the petty nobility. Joel Lipkin has found that, in the first half of the twelfth century, as many as three-quarters of all Cistercian bishops had at one time been monks at Clairvaux; "The Entrance of the Cistercians into the Church Hierarchy, 1098–1227: The Bernardine Influence," in E. Rozanne Elder and John R. Sommerfeldt, eds., *The Chimaera of His Age: Studies on Bernard of Clairvaux*, Studies in Medieval Cistercian History 5 (Kalamazoo, Mich., 1980), pp. 65–66.

[25]Burgundy seems to have been a much more reformed area than some other parts of France, however, so one cannot necessarily extrapolate from the Burgundian model. Closer to Paris, two king's sons held the abbatial office at several different monasteries from the age of six or so during the middle years of the twelfth century. See Andrew W. Lewis, *Royal Succession in Capetian France: Studies on Familial Order and the State* (Cambridge, Mass., 1981), pp. 59–60.

at the same time, all but one of the six bishops were from the ranks of the local nobility, none from a family more powerful than a family of castellans (the social origins of the sixth bishop, who originally came to Burgundy from Flanders to become a monk under Bernard of Clairvaux, are unknown). For Chalon the origins of two of the five twelfth-century bishops are known, and both are from the petty nobility; Peter (1158–1178) was indeed not even from a castellan family but rather from a family of urban knights which served the local Cluniac priory of St.-Marcel. At Langres in the same period, the eight bishops included a brother of the duke of Burgundy (Walter, 1163–1179), a brother of the count of Bar-sur-Seine (Manasses, 1179–1193), five bishops from castellan or knightly families, plus one whose origins are not known. Of the five twelfth-century bishops of Mâcon, the origins of two are known, and both were from the local petty nobility. At Nevers the eight twelfth-century bishops included two brothers of the lords of local castles and six whose origins are not known. Again, the Burgundian bishops are not unique, for it has been found that in the dioceses of Lorraine and the lower Loire more twelfth-century bishops came from lower levels of the nobility than did their eleventh-century predecessors.[26]

Overall, then, the origins of nearly two-thirds of the twelfth-century Burgundian bishops are known, and all these bishops came from the ranks of castellans, petty nobles, and knights, in striking contrast to the pattern of origins in the same dioceses in the previous century. The only exceptions are the brother of the count of Bar, which was a very small county, and the brothers of the dukes of Burgundy. Those bishops whose origins are not known most likely also came from the lower nobility of their region. When noble families sent a son into the cathedral chapter, as detailed in the preceding chapter, they generally sent him to one nearby, and these members of the regional petty aristocracy provided most twelfth-century bishops. The castellans who had been incorporated into the ranks of the nobility by the end of the eleventh century at the latest, and the knights who were well on their way to joining the nobility by the middle of the twelfth century, imitated the older nobility among other things in sending their sons into the church, a position from which they could hope to obtain high ecclesiastical office.

[26]Parisse, "La noblesse Lorraine," pp. 408–12. Boussard, "Les évêques en Neustrie," pp. 164, 191.

The Social Origins of Burgundian Abbots

There is no discernible change in the origins of Burgundian abbots between the eleventh and twelfth centuries comparable to that in the origins of bishops. Rather, the monastic houses give the impression of having been in advance of the cathedral chapters, for they elected their leaders from the middle or lower nobility even in the eleventh century. In part this impression hinges on the sources. The eleventh-century monasteries that did not follow a strict rule, the houses where one might expect the abbots to be most like the eleventh-century bishops, have very few surviving records. While the bishops of the time, no matter what their background, always became involved in enough diocesan affairs to be recorded, the abbot of a house of lax life might be ignored. Few people made gifts to unexemplary monasteries, so the monks did not have large collections of donation charters that might reveal abbatial origins. And many unreformed houses had so few monks that they would in any event have generated few documents. The few Burgundian houses that had had local counts acting as their abbots in the tenth century, such as St.-Bénigne of Dijon, were reformed and given their own abbots by the year 1000. Thus the houses where abbatial origins are known in the eleventh century are those of a reformed life, those houses where the abbots were elected by the monks rather than imposed from outside, in a manner similar to the election of bishops after the Gregorian reform. It is therefore not surprising that the men who headed regular monasteries, both before and after the Gregorian reform, were very similar to the men who headed Burgundian sees during the twelfth century.

They tended to be noble but of the middle or lower nobility. They were not burghers' or peasants' sons, but neither were they sons of great dukes or counts.[27] At Cluny, for example, the abbots were routinely the sons of castellans and knights. Odilo (994–1049) was of a noble family of the Auvergne; Hugh (1049–1109) was of the castellan family of the lords of Semur;[28] Ponce (1109–1122) was son of the count of Melgueil (a small county in Languedoc, near the Mediterranean); and Peter the Venerable (1122–1156) was of the family of the lords of Montboissier. At St.-Bénigne of Dijon, Abbot William (990–1031) was of Italian comital ancestry, but of the four other eleventh-century abbots, one was of the petty nobility of the region

[27]For the following examples, see the references in Appendix C.
[28]See Appendix A, p. 360. It has sometimes been stated that Hugh was related to the Capetian dynasty, but this is not strictly true. His sister married—and was repudiated by—the Capetian duke of Burgundy, but this is certainly not the same thing as Hugh himself being related to the kings.

(Halinard, 1031—1052), and one was of a knightly family (Jarenton, 1076—1113); the families of the other two are not known. In the twelfth century, again all the abbots whose families are known were from the lower levels of the nobility, the most powerful families being the castellans of Grancey, the relatives of Abbot Peter III (1188—1204).

The abbots of Molesme and of the houses of the Cistercian order were always of the lower levels of the nobility, at least those whose origins are known. Robert, the founder of Molesme (1075—1111), seems to have come from the petty aristocracy of Champagne; and his prior and successor, Gui (1111—1132), was of the family of the castellans of Châtel-Censoir. Bernard, abbot of Clairvaux (1115—1153) and the most famous figure of the Cistercian order, was of the family of the lords of Fontaines-lès-Dijon, who were not even important enough to have their own castle.[29] Stephen, first abbot of the Cistercian house of Les Roches, was from a somewhat more important family, that of the lords of Toucy.[30] But this castellan family was still of an appreciably lower rank than the families of viscounts or counts. Houses of canons regular too normally had abbots from families of castellans and petty nobles. For example, Milo, abbot of the Premonstratensian house of St.-Marien of Auxerre between 1155 and 1203, was son of Lord Anselm of Traînel.[31]

Both before and after the Gregorian reform, it seems to have been taken for granted—by secular nobles and by ecclesiastics themselves—that bishops and abbots should be of the nobility. Though it became more rare for members of the upper nobility to hold positions of power in the church once their secular relatives could no longer assure them whatever ecclesiastical office they wished, monks and cathedral canons still tended to elect nobles, even if from the lesser nobility. The change in the origins of church leaders should be seen as evolutionary rather than disjunctive. Thus the Gregorian reform, far from creating a separation between ecclesiastical and secular leaders, may well have strengthened the ties between the nobility and the local abbots and bishops.

[29]It has sometimes been suggested that the lords of Fontaines, Bernard's family, were first cousins of some of the more powerful Burgundian families, but the evidence does not support such a conclusion; see below, Chapter 10.

[30]Quantin I.268 (pp. 419—20).

[31]Robert of St.-Marien, *Chronicon* 1203, MGH SS XXVI:262. Theodore Evergates has studied the lords of Traînel, though he erroneously calls Milo abbot of "St.-Manin"; *Feudal Society in the Bailliage of Troyes under the Counts of Champagne, 1152—1284* (Baltimore, 1975), pp. 205—7. Otbert, abbot of the Augustinian house of Ste.-Marguerite in the 1140s, was the son of a local knight; Arch. Côte-d'Or, 20 H 674.

The Development of Ecclesiastical Dynasties

Despite the shift in social origins of ecclesiastical leaders and the general waning of secular influence, family ties of a different sort continued to have a strong impact on the ecclesiastical careers of young knights and nobles throughout the period. This was so because noble ecclesiastics, both before and after the Gregorian reform, tended to look after their younger relatives in the church. As indicated in the preceding chapter, secular families usually chose a house where an uncle or brother was already established when determining that a son should enter the church, and thus the uncle or brother could use the powers of his own office to help his young relative advance.

A cathedral canon generally left a will, disposing of his prebend— which he often tried to leave to a younger relative—as well as his personal property. Cathedral canons and local nobles could become embroiled in quarrels over a canon's inheritance if he did not specify what part of his property was to go to his ecclesiastical nephews, what part to secular relatives—a house in the cathedral close was clearly not appropriate for a secular lord, but other property might go to anyone—and what was to be given as alms to his or another church. When Albuin, a cathedral canon at Autun, was dying in 1109, he left some of his personal property to the other canons, "for his soul," with the consent of his nephew Falco, also a canon, "who was to succeed him by hereditary law." Falco's brothers, knights staying in the world, also gave their consent. Similarly, when William, dean of the chapter of Chalon, made his will in 1185, he designated his nephews Walter and William, canons in the chapter, as his principal heirs. He gave his house in the cathedral close to Walter, specifying that he should pass it on, when *he* died, to a *nepos* of his own, if the *nepos* were a canon of the cathedral. Around the same time, Warner, archdeacon of Langres, gave the church of Chevigny to St.-Étienne of Dijon in order to found his anniversary there, and the canons of St.-Étienne gave the church *in casamento* to Warner's nephew Matthew, a cathedral canon at Langres.[32] The "hereditary law," which had made Albuin designate his nephew as his heir seventy-five years earlier, thus made Dean William feel sure that the nephew to whom he gave his property would wish to pass it on to his own nephew, and made the canons of St.-Étienne grant the church Archdeacon Warner had given them to Warner's nephew.

It was scarcely questioned that a cathedral canon should help the advancement of his younger relatives. As a biographer of the bishop

---

[32]Autun/Église 1.35 (I:56—57). Chalon, pp. 112—14. St.-Étienne IV.61, 69 (pp. 75, 80—81).

of Auxerre, writing around 1140, said, "Among all the prelates of the church, of whatever order, scarcely one can be found who has not given his relatives ecclesiastical honors and benefices, even if they are not worthy"—this biographer hurried on to say that *his* subject was one of the rare exceptions in the general pattern.[33] (Interestingly, this bishop, who had been abbot of St.-Germain before his election to Auxerre, had been made abbot by his uncle, Abbot Hugh the Great of Cluny.)

The result of this promotion of ecclesiastical relatives was that virtual dynasties were established in many Burgundian churches, where a series of uncles and nephews held office in the same or neighboring churches.[34] Though no one family ever completely dominated a church, many abbeys and bishoprics were headed by men from the same family for generations. For example, in the eleventh century, a series of uncles and nephews, brothers of the viscounts of Nevers, held the episcopal office at either Nevers or Auxerre for eighty years: Bishop Hugh (1016–1069) was uncle of Bishop Geoffrey of Auxerre (1052–1076), himself the uncle of Bishop Hugh II of Nevers (1074–1096). At Langres, Bishops Harduin (1049–1065) and Hugh-Rainard (1065–1084) were first cousins, of the family of the counts of Tonnerre, and Harduin was the uncle of Bishop Robert of Auxerre (1076–1092). At Mâcon, Bishops Letbald (993–1016) and Walter (1031–1061) of Brancion were uncle and nephew; Bishop Walter was in turn uncle of another Walter, the dean of the cathedral chapter of Mâcon, and cousin of one Maiolus Poudreux, another canon at Mâcon.[35]

Ecclesiastical dynasties established in the tenth and eleventh centuries were generally made up of the relatives of powerful secular nobles. It should be noted that no Burgundian family consistently produced individuals powerful in the church over the course of the tenth and eleventh centuries unless their brothers were also powerful in the secular world. The twelfth century too had episcopal dynasties, but they were of different families than the eleventh-century dynasties. Typical are the members of the *Narbonnia* family of Toucy, a family of the lower nobility. They produced the brothers Bishop William of Auxerre (1167–1181) and Archbishop Hugh of Sens (1143–1168), as well as a third brother, Hervé, provost of the chapter of

---

[33]*Gesta pontificum*, pp. 415–16; see also Bouchard, *Spirituality and Administration*, pp. 62–63. William Mendel Newman has found a similar pattern in the cathedral of Soissons; *Les seigneurs de Nesle en Picardie (XIIᵉ–XIIIᵉ siècle)*, 2 vols. (Paris and Philadelphia, 1971), I:106–7.

[34]Constance B. Bouchard, "The Structure of a Twelfth-Century French Family: The Lords of Seignelay," *Viator*, 10 (1979), 52–53; and Bouchard, "Origins of Bishops," pp. 290–94. See also Pycke, *Le chapitre cathédrale de Tournai*, pp. 86–90.

[35]See Appendix B; and, for the lords of Brancion, Appendix A, pp. 297–302.

Sens. Similar uncle-nephew dynasties included Bishops Stephen (1112–1139) and Humbert (1140–1148) of Autun; Humbert went on to be archbishop of Lyon. They too were of the lower nobility, at most a castellan family; modern scholars sometimes refer to them as "de Bâgé."

The most powerful families in the Burgundian episcopacy in the twelfth century were not always powerful in the world: two of the most important episcopal dynasties in this period were the relatives of the dukes of Burgundy, the most powerful secular family in the region, and of the lords of Seignelay, a family of castellans whose power did not reach beyond the Auxerrois. Bishops Robert (1140) and Henry (1148–1170) of Autun were brothers, and also brothers of Bishop Walter of Langres (1163–1179) and of Duke Odo II of Burgundy; all were great-nephews of Bishop Robert of Langres (1084–1111). Gui, archbishop of Sens (1176–1193), brother of the lord of Seignelay, was uncle of the brothers William, bishop of Auxerre and Paris (1207–1220 and 1220–1223), and Manasses, bishop of Orléans (1207–1221), and of Hugh IV, bishop of Auxerre (1183–1206); William had a nephew Andreas, archdeacon under him at Auxerre. Similar twelfth-century episcopal dynasties have been found in the dioceses of Picardy, Normandy, and Lorraine.[36]

Even when the nephew did not succeed his uncle as bishop, he often attained a high position in the chapter. Such was the case with Bruno, nephew of Bishop Bruno of Langres (980–1016), who went on to be treasurer of the chapter of Langres in the 1030s.[37] Similarly, a century later, Fulk and Ulric, the nephews of Willenc of Aigremont, bishop of Langres (1125–1136), became archdeacons under him, an office Fulk held until almost 1170, while Ulric became provost of Sts.-Géosmes, a house dependent on the chapter of Langres. Ulric himself had a nephew, named Guiard, and a great-nephew, named Ulric, both of whom became canons of Langres under their uncle. At Chalon, Bishops Walter of Sercy (1126–1158) and Peter of St.-Marcel (1158–1178) both had nephews, their namesakes, in the chapter under them; young Walter of Sercy became archdeacon and eventually dean. Theobold, bishop of Nevers (1176–1188), had a nephew, also named Theobold, who served as dean of the cathedral chapter under his uncle. Manasses, bishop of Langres (1179–1193), had a relative (collateralis) in the chapter of Langres, to whom he gave the revenues of five churches in 1189.[38] These uncles whose nephews served in

36Newman, Les seigneurs de Nesle, I:100–104. Gaudemet, "Recherches sur l'épis-copat," pp. 142–43; and Gaudemet, Le gouvernement, pp. 91–92. Parisse, "La noblesse Lorraine," pp. 405–8.
37See Appendix B, p. 394.
38Langres 43 (p. 419).

Plate 2. The twelfth-century church at Bâgé

the cathedral chapter under them may have hoped their young relatives would become bishop after them. The nephews certainly seem
to have hoped so; when Bishop Humbald of Auxerre died in 1114, his
nephew Ulger, provost of the chapter, tried unsuccessfully to engineer
his own election. But an uncle could do no more than start a dynasty;
he could not ensure that it would continue.[39]

Specific episcopal dynasties in Burgundy continued either through
the eleventh century or through the twelfth, but not both; the Gregorian reform again seems to have been the watershed. This is doubtless due to the change in the way bishops were elected, for in
monasteries such as Cluny, where no such change took place, abbatial
dynasties were able to continue unbroken. The chief example is the
monastic relatives of the lords of Semur, discussed in Chapter 1.[40] In
the second half of the twelfth century, however, most monasteries—
Cluniac as well those of the new Cistercian order—began electing new
abbots not from the members of the house but rather from the abbots
of the monastery's daughter houses; the result was a weakening in the
ties that had bound members of a family to a particular monastery's
leadership over the generations.[41]

Still, even as it became more common to translate successful abbots
from house to house, and as the great reformed monasteries of Burgundy attracted a sizable number of monks from other regions, most
monks and cathedral canons continued to be related to the nobility of
their church's region and hence to each other. Not all families made
any of their sons ecclesiastics, but since most of the secular nobles of
a region were related in some degree to each other,[42] even those families that included no ecclesiastics generally had some cousins in the
church. The cathedral chapters and local monasteries were thus part

[39]When Geoffrey, abbot of St.-Martin of Autun in the late twelfth century, made his
nephew Gui prior, he may have hoped that Gui would succeed him as abbot, but the
young man did not; BN, Coll. Bourgogne 111, fol. 109r.

[40]Another important ecclesiastical dynasty was the family of Peter the Venerable; he
was abbot of Cluny; his mother and nieces were nuns at Marcigny, which was affiliated
with Cluny; his brother Herman was prior of Cluny before becoming abbot of Manglieu; his brother Jordan was abbot of Chaise-Dieu; his brother Ponce was abbot of
Vézelay; and his brother Heracleus was archbishop of Lyon. See Appendix C, pp. 411,
431.

[41]Election by the heads of daughter houses was specified in the Carta Caritatis, the
agreement between houses of the Cistercian order worked out in the first years of the
order's growth, and in subsequent Cistercian legislation. Bouton and Van Damme,
eds., Textes, p. 101. Canivez, Statuta, I:29, no. 67. Constance B. Bouchard, "Changing
Abbatial Tenure Patterns in Burgundian Monasteries during the Twelfth Century," Revue Bénédictine, 90 (1980), 251–54.

[42]Constance B. Bouchard, "The Origins of the French Nobility," American Historical
Review, 86 (1981), 523.

of the web of relationships which bound the regional nobility together in the twelfth century.

Distinctions between Noble Churchmen and Noble Laymen

In considering ecclesiastical dynasties, one should note that, just because leaders of the church had very close ties to the leaders of society, this did not mean they were pawns of their secular brothers. Even those tenth- and eleventh-century ecclesiastics whose relatives in the world obtained their office for them were on occasion model patrons of reform. Two great patrons of the Cluniac order were Bishop Bruno of Langres (980–1016), nephew of the king who had made him bishop and brother-in-law of Count Otto-William of Burgundy; and Bishop Hugh of Auxerre (999–1039), count of Chalon in his own right.[43] The brothers of the viscounts of Nevers, the series of uncles and nephews who were bishop of either Auxerre or Nevers for much of the eleventh century, were behind the monastic reform at La Charité-sur-Loire and at the houses of St.-Étienne, St.-Symphorien, and St.-Victor of Nevers—this even though one bishop of Nevers had taken office when his parents bought the bishopric for him. Bishops Hugh-Rainard (1065–1084) and Robert (1084–1111) of Langres, respectively from the families of the counts of Tonnerre and the dukes of Burgundy, were instrumental in the foundations of first Molesme and then Cîteaux in their diocese.

In the twelfth century, if the interests of an ecclesiastic's noble relatives and those of his church were in conflict, the church often took precedence. For example, in 1198, Warner, bishop of Langres, not only persuaded his uncle, Simon of Rochefort, to give up his claims to property other knights had given the Cistercian monks of Auberive, but forced his uncle to pay the monks ten pounds as a guarantee against reopening his quarrels.[44] Nobles might send their sons into the church with the expectation that they would rise to a position of power, but they could not be assured that the aims and goals of these ecclesiastics would be the same as their own.[45]

The nobility's way of life in the world was both very similar to and very different from the way of life of their brothers in the church.

[43]Martine Chauney, "Deux évêques bourguignons de l'an mil: Brunon de Langres et Hughes Ier d'Auxerre," *Cahiers de civilisation médiévale*, 21 (1978), 385–93. See also Constance B. Bouchard, "Laymen and Church Reform around the Year 1000: The Case of Otto-William, Count of Burgundy," *Journal of Medieval History*, 5 (1979), 4–5.

[44]Auberive I, fol. 159v, no. 11.

[45]Emma Mason has found a similar pattern in England; "Timeo barones et donas ferentes," in *Religious Motivation: Biographical and Sociological Problems for the Church Historian*, ed. Derek Baker, Studies in Church History 15 (Oxford, 1978), pp. 74–75.

Ecclesiastical lords, like secular lords, could have other nobles bound to them by ties of vassalage. In the twelfth century the count of Auxerre held his county in fief from the bishop of Auxerre, and the lord of Seignelay and the viscount of Sens both held their castles in fief from the abbot of St.-Remi of Sens, while in the early thirteenth century Count Hervé of Nevers held Bourbon as a fief from the bishop of Autun.[46] The bishops of Autun were feudal lords of most of the knights in the valley of the Brenne (see below, Chapter 5). The bishops of Langres had a papal confirmation, issued by Paschal II in 1105, of their lordship over nineteen castles in their region, including those of Tonnerre, Tilchâtel, Châtillon, Fouvent, Saulx, Grancey, Bar-sur-Aube, and Bar-sur-Seine.[47]

Cathedral canons were especially close to the secular nobility in that they, too, lived in their own houses and had their own personal income, might spend their days in hunting or even fighting, and were generally involved in the same sorts of administrative tasks as occupied secular nobles. Though canons regular and the monks of regular houses had neither the individual property of the cathedral canons nor their opportunity for individual initiative, the monastic life could be quite luxurious—an accusation that Bernard of Clairvaux made (somewhat unfairly) against the Cluniac way of life—and monastic officials too spent much of their energies on the mundane details of administering vast estates. But most monasteries enforced a life of strict discipline on their members, especially the Cistercian order in the twelfth century. The letters of Bernard of Clairvaux and the legislation of the Cistercian chapters general show a determination to follow "voluntary poverty" so strictly that the parents of some converts were afraid their sons would break down from deprivation and overwork, and even Bernard sent away one novice as too delicate for the Cistercian life. They ate no meat and did not use lard even for cooking, eating only bread (whole wheat or rye, made from unsifted flour, according to statute), vegetables, eggs, and cheese, and not even eggs and cheese during the numerous periods of fasting. Most of the day's labor was carried out in silence. The Cluniacs, partly in imitation of the Cistercians, enforced similarly strict rules on diet, as seen in the *Statuta* of Peter the Venerable.[48]

Even within the less strict houses, there were real differences

[46]Yves Sassier, *Recherches sur le pouvoir comtal en Auxerrois du Xe au début du XIIIe siècle* (Auxerre, 1980), pp. 177—82. Bouchard, "The Structure of a Twelfth-Century Family," p. 55. Autun/Évêqué 177 (p. 187).

[47]GC IV:153, no. 28. For examples from other areas, see Gaudemet, *Le gouvernement*, pp. 150—55.

[48]Canivez, *Statuta*, pp. 13, no. 4; 16, no. 14; 18, no. 24. Bernard of Clairvaux, Letters 1, 110, 322, 408, *Opera*, VII:1—11, 282—83; VIII:256—58, 389. Peter the Venerable, *Statuta* 11, 12, 14, PL CLXXXIX:1029.

between the secular and ecclesiastical ways of life. In joining the church, nobles were not merely moving from one mode of the luxurious life to another. Burgundian bishops and cathedral canons did not marry or produce families, and life in their individual houses was never as comfortable—except perhaps for the bishops themselves—as the life of a great lord in his castle. Monks especially were curtailed in their freedom, and, as I indicate in the following chapters, in the twelfth century it was the strictest houses, the ones whose way of life was most different from that of the secular nobility, that were the most attractive to the local nobles.

Both before and after the Investiture Controversy and Gregorian reform, the secular nobility produced most leaders of the church. But there was no set or static relationship between the leaders of the church and the leaders of society. In the eleventh century, great nobles often chose church leaders, men from their own families or from their retinues. In the twelfth century, most church leaders were still of noble origin, but they came from the lower ranks of the nobility and were chosen by other ecclesiastics rather than by their secular relatives. In spite of occasional worries by the clergy that men powerful in this world might not always be the best to lead a church whose ultimate concern was the next world, nobility, with its power and prestige, was considered a virtual prerequisite for high ecclesiastical office throughout this period.

The Gregorian reform did have a real effect in that, once its impact was felt, most powerful ecclesiastical dynasties were no longer closely related to powerful secular dynasties, as they had been in the eleventh century. The greatest lords could no longer impose their sons and favorites on the churches. But bishops and abbots continued to be men of the local nobility, who started their ecclesiastical careers under the tutelage of their older relatives and in turn helped the advancement of their nephews. The family, the essential unit of secular society, was also a vital element in the life of the church. But this intimacy of blood ties does not imply that the church was in any way "secularized." As I argue in the next section, ecclesiastical reform— that is, the establishment of church government free from outside interference and of a monastic life of individual poverty and humility—was possible only because of the active participation of the secular nobility.

PART TWO

MONASTIC REFORM

AND THE NOBILITY

One aspect of the nobility's relation to the medieval church was the entry of nobles into monasticism and into the ecclesiastical hierarchy, as described in Part One. But a second aspect was the support secular nobles gave to reformed houses. The following chapters discuss the vital role of powerful men, men who did *not* leave the world, in the spread of monastic reform in the High Middle Ages.

Reform is the keynote of the ecclesiastical history of the eleventh and twelfth centuries. Once considered to be a result of the quarrel between pope and emperor over their relative authority in Christendom, this reform movement, it is now recognized, encompassed many strands: the regulation of clerical life, adult conversions to the "apostolic life," the refoundation of old monasteries and the establishment of new ones.[1] Monastic reform had begun well before the late eleventh-century regulation of the morals, education, and mode of election of the secular clergy, and it continued to gain force throughout the twelfth century. This section examines the monastic reform movement in Burgundy and the role that the nobility played in this reform.

The word *reformare*, literally to shape anew, was used in the central Middle Ages to describe the process by which an old church, often abandoned since the time of the Viking invasions or else staffed by only a few clerics of unexemplary life, would be refounded, rebuilt, and repopulated with monks of a regular life. Modern scholars have broadened the meaning of the term "reformed" to designate any monastery or monastic order that consciously sought to follow a way

[1]For the broad reform movement, see André Vauchez, *La spiritualité du moyen âge occidental, VIIIᵉ−XIIᵉ siècles* (Paris, 1975), pp. 33−66; and Jean Leclercq, François Vandenbroucke, and Louis Bouyer, *The Spirituality of the Middle Ages*, A History of Christian Spirituality 2 (New York, 1968), pp. 101−6.

of life more rigorous than the general pattern. Monastic authors of the eleventh and twelfth centuries also spoke of a "regular" way of life, *regularis*, by which they literally meant adherence to a monastic rule (generally that of Saint Benedict). Regular (or reformed) monks followed a life based on chastity, common property, and individual poverty.

Many modern scholars, by confusing monastic reform with the issues of the Investiture Controversy, have depicted the secular nobility and ecclesiastical reformers as opposing forces. But there were several distinct aspects of the religious life which developed or altered during this period. A reform of the monastic life, an attempt to return to the *vita apostolica* of the early Church or to find new means of institutionalizing the purest way of life, was of course a process that had been continually repeated since the beginning of Christian monasticism. In Burgundy this reform process entered a new cycle in the tenth century and had grown, under various guises, to include almost all religious corporations by the early twelfth century. In contrast, another development of the eleventh century entailed an institutional separation between the property, rights, and duties of secular men and of those who, as ecclesiastics, acted as God's representatives on earth. This development took definite shape in the second half of the eleventh century, marked by what Gabriel LeBras has called "hierarchical contraction,"[2] and has been closely associated with Pope Gregory VII (1073–1085).

Gregorianism and monastic reform had both differences and similarities. Most scholars now agree that Cluny cannot be considered responsible for the issues that led to the Investiture Controversy, even though Cluny found common ground with the papacy in putting primary emphasis on remission of sins, and Gregory may well have found in Cluny precedents for his insistence on the importance of Saint Peter (Cluny's patron and the patron of Rome) as the ultimate arbiter.[3] Yet the Gregorian insistence that ecclesiastical leaders shun such worldly activities as buying their office or keeping concubines (an emphasis that actually began before Gregory, in particular with Leo

[2]Gabriel LeBras, *Institutions ecclésiastiques de la Chrétienté médiévale*, Histoire de l'Église depuis les origines jusqu'à nos jours 12 (Paris, 1959–64), p. 592. Bernard Bligny, though defining the different stages of reform somewhat differently than I, also notes that eleventh-century reform was not a monolithic entity; "L'Église et le siècle de l'an mil au début du XIIe siècle," *Cahiers de civilisation médiévale*, 27 (1984), 9, 31–32.

[3]The best recent historiographical survey of the arguments on Cluny's influence on the Gregorians is that of Barbara H. Rosenwein, *Rhinoceros Bound: Cluny in the Tenth Century* (Philadelphia, 1982), pp. 14–16, 23–26. See also H. E. J. Cowdrey, *The Cluniacs and the Gregorian Reform* (Oxford, 1970), pp. 139–42, 266–67; and Marcel Pacaut, "Structures monastiques, société et Église en Occident aux XIe et XIIe siècles," *Cahiers d'histoire*, 20 (1975), 125–26.

IX, 1049–1054), as well as the demand that ecclesiastical property be removed from the control of secular powers, helped establish regular elections of relatively chaste and pious bishops, men who were much closer to the reformed abbots of the preceding century in their way of life than many of their episcopal predecessors, and who generally helped establish new houses of reformed monks in their dioceses. Still, it must always be kept in mind that either monastic reform or the controversy between church and state was possible without the other. This book is primarily concerned with monastic reform. As I suggest in the following chapters, reform of the monastic religious life, which began well before the conscious separation of secular and ecclesiastical affairs, was carried out with the cooperation and indeed insistence of the very leaders of secular society whom extreme Gregorianism numbered among the enemy.

This section begins with a background chapter on the tenth century. In the next chapter I examine the chief features of the spread of monastic reform in Burgundy in the eleventh and twelfth centuries. The two following chapters discuss the sorts of individuals and groups of individuals who became donors to reformed monasteries. And in Part Three I analyze the types of gifts these men made and their possible reasons for making them. The division between reform of monasteries and gifts to monasteries is simply organizational; in actuality, the establishment of a house of monks and generosity to those monks were carried out by the same nobles and were part of a series of interactions between men powerful in the world and determinedly unworldly monks.

[3]

The Tenth-Century
Background of Reform

The Foundation of Cluny

The history of the reform movement in Burgundy in the High Middle Ages must begin with the foundation of Cluny.[1] Reforming existing houses and establishing new ones with a consciously more rigorous way of life than that generally practiced had of course been going on since the origins of western monasticism. One of the most important reforms for Burgundy was that initiated by Benedict of Aniane at the beginning of the ninth century, in which the Benedictine Rule was emphasized ·so strongly that in later centuries Saint Benedict's Rule came to be regarded as *the* Rule. Benedict of Aniane's reform established a tradition of regular life which was brought to Cluny at the foundation of that house a century later.[2] In the intervening century, the Viking invasions and the wars between the Carolingians and their great vassals created such political and economic chaos that very few monasteries were able to survive with their regular way of life intact. But a few did survive, and some new ones were founded. The most notable foundation was that of Cluny, established in 909 in spite of—or even because of—wars and disorder that threatened to be at least as bad in the tenth century as in the later

---

[1]The first in-depth scholarly study of Cluny was that of Ernst Sackur, *Die Cluniacenser in ihrer kirchlichen und allgemeingeschichtlichen Wirksamkeit bis zur Mitte des elften Jahrhunderts*, 2 vols. (Halle an der Saale, 1892–1894; rpt. Darmstadt, 1965). This study, which goes only to the middle of the eleventh century, was also the first to argue that the spread of Cluny's reform was carried out with the assistance of the powerful nobility; see for example I:34–35.

[2]Barbara H. Rosenwein, "Rules and the 'Rule' at Tenth-Century Cluny," *Studia monastica*, 19 (1977), 312–13. For Benedict of Aniane, see, most recently, Josef Semmler, "Benedictus II: Una regula—Una consuetudo," in *Benedictine Culture, 750–1050*, ed. W. Lourdaux and D. Verhelst, Mediaevalia Lovaniensia, Studia 11 (Louvain, 1983), pp. 28–47.

ninth. Cluny's origins were not strikingly unusual, but 909 has been taken as the beginning of the reformed monastic movement in Burgundy, because during the tenth century Cluny evolved from the single house of the foundation into a powerful reforming order that, by the eleventh century, had grown from its rather slim beginnings to embrace an exponentially growing number of monks and houses. Once this order began to spread it suffered no major setbacks.[3]

The house was founded by Duke William I of Aquitaine, who was also the count of Mâcon, on property located northwest of Mâcon.[4] The duke indicated in the foundation charter that no bishop or count would interfere in the internal affairs of the house, which would be dependent only on the pope. William himself promised not to try to influence the choice of a new abbot, instead leaving the choice to the free election of the monks, though indeed he frequently appeared in the abbey's charters, protecting, encouraging, and admonishing.[5] After the duke's death, Aquitaine went first to his nephew William II, then to the counts of Poitou, while Mâcon became a separate county under the control of an adventurer from Narbonne.[6] With the departure of the dukes of Aquitaine from the Mâconnais, Cluny developed in a virtual power vacuum in terms of the greatest secular and ecclesiastical lords: its archbishop (the archbishop of Lyon) was far away, and the region was at the very fringes of the authority of the French king (after 951 no French king appeared there in person for over two centuries). Cluny's closest ties were not with king or duke but with the local counts and noblemen of the region.[7]

Other Churches in the Tenth Century

Cluny was of course not the only great reforming center of its time. In his classic work on Gorze, Kassius Hallinger has demonstrated that in different regions different centers attracted the gifts and acquired the churches that led to the expansion of reformed monasticism.[8]

---

[3]For tenth-century Cluny, a relatively neglected scholarly topic, see, most recently, Barbara H. Rosenwein, *Rhinoceros Bound: Cluny in the Tenth Century* (Philadelphia, 1982).

[4]The choice of Mâcon seems to have been made partly by his wife, whose family had long held power there and from whose father William had acquired the county. I am presently completing a study of her family, the Bosonids.

[5]C 112 (I:124–28).

[6]Constance B. Bouchard, "The Origins of the French Nobility: A Reassessment," *American Historical Review*, 86 (1981), 517–18. See also Appendix A, pp. 261–62.

[7]Georges Duby, *La société aux XIe et XIIe siècles dans la région mâconnaise*, 2nd ed. (Paris, 1971), p. 401. Gerd Tellenbach, "Il monachesimo riformato ed i laici nei secoli XI e XII," in *I laici nella "Societas Christiana" dei secoli XI e XII*, Miscellanea del Centro di studi medioevali 5 (Milan, 1968), p. 124.

[8]Kassius Hallinger, *Gorze—Cluny: Studien zu den monastischen Lebensformen und*

Even in Burgundy, Cluny was not at first the obvious center for a new emphasis on monastic regularity. The monastery of Vézelay, though it later came into Cluny's orbit, had been founded fifty years before Cluny, with the same emphasis on a regular life for its monks and nuns (the nuns were a part of Vézelay's life for only a short time) and the same specified dependence on the pope, rather than on any bishop or secular lord, which Cluny was given at the time of its foundation. Other ninth-century houses of reformed monks were similarly freed from dependence on their (sometimes corrupt) bishops.[9] Perhaps what gave Cluny its unique position by the middle of the eleventh century was not its original dependence on Rome, but the long life and great ability of its abbots during its first centuries,[10] abbots who were supported by the goodwill of the local nobility.

If not unique in its monastic regularity in the tenth century, Cluny was certainly not typical. More typical was the ruined monastery. Most of these monasteries had a long history, going back to the eighth century or well before. There were a few foundations (including Cluny of course) made in the French countryside in the eighth through tenth centuries (most founded by a king or great duke), but in the urban areas virtually no new houses were founded between the seventh and eleventh centuries.[11] There was however no shortage of houses requiring reform or refoundation. Many of the older churches lay abandoned, having been sacked by the Vikings or Magyars, or had so few monks that the community monastic life was impossible.[12] The abbey of St.-Martin of Autun was said to be "destitute of religion" when, in 949, the Burgundian counts Giselbert and Hugh the

---

[9]The abbey of St.-Philibert of Tournus, for example, was granted immunity from all episcopal control by Pope John VIII in 878; Tournus, pp. 99—100. For the foundation of Vézelay, see the foundation charter and the twelfth-century chronicle of the monastery; Vézelay, pp. 243—48, 416; and Rosalind Kent Berlow, "Spiritual Immunity at Vézelay (Ninth to Twelfth Centuries)," Catholic Historical Review, 62 (1976), 574—77. Both St.-Germain of Auxerre and Flavigny have charters of immunity supposedly granted them by Charles the Bald in the mid-ninth century, though Yves Sassier has argued that these are forgeries from around the year 1000, after both houses had been reformed to Cluny's ordo; Sassier, "Quelques remarques sur les diplômes d'immunité octroyés par les Carolingiens à l'abbaye de Saint-Germain d'Auxerre," Bibliothèque de l'École des chartes, 139 (1981), 46—48. See also Adriaan H. Bredero, "Cluny et le monachisme carolingien: Continuité et discontinuité," in Benedictine Culture, pp. 63—65.

[10]Noreen Hunt, Cluny under Saint Hugh, 1049—1109 (London, 1967), pp. 20—21.

[11]Hartmut Atsma, "Les monastères urbaines du nord de la Gaule," Revue d'histoire de l'Église de France, 62 (1976), 163—87.

[12]In Provence, Saracen raids virtually destroyed the church—both bishoprics and monasteries—at the end of the ninth century. The reestablishment of the church began only in the middle of the tenth century, when the local princes began giving churches to Cluny, and later to the new Arlesian house of Montmajour. See Jean-Pierre Poly, La Provence et la société féodale, 879—1166 (Paris, 1976), pp. 56—69.

Black asked for monks from Cluny to settle there, under an elected abbot. When Bishop Walter of Autun confirmed the refoundation of Flavigny in 992, he noted that the few monks who had been living there no longer followed Benedict's Rule, as the monks had originally done. The debilitated state of the monastic life at Flavigny in the tenth century is further indicated by the fact that the bishop's reforming charter is the first document preserved by the monks for the entire century, in contrast to the many documents preserved from the relatively flourishing days of the ninth century.[13] Many of the houses that suffered damage in the tenth century however were not reformed until the eleventh century. The little monastery of St.-Georges of Couches, for example, which was restored in 1018 by the bishop of Autun, had only one monk left at the time.[14]

The Growth of Cluny's Order

Cluny stands in contrast to the general pattern of monastic life in the tenth century. It was a flourishing house, growing rather than declining in membership, following the Benedictine Rule with determination rather than lapsing from it. After its foundation, Cluny's possessions and position grew slowly but steadily, with an acceleration after about 980 in the amount of land it acquired.[15] Distinct from the enrichment of the monastery through pious gifts was the growth of its order, through the submission of old monasteries to Cluny and the establishment there of monks following Cluny's way of life.

During the tenth century it became relatively common for bishops or nobles to give Cluny ruined houses or houses populated by monks of dissolute life. Many of these monasteries were then settled by monks from Cluny. Some of these houses became priories in which the monks were considered part of Cluny's congregation. They were headed by priors, not by their own abbots, for they were considered to be under Cluny's abbot, even though they were located some distance from Cluny. Burgundian examples include the monastery of Paray-le-monial, discussed in the next chapter, which had monks from Cluny set in it and which became a priory at the end of the tenth century. The process of establishing Cluniac priories continued throughout the eleventh and twelfth centuries. In 1059 the long-abandoned monastery of La Charité-sur-Loire, which had been

[13]GC IV:72, no. 33. Plancher I.30 (pp. xxiv—xxv). For the original adherence to the Rule of Saint Benedict at Flavigny, see also Flavigny 22 (pp. 49—51) [Collenot, pp. 66—67].
[14]GC IV:76—77, no. 40. The charter was misdated by the editors of GC.
[15]Rosenwein, *Rhinoceros Bound*, pp. 36—37. Duby, *La société mâconnaise*, p. 68.

"harmed by the impious and had lost its dignity," according to the charter confirming its reformation, was submitted to Cluny as a priory by the bishop of Auxerre and the count of Nevers. In the following decades the house became a reforming center in its own right, with its own circle of dependent monasteries.[16] Many other monasteries adopted Cluny's customs without being given to Cluny; these retained their own abbots, and so did not become priories. They were reformed to Cluny's regular way of life, sometimes by an abbot who had been a monk at Cluny, but were not submitted to Cluny's direction.[17] The monastery of St.-Benoît-sur-Loire, for example, was reformed to Cluny's discipline in 938 (over the objections of some of its monks) by Duke Hugh the Great and the abbot of Cluny, with the consent of the pope.[18] The monastery of St.-Bénigne of Dijon, discussed in the next chapter, similarly adopted Cluny's way of life but retained its own abbot.

Cluny's *ordo*, its rule and the daily life of its monks, spread through Burgundy and beyond as it was adopted by or imposed on a growing number of monasteries. Though by the later twelfth century the Cluniac order had developed a somewhat monolithic appearance, in part in imitation of the Cistercian order,[19] in the tenth and eleventh centuries it was not clear what made a house "Cluniac," a question that in fact did not seem to concern the monks. *Ordo* for them meant regularity of life, not a closely affiliated group of monasteries.[20] Even in the region near Cluny, most religious houses were not submitted to that abbey. Cluny's order spread out not as a solid wave across Burgundy but as a series of individual and often scattered reforms of individual churches. But the chief method of reestablishing regularity at a deserted or dilapidated abbey was to give it to a reformed monastery, and Cluny's way of life was considered holy by many of those with abbeys to give.[21]

Bishops and secular nobles often gave Cluny not only ruined or

[16]La Charité 1 (pp. 1–3). Hunt, *Cluny under Saint Hugh*, p. 124.

[17]Many of the houses reformed by Cluny in the tenth century were located outside Burgundy; see the maps in Rosenwein, *Rhinoceros Bound*, pp. xiv–xv. These more distant houses usually did not become priories.

[18]Fleury 44 (pp. 110–14). See also Rosenwein, *Rhinoceros Bound*, p. 48.

[19]Adriaan H. Bredero, "Comment les institutions de l'Ordre de Cluny se sont rapprochées de Cîteaux," in *Istituzioni monastiche e istituzioni canonicali in Occidente (1123–1215)*, Miscellanea del Centro di studi medioevali 9 (Milan, 1980), pp. 166–80.

[20]Jacques Hourlier, "Cluny et la notion d'ordre religieux," in *À Cluny: Congrès scientifique, 9–11 juillet 1949* (Dijon, 1950), pp. 219–26. Giles Constable, "Cluniac Administration and Administrators in the Twelfth Century," in *Order and Innovation in the Middle Ages: Essays in Honor of Joseph R. Strayer*, ed. William C. Jordan, Bruce McNab, and Teofilo F. Ruiz (Princeton, 1976), pp. 17–18.

[21]Joachim Wollasch, *Mönchtum des Mittelalters zwischen Kirche und Welt* (Munich, 1973), pp. 147–49.

dissolute monasteries but parish churches, chapels, and small oratories as well. Occasionally such a church would become a priory, but this was rare. Cluny certainly did not "reform" all the churches it was given. In the case of parish churches and chapels, the abbot of Cluny now simply appointed the officiating priest; one might say that these churches went from being the property of a secular lord or bishop to being the property of Cluny.

Cluny and Secular Society

Both Cluny and her daughter houses received gifts from the laity which made possible the monks' continued prosperity. Although in the tenth century there was nothing like the huge flow of gifts that came to Cluny in the eleventh,[22] the abbey's cartularies still record a steady stream of pious donations. Dietrich Poeck, studying specifically the gifts laymen made to Cluny in return for burial in the abbey's cemetery, has found that both the absolute number of such gifts and their geographic spread increased steadily during the course of the tenth century. Whereas, at the beginning of the century, burial gifts (typically consisting of a *mansus* or *curtilis*, the amount of land theoretically required to support one peasant family) were usually of property located within eight kilometers of the abbey church, by the end of the century burial gifts more than thirty kilometers away had become common.[23]

Even before gifts to Cluny became common, they were often very large, sometimes consisting of large tracts of land and several churches. Typical is a gift that Count Alberic II of Mâcon made in 962, the year he succeeded his father as count. He gave Cluny, for his parents' souls, a large amount of property at Igé, eight kilometers southeast of Cluny, including three *mansi* with serfs and half the parish church, and a chapel and four more *mansi* with serfs in nearby villages. He specified that Cluny would receive the other half of the parish church when he died.[24]

The donors who gave Cluny land and churches often seem, like Alberic, to have been members of the upper aristocracy. It is difficult to do any sort of close analysis of the social standing of all the donors,

---

[22]Many of the tenth-century charters in Cluny's cartularies are not records of gifts but rather of the transactions by which some donors acquired the property they eventually gave Cluny.

[23]Dietrich Poeck, "Laienbegräbnisse in Cluny," *Frühmittelalterliche Studien*, 15 (1981), 80–121; see especially the maps on pp. 82, 88, 97, and 108–9.

[24]C 1124 (II:215–16). For Alberic, see Appendix A, pp. 264–65. For the churches given to Cluny, see also Gui de Valous, "Le domaine de l'abbaye de Cluny aux Xᵉ et XIᵉ siècles," *Annales de l'Académie de Mâcon*, 3rd ser. 22 (1920–21), 361–65.

since it was common practice in the tenth century to refer to someone
in a charter simply as *quidam vir* (or *quaedam femina*), even if the
individual is known from other evidence to have been of a noble family.[25] One certainly cannot assume that all those whose social position
the charters do not make clear must have been noble, but it would be
equally wrong, as some have maintained, to see in the *quidam viri* support for Cluny by the local "folk."[26] Many of these donors were at
any rate quite wealthy, to judge from the size of the gifts they made
Cluny, whether or not they are considered members of the nobility.
The brothers Adrald and Raimbert are typical. In 930 they, together
with their wives, gave Cluny vineyards in three different villages, two
located in the Mâconnais and one in the *pagus* of Autun, together
with appurtenant "houses, fields, woods, meadows, running and still
waters." One might consider these well-to-do free men examples of
the class that began to develop into petty lords and castellans a century later, as the number of those considered noble began to
expand.[27]

But Cluny was most consistently patronized in the tenth century by
men and women who were certainly members of the upper nobility.
One of the families that made the greatest number of gifts to Cluny in
the tenth century was that of the counts of Mâcon, mentioned above.
The counts, who acted as advocates for the monks, frequently gave
Cluny land and churches themselves and witnessed many gifts both
from other laymen and from bishops.[28] Acting as advocate meant
being involved in the internal as well as the external affairs of the
monastery. In 954 the monks of Cluny consulted with Count Leotold
before electing Maiolus as abbot.[29] A second family that supported
Cluny in the tenth century was related to Richard le Justicier, duke of
Burgundy, and was part of the group known to modern scholars as the

---

[25]For example, one Bertasia, called *nobili projenie* in a 926 charter, appeared in another charter two years later as simply *Bertazia femina;* C 271, 359 (I:265, 335). Stephen
Weinberger has suggested that, in the tenth century, people were or were not called noble in monastic documents depending on whether they acted as defenders of monastic
rights and possessions; "Nobles et noblesse dans la Provence médiévale (ca.
850–1100)," *Annales: Économies, Sociétés, Civilisations,* 36 (1981), 915–19. But this
explanation cannot have a universal application. In the first of the documents cited
above, Bertasia and her husband made a property transaction with a cleric; in the
second, where she is not called noble, she gave some property to Cluny for her
husband's soul.

[26]For example, Johannes Fechter, *Cluny, Adel und Volk* (diss., University of
Tübingen, 1966), pp. 48–50. Fechter's views have been effectively refuted by
Rosenwein, *Rhinoceros Bound,* pp. 32–34.

[27]C 403, 404 (I:387–90). Bouchard, "Origins of the Nobility," pp. 531–32.

[28]C 432, 625, 655, 680, 719, 729, 753, 768, 780, 799, 1044, 1124, 1198, 1291
(I:420–21, 582–83, 609–10, 632–34, 671–72, 685, 710–11, 723–24, 733–34, 751;
II:137–38, 215–16, 280–81, 368).

[29]C 883 (II:1–2).

Bosonids. He, with his wife, sons, and relatives—especially Raoul, king of France (923–936); Richard's nephew Louis the Blind, king of Provence (890–928) and emperor (900–928); Louis's son Charles-Constantine, count of Vienne; and Louis's second cousin Hugh, count of Vienne and king of Italy (926–947)—were extremely generous to Cluny. Hugh and his son Lothair, co-kings of Italy, even sent messengers back from Pavia in 934 to convey title to Cluny of two villages in the region of Lyon, including "chapels, houses, fields, vineyards, meadows, pastures, woods, waters, hills and valleys, and serfs of both sexes." Lothair's daughter Emma retained her family allegiance to Cluny; after marrying the Carolingian king of France, she persuaded her husband to confirm a gift to Cluny in 983/4.[30] The third of the great families that patronized Cluny in the tenth century was that of the counts of Chalon. Like the counts of Mâcon, whose power had been established two generations earlier, the counts of Chalon began making gifts to Cluny almost immediately upon reaching power and shortly founded the house of Paray-le-monial, with the assistance of the abbot of Cluny, as discussed in Chapter 4. All of these great tenth-century patrons of Cluny were quite new to their positions when they began making gifts to Cluny. The first count of Mâcon was an adventurer from Narbonne who had claimed the county by marrying the viscount's daughter. Richard le Justicier was only one generation removed from household officials in the king's court. The first count of Chalon, son of the viscount, had been confirmed in his office by the king only a short time before founding Paray.[31] In the violence of the tenth century, none of these families was assured of retaining their recently won power. As Barbara Rosenwein has argued, perhaps what attracted these powerful families to Cluny was the very stability of the monastic life. Surrounded by wars and invasions—Abbot Maiolus of Cluny was even kidnapped by the Saracens in Provence in 972—the monks continued to follow an orderly life, based on the liturgical round. Powerful men, riding high on Fortune's wheel, but always in danger of a rapid descent, found the order of Cluny immensely attractive, and they had the wealth to endow the monks they wished to have pray for them.[32] The ascent to power of such men as Count Lambert of Chalon and Count Otto-

---

[30]C 223, 229, 230, 379, 396, 397, 417 [this is the gift from Hugh and Lothair], 499, 627, 656, 1646 (I:213, 219–21, 358–61, 379–82, 403–4, 483–85, 584–85, 610–11; II:680).

[31]Bouchard, "Origins of the Nobility," pp. 512–13, 516–18.

[32]Rosenwein, *Rhinoceros Bound*, pp. 40–41, 101–2. For the capture of the abbot by the Saracens, see Syro, *Vita Sancti Maioli* 3, PL CXXXVII:765–67; and P.-A. Amargier, "La capture de Saint Maieul de Cluny et l'expulsion des Sarrasins de Provence," *Revue Bénédictine*, 73 (1963), 317–19. For the troubled situation in Provence at this period, see Poly, *La Provence*, pp. 3–29.

William of Burgundy, who took over the county of Mâcon in the 980s, was marked by generous gifts to Cluny, which were almost as clear an indication of a new position as any exercise of power.

The growth of Cluny's possessions in the century after its foundation, it must be stressed, took place without any distinctions being made between those who should and those who should not hold ecclesiastical property, including parish churches and the income from altars. The principle that laymen should not hold church property was not enunciated as a principle until the later eleventh century.[33] In its willingness to see churches in lay hands, Cluny was very much a part of the late Carolingian era. Even though the older scholarly view—that Charles Martel had seized all ecclesiastical property to distribute to his followers and create a warrior class—has been discredited as too sweeping,[34] it is clear that the need for a sharp distinction between those who could hold secular property and those who could hold church property never occurred to those in authority in the early Middle Ages.

Although the abbots of Cluny would fight at length to recover property they felt had been improperly taken from them, they were also quite willing to grant the abbey's secular friends some of the property they had been given, in return for a nominal rent. These were grants *in precaria*, made for the lifetime of the recipient and sometimes of his children. Churches and agricultural land might both be granted *in precaria*. Precarial grants were a way to reward a supporter, or even to rid oneself of the burden of managing a distant piece of property, without permanently alienating that property. In the early years of the eleventh century, for example, Abbot Odilo gave Agnes, daughter of Count Otto-William of Burgundy and duchess of Aquitaine, a large amount of land, in remembrance of the *familiaritas et pie societas* of her family, according to the charter. This precarial grant was made "not for any money or reward but for goodwill only."[35] A large proportion of the documents of the tenth century recording transactions between laymen and churchmen (bishops as well as abbots) describes not gifts but precarial grants. Written records were needed to remind the principals a generation later (especially if the grant had been made gratuitously) that such a grant did not create ownership.[36]

[33]Jean Leclercq, François Vandenbroucke, and Louis Bouyer, *The Spirituality of the Middle Ages*, A History of Christian Spirituality 2 (New York, 1968), pp. 95—98.

[34]Walter Goffart, *The Le Mans Forgeries*, Harvard Historical Series 76 (Cambridge, Mass., 1966), pp. 6—22. Bernard S. Bachrach, "Charles Martel, Mounted Shock Combat, the Stirrup, and Feudalism," *Studies in Medieval and Renaissance History*, 7 (1970), 66—72.

[35]C 2742 (III:765—66).

[36]See also Valous, "Le domaine de l'abbaye de Cluny," pp. 378—81. For grants *in precaria* from bishops, see for example M 296 (p. 175); GC IV:226, no. 6; Autun/Église 1.42 (I:69); Quantin I.73 (pp. 141—42); and Nevers/St.-Cyr 20 (pp. 42—43).

The lack of a sharp distinction at Cluny between "secular" and "ecclesiastical" sorts of property is further indicated by the fact that, when a layman gave Cluny a chapel or parish church, the monks did not insist on receiving the entire church. As Hans-Erich Mager first argued, since Cluny often accepted half a church while leaving the other share in the hands of the lay donor, or took a church without its tithes or tithes without a church, or even granted a nobleman one church in exchange for another, the abbots do not seem to have had any conscious program to remove churches from the hands of the laity.[37] The same practice may be seen at Cluny's daughter houses. Paray-le-monial, for example, in the mid-eleventh century accepted a knight's gift consisting of half of the church and revenues of St.-Léger.[38] Therefore the general passage of churches from the hands of the secular nobility to the monks of Burgundian houses, a process that began in the tenth century, cannot be considered due to a conscious stand antithetical to lay possession of any ecclesiastical property.

Rather, gifts of property from laymen and precarial grants to laymen all formed part of an ongoing association between Cluny and its secular neighbors, with property transactions serving to cement the relationship—a relationship that in some cases was more important to the monks than the actual property involved. This attitude may best be illustrated through the example of the lords of Brancion, a family whose generosity to Cluny in the tenth century was second only to that of the dukes and counts mentioned above.[39] The chapel of St.-Saturn, originally given by Letbald, lord of Brancion, to his wife Doda on their marriage in 925, became Cluny's property in 951 when Doda's children by her second husband gave it to the monks for their parents' souls. But the monks of Cluny did not keep the chapel; rather, the abbot granted it *in precaria* in 961 to Warulf, Letbald's younger brother, along with some other property located north of Cluny. Interestingly, only one year previously Warulf had been forced by the count of Mâcon to recognize that St.-Saturn was Cluny's, not his—the precarial grant may then have been made as a compromise. After Warulf died the abbot Maiolus again granted this church *in precaria* to Warulf's grandson Maiolus (probably named for the abbot although he was no relation), a canon at Mâcon.[40]

The pattern of family members granting property to Cluny which Cluny later granted to other family members could become quite

---

[37]Hans-Erich Mager, "Studien über das Verhältnis der Cluniacenser zum Eigenkirchenwesen," in *Neue Forschungen über Cluny und die Cluniacenser*, ed. Gerd Tellenbach (Freiburg, 1959), pp. 190–207. See for example C 1321, 1322 (II:296–99).
[38]Paray 21 (pp. 16–17).
[39]For the lords of Brancion, see Appendix A, pp. 295–99.
[40]C 254, 789, 941, 1087 (I:245–46, 750; II:47, 180–81).

complicated, as the example of some property at Coulanges and Boye demonstrates. (These two *villae* are located ten kilometers northeast of Cluny.) The property was originally given to Cluny in 951 by the previously mentioned widow Doda, formerly lady of Brancion, and a certain Raculph (who may have been her brother), but the abbot soon granted it to her brother-in-law Warulf. Warulf's son Letbald held it after him. Warulf's daughter Testa returned the church of Coulanges to Cluny at the beginning of the eleventh century, but her brother Letbald, now bishop of Mâcon, granted it *in precaria* to her nephew Roclenus (a cleric, son of her husband's brother); the abbot of Cluny did not dispute the right of the bishop of Mâcon to give away Cluny's property.[41] The tenth-century evidence of such transactions back and forth between a family and Cluny is perhaps better for the lords of Brancion than for any other local family, but it is clear that the abbots, in trying to maintain friendly relations with this powerful family, were quite willing to see some of their property, even churches, in secular hands.

It is necessary then to avoid reading the ideas of "reform" developed at the end of the eleventh century back into the earlier period. Many monasteries of regular life—including Cluny—were established and flourished long before a sharp distinction was drawn between those who should and should not hold ecclesiastical property. It has sometimes been maintained that the spread of Cluny's *ordo* was from the beginning in opposition to the secular world, which had somehow contaminated other tenth-century religious houses,[42] but reform was not a monolithic entity. A monastery might well observe a life of austerity and obedience, a life very different from that of secular nobles, without seeking to eliminate laymen from owning all ecclesiastical property, much less without trying to establish a separation between the monastery and the society of its noble neighbors.

Indeed, Cluny needed the friendship of those noble neighbors, for when Cluny's regular way of life was established at a monastery, it was the result of a partnership between Cluny's abbot and the local

[41]C 517, 793, 802, 1087, 1088, 1460, 2719 (I:502–3, 744–45, 754–56; II:180–82, 513–15; III:741–43). M 465, 523 (pp. 268, 308). Valous thinks that two separate *villae* named Collonge are involved; "Le domaine de l'abbaye de Cluny," p. 432. The context makes this unlikely. I think all these documents refer to one place, Coulanges, which C 793 identifies as being in the *ager* of Grevilly (fifteen kilometers northeast of Cluny). See also Maurice Chaume, *Les origines du duché de Bourgogne*, II, iii (Dijon, 1931; rpt. 1977), pp. 1127–28. For the meaning of *villa* and *ager*, see, most recently, François Bange, "L'*ager* et la *villa*: Structures du paysage et du peuplement dans la région mâconnaise à la fin du Haut Moyen Age (IXe–XIe siècles)," *Annales: Économies, Sociétés, Civilisations*, 39 (1984), 529–69.

[42]See, among many examples, Marcel Pacaut, "Structures monastiques, société et Église en Occident aux XIe et XIIe siècles," *Cahiers d'histoire*, 20 (1975), 119–22.

lords. It would be incorrect to describe Cluny as possessing a "will to expand," since the abbots seem to have been uniformly unconcerned with expansion of the order per se; and though they were usually willing to receive and reform the monasteries given to them for that purpose, there are cases in which the abbot was unwilling to establish a priory because of the difficulty in finding the dozen monks thought a necessary minimum. Laymen were eager to give their churches to Cluny even when Cluny was less eager to receive them.[43] Perhaps the chief contribution of tenth-century Cluny to the spread of the religious life in Burgundy was its establishment of a role for the secular nobility in monastic reform.[44] The intimacy thus established between reformed monasticism and the secular nobility continued throughout the eleventh and twelfth centuries, tying nobles to the new orders as they had been tied to Cluny, but its roots were in the generally unreformed tenth century.

Eleventh- and twelfth-century Cluny will be further discussed in the following chapters. With its origins in a period when the ruined church was most typical, it became a model other monasteries could use in reforming their own religious life. The religious movement that might be said to have begun, at least in Burgundy, with Cluny's foundation, underwent a number of changes in the following three centuries, but it never retreated during this time. Cluny's foundation, and the revitalization of the monastic life at many other houses, took place well before the lines were sharply drawn between the spheres of secular and ecclesiastical activity, and involved both regular monks and their noble neighbors. And Cluny established a pattern that was repeated, though in modified form, at later monastic foundations: a powerful layman who had recently attained a high position would almost immediately use that position to endow the holiest monks he could find.

[43]Mager, "Studien," pp. 170–78. Tellenbach, "Il monachesimo riformato," p. 129. Giles Constable, "Monastic Possession of Churches and 'Spiritualia' in the Age of Reform," in Il monachesimo e la riforma ecclesiastica (1049–1122), Miscellanea del Centro di studi medioevali 6 (Milan, 1971), p. 311. Hunt, Cluny under Saint Hugh, pp. 150–54.

[44]Joachim Wollasch, "Reform und Adel in Burgund," in Investiturstreit und Reichsverfassung, ed. Josef Fleckenstein (Munich, 1973), pp. 281–85.

[4]

Monastic Foundations
and Reform in Burgundy

The growth in Cluny's size and influence foreshadowed a wider trend. During the eleventh and twelfth centuries, there was an increase in the number of reformed monasteries in Burgundy, entailing both the foundation of new houses and the reformation of old, previously existing houses. Rather than a self-directed or monolithic movement, the great expansion in the number of monasteries of regular life was the product of numerous individual decisions, made by laymen and monks, to establish a house in a particular location.

Monastic Reform around the Year 1000

Much of the monastic reform of the late tenth and eleventh centuries was similar to that carried out by Cluny in the tenth century. Very few completely new monasteries were founded in Burgundy, and those few were generally the foundations of dukes or counts. New monastic communities were most commonly founded when a nobleman gave a church he had owned (or even his castle chapel) to a monastery of renowned regularity of life. Cluny helped establish more new communities of monks in the first half or three-quarters of the eleventh century than did any other single Burgundian house in the same period. Sometimes the church in which monks were set was an abandoned monastery, sometimes a chapel or rural parish church that had not before been served by monks. Some of these churches became priories, while others, though staffed at at least in part by monks from the mother house, retained their independence and their own abbots. Often only a few monks might settle in the church, too few to have sustained it had it been an independent monastery but enough to establish the mother house's claim to it and to offer prayers for the house's noble founder. A tiny church supporting only a few monks was known as a cell; monks might be rotated in and out of it from the mother church. Many other churches given to monasteries remained parish churches or chapels and housed no monks.

Both secular nobles and bishops gave churches in their control to the great reforming houses as dependencies. A donor usually gave a church he held to a nearby monastery; almost all the churches Cluny received in the eleventh century, for example, were located in Burgundy.[1] If the nobleman who helped establish a new body of monks was very powerful, he might also establish other houses, and if he was a simple castellan he might establish only one house on which his descendants' pious generosity would be focused for generations, but in any case such reforms were a matter involving only a man's family, not his neighbors. The following examples are taken from the late tenth and early eleventh centuries, a period in which a number of old Burgundian houses were restored.[2]

St.-Bénigne of Dijon was, after Cluny, one of the most important reformed monasteries of Burgundy. A very old house, it had fallen into what an eleventh-century chronicler called an "ambiguous position" after the Viking and Magyar invasions. It was reformed in 990 by Otto-William, count of Burgundy, and his brother-in-law Bruno, bishop of Langres. They asked the abbot of Cluny to send them twelve monks, headed by Otto-William's cousin William, a monk at Cluny who became the first reformed abbot. The necrology of St.-Bénigne commemorates Bishop Bruno as having reformed the house with "the great help of Count Otto-William of Burgundy."[3] St.-Bénigne, reformed to Cluny's *ordo* but not her direction, quickly became the center of its own reform movement. For example, shortly before 1000, Duke Henry of Burgundy, Otto-William's stepfather, gave St.-Bénigne the church of St.-Vivant of Vergy, and Abbot William established a priory there. Otto-William's son, Count Raynald of Burgundy, gave St.-Bénigne a small church in the castle of Vesoul,

---

[1]Noreen Hunt, *Cluny under Saint Hugh, 1049–1109* (London, 1967), pp. 126, 136.

[2]There were some twenty-five major monasteries in Burgundy in the tenth century. Most had been founded in Merovingian times and were reformed, with some assistance from Cluny's abbot, at the end of the tenth century or the beginning of the eleventh. The only important exceptions, besides Cluny itself, were Vézelay, Pouthières, and Tournus, which had all been founded only in the second half of the ninth century. The smaller monasteries, *abbatiolae*, such as St.-Eusèbe of Auxerre or St.-Amatre of Langres, which had never had more than a few monks, were reformed only in the twelfth century and then as houses of canons regular. For details on the Burgundian monasteries between the sixth and the eleventh century, see my forthcoming "Monastic Reform in Burgundy before the 'Age of Reform.'"

[3]St.-B. II.259 (pp. 48–49). Chron. St.-B., pp. 129–31. Dijon, Bibliothèque municipale, MS 591, fol. 162v. See also Constance B. Bouchard, "Laymen and Church Reform around the Year 1000: The Case of Otto-William, Count of Burgundy," *Journal of Medieval History*, 5 (1979), 1–10.

and four monks were set there.[4] St.-Bénigne continued to receive gifts from the counts and dukes of Burgundy throughout the eleventh century.

St.-Germain of Auxerre, like St.-Bénigne an old house, owed its reform to the concern of noble families long associated with the house. It had been originally founded in the fifth century as a basilica in honor of Saint Germain, bishop of Auxerre. It became a monastery in the sixth century and produced a number of scholars and bishops of Auxerre over the next three centuries. In the late ninth century, however, it lost both its regularity and its independence. Hugh, called "the Abbot," of the great noble family of Welfs which produced the kings of imperial Burgundy and who himself was the uncle of Charles the Bald, took the direction of St.-Germain by 853, even though less than twenty years earlier Louis the Pious had granted the monks the right to elect an abbot from among their own members. Hugh was succeeded by Lothair, son of Charles the Bald, and though he seems to have adopted the monastic life himself, after his death the monastery was given to Count Boso, a *fidelis* of the king. In the tenth century, St.-Germain was headed by the dukes and counts of Burgundy, beginning with Richard le Justicier, Boso's brother, who had himself married a woman of the Welf family. St.-Germain might thus be considered a classic example of decadence, of a house suffering "in the hands of the laity."[5] But it was the nobles controlling St.-Germain who brought about its eventual reform. In the 980s, Duke Henry of Burgundy, who had been lay abbot of the monastery for some twenty years, decided to reform St.-Germain. Not surprisingly, after over a century of lay rule there were few monks left at St.-Germain, and those there did not follow a strictly regular life. Henry and his half brother Heribert, bishop of Auxerre (971–996), asked Maiolus, abbot of Cluny, to send them a monk versed in strict observance of the Benedictine Rule who would restore the abbey's reputation. Maiolus agreed, and, restored to Cluny's discipline under their new abbot, though not made a dependent of Cluny, the monks of St.-Germain flourished for close to a century.[6]

[4]Chron. St.-B., pp. 135, 194. Niethard Bulst, *Untersuchungen zu den Klosterreform Wilhelms von Dijon (962–1031)* (Bonn, 1973), pp. 5–15.

[5]Franz J. Felten, in a recent revisionist study, has argued that the lay abbots, frequently found in the Frankish period, should not automatically be considered inimical to the church. While his thesis—that the monasteries of the sixth through ninth centuries should be viewed in their temporal context, rather than from the viewpoint of later reformers—is certainly valuable, the churchmen themselves, from the tenth century onward, as he himself notes, began to find lay abbots a detriment to the regular life, and it was at this point that the high medieval reform movement began. Felten, *Äbte und Laienäbte im Frankenreich: Studien zum Verhältnis von Staat und Kirche im früheren Mittelalter* (Stuttgart, 1980), pp. 1–17, 304.

[6]*Gesta pontificum*, pp. 382–83. Quantin I.82 (pp. 157–59). For the lay abbots of St.-Germain, see Quantin I.23, 34, 38, 45, 46, 56, 68, 72 (pp. 66, 72, 87, 94, 108, 133, 139).

Plate 3. The twelfth-century tower of
St.-Germain of Auxerre

But St.-Germain did not remain reformed. About a century later, the abbot, who had acquired his position at a very early age, fell into some sort of "iniquity," according to contemporary sources. The house was once again restored to a strict observance of Cluniac customs, but not by the abbot of Cluny. This reform was carried out by Bishop Humbald of Auxerre (1095–1114), whose first act as bishop was to have the current abbot of St.-Germain dismissed, and by Counts William of Nevers and Stephen of Blois, the second of whom held the advocacy of St.-Germain in fief from the duke of Burgundy. The new abbot was a Cluniac monk who was nephew of the abbot of Cluny, but before assuming his office he was absolved, at the insistence of the bishop of Auxerre, of his allegiance to his uncle and to Cluny.[7] It is clear that on the two occasions, a century apart, that St.-Germain was reformed, it was at the initiative of secular lords and bishops; these lords saw Cluny as an appropriate house from which to obtain reforming abbots, but Cluny herself neither initiated the reform nor brought St.-Germain into her order.

Another important reform that took place at the very end of the tenth century was that of Paray-le-monial. This house, one of the few new tenth-century foundations, had been founded in 973 (under the name Orval) by Lambert, count of Chalon-sur-Saône.[8] He founded it on his own land, at his own expense, "with the help of Maiolus, abbot of Cluny," according to the foundation charter. Maiolus sent monks from Cluny to live there, and Lambert specified that the house would be free of all "secular domination," but the house was not made a dependency of Cluny. It maintained its own abbot and turned to the count of Chalon rather than to the abbot of Cluny for protection. After Lambert's death around 978, Count Geoffrey Greymantle of Anjou, who married Lambert's widow and acted as count of Chalon, and Lambert's son Hugh all gave a number of churches and pieces of land to Orval. But within twenty-five years of its foundation, Orval already required reformation. It was reformed in 999 by Lambert's son Hugh, count of Chalon.

Hugh was a powerful count who also acted as bishop of Auxerre for forty years at the beginning of the eleventh century (999–1039). He is often referred to in the charters of the time as "both count and bishop." As count, he fought the king in the Burgundian wars of

---

[7]For this second reform of St.-Germain, see C 3859 (V:209–10); and Constance Brittain Bouchard, *Spirituality and Administration: The Role of the Bishop in Twelfth-Century Auxerre*, Speculum Anniversary Monographs 5 (Cambridge, Mass., 1979), pp. 26–28. For the count of Blois's advocacy of the house, see also Yves Sassier, *Recherches sur le pouvoir comtal en Auxerrois du Xe au début du XIIIe siècle* (Auxerre, 1980), pp. 50–60.

[8]Paray 2–4, 14 (pp. 2–6, 12). C 2484 (III:562–66). *Gesta pontificum*, p. 386. For the counts of Chalon, see Appendix A, pp. 307–14.

1002—1004. As bishop, he rebuilt the cathedral of Auxerre and helped restore lost property to several churches in his diocese. In both his capacities, as count and bishop, he proved himself a patron of reform and a close friend of the monastery of Cluny. It was in his role as count rather than bishop—Paray was in his county but not his diocese—that he reformed the house. The reformation charter spoke vaguely of "brotherly love declining and iniquity increasing"; Hugh, the charter said, saw that "worldly deeds will lead to ruin" and that "this house had not been able to remain in the state in which his father had established it." Though the monastery had been declared free of secular domination when founded, there was no question but that it was Hugh's to dispose of as he would, and he gave it to Odilo, abbot of Cluny, as a dependent house. Henceforth it did not have an abbot of its own but rather a prior, answerable to Cluny. Hugh had his uncle Robert, his half brother Maurice, Count Otto-William of Burgundy, and Otto-William's son Gui all confirm this reform. Unlike St.-Bénigne and St.-Germain, then, it became a priory.

The regularity of Paray was now assured. It continued to receive gifts from the counts of Chalon throughout the eleventh and twelfth centuries. Over the next forty years Hugh made numerous gifts to the monks, many of which were confirmed by his nephew Theobold, who succeeded him as count of Chalon and continued his generosity after Hugh's death. That Hugh asked for confirmation from Theobold rather than the canons of Auxerre again indicates that these gifts were made in his capacity as count, not bishop. After Theobold succeeded as count he again confirmed the abbey's rights and possessions; his daughter Ermengard, lady of Bourbon, as she was dying, gave Paray land that had been part of her dowry; and Theobold's grandson, Gui of Thiers, count of Chalon, confirmed all of his predecessors' gifts to Paray when he left on the First Crusade. His descendants in the twelfth century reiterated and reconfirmed the house's rights and privileges.[9]

St.-Marcel-lès-Chalon, a house originally founded in the sixth century but which was in ruins in the tenth century, provides another example of reform on the eve of the eleventh century. The house was reformed when Geoffrey Greymantle, Hugh's stepfather and acting count of Chalon, gave St.-Marcel to Cluny at the end of the tenth century, to become a priory. Geoffrey did so with the assistance of Abbot Maiolus of Cluny and Duke Henry of Burgundy. "The religious life was almost extinguished" there when Geoffrey reformed it, according to a charter drawn up two generations later. In 999,

[9]Paray 15, 107, 140, 180, 182—86, 193—94, 208, 209, 222 (pp. 13, 56—57, 68, 90—93, 97—99, 107—9, 119—21).

Plate 4. The south transept of Cluny. Of the church finished at the beginning of the twelfth century, this is the only substantial part that remains.

Plate 5. The old front doors of the abbey church of Cluny. This view, looking down what was once the nave to the south transept, gives an idea of the size of the church.

Geoffrey's stepson, Hugh of Chalon, confirmed the reform of St.-Marcel at the same time he gave Paray to Cluny.[10]

The reforms detailed above, and others that took place from the end of the tenth century through the late eleventh, were carried out at the initiative of and with the consent of counts, viscounts, and bishops from powerful families. The bishops who helped further the cause of monastic reform were not themselves "reformed," at least in the later eleventh-century sense of the term. Bruno of Langres had been appointed bishop by his uncle the king when still five years too young to be canonically elected; and Hugh, simultaneously bishop of Auxerre and count of Chalon, played a personal and active role in the Burgundian wars of the early eleventh century (see also above, Chapter 2). Ecclesiastics did not have to pursue the austere monastic life themselves in order to support it.

This establishment of bodies of reformed monks produced a large number of dependent houses for the great Burgundian monasteries. In 931 Pope John XI had confirmed Cluny's right to place the monasteries it had been given under the authority of Cluny's abbot, and by 937 there were already seventeen such dependent monasteries listed in papal confirmations of Cluny's possessions. This figure had increased to thirty-seven in 994 and over sixty by 1048, and even so these figures do not include those houses like St.-Bénigne which retained their own abbots nor the many churches given to Cluny where no monks were set. The number of Cluniac priories continued to increase in the twelfth century; the figure for the end of the century has been estimated at anywhere from a few hundred houses to a thousand, depending on how one defines "Cluniac."[11]

New Forms of the Religious Life

While Cluny long continued to be given churches to reform, by the twelfth century the traditional monasticism it represented was no longer seen as the only or even the chief way to holiness. A number of new forms of the religious life had appeared. It is worth summarizing briefly these different forms, because all of them had an impact on the monastic life.

The first chronologically were the hermits, who began to appear in

[10]St.-Marcel 6 (pp. 11–12). C 2484, 3341 (III:562–66; IV:429–31). See also Martine Chauney, "Les origines du prieuré clunisien de Saint-Marcel-lès-Chalon," in *Mélanges d'histoire et d'archéologie offerts au professeur Kenneth John Conant* (Mâcon, 1977), pp. 93–94.

[11]John XI, Letter 1, PL CXXXII:1057. Bede K. Lackner, *The Eleventh-Century Background of Cîteaux*, Cistercian Studies Series 8 (Washington, D.C., 1972), pp. 40–42.

significant numbers in Italy around the year 1000. Since hermits were by their very nature solitary and unorganized, it is impossible to date their appearance or spread with any exactness, but by the middle of the eleventh century men following some sort of eremetical life were becoming relatively common in France. Though some hermits lived and died in total obscurity, others attracted groups of followers, so that they slipped into the cenobitic life of a community or joined an established monastery (often at the urging of a bishop, who attempted to regularize their life), bringing with them a desire for solitude and contemplation.[12] The Carthusians, established at La Grande Chartreuse around 1080, institutionalized many eremetical elements. Even when new twelfth-century monasteries did not grow directly out of a hermitage, they often incorporated such eremetical ideals as silence and solitude.[13]

Several houses in Burgundy were founded on eremetical bases. The Benedictine abbey of St.-Rigaud, for example, was blessed by the pope in 1071, and confirmed in its adherence to Benedict's Rule, a few years after the house had been established as a hermitage by a monk from the Auvergne. The hermitage had received several gifts of land and churches from the counts of Chalon and Forez, the lords of Bourbon, and some local knights before the bishop of Autun urged the hermits gathered there to adopt a regular life, under one of their number whom they elected as abbot, and to seek the pope's confirmation.[14] Several of the Cistercian houses were also founded on sites of hermitages, as noted below.

Another form of the "apostolic life" which had a significant impact on the religious life of the twelfth century, though it never attracted many followers in Burgundy, was that of the wandering preachers, who voluntarily adopted poverty and an itinerant life in imitation of what they perceived to be the life of Jesus and the apostles.[15] Many wandering preachers, like hermits, were "regularized," persuaded to

---

[12]Henrietta Leyser, *Hermits and the New Monasticism: A Study of Religious Communities in Western Europe, 1000–1150* (London, 1984), pp. 2–5. Jean Leclercq, François Vandenbroucke, and Louis Bouyer, *The Spirituality of the Middle Ages*, A History of Christian Spirituality 2 (New York, 1968), pp. 110–19. Giles Constable, "The Study of Monastic History Today," in *Essays on the Reconstruction of Medieval History*, ed. Vaclav Mudroch and G. S. Couse (Montreal, 1974), pp. 30–32; and Constable, "Eremetical Forms of Monastic Life," in *Istituzioni monastiche e istituzioni canonicali in Occidente (1123–1215)*, Miscellanea del Centro di studi medioevali 9 (Milan, 1980), pp. 239–64.

[13]The monastery of Cîteaux, though always organized as an abbey under an abbot's direction, was originally referred to as a *heremum*, to indicate its isolation. "Exordium parvum" 3, 6, ed. Bouton and Van Damme, *Textes*, pp. 59, 63.

[14]Arch. Saône-et-Loire, H 142, nos. 1–4. M 5–6 (pp. 4–5).

[15]Herbert Grundmann, *Religiöse Bewegungen im Mittelalter*, new ed. (Hildesheim, 1961), pp. 5–17, 41–66. M.-D. Chenu, *Nature, Man, and Society in the Twelfth Century*, ed. and trans. Jerome Taylor and Lester K. Little (Chicago, 1968), pp. 219–30.

adopt a rule and settle in one place. In the twelfth century those who clung to their itinerant preaching remained on the fringes of heresy. Only in the thirteenth century, with the organization of the Franciscan and Dominican friars, was this form of the "apostolic life" given a regular place within the organization of the church.[16] The radical "apostolic" groups of the twelfth century attracted mostly young adults, including many young men (and women) from the wealthy burgher and knightly classes, who adopted a life of voluntary poverty. Many such conversions of course were not permanent; membership in the ill-defined apostolic groups was always in flux. But by the end of the twelfth century the elements of preaching and poverty had become firmly established as the essential elements of the apostolic life—which was no longer always equated with the monastic life.[17]

A form of religious life with more direct impact in Burgundy was that of the canons regular, who first appeared in the mid-eleventh century. Like monks, they followed a life of individual poverty and collective property, in obedience to their elected head (usually called a prior rather than an abbot, although, unlike the priors heading Cluniac daughter houses, the priors of houses of canons regular had no abbots over them). Rather than following the Benedictine Rule or another monastic rule, however, these canons followed a rule believed to be based on instructions left by Saint Augustine. In general (though not always), they served in a body as priests in a parish church or other church frequented by laymen (such as a castle chapel). They instructed the world, by preaching or by the example of their own lives, rather than seeking first their own way to God and praying for the world in the solitude of the cloister.[18] The preaching that was condemned in wandering teachers was encouraged in consecrated priests living as groups of canons. In the later eleventh and early twelfth centuries, when there was a renewed emphasis on apostolicity, the individual poverty, common life, and preaching of the canons regular attracted a great deal of support.

There were a variety of canons regular in the twelfth century. There were individual houses of canons, such as Oigny, founded in

[16]M.-H. Vicaire, *The Apostolic Life*, trans. William E. De Naple (Chicago, 1966), pp. 88–91. Grundmann, *Religiöse Bewegungen*, pp. 70–71, 135–36.

[17]Brenda M. Bolton, "Paupertas Christi: Old Wealth and New Poverty in the Twelfth Century," in *Renaissance and Renewal in Christian History*, ed. Derek Baker, Studies in Church History 14 (Oxford, 1977), pp. 95–96. Lester K. Little, *Religious Poverty and the Profit Economy in Medieval Europe* (Ithaca, 1978), pp. 70–83.

[18]Caroline W. Bynum, "The Spirituality of Regular Canons in the Twelfth Century: A New Approach," *Medievalia et Humanistica*, n.s. 4 (1973), 3–7, 18–19; and Bynum, *Docere verbo et exemplo: An Aspect of Twelfth-Century Spirituality*, Harvard Theological Studies 31 (Missoula, Mont., 1979), pp. 1–5, 195–96. R. W. Southern, *Western Society and the Church in the Middle Ages* (Harmondsworth, England, 1970), pp. 241–50.

1116 by Lord Gaudin of Duesme and Lord Milo of Frôlois, who, with the consent of the duke and the bishop of Autun, gave a "religious man" all the woods, meadows, fields and tithes they had at Oigny.[19] There were orders of affiliated houses of such canons, most notably the Premonstratensians. Premonstratensian canons were established in the long-abandoned churches of St.-Marien and Notre-Dame of Auxerre by the count and bishop of Auxerre between 1139 and 1141.[20] The house of Septfontaines, originally an independent house of Augustinian canons established around 1115, became absorbed into the Premonstratensian order somewhat later.[21]

Often the first bishop to encourage the establishment of these canons was also the first bishop elected "canonically" in the wake of the Gregorian reform. It is interesting to note that bishops put into office by their relatives or bishops accused of simony often supported reformed monks, as mentioned above, but showed little interest in parish churches (many of which had long been ruined); however, the bishops elected canonically set out to refound and reform most urban parish churches, even though they saw no need for a strict rule in their own cathedral chapters. Canons regular took over a large proportion of urban parish churches, often replacing chapters of secular canons, as they did at Châtillon in 1138.[22] In 1120 Pope Calixtus II urged the bishop of Auxerre to replace all the secular canons in and around the city with monks or canons regular; by the middle of the twelfth century, the only "non-reformed" body was the cathedral chapter itself.[23] By the end of the twelfth century, houses of canons regular of all types probably outnumbered French monasteries in numbers of houses if not necessarily in numbers of brothers.[24] Unfortunately, not nearly as much is known about canons regular—the canons' origins, their property, their daily activities—as about monks. Very few houses produced cartularies (perhaps because they often had little property); the only Burgundian bodies of canons

[19]GC IV:85, no. 48. This charter is misdated 1106 by the editors. Duesme is nine kilometers north of Oigny, Frôlois seven kilometers southwest.

[20]*Gesta pontificum*, p. 419. Robert of St.-Marien, *Chronicon* 1126, 1139, MGH SS XXVI:231–35. Quantin I.239 (pp. 282–83). Quantin II.134 (p. 145). See also Bouchard, *Spirituality and Administration*, pp. 56–57.

[21]Arch. Haute-Marne, 10 H 4, 10 H 12.

[22]GC IV:170, no. 46.

[23]Quantin I.135 (pp. 251–52). For the reform of the churches of Auxerre, see GC XII:134, no. 48; and Quantin I.164, 209 (pp. 284–86, 348–49). See also Bouchard, *Spirituality and Administration*, pp. 28–29, 56–57.

[24]Lester K. Little, "Evangelical Poverty, the New Money Economy, and Violence," in *Poverty in the Middle Ages*, ed. David Flood (Paderborn, 1975), pp. 15–16. Jacques Hourlier, *L'âge classique, 1140–1378: Les religieux*, Histoire du droit et des institutions de l'Église en Occident 10 (Paris, 1971), pp. 22, 81–84.

regular for whom any substantial documentation survives are St.-Étienne of Dijon, Châtillon, and Notre-Dame of Beaujeu.

Houses of canons regular were established by ecclesiastical leaders and by men from all levels of the aristocracy, sometimes as one foundation among many, sometimes as a house to which the secular founder closely attached himself and his family. St.-Étienne of Dijon, located in the duke's capital, was one of the most influential houses of canons regular in Burgundy. It was an old house that had been refounded as a house of canons in 1032 (see below, Chapter 10). The house adopted the Augustinian Rule in the twelfth century, but its reform shows that even then the forces of tradition could prevent or at least slow radical change. In 1113 Bishop Joceran of Langres ordered the house reformed, but he could not expel the current canons. Rather, he arranged that those canons who wanted to "live canonically," according to the Augustinian Rule, should separate from the rest of the brothers, living outside of town until there were at least twelve of them. Originally only four canons—one of whom died immediately—and a canon who joined them from Châtillon agreed to "amend their lives," but within three years they had gathered enough regular canons to return to Dijon. Warner, the archdeacon of Langres who had acted as abbot of St.-Étienne before 1113, insisted as part of the agreement that he keep most of St.-Étienne's property. Only after he died in 1126 was Bernard of Clairvaux able to persuade the chapter of Langres to restore the canons' property to St.-Étienne.[25] The house of Châtillon, a house of secular canons founded around the year 1000 by the bishop of Langres and reformed in the 1130s by the bishop of Langres and Bernard of Clairvaux as a house of regular canons, used the same procedure as had St.-Étienne to establish the Augustinian observance. The bishop decreed that only canons who agreed to follow the Augustinian Rule could replace canons who had died.[26]

Although neither St.-Étienne of Dijon nor Châtillon was ever identified with just one family, some houses of canons regular could have an almost exclusive arrangement with one group of relatives. The lords of Beaujeu attached themselves closely to the church of Notre-Dame of Beaujeu, a house of canons which they founded in the late tenth century and helped reform in the later eleventh century, saying that they had established the church "free of any servitude or evil exactions, retaining no spiritual [i.e., ecclesiastical] benefices" for themselves. They and the bishop of Mâcon asked the pope to take

[25]St.-Étienne II.22, 24, 31 (pp. 25–28, 31–34, 29–40). Pérard, p. 141. Bernard of Clairvaux, Letter 59, *Opera*, VII (Rome, 1974), 152.
[26]Arch. Côte-d'Or, 18 H 625. Châtillon, fol. 11v.

the church and its newly established body of canons regular under apostolic tutelage in 1070 and had the papal legate dedicate a new church edifice six years later.[27] This attachment by the lords of Beaujeu to the body of canons they helped establish in their own castle did not however preclude a continued attention over the eleventh and twelfth centuries to Cluny, a church located thirty-five kilometers to the north, or the foundation of a second house of canons regular, at Belleville, in 1158.[28] The church of Beaujeu seems to have been identified more closely with the family than the family with the church.

Similarly, Lord Gui of Saulx, whose predecessors had originally established a body of secular canons in the chapel of his castle in 1130 to carry out the divine office in grand style, replaced them with canons regular in 1197, with the consent of Bishop Warner of Langres; he made these canons a number of gifts in succeeding years.[29] Duke Hugh III of Burgundy founded the Ste.-Chapelle at Dijon and established canons regular there in 1172 to fulfill a vow he had made while coming back from Crusade.[30] These chapels were important to the families of the lords of Saulx and the dukes, but the families were more generous to the local monasteries.

Since most bodies of canons regular were quite small, and since they were often supported at least in part by their parish revenues, they needed a smaller foundation gift than did most houses of monks. Hence a noble who could not have afforded to establish a Benedictine monastery often had the necessary substance to set up a house of canons regular. The house of Longué, though it later became part of the Cistercian order, was founded around 1100 as a house of Augustinian canons, originally with only three priests. The property that supported these three, composed primarily of land at Aubepierre, across the river from the house, and rights over a few peasants, came from a series of small gifts from the lord of Rouvres, the lord of Arc, the lord of Marac, and a knight of Châtillon.[31] These were not powerful lords; they were men at the lower fringes of the nobility. Such small foundations of houses of canons regular in particular offered an avenue through which knights, who were beginning to acquire some wealth in the twelfth century, could emulate members of the longer-established nobility in founding a house of religious life and reaping

[27]Beaujeu 1, 8, a2 (pp. 9—10, 14, 38—41).
[28]M.-C. Guigue, ed., *Cartulaire Lyonnais*, I (Lyon, 1885), 53—58, no. 39.
[29]Pérard, pp. 225, 233—34. Plancher I.144—46 (pp. lxxxvi—lxxxvii).
[30]Arch. Côte-d'Or, G 1123. St.-Étienne IV.49 (pp. 65—66).
[31]Longué, fols. 91r—93v. Rouvres is ten kilometers southeast of Longué, Arc ten kilometers northeast, Marac twenty-two kilometers east, and Châtillon twenty-six kilometers to the west.

its spiritual benefits, even if they lacked the means to establish a house of Benedictine monks.[32]

Another alternative with many of the same benefits was to found an altar to a particular saint within a church. Such was the case when the heirs of the knight Bernard of Meix founded an altar in the collegial church of St.-Pierre of Tonnerre for his soul in 1156.[33] Men to whom the foundation of even a large monastery would not have been a burden also founded altars in order to cement their friendship with the members of a particular church, although their major pious gifts were made elsewhere. For example, in the later twelfth century, the count of Auxerre and his mother established an altar in the cathedral of Auxerre while the count was dying, and they stipulated that the canons who served the altar should pray daily for his soul.[34] The foundation of houses of canons or of altars was not restricted to the lower levels of the aristocracy, but such foundations did provide a means for the individual without a great deal of wealth to secure the good offices of a group of religious men who would pray for him and for his family.

The New Monastic Orders

The multiplication of forms of the religious life in the later eleventh century produced not only new varieties of the *vita apostolica* but also new forms of Benedictine monasticism. The most influential was the Cistercian order, centered in Burgundy, with all its original houses in the duchy.[35] It was once thought that the Cistercians were founded in reaction to the gradual corruption of the Cluniac life. This view is now seen as much too sweeping; the Cluniacs thrived into the thirteenth century, long after Cîteaux's foundation. Rather, the Cistercian order is now seen not as a reaction to decadence but rather to what Jean Leclercq has called a "crisis of monasticism," the realization that traditional Benedictine monasticism, even in its "regular" form, no longer satisfied the yearnings of all those in search of salvation.[36] The Cistercians set out to follow the Benedictine Rule more

[32]Little, *Religious Poverty*, p. 99. Southern, *Western Society and the Church*, pp. 245–47.

[33]M. Jolivot, ed., "Chartes de l'Église Saint-Pierre de Tonnerre," *Bulletin de la Société des sciences historiques et naturelles de l'Yonne*, 36 (1882), 192–93, no. 2.

[34]*Gesta pontificum*, pp. 422–24. GC XII:135–36, no. 51. See also Bouchard, *Spirituality and Administration*, p. 87.

[35]The only listing of all Cistercian houses remains that of Leopold Janauschek, *Originum Cisterciensium* (Vienńa, 1877; rpt. Ridgewood, N. J., 1964); only one volume ever appeared.

[36]Jean Leclercq, "The Monastic Crisis of the Eleventh and Twelfth Centuries," in *Cluniac Monasticism in the Central Middle Ages*, ed. Noreen Hunt (London, 1971), pp.

closely than they believed contemporary monks were following it, but they also studied the Bible closely, attempting to return to the *ecclesia primitiva* that was also the goal of many of the new eleventh-century forms of the religious life.[37]

One cannot of course see the Cistercians as the only form of monasticism in the twelfth century. Contemporaries were very aware of the differences between the various forms of monasticism, and representatives of each order defended their own, but there was also a sense that the different sorts of monasteries were suited for people of different temperaments.[38] Other monasteries continued to flourish in the twelfth century; indeed more houses seem to have been reformed to the Cluniac way of life in the twelfth century than in the eleventh.[39] Houses also were reformed to the Benedictine Rule in the twelfth century, as they had been in the eleventh, without necessarily joining either of the great Burgundian monastic orders. The church of St.-Martin of Langres, for example, was reformed by Duke Hugh II of Burgundy between 1102 and 1111 by the expedient of giving it to the Benedictine monks of St.-Seine. Hugh's uncle Robert, bishop of Langres, who approved this reform, said that Hugh had given the church to St.-Seine because he did not want it any more.[40] From such mundane reasons spiritual reform could come.

The Cistercian order had its roots in Molesme, a house founded in 1075, twenty-three years before Cîteaux's foundation. The first abbot of Molesme, Robert, who was later the first abbot of Cîteaux, had spent a number of years at different religious houses, seeking a progressively more rigorous and "apostolic" form of life. He and a group of monks settled at Molesme, where no monastery had stood before. The property was given to them by a large group of cousins and neighbors of the lower nobility, headed by Hugh of Maligny, each of whom held part of it as allodial land.[41] Molesme was enormously

---

217–37. Leclercq, Vandenbroucke, and Bouyer, *The Spirituality of the Middle Ages*, pp. 127–28. John Van Engen has recently argued that the word "crisis," even in the restricted sense in which Leclercq used it, implies difficulties that the black monks did not begin to feel until fifty years after Cîteaux's foundation; Van Engen, "The 'Crisis of Cenobitism' Reconsidered: Benedictine Monasticism in the Years 1050–1150," *Speculum*, 61 (1986), 269–85.

[37]Chenu, *Nature, Man, and Society*, pp. 204–13. Glenn Olsen, "The Idea of the Ecclesia Primitiva in the Writings of the Twelfth-Century Canonists," *Traditio*, 25 (1969), 61–66.

[38]Giles Constable, "Twelfth-Century Spirituality and the Late Middle Ages," *Medieval and Renaissance Studies*, 5 (1969), 40–42. Caroline Walker Bynum, "Did the Twelfth Century Discover the Individual?" *Journal of Ecclesiastical History*, 31 (1980), 5–9.

[39]Lackner, *Eleventh-Century Background*, p. 40.

[40]St.-Seine, p. 252.

[41]Molesme 1.2 (II:5–6). See also below, Chapter 10.

successful; like Cluny in the same period, it was given a large number of parish churches and unpopulated houses to make into priories. Most of these priories were nearby, such as the priory of Varennes, which Lord Rayner of Choiseul gave the monks in 1084, but a few were located some distance away, for example a church in Savoy, which Count Humbert of Maurienne gave Molesme in 1097, asking the abbot to set monks there.[42]   Jacques Laurent, who edited Molesme's cartularies, estimated that there was scarcely a noble family in northern Burgundy which did not make at least some contribution to this house.

Molesme's foundation is distinctive in several respects compared to the earlier reforms described above; many of its distinctive features are found again in the Cistercian order in the twelfth century. Molesme was an entirely new foundation, rather than the refoundation of a ruined monastery or the establishment of monks in a church that had previously housed secular canons or parish priests. And the property on which the monks built their cloister was given to them by a large group of nobles rather than one individual. Factors leading to these changes are discussed below.

Cîteaux was founded in turn by monks from Molesme in 1098, when Abbot Robert and a few of the brothers decided that even more rigor was required than prevailed at Molesme. The New Monastery was established on land given them for the purpose by the viscount of Beaune and the duke of Burgundy. Though Robert was recalled to Molesme the next year, the monastery he helped establish was able to continue in existence and even grow, and in 1113 the arrival of Bernard, the future abbot of Clairvaux, with some thirty friends and relatives, assured its success and expansion.[43]   Cîteaux quickly became the mother house of a large order, as many young men decided to become monks, and nobles invited the Cistercians to settle on their land.   Cistercian houses were never in the majority among all monasteries, even in Burgundy, where they were most concentrated, and they were only one of a number of new monastic orders that began to spread across Europe in the early twelfth century, but they

[42]Molesme 1.4, 26 (II:7—8, 36—39). It is interesting to note that Humbert's wife was the daughter of the count of Burgundy.

[43]Cîteaux/Marilier 23 (pp. 49—51). "Exordium parvum" 1—3, ed. Bouton and Van Damme, *Textes*, pp. 56—60. The story of Cîteaux's foundation and of Bernard's influence on the expansion of the order has been told many times. See for example Leclercq, Vandenbroucke, and Bouyer, *The Spirituality of the Middle Ages*, pp. 187—94; and Louis J. Lekai, *The Cistercians: Ideals and Reality* (Kent, Ohio, 1977), pp. 13—19. The traditional date for Bernard's arrival at Cîteaux is 1112, but Lekai believes that 1113 is more accurate, arguing that early biographers pushed the date up to make Bernard personally responsible for the expansion of the house, which by 1113 necessitated the founding of the first daughter house.

were the most visible of the new orders and, at least during Bernard's life (he died in 1153), the most influential.

The disagreements between the abbots Bernard of Clairvaux and Peter the Venerable of Cluny in the 1120s accentuate the differences between the Cistercian and Cluniac orders, but in practice the two orders shared many similarities. The Cistercians for example prided themselves on living from the labor of their own hands, rather than receiving income from mills, dependent peasants, or the like, but in practice the Cistercians too quickly received such sources of income. In 1147 Bernard himself welcomed Savigny into the order; the income of this old Norman house was entirely of this type. Though Bernard spoke harshly of the Cluniacs' deviations from the Benedictine Rule, the Cistercians themselves introduced such innovations as the *conversi*, the lay brothers who in practice did most of the agricultural work for the monks, and the abolition of oblates. Faced with economic embarrassments and problems with discipline, Peter the Venerable established more stringent requirements for acceptance into Cluny. By the 1140s, Bernard and Peter were much closer than their earlier rhetoric would have suggested possible.[44]

The first four daughter houses of Cîteaux, her "four oldest daughters," were all founded in Burgundy within two years of Bernard's arrival at Cîteaux. Unlike Cluniac priories, they had their own abbots, but institutionally they were bound very closely to the mother house. La Ferté was founded in 1113 on land given by the cousins William and Savaric, joint counts of Chalon, and by the lord of Brancion. Pontigny was founded the following year on the allodial land of Ansius (sometimes also called Hildebert), a cathedral canon of Auxerre, of the count of Nevers, and of a noble widow named Gilla.[45] Clairvaux, Cîteaux's third and best-known daughter, was founded in 1115 on land given by a variety of knights and members of the petty nobility who held land in the area, the most important of whom were the viscounts of La Ferté (located five kilometers to the south).[46] Morimond, the fourth daughter, was also founded in 1115, as a joint

[44]See especially Peter's famous letter no. 111 to Bernard, from around 1144, in which he says that, even though one wore a habit made from wool of a black sheep and the other a habit made from wool of a white sheep, they were both members of the same flock under the same Shepherd; *Letters*, I:274–99. See also Richard Roehl, "Plan and Reality in a Medieval Monastic Economy: The Cistercians," *Studies in Medieval and Renaissance History*, 9 (1972), 84–86, 104; and Giles Constable, "Cluniac Administration and Administrators in the Twelfth Century," in *Order and Innovation in the Middle Ages: Essays in Honor of Joseph R. Strayer*, ed. William C. Jordan, Bruce McNab, and Teofilo F. Ruiz (Princeton, 1976), pp. 19–21.

[45]La Ferté 1 (pp. 41–42). Pontigny 84 (pp. 152–54). *Gesta pontificum*, p. 406. Robert of St.-Marien, *Chronicon* 1114, MGH SS XXVI:230. See also Terryl N. Kinder, "Some Observations on the Origins of Pontigny and Its First Church," *Cîteaux*, 31 (1980), 9–12.

[46]Clairvaux/Waquet 6 (pp. 8–14). The foundation charter in Clairvaux's cartulary,

effort of several laymen and ecclesiastics. These included Lord Ulric of Aigremont and his wife, who held the land on which the house was founded; one John, described in the foundation charter as a "man of religious spirit," who originally settled as a hermit in the church of Morimond around 1110 but then invited the abbot of Cîteaux to send monks there; Willenc, dean of the cathedral of Langres, who seems to have been Ulric's uncle; Bishops Robert and Joceran of Langres; and Abbot Stephen Harding of Cîteaux.[47]

The new Cistercian houses were populated primarily by knights and members of the lower nobility. Although of course the origins of the majority of monks must always be unknown, those monks whose families *are* known were almost invariably sons of knights or petty castellans. The letters of Bernard of Clairvaux on conversion, which were saved and circulated as examples of the issues a Cistercian novice would face, always assume that the new convert is from such a family. Bernard wrote a learned young man of Chaumont, saying that He who had given the young man the gifts of "an exalted family, a strong body, an elegant form, and a quick mind" would inquire of him how he used these gifts. He wrote a noble convert's parents that they should not think that they had lost their son when he entered the monastery, for he had left one "noble life" for one of "higher nobility." In his letter of welcome to the convert Hugh, later abbot of Bonneval, Bernard said that the "wisdom" that would lead a "delicate young nobleman" to scorn the world could only be the wisdom of God.[48]

The Cistercian order quickly became tremendously popular, expanding in Burgundy even faster than Cluny's order had initially. Nobles tried to establish Cistercians on their property even over the protests of abbots who feared their order was being spread too thin. Maizières, for example, was founded at the insistence of Lord Fulk of Rahon, who gave the property for the abbey to La Ferté in 1132, asking the abbot to set a suitable number of monks there. The abbot at first refused; he gave in only when Fulk persuaded the abbot of Cîteaux, the archbishop of Tarentaise, and the bishop of Chalon to add their requests to his (the archbishop of Tarentaise had been abbot of La Ferté before his election to that see). Lay initiative here, as in many cases, was the difference in establishing this Cistercian house.[49]

---

printed in GC IV:155, no. 31, and recording gifts of land from the count of Troyes, is now considered a later production; see Clairvaux/Waquet, p. vii.

[47]Morimond's foundation charter is printed in Louis Dubois, *Histoire de l'abbaye de Morimond* (Paris, 1851), pp. 411–12. A slightly abbreviated version of this charter is printed in GC IV:159, no. 36. The original charter is Arch. Haute-Marne, 8 H 1.

[48]Bernard of Clairvaux, Letters 104, 110, 322, *Opera*, VII:261–63, 282–83; VIII (Rome, 1977), 256–58.

[49]GC IV:239, no. 22. Obit. Lyon II:625.

The houses of the Cistercian order, like Molesme in the late eleventh century, tended to be founded completely anew rather than through the refoundation of a ruined house, and were often founded by a number of nobles acting together. A few older houses (such as Savigny, mentioned above) became affiliated with the order, but if there were already religious men at a place that became Cistercian, they were generally hermits, not monks.[50] Unlike Molesme, a great many Cistercian houses did not have a formal foundation charter drawn up until several years after the arrival of the first monks, at which time they asked the bishop to confirm their foundation.

The Cistercian house of Reigny was originally founded in 1128 at Fontemois, where a small group of hermits had been living for a generation. Once Fontemois adopted the Cistercian rule, becoming a daughter of Clairvaux, the house expanded rapidly and six years later moved to Reigny. The *villa* of Reigny was given to the monks by the knight Josbert Chapel in return for a payment of seventy pounds. The transaction was quite complicated, since it required the approval of Josbert's feudal lord, Bochard Borseron, *his* lord, Peter of Fontenay (located ten kilometers to the west), *his* lord, Geoffrey, lord of Donzy (one of the most powerful men of the region), and the bishop of Auxerre, from whom the lords of Donzy held much of their property in fief.[51] The abbey of Auberive, founded as a daughter of Clairvaux in 1135, was established on land given by literally dozens of different men and women, headed by Lord Raynald of nearby Grancey and Eblo, count of Saulx, with their families, but also including a great many allodists of the petty nobility. The Cistercian abbey of Quincy, founded about the same time, was established on land given by three *milites* and rounded out by gifts from other knights, with the approval of their feudal lords, Count William of Nevers and Lord Milo of Noyers.[52]

Several factors were involved in these changes from the eleventh century.[53] By the twelfth century, there were very few old monasteries left in Burgundy which had *not* already been reformed, so

---

[50]Leyser, *Hermits and the New Monasticism*, pp. 35, 101−2.

[51]*Gesta pontificum*, pp. 406, 411. Quantin I.109, 175, 185 (pp. 208−10, 299−300, 312−13). This last document is reprinted as Quantin II.45 (pp. 49−51), where it is dated 1127, which seems more likely than the "c. 1136" of Quantin I.

[52]For Auberive, see GC IV:165−68, no. 42; the original charter is Arch. Haute-Marne, 1 H 7 bis. For Quincy, see GC IV:179−80, no. 60.

[53]In areas outside Burgundy, where Cluniac priories were still being founded in some numbers in the twelfth century, most new foundations were totally new, not reforms of old houses, and were done by castellans and lesser lords. See Philippe Racinet, "Implantation et expansion clunisiennes au nord-est de Paris (XIe−XIIe siècles)," *Le moyen âge*, 90 (1984), 9−12, 16. Hence the differences between the eleventh and twelfth centuries in Burgundy cannot be only the differences between the Cistercians and the Cluniacs.

in many cases it would have been impossible for the twelfth-century monks simply to move into a ruined monastery, even if they had wished to do so. Indeed, many monks of the twelfth century, especially the Cistercians, deliberately tried to establish their monasteries "in the desert," away from the busy urban centers where most of the old churches were located. The Mâconnais and Brionnais were already thickly settled with Cluniac monks by the beginning of the twelfth century, and hence no Cistercian houses were founded in the dioceses of Mâcon or Nevers. Rather, the greatest concentration of Cistercian houses was in the relatively unsettled diocese of Langres. Whereas in the eleventh century most reformed monks carried out the liturgy in churches where the same saint had been honored since Carolingian or even Merovingian times, in the twelfth century monasticism broke with tradition at least in the sites chosen for the monks to settle. Even if a church was already located there, the new Cistercian house was dedicated not to that church's saint but rather to Mary, Notre-Dame.

In addition to desiring suitable solitude from the cares of the world, the Cistercian monks needed fairly large tracts of land on which to carry out agriculture, for their order emphasized manual labor, with the intention that the monks raise their own food. By the end of the twelfth century few nobles owned vast tracts of empty land; thus a number of neighbors had to cooperate in the foundation of a Cistercian house. Because a foundation was a group effort, there was no single moment at which the house could be considered established, and no single powerful donor who wished to record his generosity for posterity and have his own scribe record it; hence a foundation charter came only when the monks had become settled and asked the bishop for his confirmation of what they already had. The foundation of a Cistercian house—like the foundation of a house of canons regular—was then a possibility for even a relatively poor member of the aristocracy, as long as he had the assistance of his neighbors and relatives.

Many new houses of nuns as well as those of monks were founded in the twelfth century. Jully, a house of nuns dependent on Molesme, was founded around 1115 in the old castle of Jully when Count Milo of Bar gave it to the monks of Molesme. The count's charter specified that he had inherited the castle from his ancestors, the counts of Tonnerre, but that it had been "destroyed by demons." Theobold, count of Troyes, also approved the establishment of nuns there. In 1145 the knight Geoffrey Fournier gave Molesme the Chapelle d'Oze, asking that nuns from Jully be established there. Consenting were his family, his two lords Clarembald of Chappes and Count Gui of Bar, and Bishop Geoffrey of Langres.[54] The nunnery of

---

[54]Jully, pp. 256, 263. "Vita Sancti Petri prioris Juliacensis puellarum monasterii," in

Tart, loosely affiliated with Cîteaux, was founded in the early 1120s by Arnulf Cornu (of the family of the lords of Vergy) and his wife, with the consent of Duke Hugh II of Burgundy; the nuns were to be subject to the "correction and ordering" of the abbot of Cîteaux.[55] The nunnery of Crisenon, which received a formal foundation charter from the bishop of Auxerre in 1134, was founded in a church that Lords Hugh and Narjod of Toucy had given Molesme as part of a gift of allodial land at the very end of the eleventh century. Its refoundation as a house of nuns required the approval of both the bishop and the count of Auxerre, the abbot of Molesme, and Narjod's heirs.[56] Twelfth-century nunneries, like the monasteries of the time, were often founded by several nobles acting in concert, unless the secular founder was a man like Count Milo of Bar with a large amount of property—even if in ruins—which he could give to the nuns.

Thus, at the same time as the number of religious houses and varieties of the religious life multiplied, the number of different men who helped establish such houses greatly increased. Even the dukes of Burgundy, wealthy enough to found their own individual monasteries had they wished, cooperated with members of the lesser nobility in founding Cistercian houses: Duke Odo I for example gave the viscount of Beaune a large sum of money when Cîteaux was first founded, in return for the rest of the valley in which the monks had settled, which the duke then gave the monks. And, when Cîteaux's daughter house of La Bussière was founded thirty years later, Duke Hugh II, with his wife and all his sons, recompensed the monks of St.-Vivant of Vergy for some property that had been Vergy's but that now went to the new Cistercian house. Duke Hugh's gift is recorded second in La Bussière's cartulary, after the charter recalling the foundation of the house by a group of petty nobles, of whom the most important is the castellan Warner, lord of Sombernon.[57]

The emphasis I have given here to the role of the nobility in

---

Genus illustre, p. 145 [rpt. PL CLXXXV:1263].

[55]GC IV:157, no. 34. On the Cistercian nuns in general, see Sally Thompson, "The Problem of the Cistercian Nuns in the Twelfth and Early Thirteenth Centuries," in *Medieval Women*, ed. Derek Baker, Studies in Church History, Subsidia 2 (Oxford, 1978), pp. 229–33; and Penny Schine Gold, *The Lady & the Virgin: Image, Attitude, and Experience in Twelfth-Century France* (Chicago, 1985), pp. 81–85.

[56]Quantin I.176 (pp. 301–2). Quantin II. 49 (pp. 54–55). Molesme 1.53, 54, 78, 101 (II:63–65, 83–84, 105–6). Innocent II freed Crisenon from any tie to Molesme in 1140; GC XII:112, no. 19. For the lords of Toucy, see Appendix A, pp. 372–75.

[57]Cîteaux/Marilier 15, 16, 23, 85 (pp. 39–41, 50, 90). Jules Marion, "Notice sur l'abbaye de La Bussière. Pièces justicatives," *Bibliothèque de l'École des chartes*, 4 (1842/43), 561–62, no. 1. See also Constance B. Bouchard, "Noble Piety and Reformed Monasticism: The Dukes of Burgundy in the Twelfth Century," in *Noble Piety and Reformed Monasticism: Studies in Medieval Cistercian History VII*, ed. E. Rozanne Elder (Kalamazoo, Mich., 1981), p. 5.

reformed monasticism stands in contrast to the traditional view, held by many scholars, that the church reform of the eleventh and twelfth centuries was carried out in determined opposition to the local nobility. In fact, the establishment of new houses of monks or canons generally took place because of noble initiative, not because of a monastic will to expand. Even in the middle years of the twelfth century, when groups of canons, hermits, and monks virtually roamed through Burgundy looking for a place to settle, they could scarcely establish themselves where they were not wanted. Monks could not unilaterally expand their order; they needed to be invited.

The history of monastic reform and foundation in Burgundy is a history of tremendous variety tied together by several common themes. The differences are perhaps more obvious than the similarities. In the late tenth and early eleventh centuries, great nobles gave the ruined churches they had owned to monasteries like Cluny to reform, expecting monks who had lived in the cloister since childhood to serve these reformed houses. In the later eleventh and early twelfth centuries, hermits, canons regular, Carthusians, and wandering preachers, many of whom had made a conversion to the religious life as young adults, began to appear. In the twelfth century, the new Cistercian order, established in newly formed houses, far from the old urban ecclesiastical centers, on lands donated by large groups of the petty nobility, tried to create a monastic life closer both to the Bible and to Benedict than was the Cluniac life. If participants in the wandering or eremetical apostolic movements thought the monastery was not a sufficient imitation of the life of Christ, the Cistercians still believed monasticism could be modified into a true *vita apostolica*.

In all these varieties of house and order, there were some common features. All these monks, hermits, priests, and preachers believed that it was possible to achieve holiness through one's way of life. They believed such a way of life could and should be institutionalized, so that their successors would also reach holiness by following it. And all these disparate ways of holy life depended for their institutionalization and continuation on the support of secular nobles, men who received the spiritual benefits vicariously. In the next chapters, I discuss more fully the men who patronized medieval monasteries, then turn in later chapters to a discussion of changes in the sorts of gifts that monasteries received between the eleventh and twelfth centuries.

[5]

The Patrons of
Monastic Reform

The new monastic orders and the reforms and new foundations of the eleventh and twelfth centuries were possible only because the monastery exercised an attraction for powerful local laymen. In this chapter, I discuss aspects of the patronage of Burgundian monasteries, beginning with the most formal sort of arrangement, the position of *advocatus*. I then examine the social status of the men who patronized reformed monasteries and the role of women in spreading the influence of a particular monastery. In the next chapter, I shall continue the discussion of monastic patronage by describing several families and their relationships with particular houses over the generations.

The Monastic Advocate

A noble's continuing interest in the monks of a particular house could be formalized in the office of *advocatus*. In many ways the advocate can be viewed as a compromise. On the one hand, monks insisted that a reformed house be free of outside meddling, and, on the other, the monks needed some kind of agent who was powerful enough to be respected outside the cloister walls. Hence the nobles who helped reform houses, in the eleventh century especially, and who promised to allow the monks to carry out their liturgical round without interference, frequently became the advocates of their foundations. Adopting the title *advocatus*, *custos*, or *adjutator*, secular nobles would take responsibility for collecting a house's revenues in distant areas, represent the house in legal cases, and take steps to protect the house from other laymen who had made attacks on its property. The terms *advocatus* and *custos* could be used interchangeably, or occasionally a house would have both an *advocatus* to act as its agent and a *custos* to protect it. Though these advocates left the election of a new abbot to the monks, they routinely confirmed the elevation of the abbot, promising to defend him as they had his predecessor.

The *advocatus* seems to have been an institutional development from the position of the ninth-century Carolingian kings. Though the king was not himself a member of the priestly order, members of the Frankish clergy in the ninth century believed that the royal office was divinely authorized and sanctioned and that it was necessary for the king to protect the churches of his realm, sometimes even choosing new church leaders. Once established, this duty to protect churches progressively devolved during the tenth and eleventh centuries from the king to counts and even lesser lords, as the counts also appropriated other privileges and responsibilities that in the ninth century had belonged to the king.[1]

Most monasteries had advocates in the tenth and eleventh centuries. The monks of Cluny, as noted in Chapter 3, consulted the count of Mâcon, the most powerful lord of their region, whom they referred to as their *advocatus*, before electing Maiolus as abbot in 954. Again, in 993, they invited Duke Henry of Burgundy and the counts of the region to be present when they elected Abbot Odilo, to approve and give stature to his election. When the abbot of Montier-en-Der built a church at Guindrecourt in 1059 (located ten kilometers west of Vignory), he asked Lord Gui of Vignory and his brother to accept the *advocatio* and *custodia* of the church to keep it "free from all disturbance." Molesme, founded in 1075, also had its advocates. In 1101 the count of Nevers "took the custody of Molesme's property and guarded it from harm."[2]

A lord who called himself *advocatus* or *custos* of a Burgundian house in the eleventh century seems to have taken his duties seriously. Abbots may even have asked nobles they considered a possible threat to accept the advocacy of their house—as did the abbot of Montier-en-Der in the example above—in order to forestall these nobles' attacks. The monks turned first to their advocates when they needed help against other laymen. The counts of Chalon for example normally acted as protectors of the churches of Chalon; in 1093, Geoffrey of Donzy and Gui of Thiers, the acting counts of Chalon, forced a knight named Boniface to return to the Cluniac priory of St.-Marcel-

[1] Karl Frederick Morrison, *The Two Kingdoms: Ecclesiology in Carolingian Political Thought* (Princeton, 1964), pp. 118, 152, 199. Georges Duby, *La société aux XI*e *et XII*e *siècles dans la région mâconnaise*, 2nd ed. (Paris, 1971), pp. 89–93, 104–6, 137.

[2] C 883, 1957 (II:1–2; III:174–77). Vignory 2.3–4 (pp. 171–72). Molesme 1.28 (II:40–43). See also Yves Sassier, *Recherches sur le pouvoir comtal en Auxerrois du X*e *au début du XIII*e *siècle* (Auxerre, 1980), pp. 68–69. For the lords of Vignory and counts of Nevers, see Appendix A, pp. 379–81, 346–47.

lès-Chalon the property his brother had given St.-Marcel when leaving on pilgrimage and which Boniface had claimed.[3] Overall, a great many quarrels were settled in the eleventh century with the urging of the churches' advocates, and many of the gifts that the churches received were given with the assent of these same advocates. Monasteries frequently sought royal confirmation of their possessions, and, almost invariably, when a king confirmed a house's possessions or made gifts of his own, he specified that he had done so at the request of the house's noble guardian. For example, the kings of France and of imperial Burgundy confirmed the possessions of St.-Bénigne of Dijon, early in the eleventh century, at the request of Count Otto-William of Burgundy, who acted as the house's advocate after helping restore it, and of Hugh, count of Chalon and bishop of Auxerre, who called himself the *custos* of the monastery.[4]

The advocates of a particular house might give it other churches to reform after they had originally helped reform the house itself. This continuing interest may be seen in the relations of the lords of Tilchâtel with the church of St.-Florent of Til. In 1033 Lord Aimo of Tilchâtel gave St.-Florent to the very recently reformed church of St.-Étienne of Dijon, which set canons there. Then, at the end of the eleventh century, Lord Aldo of Til, Aimo's grandson, gave the castle chapel of Til to St.-Florent as a dependent priory, with the consent of Bishop Robert of Langres, from whom the chapel had been held in fief.[5] Reform of these individual churches was part of an ongoing friendship between the lords of Til and the house of St.-Étienne of Dijon.

The churches of the eleventh century were so dependent on their advocates that, if the advocate turned on them, they were almost helpless. Fortunately for the churches, such an event was rare. One of the chief difficulties of the Burgundian churches in the middle decades of the eleventh century was dealing with Duke Robert I, first of the Capetian dukes. While he was sometimes a generous donor himself and frequently confirmed the pious gifts of other nobles,[6] he was also a man with a strong violent streak. He killed his own father-

[3]St.-Marcel 107 (p. 91). See also Appendix A, pp. 312–13.

[4]St.-B. II.260 (pp. 49–53). Constance B. Bouchard, "Laymen and Church Reform around the Year 1000: The Case of Otto-William, Count of Burgundy," *Journal of Medieval History*, 5 (1979), 5–7.

[5]St.-Étienne I.64 (pp. 86–87). Pérard, p. 75. This first charter is dated MXXXIII and also dated "in the seventh year of the reign of King Henry," which gives 1033 if one dates his reign from 1026, when he was associated as king with his father. The editor however dates it 1038. For the lords of Tilchâtel, see Appendix A, pp. 366–68.

[6]For examples from Cluny, St.-Bénigne, and St.-Étienne of Dijon, see C 2888, 2949 (IV:82–85, 149–50); St.-B. II.315, 324, 338 (pp. 95–97, 104–6, 117–18); and St.-Étienne I.77 (pp. 96–97).

in-law, the father of Abbot Hugh of Cluny, though it is not entirely clear whether this was a premeditated act; Abbot Hugh's biographer said that, rather than plotting revenge, the abbot prayed for his soul.[7] Robert seized many of the goods of St.-Bénigne of Dijon in the 1040s and of the cathedral of Autun in the 1060s, only desisting in the latter case after Abbot Hugh held a general council to preach peace.[8] Robert was sufficiently powerful that the Burgundian monks wanted his protection, but he was also powerful enough that he was hard to discourage when he decided to attack churches or laymen.

The importance of the *advocatus* diminished in the late eleventh century. In part this development was a result of the Gregorian reform, of a new consciousness of the distinction between ecclesiastical and secular positions, though it was the kings who lost the most ground. While there were still some, such as the so-called Norman Anonymous, who argued strenuously that the king was the anointed of God, the more prevalent view was expressed by Honorius of Autun. He presented a picture of society in which laymen were subject to clerics at all points: a peasant, he said, should serve a deacon, a knight should serve a priest, a great lord serve a bishop, and a king the pope.[9]

Nevertheless, even those ecclesiastics who saw the widest gap between secular and spiritual still insisted on a role for the secular nobility in the life of the church, in particular, protecting churchmen and others who could not protect themselves. Gregory VII himself berated Abbot Hugh of Cluny for welcoming Duke Hugh I of Burgundy (Robert I's grandson) as a monk in 1079, saying that the duke's conversion, which Gregory might have been expected to welcome, was a disaster that had left a hundred thousand Christians without a protector.[10] Bernard of Clairvaux expressed a similar view of the positions of *regnum* and *sacerdotium* in 1144 when he wrote to Conrad III, asking him to defend the church in Rome against the local mob. He said that king and priest were both parts of one body—that is, the Christian people—both created by God for mutual assistance.[11]

[7]Gilo, "Vita Sancti Hugonis" 1.51, ed. Cowdrey, "Studies," p. 88.
[8]Petit 31 (I:375–76). Hugh the Monk, "Vita Hugonis" 4, ed. Cowdrey, "Studies," pp. 122–23.
[9]Norman Anonymous, "Tractatus" 4, MGH Libelli de lite III:664. Honorius of Autun, "Summa gloria de apostolico et augusto" 2, PL CLXXII:1261. See also Ernst H. Kantorowicz, *The King's Two Bodies: A Study in Medieval Political Theology*, 2nd ed. (Princeton, 1966), pp. 44–46, 91–92; and R. W. Southern, *Western Society and the Church in the Middle Ages* (Harmondsworth, England, 1970), pp. 36–38, 100–105.
[10]Erich Caspar, ed., *Das Register Gregors VII*, MGH Epp. II, i:423–24, no. 6.17. See also Constance B. Bouchard, "Noble Piety and Reformed Monasticism: The Dukes of Burgundy in the Twelfth Century," in *Noble Piety and Reformed Monasticism: Studies in Medieval Cistercian History VII*, ed. E. Rozanne Elder (Kalamazoo, Mich., 1981), p. 1.
[11]Bernard of Clairvaux, Letter 244, *Opera*, VIII (Rome, 1977), 134–36.

Although by the twelfth century the king's role as advocate of the church had been consciously restricted, the monks of Burgundy still occasionally saw the kings as their best protectors. In 1119 the monks of Cluny invited King Louis VI to accept the *defensio, garda*, and *tutella* of their house. In 1139, when King Louis VII hesitated about granting the *regalia* at Langres after the disputed election there, Bernard of Clairvaux wrote the king, "This land is yours," and said that the king's delay was leading to pillage and plunder.[12] In 1166, when the abbot of Cluny asked Louis VII to come protect his abbey from the rapine of its secular neighbors—the first time a French king had actually come to southern Burgundy since the middle of the tenth century—he insisted that *Burgundia* was part of the king's realm, his to protect. It was the king's duty, the Cistercian bishop of Pavia added in his own letter to Louis, to reestablish the church's peace.[13]

While the king only occasionally appeared in Burgundy as a monastic advocate in the twelfth century, the dukes were very frequently called *advocatus* and were expected to defend the Burgundian churches. (Interestingly, between the death of Duke Henry in 1002 and Hugh I's entry into Cluny in 1079, the dukes of Burgundy rarely appear as supporters or advocates of the Burgundian monasteries, but they are often found in this role in twelfth-century documents.) In the early twelfth century the monks of St.-Bénigne gave the *custodia* of their house to Duke Hugh II; Hugh said that he would resign it and let the monks grant it to whomever they wished, but the monks apparently wanted *him* to be their *custos*, for Hugh's descendants held this office until the end of the twelfth century, as noted below.[14] In 1133 the pope asked the duke to enforce the solution of a longstanding quarrel between the houses of St.-Seine and St.-Étienne of Dijon, a resolution that had been mediated by the abbot of Cîteaux. When the count of Nevers attacked the monastery of Vézelay around 1150, the pope called on Duke Odo II as the best protector the monks could have, even though Odo had been aiding the count of Nevers in his depredations. Perhaps the monks were here hoping to convert a threat into a source of defense. In 1176 the duke led a group of mediators who settled a quarrel between the abbey and burghers of Tournus. The dukes of Burgundy held the *custodia* of St.-Bénigne of Dijon until 1193, when Duke Odo III gave it to the monks. The duchesses of Burgundy held the *custodia* of the nunnery of Tart throughout the twelfth century.[15] For the dukes as for the kings, it

---

[12]Layettes 46 (I:41). Bernard of Clairvaux, Letter 170, *Opera*, VII (1974), 383–85.
[13]RHGF XVI:129–32, nos. 397–402. See also Duby, *La société mâconnaise*, pp. 401–9.
[14]BN, Coll. Baluze 13, fol. 184.
[15]St.-Étienne II.102 (pp. 112–13). Vézelay 40, 41 (pp. 338–39). Petit 594, 1008 (II: 381; III:372–73). Arch. Côte-d'Or, 1 H 13. For Vézelay, see also Bouchard, "Noble

was taken for granted that a part of the responsibilities of being a ruler of society was the defense and support of the church.

Nobles as Patrons and Defenders

Even without being given the title of *advocatus*, a noble could be considered a chief defender of the church. By the twelfth century, the formal role of advocate was less common than informal arrangements in which bishops and abbots encouraged local nobles to protect the Church—or at least *their* church. Peter the Venerable, abbot of Cluny, spelled out the role of powerful laymen in Burgundy, which Peter likened to Israel "without king and without prince" (Hosea 3:4), or rather with men who had "the title only," who "devoured rather than defended" the people. When Lord Humbert III of Beaujeu returned from Jerusalem in the 1140s, Peter said, the clergy, monks, and peasants of the region all rejoiced, and the churches rang with song. Peter himself broke off other business to go welcome Humbert back. Now, he said, Humbert would attack all those who preyed on "countrymen, farmers, the poor, widows, orphans, monks, and churches," bringing "peace between the Saône and the Loire." It is interesting to note that churches and the poor were here explicitly linked. Peter even insisted that it was better for Humbert to fight those who attacked churches in Burgundy than it was to fight the infidel in the Holy Land,. where Humbert had briefly been a Templar. Like Gregory VII, Peter thought it often better for a powerful lord *not* to enter orders himself, since he could defend the church so much better if still a layman.[16]

During the twelfth century many nobles were treated as defenders of monastic rights and trustworthy mediators. In 1152, when Bernard of Clairvaux wrote to Count Henry of Troyes to reprimand him for stealing the pigs of the canons of Châtillon, he reminded the count that God had made him a prince on earth "to encourage the good, to restrain the evil, defend the poor, and do justice to the injured" (cf. Psalms 146:7). In 1177 the count of Joigny and the count of Sancerre mediated a quarrel between the monks of the Cluniac priory of Joigny (dependent on La Charité) and the monks of Escharlis, even though the counts of Joigny appeared most frequently in ecclesiastical

---

Piety and Reformed Monasticism," p. 2. Similarly, the count of Troyes collected revenues at Chablis (east of Auxerre) on behalf of the distant monks of St.-Martin of Tours, for whom he held the *custodia*, until 1151, when he granted this *custodia* to Anseric I, lord of Montréal; Layettes 118 (I:68).

[16]Peter the Venerable, Letters 172–73, *Letters*, I:407–11. For Humbert, see Appendix A, p. 293.

documents over the course of the twelfth century when ordered to desist in their long-standing quarrel with the nuns of St.-Julien of Auxerre. Even the Cistercian chapter general appealed to the count of Burgundy in 1192 on behalf of the Cistercian houses in the diocese of Besançon, which complained that the provost of Besançon cathedral had been devastating their possessions.[17]

Once a man had proven himself as the defender or advocate of a particular house, the monks tended to turn to him or his descendants when in need of protection or confirmation of their possessions. For example, the lords of Sombernon, who had founded the Cistercian house of La Bussière in 1131, continued to confirm gifts to it from other laymen throughout the twelfth century. In 1188, when a man agreed to give up his false claim (*calumnia*) to a certain income belonging to La Bussière, Lord Walter of Sombernon and his brother made themselves responsible to the monks (*responsales sumus*) for assuring the agreement was kept.[18] Similarly, throughout the twelfth century the counts of Nevers were generous to St.-Étienne of Nevers, which Count William I refounded as a Cluniac priory in 1097 (see below, Chapter 10). Over the space of six generations, new counts of Nevers almost invariably confirmed the house's possessions and the gifts their fathers and ancestors had made to it at the time they took office.[19] Patronage of a particular house could thus become a part of family tradition, and monks or nuns could count on this tradition as an ally in attempting to find consistent supporters and patrons among the nobility. In the next chapter, I give additional examples of a family's patronage of a particular house over the generations.

The Social Position of Monastic Patrons

While the men who patronized monasteries throughout the eleventh and twelfth centuries needed some minimum of power and wealth in order to protect and endow the monks, monastic patrons were not a homogeneous social group. The monastic patrons of the eleventh century, and the patrons of the more traditional Benedictine houses throughout the eleventh and twelfth centuries, were more likely to come from the upper levels of the nobility than were the men who patronized the new orders of the twelfth century, especially the

[17]Bernard of Clairvaux, Letter 279, *Opera*, VIII:191. La Charité 72 (pp. 166–67). Canivez, *Statuta*, I:155–56, no. 48.
[18]La Bussière 1.6 (fol. 4v). For the lords of Sombernon, see Appendix A, pp. 365–66.
[19]Nevers/St.-Étienne 2, 12, 16, 23 (pp. 76–78, 89–91, 93–95, 98). C 3724, 4297 (V:67–74, 660–62).

Cistercians. The differences between these nobles were not juridic so much as political or social—they were differences in the nobles' ancestry, wealth, and power.[20]

The frequent and generous gifts of the eleventh century, to found new houses or support reformed monks, may have been a relatively new phenomenon. Before approximately 980, noble gifts even to such monasteries as Cluny had been less frequent;[21] and there were at any rate few reformed houses to which gifts could have been made. (It may be that the documents that would have revealed generous gifts in the tenth century were lost, though the fullness of the cartularies of Cluny argues against this supposition.) A possible reason for the increase in numbers of gifts is the establishment of new lineages of viscounts or castellans at the end of the tenth century. These powerful men, once they had the property necessary to make such gifts, sought to endow monks, as kings and dukes had done earlier.[22]

In the twelfth century, in contrast to the eleventh, the great lords were largely replaced by members of the lesser nobility as the principal supporters of monasticism. Whereas, as noted in Chapter 4, the secular lords who helped found eleventh-century houses were generally of at least castellan rank, and often more powerful, in the twelfth century they were at the most of castellan rank, and generally less powerful.[23] One could not call this development a "democratization" of the process of monastic foundation, for these founders were still members of society's elite. The size of the aristocracy was constantly growing in the twelfth century, but it still constituted only a tiny fraction of society.

Some of the greatest lords, most notably the dukes, continued to help found houses in the twelfth century; they were among the most important patrons of the Cistercian order. But they *helped* found Cistercian houses; they did not initiate the foundations themselves.[24] Similarly, the dukes sometimes made the first gifts of property to

---

[20]Joachim Bumke, *The Concept of Knighthood in the Middle Ages*, trans. W. T. H. and Erika Jackson (New York, 1982), pp. 107–23. Heinrich Dormeier, studying specifically lay gifts of churches to Montecassino, has noted that in the eleventh century princes and counts predominated among the donors to the abbey; Dormeier, *Montecassino und die Laien im 11. und 12. Jahrhundert*, Schriften der MGH 27 (Stuttgart, 1979), p. 53.

[21]Duby, *La société mâconnaise*, pp. 56, 68.

[22]Jean-François Lemarignier gives a similar explanation for the increase in generosity to Norman and northern French monasteries in the eleventh century; "Le monachisme et l'encadrement religieux des campagnes du royaume de France situées au nord de la Loire, de la fin du Xe à la fin du XIe siècle," in *Le istituzioni ecclesiastiche della "Societas Christiana" dei secoli XI–XII: Diocesi, pievi e parrocchie*, Miscellanea del Centro di studi medioevali 8 (Milan, 1977), pp. 358, 381–84.

[23]Dietrich Poeck, studying specifically gifts made to Cluny for burial there, discovered a fair number of *milites* among the donors for the first time in the later eleventh century; castellans accounted for most of the rest; "Laienbegräbnisse in Cluny," *Frühmittelalterliche Studien*, 15 (1981), 153–55.

[24]For a similar pattern in England, see J. C. Ward, "Fashions in Monastic Endow-

allow the Cistercians to found a grange, but the rest of the land came from gifts of petty donors. For example, Cîteaux first obtained property at Vernolle and Civry around 1125, when Duke Hugh II and Lord Warner of Sombernon gave what they had there. But the rest of the land and the tithes were assembled from gifts from men who principally seem to have been knights, since their gifts were witnessed by the lords and ladies "of the castles where they lived."[25] The rapid spread of the Cistercian order may be due in large part to its appeal to this growing segment of the nobility.

The Cistercian houses were patronized especially by knights, that is, new men, people who had never appeared in the records before they began making small gifts to the monks of a nearby house. Because the same people keep appearing in the monastery's records—as donors, as those claiming the monastery's property, or as those witnessing others' transactions—it is relatively straightforward to establish their social position. That is, although a man may not be designated as *miles* or *dominus* in every charter in which he appears, these or other titles will probably be given to him eventually in other documents. For example, the knight Milo of Arc, a patron of the Cistercian house of Longué at the end of the twelfth century, is called in some charters Milo of Arc, *miles*, son of Clarembald, and in others simply Milo, son of Clarembald.[26]

The social composition of the group that made most of the donations to the Cistercians can be strikingly illustrated with the example of Fontenay. This daughter of Clairvaux, founded in 1119, produced two cartularies in the thirteenth century; though both are somewhat mutilated, they contain the major proportion of the twelfth-century gifts that the monks found it important to record for posterity (there is a fair amount of duplication between the two cartularies). A number of original twelfth-century charters still survive as well.[27] If one analyzes the social positions of Fontenay's patrons (and of those neighbors who tried to seize the monks' property), one finds that they were almost exclusively castellans and knights. Further, they came from a relatively small geographic area, close to Fontenay or in the

ment: The Foundations of the Clare Family, 1066–1314," *Journal of Ecclesiastical History*, 32 (1981), 442.

[25]Cîteaux/Marilier 77 (pp. 84–85). Vernolle and Civry are forty-two kilometers northwest of the abbey.

[26]Longué, fols. 98v–99r. Martine Garrigues, in the introduction to her edition of the cartulary of the Cistercian house of Pontigny, also noted that almost all donors were from the local petty nobility (*hobereaux*); Pontigny, p. 21.

[27]Fontenay's documents are in the Arch. Côte-d'Or, in the series 15 H; the two cartularies are bound together as 15 H 9.

valley of the Brenne (Fontenay is located at the source of a stream that flows from it four kilometers into the Brenne).[28]

The most important noble family that consistently appears in Fontenay's records is that of the lords of Montbard. These brothers and nephews of Bernard of Clairvaux's mother had their castle less than five kilometers from the abbey. Lord Rainard of Montbard, Bernard's uncle, helped found Fontenay originally. He made the monks several gifts, including his share of Fontaines-lès-Sèches (sixteen kilometers north of Fontenay), which he defended against the rival claims of the count of Bar, and also the woods of Planay (twelve kilometers north of Fontenay), a gift his grandson and great-grandson, both named Andreas, confirmed later in the century.[29] Rainard also helped found the nunnery of Puits d'Orbe nearby.[30] Rainard's grandson Andreas confirmed several gifts from local knights to Fontenay; he attested to a rather sizable gift from three laymen of allodial land between Fontenay and Marmagne; he agreed to a gift from a knight of pasture rights for pigs in woods the knight held from him in fief; and in 1162, when two brothers of Nesle gave Fontenay pasture rights at Nesle and in nearby communities, it was done "in the hand of Lord Andreas," according to the donation charter (Nesle is sixteen kilometers north of Fontenay).[31]

But the lords of Montbard appear less frequently than do some of their dependent knights. From the viewpoint of the monks of Fontenay, one of the most important local households was that of a knightly family who had their center at Marmagne, three kilometers south of the abbey. The members of this family held much of their land in fief from the bishop of Autun. They were important to the monks both as monastic patrons and as converts to the monastic life.[32] Three generations of this family gave Fontenay property during

[28]The monks did receive some gifts from the lords of Thil, whose castle was located twenty-eight kilometers to the south, but most of these gifts were of property that the lords of Thil owned closer to Fontenay, at Fresnes and Ménétreux, five and eleven kilometers southeast of the abbey. See, for example, Arch. Côte-d'Or, 15 H 163, nos. 2, 3.

[29]Genus illustre, pp. 540–41, no. 99 [rpt. PL CLXXXV:1461–62]. This charter was printed from a part of the cartulary of Fontenay that has become mutilated since the seventeenth century. Petit 457 (II:320–21). Jobin, St. Bernard, pp. 613–14, 641–43, nos. 46, 69. The original documents of the latter transactions are in Arch. Côte-d'Or, 15 H 156, nos. 1, 4, 5. For the lords of Montbard, see also Appendix A, pp. 334–38.

[30]GC IV:160–61, no. 38. Agnes, first abbess of Puits d'Orbe, was the sister of Geoffrey, first abbot of Fontenay; Jobin, St. Bernard, p. 635, no. 62.

[31]Fontenay II, fol. 35v, no. 32. Arch. Côte-d'Or, 15 H 156, no. 2. Petit 383 (II:282–83).

[32]A case can be made for identifying Giselbert, the first member of the family to appear in Fontenay's cartulary, as one of the sons of Aimo Bruno, a knight in the castle of the lord of Grignon who gave Flavigny his rights over the parish church of Marmagne when he died in 1100—specifying, however, that two of his nephews would still appoint the priest in the church. However, since Flavigny's cartulary ends at almost the

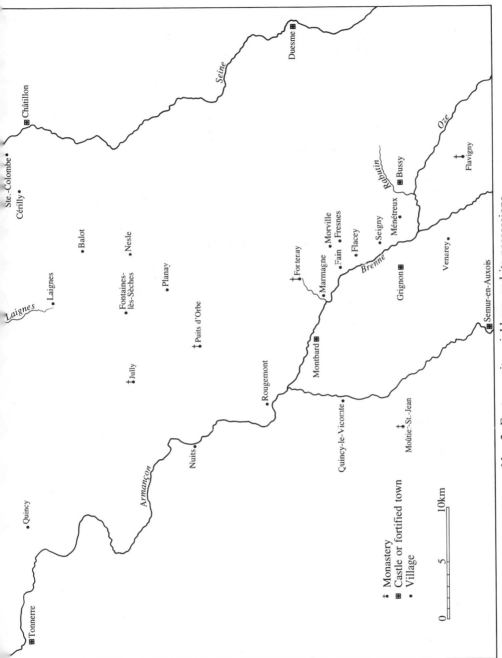

Map 2. Fontenay, its neighbors, and its possessions

Tonnerre

Quincy

Ste.-Colombe
Cérilly
Châtillon

Laignes
Laignes

Balot

Nesle

Fontaines-
lès-Sèches

Planay

Jully

Puits d'Orbe

Duesme

Fortenay

Marmagne
Morville
Fain Fresnes
Flacey
Seigny
Ménétreux
Bussy
Flavigny

Grignon

Venarey

Semur-en-Auxois

Montbard

Rougemont

Nuits

Quincy-le-Vicomte

Moûtie-St.-Jean

Seine

Oze

Rabutin

Brenne

Laignes

Armançon

‡ Monastery
⊞ Castle or fortified town
• Village

0   5   10km

the twelfth century. The first was Giselbert of Marmagne, who gave the monks some land at Seigny (ten kilometers upstream along the Brenne from Fontenay) which he had held in fief from the bishop of Autun, as well as some additional land next to the abbey. He made this gift when he fell ill and entered the monks' infirmary, where he died soon after. When his only son soon died as well, Giselbert's widow gave the monks half of all the allodial land she had at Marmagne and a small annual income to establish anniversaries for her son and husband.[33] Shortly before Giselbert's death, his nephew Aimo, after initially quarreling with the monks, gave them some land at Grignon, across the river from Seigny, in return for some land at Marmagne.[34]

After Giselbert died Aimo seems to have inherited from him. He, with his brother Geoffrey (like Aimo, called a *miles* in some of the charters) and sister Elizabeth, gave Fontenay some additional land at Seigny. Aimo received a colt, his brother thirty solidi, and his sister ten solidi, *de karitate ecclesie*, as a counter-gift from the monks.[35] At about the same time, their cousin Ermensend, who had married a knight of Venarey, eleven kilometers upstream from Marmagne, gave Fontenay all she held in fief from the bishop of Autun between Seigny and Fresne in return for a small counter-gift of thirty-five solidi and a setier of wheat, and also gave her son Aimo—apparently her only son—as an oblate (note the ready acceptance by the Cistercians of Fontenay of this child oblate).[36]

A few years later the knight Aimo decided to become a monk at Fontenay and gave the monks the rest of his property at Seigny as an entry gift, with the consent of his brother and his sister Elizabeth. She had in the meantime married Bartholomew, a knight of Châtillon.[37] Châtillon is located some thirty kilometers northeast of Fontenay, separated from it by the ridge of land that divides the Seine and Brenne/Armançon river valleys, and Bartholomew's family had never been involved with Fontenay's affairs before this marriage. Afterward, however, Bartholomew, with his wife Elizabeth and his seven children, appears frequently in Fontenay's charters. Since Aimo had left no sons when he entered Fontenay, his nephews,

---

same time as Fontenay's begins, it is impossible to be sure of this identification or to know if this knightly family continued to patronize Flavigny at the same time as Fontenay. See also Petit 98 (I:414—15).

[33]Fontenay II, fols. 13v—14r, nos. 35—37.

[34]Fontenay II, fols. 14r—v, 43v, nos. 38, 12.

[35]Fontenay I, fol. 101r, no. 12. Fontenay II, fols. 11r—v, no. 26. For the practice of counter-gifts, see below, Chapter 9.

[36]Fontenay II, fols. 3r—v, no. 45.

[37]Fontenay II, fols. 11v—12r, no. 27.

Elizabeth's sons, inherited the lordship of Marmagne and with it an interest in Fontenay's possessions. This interest was initially demonstrated in an attempt to seize the property Aimo had given the monks, but, after the monks had persuaded them to give up the quarrel, they gave the monks some tithes for the rather large payment of 300 solidi and thirty pounds.[38]

Most of Fontenay's other patrons were like these knights of Marmagne: men who had their center close to the abbey—usually no more than twenty-five kilometers, one full day's walk, away, and often closer—and who were lords of a rather restricted area. They could not be called castellans because they did not have a castle, yet their property was important enough that the bishop of Autun demanded they do homage to him for it. They were also new men, who had rarely appeared in the records before Fontenay was founded, if at all. They may well have been men originally set up as dependent agents of the bishops, men who had only recently been able to establish a position of independent power. These knightly patrons were men who alternated between the rough seizure of property which had probably marked their recent rise to power and the open-handed generosity that could validate their position as members of the aristocracy. Perhaps they had become interested for the first time in monasticism when Fontenay was founded in their neighorhood, or, alternatively, they had not had enough property or power before the twelfth century to be able either to threaten monasteries' possessions or to endow monasteries on a regular basis. In either event, Fontenay and its knightly neighbors reached prominence together.

Since the knights and members of the petty nobility who patronized Cistercian houses came from a restricted area, one might wonder what the knights did who lived in areas where there were no Cistercian houses. Presumably, there was a roughly comparable concentration of knights everywhere, and certainly they did *not* travel long distances to make pious gifts to Cistercian monks. Fontenay was the only Cistercian house in its region. To the southeast, there was no other Cistercian house until Cîteaux, eighty kilometers away, and before reaching Cîteaux one had to pass Flavigny, St.-Seine, and St.-Bénigne and St.-Étienne of Dijon. Yet these houses only rarely received gifts from knights.

It is difficult to do extensive comparisons of the donors to Cistercian houses with the donors to the more traditional Benedictine houses, since none of the latter has as large a collection of documents from the twelfth century as do many of the Cistercian houses—not because their archives survived less well, but because these houses

---

[38]Fontenay II, fols. 28r–30r, nos. 13–15. Petit 568 (II:369–70).

received fewer gifts. Cluny, with its carefully preserved archives, has far fewer documents from the twelfth century than the eleventh, and far fewer knights are found in Cluny's archives than those of the Cistercian houses. St.-Seine, located thirty-six kilometers southeast of Fontenay, has no gifts from knights recorded in its cartulary, even though it does record extensive gifts from the dukes and from castellans from a fairly wide area, including the lords of Mt.-St.-Jean, thirty-three kilometers to the southwest, and the lords of Grancey, thirty kilometers to the northeast. The old houses of Bèze and Pouthières have only a handful of documents from any donors surviving from the twelfth century (a total of three for Bèze from the second half of the century). This lack is not a matter of documents having been lost in the Revolution, for even in the mid-eighteenth century, when the monks inventoried their goods and their charters, those few documents that now exist were all they had, even though they had many charters from the late Middle Ages on. It is particularly striking to find so few charters from twelfth-century Bèze, since it has a large number of eleventh-century documents.[39] The conclusion seems inescapable that old, relatively small houses like these were simply outcompeted by the Cistercians. Perhaps then the knights of the twelfth century flocked to nearby Cistercian houses to make pious gifts, but if no Cistercian house was nearby they rarely made pious gifts at all.

Support of Multiple Houses

Though some families patronized the same houses generation after generation, it was possible for a family to change allegiance in its support of monastic houses. The wealthier families might make gifts to a large number of houses, even though a less powerful family might patronize only one or two houses. Toward the end of the twelfth century the number of different houses in whose records a particular family might be found increased. If a family made its gifts to just two different houses, it generally chose two similar ones, such as two Cistercian houses or two Cluniac houses. Members of the family of the lords of Montsaugeon, for example, who founded the Cistercian monastery of Theuley in 1130, were also among the earliest donors to the Cistercians of Auberive a few years later.[40] Family tradition helped in deciding to which house to make gifts, but family tradition was not an absolute, and each generation had to choose whether to

---

[39] Arch. Côte-d'Or, 3 H 1, 9 H 1.
[40] GC IV:163–64, 166, nos. 40, 42.

follow it. Two houses of the same order, located near each other, could even be rivals for the same patrons.

Morimond and La Crête, located thirty-one kilometers apart, were both patronized by some of the men who lived between the two houses (La Crête was a daughter of Morimond). But men whose center of power was on the side of one house away from the other almost always patronized one house (the closer one) but not the other. The lords of Clefmont (also sometimes given the title of count) took an interest in both houses. Clefmont was located thirteen kilometers northwest of Morimond and nineteen kilometers southeast of La Crête. Robert Wicard, count of Clefmont, and his wife Beatrix were among the early donors who first helped establish La Crête's possessions in the valley of the Rognon; Robert gave his allodial land at Forcey (seven kilometers south of the abbey).[41] Robert's father, Simon I, also gave the monks fishing and pasture rights—perhaps before Robert gave his land at Forcey—a gift that Robert and Beatrix confirmed in 1136. Their two sons, Simon II, lord of Clefmont, and Robert Wicard II, confirmed all these gifts in 1162. In 1175 Simon II attested to the gift of some woods to La Crête from a knight. In 1196 Simon's wife attested to the end of a quarrel between a knight and La Crête.[42]

While thus playing a steady if not spectacular role in the welfare of La Crête, the lords of Clefmont also sometimes patronized Morimond. Since the land on which Morimond was founded (by the lords of Aigremont) had been held in fief from the counts of Clefmont, they had to give their assent to the house's foundation in 1115.[43] However, they are not found again in Morimond's charters until the later twelfth century. Robert Wicard II of Clefmont witnessed a knight's gift of land and pasturage to Morimond in 1170. Simon II, lord of Clefmont, gave Morimond land near Grandrupt and Levécourt (Levécourt is seven kilometers northeast of Clefmont), with the consent of his wife and brother, in 1181; confirmed the gift of an annual *cens* to Morimond from one of his men in 1182; and gave up his claims on the tithes of Levécourt in 1185.[44] At the same time, the counts of Clefmont made their first appearance in the archives of several other Cistercian houses. Simon II pawned some pasture rights to Longué in 1187, and, while the lords of Clefmont did not make any gifts of their own to Clairvaux, located fifty-five kilometers to their

[41]Arch. Haute-Marne, 5 H 5. For the counts of Clefmont, see Appendix A, pp. 317–19.
[42]Arch. Haute-Marne, 5 H 7.
[43]Arch. Haute-Marne, 8 H 1. The foundation charter of Morimond, as printed in GC IV:159, no. 36, is abbreviated and does not mention the counts of Clefmont.
[44]Arch. Haute-Marne, 8 H 19, no. 1; 8 H 67, no. 13; 8 H 54, no. 7; 8 H 67, no. 15.

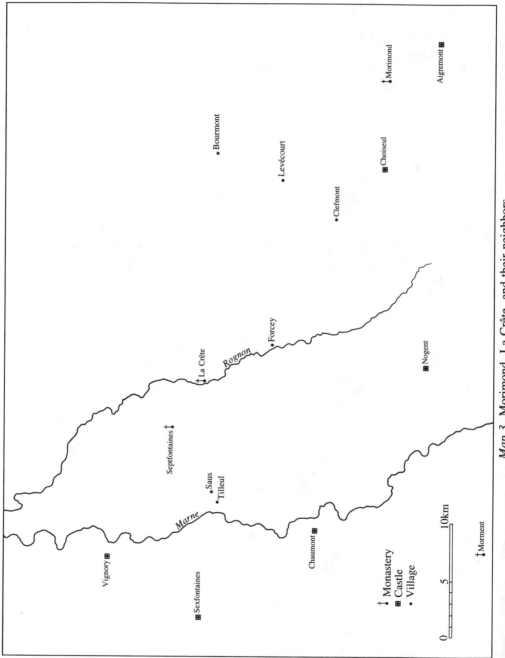

Map 3. Morimond, La Crête, and their neighbors

west, Simon, with his wife and son, confirmed in 1188 gifts other men had given: property located within twelve or fifteen kilometers of Clairvaux which had been held in fief from him. A few years later Lord Simon made a brief and unsuccessful attempt to claim some of Auberive's property as his own, property which, however, he claimed in the name of his wife, since his own predecessors had had no contact with Auberive.[45]

Besides these Cistercians houses, another house, that of Septfontaines, a body of canons regular that later joined the Premonstratensian order, was also located near Clefmont, twenty-four kilometers to the northwest. The lords of Clefmont do not seem to have made any gifts of their own to Septfontaines, in spite of its proximity, though a knight did ask Simon II, lord of Clefmont, to seal the charter attesting to his gift of arable land to the canons in about 1162. Similarly, Simon and his brother Robert Wicard granted the Hospitallers of Morment (located thirty-two kilometers southwest of Clefmont) the right to receive property held from them in fief in 1167, as Lord Simon II did again in 1189.[46]

While the lords of Clefmont patronized both La Crête and Morimond, houses that lay a short distance in either direction from their castle, the lords of Sexfontaines originally patronized only La Crête. Geography as well as family tradition appears to have played a role in such patterns of patronage. Their castle was located twenty-one kilometers west of La Crête, on its far side from Morimond. Simon of Sexfontaines gave pasturage along the Marne to the monks of La Crête when the abbey was first established, as well as giving up claims to their granges at Tilleul and Saus, on the Marne (twelve kilometers west of La Crête). In 1162, on the anniversary of his father-in-law's death and at the request of his wife, Adelaide Wicheta, and as he was himself preparing to go to Jerusalem, Simon gave up his quarrels with the monks of La Crête.[47] After his death his wife and children, after initially claiming the property he had given the monks, reconfirmed it in 1172. Lord Simon also gave pasture rights in his lands to the monks of Clairvaux (Sexfontaines is twenty kilometers northeast of Clairvaux). In 1193 this same Adelaide Wicheta and her men gave La Crête the tithes of newly cultivated land, the *novalia*, at Forcey.[48]

This Adelaide Wicheta was the daughter of Robert Wicard I of Clefmont, which may explain why she had property at Forcey to give the monks. And because of this family connection, the family of the

[45]Longué, fol. 85r, no. 17. Clairvaux I, p. 73, no. 2. Auberive I, fol. 56v, no. 12.
[46]Arch. Haute-Marne, 10 H 14. Petit 455 (II:320). Morment 50 (pp. 128–29).
[47]Arch. Haute-Marne, 5 H 5, 5 H 8. For the lords of Sexfontaines, see Appendix A, pp. 361–63.
[48]Arch. Haute-Marne, 5 H 6, 5 H 8. Clairvaux I, pp. 80–81, nos. 33–35.

lords of Sexfontaines began appearing in the records of Morimond as well as La Crête during the 1160s. After her husband's death, Adelaide, along with her children, brother, and father, gave a large amount of land to Morimond in 1165.[49] In this example family ties had carried the patronage of the lords of Sexfontaines beyond the one nearby Cistercian house that they had originally patronized exclusively.[50]

There were then several factors influencing a particular family's choice of which house or houses to patronize. A family's wealth and power helped determine to how many houses they might effectively make their pious gifts. Geographic proximity made some houses more available than others, and the reputation for holiness of different houses made some more appealing than others. Family tradition was a powerful inducement to patronize a particular house, as was the attitude of a man's wife, as I shall now discuss.

The Role of Women in Spreading Monastic Reform

It is noteworthy that in the primarily patriarchal eleventh and twelfth centuries, when office and power were almost always inherited in the male line, women still played an important role in deciding *where* a family would make its pious gifts. Their influence seems to have been wielded behind the scenes, but it was no less effective. Though nuns were never more than fractionally as common as monks and priests in the High Middle Ages, women in the secular world significantly aided the spread of church reform, as suggested in the preceding examples of Elizabeth of Marmagne and Adelaide Wicheta. When a woman married she took to her new home and new husband an interest in the monasteries she had been brought up to admire. She might introduce her husband's family to a house they had never before patronized, or she might continue to make her own gifts to the same monastery that her family—though not her husband's—had long patronized. For example, Agnes, daughter of Otto-William of Burgundy, married Duke William V of Aquitaine, and shortly after this marriage he began making gifts to Cluny, something neither he nor his immediate predecessors had done before. Though Cluny had been founded by William I of Aquitaine, the county had gone to the counts

---

[49] Arch. Haute-Marne, 8 H 107.

[50] There was a priory of St.-Bénigne of Dijon located at Sexfontaines, but since virtually no twelfth-century documents survive, it is impossible to tell what the lords of Sexfontaines's relations were with this house. This priory was established at a ruined church in 1030; St.-B. II.295 (pp. 78–79). The pope confirmed the monks' possession of their church in the 1130s; PU Champagne 29 (II:226–27).

of Poitou upon the death of his nephew William II, and the counts of
Poitou virtually ignored Cluny until Agnes married William V.
Agnes, in addition to encouraging her husband's generosity, made a
number of gifts to Cluny in her own name.[51] In about 1062 her
daughter, the empress Agnes, along with her mother, asked Pope
Alexander II to take the church of St.-Nicholas of Poitou under apostolic protection; the empress had grown up near Poitou, and it was her
concern for this church, not her husband's, which was instrumental
here.[52]

In Burgundy, Ermengard, of the family of the counts of Chalon
which had founded Paray, married the lord of Bourbon. But when she
was dying, in the late eleventh century, she gave all her dower property to Paray for the good of her soul. Similarly, Ermengard's older
sister Adelaide, who inherited the county of Chalon when their
brother Hugh II died without sons, brought an interest in Paray as
well as the county of Chalon to her husband and their heirs. Her son
came to Paray as he was leaving for the First Crusade to confirm the
gifts of previous counts of Chalon.[53] The counts of Chalon also
became involved in the eleventh century in support of the nearby
abbey of Tournus. When the previously mentioned Hugh II, count of
Chalon, married Constance, daughter of the duke of Burgundy, he
interested her in Tournus as well, so that when, after his death, she
married Alfonso VI of Castile, she continued to be involved in the
affairs of this abbey. She sent Tournus a large amount of gold and
silver, as well as assisting her new husband in making substantial gifts
of bullion to Cluny, which had been patronized by her own family,
the dukes of Burgundy, throughout the eleventh century. Maintaining
her contact with Burgundy through visits of her nephew, the duke, as
well as through messengers and letters, she carried a concern for the
monasteries of Burgundy far beyond the Burgundian borders.[54]

Constance arrived in Spain at a time when the Spanish royal family
had become very interested in the monastery of Cluny. One of the
most important results of this interest was the spread of the
Cluniac—and eventually Cistercian—orders into Spain, essentially
against the better judgment of the Burgundian abbots. Cluny had sent
some directives on the regular life to Spain in the tenth century and
received gifts from the Spanish kings in the early eleventh century,[55]

---

[51]C 2716, 2855, 3322 (III:739−40; IV:54, 414−15). For Agnes, see Appendix A, p.
270.
[52]Pflugk-Harttung, I:36−38, no. 38.
[53]Paray 87, 107, 208 (pp. 46−47, 56−57, 107−8). See also Appendix A, pp. 312−13.
[54]Tournus, pp. 134−35. C 3735 (V:83−86).
[55]Peter Segl, *Königtum und Klosterreform in Spanien: Untersuchungen über die
Cluniacenserklöster in Kastilien-León von Beginn des 11. bis zur Mitte des 12. Jahrhunderts*
(Kallmünz, 1974), pp. 23−46.

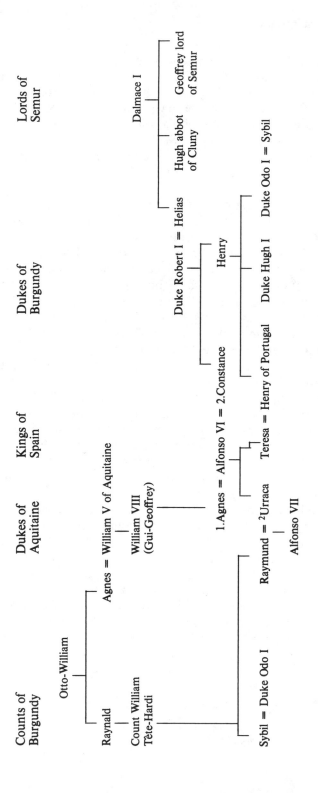

Fig. 2. Family ties between the principal patrons of Cluny

but the closest ties between Cluny and the Spanish royal house were established in the 1060s, when Abbot Hugh helped arrange the release of Alfonso VI of Castile from his brother's prison (the two were disputing their father's inheritance); in gratitude, Alfonso arranged annual shipments of Spanish ore to Cluny.[56] Shortly afterward, Alfonso married Constance, and his interest in the Burgundian monasteries intensified. Alfonso VI established the first Cluniac priories in Spain; his requests to establish such priories were in fact so numerous that the abbot of Cluny refused several of them.[57]

Constance's daughter, Urraca of Spain, and Urraca's half sister Teresa both married Burgundians; Urraca married Raymund, son of Count William Tête-Hardi of Burgundy, around 1087, and Teresa married Henry, brother of Duke Odo of Burgundy, about eight years later (Henry became count of Portugal). These marriages of course made the ties between Spain and Burgundy closer still. Alfonso VI and his daughters began marrying Burgundians, reforming Spanish houses to a Cluniac rule, making gifts of bullion to Cluny, and inviting Burgundian nobles to help fight in the *reconquista*, all within a very short time.[58] The ties between the principal patrons of Cluny may be seen in Figure 2.

As the Spaniards who befriended Cluny established close ties with that house over the generations, so the Burgundians who went to Spain remembered the Burgundian monasteries. Urraca's husband, Raymund, who took the title of count of Galicia, asked the abbot of Cluny to confirm the agreement that he and his brother-in-law, Henry of Portugal, made on dividing the spoils when they were preparing to march toward Toledo against the Muslims. Similarly, the necrology of St.-Bénigne of Dijon included prayers for Raymund. And Henry of Portugal and his Spanish wife made gifts from Spain to the Cluniac house of La Charité-sur-Loire.[59] Links of marriage thus helped carry Cluny's influence far beyond Burgundy during the eleventh century,

[56]Gilo, "Vita Sancti Hugonis" 1.9, ed. Cowdrey, "Studies," pp. 59–60.

[57]C 3343, 3540, 3735 (IV:431–40, 665–68; V:83–86). Noreen Hunt, *Cluny under Saint Hugh, 1049–1109* (London, 1967), pp. 126–28.

[58]Segl, *Königtum und Klosterreform in Spanien*, pp. 180–81. Alfonso had begun giving Cluny Spanish churches shortly before marrying Constance of Burgundy, while his first wife was still alive—but this first wife was the great-granddaughter of Otto-William; C 3508 (IV:625–26); *La chronique de Saint-Maixent, 751–1140*, ed. Jean Verdon, Les classiques de l'histoire de France au moyen âge 33 (Paris, 1979), p. 132. For Alfonso's and his daughters' alliances with the Burgundians, see also Bernard F. Reilly, *The Kingdom of León-Castilla under Queen Urraca, 1109–1126* (Princeton, 1982), pp. 10–44; and Evelyn S. Procter, *Curia and Cortes in León and Castile, 1072–1295* (Cambridge, Eng., 1980), pp. 14–15. For the family connections, see Appendix A, pp. 257–58, 273–74.

[59]*Documentos Medievais Portugueses*, I (Lisbon, 1958), 3–4, 10–11, nos. 2, 6. St.-B. II.420 (p. 198). La Charité 40 (pp. 106–9).

to the point that Cluny became very closely identified with the Spanish royal family.[60]

In the twelfth century, as the Spanish Christians and French Crusaders—many from Burgundy—gradually reconquered land from the Muslims, the Spanish nobility invited the abbots of Cîteaux and Clairvaux to send monks to settle on the recovered land. Bernard of Clairvaux was opposed to the practice; he wrote to the abbot of Pruilly that there were many good places to found daughter houses in Burgundy and Champagne, and founding one there was preferable to sending monks "into exile" for the difficult and expensive task of founding a house in Spain. But his opposition could not halt the practice.[61]

Further examples of the influence of women at the end of the eleventh century are provided by the sisters Ermentrude and Clemence, sisters of Raymund of Galicia and daughters of Count William Tête-Hardi of Burgundy; they too took an interest in Burgundian houses far beyond Burgundy. Ermentrude married Count Theoderic of Montbéliard, and his family began to make gifts to Cluny for the first time shortly after this marriage. It is striking that the counts of Montbéliard began making their gifts *then*, for this was not their first contact with Cluny. Abbot Hugh of Cluny, according to his *vita*, had once visited Theoderic's parents in their home and miraculously averted a thunderstorm during dinner.[62] Similarly, Clemence, who married Robert II, count of Flanders, took with her the family affection for Cluny. Shortly after her marriage she gave Abbot Hugh of Cluny the Flemish monastery of St.-Bertin, with the consent of the abbot of St.-Bertin but against the initial objections of both Abbot Hugh and the monks of St.-Bertin. Clemence was thus responsible for the spread of the Cluniac order in a new direction, north of the Loire for the first time, and the beginning of an active center of monastic reform in Flanders.[63] Hence the political and family ties of the Burgundian nobility—especially their ties through marriage—were sometimes responsible for establishing daughter houses of Burgundian monasteries in distant parts of Europe as well as closer to home.

[60]Segl, *Königtum und Klosterreform in Spanien*, pp. 93–99. Raymund's and Urraca's children also gave Cluny a church; C 3970 (V:327–28). See also Johannes Fechter, *Cluny, Adel und Volk* (diss., University of Tübingen, 1966), p. 109; and Marcelin Défourneaux, *Les français en Espagne aux XIe et XIIe siècles* (Paris, 1949), pp. 136–37.

[61]Bernard of Clairvaux, Letter 75, *Opera*, VII:182. For examples of Cistercian foundations in Spain, see Jobin, *St. Bernard*, pp. 593–94, 599–600, nos. 30, 35. See also Southern, *Western Society and the Church*, p. 263.

[62]C 3830 (V:190–91). Gilo, "Vita Sancti Hugonis" 1.34, ed. Cowdrey, "Studies," p. 78. See also Appendix A, pp. 274–75.

[63]C 3899, 3733 bis (V:249–50, 836–38). "Miscellanea Hugonis" 3, ed. Cowdrey, "Studies," pp. 161–62. Simon, "Gesta abbatum Sancti Bertini Sithiensium" 2.64–68, MGH SS XIII:648–49. See also H. E. J. Cowdrey, *The Cluniacs and the Gregorian Reform* (Oxford, 1970), pp. 106–7.

The role of women is perhaps not so striking in the twelfth century, since in this period one is dealing with knights whose marriages interested them in monasteries in the next river valley rather than with counts and dukes learning through their wives of monasteries in the next kingdom. But women were just as important, even if on a smaller scale, in spreading an abbey's influence beyond its immediate neighborhood. This may be seen especially with the Cistercian houses. A knightly family of Cérilly, located twenty-seven kilometers north of Fontenay, over the divide into the next river valley, appeared for the first time in Fontenay's records when Rayner of Cérilly married the daughter of Girard "the Hairy," whose own property was located within seven kilometers of Fontenay. In 1182 Rayner and his wife gave land to Fontenay which they had inherited from Girard, at Flacey, Fain, and Morville. In this case, Rayner was not merely agreeing to his wife's disposition of her father's property: clearly he himself had become convinced of Fontenay's merits because he had the monks specify in the donation charter that they would receive him as a monk if he decided to convert when dying.[64]

Similarly, Mileta of Aigremont, daughter of Lord Fulk of Aigremont, the founder of Morimond, brought an interest in Morimond to her husband, Girard of Bourmont (located seventeen kilometers northwest of the abbey, on the far side from Aigremont), whose family had not previously been found in Morimond's charters. Her three sons, Fulk, Louis, and Willenc, gave Morimond their allodial property at Levécourt (twelve kilometers northwest of the abbey) in 1176.[65] It is interesting to note that her first and third sons were named for her relatives—patronage of Morimond may have been one part of an identification with the lords of Aigremont, a more powerful family than Girard's.

This influence of women on the spread of reformed monasticism was part of the wider influence that women exercised even in the patrilinear High Middle Ages. Men always tried to improve their own position by marriage with women of more powerful families and identification with this greater power, which seems in many cases to have included patronage of the same houses the wife's more powerful family had patronized. The choice of where to make gifts to ensure prayers after death was often made by a wife for her husband if she outlived him, as many wives did. Even when husband and wife decided together where to make their pious gifts, the husbands of the eleventh and twelfth centuries often trusted their wives' judgment

---

[64]Arch. Côte-d'Or, 15 H 163, no. 5. These three *villae* are located between four and six and one-half kilometers southeast of the abbey, upstream along the Brenne.

[65]Arch. Haute-Marne, 8 H 67, no. 6. For the lords of Aigremont, see Appendix A, pp. 279–82.

more than their own, and in searching for the most holy group of monks in the area they were willing to listen to accounts of the holy monks of the next river valley. The almost exclusively male orders of the eleventh and twelfth centuries might not have expanded nearly as far or as successfully had local noble women not assisted in spreading the word of their pious way of life.

The nobility then played a vital role in the spread of reformed monasticism. Far from representing an anti-noble sentiment, the multiplication in the number of houses and their possessions grew out of noble support for these monks. The monks' attempt to find an appropriate place to attain individual salvation coincided at certain points with the nobles' desire to have holy monks praying for them and to demonstrate to the world that, as monastic supporters, they were the successors of early medieval kings and princes. Though ecclesiastics might have preferred that men powerful in the world act to protect the church as a whole, most nobles chose a few churches as *their* churches and patronized them to the exclusion of all others. From their own point of view, the nobles were not fulfilling a "useful" function in society. Rather, they were asserting or affirming a particular relationship with a particular saint and the monks who knew that saint best. For the patrons of monastic reform did more than set up an individual abbey; they established a close tie with a saint that would last throughout their lives and beyond.

The rise of the powerful castellans of the eleventh century and the outpouring of gifts to houses such as Cluny occurred together. Secular lords acted as advocates, protecting their monasteries and encouraging gifts to them, and giving their children an interest in these same houses. The role of the family was central: most nobles supported the same houses as their ancestors, once they had chosen a house to support. However, they were certainly amenable to giving their attention to new houses; thus many of the great patrons of Cluniac priories in the eleventh century turned in the twelfth century to Cistercian houses.

Yet the principal benefactors of the new Cistercian order were knights, whose position had been recently established. In some sense their monastic patronage may have been carried out in imitation of the longer-established nobility. Knights certainly imitated great lords throughout the twelfth century in establishing patrilineal dynasties and even in making their houses into miniature castles.[66] And patronizing monasteries as nobles had always done proved (to themselves or to

---

[66]Georges Duby, "The Diffusion of Cultural Patterns in Feudal Society," in *The Chivalrous Society* (Berkeley and Los Angeles, 1977), pp. 173–77.

great nobles) that they were members of the aristocracy. To be the man that monks turned to in need gave a knight an air of panache and authority that needed no actual domination of monks to be effective. The relationship between knights and the new monasteries was synergistic. The multiplying Cistercian houses benefited from the increasing numbers of knights interested in monastic patronage, men who had risen to a position in which they had property worth giving to the monks—at least if they acted in concert with other knights. The Cistercian houses were particularly attractive to these new members of the aristocracy because these houses were peopled by men like themselves, they were nearby, and they were small and poor enough that the small gifts a knight could offer would not be lost in a welter of possessions.

[6]

Monastic Patronage
over the Generations

Individual families—the group of relatives who held the same property, inherited (usually) in the male line—tended to support the same churches over the generations. If family members had founded or reformed a particular house, their descendants generally continued to support and make gifts to that house. And if family members once made gifts to an existing reformed house, then their descendants as well patronized that house. Relations between monks and a particular lineage could sometimes be ambiguous; the heirs of a donor were the most likely men to try to claim his pious gift, as detailed in Chapter 9. But the monks made every effort to settle such disputes amicably while asserting their prerogatives, wishing above all to avoid alienating the currently aggressive young representatives of such a lineage, because they were also ultimately the most likely to add to the gifts their predecessors had made. In this chapter, I examine the long-term commitment of noble families to individual houses, by using the examples of three important Burgundian families, the dukes of Burgundy, the counts of Burgundy and Mâcon, and the lords of Brancion and Uxelles.

The Dukes of Burgundy

The dukes, the most powerful of the Burgundian families, made pious gifts to a variety of different houses. Still, even their generosity was not bestowed universally. They tended to return to the same houses, and they also tended, as they patronized increasing numbers of new houses, to drop some of the old ones.

The dukes of the eleventh century had made gifts to St.-Bénigne, and in the first decades of the twelfth century Duke Hugh II too gave the monks there some property.[1] But St.-Bénigne received very few gifts from later dukes, even though, as noted in Chapter 5, the dukes continued to hold the abbey's *custodia*. Family members increasingly turned their attention instead to the new monastic orders. Hugh II's uncle, Hugh I, and his father, Odo I, had been among the first to appear in Molesme's charters after the foundation of that house in 1075. These brothers, along with a third brother, Bishop Robert of Langres, and their sister Beatrix, lady of Vignory, gave Molesme a number of churches and other property; Bishop Robert even took the habit there himself shortly before his death.[2] But even the generosity of this generation to Molesme was overshadowed in the twelfth century by the family's patronage of the Cistercian order.

Duke Odo I, before leaving for Jerusalem in 1101, made several gifts to the New Monastery of Cîteaux, founded only three years earlier. He and his successors were recorded among the abbey's principal brothers and friends in the house's necrology.[3] Duke Hugh II, his son, sometimes had Cîteaux in mind even when ostensibly patronizing St.-Bénigne, for one gift he made the monks of St.-Bénigne, consisting of some revenue sources, was made in return for their donation to Cîteaux of some land near that abbey.[4] In the next three generations, Odo II, Hugh III, and Odo III made gifts of land, pasture rights, and annual incomes to the Cistercian monks of Maizières, Auberive, Longué, Clairvaux, and Theuley, as well as Cîteaux, and also confirmed the gifts other lords had made to these houses.[5]

Throughout much of the twelfth century, until the final decades, the dukes made most of their pious gifts to houses of the Cistercian order, only rarely making gifts to any other monastery or house of reformed canons.[6] The dukes did however cultivate their relations with the bishops of Autun and Langres, confirming the bishops' rights and possessions and establishing anniversaries at the cathedrals. In 1178 the duke took the county of Langres from the lords of Saulx and

[1]St.-B. II.403, 404, 419, 459 (pp. 182–84, 196–98, 228). Arch. Côte-d'Or, 1 H 13, no. 8. For the dukes' family, see Appendix A, pp. 255–61.
[2]Molesme 1.1, 3, 5–7, 11, 103, 220, 252; 2.369 (II:3–4, 6–7, 9–13, 19, 107, 204, 235, 389–90).
[3]Obit. Lyon II:612.
[4]St.-B. II.429 (p. 206). Duke Hugh also gave the Cistercian monks of Fontenay some property at Grignon, located across the river from the abbey; Fontenay II, fols. 6v–7r, no. 9.
[5]Cîteaux/Marilier 182 (pp. 148–49). Petit 466, 887 (II:426–27; III:325–26). Arch. Haute-Marne, 1 H 88 [copy in Auberive I, fol. 176r–v, no. 102]. Longué, fols. 18v–19r, no. 10; fols. 130v–131r. Clairvaux I, p. 153, no. 1; p. 286, no. 20. Arch. Saône-et-Loire, 20 H 3; H 54, no. 16. Petit 869 (III:315–16). Theuley, fol. 27v.
[6]When in 1179 Hugh III made a gift to Cluny, consisting of a piece of land yielding ten solidi a year, he said it was only to make amends for damages he had done; C 4269 (V:630–31).

bestowed it on the bishops of Langres. (The bishop then was Walter, uncle of Duke Hugh III.)[7] These bishops, whose spiritual authority covered the same area of northern and eastern Burgundy over which the dukes wielded the principal temporal authority, were potentially either rivals or allies, and the dukes always found it worth cultivating them, even when they did *not* have a brother or uncle in one of these two sees.

There was a change toward the end of the twelfth century, as Dukes Hugh III in the 1180s and especially Odo III in the 1190s began making gifts to a great many different houses, something their predecessors had not done. No longer restricting their generosity to the Cistercians, they also began making gifts to many of the traditional Benedictine houses and the Augustinian houses in the dioceses of Langres and Autun. These gifts tended to be small, usually consisting of an annual income, or at most a mill or two *homines*, but they were gifts nonetheless. The recipient houses included St.-Bénigne, in whose archives the dukes once again appear after a long absence. Other recipients included the monks of St.-Martin of Autun and of St.-Seine, the canons regular of St.-Symphorien of Autun, St.-Étienne of Dijon and the ducal chapel in that city, and the nuns of Jully.[8] But it seems that in the twelfth century the dukes, in making gifts with the announced intention of saving their souls, considered the Cistercian houses the most likely to provide their salvation, and thus they let Cluny and St.-Bénigne, which family members had patronized in the eleventh century, fall into relative neglect.

The Counts of Burgundy and Mâcon

The eleventh- and twelfth-century counts of Burgundy and Mâcon were second in power only to the dukes. The lineage produced powerful secular lords, spouses for many of the royal and comital families of western Europe, four bishops, one of whom became pope, several crusaders, and a number of patrons of reformed monasticism. The family's original center in the duchy was between Mâcon and Dijon. They enjoyed their period of greatest power at the beginning of the eleventh century, when Otto-William was count.[9] They

---

[7] Autun/Évêché 2.16 (pp. 257–58). Autun/Église 2.7, 2.23, 3.7 (I:92–93, 111–13; II:12–13). GC IV:187–88, 192, nos. 71, 79 (the first of these is also edited as Langres 125 [p. 532]).

[8] Arch. Côte-d'Or, 1 H 13, nos. 10–11. Autun/St.-Martin 25 (p. 53). Plancher I.99–100 (p. lix). Autun/St.-Symphorien 25, 35 (pp. 59–60, 75–76). St.-Étienne IV.18, 102, 107, 116 (pp. 38, 116, 119–20, 129–30). Petit 972 (III:358). Jully, pp. 275–76.

[9] Constance B. Bouchard, "Laymen and Church Reform around the Year 1000: The Case of Otto-William, Count of Burgundy," *Journal of Medieval History*, 5 (1979), 1–10. See also Georges Duby, *La société aux XIe et XIIe siècles dans la région mâconnaise*, 2nd

extended their authority eastward after Rudolph III of imperial (trans-Saône) Burgundy died in 1032 without heirs. The western center of family power was reduced during the eleventh century as the dukes of Burgundy made Dijon their own capital, and their more eastern territories were attenuated in 1156, when the emperor Frederick Barbarossa married Beatrix, heiress of the county of Burgundy, and claimed trans-Saône Burgundy. However, Beatrix's cousins, the counts of Mâcon, continued to call themselves counts of Burgundy in their charters, and the descendants of Frederick Barbarossa and the descendants of the counts of Mâcon were reunited by marriage in the thirteenth century.

Otto-William, though he is usually described by modern scholars as a ruthless lord trying to carve out a principality for himself, was viewed with favor by his ecclesiastical contemporaries as a monastic patron, especially at Cluny and at St.-Bénigne, which he had helped reform in 990 (see above, Chapter 4).[10] Otto-William's immediate successors maintained his pattern of generosity to these churches. His son Raynald, who took the title of count of Burgundy, and grandson Otto (son of Otto-William's son Gui, who predeceased him), who took the title of count of Mâcon, often appeared with Otto-William in his donation charters in the last years of his life, and, after his death in 1026, they confirmed his pious gifts and added gifts of their own.[11] Raynald also persuaded King Rudolph III of imperial Burgundy to set Cluniac monks in a church that was under Rudolph's control, and himself made gifts to the church of St.-Anatole of Salins, gifts that King Rudolph confirmed.[12]

This rather static relationship with Cluny and a few other houses was continued in the next generation. Raynald's nephew Otto, count of Mâcon, and his wife, Elizabeth, gave Cluny a large amount of land and a *villa* during the 1030s, and Elizabeth witnessed some gifts to Cluny from other members of the Burgundian nobility.[13] These

---

ed. (Paris, 1971), pp. 137–39. The genealogies of the counts of Mâcon and Burgundy in the tenth and eleventh centuries are quite complicated. For a discussion of the problems, see Appendix A, pp. 265–79.

[10]Otto-William founded a church, Notre-Dame of Vaux-sur-Poligny, in the archdiocese of Besançon, which the archbishop gave to Cluny after Otto-William's death—apparently in the belief that his donations belonged to Burgundian churches; C 2890 (IV:86–88).

[11]Chron. St.-B., p. 193. See also M 471 (p. 271); St.-B. II.284 (pp. 72–73); and C 2694, 2736 (III:721–22, 759–61). Raynald also gave the monks of Flavigny ownership of one of the cauldrons at Salins where the water was boiled down to make salt; Flavigny 14 (pp. 33–35) [Collenot, pp. 92–93].

[12]Theodor Schieffer, ed., *Die Urkunden der burgundischen Rudolfinger* (Munich: MGH, 1977), pp. 292–95, nos. 121, 122.

[13]C 2712, 2713, 2733, 2734, 2852, 2845, 2979 (III:735–36, 756–58; IV:45–46, 52–53, 176–78).

counts also maintained the more or less cordial relations with the bishops of Mâcon which had existed since the tenth century. The bishops had enough respect for the counts' position within their city that the cathedral cartulary even included an early twelfth-century genealogy of the counts of Mâcon—none of whom, it should be noted, joined the cathedral chapter.[14] Otto gave the cathedral of Mâcon a vineyard for the good of his soul, "remembering that we need the mercy of God"; his wife and brother both agreed to this pious gift.[15] Geoffrey, Otto's son and successor as count of Mâcon, did little more during his short rule than give the canons of Mâcon a serf, "thinking of the enormity of his sins."[16]

This pattern—of keeping contact with both the local monks and the local cathedral canons through fairly small gifts and an almost paternalistic confirmation of others' generosity—continued throughout the eleventh century. The only exception was that of Otto's grandson Gui, count of Mâcon, who took his predecessors' affection for Cluny much further than they had; saying he "recognized how useless the honors of this world were," he entered the monastery himself in 1078 (his wife entered the affiliated nunnery of Marcigny).[17] Before doing so, he, like his immediate predecessors, had witnessed a few gifts to Cluny and confirmed in general terms any acquisitions the monks might make in his county, as well as giving the cathedral canons of Mâcon the land on which to build a church, after first pressing for a period a claim to receive certain dues from the canons' vineyards.[18] But by entering Cluny he took a path radically different from that of his predecessors. At Cluny he was soon given the position of prior of the dependent house of Souvigny. Gui entered Cluny at the same time as Wigo, count of Albion, and as Duke Hugh I of Burgundy, who had succeeded his grandfather as duke in 1076. All three seem to have been struck, at a critical juncture in their lives (the duke had been wounded in battle), by the need to find salvation in withdrawal from the world.

When Gui entered Cluny, the county of Mâcon was taken by his cousin, William I Tête-Hardi, Raynald's son, who already held the office of count of Burgundy. William, like his cousins at Mâcon, was in contact with the church, both cathedral canons and reformed monks, principally through a series of small gifts he made. As he had

[14]M 7 (p. 6).
[15]Otto also agreed, "for the good of his soul," to give up his claims to the property of one of the cathedral canons there; M 268, 464 (pp. 161, 266–67).
[16]M 454 (p. 260).
[17]C 3528 (IV:650–51).
[18]C 3475, 3488, 3504, 3518 (IV:583–84, 596, 618, 638–40). M 11, 192 (pp. 10–11, 124). Gui also helped the bishop establish the abbey of St.-Rigaud in the early 1070s; Arch. Saône-et-Loire, H 142, no. 1.

expanded his power east of the Saône, he made some gifts to churches there as well.[19] But perhaps William's greatest influence on the Burgundian churches was through his numerous children, including at least six sons and four daughters. (The daughters were discussed in Chapter 5.)

Two of his sons took orders, the first members of the family to begin their careers in the church and the first secular clerics. Hugh became archbishop of Besançon (1085–1101), while Gui became archbishop of Vienne (1090–1119), from which position he was elected pope under the name of Calixtus II (1119–1124). Among William's other sons, Stephen I and Raynald II went on Crusade and Raymund fought the Saracens in Spain (as noted in Chapter 5), thus taking part in the militant form of Christianity which was becoming more common at the end of the eleventh century. But they still patronized Cluny and St.-Bénigne in preference to other churches. Raynald added to his father's gift to Cluny of land east of the Saône; Stephen confirmed and encouraged his vassals' gifts to Cluny; and Raymund gave Cluny some houses located at Salins while he was still in Burgundy. After Raymund left for Spain he gave the monks several Spanish churches, with the consent of his wife and his Spanish in-laws. In addition, saying that he wished to "imitate his ancestors," Raymund made several gifts to St.-Bénigne.[20]

But in the first decades of the twelfth century, after Stephen, Raynald, and Raymund had gone to Spain or the Holy Land, several major changes took place in the ongoing relations of the counts of Burgundy and Mâcon with the local churches. They began to patronize the houses of the new Cistercian order as well as the houses to which their predecessors had always made their gifts, and they began at least occasionally to quarrel with the local churches. These changes, however, did not take place suddenly or dramatically.

William II "the German," son of Raynald II, who succeeded him as count of Mâcon, confirmed in 1107 all his predecessors' gifts to Cluny, noting specifically his uncle Stephen, his father, Raynald II, his grandfather William Tête-Hardi, his great-grandfather Raynald I, and his great-great-grandfather Otto-William. Here he was explicitly acting in the context of a long family tradition. He also confirmed the gifts of his mother, Regina, who had become a nun at Marcigny after her husband's death, and asked the monks to pray for his maternal grandfather, Cono.[21] But his son, William III, broke with his predecessors

---

[19]C 3615 (IV:776–77). C.-U.-J. Chevalier, ed., *Cartulaire de l'abbaye de Saint-André-le-Bas de Vienne* (Vienne and Lyon, 1869), p. 196, no. 256. Beatrix 175–77 (pp. 204–7).

[20]C 3614, 3735, 3743, 3773, 3774 (IV:776; V:83–86, 95–96, 124–25). St.-B. II.365 (pp. 143–44). Pérard, pp. 198–200.

[21]C 3862 (V:211–13); Marcigny 30 bis, 102 (pp. 26–28, 73–74). Cono's relatives

and attacked Cluny. Peter the Venerable's *Miracula*, written in the mid-twelfth century, describe him at length and very negatively. This count, Peter said, made it his practice to "exercise tyranny" over the men and churches of the Mâconnais, so that monks, canons, and lay-men all had to pay him tribute, until he was appropriately carried away by demons.[22]

William's cousins Raynald III (d. 1148), count of Burgundy, and William IV (d. 1156), who took the county of Mâcon after the death of William III, were, like William III, much more litigious than their predecessors. Soon after assuming power they quarreled with the bishops of Mâcon over their respective rights in that city. Raynald and Bishop Berard reached an agreement, one of the earliest of its kind, in which it was decided that the bishop should have judicial rights over all cemeteries and all clerics in the city, while the count should judge all thieves and adulterers. This agreement, which put secular and ecclesiastical relations on a new footing, each authority having its defined sphere of responsibility, did not stop the brothers from reopening the quarrel over judicial rights when Bishop Berard was replaced by Bishop Joceran in 1122.[23] The counts also claimed certain rights in Vienne, where their uncle Gui had been bishop; in 1146, when Archbishop Humbert of Vienne asked the emperor Conrad III to help him restore his rights in the city, he singled out Count William IV among the "secular powers" and asked Conrad to forbid him to interfere in the city.[24] But the counts never established a center of power in Vienne comparable to that which they acquired at Mâcon, and they do not seem to have sought one at Besançon, the other major city of trans-Saône Burgundy. Indeed, in 1148 Counts Raynald and William granted the cathedral of Besançon blanket per-mission to acquire whatever the canons could from the counts' vas-sals.[25]

In addition to quarreling with the bishops of Mâcon and Vienne, Counts Raynald III and William IV also broke with tradition in mak-ing gifts to new or newly reformed houses in their region, among them St.-Étienne of Dijon, recently reformed as a house of canons regular. Raynald, saying that he wished to redeem his soul since he

---

had founded a Cluniac priory near Neuchâtel fifteen years earlier; C 3665 (V:12–14).

[22]Peter the Venerable, *Miracula* 2.1, PL CLXXXIX:909–11; cf. "Anselmi continuatio Sigeberti" 1127, MGH SS VI:380.

[23]M 589, 590 (pp. 355–57). In the first half of the twelfth century other French counts and bishops who shared a city also became involved in prolonged quarrels over their respective rights to justice and customary dues. For parallels, see Constance Brit-tain Bouchard, *Spirituality and Administration: The Role of the Bishop in Twelfth-Century Auxerre*, Speculum Anniversary Monographs 5 (Cambridge, Mass., 1979), pp. 54–55.

[24]MGH DD regum et imperatorum Germaniae IX:265, no. 145.

[25]Beatrix 103 (pp. 122–23).

was "not worthy of the grace of God," told the canons of St.-Étienne that they would no longer have to pay certain tolls and dues in his lands. Count William confirmed the rights of the nuns of Château-Chalon (located in the diocese of Besançon) shortly before his death.[26] And, most importantly, the counts began appearing in the cartularies of Cistercian houses.

Theirs was not the first instance of family generosity to the new order, however. Bonnevaux, the first Cistercian house in the diocese of Vienne, had been founded in 1117 by Archbishop Gui of Vienne, their uncle.[27] But these counts were the first secular members of the family to help spread the Cistercian order. They were especially active in the diocese of Besançon. Around 1130, for instance, Raynald III gave the house of Cherlieu, originally a house of canons regular, to Clairvaux, to become a house of Cistercian monks. When Le Miroir, the first daughter of Cîteaux in the diocese of Lyon, was established in 1131, Count William IV gave his consent, since the land on which the house was founded had been held from him. Only a few years later, around 1136, Raynald himself founded Acey, a daughter house of Cherlieu.[28]

In addition to helping found several houses, both Raynald III and William IV made gifts to established Cistercian houses in the duchy of Burgundy and in the county of trans-Saône Burgundy. Several factors influenced the patterns in which this patronage was bestowed. For example, William married the heiress of Trier, whose family had founded the Cistercian house of La Charité, located in the diocese of Besançon, and after this marriage he and his sons made several gifts to this house as well as to Cherlieu.[29] Around 1130 his brother Raynald granted Cîteaux's men and wagons the freedom from tolls in his lands and reconfirmed this grant a decade later. He gave the Cistercians of Theuley a large amount of land in the 1140s, within ten years of the abbey's foundation. He also confirmed La Charité's possessions and also those of the Cistercian houses of Bonnevaux and Grâce-Dieu, located in his county of trans-Saône Burgundy. Raynald's confirmation of the possessions of these Cistercian houses was remembered and recalled when Frederick Barbarossa, who married Raynald's daughter Beatrix and took his county in 1156, confirmed the houses' rights himself.[30]

[26]St.-Étienne II.105 (pp. 115–16). Beatrix 111 (pp. 128–31).
[27]Cîteaux/Marilier 62 bis (p. 204).
[28]For the original establishment of Cherlieu, see GC XV:25–26, no. 22; and Jean-Pierre Kempf, *L'abbaye de Cherlieu, XIIᵉ–XIIIᵉ siècles: Économie et société* (Vesoul, 1976), pp. 16–18, 72. Cîteaux/Marilier 86 (p. 90). GC XV:31–32, no. 28.
[29]Beatrix 108–10, 115 (pp. 127–28, 133).
[30]Cîteaux/Marilier 106 (pp. 100–101). Arch. Haute-Saône, H 422. Theuley, fol. 21r. MGH DD regum et imperatorum Germaniae X:241, no. 143.

But Raynald III and William IV had not forgotten St.-Bénigne and Cluny, the houses counts of Burgundy and Mâcon had always patronized. Following family tradition, they confirmed what their uncle Raymund had given St.-Bénigne before he went to Spain, and they also gave the monks there some vineyards and fishing rights.[31] Their gifts to Cluny varied greatly and included petty income sources, the monastery of Baume, and protection of the abbey's rights. When Peter the Venerable, abbot of Cluny, reestablished the abbey's "peace" in 1153, he specifically asked Count William to help him maintain it.[32] It is noteworthy that Raynald III's heiress, Beatrix, maintained her Burgundian interests after she became empress. All the charters she issued herself after her marriage were for Burgundy, and she continued her father's and uncle's devotion to Cluny. She was generous to the Cluniac priory of Romain-Môtier, located in the Empire, even assisting in rebuilding the *burg* around the church.[33] The brothers Raynald III and William IV had quite a different relationship to the local churches than had their predecessors, but St.-Bénigne and Cluny were still important for them.

Several major changes in the temporal power of the counts of Burgundy and Mâcon occurred in the next two generations. After the county of Burgundy went to the emperor with the daughter of Raynald III, the sons of William IV were still able to make advantageous marriages that helped maintain the wealth and power of the counts of Mâcon: Stephen II (d. 1173), who called himself count of Burgundy (*comes in Burgundia*) as well as lord of Trier, married Judith of Lorraine, Frederick Barbarossa's niece; and Girard, count of Mâcon and Vienne, married the heiress of Salins, whose family had been the other major power in trans-Saône Burgundy. But there were no corresponding changes in the family's relationship with the church. Stephen II and Girard quarreled intermittently with the bishops of Mâcon and the abbot of Tournus and made a few small gifts to Cluny[34] and several more important ones to various Cistercian houses. They were especially generous with salt from their cauldrons at Lons-le-Saunier. When Stephen II went to Jerusalem in 1170, in the company of the duke of Burgundy, he granted Cîteaux and the Cistercian

[31]Pérard, pp. 227, 229—31.

[32]C 4116, 4122, 4125—27, 4141 (V:461, 465—71, 486—87). Beatrix 132 (pp. 148—49).

[33]M.-J. Gauthier, ed., *Cartulaire des comtes de Bourgogne (1166—1321)*, Mémoires et documents inédits pour servir à l'histoire de la Franche-Comté 8 (Besançon, 1908), pp. 3—4, no. 2. Heinrich Appelt, "Kaiserin Beatrix und das Erbe der Grafen von Burgund," in *Aus Kirche und Reich: Studien zu Theologie, Politik und Recht im Mittelalter, Festschrift für Friedrich Kempf*, ed. Hubert Mordek (Sigmaringen, 1983), pp. 275—83.

[34]C 4233, 4279 (V:584—86, 644—47). Alexander III, Letter 1506, PL CC:1297—98. C 3791 (V:135—37); the editor incorrectly attributes this charter to Stephen I. M 623 (pp. 377—78). Tournus, pp. 166—67.

nuns of Tart an annual revenue in salt from Lons. Stephen also gave Morimond an income in salt, and Girard gave La Ferté a similar income. While leaving on Crusade in 1170, Stephen freed the monks of the Cistercian order from paying tolls on his land. His companion the duke, who was Stephen's brother-in-law (the two had married sisters), similarly freed the Cistercian monks from paying dues and tolls in his own lands at the same time. When Stephen died in 1173 his brother Girard confirmed both the income in salt and the freedom from tolls that Stephen had given Cîteaux.[35]

In the following generation, especially in the 1190s and later, Stephen II's son, Stephen III, count of Burgundy and Auxonne, and Girard's son, William V, count of Mâcon and Vienne, seem to appear in Cluny's charters much more frequently than the counts had for several generations, making small gifts and confirming the gifts of others. Here the counts' generosity paralleled that of the dukes in the same period. But during the 1190s William also became involved in quarrels with Cluny, claiming rights to some of the monks' men and property.[36] At the same time, the counts made just a few gifts to Cistercian houses. William V had given Maizières an annual income in salt in 1174, and his cousin Stephen III gave the same house an annual income at Lons in 1199.[37]

The counts of Burgundy and Mâcon then, while varying over the generations in their relation with the church, had one fixed point, a close association with the monks of Cluny, an association closer than any between Cluny and the dukes. This closeness aside, their relations with the church changed direction every two generations or so. At the beginning of the eleventh century the family played a major role in reforming old monasteries to a regular life. In the middle decades of the century family members engaged in something of a

[35]Cîteaux/Marilier 193, 208, 222, 223 (pp. 156, 167–68, 177–78). Arch. Haute-Marne, 8 H 115. Arch. Côte-d'Or, 78 H 1042. Clairvaux I, p. 72, nos. 2–3. Auberive I, fol. 172r, no. 81. C 4233 (V:584–86). For the dukes, see Cîteaux/Marilier 192, 198 (pp. 155–56, 159–60). Stephen's father-in-law, Duke Matthew of Lorraine, similarly exempted the Cistercian house of La Crête from paying tolls; Émile Duvernoy, "Catalogue des actes des ducs de Lorraine de 1176 à 1220," *Mémoires de la Société archéologique lorraine et du Musée historique lorraine*, 64 (1914/19), 149, no. 127. Stephen, duke of Lorraine, granted this same privilege to Clairvaux in 1186; Clairvaux I, p. 291, no. 37. For gifts from these counts to the Cistercians of La Charité, Cherlieu, and Chassaigne, and the nuns of Château-Chalon and Tart, see Beatrix 109, 113–18 (pp. 127–28, 132–35); Arch. Haute-Saône, H 285; BN, Coll. Baluze 4, fol. 29r.

[36]C 4342, 4348, 4353, 4370, 4377 (V:706–7, 711–12, 715–16, 726–27, 733). For the counts' gifts to the Cluniac priory of St.-Vivant of Vergy, see Arch. Côte-d'Or, 21 H 679.

[37]In 1190 the cousins Stephen and William gave the Cistercian nuns of Tart forty sacks of salt a year, after earlier confirming Stephen II's gift of one sack to these same nuns; Arch. Côte-d'Or, 78 H 1042; Arch. Saône-et-Loire, H 54, nos. 8, 21; Plancher I.137 (p. lxxxii).

holding action, making Cluny and the cathedral chapter of Mâcon small gifts and confirming the gifts of others. In the final decades of the eleventh century family members again became more directly involved in the church, as Count Gui entered Cluny, two of his cousins became bishops, and, a few years later, members of the family began going to Spain or the Holy Land to fight the infidel. Unlike the dukes of Burgundy, the family played no role in the establishment of the Cistercian order, but they did begin making gifts to existing houses of the order and founding new ones about a generation after Cîteaux's foundation. At the same time they quarreled briefly but fiercely with their neighboring bishops over what they considered their rights. After the first few decades of the twelfth century, however, the counts returned to a rather static pattern. Some family members still went on Crusade, but otherwise their principal contact with the church was through a series of small gifts to Cistercian houses, especially ones family members had previously patronized, and always to Cluny.

The Grossi of Brancion and Uxelles

In contrast to the preceding discussion of the powerful dukes and counts of Burgundy, the following discussion of the lords of Brancion and Uxelles is intended as an example of the changing relations between a castellan family and the Burgundian monasteries over the course of nearly three centuries. These castellans were like the counts in that they owed their principal allegiance to Cluny. I refer to family members collectively as the Grossi; from the mid-eleventh century on, all male family members took the *cognomen Grossus*, or "Gros."[38] The use of this *cognomen* is perhaps justified, for this family was quite wealthy compared to most castellans, controlling a large amount of territory in the Mâconnais, as well as the castles of Brancion and Uxelles, perched on two of the highest points between the Saône and the Grosne, about eight kilometers apart (although twice that far by the road). In the eleventh century family members appear regularly in the cartulary of the cathedral of Mâcon, and in the twelfth century in the cartulary of the Cistercian house of La Ferté, but above all their activities are attested by documents from Cluny, which was located seventeen kilometers southwest of Brancion (as the crow flies,

---

[38]For this unusual *cognomen*, see Constance B. Bouchard, "The Structure of a Twelfth-Century French Family: The Lords of Seignelay," *Viator*, 10 (1979), 44 and n. 16. For the family, see Appendix A, pp. 300–307.

twenty-five kilometers by the road). The extent of their possessions—or at least the possessions they gave to Cluny—is shown in
Map 4.

In the male line the family of the Grossi begins at the end of the
tenth century with Joceran I, lord of Uxelles, who married Rotrudis,
daughter of the lord of Brancion, a castle that Joceran's descendants
eventually acquired. Rotrudis' ancestors had been generous to Cluny
practically since its foundation in 909, and she not only followed her
own family tradition but interested Joceran in Cluny as well. She and
Joceran gave Cluny several *mansi*, vineyards, two churches, and at
least one serf, and also witnessed gifts of land in the Mâconnais which
several other people gave to Cluny.[39]

The sons of Joceran and Rotrudis continued their parents' generosity. Maiolus Poudreux, a canon at the cathedral of Mâcon, was especially generous. About 990 he gave Cluny a *mansus* at Mont, specifying that he would be buried at Cluny. He stated that anyone who
tried to claim this burial gift would "incur the wrath of God and all
the saints and be compelled to pay a fine of four pounds in gold."[40]
Maiolus lived for quite some time after this, however, and during the
next decades made Cluny several gifts of serfs and *mansi*, also giving
the monks some land both he and they had claimed as theirs.[41] In
1030, when he was dying, Maiolus took the monastic habit at Cluny
and increased his earlier gifts by giving the monks a great deal of land
around Taizé. After his death his nephew Joceran II gave Cluny some
land he had inherited from Maiolus, for his uncle's soul.[42] Though
Maiolus' brothers were not as generous as he, they too made gifts to
Cluny; his brothers Bernard I and Israel (who had witnessed his gift of
the *mansus* at Mont), along with Bernard's wife, Emma, and Israel's
son Joceran, over a period of time gave the monks land located at six
different *villae*.[43]

---

[39]C 898, 1521, 1538, 1577, 2493, 2896 (II:13–14, 570–71, 588–89, 622–23;
III:572–73; IV:98–99).

[40]C 1845 (III:88–89). Mont is a common place name in the mountainous Mâconnais
and Beaujolais regions. Guy de Valous identified this Mont, said to be in the *pagus* of
Lyon, as one near St.-Germain-sur-l'Arbresle, twenty kilometers northwest of Lyon
and sixty-seven kilometers south of Cluny; Valous, "Le domaine de l'abbaye de Cluny
aux Xᵉ et XIᵉ siècles," *Annales de l'Académie de Mâcon*, ser. 3, 22 (1920–1921), 454.
But since the *pagus* of Lyon extends quite far north from Lyon, nearly to Mâcon, I
would prefer to place this Mont somewhere closer to Cluny.

[41]C 2202, 2406, 2508, 2552, 2904 (III:351–52, 497–98, 585, 617; IV:103–4). See
also Dietrich Poeck, "Laienbegräbnisse in Cluny," *Frühmittelalterliche Studien*, 15
(1981), 102–3.

[42]C 2445, 2827 (III:526–27; IV:31). The first document cited here is Joceran's gift;
the documents of the Grossi family are not in chronological order within the edition of
Cluny's charters. Taizé is nine kilometers north of Cluny.

[43]C 2322, 2351, 2486, 2617, 2959, 3132 (III:442, 461, 568–69, 664–65; IV:157–58,
297).

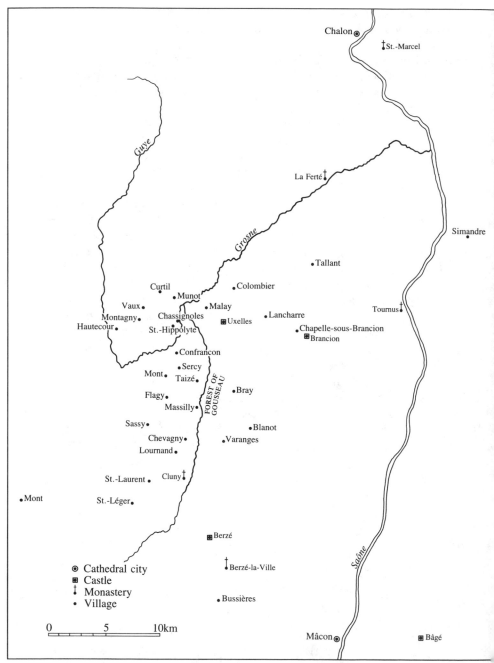

Map 4. The possessions of the Grossi of Brancion and Uxelles

Thus the family of the Grossi was generous to Cluny, individually and collectively, from the time the family first appears as a cohesive unit. The property this family gave the monks was generally located no more than twenty kilometers from the abbey, and often less than ten. This proximity, however, may indicate not so much an interest in giving the monks convenient land as that this is where the Grossi themselves happened to own *villae* and *mansi*. These early gifts by Rotrudis, Joceran, and their sons were primarily gifts of land from the family's hereditary possessions in a rather compact area between the Guye and the Grison, north and northwest of Cluny. Most of the land was allodial; some was specified as *allodium*, and much of the rest can be assumed to be allodial, since the donor said explicitly that it was his by right and by inheritance, and there seems to have been no lord whose permission the Grossi had to seek to make the gifts. As Georges Duby's work has made clear, the practice of holding land in fief did not become prevalent in the Mâconnais until well into the eleventh century.[44]

The gifts the Grossi made to Cluny in the tenth and early eleventh centuries were generally made with the specification that they were given to Saint Peter, the patron of Cluny and the saint who held the keys of heaven, for the good of the souls of the donor and his relatives. A large number of family members were indeed buried at Cluny over the generations.[45] Joceran, Rotrudis, and their sons showed an eagerness for salvation that seems to have ignored any economic considerations. Yet, in spite of their wealth at the end of the tenth century, members of the family clearly could not have continued to give their land away in this manner without eventually impoverishing themselves. And indeed, from the 1030s onward, a note of caution begins to creep into the documents. The Grossi were still eager to be on good terms with the monks of Cluny and, through them, with Saint Peter and with God. But they sought to obtain this goodwill through somewhat smaller gifts.

For example, sometime around 1050 Bernard III Grossus gave the monks of Cluny not a large piece of land and its serfs but rather the income he had been receiving from one serf. He also gave Cluny a

[44]Duby, *La société mâconnaise*, pp. 58–59, 102, 149. Indeed, since a number of regional studies (of the Narbonnais, Champagne, Bordelais, Bazadez, and Catalonia, as well as the Mâconnais) have indicated that "feudalism was late" in reaching these regions, it would probably be good to change the prevailing opinion that fief-holding was the common pattern from the early eleventh century on and accept instead that in the eleventh century and perhaps the twelfth a large amount of land was allodial. See Constance B. Bouchard, "The Origins of the French Nobility: A Reassessment," *American Historical Review*, 86 (1981), 531, n. 91.

[45]See for example C 1845, 2322, 2904, 3073, 4664 (III:88–89, 442; IV:103–4, 255–56; VI:190–91).

female serf, a gift that his son Landric initially claimed but then
returned to Cluny. In 1070 Bernard's sons gave Cluny one vineyard
for their father's soul.[46] While Bernard III's gifts were smaller than
those of his predecessors, he was still interested in gaining the friendship of the monks of Cluny, as Peter the Venerable's *Miracula* illustrate. The story tells how Bernard, who had gone on pilgrimage to
Rome around 1070 and died on the journey, continued to seek the
friendship of Cluny's monks even after his death, appearing to them
as a ghost, asking for their prayers.[47] (Contrast this story to Peter's
description of Count William III of Mâcon, mentioned above.) The
monks at least had little doubt that the Grossi, out of a strong hope
for intercessory prayers, gave them whatever they could over the generations.

Landric Grossus, son of Bernard III, made several small gifts of
land and serfs to Cluny toward the end of the eleventh century; but
he also sold Cluny a house at Sercy for 100 solidi, clearly interested in
financial arrangements as well as pious gifts.[48] By the early twelfth
century the gifts to Cluny from the Grossi had become much smaller
than those of earlier generations—a source of income rather than
land, or only enough land to support one serf. But of course one cannot say that the Grossi family had begun trying to find a cut-rate route
to salvation. For a family that had become less wealthy as a result of
several generations of partible inheritance as well as ancestral generosity to Cluny, such a relatively small gift was probably as much of a
financial wrench as a gift of a large number of *mansi* had been a century earlier.

After the first decades of the twelfth century, the Grossi appear
much less frequently in Cluny's cartulary than they had earlier. Their
gifts, even small ones, were few, although they continued to confirm
donations made previously. Bernard V Grossus, who went twice to
the Holy Land and made gifts to Cluny on each occasion, was one of
the last family members to make gifts of any substance to Cluny. In
1110 he gave the monks a woods at Bray; in 1117 he gave the monks
a number of serfs; in 1124 he gave whatever he had, "justly or
unjustly," at Mont, for his father's soul; and in 1147 he freed the
peasants belonging to the monks from paying certain dues to him.[49]
Even so, he quarreled with the abbot of Cluny when he began
demanding tolls from the merchants and pilgrims coming into Cluny
(the road to Cluny from the northeast passes by Brancion and

[46]C 2881, 3428, 3753, 3754 (IV:75–76, 539–40; V:106–8).
[47]Peter the Venerable, *Miracula* 1.9, PL CLXXXIX:874–76. Abbot Hugh is mentioned in this story, which makes it clear that Bernard III is the subject.
[48]C 3034, 3074, 3621 (IV:227–29, 255–56, 786–89).
[49]C 3896, 3926, 3929, 3972, 4131 (V:246–48, 278–79, 282–83, 330, 473–74).

Plate 6. The village of Brancion and the twelfth-century church, as seen from the castle

Uxelles). He had originally given up his claim to *peagium*, giving hostages to his agreement, but started extorting tolls again, under the name of *conductum*. After the abbot of Cluny threatened to excommunicate him, Bernard made peace, in an agreement mediated by the bishop of Autun.[50] Bernard's son Joceran IV appears chiefly in the monastery's charters trying to reappropriate earlier family gifts, although, around 1175, when he was dying, he did give the monks some of his allodial land.[51]

Even when gifts from the Grossi to Cluny had slowed to a trickle and quarrels with Cluny became common, family members continued to make gifts to La Ferté-sur-Grosne, a Cistercian house founded in 1113, fourteen kilometers north of Brancion. Their decreasing generosity to Cluny was thus due in part to a switch of allegiance. Bernard V Grossus and his son Joceran IV gave several sizable gifts of land to the monks of La Ferté in the 1140s and also confirmed several gifts that other laymen made the monks.[52] From the time the family first emerged until they were forced to sell off their property, they maintained close ties with their neighbors at Cluny, but, in the twelfth century, when their supply of allodial land and of serfs grew smaller, they fastened on the most holy of the nearby monasteries—which in this case was a Cistercian house—when making their largest gifts.

During the rest of the twelfth century and the first half of the thirteenth, until the lineage ended, the intermittent appearance of the Grossi in Cluny's documents often involved a cease-and-desist order, in which family members were persuaded that their claims to Cluny's men and property were unjust. For example, at the beginning of the thirteenth century family members agreed to stop bearing arms within Cluny's *bannum*; in 1213 the duke of Burgundy agreed to protect Cluny's land, specifically against Joceran V Grossus; and in 1214 Joceran and his brother agreed to give up their claims to certain dues from Cluny's men, in an agreement mediated by the archbishop of Lyon.[53] However, in the early thirteenth century the monks of Cluny

[50]C 3920 (V:270—72).

[51]C 4106, 4131, 4253 (V:455—56, 473—74, 587—88). See also Marguerite Rebouillat, "La lutte entre les seigneurs de Brancion et Cluny," in *La guerre et la paix: Frontières et violences au moyen âge*, Actes du 101ᵉ Congrès national des sociétés savantes (Paris, 1978), pp. 342—43.

[52]La Ferté 2, 99, 103, 116, 145 (pp. 42—43, 100, 102—3, 110—12, 126—28). The last two are the confirmations of gifts from others. Henry, the last lord of Brancion, continued this tradition a century later when he gave La Ferté a mill on the Grosne in 1239, before he left on Crusade; J. Louis Bazin, *Brancion: Les seigneurs, la paroisse, la ville* (Paris, 1908), pp. 212—13, no. 9. The Grossi did however quarrel with La Ferté at the very end of the twelfth century as they had earlier quarreled with Cluny; Arch. Saône-et-Loire, H 25, nos. 40, 50.

[53]C 4410, 4472, 4481, 4482 (V:785—87; VI:27—28, 34—38). The Grossi made similar claims on the property of other churches besides Cluny in the later twelfth century. Joceran IV Grossus was persuaded to give up property belonging to the cathedral

still considered the lords of Brancion important neighbors. Joceran V
almost always drew up the charters attesting to the agreements
between Cluny and the local knights on financial matters or fief-
holding drawn up in the 1230s, and confirmed many of the gifts from
these knights to the monks.[54] But the family made scarcely any gifts
of their own to the abbey after the middle of the twelfth century.
Bartholomew, bishop of Pécs (Fünfkirchen) in Hungary, who made a
large payment to Cluny in 1234 to assure burial there as his ancestors
had first done almost two hundred and fifty years earlier, stands
almost alone among the thirteenth-century Grossi.[55]

In part, the family had incurred serious financial difficulties that precluded large pious gifts. Their growing impoverishment is marked by
the gradual selling of their possessions. Joceran V was forced to sell
about half his property between 1224 and 1237; but even here he
acted within the context of long family ties to Cluny, for he sold the
property to the monks.[56] The money raised however was not sufficient to end the family's difficulties. In 1259 Joceran's son Henry III
sold Brancion and Uxelles to the duke of Burgundy, and the family's
fortunes ended. Financial problems, which had been reflected in the
decreasing volume of gifts to Cluny for over a century, had finally
caught up with the Grossi.

In this overview of the relations between Cluny and the Grossi, it
should be noted that over the generations family members tended to
give the monks property located in the same *villae* as the gifts of their
ancestors. For example, Bernard I agreed to a gift of land at Lournand (three kilometers northwest of the abbey) to Cluny at the end of
the tenth century, a gift made by his uncle Odo. Bernard's brother
Maiolus Poudreux gave Cluny his right to certain *consuetudines* at
Lournand a few years later, and two centuries later lord Joceran V of
Brancion gave up some claims to Cluny's property at Lournand and
sold the monks additional rights there.[57] Three sons of Joceran I,
Bernard, Joceran, and Maiolus Poudreux, gave an allod at Bussières to
Cluny in three separate portions between 999 and 1005 (Bussières is
eleven kilometers southeast of the abbey).[58] Cluny also acquired land
at Taizé from the Grossi in piecemeal fashion over the generations.
Maiolus Poudreux gave the monks some land there when he took the

---

chapter of Chalon only in 1171 when King Louis VII pressured him to do so (Chalon is
twenty-eight kilometers north of Brancion); GC IV:242–43, nos. 27, 28.
[54]C 4603, 4604, 4614, 4617, 4652, 4653, 4655, 4671, 4673, 4674, 4675, 4681, 4700,
5002 (VI:150–51, 156, 159, 180–81, 183–84, 194–97, 203, 218–29, 467).
[55]C 4664, 4669 (VI:190–93).
[56]C 4544, 4711 (VI:93, 230–34).
[57]C 2351, 2406, 2552, 4447, 4544 (III:461, 497–98, 617; V:820; VI:93).
[58]C 2486, 2532, 2617 (III:568–69, 603–4, 664–65).

habit at the end of his life; the brothers Joceran III Grossus and Landric Grossus gave the monks some additional land and a serf at Taizé at the end of the eleventh century; and in 1231 Joceran V confirmed a gift there from a certain canon of Mâcon.[59] Similarly, the family sometimes disputed Cluny's ownership of the same piece of property over the generations. Joceran I for example originally gave Cluny the church of St.-Hippolyte (fifteen kilometers northwest of the abbey) around the year 1000, but around 1060 his great-grandson, Bernard III Grossus, claimed the church's men. Around 1110 Bernard V Grossus gave up his claims to St.-Hippolyte, "whatever his ancestors had given Cluny," while preparing to go on Crusade. In 1214 Joceran V Grossus made peace with Cluny by giving up his own claims to St.-Hippolyte.[60]

The picture that emerges from this survey of the Grossi is one of a family that was very conservative in its relations with religious houses: for nearly three centuries, in spite of changing economic conditions and the appearance of the Cistercian order, they never forgot their family's ties with Cluny. Although the size of the pious gifts family members made varied over the generations, the property they gave was always located in the same area, the area of the family's power. As long as the Grossi continued to hold land, in fief or allod, in the Mâconnais, they continued the long family tradition of seeking salvation through support of the local monasteries, especially Cluny.

The dukes and the counts of Burgundy and the Grossi of Brancion and Uxelles all maintained close ties with Cluny even while their political situations, their fortunes, and their monastic neighbors all changed. Part of inheriting the duchy or the county of Burgundy or the lordship of Uxelles was, for each new generation, inheriting an interest in the monks of Cluny. In some ways this relationship is easiest to understand with the Grossi, whose center was only seventeen kilometers from Cluny; whether they acted as donors, economic entrepreneurs, or attackers of monastic property, they always had to deal with their powerful monastic neighbors. The counts of Burgundy however illustrate that family tradition as well as geography could maintain a family's relations with a particular house. When Otto-William became count of Mâcon, twenty kilometers southeast of Cluny, it was natural that he would immediately follow the example of the tenth-century counts of Mâcon in establishing close ties with that abbey, and the ties that he established were so strong that they persisted even after his twelfth-century descendants had moved their

[59]C 2827, 3066, 4603 (IV:31, 251–52; VI:150).
[60]C 2493, 3474, 3920, 4481, 4482 (III:572–73; IV:582–83; V:270–72; VI:34–38).

center of power east of the Saône. But in each generation nobles had
to strike a balance between following family tradition and setting
themselves up as the patrons of new houses, which might seem to
offer an even greater holiness of life.

In the eleventh and twelfth centuries monasticism flourished to a
large degree because support of the local monasteries became an
essential part of the family life of the Burgundian nobility. Nobles
supported the houses reformed by their ancestors, through gifts and
by acting as advocates. By making friends with their secular neighbors, monks were able to found and reform additional monasteries—
though more often following the schedule of the secular donors than
their own. Founding a house and protecting it against its neighbors
were of course not enough to maintain a group of monks. The monks
needed a sustained inflow of goods and property to pay for their
upkeep. In the following section, I discuss in more detail gifts from
nobles to reformed monasteries, the types of property the monks
received, and when and where they received it.

PART THREE

NOBLE GENEROSITY TO

REFORMED MONASTERIES

A noble could share in the spiritual benefits of a monastery by founding a new house or by making gifts to an already established house. In the documents of the eleventh and twelfth centuries both practices were described as entailing a gift of one's goods to a saint. While the *purpose* of reformed monasticism was of course considered to be the preparation of the soul for God, one of the monks' *functions*, and a necessary one, was the acquisition of property. The material well-being of a house was a prerequisite for the well-ordered religious life within it. Virtuous Benedictine abbots were always praised for increasing their houses' prosperity.[1] The Cistercians, in spite of their polemic against wealthy houses, could not themselves have survived without substantial property holdings. When Pope Innocent II issued the first great papal confirmation of the rights of the Cistercian order in 1132, he began in the traditional manner by confirming whatever possessions the houses already had or might acquire in the future, "by the grants of bishops, the generosity of kings or princes, and the offerings of the faithful."[2] Even the most unworldly monks were constantly concerned with property: acquiring it, keeping it, managing it, deciding whether a certain sort of property was even suitable.

Since a gift was made as much to the saint as to the monks, houses of a somewhat disreputable life as well as those of exemplary life might receive gifts from the local nobility. Cathedral canons, whose holiness was more apparent in their position of spiritual authority than their mode of life, also received a number of pious gifts, especially in the eleventh century. But the regular houses always received more; monks were expected to intercede for the noble donor with the saint,

[1] John Van Engen, "The 'Crisis of Cenobitism' Reconsidered: Benedictine Monasticism in the Years 1050–1150," *Speculum*, 61 (1986), 285–92.
[2] Cîteaux/Marilier 90 (pp. 92–93).

and the prayers of monks of more striking holiness were naturally considered more efficacious. In this part, I discuss the sorts of gifts that nobles made to reformed monasteries, beginning with the gifts themselves, and continuing with the timing and location of these gifts, claims against pious donations and other sorts of transactions involving monks and nobles, and finally some suggestions as to the motivations behind these gifts.

[7]

Types of Noble Gifts
to Reformed Monasteries

Generosity to nearby monastic houses was almost a universal phenomenon among the nobility of Burgundy. Though monastic archives also included records of gifts from members of the secular clergy and confirmations of possessions by pope, bishop, or king, records of the local nobility predominate. When the pope listed and confirmed Cîteaux's possessions in 1165, he put the donations from the duke of Burgundy first.[1] From the rather stylized records of transactions that constitute the charters, one can gain an overall impression of the types of gifts that nobles made to Burgundian monasteries.

At first glance it might appear that there was no difference in the patterns of pious gifts before and after the Gregorian reform. In both the eleventh and twelfth centuries nobles gave the local houses an eclectic assortment of churches, land, and miscellaneous sources of income. Yet from the early eleventh century to the end of the twelfth real changes occurred, changes in the size of the standard pious gift and in the relative frequency of different sorts of gift.

In the eleventh century gifts were usually large, in many cases consisting of at least one *mansus* and sometimes numerous pieces of land, meadows, vineyards, and *mansi*, given together with the men who cultivated them. In a fair number of cases, especially early in the century, a man would give some property to a monastery and then receive it back in benefice for his life, or else the monks would give it in benefice to a relative. In this case the donor generally gave the monks some sort of payment *in vestitura* immediately to symbolize that the property was indeed theirs.[2]

---

[1]Cîteaux/Marilier 175 (pp. 140–42).

[2]See, for example, the charter in which Artald, count of Lyon, gave Cluny a church in 995, specifying however that he would keep it for his lifetime, paying the monks five solidi a year *in vestitura* on the feast of Saint Peter; C 2292 (III:419–20). In 1002 a cleric confirmed that a *mansus* he held had actually been been granted to Flavigny by his fa-

In the twelfth century the gifts that were recorded in the archives of Burgundian houses were generally somewhat smaller than in the eleventh century. A gift of land usually involved only one small piece, a pasture or field, or half a *mansus*. It also became more common to make gifts of an annual income, rather than land itself. Gifts were rarely returned *in beneficio* to the donors. Twelfth-century gifts were smaller than those of the eleventh century in part because they were made more frequently by knights and men at the lower fringes of the nobility, as detailed in Chapter 5, and in part because the great noble families were becoming poorer, after generations of partible inheritance and pious donations, in a time of rising prices.

But what the gifts of the twelfth century lacked in size they made up for in quantity. While some more traditional houses, like Cluny, received fewer gifts in the twelfth century than they had in the eleventh, the houses of the new Cistercian order received an enormous number of gifts. The sheer quantity of smaller gifts made possible an overall transfer of property from the secular aristocracy to reformed monks at least as large in the twelfth century as in the eleventh. These differences between the eleventh and twelfth centuries will be further discussed in the following analysis of the different types of gifts laymen made to Burgundian monasteries.

Land

Land was always the most common sort of gift. In the eleventh century donors generally gave the monks one *mansus* (or *curtilis*), often including the servile family living on it. Gifts of land almost always involved cultivated land (or pastures); gifts of unworked, empty land were extremely rare.[3] Such a gift of land was generally stated to include "all appurtenances, that is, fields, vineyards, meadows, woods, land cultivated and uncultivated, ponds and running water."[4] The donor often specified the borders of the donated land in terms of who held the adjoining land.[5]

---

ther and was his only in benefice from the monks. He agreed to pay two denarii a year from then on to indicate that the *mansus* was indeed held in benefice; Petit 202 (I:484–85). For a late eleventh-century example, see Marcigny 41 (p. 35).

[3]Guy de Valous, *Le temporel et la situation financière des établissements de l'ordre de Cluny du XIIe au XIVe siècle*, Archives de la France monastique 41 (Paris, 1935), pp. 16–17. Dietrich Poeck, studying in particular gifts made to Cluny in return for burial there, discovered that throughout the eleventh century such gifts almost always consisted of a single *mansus*; Poeck, "Laienbegräbnisse in Cluny," *Frühmittelalterliche Studien*, 15 (1981), 122, 152.

[4]This particular quote is from an early eleventh-century charter of Cluny; there are dozens of similar examples; C 2094 (III:287–88).

[5]See, for example, the early twelfth-century gift to the brothers of Fontemois (the

In the eleventh century the donated property was usually allodial; the donor typically specified that he had inherited it, or occasionally mentioned the people he had bought it from—a pattern more common in the earlier than the later eleventh century. If the donor was a wealthy man, he might give several *mansi* at once, though there was no necessary correlation between the donor's wealth and the size of the gift. Typical of many eleventh-century gifts to Cluny was that of Count Raynald of Nevers, made sometime around 1030; he gave the monks several *mansi* near Nevers, consisting of fields, streams, vineyards, and pasture land, specifying that he did so for the souls of his parents, wife, son, and brother. Similarly, in 1075 the noble brothers William and Raynald gave St.-Marcel-lès-Chalon all the property they had inherited from their father, located in several different *villae*.[6]

Sometimes eleventh-century monks acquired large tracts of land but only over an extended period of time, because separate heirs to the property would need to make their own donations. In the early eleventh century Cluny very gradually acquired some land at Dommartin from the four sons of one Frotgar, who had left it to them in equal shares. The first son became a monk at Cluny when young and gave his portion to the house at that time; the second gave Cluny his share of the property out of gratitude to Abbot Odilo, who was instrumental in having him released from captivity after a local war; the third gave Cluny his portion when he became a monk in his old age; and the fourth, who had received all his brothers' portions from Cluny to hold in benefice during his lifetime—perhaps because Dommartin is located twenty-eight kilometers southeast of Cluny, on the far side of the Saône—specified that his portion should go to Cluny on his own death.[7] In this case, it took almost two generations before this property completely left the family's hands and passed to Cluny.

In the twelfth century land was still the most common sort of gift. While the *mansi* of the eleventh century had usually been donated complete with dependent peasants, the Cistercians preferred to receive their land empty of all inhabitants. When two knights of Bouilly gave the Cistercian monks of Pontigny some land for their grange at St.-Procaire in 1146, the donors specified that they would not allow any of

---

house that later became Reigny), in which the donors specified that the borders were located where the property adjoined the possessions of the monks of Pontigny, the monks of St.-Germain, the lords of Châtel-Censoir, and the lords of Noyers; Petit 266 (II:223–25).

[6]For Count Raynald of Nevers, see Appendix A, pp. 343–45. C 2811 (IV:13–14). St.-Marcel 55 (pp. 57–58). Though the brothers are not specifically called noble in this charter, their mother is called *nobilissima domina* in a slightly later charter recording a gift she made herself; St.-Marcel 56 (p. 58).

[7]C 2118 (III:304–5).

their men to pass over or cultivate the donated land, and indeed they promised that they would tear down the houses presently standing on it.[8] Although some twelfth-century nobles did give large tracts of land, the most common gift was a somewhat smaller piece of property. When in 1176 Count Gui of Nevers became concerned with the salvation of his soul, for example, he gave the monks of Pontigny a single vineyard at Auxerre; in spite of the apparent smallness of this gift, the count considered it important enough to have the bishops of Auxerre and Nevers and the apostolic legate all confirm it. In 1187 Lord Hervé of Donzy gave the monks of La Charité one meadow, and the monks agreed in turn to pray for his soul.[9]

The few large gifts that monks still received in the twelfth century, the ones consisting of broad expanses of land, were now generally the joint gifts of several different donors. For example, four knights gave Cluny the vineyards and fields of Mohel in 1100, with the consent of Count Stephen I of Mâcon, from whom they had held the land in fief. The gifts that established the initial possessions of the monastery of La Ferté and gave the monks ownership of the surrounding forest of Bragny were made initially by the counts of Chalon and the lords of Brancion in 1113 but were built up in the first twenty years or so of the house's existence by small gifts from knights and petty allodists of the region, men who lived no more than sixteen kilometers away and usually closer. The monks of Morimond acquired land at Levécourt (thirteen kilometers northeast of the abbey) in 1176 and 1177 through a series of small gifts of allodial land from the lady of Aigremont, a knight of Clefmont, and the brother of the lord of Choiseul.[10]

The relative smallness of a particular piece of donated property did not mean that it had only a small value to the monks. Any piece of property that rounded out their possessions in a particular area was always valuable. Especially in the later twelfth century, when the growing wine trade made wine grapes a good cash crop, a vineyard, or even a place where the monks could plant a vineyard, always seems to have been highly valued.[11] Whatever the size of the gift, even if it were a relatively small gift from a wealthy man such as the count of Nevers or the lord of Donzy, the monks were happy to accept it.

---

[8]Pontigny 88 (p. 160).

[9]Pontigny 8 (pp. 89–90). La Charité 76 (pp. 171–72). For the counts of Nevers and the lords of Donzy, see Appendix A, pp. 347–49, 327–29.

[10]C 3743 (V:95–96)., La Ferté 1–16 (pp. 41–51). Arch. Haute-Marne, 8 H 67. For the families of the lords of Aigremont and of Choiseul, see Appendix A, pp. 279–83, 314–16.

[11]See for example La Bussière 6.1 (fol. 42r); and C 3972 (V:330).

Churches and Tithes

Churches and tithes constituted another type of gift made to monasteries and houses of canons regular throughout the eleventh and twelfth centuries: entire churches that could be made into priories, parish churches, partial shares in churches, tithes without churches or vice-versa. Most of these churches never became priories, but the monks or canons selected the priests and presented them to the bishop.[12] Modern scholars commonly suggest that churchmen were aggressively trying to recover all parish churches from laymen.[13] But until the end of the eleventh century, the charters that record the donations of churches are generally cast in terms identical to those which recorded transfers of other sorts of property. Since the bishop or the monks themselves generally drew up these donation charters, it seems that these ecclesiastics did not see gifts of churches as essentially different from any other donations; they were recording gifts that enriched their monastery, not recovering ecclesiastical property that had improperly fallen into lay hands.[14]

As the monks of tenth-century Cluny had been willing to receive partial shares in churches or tithes, rather than insisting on principle that a layman entirely give up any ecclesiastical possessions, other Burgundian monasteries readily accepted even piecemeal donations of churches throughout the eleventh century. The monks of St.-Marcel-lès-Chalon, for example, received a partial share of a church from Lord Gui of Verdun-sur-le-Doubs at the end of the eleventh century. The monks had had a cell near Gui's capital, and he had burned it down (apparently intentionally). Wishing to make amends somewhat later, he offered to give the monks a partial share in the parish church of St.-Laurent, located near the destroyed cell: the altar offerings, the burial and baptismal fees, and the third part of the tithes, retaining the rest for himself. "Thinking of my poverty," Gui's charter said, "I cannot make amends for everything, but out of my own free will I

[12]For examples of presentation of the priest by the black monks of St.-Michel of Tonnerre, the canons of Notre-Dame of Beaune, and the Cistercian nuns of Colonge, see Tonnerre, Bibliothèque municipale, MS 40 [on microfilm at the Arch. Yonne as 1 Mi 395]; Arch. Côte-d'Or, G 2847; and Arch. Haute-Saône, H 933.

[13]Bede K. Lackner, for example, stated that Cluny had to "fight" to "wrest private churches from the laity"; *The Eleventh-Century Background of Cîteaux*, Cistercian Studies Series 8 (Washington, D.C., 1972), p. 74. Jon N. Sutherland described the process by which the bishop of Grenoble acquired churches and land in the first decades of the twelfth century as an effort "to extricate the Church from its dependence on the laity; the long and short of it was that he determined to remove lay influence in church land"; Sutherland, "The Recovery of Land in the Diocese of Grenoble during the Gregorian Reform Epoch," *Catholic Historical Review*, 64 (1978), 377–89, esp. p. 381.

[14]See also B. R. Kemp, "Monastic Possession of Parish Churches in England in the Twelfth Century," *Journal of Ecclesiastical History*, 31 (1980), 135–36.

Plate 7. A noble gives a church to a bishop. (From the mid-twelfth-century carvings at Autun. Note the angel, above.)

wish to give some little thing." He also promised to give the monks another church, "if they can recover it from those who hold it from me."[15] The Cluniac monks of St.-Marcel accepted Lord Gui's profession of poverty and did not insist on receiving the entire church of St.-Laurent; they were happy to take what they could.

Many different monasteries received gifts of churches and tithes during the eleventh century. These churches were usually given as part of a larger gift, consisting of several sorts of property. To cite a few examples, around 1004, when Count Aimo I of Auxois was dying, he made his testament in favor of Flavigny, where he wished to be buried, and gave the monks there a large piece of property by the forest of Chanceaux, including serfs, wooded and cultivated land, and an oratory dedicated to St.-Germain (Chanceaux is fourteen kilometers east of Flavigny). In the mid-eleventh century, the knight Hugh of Château-Pierre, with his wife and sons, gave Paray-le-monial half the cemetery, tithes, and altar dues of a church, in addition to some meadows and fields, for the soul of his brother, who had been killed. In 1075 Lord Ulric of Bâgé gave the monks of Tournus a chapel that he specified was his own allodial property. Around the same time Duke Hugh I of Burgundy, with Count William Tête-Hardi of Burgundy and Count Hugh II of Chalon, gave St.-Marcel-lès-Chalon the church of Fleury-la-Vallée (thirteen kilometers northwest of Auxerre) because Duke Robert I had died there and "many were afraid of it." And toward the end of the eleventh century three noble brothers of Saxole and their cousin jointly gave Cluny a parish church with its tithes, the chapel in their castle with the priest's lands, and the right to pasture thirty pigs in the woods of Saxole.[16] In all these cases, which involved parish churches or chapels rather than old monasteries that could become priories and in which the recipient monasteries included houses of the Cluniac order and other Benedictine houses, there seems to have been no question in the minds of the donors or the monks themselves that the churches were the laymen's to give.

But the Gregorian reform eventually had an impact on lay ownership of churches, though it was not felt until a generation after Gregory VII. Not long after becoming pope in 1073, Gregory held a council at Rome of which the opening canon declared, "No layman may

[15]St.-Marcel 42 (p. 47). Heinrich Dormeier has found that gifts of partial churches were often made to Montecassino in the eleventh and twelfth centuries in spite of the close ties this house had with the reformed papacy; *Montecassino und die Laien im 11. und 12. Jahrhundert*, Schriften der MGH 27 (Stuttgart, 1979), p. 81. Dormeier argues that such gifts were common because the lay donor himself owned only part of a church in the first place.

[16]Flavigny 39 (pp. 80–84) [Collenot, pp. 86–87]. Paray 18 (p. 15). Tournus, pp. 131–33. St.-Marcel 33 (pp. 36–38). C 3046 (IV:236–37). For Aimo of Auxois, see Appendix A, p. 284.

hold a church or an ecclesiastical benefice, nor the altar offerings, or
the fees from burial or baptism, except for those things which pertain
to the priest's fief or the third part of the tithes. Neither may a cleric
or monk receive churches from these laymen, by gift or purchase,
except through the bishop."[17] This canon began to be observed only
after it had been frequently repeated. From the very end of the
eleventh century on, both secular nobles and monks began to feel
somewhat uneasy about churches in lay hands. The example of four
brothers of Montgerbert illustrates this uneasiness and one solution to
the problem. Around 1096, shortly after Pope Urban II preached
against lay possession of churches at the Council of Clermont, Bishop
Berard of Mâcon told these four brothers that it was to the detriment
of their souls for them to continue to hold a certain church. They
were able to get around this difficulty by making one of their number
a canon at the cathedral of Mâcon and giving the church entirely to
him, with the bishop's approval.[18] In this case, the church had certainly been removed from secular control, even though it still
remained under family control.

The Burgundian monasteries were given far fewer churches in the
twelfth century than in the eleventh. Most laymen seem to have
parted with their churches (voluntarily or under coercion) by the early
decades of the twelfth century. The brothers of Montgerbert were not
the only laymen persuaded that it was improper for them to hold
churches. In 1113, for example, the monks of Molesme received a
church from Milo, brother of the lord of Montbard, having told him
he "possessed it unjustly, since such possessions are not for laymen."[19] But laymen continued to give some parish churches to
monasteries throughout the century; this continuation indicates that
ecclesiastics, instead of pursuing a vigorous program aimed at wresting
these churches from laymen, were willing to wait for laymen to
present them as gifts.[20]

The original Cistercian legislation forbade possession of churches, as
Saint Benedict had made no provision for them in his Rule, and this
prohibition too lowered the overall number of churches that

[17]Pflugk-Harttung, II:125, no. 161.
[18]M 536 (p. 314).
[19]Molesme 1.242 (II:226–27). For the lords of Montbard, see Appendix A, pp.
334–38.
[20]Bernard Chevalier has similarly demonstrated that in the diocese of Tours a
number of parish churches were given to the heads of the local Cluniac priories at the
initiative of the nobles who held those parish churches; Chevalier, "Les restitutions
d'églises dans le diocèse de Tours du Xe au XIIe siècle," in *Études de civilisation
médiévale (IXe–XIIe siècle): Mélanges offerts à Edmond-René Labande* (Poitiers, 1974),
pp. 129–41. Sutherland's evidence—contrary to his conclusions—shows that the
bishops of Grenoble peacefully obtained churches and other property from the counts
and other nobles of the region; "Recovery of Land," p. 381.

monasteries received as gifts.[21]   The Cistercians in Burgundy maintained their stance against churches throughout the twelfth century. It
is revealing to compare papal confirmations of the possessions of the
Cistercian monasteries, in which no parish churches are listed, with
those of other Benedictine and Augustinian houses, in which the pope
confirmed monastic ownership of dozens of churches scattered over
several dioceses.[22]   The Cistercians often had the popes list their
daughter abbeys and usually their granges, but parish churches, which
were set up to serve secular society and from which the monks would
receive an income although the churches did not serve the spiritual
needs of the monks themselves, were not usually found in twelfth-
century papal bulls for the Cistercians.[23]

The Cistercians however were not opposed on principle to any
monastic ownership of churches, even if they tried to avoid owning
churches themselves.   In a letter written in the 1130s Bernard of
Clairvaux chided the archbishop of Sens for being slow to approve the
donation, of an inherited church, which a knight wanted to make to a
non-Cistercian house.   "When laymen wish to relinquish churches or
ecclesiastical benefices, which it is wrong for them to hold, it is one
good act," said Bernard, "and when they wish to transfer the
churches to the use of the servants of God, it doubles the good deed.
But as they cannot do this, except by the hand of the bishop, the
bishop causes either two evil or two good acts, depending on whether
he gives his assent or not."[24]   Here Bernard assumed the bishop
would act as an intermediary, as Gregory VII said the bishop must,
although most gifts of churches to Burgundian monasteries did not
mention the bishop.

By the beginning of the twelfth century most laymen had given
their churches to reformed monks, but they tended to hold onto their

---

[21]"Exordium parvum" 15, ed. Bouton and Van Damme, *Textes*, p. 77. Canivez, *Statuta*, I:14—15, no. 9.

[22]See, for example, Paschal II's confirmation of St.-Bénigne's possessions in 1105,
which included churches in the dioceses of Langres, Toul, Autun, Besançon, Chalon,
Valence, Die, Bayeux, and Sens. Two years later, Paschal confirmed that the Cluniac
priory of La Charité had churches in an equally large number of dioceses. In 1136,
when Innocent II confirmed Molesme's possessions, the bull listed churches in the
dioceses of Langres (where most were located), Toul, Troyes, Châlons, Meaux, Reims,
Beauvais, Sens, and Auxerre; Pflugk-Harttung, I:83—84, 89—90, 152—53, nos. 91, 98,
174. Eugenius III's confirmation of the possessions of Vézelay in 1152 and Alexander
III's confirmations of the goods of the Benedictines of Moûtier-St.-Jean and of the Au-
gustinians of Ste.-Marguerite in 1164 consisted almost entirely of churches; PU Berry,
pp. 57—58, no. 26; Reomaus, pp. 208—11; Arch. Côte-d'Or, 200 H 674.

[23]See for example Alexander III's confirmations of the possessions of Cîteaux and
Clairvaux; Pflugk-Harttung, I:236—38, 340—42, nos. 254, 392. See also Dietrich
Lohrmann, *Kirchengut im nördlichen Frankreich: Besitz, Verfassung und Wirtschaft im
Spiegel der Papstprivilegien des 11.—12. Jahrhunderts* (Bonn, 1983), pp. 199—202.

[24]Bernard of Clairvaux, Letter 316, *Opera*, VIII (Rome, 1977), 249.

tithes for a long time.[25] At the end of the twelfth century laymen still seem to have had a great many tithes, for they continued to give them to the local monks with some frequency. Indeed, since laymen who had held tithes usually gave them to reformed monasteries, rather than to the priests of the parish churches to which they had originally been attached, the monks were not "recovering" them so much as receiving a new sort of revenue.[26] Sometimes tithes that had been divided up between several noble families were reunited in the possession of one monastery, as was the case with the tithes of Sermoise, which several members of the lower nobility gave piecemeal to the Cluniac monks of St.-Étienne of Nevers in the early 1140s. One of the knights added an income of seventeen solidi a year from his mill to his gift of tithes, an indication of how small were the perceived differences between these income sources.[27]

Indeed, in the twelfth century tithes were not considered a purely ecclesiastical source of income. Laymen were always entitled to one portion (a theoretic quarter) even of ecclesiastical tithes, the *tertiam* or "third part" that Gregory VII mentioned at the Council of Rome. The first and second portions were destined for the bishop and for the priest of the church, the third for guests and needy laymen, and the fourth for the upkeep of the church.[28] In practice local lords had long taken the *tertiam*. The term *decimas* could be and frequently was applied to any sort of income levied as a percentage of a crop or yield. Hence, if a layman possessed tithes, one cannot be sure that he possessed property that rightfully belonged to the church. Further, the confusion in terms reflects a confusion in principle. Churchmen had no firm opposition to laymen owning tithes comparable to the late eleventh- and early twelfth-century opposition to laymen owning churches. Churchmen sometimes even gave tithes to laymen themselves, as did Alain, bishop of Auxerre and a Cistercian monk. In 1159 he assigned to two sons of a knight the tithes that their father and the nuns of Crisenon had been disputing, with the stipulation that, on the sons' deaths, the nuns would receive the tithes. The copy of the agreement preserved at Crisenon says Alain had made this arrangement "to reach peace."[29] Here, both the nuns and the bishop

[25]Giles Constable, "Monastic Possession of Churches and 'Spiritualia' in the Age of Reform," in *Il Monachesimo e la riforma ecclesiastica (1049–1122)*, Miscellanea del Centro di studi medioevali 6 (Milan, 1971), pp. 317–18.

[26]Giles Constable, *Monastic Tithes from Their Origins to the Twelfth Century* (Cambridge, Eng., 1964), pp. 66, 83–84. Chr. Renardy, "Recherches sur la restitution ou la cession de dîmes aux églises dans le diocèse de Liège du XIe au début du XIVe siècle," *Le moyen âge*, 76 (1970), 208, 240.

[27]Nevers/St.-Étienne 5–6 (pp. 80–83). Sermoise is five kilometers south of Nevers.

[28]"Exordium parvum" 15, ed. Bouton and Van Damme, *Textes*, p. 77.

[29]Crisenon 65 (fol. 25r); repeated at 144 (fols. 73v–74r).

seem to have been more concerned with the practical achievement of peace than with any abstract principle on tithe-holding. The Cistercians originally forebade possession of tithes, as they did the possession of any source of annual income, but after the initial decades of the twelfth century they do not seem to have hesitated to accept gifts of tithes.[30]

Though nobles were most likely to give their churches and tithes to a monastic house, they sometimes gave them to a cathedral instead, as did Lord Humbert II of Beaujeu, who at the end of the eleventh century gave the cathedral canons of Mâcon two parish churches and a chapel.[31] Further, bishops and cathedral canons, like members of the secular nobility, also gave the churches they held personally to reformed monks. Such donations were often phrased in the same terms a secular donor would use; for example, in 1114 Bishop Walter of Chalon and his chapter gave a rural parish church to the Cluniac priory of St.-Marcel-lès-Chalon, specifying that they did so out of a desire to save their souls.[32] Members of the secular clergy as well as their brothers and cousins in the world saw churches and tithes as an appropriate gift to win salvation through association with regular monks.

Annual Incomes

In addition to giving the Burgundian monasteries scattered pieces of land and churches or shares in churches, nobles also made gifts consisting of an annual income, especially during the twelfth century.[33] Such a *cens* might entail several solidi a year to be paid from the donor's tolls on a certain bridge, or half the income from one of the mills he controlled, or two measures of grain or of wine to come from specified fields or vineyards. Sometimes the donor indicated what the monks would do with the income; Duke Hugh III specified that the forty solidi a year he gave the canons regular of Châtillon for his soul should be used to buy the brothers new sandals during Lent.[34] During the twelfth century all nobles increasingly relied on such income

[30]For examples from La Ferté, La Crête, Beaulieu, and Clairvaux, from between 1147 and 1198, see GC IV:241, no. 25; Arch. Haute-Marne, 5 H 9; Langres 41 (p. 416); and Clairvaux I, p. 64, no. 47. For parallels in southern France, see Constance H. Berman, "Cistercian Development and the Order's Acquisition of Churches and Tithes in Southwestern France," *Revue Bénédictine*, 91 (1981), pp. 201–2.

[31]M 21 (p. 18). For Humbert, see Appendix A, p. 292.

[32]St.-Marcel 75 (pp. 71–72).

[33]See also Valous, *Le temporel de l'ordre de Cluny*, p. 102.

[34]Petit 825 (III:295–96). In 1176, as Count Gui of Nevers was dying, he gave the nuns of Crisenon an annual *cens* of 100 solidi, from his tolls at Auxerre, to buy chemises; Crisenon 10 (fol. 6r). This charter is summarized as Petit 598 (II:382–83).

sources,[35] so it is natural that they should have made such gifts to the monks.

Although the original Cistercian legislation specified that the monks should not receive annual revenues or revenue sources, in practice most of the houses of the Cistercian order began receiving such gifts almost as soon as they were founded. The first major Cistercian legislation, that coming out of the chapter general of 1134, specified that the monks were to live "from the labor of their own hands, from cultivation and from their flocks, whence it is proper that we possess for our own use waters, woods, vineyards, meadows, and fields, remote from the dwellings of secular men." The *Statuta* went on to say that the monks were not to have any possessions "contrary to monastic purity," that is, "churches, altars, burial fees, tithes of the labor or food of others, villages, villagers, the income from land, or the revenues from ovens or mills."[36] That such sources of income were expressly forbidden in 1134 indicates that they had probably already become common. Just the year before, for example, the Cistercian monks of Pontigny had worked out an elaborate agreement with the Cluniac monks of nearby St.-Germain on how the revenues of a certain mill were to be divided.[37] Clairvaux is one exception to the general pattern of accepting such revenues; at least until Bernard's death in 1153 the cartulary records no such gifts, though the phrase "He gave whatever he had there," used in most donation charters at Clairvaux, may cover revenues as well as land.[38] In practice all the Burgundian houses of whatever order received gifts of an annual income at some point during the twelfth century.[39] Such gifts, which would not require a large initial investment, would still assure perpetual friendship between the donor and the monks.

Often an annual *cens* consisted of only a few measures of grain or wine or ten or twenty solidi a year, but in a few cases gifts of annual

[35]Georges Duby, *The Early Growth of the European Economy: Warriors and Peasants from the Seventh to the Twelfth Century*, trans. Howard B. Clarke (Ithaca, 1974), pp. 227–30.

[36]Canivez, *Statuta*, I:14–15, no. 9.

[37]Pontigny 101 (pp. 171–72). The monks of La Ferté acquired several mills in the area of their monastery at about the same time; La Ferté 5–8 (pp. 44–46).

[38]When Lord Josbert of La Ferté (six kilometers south of Clairvaux) left for Jerusalem in 1145, he gave Clairvaux whatever he had at Perrecin (just south of the abbey), "retaining nothing except rights of justice," which he said he would take back if he returned alive. That the rights of justice were here included in "whatever he had" suggests that they may also have been included in other donations. Clairvaux/Waquet 10 (pp. 16–17). Shortly after Bernard's death Count Walter of Brienne gave Clairvaux 100 solidi a year from the tolls of Brienne; Clairvaux/Waquet 33 (pp. 56–57).

[39]For examples from the nunneries of Jully and Crisenon, from Cluny and the Cluniac priory of La Charité, and from the Cistercian houses of Cîteaux and Fontenay, see Jully, p. 264; Quantin II.435 (p. 441); C 4339 (V:704–5); La Charité 65 (pp. 154–56); Cîteaux I, fol. 33r; and Autun/Évêché 15 (p. 257).

income were substantial. For example, in 1164 Count William IV of Nevers gave the Cluniac priory of St.-Étienne of Nevers the right to collect and keep the *questam* that William had the right to collect from the townsmen of Nevers; this could total as much as 3000 solidi a year. William said that he would claim this *questam* only if he were going on Crusade, or to pay for the marriage of his oldest daughter or his own ransom. In 1185 Count Peter of Nevers confirmed this gift (after initially refusing to honor it) and added that he would claim the 3000 solidi for only the first two causes, but not for his own ransom. This gift was so substantial that the monks had both the king and the pope reconfirm it, in 1186 and 1187. Peter's daughter, the heiress of Nevers, and her husband issued a similar charter when she inherited.[40]

Twelfth-century nobles gave the local monasteries not only set incomes but often sources from which they could expect some income. Such gifts as ovens and mills, for example, were common. Some gifts of mills were made in the eleventh century, generally given as part of a larger gift of property,[41] and some were also given in this way in the twelfth century, but mills and ovens increasingly became gifts in their own right.[42] Though Bernard of Clairvaux gave the black monks of Montier-la-Celle an oven at Troyes which the Cistercian monks of Mores had acquired, saying "our brothers cannot receive income acquired in this manner,"[43] in the final decades of the twelfth century the Cistercians too began acquiring such property with some frequency. In 1188 Lord Hugh of Vergy attested to the gift to the Cistercian monks of La Bussière of some mill rights; and at the end of the twelfth century the sister of the lord of Aigremont gave the mills of Aigremont to Morimond—over the objections of the parish churches of Aigremont and Arnoncourt, which claimed the tithes of the mills. (Arnoncourt and Aigremont are three kilometers apart, a short distance south of Morimond.)[44]

[40]Nevers/St.-Étienne 9, 16 (pp. 86–88, 93–95). C 4312, 4426 (V:671–72, 798–800). GC XII:345–46, no. 55. See also Appendix A, pp. 348–50.

[41]See, for example, the charter that Geoffrey III of Semur granted when he took the habit in 1088; he gave Cluny and Marcigny a mill as part of his gift of whatever he held in the *villae* of Baugy and Charency; Marcigny 15 (pp. 15–17). About twenty years later, when a knight named Stephen entered Cluny, he gave as his entry gift a large amount of allodial property, including a *mansus*, half a forest, and a mill, with the consent of his wife and sons; C 3030 (IV:223–24).

[42]For examples of gifts of ovens and mills in the second half of the twelfth century, see Jully, p. 268; Tournus, pp. 161–63; La Charité 70 (pp. 164–65); and Arch. Côte-d'Or, 8 H 505 (the gift of a mill from the duke to Moûtier-St.-Jean).

[43]Mores 3 (pp. 49–50). In 1146, however, a comparable transaction went the other way, when the Cistercians of Quincy acquired half a mill from the black monks of Molosmes; Arch. Côte-d'Or, 17 H 620.

[44]La Bussière 1.4 (fols. 3v–4r). Arch. Haute-Marne, 8 H 9, no. 4.

Dependent peasants were also considered sources of income. They represented a source of rents, fees, and judicial fines, all of which would be paid to their new lord. Cluniac houses, traditional Benedictine houses, Molesme, and houses of nuns all received *servi* (or *homines*, as they were called in preference in the twelfth century).[45] The Cistercians received peasants much less often—indeed such gifts were forbidden—but gifts of peasants were recorded at least occasionally from the time of the order's foundation on. When Raynald, viscount of Beaune, gave the monks from Molesme their original property at Cîteaux in 1098, he retained two *servi* and an *ancilla* for himself; his sons gave these three dependent peasants to the monks after his death (at which time they were identified as two *homines* and an *ancilla*).[46] Here the Cistercians faced a problem that recurred throughout the twelfth century: they were given what their noble donors, not they, thought appropriate.[47]

A negative form of the gift of a regular income or source of income was to free the monks of a house from certain obligations, such as paying tolls to the king, duke, or local lord whenever the monks or their men and animals crossed his land. For example, the first charter in Pontigny's cartulary is an immunity from tolls on royal land which Louis VI granted the monks in 1131. In 1188 Lord Humbert the Young of Beaujeu, on the death of his mother, exempted the monks of Cluny from certain tolls on his land, a gift reconfirmed about twenty years later by his son Guichard.[48] By the end of the twelfth century a regular income, an income source, or exemptions from tolls had become a very common sort of gift, something that would have continuing value to the monks and would remind them yearly of the donor for whom they were praying.

Pasture and Forest Rights

One of the most frequent sorts of gifts during the twelfth century was the gift of pasture rights: the right for the monks to use the meadows for their sheep and the woods for their pigs. Sometimes

[45]C 3753, 3754, 4314 (V:106–8, 673–75). Reomaus, pp. 223–24. Molesme 1.145 (II:143). Crisenon 141 (fols. 72v–73r).

[46]Cîteaux/Marilier 101 (p. 98).

[47]Nobles continued to make gifts of dependent men into the thirteenth century; in 1204 Count Peter of Auxerre established anniversaries for himself and his first and second wives by giving the Cistercian monks of Reigny two dependent families along with rights of justice at Vermenton; Quantin III.32 (p. 16).

[48]Pontigny 1 (p. 85). C 4332, 4456 (V:720–21, 830). The various Cluniac houses were often freed from tolls in this way; see Valous, *Le temporel de l'ordre de Cluny*, p. 115. For the lord of Beaujeu, see Appendix A, pp. 293–94.

pasturage was granted for only one sort of animal; sometimes it was specified that any sort of animal might be pastured in the area in question, as when Lord Fulk of Choiseul gave the nuns of Belfays pasture rights in 1176 for "all their animals, steers, cows, sheep, goats, pigs, and horses."[49] Forest or woods usage, the right to gather wood for building or for fires, as well as rights to the berries and honey and other forest products, was also a frequent gift. When the Cistercian house of La Ferté was founded in 1113, the founders, the counts of Chalon, gave the monks from Cîteaux one-quarter of the forest of Bragny for their monastery but gave them usage rights in the rest of the forest.[50]

Houses of all orders received woods usage and pasture rights as gifts. In 1110, when Bernard V Grossus confirmed that his father and grandfather had given Cluny usage in certain woods on the Grosne, he specified that the monks could use it for gathering firewood every day, but that they were not to use the wood to make lime or charcoal. The family of the lords of Aigremont, who founded Morimond, specified in the foundation charter that they had given the monks pasture rights for their animals and the right to gather firewood. Successive lords of Aigremont confirmed these usage rights over the next century—even if they confirmed nothing else.[51] The monks of Clairvaux received pasture rights intermittently throughout the second half of the century, often from men who did not give Clairvaux land. The gifts included those from the bishop of Langres, the lord of Sexfontaines (twenty kilometers northeast of Clairvaux), and from the lord of Vignory (twenty-eight kilometers northeast of Clairvaux).[52] The Cistercian house of Beaulieu, founded in 1166, received primarily gifts of land for the first decade of its existence (and not many gifts at that), but, beginning in the late 1170s, it began to receive gifts of pasture rights, especially at Bussières-lès-Belmont and Chaudenay (respectively nine kilometers south and six kilometers west of the abbey). These gifts came both from laymen and members of the cathedral chapter of Langres (Langres is eighteen kilometers west of Beaulieu).[53] That these gifts of pasture rights were often so close to the abbey may indicate that the brothers were actively soliciting such gifts in an area convenient for pasturage.

[49] Arch. Haute-Marne, 8 H 22. For Fulk, see Appendix A, p. 316.
[50] La Ferté 1 (pp. 41–42).
[51] C 3896 (V:246–48). Arch. Haute-Marne, 8 H 1, nos. 2–5. For Bernard Grossus and the lords of Aigremont, see Appendix A, pp. 304–5, 279–83. For another example of woods usage, which Geoffrey of Arcy gave the nuns of Crisenon in 1182, see PU Berry, pp. 123–24, no. 101.
[52] Clairvaux/Waquet 41, 45 (pp. 62, 71). Clairvaux I, pp. 80–81, 153–54, nos. 33, 35, 39. Vignory 2.54–55 (pp. 196–97).
[53] Arch. Haute-Marne, 2 H 2, 2 H 5.

For the Cistercians of the late twelfth century, whose economy was increasingly based on raising flocks of sheep, pasture rights were a necessary addition to the agricultural land on which the monks and their *conversi* raised their crops. For laymen, pasture rights were a gift that did not require the outlay of great capital. The lay donor could still keep the land on which the monks pastured their flocks, and in fact he often put his own sheep or pigs on the same land. Yet, since such a gift was so necessary to the monks, they would always receive it with the gratitude the laymen expected.

No single type of gift was considered most suitable for regular monks. In the eleventh century nobles generally held large tracts of land, and in the twelfth century they derived much of their income from sources such as mills and ovens, and they gave the monks whatever they had to give. Robert, son of Lord Gui IV of Vignory, even gave Molesme his warhorse when he was dying; his mother and brother, however, decided that this was an unsuitable possession for peaceful monks and substituted a vineyard after his death.[54] Just such eclectic mixtures of gifts as those described above—land, churches, *cens*, mills and ovens, pasture rights, juridic rights, dependent peasants, tithes, and freedom from tolls—are recorded in the archives of almost all Burgundian monasteries, both the older houses and the new foundations of the twelfth century.

In general, laymen did not seem to appreciate the distinction between Cistercian ideas of suitable monastic property and those of the more traditional monasteries. They continued to endow the new houses, whose special holiness of life they acknowledged by the sheer volume of their gifts, with the same kind of donation their ancestors had always made. The Cistercian chapter general recognized the difficulty the monasteries of the order had in receiving what they wanted, rather than what laymen wanted to give them. When the chapter general, trying to reduce the number of town houses the monks had been given, ordained in 1189 that no monastery should own more than one house in a particular place, the legislation recognized that laymen might still want to give the monks such houses: "If someone gives another house in alms, the monks should sell it within one year."[55] Whether they felt they could not refuse any gift made with a good will, or whether they themselves were not fully aware of the chapter general's proscriptions on this point, the abbots of most Cistercian houses accepted what they were offered, so that

---

[54]Molesme 1.252 (II:235). For Robert of Vignory, see Appendix A, p. 382.
[55]Canivez, *Statuta*, I:112, no. 11.

refusal of certain types of gifts was the exception.[56] Though the houses of the twelfth century did not receive parish churches or grants of great blocks of land as had many houses in the eleventh century—obtaining their property from a number of different donors instead—there is little in the archives of the Cistercian houses to distinguish them from other twelfth-century houses.

No sharp break in the pattern of noble gifts to monasteries occurred either with the Gregorian reform or with the foundation of the Cistercian order. Nonetheless, there are significant differences between the eleventh century and the twelfth. In the eleventh century many gifts were made by counts, dukes, and powerful castellans, men with churches and large amounts of land to give. In the twelfth century, monasteries, both old and new, continued to receive gifts of land and churches from well-established nobles, but they also began to receive a greater variety of gifts, including gifts of a *cens* or exemption from certain tolls, and from a greater variety of men, including knights and men at the lower fringes of the nobility. Though the average twelfth-century gift was smaller than the typical gift of the eleventh century, the monks received a much greater *volume* of gifts. This greater volume gave the monks much more to supervise and remember—which may be why most older houses drew up their first cartularies in the early twelfth century. The gifts of mills, bridges, tolls, market stalls, and the like also required more complex management than did agricultural land. The monks in general seem to have been successful in their new role as managers—the role Bernard of Clairvaux had wished the Cistercians to avoid.

[56]Louis J. Lekai, "Ideals and Reality in Early Cistercian Life and Legislation," in *Cistercian Ideals and Reality*, ed. John R. Sommerfeldt, Cistercian Studies Series 60 (Kalamazoo, Mich., 1978), pp. 5—11. For an example of a Cistercian house in southern France that received a variety of tithes and churches, see Constance H. Berman, "The Foundation of the Monastery of Silvanès: The Economic Reality," ibid., pp. 289—90.

[8]

The Timing and Location of Gifts

While there was an enormous variety in the type of gift a noble might make to reformed monks, nobles normally made such gifts only at certain times and only to certain houses. Although theoretically a noble could make a pious gift at any time of his life, he was most apt to do so in periods of personal crisis. The crisis could be the decision to leave the world for the monastic life, or the deepest of human crises, death.

Gifts in Time of Death

Asking for prayers for the souls of the dead was a common practice from the early Middle Ages on. A great many of the gifts made to the Burgundian monasteries in the eleventh and twelfth centuries were made when the donor felt he was dying or when one of his relatives or close friends had just died. In 1174 Count William II of Chalon freed the monks of St.-Benoît-sur-Loire from certain customary dues, specifying that he felt his end was near.[1] The death of a person close to the donor could elicit as many gifts as his own imminent demise. For example, when Girard of Rahon, friend and vassal of Duke Hugh III, died in 1187, the duke made gifts for his soul to the Cistercian monks of Maizières, to whom he gave a *mansus* and four measures of wine; of La Bussière, to whom he gave ten measures of wine a year; of Quincy, to whom he gave pasture rights; and of Cîteaux, to whom he gave 120 setiers of grain a year. He also gave the cathedral of Chalon an annual income of 100 solidi to establish Girard's anniversary there; gave Cluny half the proceeds from his

[1]Fleury 206 (II:57–59).

[190]

sales tax in return for a daily mass for Girard's soul; and gave the nuns of Tart an annual income of grain for Girard's soul.[2]

Many members of the lesser nobility also made their gifts in times of imminent or recent death. When Jocelin of Arcy died in 1147, his wife and nephews went directly from the funeral to Reigny to confirm his dying gifts to the monks there.[3] The salvation that the monks promised in return for a gift was naturally of most interest at these times. The link between death and pious donations is made explicitly in the foundation charter of the Cistercian house of Theuley. The lord of Montsaugeon and Mirebeau, the story went, appeared after his own death, in a vision, and told an old friend in the cathedral chapter of Langres, "If you wish to save my soul, give Theuley to the White Monks." The cathedral canon quickly contacted the lord's sons to arrange for this foundation.[4]

Those who made gifts as they were dying (or, like the lord of Montsaugeon, when already dead) would choose to endow the most holy monks in the vicinity. In the twelfth century the Cistercians especially received an enormous number of gifts from the dying and from their relatives. When Lord Osmund of Rougemont was dying in 1197, for example, he gave pasture rights to the Cistercian monks of Fontenay, for the good of his soul, even though he was actually lying ill at the old Benedictine monastery of Moûtier-St.-Jean, a house without the prestige of Fontenay. The monks he trusted to nurse him were not necessarily those whose prayers he considered the most efficacious.[5]

A number of donors did not want to give their property away until they were actually dead. Especially in the eleventh century, *post obitum* gifts were quite common. In such a case the donor would arrange to have a gift made on his death, to ensure prayers and often burial, but he would retain the property while he was alive and could still enjoy its economic advantages. Often he would pay the monks a small annual fee *in vestitura*, as mentioned in Chapter 7, to indicate that the monks were legally invested with the property. While some scholars have thought that the frequency of such *post obitum* gifts in Cluny's eleventh-century charters indicates a large proportion of peasants and non-nobles among Cluny's donors,[6] a desire to retain such an

---

[2]Petit 760, 761, 769, 772, 842 (III:270–71, 273–74, 275–76, 302). Chalon, pp. 63–64 (summarized as Petit 765 [III:272]). C 4313 (V:672–73). Plancher I.110 (p. lxii) (summarized as Petit 766 [III:272]). See also Quantin II.395 (pp. 63–64).

[3]Quantin I.279 (p. 430): "Cum autem redissent ob officio funeris venerunt ad portam Reigniaci."

[4]GC IV:163–64, no. 40.

[5]Petit 908 (III:331–32).

[6]See, for example, Johannes Fechter, *Cluny, Adel und Volk* (diss., University of Tübingen, 1966), pp. 14, 22, 30.

economic advantage need not imply that the donors were from any particular economic class. Indeed, even such powerful persons as Otto, count of Mâcon in the first half of the eleventh century, and his wife, Elizabeth, gave Cluny a large amount of land, "including vineyards, fields, meadows, woods, and water," with the specification that they would retain it for their lives.[7] Death was considered the appropriate time for gifts, whatever one's economic position.

Burial

The surest way to be associated with holy monks after death was to be buried at the monastery. Someone who made a deathbed conversion and put on the monastic habit would be buried in the monks' cemetery, close to the saint's special friends, and often a layman could arrange to be buried there as well. For example, when Lord Humbert of Bourbon gave up some claims against Cluny's property in the late eleventh century, the monks promised that in return they would bury him if he died in the world and receive him in the cloister if he decided to become a monk.[8] The ecclesiastical hierarchy tried to draw a distinction between a fee for burial, which as a sacrament should have been free, and alms for one's soul, which a layman would be expected to give. But it was hard to draw the line, as is clear in the identical bulls Paschal II sent the bishops of Autun and Mâcon in 1100. "We decree," he said, "that no fee shall be charged for burial by any house; but for the redemption of sins, we institute and confirm by apostolic decree that those dying in a church in which they have received the sacraments shall give alms."[9] In practice no powerful layman would have thought of requesting burial at a monastery of any order without a suitable gift.

Because a legal transaction had to be completed between living people, a man either had to make a burial gift while alive or hope his relatives would make such a gift for him after his death. A description of the usual arrangement of burial gifts is found in an 1142 charter of the priory of St.-Florentin, a dependency of St.-Germain of Auxerre. The charter anticipated that someone "in his last days" would arrange to give something to a church "for his burial," unless he "died intestate" or had "little concern for his soul." Even in this

---

[7] C 2733 (III:756–57). For Otto of Mâcon, see Appendix A, pp. 270–71. See also Barbara H. Rosenwein, *Rhinoceros Bound: Cluny in the Tenth Century* (Philadelphia, 1982), pp. 33–34.
[8] C 3806 (V:153–55).
[9] PL CLXIII:39–42, nos. 18, 19.

case, the monks assumed that someone else would quickly arrange to "make a gift for him."[10]

Cluny, like many other monasteries, regularly buried its patrons in the eleventh century.[11] A charter from the first half of the century begins, "It is sanctified by religious men of old, that, after the course of this uncertain life, the inanimate body should be taken to and buried at a place where the saints are commemorated, so that the saints may remove some of one's sins and transgressions. Faith urges us therefore to this holy custom, and, because of sin, the dead man's relatives and friends should, as much as possible, make gifts in alms to these holy places."[12] Throughout the tenth and eleventh centuries, as Dietrich Poeck's analysis has shown, roughly 10 percent of all gifts made to Cluny were made specifically in return for burial there; the highest percentage was 17 percent, in the first half of the eleventh century.[13] The popularity of the house and its aura of sanctity were such that in the middle of the century the monks were often asked to bury people from some distance away, further than the body could be conveniently transported. To avoid this problem, those who knew they were dying were often transported to Cluny at once.[14]

Other Benedictine houses also received many gifts in return for burial in the eleventh century. Around 1000 a certain Milo of Thil, called *nobilis* in the charter, made a gift to Flavigny for the soul of his nephew, Aimo Pilo, who had just died. Before his death, Aimo had requested burial at Flavigny, and his uncle Milo gave the monks a *mansus* as payment for this burial, with the confirmation of the count of Auxois. Milo himself gave the monks of Flavigny some allodial land in the Morvan around the same time for his own burial, a gift that his son Gui confirmed after Milo died.[15] Sometimes members of a particular family were almost all buried at a particular monastery; in the eleventh century the counts of Tonnerre were buried at St.-Michel of Tonnerre, a house that their ancestors had reformed.[16] Women too were often buried at monasteries during the eleventh century.

[10]Quantin I.215 (pp. 357–58).

[11]A typical example is provided by Guichard I, Lord of Beaujeu, who made gifts of several *mansi* to Cluny to assure that he and his wife and son would be buried there; C 2040 (III:246–47).

[12]C 2042 (III:248–49).

[13]Dietrich Poeck, "Laienbegräbnisse in Cluny," *Frühmittelalterliche Studien*, 15 (1981), 85, 92, 101, 122, 152.

[14]Even someone who lived near Cluny might wish to arrive at the abbey while still alive. In the mid-eleventh century, one Richard of Ruffey (just west of Cluny) had himself carried to Cluny when he felt he was in his final days, and he gathered all his relatives around him to attest to his gift of land and serfs to the monks in return for his burial; C 2008, 2009 (III:221–22).

[15]Flavigny 36 (pp. 76–77) [Collenot, p. 83]. Petit 4, 7 (I:344–45, 348–49).

[16]Quantin I.90, 92 (pp. 171–73, 177–78).

Around 1100 the knight Hugh Burdin, saying that "since he had no carnal sons to inherit from him, he chose instead spiritual sons as his heirs, that is God, the apostles Peter and Paul, and the monks of Cluny," gave Cluny property at Lournand (three kilometers northwest) for his wife's burial and the reception of his stepson as an oblate.[17]

Molesme, founded in 1075, followed the same pattern as most eleventh-century houses in burying its greatest patrons and agreeing to bury other men and women who made substantial gifts.[18] The Cistercian order however initially broke with Molesme over the practice of burial and officially forbade the burial of any laymen within the monastery walls.[19] In practice, however, after the first decades Cistercian houses regularly buried the most powerful of their noble friends. Cîteaux herself buried the twelfth-century dukes of Burgundy and their relatives, perhaps because of their role in founding the house, and Pontigny, Cîteaux's second daughter, buried all the relatives of the lords of Seignelay throughout the twelfth century.[20] Around the middle of the twelfth century the Cistercian monks of Theuley agreed to bury Lord Fulk of Mailly, after Fulk's widow and son had given them a substantial gift of land at Bourberain. The bishop of Autun had forbidden Fulk to be buried in consecrated ground because of the damages he had inflicted on his church's property, but the monks paid for the damages themselves in order that the ban might be lifted. (Bourberain, located seventeen kilometers west-southwest of Theuley, became an important grange.)[21] The chapter general of the Cistercian order repeatedly forbade any further burials of secular nobles, though in 1157 an exception was made for a monastery's founder; the very frequency of the bans on this practice attests to its popularity.[22]

---

[17]C 3713 (V:60–61). For another example of the burial of a woman, see St.-Marcel 77 (p. 73).

[18]See for example Molesme 1.220, 227, 272 (II:204, 211, 251).

[19]The legislation of 1134 ordered that no one external to the monastery be buried in the house, except for two of the house's greatest benefactors; Canivez, *Statuta*, I:19, no. 27.

[20]Cîteaux/Marilier 198 (pp. 159–60). Petit 669 (II:411–12). For the lords of Seignelay, see Appendix A, pp. 355–57; *Gesta pontificum*, pp. 451–53, 485; and Constance Brittain Bouchard, *Spirituality and Administration: The Role of the Bishop in Twelfth-Century Auxerre*, Speculum Anniversary Monographs 5 (Cambridge, Mass., 1979), p. 124. See also Richard Roehl, "Plan and Reality in a Medieval Monastic Economy: The Cistercians," *Studies in Medieval and Renaissance History*, 9 (1972), 99.

[21]Theuley, fols. 22v–23r.

[22]Canivez, *Statuta*, I:68, no. 63. In 1190 the monks of Clairvaux obtained papal permission to bury the count of Flanders and his wife; PU Champagne 272 (II:390). Other examples of Cistercians burying their patrons include Fontenay II, fols. 1r–v, no. 36, the burial of a woman; Petit 386 (II:284–85), the burial of a woman at La Bussière in the 1160s; and Arch. Saône-et-Loire, 20 H 17, the burial of three men at Maizières in 1173.

Monastic burial continued to be popular in houses of every order throughout the twelfth century. Where a man was buried was an important part of his identity to future generations. The counts of Nevers in the late twelfth century referred to Counts William II, William III, and William IV, who had succeeded each other, not by any ordinal numbers, but as the Count William buried at La Grande Chartreuse, the one buried at St.-Germain of Auxerre, and the one buried at Bethlehem.

Anniversaries

A gift made with an eye toward death might also be made to a house other than the one where the noble chose to be buried. Frequently a gift was made with the stipulation that in return the monks would offer annual prayers for the soul of the donor (or the person he specified) in an "anniversary," as mentioned above in connection with the duke's gifts for Girard of Rahon. On this day, usually the date of his death, though it could also be his birthday or a special saint's day, the monks offered prayers for him each year. Anniversaries, which did not become common until the final decades of the eleventh century, were very commmon in the twelfth. Their popularity is attested by the necrologies kept by the Burgundian houses. These often took the form of calendars in which names would be entered according to the date on which their anniversary was celebrated.[23]

By being entered in a monastery's necrology, a noble entered into the "society and fraternity" of the monks, as the documents put it. This *societas et fraternitas* was more than just a vague association. It meant that someone was included with the members of the abbey (living and dead) for whom prayers were offered, generally every day. Bishops and the abbots of other houses also often asked to be included in the "society" of a particular house.[24] A donor thus hoped to obtain the same spiritual benefits the monks won through their holy life and their prayers. For example, in the late eleventh century, a

---

[23]For the central position of the "books of the dead" in relations between monasteries and secular society, see Karl Schmid and Joachim Wollasch, "Die Gemeinschaft der Lebenden und Verstorbenen in Zeugnissen des Mittelalters," *Frühmittelalterliche Studien*, 1 (1967), 365–405. For southern Italian parallels, see Heinrich Dormeier, *Montecassino und die Laien im 11. und 12. Jahrhundert*, Schriften der MGH 27 (Stuttgart, 1979), pp. 164–95.

[24]For example, Bishop William of Auxerre established his anniversary at the Premonstratensian house of St.-Marien in 1180, by giving the brothers two churches, and Bishop Stephen II of Autun gave the same house a vineyard at Chastellux in 1186 for his own anniversary; Lebeuf IV.72 (p. 54); Quantin II.355 (pp. 366–67).

large group of nobles, with their wives, gave Cluny a church, asking that the monks "intercede for them with God," and asking to be entered in the house's necrology (*martirlogium*), "so that by the monks' prayers they might gain eternal life." The donation charter specified the death dates of their relatives, to facilitate entry into the necrology.[25]

An anniversary was often established by the gift of an annual *cens*; sometimes the donor specified that the revenues would pay for a meal that the canons or monks would eat together on the day they celebrated the anniversary. In the early twelfth century, when Lord Galcher of Salins gave Cluny some salt pans that he said produced salt worth four solidi a week, he specified that the money be used to buy the bread, wine, beans, and fish for the dinner of the monks— including those in the infirmary—on his anniversary.[26] One might give the annual income directly, or give some land that would produce it; in the late eleventh century, the knight Richard of Iguerande gave Cluny some allodial property in the *pagus* of Autun in return for an anniversary for his mother.[27]

It was possible to establish an anniversary with a fairly small gift, but some nobles made up for this apparent stinginess by establishing anniversaries at a number of different churches. One of the most prolific in this respect was Mathilda, countess of Nevers and Tonnerre. In 1176 she established an anniversary for her father at the Cistercian house of La Bussière. In 1177 she made gifts to the canons regular of Oigny for the souls of her first two husbands, Odo of Issoudun and Count Gui of Nevers. When her infant son died in 1182 she took the opportunity to establish anniversaries for him, herself, and her three late husbands at Jully and Cîteaux. In 1186 she established her anniversary in the cathedral of Langres and in the convent of Crisenon. In 1191 she established her husband's anniversary at the cathedral of Auxerre, anniversaries for herself and Count Gui at St.-Germain and St.-Marien of Auxerre, and her own anniversary at Cluny. In 1195 she established an anniversary at the Cistercian house of Reigny; and in 1196 she established her anniversary at St.-Denis of Vergy.[28] Guichard IV of Beaujeu similarly made gifts to a number of

[25]C 3312 (IV:405−6).

[26]C 3776 (V:126−27).

[27]C 3373 (IV:468−69). The donation charter specified that the income from the land's serfs, vineyards, meadows, and woods would pay for the monks' meal on the day of the anniversary. It is interesting, however, that Richard kept the property during his lifetime, paying only two solidi a year *pro investitura*. For another example, see St.-Marcel 85 (p. 77).

[28]For Mathilda, see Appendix A, pp. 348−49. La Bussière 15.6 [fol. 141v] (this charter is printed as Petit 599 [II:383]). GC IV:92, no. 58. Jully, p. 273. Cîteaux/Marilier 248 (pp. 196−97). Langres 144 (p. 563). Quantin II.356, 431 (pp. 367, 435−36). C 4350, 4358, (V:712, 718−19). Arch. Yonne, H 1562. Petit 937, 938 (III:342−43).

different churches to establish his anniversary. When he made his testament, toward the end of the twelfth century, he specified the gifts to be made after his death: to Cluny above all but also to the churches of Beaujeu, Belleville, Joux, Grandmont, and many others.[29] Mathilda, who came from the family of the dukes of Burgundy, and the wealthy lord of Beaujeu established more anniversaries than did most nobles, but a number of other nobles also sought to have as many monks as possible praying for their relatives and themselves.

The number of anniversaries reached impressive proportions at many houses. In 1192 the Cistercian chapter general ordained that no more annual or daily masses should be established for one person's soul,[30] but the legislation was widely ignored. Anniversaries offered the hope of salvation to laymen and a regular source of income to ecclesiastics; they were too beneficial to both to be eliminated.

The Crusades

In addition to making gifts with an eye toward natural death, the Burgundian nobles made many pious gifts when starting on dangerous enterprises. Men leaving on Crusade, and knowing that their chances for return were slight, poured out gifts to the local monasteries throughout the twelfth century. The word used for what is now called a Crusade was *peregrinatio*, the same word used for a pilgrimage, and in both cases, before they left, those going to visit a holy place felt compelled to make friends with local saints.[31] Duke Odo I of Burgundy, when leaving for Jerusalem in 1100, even turned back after he had already started out to make peace with Cluny over some injuries the monks said he had caused them.[32]

The monks of Burgundy received a large number of gifts between 1095 and 1101, when the Crusaders left for the successful siege of Jerusalem or went to join the victors;[33] in 1147, when a number of

---

Mathilda also made gifts for the soul of her son William and her husband Gui to Pontigny in 1182, though she did not establish an anniversary there; Pontigny 13, 14 (pp. 93–94). She was still not as assiduous as her granddaughter, also named Mathilda, who established her anniversary at forty-four separate churches when she died in 1257; Lebeuf IV.191 (pp. 110–11).

[29]Beaujeu a8 (pp. 50–52). See also Appendix A, pp. 294–95.

[30]Canivez, *Statuta*, I:147, no. 3.

[31]Jonathan Sumption, *Pilgrimage* (Totowa, N. J., 1975), pp. 122–37. Bernard McGinn, "*Iter Sancti Sepulchri*: The Piety of the First Crusaders," in *Essays on Medieval Civilization*, ed. Bede Karl Lackner and Kenneth Roy Philip, The Walter Prescott Webb Memorial Lectures 12 (Austin, Texas, 1978), pp. 33–55.

[32]C 3809 (V:156–59).

[33]Orderic Vitalis refers to the rush of Crusaders to Jerusalem after that city was captured by the Franks; *Historia ecclesiastica* 10.20, ed. Marjorie Chibnall, V (Oxford, 1975), 322–26. Those who went in 1101 included the duke and Counts Stephen of

Burgundians followed Louis VII on the Crusade preached at Vézelay;[34] and in 1189 and 1190, when the Third Crusade was launched. The Cistercians established daily masses for the souls of all Crusaders in 1190.[35] Burgundian nobles also went to the Holy Land between major Crusades, most notably in 1171, when Duke Hugh III and Count Stephen II of Burgundy led a group of Crusaders. "I wish to become a participant in the prayers and spiritual benefits of the brothers of Cîteaux, where my predecessors are buried," said Duke Hugh III in 1171, granting the Cistercians freedom from tolls before leaving for Jerusalem.[36] A smaller number of Burgundian nobles went to fight the infidel in Spain; and like those leaving for Jerusalem they too made pious gifts before departing.[37] Those few Crusaders who returned to Burgundy alive were usually so grateful that they too made generous gifts.[38] The gifts which the Crusaders made were of the same variety as other pious gifts made during the twelfth century: a mixture of land, income sources, or exemptions from certain dues.[39]

By the end of the twelfth century three generations of experience had shown that many Crusaders never returned home, so leaving for the Holy Land was indeed a turning point. It was not however always the last opportunity Burgundian nobles might have to gain the prayers of Burgundian monks, those they knew and trusted. A great many nobles from Burgundy were at the devastating siege of Acre in 1191, and as they were dying they sent instructions home to make final gifts to the monks they had known. Gui of Pierre-Pertuis wrote his wife from Acre to urge her to give the nuns of Crisenon the mill at

Burgundy and William of Nevers; Alberic of Aix, *Historia Hierosolymitanae expeditionis* 8.25, PL CLXVI:618; Fulcher of Chartres, *Historia Hierosolymitana (1095–1127)* 2.16, ed. Heinrich Hagenmeyer (Heidelberg, 1913), pp. 428–30.

[34] Alberic of Aix, *Historia Hierosolymitanae expeditionis* 8.6, 8.25, 8.30, PL CLXVI:608, 618, 620. Odo of Deuil, *De profectione Ludovici VII in Orientem* 1, ed. Virginia Gingerick Berry (New York, 1948), p. 9. See also Bernard of Clairvaux, Letter 256, *Opera*, VIII (Rome, 1977), 163–65.

[35] Canivez, *Statuta*, I:122, no. 16. Among the powerful men of Burgundy who went on the Third Crusade, along with the kings of France, England, and Germany, were the duke of Burgundy, the count of Nevers, the count of Chalon, the count of Joigny, the lord of Montréal, the lord of Seignelay, the lord of Noyers, the lord of Donzy, the lord of Toucy, the lord of Grancey, the lord of Vignory, the lord of Sombernon, the lord of Semur, and the lord of Chacenay. See Petit 799, 809, 848, 852, 867 (III:286–87, 290–91, 305–7, 314–15); Quantin II. 405, 407, 409, 410, 429 (pp. 411–16, 433–34); Vignory 2.46 (p. 192); La Charité 76 (pp. 171–72); Arch. Saône-et-Loire, H 25, no. 52; Clairvaux II, p. 176, no. 34.

[36] Cîteaux/Marilier 198 (pp. 159–60).

[37] For example, when the knight Gui Rufin left to fight in Spain in 1092, he gave St.-Marcel-lès-Chalon a *mansus* and some serfs; St.-Marcel 115 (pp. 94–95).

[38] See for example C 3765 (V:117–18).

[39] For examples, see Vignory xxxiv bis (pp. 82–83); Cîteaux/Marilier 121, 192–94, 198 (pp. 109, 155–57, 159–60); Corbigny 3 (pp. 6–7); Arch. Côte-d'Or, 15 H 130, no. 7; and Petit 843 (III:303).

Pierre-Pertuis for the good of his soul. His family had long supported Crisenon, and he had his letter sealed by his nephew and by Lord Narjod of Toucy, both of whom were with him; the lords of Toucy had helped found Crisenon sixty years earlier.[40] Also writing from the seige of Acre were Clarembald, lord of Noyers, who made gifts to the Hospitallers; and Rainard of Grancey, who asked his children to give the Templars everything he had either at Gessey-le-Franc or at Bussière, leaving the choice to them. Duke Hugh III, whose second crusading trip in twenty years took him to Acre, wrote both his son and King Philip, back in France, to make sure that a gift of ten pounds a year he had intended to make to St.-Étienne of Dijon was indeed made.[41]

Dying in the Holy Land, the Burgundian Crusaders made their last gifts either to the military crusading orders, the Hospitallers and the Templars, or else to the same houses they would have endowed had they stayed home. Their relatives at home regularly made gifts to these same houses for the Crusaders' souls, even without specific instructions from the east. Around 1100 the wife of a knight named Berengar, who had died in Jerusalem, gave Cluny a small annual payment for the good of his soul, and herself entered Marcigny, Cluny's sister house. A few years later Duke Hugh II of Burgundy gave all the land he had claimed at Ahuy, *sive juste sive injuste*, to St.-Étienne of Dijon for the soul of his father Odo, also dead on Crusade (Ahuy is six kilometers north of Dijon). In 1193, after Duke Hugh III had died at Acre, his son Odo confirmed all the rights and possessions of St.-Bénigne of Dijon for his father's soul.[42] A friendship between a nobleman and the monks of a particular house might be built up slowly (and, from the monks' point of view, painfully), but, once established, those monks were to the noble *his* monks, men he could count on to pray for his soul, monks he would turn to though half a world away.

---

[40]Quantin II.429 (pp. 433−34). Lord Narjod, who died himself the following year, gave Crisenon an annual income of two measures of wine; Quantin II.435 (p. 441). For the lords of Pierre-Pertuis and Toucy, see Appendix A, pp. 356, 375.

[41]Petit 852 (III:306−7). Quantin II.405 (pp. 411−12); this document is misdated in the edition. St.-Étienne IV.102−3 (pp. 116−17). For Rainard of Grancey and Duke Hugh, see Appendix A, pp. 334, 260−61.

[42]C 3804 (V:152). St.-Étienne II.17 (pp. 21−22). Arch. Côte-d'Or, 1 H 13.

The Geographic Location of Gifts

The cartularies of Cluny, St.-Bénigne, Molesme, and Clairvaux record gifts from dozens of different noble and knightly lineages of the region. A house of good reputation might receive gifts from nobles from all over western Europe. Cluny and St.-Bénigne received gifts of land in Champagne, Savoy, Provence, Lombardy, and even England, as well as the Spanish priories mentioned in Chapter 5, and during its first decades Molesme received gifts of churches located in many parts of Europe. It should be noted that, in the case of Cluny and St.-Bénigne, the monks began to receive gifts in distant areas only during the 1060s or 1070s, around the time that Molesme was founded.[43] But most of the noble donors to Burgundian monasteries were themselves Burgundian.

Indeed, the patterns of patronage were generally more local still. All monasteries had what might be called an "area of greatest influence" surrounding them, an area in which most of their property lay and where most of their donors lived. As already noted in Chapter 5, in the example of Fontenay's patrons, this area tended to be quite compact, stretching no more than twenty-five or thirty kilometers from the abbey, the distance of a long day's walk or a one-day round-trip on horseback (i.e., the abbey was the center of a rough circle no more than sixty kilometers across).[44] An abbey's property however did not spread in a perfect circle around it; it tended to be modified by both geographic and sociological features. Abbeys were almost invariably built on rivers, often near their source (Bèze and Fontenay are located where fountains well up from the limestone, as was Clairvaux until the original site proved too narrow, and the monks moved a few kilometers downstream; Auberive is a short distance below the source of the Aube, and Bourras is a short distance below the source of the Nièvre), and an abbey's area of influence generally stretched a greater distance downstream than in any other single direction. Rivers could also act as boundaries; Fontenay had many more possessions on the north side of the Brenne (the river into which Fontenay's stream flowed), the abbey's side, than on the south. Hills, even though they do not seem like major barriers to the modern

---

[43]In a short period in 1080–1081, Cluny received gifts of churches in England (confirmed by the English king); at Bar, in the county of Champagne; at Saintes, near the Atlantic coast (a gift from the duke of Aquitaine); in Lombardy (from the count of Bergamo); and at Burgos, in Spain (from the Spanish king); C 3558, 3579–82 (IV: 687–88, 714–22). Molesme 1.3–6, 20, 119; 2.283 (II:6–13, 31–32, 120–21, 353–55).

[44]Philippe Racinet found a similar pattern in the possessions of Cluniac priories of northeastern France; "Implantation et expansion clunisiennes au nord-est de Paris (XIᵉ–XIIᵉ siècles)," Le moyen âge, 90 (1984), 23–33.

eye, could keep an abbey's influence from spreading in a particular direction.

An abbey's area of influence was usually smallest in its first generation or so of existence, before its reputation had spread out of the immediate neighborhood. Most Cistercian houses initially received property located only a few kilometers from the abbey church. Pontigny, for example, acquired only property located along the Serein river and less than five kilometers away for the first twenty years or so after its 1114 foundation; only in the 1130s did the monks begin to acquire land and establish granges in the Armançon valley, eight or nine kilometers to the northwest.[45] The few examples of noble patrons who came from further away were men whose families had ties to Pontigny's immediate region. For example, Stephen, lord of Pierre-Pertuis in the mid-twelfth century, had gained that property by marrying an heiress, and he continued to make gifts to Pontigny, just as his family, the lords of Seignelay, had always done (Seignelay is eight kilometers west of Pontigny). Stephen ignored Vézelay, clearly visible from the castle of Pierre-Pertuis, looking instead directly past it, fifty kilometers north to Pontigny.[46]

The Cistercians of the twelfth century may have had more compact areas of influence than some of the eleventh-century houses in part because they made a conscious effort to acquire property next to the abbey or next to their granges. Much of the land they received as gifts or in pawn consisted of "whatever the donor had within one league (leuga) of the abbey."[47] Aside from the Cistercians' own attempts to acquire coherent pieces of property, these monks may also have had less scattered possessions than did some late eleventh-century houses simply because there were more abbeys in Burgundy in the twelfth century than in the eleventh, and landowners and potential donors did not have to travel as far to find monks to whom to make their gifts.

It is possible to draw the most detailed maps of an area of influence for Cluny and for several of the Cistercian houses, those with the greatest number of surviving charters. In the case of Cluny, though scholars have often remarked how far-flung some of its possessions were, in total numbers the gifts the monks received in the Mâconnais far outweighed those anywhere else, even in the later eleventh century, at the height of the abbey's prestige. In general, if one excludes the gifts from Spain and Lombardy, the property the monks were given was no more than thirty kilometers from the abbey and often

[45]See Garrigues' map in Pontigny, p. 23.
[46]For Stephen, see Appendix A, p. 356.
[47]See for example Arch. Haute-Marne, 2 H 1, 2 H 6, documents from Beaulieu.

much less. They were given very little property east of the Saône, twenty kilometers east of Cluny, or southeast of Mâcon, twenty-five kilometers away. Cluny's area of influence stopped well before reaching Tournus to the northeast, thirty-seven kilometers by the road, or Paray to the west, fifty kilometers away. Their possessions were most concentrated in the region immediately to the northwest of the abbey, between the Grosne and the Guye, no more than ten or fifteen kilometers away.[48] Cluny's *bannum*, the area in which no one but the monks had authority, as delineated and confirmed by Urban II in 1095, was even smaller, a rough circle around the abbey with a radius of five kilometers.[49]

Not only did the monks receive property relatively close to the monastery but they tended to receive it in *villae* where they already owned property. Many eleventh-century donation charters state that a piece of property "adjoins the land belonging to Saint Peter."[50] Thus Cluny's possessions were spread out as a series of scattered *villae*— within each of which however the monks might own substantial property—over an area roughly a day's journey from the abbey. On the few occasions when the monks received property a substantial distance from Cluny, it was almost always the gift of a very wealthy and powerful person. Less powerful donors made their gifts to monasteries closer to their own homes.

When Cîteaux was first founded and began to establish its granges, in the first decades of the twelfth century, its patrons came from a region within a fairly small distance of the monastery. The abbey's first major patrons were the viscount of Beaune, whose capital was twenty-three kilometers southwest of the abbey, and the duke of Burgundy, whose capital at Dijon was twenty-two kilometers to the north. In the first fifteen years or so after the abbey's foundation, the monks established vineyards at Gilly, located ten kilometers to the north; founded a grange at the borders of Brétigny and Gémigny, seven kilometers to the northwest; and established a grange at Moisey, sixteen kilometers to the southwest. The grange at Moisey is an example of a grange that became a miniature center of monastic influence, attracting gifts from petty lords of the immediate region. The men who gave the land to establish the grange included the lord of Reullée (two kilometers west of Moisey), the lord of Chaublanc (six

[48]See also Poeck, "Laienbegräbnisse in Cluny," pp. 80, 88, 97, 106, 129.

[49]Urban II, Sermon 1, PL CLI:563–64. Georges Duby, *La société aux XIe et XIIe siècles dans la région mâconnaise*, 2nd ed. (Paris, 1971), p. 186. For the extent of the *bannum* and of Cluny's wider *seigneurie*, see Duby's Map 11, pp. 518–19.

[50]See, for example, C 3146 (IV:308). This is a late eleventh-century gift of land at Lournand (three kilometers northwest of the abbey), bordered on three sides by Saint Peter's land and on the fourth by the public road; it was a missing piece in the monks' possessions.

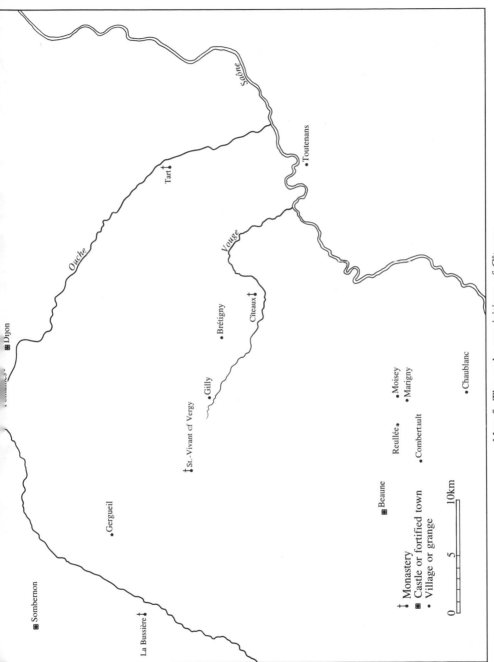

Map 5. The early acquisitions of Cîteaux

Monastery †
Castle or fortified town ▣
Village or grange •

0   5   10km

Sombernon ▣
La Bussière †
Gergueil •
Dijon ▣
Ouche
Saône
St.-Vivant of Vergy †
Gilly •
Brétigny •
Tart †
Vouge
Cîteaux †
Toutenans •
Beaune ▣
Reullée •
Moisey •
Combertault •
Marigny •
Chaublanc •

kilometers south), the family of the lords of Combertault (six kilometers southwest), the canons of Beaune (eleven kilometers to the
west), and the priests of Marigny (one and one-half kilometers west),
who needed the permission of the bishop of Autun to give Cîteaux
the tithes of Moisey.[51]

One of the Cistercians' most important early granges was Gergueil,
located twenty-four kilometers northwest of the abbey. Since Gergueil was on the far side of St.-Vivant of Vergy from Cîteaux, the
canons of Vergy (located seventeen kilometers west-northwest of
Clairvaux) initially contended with the monks of Cîteaux over this
property, which they considered to be theirs—or at least they considered the tithes to be theirs. The monks finally obtained the tithes
of Gergueil from the canons around 1110 and about a decade later
persuaded the canons not to charge them any further *cens* for the
land. Although in the following few years the monks had to defend
their property at Gergueil against several lay claimants, their chief
adversaries for it had been other ecclesiastics, whose area of influence
overlapped with theirs.[52]

But the consolidation of compact territories could also be an opportunity for cooperation among churches, or an occasion for churches to
dispense with property that they had somehow acquired far from their
own center. Around 1130 the monks of St.-Jean-d'Angéley, located
on the far west side of France, gave Cîteaux their grange at
Toutenans, located eleven kilometers southeast of Cîteaux but some
450 kilometers from St.-Jean. The monks of Cîteaux soon acquired
additional property in the area and were given the tithes by the
archbishop of Besançon.[53] The monks acquired additional land
between Cîteaux and their grange at Toutenans in the following years
when the canons of Vergy, in spite of their early conflicts, gave the
monks the land there, which lay on the far side of Cîteaux from
Vergy, for a payment of eight solidi.[54] Laymen tended to give nearby
property to the monks, since they usually patronized the closest
houses, but the ecclesiastics themselves sometimes had to sort out
conflicting claims to the land.

The abbey of Clairvaux had a similarly narrow geographic area of
influence. The abbey was located where the Aube and Aujon rivers
meet. (A third stream, now called St. Bernard's stream because the
house was originally founded at its source, also joins the Aube at
Clairvaux.) Many of the early gifts the abbey received were located in
these river valleys or in the wooded land between them. South of

[51]Cîteaux/Marilier 39, 41, 58–59, 61–62 (pp. 62–63, 65, 68–70, 73–77).
[52]Cîteaux/Marilier 37, 55, 70, 79 (pp. 58–59, 71, 82–83, 86–87).
[53]Cîteaux/Marilier 89, 93–94, 100 (pp. 91, 95, 97–98).
[54]Cîteaux/Marilier 81 (pp. 87–88).

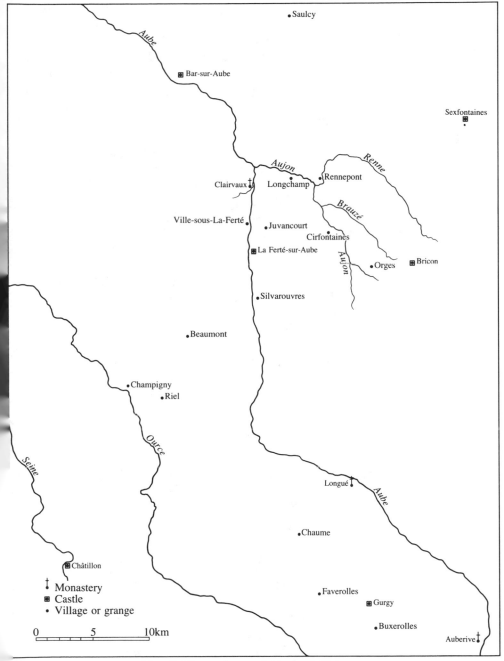

• Saulcy

🔳 Bar-sur-Aube

Sexfontaines
🔳

Aujon

Renne

Clairvaux ✝ Longchamp • Rennepont

Ville-sous-La-Ferté • • Juvancourt

Brauzé

Cirfontaines

🔳 La Ferté-sur-Aube

Aujon

• Orges 🔳 Bricon

• Silvarouvres

• Beaumont

• Champigny
• Riel

* Source*

Seine

Longué ✝

Aube

• Chaume

🔳 Châtillon

✝ Monastery
🔳 Castle
• Village or grange

• Faverolles

🔳 Gurgy

0   5   10km

• Buxerolles

Auberive ✝

Map 6. The early acquisitions of Clairvaux

Clairvaux, along the Aube, the house's property in the twelfth century stretched to Ville-sous-la-Ferté, Juvancourt, La Ferté-sur-Aube, and finally to Silvarouvres, ten kilometers to the south. To the southeast, along the Aujon and its tributary, the Brauzé, Clairvaux's area of influence reached first to Longchamp (three kilometers east) and Rennepont (five kilometers southeast) and eventually to Cirfontaines, Orges, and Bricon (sixteen kilometers southeast). To the southwest, in wooded territory, the monks owned property in the forest of Beaumont (fifteen kilometers away) and, past that, at Riel and Champigny, on the Ource, in the next river valley (twenty-two kilometers away). By the second half of the twelfth century, Clairvaux's overall area of influence stretched further west—including northwest and southwest—than it did in any other direction. To the east, Clairvaux's monks met those of La Crête, and to the southeast, their area of influence met that of Longué and Auberive. Men closer to these other Cistercian houses generally patronized them in preference to Clairvaux.

Since the monks never owned all the property within their area of greatest influence, and since some of their possessions were outside it, one cannot divide the Burgundian map into tidy zones. For the monks, their boundaries were defined most sharply when two monastic areas overlapped. The abbots of Morimond and La Crête (a daughter of Morimond, located thirty kilometers away) sometimes disputed land they both thought was theirs; in 1164 they erected boundary markers between their respective property at Grandrupt to leave no question there at least.[55] The quarrels over pasture rights between the Cistercian houses of Pontigny and Reigny (located twenty-nine kilometers apart) were settled only in the middle of the twelfth century when the bishops of Auxerre and Troyes and the abbot of Cîteaux established a boundary line between their pastures. Similarly, at the end of the twelfth century Clairvaux and Auberive (forty-four kilometers southeast of Clairvaux) quarreled over pasture rights at Gurgy-le-Château, Faverolles, and Buxerolles (located between the two abbeys though much closer to Auberive, ten to fifteen kilometers to its northwest), a quarrel settled in 1198 when the abbot of Clairvaux agreed to a division of pasture rights, the boundary being the road between Chaume and Gurgy-le-Château.[56] The

---

[55] Arch. Haute-Marne, 5 H 7; 8 H 54, no. 5. See also above, p. 139. Their quarrels continued intermittently, however, even reaching the Cistercian chapter general in 1193; Canivez, *Statuta*, I:165, no. 42. Boundary markers were a traditional method of delineating possessions. There still exists, at the archeological museum of Dijon, the large stone the monks of Flavigny and of St.-Seine erected between their respective lands in the eleventh century, with Saint Seine carved on one side, pointing toward *his* property, and Saint Peter of Flavigny on the other (the two abbeys are twenty-one kilometers apart).

[56] Pontigny 45 (pp. 118–19). Longué, fols. 19r–v, no. 12.

Cistercian chapters general tried to avoid such difficulties by legislating that houses of the order and granges belonging to different houses had to be at least a certain distance apart, ten leagues for houses and two leagues for granges,[57] but they were hampered by the donors, who did not make gifts according to any Cistercian plan but according to their own wishes.

If it was sometimes difficult for the Cistercians to sort out their respective claims, it was even more difficult for houses of different orders to do so, especially since an old Benedictine house might have always considered a region its own until the sudden arrival of the Cistercians.[58] Even when the reputation of the Cistercian order was at its height, nobles tended to patronize nearby houses, rather than deliberately bypassing them to reach the Cistercians. This may be seen for example in the southern Tonnerrois, a region about forty-five kilometers across, of which the old Benedictine houses of St.-Michel of Tonnerre, Flavigny, and Moûtier-St.-Jean had once formed the boundaries, but which were joined in the twelfth century by the nuns of Jully, the canons regular of Châtillon, and the Cistercians of Fontenay. (See Map 2, p. 135.) Fontenay especially was located in the center of the areas of influence of other houses, with St.-Michel thirty-nine kilometers and Jully eighteen kilometers to the northwest, Châtillon thirty kilometers to the northeast, Flavigny eighteen kilometers to the southeast, and Moûtier-St.-Jean sixteen kilometers to the southwest. Since Fontenay has by far the fullest archives of these houses, one cannot map as clearly the extent of their influence, or draw a line between their areas and those of Fontenay. But one can still note that Fontenay's area of influence never went *past* these houses. The abbey owned property nearly at the gates of Jully, Flavigny, Moûtier-St.-Jean, and Châtillon, but not beyond them.

To the north, Fontenay's possessions originally stopped at Fontaines-lès-Sèches, five kilometers short of Jully, and only reached as far northeast as Ste.-Colombe and Châtillon a generation after the abbey's foundation, after the daughters of men living close to Fontenay had married men living further north. To the southeast, Fontenay's possessions stopped at Bussy, five kilometers short of Flavigny, and to the southwest at Quincy-le-Vicomte, six kilometers short of Moûtier-St.-Jean. One can thus see Fontenay's influence spreading easily across the relatively unsettled territory to its north, but only with difficulty south of the river. Its boundaries were marked

[57]Canivez, *Statuta*, I:20, no. 32; 32–33, no. 6.
[58]For example, in the 1170s there were long quarrels over tithes between the Cistercians of Theuley and the black monks of Bèze, and between the Cistercians of La Ferté and the canons of St.-Symphorien of Autun; Arch. Haute-Saône, H 406; Arch. Côte-d'Or, 14 H 18.

not only by geographic features but also by the location of other houses.

Mathilda, both countess of Tonnerre and lady of Grignon at the end of the twelfth century, made a number of gifts both to Fontenay and to Jully (among many other houses, as noted above), but in each case she gave property that was closer to the recipient house than to the other. Fontenay, which was eighteen kilometers southeast of Jully, was in turn nine kilometers north of Grignon, and Mathilda's pious gifts of property at Grignon and of land further to the east were all to Fontenay. When Mathilda made a gift of property located at Tonnerre, on the other hand, twenty-five kilometers past Jully from Fontenay, she gave it not to the Cistercians but to the nuns of Jully.[59] Owning different pieces of property in her capacities as countess of Tonnerre and lady of Grignon, Mathilda gave property attached to Grignon to Fontenay, as had lords of Grignon since its foundation; and made gifts to Jully, as had earlier counts and countesses, of property close to Tonnerre. Petty landowners seem to have been influenced particularly by the relative closeness of different houses, but even the more powerful were affected by geography as well as family tradition.

No members of the nobility displayed disinterested generosity to reformed monks throughout their lives; there were certain times for this generosity. Nobles generally made their gifts when they were making a child an oblate or entering the cloister themselves, as indicated in Chapter 1, when they were dying, when a relative had just died, or they were embarking on a perilous enterprise. At the major turning points in their lives, the Burgundian nobles were most likely to endow their monastic neighbors with their own property, turning especially to the monks whom they knew best because they *were* their neighbors. From the monks' point of view, the local lords were their best source of new property, but also, as I detail in the next chapter, the source of most of the claims against them.

[59]Jully, p. 271. Petit 948 (pp. 347–48). *Genus illustre*, p. 557, no. 117 [rpt. PL CLXXXV:1470].

[9]

Gifts, Claims,
and Other Transactions

So far I have primarily discussed gifts to monasteries, offerings by laymen to monks who promised to pray for them and their relatives. Yet the documents also record other sorts of dealings between monks and their noble neighbors. Charters recording that a layman gave up a claim to monastic property are very common. From the middle of the twelfth century on, monasteries also became frequently involved in such transactions as pawn-broking and leasing. This chapter examines the various relations between monks and secular nobles other than the transfer of free gifts.

Gifts and Claims

A great many charters, though cast in terms similar to those of donation charters, record not gifts but rather a return to the monks of something that had actually been theirs all along. For example, around 1070 Stephen of Beaujeu gave up some claims to Cluny's possessions "for the remission of my sins"; and, around 1165, a knight made a gift "in alms" (*in eleemosinam*) to the Cistercians of Auberive of their tithes he had tried to claim.[1] Sometimes a man might even give up a claim for a relative's soul.[2] It should not be surprising that many charters attesting to the end of a quarrel are cast in terms similar to those of a donation charter. Nobles gave whatever they had to give, even if it was not always what the monks wanted, and one thing they always had to give was property they had claimed from the monks. Although at one stage of his life a man might feel no

[1]C 3431 (IV:541−42). Petit 427 (II:308−9).
[2]See for example Petit 624 (II:395−96), a knight who gave up a claim against the Cistercians of Quincy for his father's soul.

compunction in seizing ecclesiastical property, at another stage he might wish to make friends with the monks.

Claims against monastic property were called *calumniae* (or sometimes *querelae*), a term that meant specifically *false* claims (from the monks' point of view). Such *calumniae* might be raised by a neighbor, someone genuinely confused about the boundaries between their property, but, more frequently, the claimant was a relative of the original donor of the property in question. Often the claimant questioned the donor's right to alienate part of the family patrimony and claimed that his permission had not been properly obtained. Whether the claimants were relatives of a donor or just neighbors, in the eleventh and twelfth centuries there was no standard way for the monks to deal with them. Monks at different times or monks of different houses developed different approaches.[3]

The easiest way to deal with claims was to forestall them before they arose. Thus monks often tried to make possible claimants confirm the monastery's possessions. Sometimes the monks were willing to treat the confirmation of an earlier gift as a gift itself; they would offer spiritual benefits to someone for such a confirmation. For example, in 1037 Viscount Archimbald of Mâcon, who had returned safely from Jerusalem, in gratitude confirmed the gifts of land and of a chapel at Montmelard (twenty-three kilometers southwest of Cluny), which his grandfather Hugh and father Artald had made, and the gift of the church of St.-Laurent which he himself had given Cluny before leaving for Jerusalem.[4]

Usually the monks tried to obtain such a confirmation when a gift was originally given. The family of a donor generally had to agree to his gift, approve it, *laudare* in the Latin of the charters. The *laudatio* of family members and of the property's feudal lord, if it were held in fief from someone else, are almost always specified in the donation charter.[5] While in the eleventh and twelfth centuries there does not seem to have been any firm legal principle that an alienation required the approval of family members, this was certainly a moral norm, and

---

[3]Patrick J. Geary, "Vivre en conflit dans une France sans état: Typologie des mecanismes de reglementation des conflits, 1050–1200," *Annales: Économies, Sociétés, Civilisations* (in press).

[4]C 1672, 1673, 2922, 2932 (II:700–702; IV:123–24, 133–34).

[5]See, for example, the donation charter issued for Cluny when the *miles* Oliver became a monk around 1100 and gave the abbot a mill: he had his uncle, Dalmace of Gigny, confirm, since he had held the mill in fief from him; Dalmace had Waldric of Couches, from whom *he* had held the mill, confirm; and the bishop of Autun also agreed, "de cujus capite erat"; C 2994 (IV:192–93). After a knight gave the Cistercian monks of Les Roches a large amount of land in 1147, the monks obtained the approval first of his feudal lord, Gimo of Château-Censoir, and then of *his* lord, Geoffrey III of Donzy; Cte. de Soultrait, ed., *Inventaire des titres de Nevers* (Nevers, 1873), cols. 748–51.

the monks at any rate tried to obtain such approval to avoid the difficulty of later claims. In practice married men normally appeared in donation charters with their wives.[6] Any children who had reached the "age of reason" (twelve or fourteen) were expected to confirm their parents' donations. If a man's children did not formally confirm a gift—either because he did not have any or because they were still too young—this fact was noted.[7] If a gift were especially valuable, or if it entailed the abandonment of a claim, the monks often asked the donor to provide *fidejussores* or *adjutatores* who would be responsible for his good faith. These *fidejussores* were often the secular relatives, neighbors, or lords of the donor.[8] The *fidejussores*, like the family members who had consented, were generally listed in the donation charter.

While the consent of relatives was generally sought at the time of a gift, in the case of great feudal lords the monks often went a step beyond, encouraging counts and castellans to agree ahead of time to pious gifts of property that was held from them in fief (*in feudum* or *in casamentum*). Such a confirmation would allow the monks to receive the property at some point in the future without seeking out the feudal lord. Among many examples, Count Theobold of Chalon gave such a prior approval to Marcigny in the mid-eleventh century, shortly after that house was founded; and in 1179 Duke Hugh III granted Cluny the right to whatever the monks might acquire from property others had held from him in fief. (It is interesting to note, however, that in the eleventh century Count Theobold had contemplated only *gifts* from his knights and men, whereas, in the final decades of the twelfth century, Duke Hugh specified any property that Cluny might acquire "by gift or purchase.")[9]

Curses and financial penalties were often written together into the charter as a deterrent against claimants, who would thus be threatened whether they feared God or Mammon more. For example, when Dalmace of Vernay (five kilometers west of Beaujeu) gave some land to the canons of Notre-Dame of Beaujeu on his deathbed in 1090, he had his heirs swear to observe his gift and specified that, if they did

[6]Stephen D. White, "*Pactum . . . Legem Vincit et Amor Judicium*: The Settlement of Disputes by Compromise in Eleventh-Century Western France," *American Journal of Legal History*, 22 (1978), 305–8. Penny Schine Gold, *The Lady & the Virgin: Image, Attitude, and Experience in Twelfth-Century France* (Chicago, 1985), pp. 116–27.

[7]See, for example, Petit 606 (II:385–86), recording a man's gift to the canons of Oigny, "tunc temporis sine filiis et filiabus existebat." For another example, when the donor's sisters were said to be too young to confirm, see Cîteaux/Marilier 79 (pp. 86–87). A charter from the end of the twelfth century specifies twelve as "the age at which one can take an oath"; Quantin II.450 (p. 461).

[8]When five brothers gave up their claims to the church of St.-Julien-de-Civry in 1106, each one provided his own *fidejussor*; Marcigny 110, 114 (pp. 80–81, 83–84).

[9]Marcigny 35 (pp. 31–32). C 4269 (V:630–31).

not, they would "incur the wrath of God" *and* have to pay a penalty of seven pounds in gold.[10] A curse common in Cluny's cartularies is a reference to Dathan and Abiron. "If anyone raises *calumnias*, may he incur the wrath of almighty God and be in hell with Dathan and Abiron [cf. Numbers 6:1—34 and Psalms 106:17], and with those of whom the Lord God said, 'Depart from me' [Matt. 7:23], and may he pay a fine of five pounds in gold."[11] In the middle of the twelfth century the Cistercian monks of La Ferté had the bishop of Chalon write threats of excommunication against claimants into the pancartes in which he summarized and confirmed the monks' possessions.[12] The efficacy of the monks' prayers was highly enough regarded that a threat by the monks to cut off the prayers for a noble or his late relatives was often the chief—or even sufficient—weapon in encouraging recalcitrant laymen to give up a claim.[13] Such determined insistence that a gift not be reclaimed was necessary both for the donor, who considered the salvation of his soul to rest on the friendship of the monks won by his gift, and by the monks themselves, whose livelihood depended on such gifts.

In spite of the monks' best efforts to avoid claims, *calumniae* were common throughout the eleventh and twelfth centuries. The monks were more successful in recovering their property in the twelfth century than in the eleventh. In the late tenth century churches had been able to bring suit against laymen in the local comital courts. Both sides gave their position under oath, and the count would decide who actually possessed a particular piece of property. For example, Cluny successfully regained property through a formal surrender of claims (*guerpitio*) before the count of Chalon in 988 and before the count of Mâcon around 1000. But such comital courts disappeared after the first decades of the eleventh century.[14]

[10]Beaujeu 20 (pp. 22—23).

[11]This curse is from the very end of the tenth century; C 1756 (III:22). There are numerous other examples, and the reference to Dathan and Abiron also appears in the charters of Cluniac priories; see for example St.-Marcel 30 (pp. 32—33). Curses of various sorts are found in the charters of many houses; see Lester K. Little, "La morphologie des maledictions monastiques," *Annales: Économies, Sociétés, Civilisations*, 34 (1979), 47—48.

[12]La Ferté 16, 19, 28 (pp. 51, 55, 62).

[13]Patrick Geary, "L'humiliation des saints," *Annales: Économies, Sociétés, Civilisations*, 34 (1979), 27—36.

[14]C 1789, 2406 (III:45—46, 497—98). Georges Duby, *La société aux XI⁰ et XI⁰ siècles dans la région mâconnaise*, 2nd ed. (Paris, 1971), pp. 141—45. See also Stephen Weinberger, "Cours judiciaires, justice et responsabilité sociale dans la Provence médiévale: IXᵉ—XIᵉ siècle," *Revue historique*, 542 (1982), 282—83. In northwestern France, the comital courts continued to function through the end of the eleventh century, but even so the monks of Marmoutier still settled two-thirds of their disputes by compromise rather than judicial decision during this period; White, "*Pactum . . . Legem Vincit*," pp. 285—92.

In the eleventh century a layman was often able to claim ecclesiastical property successfully; several years or even several generations might have elapsed before the church recovered it. For example, around 1035 Duke Robert I of Burgundy gave the property of Veuvey to the monastery of St.-Bénigne of Dijon, property originally given the monks thirty years earlier by Count Otto-William but which Robert had claimed to have inherited from his great-uncle, Duke Henry of Burgundy (Otto-William's stepfather). (Veuvey is twenty-eight kilometers southwest of Dijon.) Similarly, St.-Cyr of Nevers received some allodial land from the widow of Herman of Tronsanges around 980, which she stipulated was a donation for the good of her husband's soul, but the property was reappropriated by Herman's relatives, and the canons of St.-Cyr did not recover it until a century later, though they always remembered that the land was rightfully theirs.[15] The relatives of the knight Otto of Berzé proved especially cantankerous. When Otto was dying, in the second half of the eleventh century, he gave Cluny a mill, saying in the donation charter that he wished "all the curses of the Old and New Testaments" to fall on any of his relatives who tried to reclaim his gifts. But these curses do not seem to have been effective, for Otto's brother Wigo claimed the mill, returning it to Cluny only when he was on his own deathbed. In the meantime Wigo had given it to his sister as part of her dowry, so that her son, who had inherited the mill, also had to agree to its final return to Cluny, more than a generation after it was originally given.[16]

Even when there is no direct evidence that a donor's relatives seized property given to a church, in eleventh-century documents one often finds that a series of relatives had given the same church the same property. It is not entirely clear whether both the nobles and the monks had forgotten the earlier donations, or, as seems more likely, a charter cast in the form of a gift actually represents the end of a quarrel over a piece of property. A good example of a constantly repeated gift is that of the *villa* and church of Laizé. The noble couple Milo and Ermengard first gave Cluny some arable land and the church of St.-Sulpice of Laizé, with the *villa* of Laizé, around the end of the tenth century. (Laizé is twelve kilometers southeast of Cluny.) The bishop of Mâcon confirmed this gift in 1019. In the middle of the eleventh century this couple's son Hugh gave Cluny the *villa* of Laizé, as though it were still his to give, for the soul of a son who had just died. A few years later, when he himself was dying, Hugh once again

[15]St.-B. II.228, 315 (pp. 24–25, 95–97). Nevers/St.-Cyr 11, 76 (pp. 26, 126–28). Tronsanges is twenty-six kilometers northwest of Nevers.
[16]C 3301, 3504 (IV:396–97, 618).

gave Cluny the church of St.-Sulpice of Laizé, with the confirmation of his two surviving sons and his grandsons. The monks of Cluny received each gift without any recorded remark; each donation charter is worded as though it were the first.[17]

In the twelfth century, by contrast, it is rare to find charters of this type, in which a series of relatives gave a monastery the same piece of property. On the other hand, there are many more charters openly acknowledging that a noble had raised a claim against a church's property and was seeking to end the quarrel. Overall, the twelfth century seems more litigious than the eleventh; the charters that record a quarrel between a layman and the church grew increasingly common. In the cartularies of the Cistercian houses settlements of *calumniae* fill at least half the charters of the second half of the twelfth century.[18] At Cluny, where there are far fewer twelfth- than eleventh-century charters, there are still many examples of noble claims against the abbey's property.[19] Since these charters generally record the *settlement* of a quarrel, it is possible that claims against monastic property were no more common in the twelfth century than in the eleventh, but that the monks were more efficient in having these quarrels settled— especially as the quarrels normally seem to have been settled within a few years after they arose, rather than within a few generations, as in the eleventh century.

The monks of the late eleventh and the twelfth centuries typically settled their quarrels through a mediated agreement or through compromise. This sort of settlement was based less on legal principles than on social and moral suasion. Sometimes both parties would appoint *amici* who would hear the relative merits of their claims and arrange a mutually-acceptable settlement (*compositio* or *placitum*). When the Cistercian monks of Fontenay settled their quarrel with Calo of Lucenay in 1180, each side appointed three men to hear the arguments; the monks chose a Cistercian monk of Bourras, plus the priors of the (non-Cistercian) houses of Flavigny and Semur-en-Auxois, while Calo chose the powerful lord Wiard Morhier as well as his chaplain and one of his knights.[20] Three men from each side was the typical number, but there was no firm rule, and sometimes the two sides would agree on just one mediator, if he was a highly

[17]C 1959, 2110, 2111, 2267, 2721 (III:179, 298—99, 398—99, 744—45).

[18]Constance B. Bouchard, "Property Transactions and the Twelfth-Century Cistercians," in *Proceedings of the Eleventh Annual Meeting of the Western Society for French History*, ed. John F. Sweets (Lawrence, Kans., 1984), pp. 1—3.

[19]See, for example, C 3983, 4069 (V:339—40, 419—21).

[20]Arch. Côte-d'Or, 15 H 130, no. 3. Similarly, Lord Hugh of Berzé and the monks of Cluny each appointed three men to act as judges in their quarrel in 1190; C 4346 (V:710—11). See also White, "*Pactum . . . Legem. Vincit*," pp. 293, 300; and Fredric L. Cheyette, "Suum cuique tribuere," *French Historical Studies*, 6 (1970), 291—95.

respected member of the community, such as a local ecclesiastical or secular leader.[21] Such men would command respect from both churchmen and laymen. They acted in effect as both judge and jury—or, perhaps more accurately, as mediators in binding arbitration. The *amici* would hear witnesses to the original donation, if any were available,[22] for evidence of what had actually taken place. At other times the monks and the lay claimant would themselves reach a compromise, an agreement acceptable to both. Such an agreement was also sometimes called a *placitum*.[23] Neither side could expect a clear victory, but a compromise would provide a solution that offered advantages to both sides. These compromises, arbitrated or not, seem to have been effective; among the many quarrels recorded in monastic archives, only a few were the reopening of a quarrel previously settled.[24]

The Cistercians, in their desire to avoid the affairs of the world, legislated in 1134 that no member of the order should act as judge or advocate (*prolocutor*) in *causis* or *placitis*.[25] This legislation however was not observed for long. Bernard of Clairvaux himself acted as mediator in 1145 in the long quarrel between the count and bishop of Auxerre over their respective rights in that city.[26] About ten years later a quarrel between Alain, the Cistercian bishop of Auxerre, and Count William IV was ended by the mediation of Geoffrey, the retired Cistercian bishop of Langres, and the abbots of Pontigny and Clairvaux.[27] Conflicts and conflict resolution were a constant part of the relations between monasteries and laymen, and no monastic order could distance itself from either.

In both the eleventh and twelfth centuries a great many of the claims against monastic property were brought by the relatives of the donors. When a knight promised the monks of Theuley that he himself would conduct the legal defense if anyone claimed the tithes he had just given them, he said specifically that he would defend them against his *consanguineos* and *consanguineas*. All the cartularies of Burgundian monasteries record a number of instances in which a man

---

[21]The monks of St.-Germain of Auxerre and the lord of Seignelay had the count of Nevers and Auxerre mediate their quarrel over their respective rights in the northern Auxerrois; Maximilien Quantin, ed., "Une sentence de Guillaume Ier, comte de Nevers, de l'an 1106," *Bulletin de la Société des sciences historiques et naturelles de l'Yonne*, 40 (1886), 231—34.

[22]See, for example, Cîteaux/Marilier 112 (pp. 103—4).

[23]See, for example, Petit 219 (I:495—96).

[24]See also Weinberger, "Cours judiciaires," pp. 284—85.

[25]Canivez, *Statuta*, I:26—27, no. 60.

[26]Quantin I.247 (pp. 393—97). See also Constance Brittain Bouchard, *Spirituality and Administration: The Role of the Bishop in Twelfth-Century Auxerre*, Speculum Anniversary Monographs 5 (Cambridge, Mass., 1979), pp. 54—55.

[27]Alain, Letter 5, PL CCI:1386. Quantin II.149 (pp. 164—65).

made a gift in his old age or when he was dying, and his sons refused to honor it.[28] Typical is a charter of Molesme from the first decades of the twelfth century: the knight Milo of Avalleur recalled his father's gifts to Molesme, where he had taken the habit in his final days, and Milo and his sister now gave up all their claims to these gifts.[29] Since the charter recording the confirmation of an earlier gift and the abandonment of claims against it is generally the first indication in the records that the monks were not freely enjoying the use of the donated property, there may have been many instances in which the heirs reappropriated their father's gift and never returned it.[30]

Monasteries had a rather ambivalent attitude toward the heirs of their patrons, for a man's sons were the most likely to try to claim his pious gifts, but they were also the most likely to become donors to that same monastery later in their own lives. The Grossi of Uxelles and Brancion, discussed in Chapter 6, were both major donors to and major claimants of Cluny's property in the eleventh century. For example, in the 1030s, Odo Poudreux, son of Maiolus Poudreux, a man who had made a number of gifts to Cluny, gave up his claims to land at Bassy (ten kilometers northeast of Cluny) at the same time that he gave Cluny some serfs. Around 1035 Bernard I of Uxelles gave up his claims to the church of St.-Gengoux, before Counts Hugh and Theobold of Chalon, and at the same time confirmed his mother-in-law's previous gift of several *mansi* to Cluny. (St.-Gengoux is twenty kilometers north of Cluny.) He reconfirmed this gift shortly before his death, thus gaining the spiritual benefits of a gift without having actually given the monks any hereditary property.[31]

As some families made gifts to the same monasteries over the generations, other families repeatedly attacked the same houses. The counts of Nevers, discussed in Chapter 5 as an example of a lineage that consistently protected and confirmed the rights of the family foundation of St.-Étienne of Nevers, also made claims against certain monasteries over the generations, especially Vézelay. Count Landric

----

[28]Theuley, fols. 17v–18r. For a similar pattern in England, see Emma Mason, "Timeo barones et donas ferentes," in *Religious Motivation: Biographical and Sociological Problems for the Church Historian*, ed. Derek Baker, Studies in Church History 15 (Oxford, 1978), p. 69. For northwestern France, see White, "*Pactum . . . Legem Vincit*," p. 290.

[29]Molesme 1.203 (II:187).

[30]It must have been a welcome change for the brothers of the Hospital of Morment to have the knights Widric and Rudolph of Faverolles, sons and heirs of Theoderic, who had converted and died at Morment, to declare in the mid-twelfth century that they "did not wish to defraud the house of the alms of their father, but sought to increase rather than diminish his gifts"; Morment 18 (pp. 117–18). The castle of Faverolles is seven kilometers southeast of Morment.

[31]C 2905, 2908, 3367 (IV:104–5, 108, 463). For the Grossi, see Appendix A, pp. 300–307.

began the quarrels in 1027 when he drove out the monks and asked the abbot of Cluny to send him some new ones, apparently with the specious excuse that he was going to "reform" Vézelay.[32] Later counts continued to claim an authority over the monastery which the monks denied. A century later Count William II began to impose what Hugh of Poitiers, the twelfth-century historian of Vézelay, called "unheard of exactions" on the monks' commerce. Hugh commented that the death of William II's son Raynald as a prisoner in the Holy Land, on the Second Crusade, was a judgment on his father. Yet Raynald's brother William III was again "led astray by wicked men," according to Hugh. Though the king forced this "tyrant" to give up his quarrels in 1155, his son William IV began his rule as count by complaining that the monks should not have dared elect a new abbot without his permission. Though when he fell sick a short time later he sought the abbot's forgiveness, as soon as he recovered, according to Hugh, he again attacked the abbey's goods, aided by his mother, "a modern Herodias [cf. Matthew 14:3] and a daughter of Jezebel." This quarrel was settled for good only when the count left for Jerusalem in 1167.[33] Conflicts broke out again at the beginning of the thirteenth century, when Lord Hervé of Donzy, who had become count of Nevers by marriage, seized property of the monks of Vézelay until the monks complained to the pope. Hervé had taken up not only the county of Nevers but the quarrels of its previous counts.[34] As family tradition could urge new generations to make gifts to the same monastery as their ancestors patronized, so tradition could also encourage new generations to claim the property of the same monks their predecessors had attacked.

Counter-Gifts

Once the monks had settled a quarrel, it was very common for them to give something to the claimants in return for the retraction of their *calumniae*. The counter-gift seems to have been intended to forestall any further renewal of the quarrel. When the prior of Marcigny reached an agreement around 1095 with Roland of Pommiers, who had earlier given the house some woods but had reclaimed the gift when the previous prior had died, he paid Roland twenty solidi, saying he did so "lest the unstable man try to change again what should not

[32]Quantin I.87 (pp. 166–67).
[33]Vézelay, pp. 239, 419–24, 430–31, 515, 523–24, 538, 542–45, 568, 580–81, 605–6.
[34]Innocent III, Letter 16.22, PL CCXVI:810. For the counts of Nevers, see Appendix A, pp. 340–51.

be changed."[35]   In 1163 Rayner, who had recently succeeded as lord of Salcy, reached a compromise with the Cistercian monks of La Bussière and confirmed what his father had given the monks. He did not admit however that his father had given as much as the monks claimed: the charter says, "He recognized whatever gifts of his father he had unjustly claimed and gave it even if his father had not already given it." The monks gave him sixty solidi and a palfrey. Twenty-five years later Rayner renewed his quarrels but then, "recalling the sixty solidi," gave them up.[36] In 1189 when the Cistercian monks of Mores said they "wished to reestablish peace" with one of their neighbors who had seized some of their property, they "gave him twenty solidi from the goodness of their hearts, even though his claim was unjust."[37] Sometimes the monks made a small, token payment, sometimes a rather substantial sum. When in 1196 a knight, with his wife and five children, gave up his claims to the property of the Cistercian house of La Crête, the monks gave him and his family forty solidi, an ox, a dun cow, and some blue cloth.[38]

Sometimes such counter-gifts were made not only for the abandonment of a claim but also in return for an outright gift. As the Cistercian monks of Fontenay said early in the twelfth century, as they gave a donor eight pounds and his brother four, "He gave a great deal to the church; therefore it is just that he should receive some secular return."[39] When the knight Hugh of Pierre-Pertuis gave his share of the tithes of Sermoise to the monks of St.-Étienne of Nevers in 1143, he said that he had done so "for my soul and those of my ancestors and successors and for temporal gain" (the monks gave him eighty pounds).[40]

These counter-gifts might be seen as formalizing agreements between the monks and their secular neighbors. In a period in which all gifts were made by means of a symbolic gesture (such as putting a book on the altar), a gift from the monks symbolized that they had received the layman into their spiritual community. Counter-gifts may also be seen as an indication that the monks were eager to

[35]Marcigny 63 (pp. 48–49).

[36]La Bussière 2.16, fols. 17v–18r. See also Bouchard, "Property Transactions and the Cistercians," pp. 2–3.

[37]Mores 34 (p. 63).

[38]Arch. Haute-Marne, 5 H 7. In 1179 the black monks of St.-Michel of Tonnerre gave some knights 1000 solidi in return for their withdrawal of their claims; Tonnerre, Bibliothèque municipale, MS 40 (on microfilm at the Arch. Yonne, 1 Mi 395).

[39]Jobin, *St. Bernard*, pp. 580–81, no. 21.

[40]Nevers/St.-Étienne 6 (pp. 81–83). Such counter-gifts were not limited to laymen; at the beginning of the eleventh century, the priest Blandin gave some property he had inherited at Viré to the canons of Mâcon and the church of St.-Didier of Viré, their dependency, "for the love of God, the salvation of my relatives, and the money Bishop Letbald and the canons have given me"; M 199 (p. 128).

maintain close relations with their nearest powerful neighbors, men who could easily become their enemies if friendly ties were broken.[41] Further, the gifts may have been made when settling *calumniae* because the monks recognized that they would never be able to force these neighbors to capitulate outright. Unfortunately for the monks, however, counter-gifts also seem to have acted as an economic incentive for the nobles to seize monastic property. If one succeeded in claiming monastic property, it was all to the good, and, if not, one was still likely to receive something from the monks.

It should be noted that, if someone made a gift on his deathbed, he very rarely received any sort of counter-gift from the monks. The claims that a counter-gift was supposed to avert were not an issue when the donor was dying. He did not need money or animals; he needed the monks' prayers, and these were often symbolized by preparations for his burial or anniversary or even (especially in the eleventh century) by his assumption of the monastic habit, which made any further symbols unnecessary.[42] It should also be stressed that the counter-gifts that monks made to those who gave up their claims were considerably less than what they would have paid for *buying* a comparable piece of property outright. The cheeses, capes, and new shoes that the monks of La Ferté gave as counter-gifts to some of the people who gave them land for a new grange in the mid-twelfth century certainly had more symbolic than monetary value.[43]

Even if the monks did not make any sort of counter-gift to a man who made a gift for his soul, they often gave a small payment to his relatives in return for their confirmation. Such was the case when, around 1110, Lord Aimo of Marigny gave the New Monastery of Cîteaux some land for a vineyard at Gilly (ten kilometers northwest of the abbey), and the monks gave his stepsons twenty solidi "in memory" of their confirmation, "since they had hoped to inherit this land." In the 1130s, when a knight of Semur gave some land to Marcigny, where both his wife and daughter were nuns, the prior of the house gave his sons and other relatives a payment, for, as the donation charter specified, "otherwise they would not have consented to

[41]The Grossi provide one example of an ongoing series of transactions. In 1116 the monks of Cluny gave Landric Grossus and his brother Gui a mule and a horse, in return for the brothers' confirmation of the gift of a woods their brother Bernard V Grossus had given the monks six years earlier; C 3826 (V:246—48). For these brothers, see Appendix A, p. 304.

[42]See for example La Bussière 6.16, fol. 45v. In this charter of 1196 Philibert, son of the provost of Beaune, gave the monks an annual income for the good of his soul and to establish an anniversary observance. The monks of La Bussière generally gave a monetary gift—and often a horse—to their donors, but not when someone was dying. This charter was given "imminente die obitus sui."

[43]La Ferté 36, 41, 46, 51, 57 (pp. 68—69, 71, 73, 75, 78).

the gift."[44] Since the heirs of a donor were the most likely claimants to his gifts, the monks always needed to gain their confirmation, by counter-gift if they could not obtain it freely.

Other Types of Transactions

Gifts to monasteries and claims against such gifts were by no means the only sort of transaction between churches and nobles. During the eleventh and twelfth centuries other sorts of arrangements, especially the pawning or leasing of property, became progressively more frequent. Since this book deals primarily with the role of the nobility in the spread of monasticism, not the role of monasteries in the medieval system of economic exchange, I treat these other sorts of transactions somewhat summarily here. It should be kept in mind however that by the thirteenth century such transactions were a major part of most monasteries' interactions with the secular world.[45]

One of the most common forms of economic exchange involving monasteries was the lease, a transfer of property in return for an annual *cens*. Occasionally, in the eleventh century, a church rented its property to a layman for such a *cens*. More commonly, especially in the twelfth century, a layman gave a piece of his property to the monks in return for such a payment. Such a lease was open-ended and presumed perpetual, usually passing to the heirs of the man who had set up the original lease. Depending on the size of the property, the payment might range from a few solidi to a number of pounds a year. Usually the *cens* was paid in coin but sometimes in kind; both sorts of payment are found throughout the twelfth century. Leasing was important enough to the Cluniac monks of La Charité that they obtained a special bull from Pope Lucius III in the early 1180s, confirming their right to lease both "moveable and immobile goods" in return for an annual *cens*.[46] It was most common for the monks to lease land, but it was also possible to lease other rights. For example, around 1170 Duke Hugh III leased the canons of St.-Étienne of Dijon his juridic rights over certain men of Dijon.[47]

[44]Cîteaux/Marilier 41 (p. 64). Marcigny 213 (pp. 121–22). When a knight gave the monks of Pouthières some land in 1160 for his son's soul, the monks made monetary gifts to him, his wife, his brother, his wife's brother, and the latter's wife and children; Arch. Côte-d'Or, 9 H 7.

[45]For these transactions, see also Bouchard, "Property Transactions and the Cistercians," pp. 3–4; and Constance Hoffman Berman, "Land Acquisition and the Use of Mortgage Contract by the Cistercians of Berdoues," *Speculum*, 57 (1982), 250–66. I intend to examine the financial transactions of the twelfth-century Cistercians more fully in a later study.

[46]La Charité 3 (pp. 6–7).

[47]St.-Étienne IV.43 (pp. 58–59).

When the monks wished to build up a coherent piece of property, such as a grange or vineyard, or to acquire pasture rights in a certain area, it was quite common for them to offer a rent to those petty land-owners who did not wish to give their share to the monks freely. The rent replaced at least part of the income the layman might have received from the property. The Cistercians especially received property in return for a rent in the second half of the twelfth century. For example, in the 1120s, after the monks of Cîteaux received some land at Civry and Vernolle (forty-two kilometers northwest of the abbey) from the duke and the lord of Sombernon "for the redemption of their souls," they acquired adjacent pieces of land from the knights who owned them by offering a rent in grain. They promised each knight two setiers of grain a year, half wheat and half barley, "neither better nor worse than the grain grown there, but of middle quality."[48]

Another sort of transaction was the exchange, more common in the eleventh century than in the twelfth. The monks of Cluny especially seem to have used exchange as a method of consolidating their property. In the final years of the tenth century and the first decades of the eleventh, they exchanged property both with laymen and with the bishops of Mâcon, in many of the same locations.[49] In the twelfth century the most common exchanges recorded in monastic archives were those involving the exchange of property between two churches, usually to give each a more compact set of possessions. For example, in 1134 the houses of Pontigny and St.-Martin of Chablis exchanged some property that laymen had given to the two abbeys, located between them, each house taking that which was closer; the two houses are only thirteen kilometers apart, but neither wished to go around the other's property to get to their own.[50]

Sales, like leases and exchanges, could be mutually beneficial for monks and nobles. They were always relatively uncommon, though sometimes, especially in the early twelfth century, Crusaders in need of cash for their expedition sold their property to local monasteries. When Lord Ascelin of Châtel-Censoir, for example, was preparing to leave on the First Crusade, he gave the monks of Molesme his land and rights at Nitry for twenty-seven pounds. When the knight Robert Dalmace was leaving for Jerusalem in 1106, he gave the chamberlain of Cluny a *mansus* in return for a pound of gold. When the knight Girard of Semur was leaving for Jerusalem in 1118, he gave Marcigny a *mansus* and received ten pounds from the prior "to help me in my

[48]Cîteaux/Marilier 77 (pp. 84–85). For other examples, see Arch. Côte-d'Or, 14 H 5; Petit 940, 964 (III:344, 354–57); and Clairvaux I, pp. 106–7, nos. 9–10 (summarized as Vignory 2.49 [p. 194]).
[49]C 1870, 1943, 2165, 2313, 2783 (III:104, 159–60, 332, 435–36, 808–9).
[50]Pontigny 102 (pp. 172–73). For another example, see Theuley, fol. 20r.

journey.''[51] Only at the end of the twelfth century did monks begin to buy property with any regularity, and then usually either a vineyard or a piece of property that rounded out monastic possessions in an area.[52]

But a sale was not the only way for a layman to raise money. From the middle of the twelfth century on, it became quite common for laymen to mortgage or pawn their property to monks, *impignare* or *invadiare*,[53] for even when nobles needed money they hated to alienate their property permanently, and they probably hoped to be able to redeem a pawn in the future. In such an arrangement the monks gave the layman a ''gage,'' or large lump sum payment, in return for a piece of property, the *pignus*. The ''gage'' seems to have been appreciably less than the layman would have received for actually selling the property. If the layman wished his *pignus* back, he would have to redeem the ''gage,'' generally within a specified period of a few years, and in coinage worth no less than what the gage had originally been worth.[54] Otherwise, the property became the monks' outright.

This arrangement first appears in the charters with any regularity at the time of the First Crusade. For example, when a knight of the castle Montmerle (twenty-three kilometers south of Mâcon) was leaving for Jerusalem in 1096, he gave the monks of Cluny his entire heredity *in convadimonium* for 2000 solidi, specifying that only he would be able to redeem it; if he died on his trip or returned but died without legitimate heirs before redeeming it, the property would become a gift for his soul. A few years later, as Lord Narjod of Toucy was leaving for Jerusalem, he gave the monks of Molesme, to whom he and his brother had earlier given two-thirds of their allodial property at Crisenon for their souls, the final one-third share of Crisenon, *in vadimonio*, for twenty marks of silver and a mule worth seven marks. He and his wife made a gift, ''for their souls,'' of whatever the monks would realize from the pawned property while they held it.[55]

The Crusaders of the later twelfth century often raised the money

[51]Molesme 1.33 (II:48). C 3840 (V:199). Marcigny 161 (pp. 95–96).

[52]For example, in 1176 the monks of Pontigny bought a vineyard from the provost of the count of Nevers for twenty pounds, and in 1197 the monks of La Bussière bought a vineyard from a family for twenty pounds, ten solidi; Pontigny 9 (pp. 90–91); La Bussière 6.6 (fol. 43v).

[53]A purported ''sale'' of property to Marcigny in the 1130s (a knight *vendidit* some land to the prior) was actually a pawning, for the knight specified that he could redeem the property during his life for the same amount that the prior had advanced him; Marcigny 248 (pp. 133–34).

[54]When John, viscount of Ligny, and his mother gave St.-Germain, *in gageria*, all they had at Rouvray for thirty pounds in 1165, they specified that, if the coinage had been devalued by the time they repaid the gage, the monks could choose to receive forty silver marks instead of the thirty pounds. Lebeuf IV.57 (p. 47).

[55]C 3703 (V:51–53). Molesme 1.53, 54 (II:63–65).

they needed through this sort of arrangement. The money they received was sometimes called a *guagiriam pelerini*.[56] The Cistercians especially were involved in such transactions. In 1189 the knight Adam of Savoisy, heir to Planay, while leaving for Jerusalem with his lord Andreas, pawned (*invadiavit*) to Fontenay everything he had at Planay for ten pounds, specifying that he would redeem it if he returned alive from Crusade.[57] Since few ever returned home to redeem their property, the monks thus acquired a good deal of land and other goods, some of which they could use to raise money to advance to other Crusaders.[58]

Pawning became increasingly common during the course of the twelfth century. However, serious questions about its legitimacy began to arise. Around 1150 Pope Eugenius III stated that it was usurious for someone to keep the fruits and income (usufruct) of a piece of property held as a *pignus*, rather than repay the owner once the gage was redeemed, even though keeping the usufruct was standard pawning practice.[59] One way around the intimations of usury was to make the usufruct of the property that was given in pawn a gift for the pawner's soul. Such was the case around 1180 when a noble lady gave Cluny all she and her sons had at Ruffey (three kilometers from the abbey), "in fields, meadows, vineyards, and woods," as the *pignus* for a gage of twenty pounds, specifying that she gave the monks the income from the property for her soul.[60]

In 1157 the chapter general of the Cistercian order proclaimed that Cistercian monks should not "receive property in pawn [*vadimonia sive gageriae*] any more, except for the tithes of our own fiefs and pastures," but the monks were fighting a losing rearguard action. In 1180 the chapter general ordered that those abbots who had received property for a gage should return it by the next year.[61] These repeated prohibitions had little effect. Cistercian houses such as Fontenay continued to take property in pawn, so that by the end of the twelfth century property received *in vadimonium* outweighed that received *in eleemosynam*.

---

[56]See, for example, Arch. Saône-et-Loire, H 54, no. 4.

[57]Arch. Côte-d'Or, 15 H 249, no. 3.

[58]Similar patterns have been found in many regions. See for example Patricia A. Lewis, "Mortgages in the Bordelais and Bazadais," *Viator*, 10 (1979), 27–31; Victoria Chandler, "Politics and Piety: Influences on Charitable Donations during the Anglo-Norman Period," *Revue Bénédictine*, 90 (1980), 65; Berman, "Land Acquisition," p. 251; and Penelope D. Johnson, *Prayer, Patronage, and Power: The Abbey of la Trinité, Vendôme* (New York, 1981), p. 60.

[59]Eugenius III, Letter 550, PL CLXXX:1567. See also Berman, "Land Acquisition," p. 252.

[60]C 4270 (V:632).

[61]Canivez, *Statuta*, I:60, no. 6; 88, no. 12.

Monks resisted claims against their property much more effectively in the twelfth century than in the eleventh, even though this effort required more frequent and more valuable counter-gifts to the donors and their relatives. In becoming lenders and pawn-brokers, monks also became efficient financial managers. In becoming involved in mortgages and loans, the Cistercians quickly lost some of the unworldliness that originally distinguished them. Yet, for the most part, they retained their aura of holiness throughout the twelfth century—at least for most men at some stage in their lives.

Relations between reformed monasteries and their noble neighbors showed a tremendous variety. A noble might, at different times or in different circumstances, try to appropriate monastic property, pawn some land to the monks, or make a large gift to ensure burial at the house. The nobles seem to have been well aware of the probable return on their activity: a gift from the monks in exchange for withdrawing a claim, a substantial "gage" of money, or prayers for their soul. In the following chapter, I discuss further the return nobles expected and the motives behind their pious gifts.

[10]

Motivations for Noble Generosity
to Reformed Monasteries

So far I have taken it for granted that the ostensible reason for the nobles' willingness to support monasticism was the real reason: that they often gave part of their property to a body of regular monks or asked such monks to settle on their property because they were indeed concerned for their souls, as specified in the donation charters. The very fact that those monasteries which received the most from the Burgundian nobility were the reformed houses—those which sought to follow what they believed to be the holy way of life prescribed by the Bible and the early saints—would make the conclusion seem inescapable that noble donors were most interested in associating with monks of holy life. Yet many modern scholars have suggested that the noble concern for salvation may have been mixed with more secular considerations. It is of course impossible to know the inner workings of the minds of medieval men, so no absolute conclusions are possible, but one may examine the factors that would have influenced their decisions in an attempt to determine which elements might have been of consequence to eleventh- and twelfth-century nobles. Such an examination is the purpose of this chapter.

The Charters Specify Salvation

There can be no doubt that the monks themselves depicted pious gifts and foundations as avenues to salvation. Although the monks who would receive the gifts could hardly be disinterested in urging the local nobility to save their souls, the spiritual advantages of pious gifts must have been impressed upon the nobles all their lives by their ecclesiastical neighbors and relatives. The prologues to donation charters, often drawn up by the monks themselves, sometimes give elaborate statements of the monastic position that sinful men may escape

[225]

damnation by following Christ's teachings and giving their property to men of God and to "the poor," who were identified (at least through the middle of the twelfth century) with monks who followed a life of individual poverty. In many charters from the eleventh century the donor said he had "thought of the enormity of his sins" or "contemplated human fragility." One charter from the first half of the eleventh century begins, "Whosoever gives God and His saints something of his heredity in this present world is preparing the reward of eternal life for himself in the life to come." The prologue to a 1080 charter of the count of Joigny, in which he gave the Cluniac priory of La Charité a dependent house and two parish churches, is even more explicit. It said that the count "did not wish to obtain perfection by heeding the Lord's command to give up worldly things and follow Him [cf. Matt. 19:21], but still wished to share in the heredity of Christ [cf. Rom. 8:17] in the life of heaven, by being a participant in this life with those who imitate Him [i.e., the monks]."[1]

The charters from eleventh- and twelfth-century Cluny (especially those from the eleventh century) commonly included one or more biblical quotations, which were interpreted as stating the spiritual advantages of making gifts to the saints and to the monks who served them. Generally, the more important a gift, the larger the collection of quotations. One of the most common was, "Make to yourself friends of the mammon of unrighteousness, that . . . they may receive you into everlasting habitations" (Luke 16:9).[2] This phrase was always interpreted to mean that a man might use Mammon (his wealth) to make friends among the saints, and that these friends would make a place for him in heaven. Other commonly used quotations included, "Lay up for yourselves treasures in heaven, where neither moth nor dust doth corrupt, and where thieves do not break through nor steal" (Matt. 6:20; cf. Luke 12:21);[3] "If thou wilt be perfect, go and sell that thou hast, and give to the poor, and thou shalt have treasure in heaven: and come and follow me" (Matt. 19:21);[4] "The ransom of a man's life are his riches" (Prov. 13:8);[5] "Whosoever he be of you that forsaketh not all that he hath, he cannot be my disciple" (Luke 14:33);[6] "Alms deliver . . . from death, and will not suffer the soul to go into darkness" (Tobias 4:11);[7] "Alms shall be a

---

[1]C 2171 (III:335). Quantin II.34 (pp. 34—35).

[2]See, for example, C 1993, 2029, 2065, 2084, 2322, 2360, 2747, 2834, 3679, 3724 (III:205—7, 237—38, 264—65, 279—80, 442, 466—67, 771—72; IV:37; V:32, 67—74).

[3]C 2445, 2815 (III:526—27; IV:18—19).

[4]C 2807 (IV:10—11).

[5]C 2083, 2096, 2484, 2884, 2983, 4072 (III:278—79, 289—91, 563; IV:78—79, 181—82; V:423—26).

[6]C 3537 (IV:660—61).

[7]C 2191 (III:345—469); cf. Tobias 12:9. This same quotation was used in 1147 in a donation charter for the Cistercian house of Reigny; Arch. Yonne, H 1566.

great confidence before the most high God, to all them that give it" (Tobias 4:12);[8] "Water quencheth a flaming fire, and alms resisteth sins" (Ecclesiasticus 3:33);[9] and "Give alms . . . and, behold, all things are clean unto you" (Luke 11:41).[10]

The monks knew that one could not buy salvation, that man could not be reborn in God's image simply by making a gift. Still, these biblical passages came close to saying that the proper distribution of one's goods could obliterate sins. From a theological· viewpoint, material goods themselves could not save; they only made an appropriate symbol of the sinner's contrite desire to establish himself in the grace of God. Yet this was a distinction too subtle for many laymen—and one the monks themselves may not have wanted to press too strongly. The prologue to the foundation charter of Molesme spells out explicitly the monastic viewpoint and so is worth quoting in full. Though the prologues to most foundation charters were shorter, they contained the same ideas.

In the name of the holy and undivided Trinity, the Father and the Son and the Holy Spirit, Amen. When our first father sinned, all of us were made sinners with him, since we all exist in him, in our bodies if not in our persons [cf. Rom. 5:12—14]. Therefore, when he was hurled down from the height of blessedness to the abyss of wretchedness, we too were all hurled down by the just judgment of God. Hence it is that both our inner and our outer man are subject to a great many passions from the Tree of Knowledge, that our flesh is afflicted by many very bitter sufferings, that our spirit too daily suffers many grievous assaults from the flesh to which it is joined, so that it can scarcely resist and is many times overcome by the flesh. But merciful God, having pity on the multitude of our infirmities, lest what He had made should perish, sent His Son to earth, to take the form of a servant, and to remain obedient to Him unto death. By His humility, our pride was overcome; by His resurrection, a man filled with faith may rise again from the death of sin; and by observing His teachings, he may return to his original state. He also grants us an abundance of temporal goods in our precarious life and does so daily, so that, observing Christ's teachings and giving from our superfluity to the poor, we may from these transitory goods obtain eternal life. With the grace of God, may this life attend Hugh of Maligny, his sisters, nephews, and nieces with their husbands, and Raynald of Molesme, and Odo Payen, and Gui, and Hugh of Courteron and his wife Gersendis, with her sister the lady of Chacenay and their children, and Odo of Fulvy, and Odo, son of Engilbald, and their wives. Considering with the single and sincere eye of reason that they came naked from

[8]C 2938 (IV:123—40).
[9]C 2279, 2880, 2997 (III:408—9; IV:74—75, 194—95). St.-Marcel 16 (p. 19).
[10]C 1792, 1829, 2067, 2895, 3472, 3679, 4235 (III:47—48, 73—74, 267; IV:97—98, 581—82; V:32, 587—88).

their mothers' wombs, and that they will go out from this world into miserable exile unless they do good, whereas if they persist in goodness they shall enter into the heavenly kingdom, and remembering the teachings of the Lord which say, "Give and it shall be given unto you" [Luke 6:38], they have chosen to do something very advantageous for themselves by making "friends of the mammon of unrighteousness," friends who will receive them "into everlasting habitations" [Luke 16:9]. Therefore all the above named, to conclude briefly, gave all the allodial land they had at Molesme to God and to Saint Mary and to the brothers serving them there, completely free of any other dominion.[11]

This preamble then (the rest of the charter goes on to detail the woods, meadows, mills, and so forth included in the gift and the witnesses to the donation) states the view frequently expressed in the eleventh and twelfth centuries that sinful man may make friends with the saints by giving a monastery part of his wealth.

This theme recurs throughout the records of the transactions between monks and their secular neighbors. Ecclesiastics seem to have used such biblical quotations to help persuade laymen of their proper attitude toward the church. When Count William I of Nevers rebuilt the church of St.-Étienne of Nevers and gave it to Cluny as a priory in 1097 (as discussed further below), his charter said that he did so in the recollection that, "As for man, his days are as grass: as a flower of the field, so he flourisheth" (Psalms 103:15), and "He cometh forth like a flower, and is cut down: he fleeth also as a shadow" (Job 14:2). William commented, "With these and similar sermons and *exempla* of this type I have been taught and instructed by religious and learned men and have begun to think of my soul's salvation, and how, through alms and good works, I might redeem my soul and store up 'treasures in heaven.'"[12] Bernard of Clairvaux, writing in the 1140s, again evoked the "treasures in heaven" of Matt. 6:20, "where thiefs do not break through or steal." In a letter to a noble couple he expanded on this passage and Matt. 19:21, saying that they would certainly lose what they owned on earth, unless they gave it to monks, "the poor," who would take it to heaven and store it up for them there. He managed to make pious gifts sound like an investment plan.[13]

There are indications that such exhortations were heeded and that concern for salvation did influence many nobles in their relations with the church. The prime evidence of course is the fact that so many

---

[11]Molesme 1.2 (II:5–6). Maligny is forty-four kilometers west of Molesme; Courteron is twelve kilometers northeast; Chacenay is twenty-four kilometers northeast; and Fulvy is twenty-six kilometers southwest.

[12]C 3724 (V:67–74).

[13]Bernard of Clairvaux, Letter 421, *Opera*, VIII (Rome, 1977), 405.

gifts were made when the donor was near death or had just experienced a relative's death, as detailed in Chapter 8. At such times the hereafter was of immediate concern, and secular considerations were of secondary interest. The close coincidence over the years between pious gifts and situations in which nobles would be especially concerned for the welfare of their souls should make it clear that the promise of salvation through the prayers of holy monks must have been at least a factor in noble support for reformed monasticism.

A rare direct indication of noble belief in the role monks played in providing salvation is a long poem in Old French written at the very beginning of the thirteenth century by the lord of Berzé (located in the Mâconnais, six kilometers southeast of Cluny). This secular lord provided a picture of man's sinful nature and the inevitability of death very similar to the picture presented by ecclesiastical writers. Like them, too, he spoke of monks amending the ills of the world in obedience to Christ and providing expiation for the sins of Adam. Though the monks of Burgundian houses could not have agreed with him when he described the Cistercians as often greedy for land, nuns as frequently unchaste, and the Cluniacs as inordinately wealthy—only the Carthusians gave him little to criticize—he and the monks concurred that the monastic life, when properly led, was the most holy, and that the best way for a layman to achieve salvation was to use his wealth in alms. Here, at least one noble layman explicitly acknowledged the spiritual necessity of making friends with monks, the same necessity expressed in the foundation charter of Molesme and numerous other monastic charters.[14]

Suggested Political Motives

A number of other motives besides concern for the hereafter have been adduced by modern scholars to explain noble support for reformed houses.[15] Though political considerations have not always been argued directly, scholars so often take them for granted that it is worth reexamining them to determine whether the evidence supports them as major influences. The most commonly held assumption is that a noble of the eleventh or twelfth century often reformed a house

[14]La "Bible" au seigneur de Berzé, ed. Félix Lecoy (Paris, 1938), esp. ll. 237–38, 796–99, pp. 33–37, 50.

[15]For example, Victoria Chandler states, "[This] type of motivations are [sic] more interesting because they are seldom expressed . . . Included here are social and economic reasons . . . the love of prestige or the need for money"; Chandler, "Politics and Piety: Influences on Charitable Donations during the Anglo-Norman Period," Revue Bénédictine, 90 (1980), 65.

or gave it a large amount of property to increase his "control" over the house or its region.[16] For example, Francis Hartigan has suggested that St.-Nicholas of Poitou, which was founded in the early eleventh century and then reformed a generation later, was both founded and reformed as part of the political machinations that absorbed the counts of Poitou and Anjou. The moral purposes for the foundation and subsequent reform, as stated in the documents, should, according to Hartigan, be disregarded in favor of the "less obvious though at times more important . . . motives of an economic or political nature." Hartigan is here following the pattern established by Jean-François Lemarignier, who treated the nobles' involvement in reforming monasteries as signifying their effort to preempt the king and seize political control of their regions, especially their churches.[17]

The difficulty with this interpretation is that it requires a considerable stretch of the imagination to perceive how an increase in control over a church or vacant land could result from a nobleman's gift of a church to a great reforming center or of land to a group of regular monks. According to the Rule of Saint Benedict, and as was usually specified in charters of foundation or reformation, the abbot would be chosen by the monks from among their number, once the initial reforming abbot had died, instead of being appointed by the local lord.[18] A layman who had once been able to appoint his favorites to head a monastery under his control, if indeed he did not hold the office and revenues of the abbot himself, would no longer be able to do so. Similarly, the produce of the land he had given the monks would no longer be his. Thus, in the case of St.-Nicholas of Poitou, though Count Gui of Poitou may have given the church to Cluny in part to keep it out of the hands of the Angevins, by making this gift he also gave up any control he himself may have had over the house,

---

[16]Penelope Johnson has suggested that King Richard's foundation of the Cistercian house of Bonport in Normandy may have been designed to control the passages of the Seine at that point—though she has difficulty explaining how a Cistercian monastery could house armed men; Johnson, "Pious Legends and Historical Realities: The Foundations of la Trinité de Vendôme, Bonport and Holyrood," *Revue Bénédictine*, 91 (1981), 189–91.

[17]Francis X. Hartigan, "Reform of the Collegiate Clergy in the Eleventh Century: The Case of Saint-Nicholas of Poitou," *Studies in Medieval Culture*, 6/7 (1976), 52–62. Jean-François Lemarignier, "Les institutions ecclésiastiques en France de la fin du Xe au milieu du XIIIe siècle," in *Institutions ecclésiastiques*, ed. Ferdinand Lot and Robert Fawtier, Histoire des institutions françaises au moyen âge 3 (Paris, 1962), pp. 62–64.

[18]The Benedictine Rule specified election by the community, preferably by unanimous decision; *Regula Sancti Benedicti* 64, ed. Adalbert de Vogüé and Jean Neufville, *La règle de Saint Benoît*, II, Sources chrétiennes 182 (Paris, 1972), p. 648. The Cistercians further instituted that new abbots be elected by the monks of the house acting with the abbots of any daughter houses, a practice they had Pope Innocent II confirm in 1132. Cîteaux/Marilier 90 (pp. 92–93); Canivez, *Statuta*, I:29, no. 67.

and thus can scarcely be considered to have carried out a political coup.

In fact, relinquishing political control over a church seems to have been an actual goal of the nobility in having an old church reformed. The degree to which the laity gave up any say in the monastery's internal affairs was an index to the regularity and sanctity of its life. For example, in 1004, when the viscount of Beaune and his wife gave the long-ruined church of Beaune to St.-Bénigne of Dijon so that regular monks might be set there, they carefully specified that they would retain no rights in this church or its tithes. Since the viscount had held the land on which the church was located in fief from the count of Burgundy (his stepbrother), who had in turn held it from the king of France, he asked both the count and the king to confirm his gift.[19] He seems in fact to have gone out of his way to establish the refounded house's independence and to confirm its possessions so that neither he nor any other lay lord could make any further claims on the church. Similarly, when Cîteaux was founded at the end of the eleventh century, Viscount Raynald of Beaune (who seems to have been the descendant of the man who gave the church of Beaune to St.-Bénigne) insisted in the charter in which he gave his allodial land at Cîteaux to the monks from Molesme that it would not be proper for the monks to hold their property "from secular hands," and therefore he renounced any "future control" of the land.[20] All the details of these donations, which are quite typical, suggest a determined intention to *decrease* control over the church.[21]

Suggested Economic Motives

"Control" is in any event a somewhat nebulous word. A number of scholars have preferred to adduce economics rather than politics as the chief motive principle for noble generosity, suggesting that gifts to monasteries were almost an investment. (Here of course scholars have argued for an economic return rather than the return in heaven that Bernard of Clairvaux promised.) Certainly, as noted in the previous chapter, some of the transactions between laymen and their monastic neighbors, such as the leasing or pawning of property, were

---

[19]St.-B. II.227, 233 (pp. 23–24, 28–30). Chron. St.-B., p. 164.

[20]Cîteaux/Marilier 23 (pp. 49–51).

[21]Joel T. Rosenthal, in studying noble donors in late medieval England, similarly found that these donors, far from attempting to control the monasteries out of any "class interest," failed to exploit any political advantages their gifts might have given them, "obtuse in regard to the manipulative value of a critical form of action"; Rosenthal, *The Purchase of Paradise: Gift Giving and the Aristocracy, 1307–1485* (London, 1972), pp. 128–31.

made specifically for economic purposes. But some scholars have concluded that a disguised economic motive lay behind the gifts made *in
eleemosinam* as well. For example, Bennett Hill, in his analysis of the
nobles who helped found Cistercian houses in early twelfth-century
England, suggests that the driving force behind those foundations was
economic gain. To accept this interpretation, however, one would
have to postulate a remarkable farsightedness among the donors. As
Hill indicates, most of the English Cistercian monasteries were
founded within a twenty-year period, before the order had shown
more than the first signs of the economic success it would manifest
later in the century; economic advantages would have been very
difficult to anticipate at the time.[22]

Indeed, nobles who made gifts to regular monasteries acted in a
manner that can only be considered unwise if economic return were
their goal. Donors very often made their gifts to the great reformed
houses only toward the end of their lives, when they could not expect
to benefit from any material gain. In fact, if the donor lived, he often
wanted the property back. For example, when Humbert of Senecé
and his friend Rainulph of Audenas (a priest) went on pilgrimage to
Jerusalem in 1087, they gave Notre-Dame of Beaujeu a great deal of
land in the area, specifying that the canons could enjoy the income of
the property only until their return, though if they did not come back
the monks would be able to keep it.[23] Many gifts to Cluny in the
eleventh century were made with the stipulation that the donor continue to receive the income from the donated property until his own
death (see above, Chapter 8).[24] Here economic considerations seem
to have argued *against* rather than for turning the property over to the
monks. In those cases when nobles were influenced by economic
motivations, they were motivated to use worldly prudence, not to give
their possessions to the church. While the donors were still alive and
still capable of enjoying economic advantages, they preferred to keep
the property themselves.[25]

In addition, the frequency with which heirs repudiated their parents'

[22]Bennett D. Hill, *English Cistercian Monasteries and Their Patrons in the Twelfth Century* (Urbana, Ill., 1968), esp. pp. 53–55. Hill argues his point even though he also de-
plores the efforts of many scholars to reduce religious phenomena to economic activities (pp. 9–10).

[23]Beaujeu 7, 12 (pp. 13–14, 17).

[24]For example, C 1291, 1890 (II:368; III:119–20).

[25]B. R. Kemp has suggested however that many nobles made gifts of parish churches
to monasteries in the twelfth century because these churches were of little economic advantage to their secular owners once the Gregorian reform had reduced the role these
owners could play; Kemp, "Monastic Possession of Parish Churches in England in the
Twelfth Century," *Journal of Ecclesiastical History*, 31 (1980), 134–35. A similar argument is made by J. C. Ward, "Fashions in Monastic Endowment: The Clare Family,
1066–1314," *Journal of Ecclesiastical History*, 32 (1981), 428.

dying gifts strongly suggests that they saw no material advantage in such gifts (see above, Chapter 9). Typical is Walter of Berzé, who in the middle of the eleventh century was finally persuaded to recognize his father's dying gifts to Cluny, but only after what the monks described as a long period of devastation.[26] A century later the Cistercian house of La Crête finally obtained full possession of some land—originally given to the monks by the knight Wiard the Blind of Riaucourt in 1149—but only after many years. Wiard's son, Wiard Junior, originally claimed his father's gifts, not confirming them until 1166 and still raising new claims in 1187. His cousin Alberic, a knight of Reynel (ten kilometers north of La Crête), originally claimed the gifts of both Wiard the Blind and Wiard Junior.[27] If the original donors had perceived an economic advantage in such deathbed gifts, they apparently neglected to inform their heirs of it.

Most donors and donors' children, then, did not consider pious donations economically advantageous. Indeed, in some cases pious gifts caused financial disaster. Hugh of Marney, for example, gave *all* his allodial land to St.-Marcel-lès-Chalon in the early twelfth century, several years before his own death. His nephews and his niece's husband, who considered themselves his heirs (he was childless), were furious at this apparent waste and tried to recover the property. The monks persuaded them only with difficulty to give up their claims.[28] The evidence thus suggests that generous monastic patrons among the nobility were investing in the next world rather than in this one. In the words of Emma Mason, "salvation was something to be bought on an instalment plan."[29] Nobles may well have expected something in return for their generosity, rather than engaging in disinterested charity for the good of the monks, but they made their gifts as though expecting a spiritual rather than a material return. The very variation in the timing of the occasions on which different family members felt impelled to endow monastic houses or even take the habit themselves argues that the driving force was each individual's awakened concern for his soul rather than political or economic concerns on which the whole family could agree.

[26]C 3324, 3325 (IV:417—18).

[27]Arch. Haute-Marne, 5 H 10. Riaucourt is ten kilometers north of La Crête.

[28]St.-Marcel 60, 63 (pp. 60, 62—63). Janet Meisel has discovered that some of the Welsh marchers of the twelfth century progressively ruined themselves by a long series of pious gifts; Meisel, *Barons of the Welsh Frontier: The Corbet, Pantulf, and Fitz Warin Families, 1066—1272* (Lincoln, Nebr., 1980), pp. 23, 33. See also Georges Duby, *The Early Growth of the European Economy: Warriors and Peasants from the Seventh to the Twelfth Century*, trans. Howard B. Clarke (Ithaca, 1974), pp. 169—71.

[29]Emma Mason, "Timeo barones et donas ferentes," in *Religious Motivation: Biographical and Sociological Problems for the Church Historian*, ed. Derek Baker, Studies in Church History 15 (Oxford, 1978), p. 74.

The Role of Ecclesiastical Relatives

The evidence also argues against a blanket assumption that gifts to reformed monasteries were intended primarily to benefit the donor's relative(s) within the cloister.[30] Certainly eleventh- and twelfth-century noble families would make a pious gift to a monastery at the time that a family member entered the house; such an entry gift might be the largest single gift a family made to any house. For example, when a knight named Alberic decided to become a monk at St.-Marcel-lès-Chalon in 1093, he gave the monks two *mansi* at Servigny and an allod at Ouroux, with the consent of his sons, whom he was in effect disinheriting.[31] But this sort of entry gift did not assure that family members would continue to make gifts for the monk's benefit.

In fact, the most common sort of charter in which an ecclesiastic and his secular relatives appear together is one in which the ecclesiastic has persuaded his relatives to give back church property they had appropriated. For example, around 1115 Lord Ascelin of Châtel-Censoir tried to claim the entry gift that his younger brother had made to Molesme when becoming a monk, after this brother had died, even though Gui, the abbot of Molesme, was *also* his brother; Abbot Gui and the monks had to give Ascelin ten pounds before he would give up his *calumpnia*. In the mid-twelfth century the monk Gui, of the Cistercian house of Fontenay, had to persuade his niece's husband, Oliver of Fresnes (five kilometers southeast), to give up some *calumniae* against Fontenay.[32] The presence of a relative in the church does not in itself seem to have guaranteed that family members would make no claims on that church's property; nor was this presence a necessary incentive for further generosity.

While the presence of a relative within a particular house could make a noble aware of the spiritual merits of the monks and dispose him favorably toward them, it might influence him only to the extent that he would make that house his first choice when making a pious gift. Many of the gifts nobles made to the houses where they had relatives were for purposes other than the support of those relatives. In 1111 for example Bartholomew de Mur gave a large amount of land

---

[30]As Joachim Wollasch suggests, "Parenté noble et monachisme réformateur. Observations sur les 'conversions' à la vie monastique aux XIe et XIIe siècles," *Revue historique*, 535 (1980), 14–15.

[31]St.-Marcel 113, 114 (pp. 93–94). Both of these are located seven kilometers southeast of St.-Marcel, about two kilometers apart. See also Joseph H. Lynch, *Simoniacal Entry into Religious Life from 1000 to 1260* (Columbus, Ohio, 1976), pp. 11–18.

[32]Molesme 1.238 (II:222). Fontenay II, fol. 16r, no. 42. For Abbot Gui and his brother, see also Appendix C, p. 419.

near Bourges to the Cluniac priory of La Charité-sur-Loire, where his
son Robert was a monk, but not for the purpose of bettering Robert's
lot. Indeed, this gift was made on the condition that Bartholomew
himself be accepted as a monk there. According to his donation charter, he had tried to persuade his second son, Odo, to accompany him
to the cloister, but Odo refused; in fact, the monks had to pay him
100 pounds before he would agree to his father's gift, an indication
that he had been no more eager to see family property pass to La
Charité, even with his own father and brother monks there, than he
had been to become a monk himself.[33] Similarly, around 1147, Lord
Artald of Château Loup and his wife gave the Benedictine abbey of
St.-Rigaud everything they had at a certain *villa*, noting that Artald's
uncle Robert was a monk there; however, Artald was not thinking of
Robert's welfare but of his own salvation, for his charter specified that
he was leaving on Crusade with Louis VII.[34] William, viscount of
St.-Florentin, provides a final example. In 1189 he gave St.-Germain
of Auxerre an annual income of 100 solidi and three measures of
grain from his hereditary property at Villiers-Vineux, saying he did
this for the good of his son Gui, a monk at St.-Germain, but Gui's
welfare was scarcely his principal concern, for the donation charter
went on to specify that the income would pay for an anniversary cele-
bration for William himself.[35]

Even when family feeling *did* motivate a gift to a particular church,
it was generally mixed with other considerations. A good example is
the annual revenue of sixty solidi that Stephen of Brive gave his sister
Sara, a nun at Crisenon, in 1189, indicating that it was for her use,
though it would pass to the convent as a whole on her death. But
while thinking of his sister's welfare, Stephen was also considering his
own salvation; he made the gift on the eve of his departure to the
Holy Land—from which he never returned—and specified that the
nuns would celebrate his anniversary after his death.[36] When nobles
made gifts to a house where their relatives were monks, they seem to
have done so because they already knew the house and could be
assured of its holy way of life, rather than because the nobles simply
wanted to assist their relatives.

Additionally, a great many families that had no relatives in the
church at all, or only in the cathedral chapter, still made gifts to
monastic houses. Since they were often as generous as families that
regularly produced monks, the presence of relatives in the cloister

---

[33]La Charité 48 (pp. 119–24).
[34]Arch. Saône-et-Loire, H 142.
[35]Quantin II.388 (pp. 395–96).
[36]Crisenon 161 (fol. 78v). Sara is probably identical with the Abbess Sara who took
office a short time later; see Appendix A, p. 356.

cannot in itself have been a major inducement for gift-giving. For example, Lord Roger of Vignory gave the cell of St.-Étienne, near his castle of Vignory, to the monks of St.-Bénigne in the mid-eleventh century, with the consent of Bishops Hugh and Harduin of Langres and of Count Raynald of Burgundy. The cell became a flourishing monastery, well-endowed by Roger and his descendants; but the only clerics in Roger's family, his brother and his son, were both canons in the cathedral chapter of Langres.[37] Similarly, the dukes of Burgundy were among the most generous patrons of reformed Burgundian houses throughout the twelfth century, but their family included no monks, only bishops and nuns. Clearly, then, there are enough examples of laymen who made gifts to churches where they had no relatives, and of gifts destined for purposes other than a relative's support, to indicate that the presence of relatives in the church was not in itself enough to motivate noble gifts.

It should also be noted that almost never during the late eleventh and twelfth centuries would a secular nobleman found or reform a house and then make his son the first abbot. However, in some cases at the end of the tenth century and in the early years of the eleventh, the first abbot of a newly reformed house and the secular nobles who made the reform possible were related. The Ottonian kings of Germany established several houses of reformed nuns, making their sisters or daughters the abbesses.[38] In Burgundy, St.-Bénigne of Dijon was reformed in 990 at the request of Count Otto-William of Burgundy and his brother-in-law Bruno, bishop of Langres; the first abbot was Otto-William's cousin William (see above, Chapter 4). Although Otto-William was surely pleased to see his cousin as the abbot of an important house in his capital, one should not assume that Otto-William's only concern was providing a sinecure for his relative. Indeed, William had been chosen as the new abbot of St.-Bénigne by Abbot Maiolus of Cluny, who was perfectly capable of resisting improper pressures from the secular nobility. Similarly, St.-Étienne of Dijon, an old house where the monks no longer followed a regular life, was reformed in 1032 under Warner, brother of the viscount of Dijon, who had been first provost and then abbot. Lords Humbert of Mailly and Hugh of Beaumont, the second of whom was a cousin of Warner's father, gave most of the property that enabled a body of reformed clerics there to be self-sustaining. Warner's father, Gui the Rich, asked the bishop of Langres to confirm this establishment of canons. But, again, the secular nobles who made the reform possible

[37]St.-B. II.332 (pp. 111–13). For the lords of Vignory, see Appendix A, pp. 379–84.
[38]K. J. Leyser, *Rule and Conflict in an Early Medieval Society: Ottonian Saxony* (London, 1979), pp. 63–73.

were doing more than setting up a house that might provide a position of dignity for a young relative. It seems that Warner, who initiated the reform himself, persuaded his secular relatives to help him reestablish St.-Étienne; they did not decide to refound St.-Étienne to have an appropriate place to put him.[39] Though ecclesiastical and secular relatives often worked together in church reform during the eleventh century, the nobles did more than provide appropriate positions for their sons and nephews.

In the twelfth century, in fact, all or almost all of the new houses of regular life established in Burgundy had secular founders who were not related to the first abbots of these houses. The only house of the period cited by modern scholars as a family foundation, made for the benefit of family members, is Clairvaux, and such an identification comes from a misreading of the sources. Unfortunately, the reputation of this house has caused the presumed "family" nature of its foundation to be accepted as a commonplace. It is therefore worthwhile to examine Clairvaux's origins in some detail.

Clairvaux was founded in part by the lords of La Ferté-sur-Aube (not to be confused with the Cistercian house of La Ferté-sur-Grosne) and of Châtillon. Tescelin Sorus, the father of Clairvaux's first abbot, Bernard, spent most of his adult life at the castle of the lords of Châtillon, and it is often maintained that he might somehow be related to them. Since the seventeenth century there has been a concerted effort to prove that Bernard's family was of the highest nobility, not just a group of knights or petty nobles, and attaching them to the lords of Châtillon has proved the easiest way to give him noble relatives on the paternal side.[40] More recently, Jean Richard has suggested that Tescelin and the lord of Châtillon were cousins (a suggestion based on a theory of Maurice Chaume). Although Richard admits that the little evidence there is indicates that Tescelin was a *miles castri*, a dependent knight with no family ties to his lord,[41] his

[39]Pérard, pp. 124–34, 181–82. St.-Étienne I.62, 75 (pp. 84–85, 94–95). For St.-Étienne's second reform, in 1113, see above, Chapter 4. For the viscounts of Dijon, see Appendix A, pp. 324–26.

[40]For the seventeenth-century scholarship, see Chifflet, *Genus illustre*. In the nineteenth century, the fullest discussion was by Jobin, *St. Bernard*.

[41]Jean Richard, "Le milieu familial," in *Bernard de Clairvaux*, ed. Commission d'histoire de l'ordre de Cîteaux (Paris, 1953), pp. 9–10, 558. On Bernard's father's position, see the *Vita prima Sancti Bernardi* 1.1, and the *Vita tertia* 1, PL CLXXXV:227, 523–24. Maurice Chaume had suggested that all the early daughters of Cîteaux must have been founded by men related to Bernard because some bear the same names as Bernard's presumed relatives; "Les origines familiales de Saint Bernard," in *Recherches d'histoire chrétienne et médiévale* (Dijon, 1947), pp. 110–40. It seems more likely that he has discovered which names were popular in northern Burgundy than a previously unsuspected group of relatives who were alone responsible for the spread of the Cistercian order.

suggestion has now been accepted as fact. Robert Fossier, for example, has made Bernard's father a first cousin of the lords of Châtillon, has emphasized their role in the foundation of Clairvaux (discounting the central role the documents give other families), and assumed that, if Bernard's (presumed) second cousins gave the land that he later ruled as abbot, the motive must have been family feeling for him. He thus concludes that Clairvaux was a "family foundation."[42] But this conclusion does not follow from the evidence.

The meager indications that Clairvaux had been founded by family members, for a family member, are further attenuated by the fact that for no other Cistercian house in Burgundy can this claim be made; René Locatelli marked this for the county of Burgundy, finding it somewhat difficult to reconcile with what was assumed about Clairvaux, though he was actually observing the usual pattern.[43] Though family members often collaborated on the reform or foundation of a particular monastery in the twelfth century, it seems difficult to accept the theory that what concerned them was the career of a family member; concern for their collective souls, the concern expressed in the foundation charters, seems a much more credible alternative.[44] The attempt to discover ubiquitous political and economic motivations in sources that express nothing of the kind seems more an artifact of the modern, secular and suspicious age than an insight into the way that medieval men behaved.

Crisis as Motivation

The preceding discussion has focused primarily on motivations that I believe should *not* be attributed to the medieval nobles who made gifts to reformed monasteries. In many ways such motivations are easier to disprove than to prove. Being able to argue against a desire for political power or economic gain as motivating factors does not necessarily enable one to say with confidence what the donors actually were thinking. But speculation is certainly possible. As the following

[42]Robert Fossier, "L'installation et les premières années de Clairvaux," in *Bernard de Clairvaux*, pp. 77–78; "La fondation de Clairvaux et la famille de Saint Bernard," in *Mélanges Saint Bernard*, XXIVe Congrès de l'Association bourguignonne des sociétés savantes (Dijon, 1954), pp. 22–25.

[43]René Locatelli, "L'implantation cistercienne dans le comté de Bourgogne jusqu'au milieu du XVIe siècle," *Cahiers d'histoire*, 20 (1975); see especially his discussion with Fossier, p. 221.

[44]It has also been suggested, though more tentatively, that Molesme was a "family" foundation of this sort; see Bede K. Lackner, *The Eleventh-Century Background of Cîteaux*, Cistercian Studies Series 8 (Washington, D.C., 1972), pp. 218–20 and n. 3. But there is no evidence of who Abbot Robert of Molesme's relatives were.

examples should indicate, in the eleventh and twelfth centuries, both those families whose fortunes had run out and those families which were rapidly expanding their political power reformed monasteries and gave the monks property. Perhaps the only common motivating factor was a sense of crisis.

In 1068 a small group of relatives, representing the final generation of the direct descendants of the counts of Bar and Tonnerre, gave the little church in the castle of Bar-sur-Seine and the church of Ste.-Colombe of Tonnerre to the Benedictine monastery of St.-Michel of Tonnerre. This group of relatives was headed by Hugh-Rainard, bishop of Langres (1065–1084) and last acting count; Bar would go to the counts of Brienne with the marriage of his sister, and Tonnerre to the counts of Nevers with the marriage of his first cousin Ermengard. St.-Michel of Tonnerre had been reformed to the Benedictine Rule in 980 by Hugh-Rainard's great-great-grandfather, Count Milo I, and submitted to the governance of St.-Bénigne of Dijon about twenty years later.[45] Milo's descendants had always been generous to St.-Michel, a monastery that faced their castle from a hill on the opposite side of Tonnerre's valley. The family however had produced no monks: Hugh-Rainard and his cousin Harduin, who preceded him in the see of Langres, are the only known clerics in the family. Now, with their family fortunes on the wane, Hugh-Rainard and his relatives seemed interested not in establishing any new power base but rather in reforming the last churches that remained in family control. Hugh-Rainard gave to the monks of St.-Michel who settled at Bar some land that he had inherited, and his mother added some more land and two mills, to be given to the monks on her death.[46] A few years later, Hugh-Rainard, acting this time in his capacity as bishop, helped establish the monastery of Molesme in his diocese; the next generation of monks there remembered him as their "glorious founder."[47] The considerable energy of the last male descendant of the counts of Tonnerre thus seems to have been concentrated especially on the secure establishment of houses of monks which would survive him.

Another noble interested in establishing regular monks was Count William I of Nevers. He however was of a family whose wealth and power were rapidly increasing. William inherited the counties of Nevers and Auxerre, and, by marrying Hugh-Rainard's cousin, he also obtained the county of Tonnerre. He refounded the church of St.-

[45]Quantin I.76 (pp. 146–48). Chron. St.-B., p. 136. For the counts of Tonnerre, see Appendix A, pp. 369–72.

[46]Quantin I.98, 99 (pp. 188–92).

[47]Molesme 1.1, 1.3, 2.7 (II:3, 6–7, 264). Interestingly, St.-Michel of Tonnerre came under Molesme's direction in the mid-twelfth century; Molesme 2.17 (II:269).

Victor of Nevers in 1055, near the beginning of his long rule,[48] but it was forty years before he again refounded a church. Finally, in 1097, near the end of a long and active life (he outlived all his sons), he had the church of St.-Étienne of Nevers rededicated and invited monks of Cluny to settle there, having just completed rebuilding the church himself. It is significant that he had had plenty of opportunities in the preceding thirty years to rebuild and reform this church had he wanted to or had he seen any secular advantage in doing so. As lord of the church he had approved its donation by the bishop to the cathedral canons of Nevers in 1063, and in 1068 he and the canons together gave the church to Cluny, but no one made any move to restore it so that monks might live there. In 1097, when the church was finally dedicated, he commented that he had been urged to carry out the restoration by Bishop Hugh while Hugh was still dean, but since Hugh had been elected bishop in 1074 and indeed had died in 1096, William had apparently not found his urgings very pressing.[49] But when the first of William's sons died around 1089, and the other two in the next few years, he seems to have finally turned to the project. The decision of his son Robert, bishop of Auxerre, to be buried at St.-Étienne in 1092 was probably the final impetus he needed.[50]

Once he put his mind to it, William was remarkably thorough. He had the monks of Cluny and the bishops and secular nobles of Burgundy assemble to witness the arrival of the Cluniac monks who were to live in the cloister he had built, hold services in the church he had built, use the large number of vestments, crosses, and candelabras he had provided, and enjoy the security of the walls he had built for them, as well as the comital rights over all the men living near St.-Étienne, which he had given them. These monks, the charter of 1097 specified, would be "mediators" between William and God. Though the political fortunes of the counts of Nevers were rising rapidly at the end of the eleventh century—William's grandson succeeded him as count and enjoyed a long and prosperous rule—William, at the end of his own life, was as interested as the counts of Tonnerre had been a generation earlier in giving a church that had been a family possession into the hands of reformed monks.[51] It is difficult to escape the conclusion that the advantages sought in such reforms would be found not in this world but in the next.

[48]Edmund Martène and Ursin Durand, eds., *Veterum scriptorum et monumentorum historicorum amplissima*, I (Paris, 1724), 434–36. For William of Nevers, see Appendix A, pp. 345–46.
[49]C 3388, 3417, 3724 (IV:487–91, 528–29; V:67–74).
[50]*Gesta pontificum*, p. 401.
[51]For William's descendants' relations with St.-Étienne, see above, Chapter 5.

For the Good of My Soul

A great many donation charters state that the donor made the gift *pro anima mea* or *pro animis antecessorum nostrorum*. Some scholars have dismissed this phrase as a mere stereotype, a commonplace without meaning. Others however have argued that the very frequency with which this phrase was used underlines rather than detracts from its validity.[52] But to understand the phrase "For the good of my soul," it is necessary to note that its use was far from universal. A great many charters record the interactions of secular nobles and reformed monks without mentioning the soul's welfare at all. This omission is especially striking in the Cistercian charters of the second half of the twelfth century. Here a growing attention to legal niceties meant that each document stated, in no uncertain detail, exactly what each party to a transaction would receive. Depending on the type of transaction, different words would be used. The monks of Cîteaux, for example, made a very clear distinction between different sorts of transactions when, just after the middle of the twelfth century, they drew up a list of the men from whom they had acquired their meadows at Orsans (ten kilometers southeast of the abbey). Next to each name they noted what the layman had received in return for his share, whether two solidi, or ten solidi and a cape, or two solidi, six denarii, and a setier of wine. In one-third of the cases, however, the monastic scribe noted that the layman had given the property *pro anima sua*.[53] From the point of view of the monks recording the transactions, a soul's salvation was just as real and solid as any other return. The fact that sales, pawns, leases, and the like were noted and recorded as such argues that those transactions recorded simply as gifts were just that, not concealed economic activities.

If a nobleman sold (*vendere*) some property, the amount of money the monks gave him was specified. If he pawned (*impignare* or *invadiare*) some property, the terms under which he could redeem the property were clearly stated. If, however, he gave (*dare*) property to the monks (also *concessere*, or *dare in eleemosinam*), the return was the specified salvation of his soul.[54] *Pro anima mea* was therefore neither

[52]See, for example, Richard Mortimer, "Religious and Secular Motives for Some English Monastic Foundations," in *Religious Motivation*, ed. Baker, p. 77.

[53]Cîteaux/Marilier 83 (pp. 88–89).

[54]Constance B. Bouchard, "Property Transactions and the Twelfth-Century Cistercians," in *Proceedings of the Eleventh Annual Meeting of the Western Society for French History*, ed. John F. Sweets (Lawrence, Kans., 1984), pp. 4–6. The soul's salvation cannot be equated with burial at the monastery, for most nobles made at least some gifts for their souls to houses other than the one where they were buried.

Plate 8. The weighing of souls. (From the tympanum
at Autun. Note the demon trying to fiddle the scales.)

a well-worn cliché nor a concern behind every lay-ecclesiastic transaction. It was rather a *technical phrase*.

This phrase indicated the customary return expected from one particular sort of transaction. Noble donors made clear distinctions between gifts—made for their souls—and purely financial transactions. When Lord Gaudin of Brémur gave the black monks of Molosmes a *villa* in 1146, he specified that he gave it "partly in alms, partly as a sale" (*partim in elemosinam, partim in venditionem*), and would receive spiritual benefits for himself, his children, and ancestors for the alms, and forty-six pounds for the sale. Even in transactions made explicitly for economic purposes, laymen did not forget they were dealing with holy monks. In the middle of the twelfth century, when the knight Robert of Aisy pawned (*impignaverit*) pasture rights at Gigny and Laignes to the Cistercian monks of Fontenay for 100 solidi, he specified that, if he died without heirs before redeeming the pasture rights, then and only then would these rights become a gift for his soul. In effect, while making a transaction for material gain, Robert was at the same time keeping open the option that he would be able to make a gift (consisting of these same pasture rights) for spiritual gain.[55] Rather than saying that hidden economic considerations lay behind apparently pious donations, one might better say that in cases such as Robert's a potential spiritual return lay behind an ostensibly economic transaction.

But even when gifts were made for spiritual benefits only, rather than for money, one can still see laymen calculating cost versus expected "return." This is especially evident in the establishment of multiple anniversaries, where someone could in effect amortize his risk by diversifying his portfolio, establishing anniversaries at as many churches as possible. Bernard of Clairvaux, for one, realized that the nobles of his time could conceive of spiritual benefits in terms of an investment. Exhorting the "strong knights" of Franconia and Bavaria to go on the Second Crusade, he said that any "prudent merchant" (*prudens mercator*) would recognize the value in taking up the sign of the Cross and receiving indulgence for his sins.[56] One can thus conclude that spiritual benefits were considered assets in themselves, whose worth, like that of any other investment, was calculable.

Gift-giving and claims against monastic property were the two activities that most frequently brought the secular nobility into contact with reformed monasteries. Perhaps ironically, material goods were usually at issue when a layman arrived at the monastery gate, even

---

[55] Arch. Côte-d'Or, 17 H 620, 15 H 193, no. 1.
[56] Bernard of Clairvaux, Letter 363, *Opera*, VIII:311–17.

though, if he had come to make gift, his motive was rarely economic gain. Laymen established ongoing relationships with their monastic neighbors in which they tried to calculate the probable return from different sorts of transactions. If they needed a loan or felt they had been cheated out of their inheritance, or if they wanted to sell or exchange an unprofitable piece of property, they could turn to the monks, but they went to their monastic neighbors particularly when they wanted prayers for their own or their relatives' souls.

Even though the nobility made most of the gifts to reformed monks in the eleventh and twelfth centuries, all levels of society must have experienced the sorts of crises—the death of a relative, the imminence of one's own death, or the risk of undertaking an enterprise such as a Crusade—that often prompted pious gifts. But if other sectors of society were equally concerned for their souls, they did not show it in the same way—in part because of course only the nobility had the wealth that made large-scale monastic endowment possible. In addition, nobles may well have received a more thorough religious training than did members of other classes, at least in the lesson that a sinner can buy salvation through gifts to religious men.

One might also suggest that the reformed church of the twelfth century, staffed and led primarily by nobles, appealed in particular to the situation of the nobility. Protecting the church had been a royal prerogative since the time of Constantine, and the nobles of the High Middle Ages—the counts who during the tenth and eleventh centuries had assumed much of the power that had been the kings', as well as the castellans and knights who struggled to keep their hold in the eleventh and twelfth centuries—were eager to share in this activity. Penelope Johnson offers an additional explanation, using the example of the nobility of Vendôme. She argues that a desire for independent action or a grand gesture may well have influenced many donors. The stability that Barbara Rosenwein concluded was a prime attraction of tenth-century Cluny no doubt continued to attract the upwardly mobile and inherently unstable nobles of the following two centuries.[57]

But I would argue that there was more to the special relationship between the nobility and the monks, that the life of the reformed monastery appealed exactly because it was so diametric to the normal noble life in the world. The donors were independent agents, wealthy, living a life in which family ties and the begetting of heirs were of major importance; and they rushed to make gifts to

[57]Penelope D. Johnson, *Prayer, Patronage, and Power: The Abbey of la Trinité, Vendôme, 1032–1187* (New York, 1981), pp. 13–14. Barbara H. Rosenwein, *Rhinoceros Bound: Cluny in the Tenth Century* (Philadelphia, 1982), pp. 44, 55–56, 105–6.

Plate 9. Two knights fighting. (From a twelfth-century capital at Vézelay.)

monasteries where the monks relinquished their self-will for humble obedience and forsook all personal possessions for an austere life in which the only "family" that mattered was the brotherhood of the community. Because knights and nobles knew well that their lives were not the holy life Christ had recommended, the reformed monastic life that was opposed so thoroughly to their own seemed almost by definition a holy life, and the monks those men most likely to have the ear of God.

Conclusions

In the eleventh and twelfth centuries leaders of the church and leaders of society were socially and biologically one. Bishops and abbots were almost invariably brothers of dukes and counts, viscounts and castellans, members of powerful families proud of their noble heritage. Yet the leaders of the church did not come from the same noble families throughout this entire period. In the eleventh century, when dukes and counts dominated Burgundian politics, a great many church leaders came either from the families of these lords or else from the ranks of those who served them. In the twelfth century, however, when the members of the upper nobility had lost some of their political predominance as a result of the resurgence of the French king on the one hand and the growing power of the petty nobility on the other, and when secular control over the internal affairs of the local churches had been blunted by the Gregorian reform, families of the greatest lords no longer supplied the majority of bishops and abbots. These tended to come instead from the lower levels of the nobility.

The Burgundian nobility did not act as a unit in sending their sons into the church. The basic unit of society was the family, and different noble families took different positions in regard to the church. Overall, or from a distance, there may appear to be relative uniformity, yet closer inspection reveals a great variety. Some noble families went through the eleventh and twelfth centuries producing scarcely any ecclesiastics at all. Of those who did send their sons into the church, some sent them exclusively into a monastery, some into a cathedral chapter—and in either case they tended to choose a church that older relatives had already entered. Some important Burgundian families, such as the viscounts of Nevers, produced several bishops in the eleventh century but no ecclesiastics in the twelfth century. Others, like the dukes, produced almost all their ecclesiastics in the twelfth century. Similarly, although families of the lesser nobility produced most of the monks for the new reformed monastic houses of the twelfth century, many families in this group never sent any sons into the monastery. Though a major proportion of all ecclesiastics were noble, noble families did not uniformly make a certain number of their members ecclesiastics.

In the same way, the spread of monasticism, one of the most important aspects of the religious life of the eleventh and twelfth centuries, was dependent on the goodwill and support of the local nobility, but different noble families patronized different monastic houses. In the eleventh century dukes and counts founded new monasteries and made them gifts, while in the twelfth century there were many knights and castellans who, acting in concert, were able to give reformed monks a large piece of land on which to establish a new house, and whose small gifts, taken together, represented a sizable addition to a monastery's possessions. While the dukes patronized most of the Burgundian houses at one time or another, most other families chose one or two houses and made most of their gifts to those monks over the generations. The decision to support certain monasteries was not made by the nobility as an order but by individual noble families.

Indeed, such a decision was usually made not even by an entire family but by one individual. Throughout the eleventh and twelfth centuries a large number of the quarrels into which monastic houses were drawn were the result of a noble making gifts that his heirs refused to acknowledge. Members of the nobility, especially in the twelfth century, treated local monasteries as an excellent source of revenue when they needed to lease or pawn some property, but when the return from pious gifts was prayers for the donor's soul, often only the actual donor saw the prayers as of immediate value. Thus the Burgundian churches could not rely on the nobility as a whole, or even on families as units—although they always put their hopes in the relatives of men who had helped them in the past. Rather, the relationship between a particular church and a particular member of the aristocracy was always intensely personal.

To some extent the changes in the monastic reform movement from the early eleventh century to the late twelfth can be correlated with the changing structure of the noble class and the changing needs of the noble families that made gifts to monasteries and provided their members. At the end of the eleventh century new monastic orders, exemplified by the Cistercians, took on a much more severe tone, placing greater emphasis on individual striving for holiness than on performance of the liturgical round. These new orders arose just when the lesser nobility had consolidated its position and members began sending their sons into the cloister and making pious gifts on a regular basis. Yet it would be wrong to consider the church a product of the nobility's secular interests. Throughout the eleventh and twelfth centuries the hallmark of noble involvement with the reformed church was a conscious *rejection* of the nobility's powers.

Nobles reformed old churches or founded new ones by inviting monks from monasteries that were not under their control to settle in a church or on a piece of land that had once been their own, but which they now relinquished to monastic authority. They stipulated that the monks in the newly reformed or founded monastery should live governed by the unchanging principles of a written rule (usually the Benedictine or the so-called Augustinian Rule), rather than by whim. They supported these monasteries by alienating their own fields, meadows, toll-bridges, and mills. They sought out monasteries where the holiness of life was guaranteed by the deliberate rejection of the pride, power, and wealth that characterized noble life in the world.

In the tenth century and much of the eleventh the Burgundian dukes and counts who had replaced the kings as local political authorities also sought to replace them as protectors of the church. At least since the time of Charlemagne, the church had considered kings as the chief protectors of ecclesiastical possessions and liberties. There was always some tension between a monastery and its secular neighbors, since those who were in a position powerful enough to protect the monks were also well situated to do them serious damage if they wished. Great lords who emulated the kings in protecting rather than attacking monastic houses gained a uniformly recognized respectability and even some assurance of salvation. In this period such reformed centers as Cluny stood as islands of stability where the strictly regulated liturgical round provided an alternative to the turbulence of the secular world.[1]

In the late eleventh century, however, at a time when secular life had become somewhat more orderly, Cluny and other traditional Benedictine houses no longer provided an adequate alternative to the world for all of those who saw in monasticism the main path to salvation. Though many monasteries of the eleventh century, including Cluny, continued in relative prosperity throughout the twelfth century, new orders also appeared and flourished, most notably the Cistercians, an order that emphasized the individual striving of the soul for God. This new form of spirituality of course had many roots, especially in a reexamination of the life of the apostles described in the New Testament and of the monastic life described by Saint Benedict. But this form of spirituality also met a need within the

[1]Barbara H. Rosenwein, *Rhinoceros Bound: Cluny in the Tenth Century* (Philadelphia, 1982), pp. 106–10.

secular nobility. During the eleventh century many lineages had joined the nobility, taking or being delegated positions of power, imitating the older nobility by their displays of wealth. By the beginning of the twelfth century these castellans and even lesser knights had reached a position of eminence and wealth in secular society and had enough military strength to maintain that position. Yet their power did not satisfy these recently established nobles. The new monastic orders of the early twelfth century provided a way of life uniquely suited to the spiritual needs of the nobility of the period.

Relations between the Burgundian church and the nobility in the High Middle Ages varied both with the needs of the nobles and with the changes in monastic attempts to mold noble strength and violence into more acceptable patterns. In the tenth and early eleventh centuries, when the older lineages were kept occupied with their wars with the Vikings and with each other, and the new lineages were struggling to establish themselves, the enforced calm and the opportunity for what Barbara Rosenwein has called "ritual aggression" at such monasteries as Cluny were in sharp opposition to the life of the secular world.[2] This enforced calm could be very appealing to those who had become world-weary in trying to reach or maintain a new position of power.

In this period the monks often tried to make the great lords their advocates, seeking both to forestall attacks from these lords and hoping for protection against other powerful men. The bishops of the early eleventh century went further still, leading the Peace of God and Truce of God movements. While the bishops recognized that nobles could not be stopped from fighting, they hoped to restrict *whom* the nobles would fight, and urged all knights and nobles to swear to refrain from attacks on churchmen and the defenseless, and even to restrict their wars on each other to certain periods.[3]

Toward the end of the eleventh century churchmen further defined

---

[2]Barbara H. Rosenwein, "Feudal War and Monastic Peace: Cluniac Liturgy as Ritual Aggression," *Viator*, 2 (1971), 145—57. In this article, Professor Rosenwein unfortunately uses the term "knights" when she means "nobles."

[3]The Peace of God was first preached in Burgundy at a council which Hugh, count of Chalon and bishop of Auxerre, held at Verdun-sur-le-Doubs, located in the county of Chalon, between about 1016 and 1020. Surviving from this council are the oaths required of nobles and knights (called *caballarii*), or those who bore *arma saecularia*. They promised "not to invade any church, or a church's courtyard, except to catch a malefactor; not to assail a cleric or monk, nor those walking with them, nor take their goods; not to seize anyone's ox, cow, pig, sheep, lamb, goat, or ass"; Hefele-Leclercq, IV, ii:1409—10. See also *Gesta pontificum*, p. 388; H. E. J. Cowdrey, "The Peace and the Truce of God in the Eleventh Century," *Past and Present*, 46 (1970), 42—67; and Georges Duby, *The Three Orders: Feudal Society Imagined*, trans. Arthur Goldhammer (Chicago, 1980), pp. 134—39. The Peace of God was promulgated at a number of successive Burgundian councils, including one Hugh held at Anse, in the diocese of Auxerre, in 1025; Hefele-Leclercq, IV, ii:938—39.

the suitable targets for noble aggression as excluding all Christians. Now, from the ecclesiastical viewpoint, fighting even other powerful laymen was not acceptable, whereas fighting the infidel was. Monastic houses readily advanced Crusaders the money they needed to go fight the "enemies of Christ" in the Holy Land. A few decades into the twelfth century, there was even an attempt to monasticize the nobles on Crusade, to make them live together under a rule and a master, as Templars and Hospitallers. This idea was backed by Bernard of Clairvaux, who helped write the Templars' rule. It is indicative of how far relations between church and nobility had evolved in a century that, rather than merely hoping to keep the nobles from attacking the defenseless, some ecclesiastics could dream of remaking the military class into a group of men who followed an almost monastic life. But the Templars and Hospitallers never became a viable model for more than a small part of the nobility. In Burgundy their houses were essentially indistinguishable from Benedictine or Augustinian establishments. In the Holy Land Crusaders sometimes joined these orders, but most of the monks back home hoped they would resume secular life on their return. Of course, it was hoped that a love of God and his saints would remain, but a secular noble was in a much better position than a cloistered member of a military order to act as a monastic advocate and defender, to fight off claimants with force, even if the claimants were (nominally) Christians.

Meanwhile, by the year 1100, private war was not nearly as prevalent as it had been a century earlier, and the new nobles had attained the position for which they had been striving for a century. Cluny and other traditional Benedictine houses no longer provided a clear enough contrast to the life of the world.[4] When making pious gifts or taking the habit themselves, the world-weary among the nobility sought out especially the Cistercian houses, which had been founded "in the desert." These houses were both close to and very distant from their noble patrons. The monks were well known to their neighbors, the members of the rural aristocracy, but they followed an austere life that provided the sharpest contrast to the nobles' own. The nobles preferred the Cistercians to the older Benedictine houses not because of any decadence in the latter, which were indeed at the peak of their flowering, but because the aspirations of the nobles themselves had changed. The nobles were powerful, and they endowed monasteries where the abbots would carry out their affairs

[4]Bernard of Clairvaux savagely attacked the abbots of traditional houses who rode around with a large number of mounted companions; "If you saw them you would say they were not the fathers of monasteries but the lords of castles, not the rectors of souls but the princes of whole provinces." Bernard of Clairvaux, *Apologia* 11.27, *Opera*, III (Rome, 1963), 103.

without any secular interference. They were independent, and they sought monasteries where the monks lived in common, in absolute obedience to a rule and the abbot. They were wealthy, and they flocked to join the monasteries where the monks practiced a life of voluntary poverty, even doing their own agricultural labor. They came from families that routinely produced large numbers of children, and they patronized houses where chastity was strictly observed. I suggest that the appeal of the new monastic orders of the late eleventh and twelfth centuries to the secular aristocracy was the fact that the monks' way of life stood in such diametric contrast to that of the aristocracy. Members especially of the relatively new nobility that took shape in the eleventh century had struggled for generations to attain their position, only to decide when they reached it that holiness lay in the opposite direction.

It has long been recognized that the changes in the religious life which took place between the end of the tenth century and the beginning of the thirteenth were correlated to some extent with changes in society. Lester Little especially has argued that the houses of canons regular or bodies of friars which became very numerous in the late twelfth and thirteenth centuries could have developed only in a society with large urban conglomerations and a form of market economy unknown in the year 1000.[5] But the society of the rural aristocracy was also evolving during the High Middle Ages, and with it changed many features of Benedictine monasticism.

There is certainly no question that the friars presented a change in the religious life much more radical than the difference between the Cluniacs and the Cistercians. The issue here rather is whether the spiritual reform that preceded the rise of the friars involved more than simply the removal of direct secular influence over the monks' internal affairs. The term "feudal church"—in the sense of a church peopled by, and acting in concert with, members of the local nobility— has been used pejoratively by most scholars, usually as an antithesis to "reformed church." Although the question of whether a particular church was "feudal" (as mentioned in the Introduction) can of course be manipulated by redefining the term, there is a remarkable consensus among historians of the church that to be feudal was somehow to be backward, unspiritual, and unreformed. I myself prefer to avoid the term "feudal" altogether in this context, where its pejorative usage has left it void of any other content. In this regard it should be

[5]Lester K. Little, *Religious Poverty and the Profit Economy in Medieval Europe* (Ithaca, 1978), esp. pp. xi, 84–94. Barbara H. Rosenwein and Lester K. Little, "Social Meaning in the Monastic and Mendicant Spiritualities," *Past and Present*, 63 (1974), 4, 20–32. In this article "monastic" spirituality is treated as essentially Cluniac, a consequence of the two-century gap between the the the two authors' fields of expertise.

noted that most scholars who have considered Cluny the beginning of a new form of reformed religious life, the forerunner of the movement that led to the Gregorians, Cîteaux, and to canons regular, have called Cluny "anti-feudal," while those who have seen Cîteaux and the canons as representing a sharp break with the past have called Cluny "feudal" to distinguish it from "anti-feudal" Cîteaux.

But if one goes beyond such labels to examine monks' relations with their secular neighbors, it is clear that all reformed monasteries, Cluniac and Cistercian alike, were dependent on the goodwill of the nobility. Nobles made possible their foundations, endowed them with a variety of gifts, and provided most of their members. Even the friars provide no contrast here; a major proportion of their leaders too were nobles and knights.[6] The new monastic orders certainly did not try to avoid the nobility; their concern was to try (fairly unsuccessfully) to make them understand that white monks did not want to receive the same sorts of gifts nobles had long given the black monks. The question was not how to distance themselves from the aristocracy so much as how to make sure the monks avoided the excesses of the secular nobility in their own houses. Yet the intimate ties between church and nobility do not imply that the churches were the pawns of secular ambition. The attraction of reformed monasticism for the nobility was always its contrast to the life of the world. There are essential continuities in noble-monastic relations between the eleventh and twelfth centuries, in that the friendship of the nobility was always necessary to the monks; yet around 1100 there was also a change of emphasis, when many nobles began to seek a form of religious life even more radically different from their own. The quite real differences between Cluny and Cîteaux are not those between a "feudal" and an "anti-feudal" church; rather, they are differences in the degree to which the monastic life in each offered a contrast to the life of the secular nobility.

This intimacy with the nobility carried with it however the ultimate inability of any form of medieval monasticism to provide a permanent form of unassailably pure religious life. This was not because friendship with nobles per se tainted religion, but because no monastery or monastic order could continue indefinitely to receive fortunes in wellmeant gifts and waves of (perhaps only temporarily) enthusiastic converts and still maintain the strict ideals of a religious life based on poverty and individual striving for perfection. Those monasteries (most notably the Carthusians) which were able to maintain the rigor of their life and the purity of their goals more or less unchanged throughout the twelfth century were also those which least influenced

[6]Little, *Religious Poverty*, pp. 160–61.

and were least noticed by the nobility. New monastic orders could not have spread beyond a few houses without the nobility, but ironically the holiness of life that nobles admired and sought to advance with their gifts was weakened by their overwhelming good intentions.

Reformed monastic orders and the orders of friars always intended to help the world as well as provide an alternative to the life of the world. The nobility, as is evident from the eagerness with which they embraced each new order and provided generous gifts, felt that they needed help in reaching salvation, and they found it in association with these holy men. But as the wealth and property that nobles gave the monks made these monks in many respects indistinguishable from other powerful landowners, the monastic alternative to the world became less distinctive. The thinkers of the eleventh and twelfth centuries who participated in the foundation of new orders recognized the difficulty; they repeatedly attempted a new definition of spirituality and of the relation between the secular nobility and their ecclesiastical brothers and cousins. They spoke of "reform" in the sense of returning to the early roots of monasticism, but the reform movements of the eleventh and twelfth centuries consisted not so much of restoration of old patterns as of successive attempts to find a way of setting the religious life apart from the world without losing the original goal of bringing the world salvation. The energy for these continual attempts at renewal sprang from the tension between irreconcilable goals, and no monastic order could long inspire spiritual aspirations in the secular nobility without also assuming some of the world's concerns. But the monks of the eleventh and twelfth centuries and the nobles who supported them should be seen as representing a sustained effort, which has not been duplicated since, to make spiritual issues the chief priority of the rulers of secular society.

APPENDIX A

Family Trees

The following are the family trees of the most important—or best-documented—noble families in Burgundy. Here is much of the information on family relationships referred to in the text. In constructing the family trees I have gone somewhat beyond the chronological limits of the book; if a family has roots in the tenth century, I have traced those ancestors, and I have also followed some families down to the middle of the thirteenth century, though with a less thorough treatment than for the twelfth century. The genealogies are arranged with the dukes first, the counts of Burgundy and Mâcon second, followed by the other counts and castellans, arranged alphabetically.

None of the family trees can be considered definitively set, and there has been much scholarly debate on some of the branches. In the essay that accompanies each family tree I have given my reasons for constructing the tree as I have. In this section most references to primary sources are given in parentheses; footnotes are reserved for longer references and for secondary authors. While not everyone may agree on all my details of the family trees, I hope that, in going back over the sources, they may construct their own more easily. Although I have cited the major authors who have written on a particular family, I have not tried to be exhaustive. Specifically, I have for the most part passed over in silence the authors who wrote before the accumulation of printed sources in the later nineteenth century, such as the editors of the notoriously unreliable *Art de vérifier les dates*.

The Dukes of Burgundy

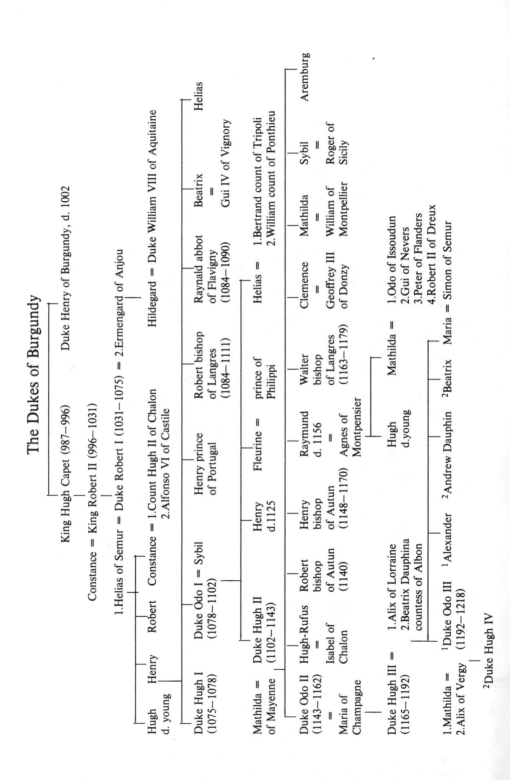

The Dukes of Burgundy

The fullest study of the dukes of Burgundy was by Ernest Petit. In the first five volumes of his monumental *Histoire des ducs de Bourgogne* he traced the dukes from the eleventh century to the late thirteenth century, giving an overview of the family's history and at the same time editing or summarizing close to 4000 documents (1500 from the early eleventh to the beginning of the thirteenth century, another 2500 from the thirteenth century). While Petit was fairly thorough, he was not always careful in his use of the sources, so in a few places I would disagree with his reconstruction of the family tree.

Henry, brother of Hugh Capet, was duke of Burgundy in the late tenth century. After his death in 1002, the duchy went (after some fighting) to his nephew, King Robert II. The dukes of Burgundy of the eleventh and twelfth century were descended from Robert II. His third son (the second to reach adulthood), Robert, became duke around 1031.[1] After the death of King Robert, Duke Robert I married Helias of Semur, the sister of Geoffrey I of Semur and of Hugh the Great, abbot of Cluny (1049–1109) (C 2949 [IV:149–50]; Petit 29 [I:371–72]; Gilo, "Vita Sancti Hugonis" 1.51, ed. Cowdrey, "Studies," p. 88; Obit. Sens III:233). He seems to have repudiated her around 1050, for John of Fécamp wrote to Leo IX to tell him he had heard that the duke had left his legitimate wife to enter into a consanguineous union with another woman (PL CXLIII:799–800). The other woman was named Ermengard, for Duke Robert is commemorated in the thirteenth-century obituary of Molesme with a wife named Ermengard (Petit V:386). According to genealogies drawn up at Anjou in the late eleventh century, she was identical with Ermengard of Anjou, daughter of Count Fulk Nerra.[2]

Duke Robert I had at least three sons, maybe four, and two daughters. He outlived all his sons ("Annales S. Benigni Divionensis" 1075, MGH SS V:42). Hugh, the oldest son, died without heirs. Henry, the second, was the father of the succeeding dukes. The name of Henry's wife is unknown. Of the two younger sons of Robert I, Robert sought his fortune in Sicily, and Simon is known only from Orderic Vitalis.[3] Robert I's daughter Constance

[1]Raoul Glaber, *Historia* 3.9, pp. 36–37. See also Andrew W. Lewis, *Royal Succession in Capetian France: Studies on Familial Order and the State* (Cambridge, Mass., 1981), pp. 25–27.

[2]"Genealogiae comitum Andegavensium" 1, ed. Louis Halphen and René Poupardin, *Chroniques des comtes d'Anjou et des seigneurs d'Amboise* (Paris, 1913), p. 247. Ermengard of Anjou and Duke Robert were second cousins. See also Georges Duby, *The Knight, the Lady and the Priest: The Making of Modern Marriage in Medieval France*, trans. Barbara Bray (New York, 1983), p. 90.

[3]Orderic Vitalis, *Historia ecclesiastica* 7.1, 13.15, ed. Marjorie Chibnall, IV (Oxford, 1973), 350; VI (Oxford, 1978), 428–32. Robert, though not Simon, is also found in a

married first Hugh II, count of Chalon, and, after his death, Alfonso VI, king of Castile.[4] Robert's second daughter, Hildegard, married Duke William VIII of Aquitaine. Hildegard is the only child definitely known to have been born to Robert's union with Ermengard.[5]

When Duke Robert died in 1075, his son Henry had been dead for some six years. Henry and his anonymous wife had, however, produced a large family. Their two oldest sons, Hugh I and Odo I, succeeded each other as dukes of Burgundy (1075–1078 and 1078–1102).[6] Odo succeeded to the duchy when his older brother retired to Cluny in 1078 (C 3531 [IV:653]), where he died in 1093 (St.-Seine, pp. 248–49).[7] Henry, a third son (Petit 62 [I:399]), became prince of Portugal after marrying Teresa, daughter of Alfonso VI of Castile (an illegitimate daughter, not the offspring of Henry's aunt Constance).[8] Two more of Henry's sons entered the church, Robert, bishop of Langres (1084–1111) (Chron. St.-B., p. 376, 378, 390), and Raynald, abbot of Flavigny (1084–1090) (Hugh of Flavigny, "Series abbatum Flaviniacensium," MGH SS VIII:503). Their sister Beatrix married Gui IV, lord of Vignory (Molesme 1.10, 103, 220 [II:18, 107, 204]). (For the lords of Vignory, see below, pp. 379–84.) They also had a sister named Helias (Molesme 1.6, 12 [II:12, 20]).

Odo I married Sybil, daughter of Count William Tête-Hardi of Burgundy (C 3516 [IV:632–33]) (see below, p. 275).[9] They had two

---

charter for Tournus; Tournus, pp. 134–35, summarized as Petit 77 (I:406). Since Orderic did not mention Duke Robert's son Hugh, saying that Robert had three sons, Henry, Robert, and Simon, it is possible that he simply called Hugh "Simon" by mistake.

[4]Falco, "Chronicon Trenorchiense" 49, ed. Arthur Giry and René Poupardin, *Monuments de l'histoire des abbayes de Saint-Philibert* (Paris, 1905), pp. 104–5. Constance was married to Alfonso by 1079; for the date, see Bernard F. Reilly, *The Kingdom of León-Castilla under Queen Urraca, 1109–1126* (Princeton, 1982), p. 11.

[5]*La chronique de Saint-Maixent, 751–1140,* ed. Jean Verdon, Les classiques de l'histoire de France au moyen âge 33 (Paris, 1979), p. 138. "Genealogiae comitum Andegavensium" 1, ed. Halphen and Poupardin, p. 247. This marriage is the link between the Capetians and the dukes of Aquitaine which made consanguineous the marriage between Louis VII and Eleanor of Aquitaine a century later. Jean Richard suggests that Robert I's sons Robert and Simon were also born to Ermengard; *Les ducs de Bourgogne et la formation du duché du XIe au XIVe siècle* (Paris, 1954), p. 14.

[6]Orderic Vitalis, *Historia ecclesiastica* 7.1, 13.15, ed. Chibnall, IV:350; VI:430.

[7]See also Erich Caspar, ed., *Das Register Gregors VII* 6.17, MGH Epp. II, ii:423–24.

[8]*Portugaliae monumenta historica, Diplomata et chartae* (Lisbon, 1867; rpt. 1967), pp. 512–13, 542, nos. 864, 914.

[9]See also Orderic Vitalis, *Historia ecclesiastica* 13.15, ed. Chibnall, VI:430. Chibnall erroneously states that Sybil was the sister rather than the daughter of Count William. The editor of the Cluny charter "corrected" *Oddo* to *Hugo*, while noting that the charter quite clearly indicated Odo. Editorial emendations like this have confused the genealogy of both the dukes and the counts. Jean Richard has described how these errors initially began; "Sur les alliances familiales des ducs de Bourgogne aux XIIe et XIIIe siècles," *Annales de Bourgogne,* 30 (1958), 37–46, 232.

sons and two daughters. The sons were named Hugh and Henry (C 3809 [V:156–59]; Chron. St.-B., pp. 427–28). Hugh II (1102–1143) succeeded his father as duke after Odo I died on Crusade (St.-Étienne II.17 [pp. 21–22]; Molesme 1.7, 13 [II:13, 20–21]). He is sometimes called "Hugh Borel" (Molesme 2.173 [II:321]). Virtually nothing is known of Henry, who died in 1125. Scholars have sometimes called him a Cistercian monk, but this seems to be an error based on the fact that his brother made gifts for his soul at Cistercian houses.[10] Their sisters married lords of Outremer. Fleurine married the prince of Philippi (Alberic of Aix, "Historia Hierosalymitanae expeditionis" 3.54, PL CLXVI:469–70), and Helias married Bertrand, count of Tripoli, and bore his heir, Ponce. After Bertrand's death, Helias married William, count of Ponthieu.[11]

Hugh II married Mathilda, daughter of Walter of Mayenne. She is sometimes referred to as "Mathilda of Mayenne" (Petit 281, 805, 986 [II:230; III:289–90, 363–64]).[12] They too had a large family. In 1131, when Hugh made a gift to the Cistercians of La Bussière, he specified that his gift was made with the consent of his wife and of "all his sons," Odo, Hugh, Robert, Henry, Raymund, and Walter (La Bussière 1.2 [fols. 2v–3r]).[13] Odo II, their oldest son, succeeded his father as duke of Burgundy (1143–1162).

Of the other sons of Hugh II, Hugh, usually known as Hugh-Rufus, married Isabel of Chalon and became lord of Châtelet-Chalon (Petit 466 [II:326–27]) (see also below, p. 313). His father had bought Châtelet-Chalon from the count of Chalon (La Ferté 82 [p. 90]). Hugh-Rufus was the father of Sybil, lady of Montréal, who married Lord Anseric II around 1161.[14] (For the lords of Montréal, see below, pp. 338–40.) Hugh-Rufus also had a son named William, who succeeded when his father died in 1171; in 1186 William called himself nephew and grandson of counts of Chalon (Petit 516, 741 [II:345–46; III:265]). After the death of Isabel of Chalon, Hugh-Rufus married Marguerite, daughter and heiress of Lord Walter of Navilly, whose first husband had died in 1166 (La Ferté 263 [pp. 205–6]; see also below, p. 326).

---

[10]Henry was first called a Cistercian by André Duchesne; *Histoire des roys, ducs, et comtes de Bourgogne et d'Arles* (Paris, 1619), p. 254. Hugh II also made gifts for Henry's soul to St.-Bénigne; Pérard, pp. 221–22.

[11]Orderic Vitalis, *Historia ecclesiastica* 13.15, ed. Chibnall, VI:430. Odo I may also have been the father of Agnes, wife of Raynald II of Grancey; see below, p. 332.

[12]Petit however calls her "de Magny-les-Villers," a community south of Dijon (II:43, n. 2).

[13]This charter was edited by Jules Marion, "Notice sur l'abbaye de La Bussière. Pièces justificatives," *Bibliothèque de l'École des chartes*, 4 (1842/43), 561, no. 1.

[14]Alberic de Trois-Fontaines, *Chronica* 1161, MGH SS XXIII:845. Petit 557 (II:362–63). H.-P.-C. de Chastellux, ed., *Histoire généalogique de la maison de Chastellux* (Auxerre, 1869), pp. 280–81; summarized as Petit 755 (III:269).

Odo II's brother Raymund married Agnes of Montpensier (Petit 357 [II:269]). Raymund died in 1156, on 28 June (Obit Lyon II:606; Petit 355 [II:268−69]; see also Plancher I.74 [pp. xlix−l], summarized as Petit 356 [II:269]). Agnes later married Lord Humbert IV of Beaujeu (Alberic de Trois-Fontaines, *Chronica* 1222, MGH SS XXIII:912; see also below, p. 293). Raymund and Agnes had a son, Hugh, who died young (Petit 357 [II:269]), and one daughter, Mathilda, who had four husbands, the most important of whom was Count Gui of Nevers (Petit 599 [II:383]; see also below, pp. 348−49). Three of Hugh II's sons become bishops, Robert, bishop of Autun (1140) ("Annales S. Benigni Divionensis" 1140, MGH SS V:44), Henry, first archdeacon and then bishop of Autun (1148−1170),[15] and Walter, archbishop of Besançon and bishop of Langres (1163−1179) ("Annales S. Benigni Divionensis" 1163, MGH SS V:45; Alberic de Trois-Fontaines, *Chronica* 1161, MGH SS XXIII:845). Of Hugh II's and Mathilda's daughters, Clemence married the lord of Donzy, probably Geoffrey III,[16] Mathilda married Lord William of Montpellier in 1156,[17] Sybil married King Roger of Sicily but died almost immediately afterward (Romoald, *Annales* 1148, MGH SS XIX:425), and Aremburg became a nun at Larrey in 1123 (Petit 198 [I:481]). Alberic de Trois-Fontaines says that one of the daughters married Hugh of Vaudemont and became the mother of Count Girard (*Chronica* 1161, MGH SS XXIII:845); it is not clear which daughter this might have been.

Odo II and his wife Maria, sister of Henry, count of Troyes,[18] had only one son, Duke Hugh III (1165−1192) (Petit 370 [II:275]).[19] Maria acted as regent of Burgundy between Odo II's death in 1162 and Hugh III's accession to power in 1165. Duke Hugh III went twice to the Holy Land. His first trip was in 1170 (Cîteaux/Marilier 192, 198 [pp. 155−56, 159−60]) and his second the Third Crusade, as indicated below.

Hugh III married twice. His first wife was Alix or Adelaide, the

[15]See the account of his election in the letter the dean and chapter wrote Suger in 1148 (while Suger was acting as regent of France); Letter 10, RHGF XV:487. See also Corbigny 4 (pp. 7−8). He had been archdeacon since at least 1142; Plancher I.66 (p. xliv).

[16]See the text quoted by Richard, "Sur les alliances familiales," p. 41, n. 4.

[17]*Liber instrumentorum memorialium: Cartulaire des Guillems de Montpellier*, ed. A. Germain (Montpellier, 1884−1886), pp. 263−65, no. 129. She and William had at least nine children: two sons named William, Gui, Raymund, Sybil, Wilma, Adelaide, Maria, and Clemence. Mathilda, who is called "duchess" in her oldest son's charters, had already died when her husband drew up his testament in 1172; ibid., pp. 160−61, 167−68, 184−89, 195−206, nos. 87, 90, 96, 99.

[18]H. d'Arbois de Jubainville, *Histoire des ducs et des comtes de Champagne*, III (Paris, 1861), 464, no. 144.

[19]Petit gives them two daughters as well, Mathilda, wife of Robert IV of Auvergne, and Alix, wife of Archembald of Bourbon; Petit II:134.

daughter of Duke Matthew of Lorraine and of Bertha, sister of Frederick Barbarossa (Alberic de Trois-Fontaines, *Chronica* 1193, MGH SS XXIII:871). He had married her by 1169 (Petit 484 [II:323–33]). They had Duke Odo III, who succeeded his father (1192–1218), and Alexander (Petit 891 [III:327]). In 1186 Hugh appeared in a charter for St.-Bénigne with sons Odo, who had just been knighted, and Alexander (Pérard, pp. 260–62; summarized as Petit 748 [III:267]). According to Alberic de Trois-Fontaines, how-ever, he divorced Alix as soon as a more eligible wife appeared. This was Beatrix Dauphina, countess of Albon, daughter of Count Dauphin of Albon, who was widowed in 1184 when her first husband, Count Alberic of Toulouse, died (Alberic de Trois-Fontaines, *Chronica* 1184, MGH SS XXIII:858; "Annales S. Benigni Divionensis" 1183, MGH SS V:46). By Beatrix, Hugh had Andrew Dauphin, born within the first year Hugh and Beatrix were married, and a daughter named Beatrix (Petit 683, 879 [III:319, 417–18]). Duke Hugh also had a daughter named Maria, who married Simon, lord of Semur (Arch. Allier, H 140). Hugh died on the Third Crusade (Alberic de Trois-Fontaines, *Chronica* 1191, MGH SS XXIII:868), and his son Odo III succeeded.

Odo III married twice, first Mathilda and then Alix of Vergy. Mathilda seems to have been of a royal family, for she is sometimes called *regina* (Plancher I.139 [pp. lxxxii–lxxxiii], summarized as Petit 902 [III:330]). He was divorced from Mathilda in 1195. When she promised the king not to marry again without his permission, she was designated as both *regina* and as countess of Flanders (Layettes 428 [I:181]). His second wife, Alix, was daughter of Lord Hugh of Vergy (Obit Lyon II:621) (see also below, p. 379). Odo and Alix had Duke Hugh IV. Odo's brother Alexander, who died in 1206, married Beatrix of Montaigu (Petit 1125–26 [III:405–6]). Alexander and Beatrix had a son named Odo, who married the daughter of Peter of Courtenay, count of Auxerre, and of Yolendis, his second wife (Alberic de Trois-Fontaines, *Chronica* 1218, MGH SS XXIII:906).

The Counts of Burgundy and Mâcon

Duke William the Pious, duke of Aquitaine in the late ninth and early tenth centuries, had also been count of Mâcon. His father had obtained the county in 880 during the wars between the Carolingians and the Bosonids (*Annales Fuldenses* 880, MGH SS I:394). In 893 the duke had his viscount there, Raculf, witness a charter (C 53 [I:61–63]). By the final years of the century, however, this Raculf was "known as count," *vocatus comes* (M 284 [pp. 169–70]). The hereditary counts of Mâcon, who began with Raculf's son-in-law, Alberic, seem to have taken the title of count at some point after the death of William II of Aquitaine. The key document for this family's history is a list of counts of Mâcon drawn up in the early twelfth century and preserved in the cartulary of the cathedral of Mâcon (M 7 [p. 6]). "First Alberic of Narbonne, who married the daughter of Viscount Raculf, made himself count after the death of Bishop Berno of Mâcon [928–937]. Then his son Leotold succeeded, and after him Count Leotold's son Alberic. When this second Alberic died, Count William married his wife." In fact, Alberic I may have called himself count while Bishop Berno was still alive, for some charters issued around 930 include both "Berno episcopus" and "Albericus comes" (M 8, 404, 496 [pp. 6–7, 232–33, 288–89]).

Alberic, known as "of Narbonne," may be the son of the viscount of Narbonne. In 911 the archbishop of Narbonne drew up a charter for Walcher and Alberic, the two sons of Maiolus, viscount of Narbonne, and his wife Raymunda.[20] Although some scholars have attempted to establish Viscount Maiolus's ancestors, the evidence is very tentative.[21] If Alberic, first count of Mâcon, is identical with Alberic, son of the viscount of Narbonne, he may have come north to Mâcon with the duke of Aquitaine.[22]

Alberic's wife Tolana is only known by name from some charters of her son (C 432, 976 [I:420–21; II:72–73]; M 488 [pp. 283–84]). Alberic had two sons, Leotold and Humbert (M 8, 38, 206, 404 [pp. 6–7, 31–32, 132, 232–33]).[23] He also had a daughter, named Attala or Tolana, after her mother (C 655 [I:609–10]). Humbert, the younger son, is usually called "of Salins" by modern scholars. He is probably the Humbert whose wife Wandelmodis, a *nobilis mulier*, made gifts to Bèze for his soul (Chron. St.-B., pp. 275–76). He had a son, also named Humbert, mentioned in 958 (C 1044 [II:137–38]), and a

---

[20]Cl. Devic and J. Vaissete, eds., *Histoire générale de Languedoc*, new ed. by Emile Mabille and Eduard Barry, V (Toulouse, 1875), cols. 130–31, no. 38. This identification was made by Mgr. Rameau, "Les comtes héréditaires de Mâcon," *Annales de l'Académie de Mâcon*, 3rd ser. 6 (1901), 128. Although I disagree on many points with this article, it is still valuable because of the author's extensive footnotes to the primary sources.

[21]See, for example, Jean Barruol, "L'influence de Saint Mayeul et de sa famille dans la renaissance méridionale du XIe siècle, d'après une documentation nouvelle du Cartulaire d'Apt," in *Cartulaire de l'Église d'Apt (835–1130?)*, ed. Noël Didier (Paris, 1967), pp. 67–83. Barruol increases the confusion by erroneously identifying Humbert II of Salins, discussed below, with Humbert I of Beaujeu.

[22]See also Jean-Pierre Poly, *La Provence et la société féodale, 879–1166* (Paris, 1976), p. 19 and n. 71.

[23]See also Theodor Schieffer, ed., *Die Urkunden der burgundischen Rudolfinger* (Munich: MGH, 1977), pp. 206–8, no. 64.

The Tenth-Century Counts of Mâcon

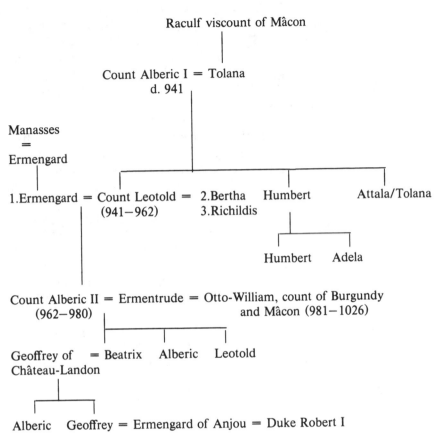

Raculf viscount of Mâcon

Count Alberic I = Tolana
d. 941

Manasses
=
Ermengard

1.Ermengard = Count Leotold = 2.Bertha   Humbert   Attala/Tolana
              (941–962)   3.Richildis

                                          Humbert   Adela

Count Alberic II = Ermentrude = Otto-William, count of Burgundy
   (962–980)   and Mâcon (981–1026)

Geoffrey of   = Beatrix   Alberic   Leotold
Château-Landon

Alberic   Geoffrey = Ermengard of Anjou = Duke Robert I

daughter named Adela, the mother of one Wandelmodis and the grandmother of Count Ingelbert I of Brienne.[24]

Leotold, oldest son of Alberic I, succeeded his father as count in 941. This is the date that Leotold, with his wife Bertha, made gifts for his parents' souls (M 488 [pp. 283–84]; C 625 [I:582–83]; see also C 655, 680 [I:609–10, 632–34]). Leotold married three times. His first wife, Ermengard, was the daughter of Manasses and Ermengard, apparently the Count Manasses who was connected to the family of the tenth-century dukes of Burgundy (C 432 [I:420–21]). Ermengard seems to have died soon, however, and Leotold married his second wife, Bertha, while his father was still alive (M 496 [pp. 288–89]). By 949 Leotold is recorded with a wife named Richildis (C 729, 753, 976 [I:685, 710–11; II:72–73]). Nothing is known of the families of his second two wives.[25]

Leotold's son Alberic II was the son of his father's first wife, Ermengard (C 1124 [II:215–16]; M 76, 488 [pp. 63, 283–84]). Leotold last appears in a charter in 961 (C 1100 [II:193–94]), and in 962 Alberic II made gifts for his parents' souls (C 1124 [II:215–16]). Before 971 he married Ermentrude, who later married Otto-William; Otto-William first appears as count around 981, so Alberic must have died by that date (C 1291, 1580 [II:368, 624–25]). Alberic and Ermentrude had at least three children, although the two boys, Alberic and Leotold, disappear from the records along with their father (Tournus, pp. 116–18; M 111 [p. 86—mistakenly assigned to Alberic I rather than Alberic II by the editor]; C 1291 [II:368]).[26] Alberic II's daughter Beatrix married Geoffrey of Château-Landon, in

---

[24]"Genealogiae comitum Andegavensium" 5, ed. Halphen and Poupardin, p. 249. It is possible that Berard of Beaujeu's wife Wandelmodis was also a daughter of Humbert I of Salins; see below, p. 289, n. 78.

[25]Maurice Chaume makes the unsubstantiated suggestion that Bertha was a daughter of Hugh the Black; *Les origines du duché de Bourgogne*, I (Dijon, 1925), 437, n. 3. But in his family tree of the relatives of Hugh the Black, he makes Richildis instead Hugh's daughter; ibid., p. 545. Elsewhere he suggests that Richildis might have "issued from one of the many sisters of Louis IV"; ibid., p. 438, n. 3. Szabolcs de Vajay suggests that Bertha was a daughter of Warner, viscount of Troyes; "À propos de la 'Guerre de Bourgogne': Note sur les successions de Bourgogne et de Mâcon aux Xe et XIe siècles," *Annales de Bourgogne*, 34 (1962), 160, n. 1.

[26]At one time I doubted the existence of these two sons; Constance B. Bouchard, "The Origins of the French Nobility: A Reassessment," *American Historical Review*, 86 (1981), 518, n. 50. This was because I had not yet seen the Tournus documents in which two individuals named Alberic and Leotold sign a charter after Alberic II and before Ermentrude; they must be their sons. The editor dates these charters 971; they are given "in the twentieth year of King Lothair," so 974 is more likely. Vajay argues, without evidence, that Alberic became abbot of St.-Paul of Besançon and Leotold archbishop of Besançon; "'Guerre de Bourgogne,'" p. 162, n. 3. It is possible, however, that they entered the church, since in one charter of Alberic and Ermentrude the first witness was Leotold, presumably their son, and he signed as "subdeacon"; Tournus, p. 118.

the Gâtinais, and had two sons, Alberic and Geoffrey. The younger Geoffrey married Ermengard of Anjou, daughter of Count Fulk Nerra and the heiress of the county of Anjou after the death of her brother Geoffrey Martel in 1060.[27]

The basic source for the succession to the county of Mâcon after the death of Alberic II is the same genealogy from the cathedral cartulary which lists the tenth-century counts. According to this source, "Count William" married Alberic II's widow and succeeded him (M 7 [p. 6]). This is Otto-William (called both Otto and William, as well as *Otto cognomento Guillelmo* in the sources), who ruled Mâcon from around 981 until his death in 1026.[28]

Otto-William was the son of Adalbert, last king of Italy, who was driven out by Otto I in 962 (MGH DD regum et imperatorum Germaniae III [1957], 381, no. 305; Raoul Glaber, *Historia* 3.2 [pp. 56–57]). His mother was named Gerberge, as his own documents testify; after Adalbert's death, she married Duke Henry of Burgundy, brother of Hugh Capet. The duke adopted Otto-William; he had no legitimate sons of his own. Otto-William's double name may indeed date from this adoption; it seems most likely that his original name was William—his grandmother was named Willa, and a cousin was also named William—and that he took the Otto in remembrance of Duke Henry's late brother Odo. Henry also named one of his illegitimate sons Odo, and he himself is referred to as Odo in at least one source.[29] Designated as heir by his stepfather, Otto-William adopted the title of "count of Burgundy," though there was no county of that name, only the county of Mâcon and apparently Otto-William's expectation of inheriting the duchy of Burgundy.[30]

There has been a great deal of scholarly controversy over the family

[27]Fulk Réchin, "Fragmentum historiae Andegavensis," and "Genealogiae comitum Andegavensium," both ed. Halphen and Poupardin, in *Chroniques des comtes d'Anjou*, pp. 232, 249. M. Guérard, ed., *Cartulaire de l'église Notre-Dame de Paris*, I (Paris, 1850), 326–27, no. 19. See also Bouchard, "Origins of the Nobility," p. 518 and n. 51. This Ermengard of Anjou is the woman for whom Duke Robert I repudiated his wife; see above, p. 257.

[28]Scholars have sometimes been confused by a reference to a "William Dirty Beard," count of Mâcon at the beginning of the eleventh century; see, for example, Rameau, "Comtes de Mâcon," p. 139. This individual, found only in the chronicle of Ademar of Chabannes, is Otto-William in garbled form; Ademar of Chabannes, *Chronicon* 3.50, ed. Jules Chavanon (Paris, 1897), p. 173. Ademar is a notoriously unreliable chronicler; see John Gillingham, "Ademar of Chabannes and the History of Aquitaine in the Reign of Charles the Bald," in *Charles the Bald: Court and Kingdom*, ed. Margaret Gibson and Janet Nelson, British Archaeological Reports, International Series 101 (Oxford, 1981), pp. 3–14.

[29]Flodoard, *Annales* 965, ed. Ph. Lauer (Paris, 1905), p. 156.

[30]The title *comes Burgundiae* may have meant simply a count within the duchy of Burgundy. Leotold, count of Mâcon, had been called *Burgundiae comes* in a royal charter of 955; *Recueil des actes de Lothaire et de Louis V, rois de France (954–987)*, ed. Louis Halphen and Ferdinand Lot (Paris, 1908), p. 16, no. 7.

The Eleventh- and Early Twelfth-Century Counts of Burgundy and Mâcon

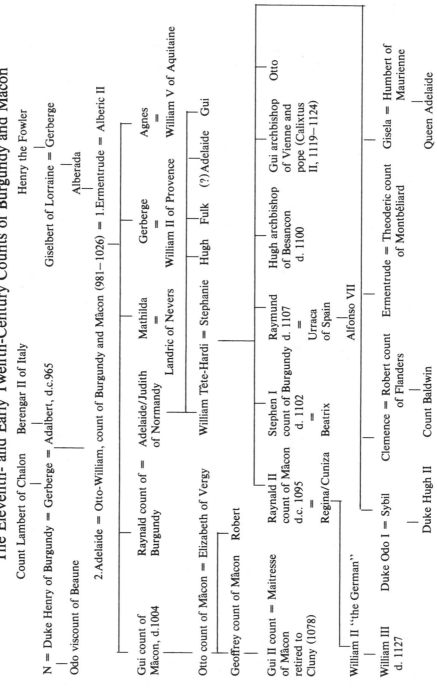

of his mother, Gerberge. I believe that she was daughter of Lambert, first hereditary count of Chalon; a *vita* of Lambert's son Hugh of Chalon said that his sister married the duke of Burgundy, and, while this sister is not named, it seems probable that Gerberge is meant (see also below, pp. 310–11).[31] Many scholars, however, have objected that, if Otto-William had no hereditary claim to Mâcon, his accession to the title merely through marriage to the widow of the last hereditary count would amount to a usurpation, something they seem eager to disprove.[32] Since Adalbert, king of Italy, had no hereditary claim to Mâcon, scholars have attempted to prove that Gerberge did. And there is a document that seems to suggest something of the sort. Sometime in the 1020s Otto-William's grandson Otto, count of Mâcon, issued a charter in which he recalled the pious generosity of his *pater* Gui, *avus* Otto-William, and *atavus* Leotold, count of Mâcon (C 2712 [III:735–36]). I myself would translate *atavus* as "great-grandfather-in-law" (since Otto's grandmother Ermentrude had been daughter-in-law of Count Leotold before marrying Otto's grandfather) or more generally as "predecessor." Several scholars however have used this term to argue that Gerberge was related to the counts of Mâcon. Most have made her a daughter of Leotold (translating *atavus* as great-great-grandfather), though Vajay prefers to make her a granddaughter of Leotold (translating *atavus* in its strictly classical sense as great-great-great-grandfather).[33] Vajay claims that documents, now lost but still in existence in the seventeenth century, gave Count Leotold a son Otto, whom Vajay would make Gerberge's father; according to him, Gerberge named her son Otto-William for her own father. As evidence for these "lost documents," Vajay cites a seventeenth-century manuscript of Pierre Chifflet. In this manuscript, however, Chifflet did not cite documents but only speculated about the family tree of the counts of Mâcon, and it is clear from the context that he was again using this same reference in C 2712 to an *atavus* Leotold

---

[31]Vajay makes the curious suggestion that Otto-William's son Gui married a sister of Hugh of Chalon. He bases this suggestion on the fact that Hugh of Chalon called Gui's son his *nepos* (Paray 184 [pp. 91–92]; C 2729 [III:752–54]). However, this document seems rather to indicate that Gui's son was the great-grandson of Hugh's sister and thus Hugh's great-nephew (*nepos* can mean great-nephew as well as nephew). Vajay, believing that Gui married a sister of Hugh of Chalon, denies that Gerberge was the sister of Hugh of Chalon, saying Gui "would not have married the sister of his own grandmother!" This argument however works the other way; since the sources attest that Gerberge was Hugh of Chalon's sister, Vajay's suggested wife for Gui must be rejected. Vajay, " 'Guerre de Bourgogne,' " pp. 160–61 and n. 4.

[32]See, for example, Vajay, " 'Guerre de Bourgogne,' " p. 153.

[33]Vajay, " 'Guerre de Bourgogne,' " pp. 159–60; see also p. 155, n. 1. The classical procession of ancestors was *pater, avus, proavus, abavus, atavus*. But I see no reason to hold the eleventh-century Count Otto to a knowledge of the exact terminology; I have seen medieval Latin authors use *proavus, abavus,* and *atavus* more or less indiscriminately for ancestors more distant than a grandfather.

(which he here translated as "great-grandfather") as the source for his speculation that Leotold had a son Otto, grandfather of the Count Otto who drew up this charter.[34]

The question of Gerberge and her family is further complicated by the attempt by some scholars to argue that Duke Henry married twice, first Gerberge and then a woman named Gersendis. Henry does indeed appear in the documents with a wife named Gersendis at the very end of the tenth century (Autun/St.-Symphorien 15, 17 [pp. 37–39, 42–44]). In a charter for Paray-le-monial, also from the very end of the tenth century, Duke Henry's wife is known as Garlindis (Paray 193 [pp. 97–98]). But it seems most likely that these are only variant spellings of Gerberge. Since Otto-William made gifts for his mother Gerberge's soul only at the beginning of the eleventh century, around the same time that Duke Henry died, one can conclude that she had lived until then; when her death was recorded on 11 December, she was described as "wife of Duke Henry," not "first wife" or anything similar (St.-B. II.228 [pp. 24–25]; Chron. St.-B., pp. 162–64; Obit. Sens III:246). The only other source to suggest that Henry may have had two wives is a satirical poem written about Landric of Nevers, in which there is an obscure reference to a wife who felt distressed and "sought Gascony." But it is difficult to draw accurate family trees from satirical literature; furthermore, the wording of the poem seems to suggest that it was Landric's wife, not Henry's, who was so distressed that she fled south, though Henry does appear in that part of the poem. All scholars, however, have taken this obscure wife to be Henry's. A few have therefore made Gerberge come from Gascony, but more commonly scholars have assumed that the poem refers to Henry's "second" wife, and that "Gersendis" was thus from Gascony.[35]

There has also been some question about the family of Ermentrude, wife of Alberic II and of Otto-William.[36] Raoul Glaber says that she

[34]Vajay, "'Guerre de Bourgogne,'" p. 160. BN, MS lat. 9866, fols. 46r–v. Chifflet discussed the presumptive "Otto son of Leotold" as a suggestion of Jacobus Severtius, the seventeenth-century historian of Mâcon—who also based his suggestion on C 2712. Chifflet's own reading of the documents led him—like me—to believe Gerberge was a daughter of Lambert, count of Chalon, not of any count of Mâcon.

[35]Adalbero of Laon, *Rhythmus satyricus* 14–15, ed. Claude Hohl, "Le comte Landri de Nevers dans l'histoire et dans la Geste de *Girart de Roussillon*," in *La chanson de geste et le mythe carolingien. Mélanges René Louis* (St.-Père-sous-Vézelay, 1982), p. 794. Hohl confuses the issue even further by saying at one point that Henry divorced Gersendis in order to marry Gerberge, when in fact the evidence indicates that, if Henry did marry a Gersendis, it was only after Gerberge's death; ibid., p. 783.

[36]Some scholars, including Vajay, have been bothered by the appearance of Otto-William's grandson Otto in documents around 1005, only twenty-five years or so after Alberic II of Mâcon died and Otto-William married his widow (C 2736 [III:759–61]). Vajay therefore concludes that Otto-William's wife Ermentrude was a different person than Alberic II's wife Ermentrude—ignoring the Mâcon cathedral genealogy that says they are the same—and puts Otto-William's marriage appreciably before 981; Vajay,

was the sister of Bruno, bishop of Langres (Raoul Glaber, *Historia* 3.2 [pp. 56–57]). She and Bruno also had a brother named Giselbert, a count.[37] Scholars have called this family "of Roucy," following the work of Ferdinand Lot at the end of the last century.[38] Lot suggested that Ermentrude must be the daughter of Raynald of Roucy because she named her own son Raynald, an argument that is scarcely convincing. All that can definitely be said of Ermentrude is that she and her brothers were the children of Alberada, daughter of Duke Giselbert of Lorraine and of Gerberge, the sister of Emperor Otto I. Since Raynald of Roucy is well known to tenth-century chroniclers, their silence on his marriage would have to be considered very odd if he had indeed married such a well-placed woman as Alberada. Instead, the name of Alberada's husband, her children's father, must remain unknown.[39]

Otto-William and Ermentrude had at least five children. Four are listed by Raoul Glaber: three girls who married the counts of Nevers, of Poitou, and of Provence, and Raynald, who married Adelaide, daughter of Duke Richard of Normandy (Raoul Glaber, *Historia* 3.2 [pp. 56–57]). A fifth is known from Otto-William's charters, Gui, who died in 1004, predeceasing his father. Gui left a son, Otto, who succeeded his grandfather as count of Mâcon (Chron. St.-B., p. 181). Gui was probably the older son; he appeared in charters with his father in 997 and 999, and he was also the only child to appear with his parents in a charter from 1002 (C 2387, 2484, 2552 [III:484–85, 562–66, 617]; Paray 213 [pp. 111–14]). Some scholars assign them a sixth child, Bruno, the *nepos* of Bishop Bruno who served in the

---

" 'Guerre de Bourgogne,' " pp. 161–62. However, Otto could quite easily have been six or so by 1005 if his father was born in 982. Just because Otto appeared in the documents does not mean he had attained his majority; indeed, the fact that he only married ten or more years later, as indicated below, suggests he was quite young when his father died. Vajay cited a charter of Mâcon cathedral that refers to Otto as *adolescens comes* to argue that Otto must have been in his teens by 1004 or 1005 (M 487 [p. 283]), but *adolescens* does not mean "adolescent" in the modern sense; the scribe doubtless used the term to mean "the younger," or "junior," to distinguish Otto from his grandfather, Count Otto [William]. Since Otto's father had died in 1004, it was reasonable that he, as the heir, start appearing in documents then.

[37]Council of St.-Basle [991] 5, MGH SS III:661.

[38]Ferdinand Lot, *Les derniers Carolingiens* (Paris, 1891), p. 10 and n. 5.

[39]For Alberada, see Siegfried of Gorze, letter to Poppo of Stablo, edited by Wilhelm von Giesebrecht, *Geschichte der deutschen Kaiserzeit*, 5th ed., II (Leipzig, 1885), 714–18; and Flodoard, *Annales*, ed. Lauer, pp. 158–59. See also Bouchard, "Origins of the Nobility," p. 518, n. 49. It is possible that Alberada's husband is not given in any source because she never married, and her children were illegitimate. She certainly named her sons for her own relatives rather than a husband's: Giselbert for her father, Duke Giselbert of Lorraine, and Bruno for her maternal uncle, Archbishop Bruno of Cologne. Ermentrude may be named for the sister of her stepfather, Louis IV of France. Even Ermentrude's son Raynald may have been named for Reginald of Lorraine, Duke Giselbert's father.

cathedral chapter of Langres under him (Chron. St.-B., p. 295). It is not clear, however, whether this nephew was the son of Otto-William and Ermentrude or of Ermentrude's brother Giselbert—or perhaps was related in some other way. Of the daughters of Otto-William and Ermentrude, Agnes, wife of William V, duke of Aquitaine and count of Poitou, is known to be their daughter because of her own charters (C 2742 [III:765−66]). The daughter who married Count Landric of Nevers was named Mathilda (C 2811 [IV:13−14]) (see also below, p. 343). The daughter who married the count of Provence was named Gerberge.[40] After Duke Henry of Burgundy died in 1002, on 15 October (Obit. Sens III:242), Otto-William fought unsuccessfully against the king for control of the duchy but retained a good deal of territory, if not the title of duke.

Ermentrude predeceased her husband. She must have been at least eight years older than he, for she and her first child appear in the documents around 971, when Otto-William was probably still quite young. Bearing three children to Alberic II of Mâcon and five or six to Otto-William must have been wearying. After Ermentrude's death, Otto-William married a woman named Adelaide (M 471, 490 [pp. 271, 284−85]; C 2694 [IV:721−22]).[41] It is possible that she is the same as the Adelaide-Blanche, sister of Count Geoffrey Greymantle of Anjou, who had married Count William I of Provence, bearing William II, whom Otto-William's daughter Gerberge married, and also Queen Constance of France. The evidence for such an identification is that the pope, in addressing Otto-William and his family in 1016, referred to "Adelaide-Blanche," countess, and her ward (*nurui*) Countess Gerberge (Benedict VIII, Letter 16, PL CXXXIX:1603). Otto-William may then have married his second wife after they had both been widowed and at the same time as their children married. The countess Adelaide was referred to as "regali progenie orta" in the obituary of St.-Pierre of Mâcon (Obit. Lyon II:492).

When Otto-William died in 1026 (*Annales S. Benigni Divionensis* 1026, MGH SS V:41), Raynald succeeded him as count of Burgundy and Otto succeeded as count of Mâcon. According to the genealogy of the counts of Mâcon in the cathedral cartulary, the county of Mâcon went first to Otto, then to Geoffrey, then Gui, and then, after him, to Raynald, son of William (M 7 [p. 6]). Otto was son of Gui,

---

[40]*Cartulaire de l'abbaye de Saint-Victor de Marseille*, ėd. M. Guérard, I (Paris, 1857), 158−59, 626−27, 641−42, nos. 133, 630, 649. Benedict VIII, Letter 16, PL CXXXIX:1603.

[41]Rameau incorrectly calls Ermentrude and Adelaide the same person; "Comtes de Mâcon," p. 141.

Otto-William's oldest son, as indicated above. His mother's name is not known.[42]

Count Otto, Otto-William's grandson, may have had a brother William; in one charter he issued for the cathedral of Mâcon, there is a "brother William" (S. Willelmi fratris ejus) among the signers, although it is not entirely clear whether Otto's brother or the brother of Viscount Hugh is meant (M 268 [p. 161]).[43] Otto married Elizabeth, the sister of Humbert of Vergy, archdeacon of Autun, and later bishop of Paris under the name of Enzelin (see below, p. 375). Elizabeth first appears with her husband in charters that can be dated no earlier than 1016 (M 268, 464 [pp. 161, 266–67]; C 2713 [III:736]), and they had had two children by 1023. When Humbert of Vergy and his sister established a church in the castle of Vergy in 1023 (Petit 19, 23 [I:360–61, 363–64; the first charter is also printed as GC IV:77–78, no. 41]; cf. Autun/Église 1.14 [pp. 22–24]), Elizabeth's sons Robert and Geoffrey signed the foundation charter.[44]

Geoffrey, son of Otto, succeeded his father as count. He is sometimes said to have married a woman named Beatrix, though I have seen no direct evidence of this. He had a son named Gui II, who first appeared in a charter with his father in 1031, while his grandfather Otto was still count (C 2852 [IV:52–53]). Gui II was the last count of Mâcon of his line. He married a woman named Maitresse but had no children and retired to Cluny in 1078 (M 11 [pp. 10–11]; C 3528, 3610 [IV:650–51, 770–71]). Maitresse may have entered Marcigny; there is a nun with this rather unusual name in the house's necrology.[45] Maitresse may be the sister of one Wigo (apparently of the

---

[42]Chaume makes Gui's wife a daughter of Beatrix, the daughter of Alberic II of Mâcon, and of her husband, Geoffrey of Château-Landon; Origines de Bourgogne, I:465, n. 2, 533. He does this in order to give Gui's son, Count Otto, an atavus Count Leotold (which he translates as great-great-grandfather). The great advantage of this hypothesis is that it explains Count Otto's reference to an atavus Leotold without having to deny that Gerberge was the daughter of the count of Chalon. It would have made good political sense for Otto-William to marry his oldest son to the daughter of a woman who might have considered herself heiress to Mâcon. This hypothesis would also explain why Count Otto named his own heir Geoffrey. The chief difficulty with this hypothesis, however, is that Gui was Beatrix's half brother.

[43]In another charter from about the same time, one William and his wife Gertrude made a gift to Mâcon with Countess Elizabeth, Otto's wife, among the witnesses; M 220 (pp. 138–39).

[44]The editor of the Cluny cartularies was confused by a charter of Otto-William and Adelaide, his second wife, in which Otto-William referred to his son Raynald and grandson (nepos) Otto. The editor thought the charter referred to Count Otto rather than to Otto-William; C 2694 (IV:721–22 and n. 4). He therefore tried to give Otto another wife, named Adelaide, in addition to Elizabeth, and a son named Raynald by her, although the nepos Otto (which he translated as nephew) further confused him.

[45]Maitresse's conversion was discovered by members of the Institut für Frühmittelalterforschung in Münster in their study of the Cluniac necrologies. Rameau suggests that Gui and Maitresse had sons named Gui and Ponce, who entered the cloister with their parents; "Comtes de Mâcon," p. 155.

family of the viscounts of Lyon) mentioned in a charter at Cluny tentatively dated from the second half of the eleventh century. In that
charter the "count of Mâcon" gave up his claims to some property
that Wigo had given Cluny, but which the count had claimed after
marrying Wigo's sister (C 3577 [IV:711–13]).

While four generations of counts were at least titular counts of
Mâcon between the beginning of the eleventh century and 1078 (Gui,
Otto, Geoffrey, Gui), there were only two contemporary counts of
Burgundy, Raynald I, son of Otto-William, and his son William. Raynald gained extensive control in the kingdom of Burgundy, east of the
Saône, after the death of the last king, Rudolph III, in 1032. While
this kingdom was supposedly absorbed into the empire at this point, in
practice the German kings paid no attention to Burgundy until the
twelfth century. While Raynald and his descendants called themselves
"counts of Burgundy," there was not yet a county of Burgundy per
se; they were rather men who held the title of count and who also
held power in Burgundy. Raynald was known simply as "count of the
region" in a charter for Bèze (Chron. St.-B., p. 299), and, in the time
of his son William, the area east of the Saône was sometimes known
just as "Count William's county" (C 3450 [IV:559–60]).

Raynald had married Adelaide (also called Judith in some sources),
daughter of Richard, duke of Normandy.[46] Because Richard of Normandy had been one of the king's chief allies in the Burgundian wars,
the marriage of his daughter to Otto-William's son may have been
part of the reconciliation at the end of the war—to which the marriage
of King Robert to Constance of Provence, the daughter of Otto-
William's second wife, may also perhaps be attributed. In addition to
their heir, William, who is known as William Tête-Hardi to modern
scholars, Raynald and Adelaide had a son named Gui, who unsuccessfully tried to challenge his cousin William the Conqueror for control
of Normandy.[47] They also had sons named Hugh and Fulk, known
only from one mention each (Beatrix 174–75 [pp. 202–5]; the first
charter is also Flavigny 14 [pp. 33–35; Collenot, pp. 92–93]).[48] They
may also have been the parents of the Adelaide who married Geoffrey
II of Semur and who is called "daughter of count Raynald" (Marcigny
1 [p. 1]), unless she was daughter of Count Raynald of Nevers.

---

[46]The Norman chronicles call her Adelaide; William of Jumièges, *Gesta normannorum
ducum* 5.16, ed. Jean Marx (Paris, 1914), p. 95; Orderic Vitalis, *Historia ecclesiastica*
7.15, 12.9, ed. Chibnall, IV:82; VI:210. She is known as Adelaide in a charter of 1023;
C 2782 (III:807–8). A charter of 1037 [misdated 1043 by Collenot] calls her Judith;
Flavigny 14 (pp. 33–35) [Collenot, pp. 92–93]; printed as Beatrix 174 (pp. 202–4).

[47]Orderic Vitalis, *Historia ecclesiastica* 7.15, ed. Chibnall, IV:82.

[48]It is possible that Fulk is identical with Fulk of Joux, whom Herman of Laon calls
princeps in Burgundia, and who married one of the seven sisters of Eblo II of Roucy;
Herman of Laon, "De miraculis S. Mariae Laudunensis" 1, PL CLVI:965–66.

William Tête-Hardi became count of Burgundy after his father's death; he was powerful enough that Pope Gregory VII called on him in 1074, along with several other princes, to help defend Saint Peter.[49] William took over Mâcon in 1078 when his cousin Gui entered Cluny; his oldest son, Raynald, took the title of count of Mâcon during his father's lifetime (C 3592, 3610, 3614 [IV:748–49, 770–71, 776]). William married a woman named Stephanie, whom most scholars have erroneously called "of Vienne." The confusion arises from charters in which counts of Burgundy and Mâcon are called counts of Vienne. All these charters, however, date from the second half of the twelfth century. Girard, called count of Vienne from 1168 on, is the first of the family to be given this title (Tournus, pp. 168–69; Beatrix 116, 139 [pp. 134, 154]). In the eleventh century the county of Vienne was held by the archbishop of Vienne, to whom Rudolph III of Burgundy had given it in 1023.[50] An epitaph of Stephanie referred to her as being "countess of the Allobrogians," but this term was used in the tenth and eleventh century simply to mean Burgundians, not specifically men of Vienne (Beatrix, p. 207). Lambert, count of Chalon in the later tenth century, is in fact referred to in one charter as "count of the Allobrogians" as well (Fleury 51 [pp. 127–30]).

William Tête-Hardi and Stephanie had a large family, of at least ten children, who first begin to appear in the documents with their parents in the 1080s. Of the boys, Raynald II succeeded his father as count of Mâcon, Stephen I took the title of count of Burgundy, Raymund married the daughter of the Spanish king, Hugh and Gui became archbishops (at Besançon and Vienne respectively), and Otto is known only from brief mentions. Of the girls, Sybil married the duke of Burgundy, Clemence married the count of Flanders, Ermentrude married the count of Montbéliard, and Gisela married the count of Maurienne. Details on these offspring are given below.[51]

Raynald II, according to the genealogy of the counts at the cathedral

[49]Caspar, ed., *Das Register Gregors VII*, pp. 70–71, no. 1.46.

[50]Schieffer, ed., *Die Urkunden der Rudolfinger*, pp. 281–83, no. 115. Szabolcs de Vajay makes the mistaken suggestion that Stephanie's mother was from Lorraine and her father from Poitou; "Bourgogne, Lorraine et Espagne au XIe siècle: Étiennette, dite de Vienne, comtesse de Bourgogne," *Annales de Bourgogne*, 32 (1960), 234–35, 247–48. The reason for bringing in Lorraine, according to Vajay, is that a seventeenth-century manuscript written by Pierre Chifflet refers to one of Stephanie's sons as being "both Burgundian and Lotharingian"; BN, MS lat. 9866, fol. 49r. In fact, Chifflet refers to one of Stephanie's *grandsons* as being both Lotharingian and Burgundian, scarcely surprising since his mother (Stephanie's daughter) was Burgundian and his father of the Lotharingian family of Montbéliard.

[51] Vajay gives them two more daughters, Bertha, the fourth and final wife of Alfonso VI of Castile, and Stephanie, wife of Lambert Franco of Royans; Vajay, "Bourgogne, Lorraine et Espagne," pp. 233–34, n. 1. He must be mistaken about Bertha at least, because the Spanish sources call her an Italian; see Reilly, *The Kingdom of León-Castilla*, p. 25.

of Mâcon, was succeeded in this title first by Stephen, his brother, and then by William "the German" (M 7 [p. 6]). This is as far as the genealogy extends. Raynald II married Regina, daughter of Cono, count of Neuchâtel; she entered Marcigny in 1088, apparently while her husband was still alive (Marcigny 30 bis [pp. 26—28]; C 3862 [V:212]; cf. C 3665 [V:14]). Regina is also called Cuniza in a charter of her son William from 1095 (Marcigny 102 [pp. 73—74]); Raynald had died by this year. William, his heir, was probably called "the German" because he was raised in the country of his mother's family. William the German called himself count of both Burgundy and Mâcon in 1106 and 1107 (C 3841, 3862, 3867 [V:200, 212—13, 217—18]). He had a son named William (M 590 [p. 357]), who was alive during the reign of Bishop Joceran of Mâcon (1122—1143), but the line ends with him. Young William III was probably the Burgundian Count William whom Anselm of Gembloux said was murdered in a church in 1127, at the instigation of demons ("Anselmi continuatio Sigeberti" 1127, MGH SS VI:380).

Raymund, brother of Raynald II, married Urraca, daughter of Alfonso VI of Castile, and became count of Galicia. This marriage may have taken place around 1087, when Raymund seems to have come to Spain for the first time with a group of Burgundians. Raymund and Urraca had Alfonso VII as well as a girl named Sancia (C 3900, 3970 [V:250—53, 327—28]).[52] Raymund died in 1107 (St.-B. II.420 [p. 198]).

The three brothers Raymund, Stephen, and Hugh, archbishop of Besançon, called themselves sons of the "most noble count" William toward the end of the eleventh century (St.-B. II.365 [pp. 143—44]). The pope Calixtus II, who had begun his ecclesiastical career as Gui, archbishop of Vienne, was son of William Tête-Hardi, according to Orderic Vitalis. Calixtus referred in his own letters to his brother Hugh, archbishop of Besançon, who died on Crusade in 1100. A contemporary chronicle also speaks of Calixtus as brother of Clemence, countess of Flanders, and of Stephen, count of Burgundy.[53] Otto is known only from a charter in which William Tête-Hardi gave a *villa* to the cathedral of Besançon, with the consent of his sons, Raynald,

---

[52]For the date 1087, see Bernard F. Reilly, "Santiago and Saint Denis: The French Presence in Eleventh-Century Spain," *Catholic Historical Review*, 54 (1968), 473—74; and *The Kingdom of León-Castilla*, pp. 13—16. See also Evelyn S. Procter, *Curia and Cortes in León and Castile, 1072—1295* (Cambridge, 1980), p. 11.

[53]Orderic Vitalis, *Historia ecclesiastica* 12.9, ed. Chibnall, VI:210. Calixtus II, Letters 15, 170, PL CLXIII:1107, 1237. "Sigiberti continuatio Premonstratensis" 1119, MGH SS VI:448.

Raymund, Hugh, and Stephen, and in memory of his late son Otto (Beatrix 175 [pp. 204–5]).

Ermentrude called herself daughter of Count William in a charter of 1105 in which she gave Cluny a church for the soul of her husband, Theoderic, count of Montbéliard, his parents, Louis and Sophia, and their own children, Louis, William, Hugh, Frederick, Rainard, and Theoderic (C 2830 [V:190–92]). Clemence, daughter of William Tête-Hardi of Burgundy, according to a "Genealogia" of the counts of Flanders and some letters of her brother Calixtus II, married Robert, count of Flanders, and bore his heir Baldwin ("Genealogia comitum Flandriae Bertiniana," MGH SS IX:306; Calixtus II, Letter 36, PL CLXIII:1127–29). Calixtus II was also the uncle of Queen Adelaide, wife of Louis VII, according to Louis's biographer Suger. Adelaide was daughter of Humbert, count of Maurienne,[54] and his wife Gisela, Calixtus's sister. Sybil married Duke Odo I of Burgundy, brother and heir of Duke Hugh I (there has been confusion in the scholarly literature about her; sometimes she is erroneously called Mathilda).[55]

The entire generation of the sons of William Tête-Hardi died not long after he did, Stephen on Crusade.[56] Gui, archbishop of Vienne, acted as regent of Burgundy until Stephen's sons grew up.[57] These sons also took the title of count of Mâcon after the death of William the German and his son William III (M 590 [p. 357]).

Stephen I had married a woman named Beatrix (Beatrix 101 [pp. 119–20]) and had at least three sons and a daughter. Of his sons, Raynald III was count of Burgundy, and William IV was count of Mâcon. William, like his father, went to the Holy Land, where he distinguished himself on the Second Crusade—and, unlike many Crusaders, returned home alive.[58] Humbert was archbishop of Besançon (1134–1162) (Beatrix 111 [pp. 128–31]). Stephen's daughter Elizabeth married Hugh, count of Champagne, and bore Odo of Champlitte, whom the count repudiated as his heir (Alberic de

[54]Suger, *Vita Ludovici Grossi regis* 27, ed. Henri Waquet (Paris, 1929), p. 204. Orderic Vitalis, *Historia ecclesiastica* 11.35, ed. Chibnall, VI:154.

[55]For Sybil, see Jean Richard's detailed discussion of the evidence and how some scholars have gone astray, "Sur les alliances familiales," pp. 34–46.

[56]Stephen left for the Holy Land in 1101 and was killed there in battle in 1102; Fulcher of Chartres, *Historia Hierosolymitana (1095–1127)* 2.16, 2.19, ed. Heinrich Hagenmeyer (Heidelberg, 1913), pp. 430, 433; Orderic Vitalis, *Historia ecclesiastica* 10.20, ed. Chibnall, V:324–26. Chibnall incorrectly calls Stephen Raynald II's son rather than brother. Orderic, perhaps confused by Alberic of Aix, who consistently called Stephen a duke rather than a count, makes Stephen into two people, Duke Stephen and Count Stephen; Alberic of Aix, "Historia Hierosalymitanae expeditionis" 8.6, 22, 41, PL CLXVI:608, 617, 623.

[57]Mary Stroll, "New Perspectives on the Struggle between Gui of Vienne and Henry V," *Archivum historiae pontificiae*, 18 (1980), 103–4.

[58]Odo of Deuil, *De profectione Ludovici VII in Orientem* 6, ed. Virginia Gingerick Berry (New York, 1948), p. 110.

The Twelfth-Century Counts of Burgundy and Mâcon

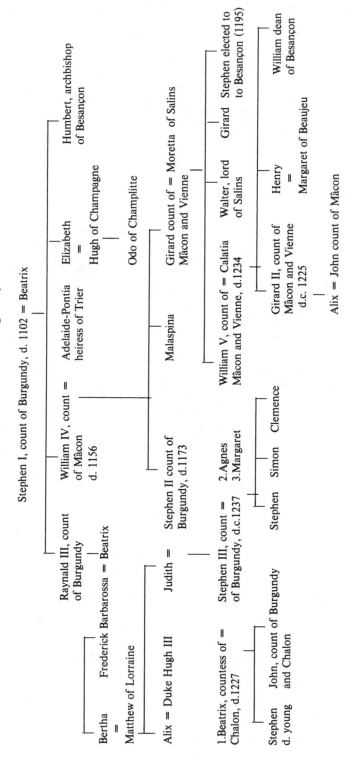

Trois Fontaines, *Chronica* 1125, MGH SS XXIII:826). In charters of the archbishop of Besançon, Odo of Champlitte is called the nephew of Count William IV of Burgundy and of Count Raynald III.[59] Odo of Champlitte married the niece of the viscount of Dijon (see below, p. 326).

The name of Raynald III's wife is not known.[60] Raynald had no sons, only a daughter named Beatrix. Raynald died in 1148 (BN, Coll. Baluze 144, fol. 105r), and his younger brother William IV acted as count of Burgundy as well as count of Mâcon, officially in his niece's name.[61] But in 1156, after William died (apparently in the Holy Land, M 623 [pp. 377–78]), Frederick Barbarossa married Beatrix and claimed the county of Burgundy—essentially the old kingdom of Burgundy—for himself (Beatrix 56 [pp. 88–89]; Alberic de Trois-Fontaines, *Chronica* 1190, MGH SS XXIII:863). He made Otto, his son by Beatrix, count palatine of Burgundy (Beatrix 55 [pp. 86–87]).[62]

However, Beatrix's cousins, the sons of William IV, also continued to call themselves counts of Burgundy. William's son Stephen II appears in a charter with the title of count of Burgundy shortly after Frederick and Beatrix married; they appear with him in the same charter (Beatrix 56 [pp. 88–89]). William had married Adelaide-Pontia, the heiress of Trier, daughter of Lord Theobold of Trier and his wife Adelaide (Beatrix 108, 109 [pp. 127–28]). According to Alberic de Trois-Fontaines, Adelaide-Pontia was the widow of Theobold, lord of Rougemont (*Chronica* 1190, MGH SS XXIII:863), though Alberic must be mistaken, for Theobold was still alive after Adelaide married William (BN, Coll. Baluze 144, fol. 105r); he may have confused Adelaide-Pontia with her mother. William and Adelaide-Pontia had sons Stephen II, count of Burgundy and lord of Trier, and Girard, count of Mâcon; Stephen was the older (M 615, 631 [pp. 373–74, 383–84]; C 4122, 4127 [V:465, 469–71]). These sons appeared with their parents in charters for Cluny in 1147. William also had a third son (perhaps illegitimate), with the unusual name of Malaspina

[59]Gabriel Dumay, "Les origines de la maison de Pontailler. Les sires de Talmay (1125–1385), Documents et pièces justificatives," *Mémoires de Société bourguignonne de géographie et d'histoire*, 26 (1910), 225, no. 8; cf. pp. 227–29, no. 11.

[60]Michel Parisse says that he married Agatha of Lorraine, a conclusion apparently based on a charter in which Raynald referred to his *collateralis* Agatha, daughter of the duke of Lorraine; Beatrix 103 (pp. 122–23); Parisse, "La noblesse Lorraine, XIe–XIIe s." (diss., Université de Nancy II, 1975), pp. 400, 864–65. However, *collateralis* was not generally used to mean "wife"; Parisse is perhaps reading it as *collectalis*.

[61]He is called count of Burgundy in charters of Frederick Barbarossa from 1152 and 1153; MGH DD regum et imperatorum Germaniae X, i:22–24, 98–99, nos. 12, 58.

[62]See also Jean-Yves Mariotte, *Le comté de Bourgogne sous les Hohenstaufen, 1156–1208*, Cahiers d'Études Comtoises 4 (Paris, 1963), pp. 46–50.

(C 4122, 4126, 4233 [V: 465, 468—69, 584—86]; Arch. Saône-et-Loire, H 25, no. 13).

Stephen II married Judith, daughter of Duke Matthew of Lorraine and of Bertha, the sister of Frederick Barbarossa (Beatrix 117, 118 [pp. 134—35]; Alberic de Trois-Fontaines, *Chronica* 1193, MGH SS XXIII:871). I shall follow the line of his descendants before returning to Stephen's brother Girard. Stephen died in 1173, when both his brother and his son Stephen III—his only known child—made gifts for his soul (Cîteaux/Marilier 223 [p. 178]; Clairvaux I, p. 72, nos. 2—3). Stephen III married Beatrix, countess of Chalon, by 1188 (Beatrix 52 [pp. 82—83]; Petit 799 [III:286—87]). (See also below, p. 314.) He received the county of Auxonne in fief from the duke of Burgundy in 1197; in documents from that year and 1201 he had a son named Stephen (Layettes 470 [I:193—94]; C 4401 [V:765—66]). This son Stephen seems to have died young, for he disappeared from the charters not long thereafter. The only surviving son of Stephen and Beatrix was John, who in 1214 was recorded as "son of Countess Beatrix of Chalon" (C 4476, 4487 [VI:29—30, 40]).

Stephen III divorced Beatrix, after their heir John was born, to marry Agnes, daughter of the count of Brienne (Beatrix 67, 76 [pp. 101, 107—8]; Alberic de Trois-Fontaines, *Chronica* 1168, MGH SS XXIII:852). They were married by 1214 (Beatrix 31 [p.71]). By 1218, Stephen had been married for a third time, to Margaret, lady of Oyselles and sister of Lady Isabel of Amboise (BN, Coll. Baluze 144, fol. 103r). By his second or third wife, Stephen had sons named Stephen and Simon. He also had a daughter named Clemence, who married the duke of Zähringen (Beatrix 90 [p. 113]). Stephen III's son Stephen became lord of Joinville and seneschal of Champagne, and Simon took the title of lord of Oyselles (Beatrix 91, 95—97 [pp. 114, 117—18]). Stephen III probably stepped down in 1234, when he last appears as count in the charters and when his son John first took the title of count of Burgundy and Chalon (C 4648, 4657 [VI:177—78, 186—87]).

In the meantime, Girard, son of Count William IV and brother of Stephen II, acted as founder of a separate line of counts of Mâcon (C 4233 [V:584—86]; M 631 [pp. 383—84]). Girard married Moretta, the heiress of Walter of Salins, by 1172. They had four sons, William V, count of Mâcon and Vienne; Walter, lord of Salins; Girard; and Stephen, who was elected archbishop of Besançon in 1195 but died before taking office. Alberic de Trois-Fontaines says that they also had daughters but does not name them, other than to say that one married the count of Savoy (Beatrix 139—42, 144 [pp. 154—58, 160]; BN, Coll. Baluze 144, fol. 92r; Alberic de Trois-Fontaines, *Chronica* 1190, 1195, MGH SS XXIII:863, 872).

Girard's son William V married Calatia, sister of Count Henry of

Champagne (Alberic de Trois-Fontaines, *Chronica* 1198, MGH SS XXIII:876). She is sometimes also called Scholastica (Plancher II.9 [p. iii]). In 1199 he called himself "count palatine" of Vienne and Mâcon (C 4377 [V:733]). His brother Walter, lord of Salins, married Mathilda, heiress of Bourbon (C 4337 [V:703—4]; BN, Coll. Baluze 144, fol. 99r), though in 1195 they were forced to separate on grounds of consanguinity, being related within "four or five" degrees (GC IV:93—94, no. 61). He then married a woman named Adelaide and died by 1219 (BN, Coll. Baluze 144, fol. 95r). She is doubtless the same Adelaide, lady of Salins, who married Rainard II of Choiseul in 1221 (see below, p. 316).

William V is the only one of his generation known to have had children. His son Girard II, the oldest (C 4526 [VI:79]), took the titles of count of Mâcon and lord of Vienne while his father was still alive (Tournus, pp. 183—84, 186; C 4526 [VI:79]). William V's son Henry was engaged in 1216 to Margaret, daughter of Guichard IV of Beaujeu, and died in 1233.[63] William V was also apparently the father of William, who became dean of the cathedral chapter of Besançon (Obit. Lyon II:407).

Girard II married the sister of Wigo, count of Forez. Their daughter Alix married John, brother of Count Peter of Brittany; they were married by 1228 (Arch. nat., J 259, no. 1; Tournus, p. 195; Layettes 2303 [II:269]; Alberic de Trois-Fontaines, *Chronica* 1222, MGH SS XXIII:912; C 46990 [VI:209—20]). John and Alix had no sons. John sold the king the county of Mâcon in 1239, thus ending the line of hereditary counts of Mâcon (Layettes 2776 [II:400—401]).

The Lords of Aigremont and Bourbonne

The lords of Aigremont are best known as the founders of Morimond. The lords of Bourbonne were a collateral branch of the lords of Aigremont. They were studied by H. de Faget de Casteljau as part of his study of the lords of Choiseul; "Recherches sur la maison de Choiseul. IV. Les seigneurs de Bourbonne," *Cahiers haut-marnais*, 110 (1972), 154—63 [hereafter cited as "Les seigneurs de Bourbonne"].

The lords of Aigremont were related by affinity to the lords of Fontaines, the family of Bernard of Clairvaux (see below, pp. 329—31). According to Alberic de Trois-Fontaines, who wrote in the thirteenth

[63]M.-C. Guigue, ed., "Testament de Guichard III [IV] de Beaujeu," *Bibliothèque de l'École des chartes*, 18 (1856/7), 161—67. Tournus, p. 188.

The Lords of Aigremont and Bourbonne

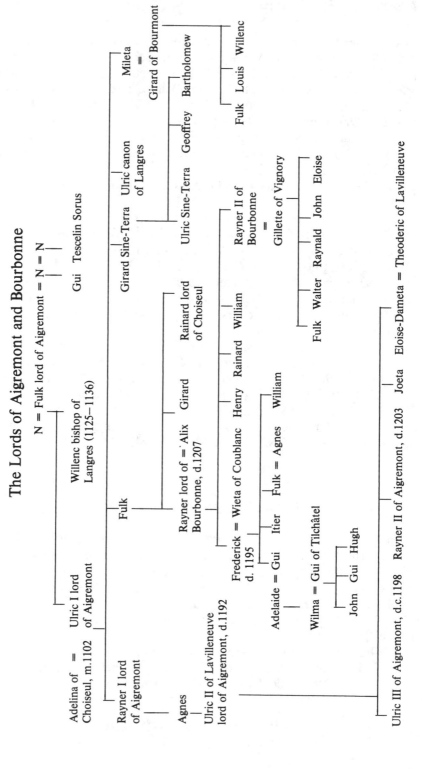

century, Tescelin Sorus's mother married Fulk, lord of Aigremont, as well as Tescelin's father, though Fulk had his heir Ulric by another woman. Fulk and Tescelin's mother had a son named Gui. This Gui, according to Alberic, married Escelina, lady of Milly, the daughter of Holduin of Joinville, brother of Geoffrey II of Joinville. Gui and Escelina had a son named Werric, who was in turn father of Walter, lord of Milly (Alberic de Trois-Fontaines, *Chronica* 1110, MGH SS XXIII:818).[64]

The real history of the lords of Aigremont begins with Ulric I, the founder of Morimond, and Fulk's son and heir by an unnamed woman. Lord Ulric had a brother Willenc, who was dean and archdeacon of Langres and went on to become bishop of Langres (1125—1136) (GC IV:168, no. 43) (see also Appendix B, p. 395). Willenc and Ulric were both sons of Fulk, but it is not clear whether they were the sons of the same mother.[65] Willenc's nephew Fulk was archdeacon of Langres under him (GC IV:161, no. 38). He also had a nephew Werric (probably a variant of Ulric).[66]

Ulric I, the founder of Morimond, married a woman named Adelina. At the time that they helped found Morimond in 1115 they appeared with sons Fulk, Roger (or Rayner), and Girard (GC IV:159, no. 36). Adelina was the daughter of Lord Rayner I of Choiseul (for the lords of Choiseul, see below, pp. 314—16); she appears in Rayner's charters, and in one charter of 1102 she is called wife of Ulric of Aigremont (Molesme 2.370 [II:390—91]). Adelina and Ulric were thus probably married in 1102. Adelina was the heiress of Choiseul; her brother Roger, their father's heir, seems to have never married, and the next independent lord of Choiseul was Adelina's grandson. Adelina and Ulric had at least four sons, Rayner I, who succeeded his father, Fulk, Girard, sometimes called "Sine-Terra," and Ulric, a canon at Langres (GC IV:159, no. 36; *Genus illustre*, pp. 506—7, nos. 69—71 [rpt. PL CLXXXV:1443—44]; Molesme 2.378 [II:394]). They also had at least one daughter, named Mileta. I shall discuss Lord Rayner I's brothers and sister before returning to him.

Fulk, brother of Lord Rayner, had a son named Rayner who became lord of Bourbonne in the mid-twelfth century (for the lords of Bourbonne, see below).[67] He probably also had a son named Rainard,

[64]Tescelin's mother is often called Eve of Grancey; see, for example, Jobin, *St. Bernard*, p. ix.

[65]H. de Faget de Casteljau makes the canon Willenc son of "Eve of Grancey" and also gives her and Fulk two more sons, named Holduin and Aimo, but without evidence; "Recherches sur la maison de Choiseul. I," *Cahiers haut-marnais*, 102 (1970), 150.

[66]Bernard of Clairvaux, Letter 2, *Opera*, VII (Rome, 1977), 12—22.

[67]Charter 11 of Remiremont, ed. Eduard Hlawitschka, *Studien zur Äbtissinnenreihe von Remiremont (7.—13. Jh.)* (Saarbrücken, 1963), pp. 153—54.

because Fulk's brother, lord Rayner of Aigremont, said that he had nephews (*nepotes*), brothers, Rayner and Rainard (*Genus illustre*, p. 506, no. 69 [rpt. PL CLXXXV:1443]). Since Adelina, wife of Ulric I of Aigremont, had been the heiress of Choiseul, it seems most likely that these brothers are identical with Lord Rainard of Choiseul and his brother Rayner (Molesme 2.362 [II:387]). Girard Sine-Terra of Aigremont married a woman named Elizabeth or Dameta (Arch. Côte-d'Or, 7 H 7, fol. 72r; summarized as Molesme 2.360 [II:386]). He was the father of the three brothers Ulric Sine-Terra, usually called "of Aigremont," Geoffrey, and Bartholomew (Arch. Haute-Marne, 5 H 6; 8 H 9, no. 1). Ulric Sine-Terra married a woman named Dameta, like his mother, and by 1189 had children named Girard and Maria (Arch. Haute-Saône, H 324).

Lord Rayner I's brother Ulric, the canon of Langres, is probably the same as the Werric, nephew of Bishop Willenc, mentioned by Bernard of Clairvaux. He became archdeacon of Langres and also served as provost of Sts.-Géosmes, just south of Langres (Quantin I.297 [pp. 451–52]; Molesme 2.361, 362 [II:386–87]). He had a nephew named Guiard, a canon at Langres (Pérard, p. 241). (It is not clear how he was related.) He also had a great-nephew Ulric of Choiseul, another canon of Langres (see below, p. 316). Lord Rayner, Girard Sine-Terra, and Ulric had a sister named Mileta. She married Girard of Bourmont, who died by 1176, and had sons named Fulk, Louis, and Willenc (Arch. Haute-Marne, 8 H 67, nos. 6, 9–10).

Lord Rayner I of Aigremont and his wife (whose name is not known) had a daughter named Agnes, their only known child (*Genus illustre*, p. 507, no. 71 [rpt. PL CLXXXV:1444]; Pérard, p. 241). Rayner was still alive in 1168 (Arch. Haute-Marne, 8 H 107). But in the following decade there is no record of a lord of Aigremont. Rayner's date of death is not known, but it seems most likely that the lordship went to his daughter Agnes and that she married the lord of Lavilleneuve.

Lord Ulric II, "of Lavilleneuve," probably Agnes's son, inherited the lordship of Aigremont in 1184. He had a *nepos* Theoderic, also called of Lavilleneuve (Arch. Haute-Marne, 8 H 7, no. 4; 8 H 77, no. 2). He had daughters named Joeta and Eloise-Dameta, as well as the sons mentioned below. Eloise-Dameta married Theoderic of Lavilleneuve, whom her brothers called their *nepos* (Arch. Haute-Marne, 8 H 7, nos. 4–5; 8 H 107). The exact degree of relationship with this Theoderic, who seems the same as the Theoderic their father called *his nepos*, is not clear; perhaps son-in-law or brother-in-law rather than nephew would be the best translation. Dameta was called *nobilis matrona* in 1199 (Arch. Haute-Marne, 8 H 9, no. 4).

Lord Ulric II died in 1192, excommunicated for his quarrels with Morimond, and was succeeded by his two sons, Ulric III and Rayner

II (Arch. Haute-Marne, 8 H 107). Ulric seems to have been the oldest of these two sons, but Rayner II was lord of Aigremont from at
least 1198. He died in 1203 (Arch. Haute-Marne, 8 H 7, nos. 5–6).
Rayner had called Rainard of Choiseul his *cognatus* (Arch. Haute-
Marne, 8 H 7), and apparently Aigremont went to the lords of
Choiseul after Rayner's death (Arch. Haute-Marne, 8 H 7, no. 6;
8 H 23; 8 H 103, no. 2).

The lords of Bourbonne, cousins of the lords of Aigremont, first
appear in the second half of the twelfth century, with Lord Rayner I
of Bourbonne and his brother Girard (Arch. Haute-Marne, 8 H 79).
They were the sons of Fulk of Aigremont and grandsons of Ulric I of
Aigremont, and the uncles of Fulk of Choiseul. Rayner I seems to
have been lord for a good fifty years, from the middle of the twelfth
century to about 1207 (Arch. Haute-Marne, 2 H 4; 8 H 67, no. 10;
8 H 93). Rayner married a woman named Alix, sister of Amadeus,
who became archbishop of Besançon at the beginning of the thirteenth
century (Arch. Haute-Marne, 8 H 15). Frederick, son of Rayner I of
Bourbonne, is mentioned in 1168 (Arch. Haute-Marne, 8 H 107). By
1179 at the latest he had married a woman named Wieta or Givera,
and their son William appeared in the charters by 1197. Lord
Rayner's other four sons were named Henry, Rainard, William, and
Rayner (Arch. Haute-Marne, 2 H 4; 8 H 15; 8 H 79; Theuley, fol.
18v).[68]

It is likely that Frederick, son of Rayner I of Bourbonne, was identical with Frederick of Coublanc, and therefore one can say that his
wife Wieta was the heiress of Coublanc, perhaps the daughter of the
Lord Gui of Coublanc who in the 1160s recalled the gifts of his father
Itier when he himself was dying (Langres 37 [p. 411]).[69] In 1179
Frederick, lord of Coublanc, was married to a woman named Gui-
donia (probably Wieta is a variant of this name), and made gifts to
Auberive with his sons Gui, Itier, Fulk, and William, the last of
whom was too young to give his assent to his father's gift (Auberive
I, fol. 6v, no. 7). Gui succeeded as lord of Coublanc; he appears with
this title in 1195, and by 1196 he was married to a woman named
Adelaide and had a daughter named Wilma. Wilma married Gui II,
lord of Tilchâtel (see below, p. 369) (Arch. Haute-Saône, H 417;
Langres 191, 302 [pp. 620, 765]).[70] Frederick of Bourbonne's son

---

[68]Faget de Casteljau also gives Rayner a son named Fulk whom he says was called a
cleric in 1134; the date makes it clear that he is mistaken; Faget de Casteljau, "Les
seigneurs de Bourbonne," pp. 154–55.

[69]Faget de Casteljau makes this identification; "Les seigneurs de Bourbonne," p. 156.
Gui of Coublanc had been orphaned young and raised by his father Itier's younger
brother, Hugh; Morment 24 (pp. 120–21).

[70]Faget de Casteljau says that Wilma took Bourbonne with her to her husband; "Les
seigneurs de Bourbonne," pp. 158–59.

Fulk, called *nepos* (great-nephew) of Archbishop Amadeus in 1214, married a woman named Agnes (Arch. Haute-Marne, 8 H 15).

Lord Rayner I of Bourbonne probably died in 1207, after a long career, for in 1207 and 1208 Rayner II, lord of Bourbonne, appeared in the documents with his brother Henry, recalling their parents, Rayner and Alix. Lord Rayner II's wife was named Gillette, and his sons were Fulk, Walter, Raynald, and John. He also had a daughter, Eloise (Arch. Haute-Marne, 8 H 15).[71] Gillette was doubtless of the family of the lords of Vignory, as, when Lord Walter of Vignory made a gift to Clairvaux around the beginning of the thirteenth century, Gillette had to agree, "as it concerned her inheritance" (Clairvaux II, p. 396, no. 24). The names Walter and Eloise among her children come from the lords of Vignory (see also below, pp. 382–83).

The Counts of Auxois

The counts of Auxois acted in the area north of Dijon during the eleventh century. They were certainly related to the lords of Salmaise and of Fouvent and may also have been connected to the lords of Sexfontaines, Sombernon, and Tilchâtel, though these connections are not clear.

Aimo I was the first known count. In the 980s he appeared with his son Walo in a charter of Duke Hugh of Burgundy, and in 992 he was called count of Auxois (Autun/St.-Symphorien 14 [pp. 35–37]; Plancher I.30 [pp. xxiv–xxv]). Count Aimo made his testament in 1004, with his sons Walo and Walter and his *nepotes* Hubert, Girard, and Halinard (Flavigny 39 [pp. 30–84; summarized Collenot, pp. 86–87, misdated 1012/3]). It is likely that his nephews Hubert and Girard are identical with Humbert and Girard, sons of Girard of Fouvent, and hence that Aimo of Auxois was Lord Girard's brother or brother-in-law (for Girard of Fouvent, see below). Aimo's sons Walo, who acted as count after his father, and Walter appeared at Salmaise in 1020, acting with Humbert and Girard, their cousins. At this time Walo had a wife named Judith and sons Aimo and Hugh (St.-B. II.272 [pp. 63–64]; cf. Chron. St.-B., p. 171). Walo was called a *miles nobilis* (Flavigny 40 [pp. 84–85; summarized Collenot, p. 99]). Count Walo's son Hugh appeared in a charter with the duke in 1052 (Petit 35 [I:378–80]).

Girard of Fouvent, probable brother of Aimo I of Auxois, married a

---

[71]Faget de Casteljau also gives them children named Gui, Alix, and Mathilda; "Les seigneurs de Bourbonne," p. 161.

The Counts of Auxois

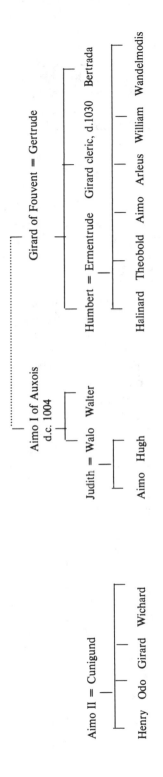

woman named Gertrude. She was probably the heiress of Fouvent,
because when Girard built a church at Fouvent early in the eleventh
century he said he was doing so on land that was his wife Gertrude's
inheritance (GC IV:141, no. 16; Chron. St.-B., pp. 308–10). They
had at least two sons, Humbert and Girard, a cleric (Chron. St.-B., pp.
294, 310–11, 345). They also had a daughter named Bertrada (St.-B.
II.272 [pp. 63–64]); she or another daughter married Count Arnulf of
Reynel (Chron. St.-B., pp. 380–82). Their son Humbert is probably
identical with Humbert of Salmaise, who appears in the documents
with that title from 1013 on (Chron. St.-B., p. 165). Humbert of Salmaise married a woman named Ermentrude and had at least six children, Halinard, Theobold, Aimo, Arleus, William, and Wandelmodis.
He also had a nephew named Theobold (St.-B. II.272, 294 [pp.
63–64, 77–78]). Humbert's brother Girard was killed in 1030 (St.-B.
II.294 [pp. 77–78]).

At the same time that this group of relatives held power, another
man, named Aimo, also seems to have been count of Auxois, perhaps
taking the title only in the 1020s or 1030s, after Walo's death.[72] In
1019 this Aimo II, a *fidelis* of the bishop of Langres, received the
church of Sexfontaines from the bishop. At that time he had a wife
named Cunigund and heirs Henry and Odo (St. B. II.266 [pp.
56–58]). Aimo II gave the church of Sexfontaines to St.-Bénigne in
1030, a gift that he confirmed (this time as a count) in 1034, along
with his wife Cunigund and sons Girard, Odo, and Wichard (St.-B.
II.295, 314 [pp. 78–79, 94–95]; Chron. St.-B., pp. 174–75). His son
Henry had presumably died by then. His son Odo, who succeeded
Aimo II as count, confirmed somewhat later (St.-B. II.316 [p. 97]).

[72]A charter of Flavigny printed by André Duchesne and reprinted by Petit calls Aimo
II the brother of Walo in its closing lines; Duchesne, *Histoire généalogique de la maison
de Vergy* (Paris, 1625), p. 49; Petit 201 (I:483–84). It is not at all clear, however, where
Duchesne got these closing lines, as they are not in the copy of the charter he himself
made from the (now lost) cartulary of Flavigny as a basis for the "Preuves" of his *Histoire de Vergy*; BN, Coll. Baluze 40, fols. 39v, 42v. Nor are they in any of the other
copies of the cartulary of Flavigny made in the seventeenth and eighteenth centuries;
Flavigny 40 (pp. 84–85); Brussels, Bibliothèque royale, MS 7827–74, fols. 286v–87r;
Châtillon, Bibliothèque municipale, MS 6, pp. 492–93; summarized by Collenot, p. 99.
Since no other source calls Aimo II the brother of Walo, it is safest to assume that he
was not and that Duchesne was mistaken or confused.

The Lords of Bâgé

The first known lord of Bâgé is Tetbert, whose wife Raimodis died around 980. He is called *illuster vir* and *vir nobilis* in the documents (C 919, 1521 [II:31−32, 57−71]; M 265 [p. 159]). He may be the same as the Tetbert, son of Rather and Trisburga, who appears in Cluny's charters in 957 (C 1037 [II:130−31]). At any rate, Tetbert and Raimodis had two sons, Ulric I and Rather (M 265, 330 [pp. 159, 191−92]; C 1521, 2265 [II:570−71; III:395−97]; M 465 [pp. 267−68]).

Ulric I was called a *vir nobilissimus* (M 543 [p. 319]). He first married a woman named Aremburg (C 1958 [III:177]). Ulric married a woman named Ermengard in 994, the year after he appears with Aremburg; she had presumably died (C 2265, 2605 [III:395−97, 656−57]). His brother Rather is probably the same as the Rather who by 993 had married a woman named Bertha (C 1944 [III:160−61]). In 1018 Ulric is referred to in a charter as "son of Tetbert" and was accompanied by his son Ulric II, designated as *puer* (M 142 [pp. 100−101]). The couple Ermengard and Ulric I appeared together for a total of some thirty-five years, until around 1030, when Ermengard and their son Ulric II made gifts for Ulric I's soul (M 430, 458, 489 [pp. 248−49, 262−63, 284]). In addition to Ulric II, Ulric I had a son named Walter, who was a cathedral canon at Mâcon (M 201 [p. 129]).

Ulric II married a woman named Beatrix (C 2370 [III:473]). Their son Ulric III was lord of Bâgé by 1075 (Tournus, p. 130; M 456 [p. 261]). A Joceran of Bâgé was a canon of Mâcon in the early years of the twelfth century; he may be a son of Ulric III (M 564, 577, 578 [pp. 336, 344−46]). Ulric IV, apparently son of Ulric III, was lord of Bâgé in 1118. His sons were Ulric, who seems to have died young, and Raynald, who was lord of Bâgé by 1149 at the latest and died in 1169 (M 577, 622 [pp. 344−45, 377]; Arch. Saône-et-Loire, G 222). Raynald had two sons, Ulric V, who succeeded, and Raynald. Both confirmed their father's dying gifts to the chapter of Mâcon.[73] Raynald may possibly be the father of Humbert, bishop of Autun (1140−1148); Humbert attended Raynald's funeral (M 622 [p. 377]). In this case, Raynald may also be the brother of Bishop Humbert's uncle and predecessor at Autun, Stephen I (1112−1139). A Hugh of Bâgé was a canon of Mâcon around the mid to late twelfth century; he may also be a relative (M 627 [p. 380]).

Ulric V married twice, first the lady of Mirebeau, who died by 1187,[74] and then the daughter of the count of Chalon (see below, p.

---

[73] Arch. Saône-et-Loire, G 222. M 622 (p. 377). Samuel Guichenon, *Histoire de Bresse et de Bugey* (Lyon, 1650), preuves pp. 8−9.

[74] Guichenon, *Histoire de Bresse*, preuves pp. 9−10. Although this charter does not

The Lords of Bâgé

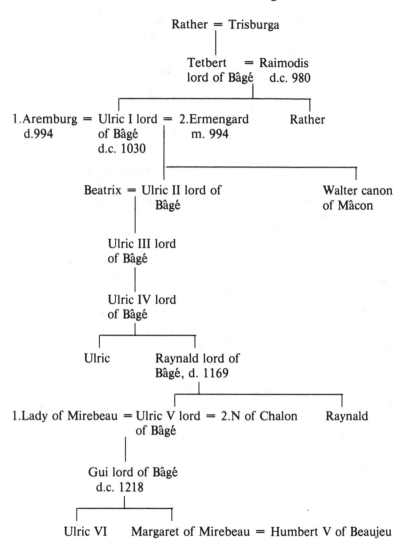

314), who had been earlier married to Joceran IV Grossus, lord of Brancion and Uxelles (C 4410 [V:785–87]). By his first wife, Ulric V had Gui, lord of Bâgé and Mirebeau, who first appeared with his father in 1180.[75] Gui died around 1218, on pilgrimage, leaving a son who succeeded to Bâgé, Ulric VI, and a daughter, Margaret, who married Lord Humbert V of Beaujeu, taking with her the lordship of Mirebeau (see below, p. 295).[76]

The Lords of Beaujeu

The lords of Beaujeu are one of the best-documented castellan families of the eleventh and twelfth centuries because of their generosity to Cluny and to the collegial church Notre-Dame of Beaujeu. The most important study of this family is the work of M.-C. Guigue, who edited the cartulary of Beaujeu (pp. 57–64). More recently, these lords have been discussed by Matthieu Méras, *Le Beaujolais au moyen âge*, 2nd ed. (Villefranche-en-Beaujolais, 1979); the discussion of the eleventh- and twelfth-century lords is on pp. 5–49.

Though Guigue and all earlier scholars of this family attempted to establish their descendance from the counts of Forez,[77] nothing firm is known about them before the time of Berard, who died before 966, when his son Humbert first appeared without him (C 1218 [II:299]). In 957 Berard had appeared with his wife Wandelmodis in a charter for Cluny with the designation *venerabilis* (C 1039 [II:133]).[78] Berard and Wandelmodis, with their son Humbert I, founded the church of Beaujeu by establishing canons in their castle chapel (Beaujeu 3 [p. 11]; Obit. Lyon II:510).

In addition to Humbert I, who appeared in the documents at the end of the tenth century (Beaujeu a1 [pp. 35–36]; C 889 [II:6–7]; M 27 [pp. 23–24]), Berard and Wandelmodis also had a son named Hugh, who appeared in one of his brother's charters (C 2005 [III:216–17]).[79] Humbert I married a woman named Emeldis; they

---

give the lady's name, it is perhaps Elizabeth, for in 1174 Odo, lord of Mirebeau, and his wife Aegidia had had children named Raynald and Elizabeth; Arch. Haute-Saône, H 422.

[75]Guichenon, *Histoire de Bresse*, preuves pp. 9–10.

[76]Ibid., p. 10. M.-C. Guigue, ed., *Cartulaire Lyonnais*, I (Lyon, 1885), 169, no. 122.

[77]See also Samuel Guichenon, *Histoire de la souveraineté de Dombes*, ed. M.-C. Guigue, I (Lyon, 1874), 162.

[78]See also Savigny 244 (pp. 164–65). Maurice Chaume makes Wandelmodis the daughter of Humbert of Salins, the brother of Count Leotold of Mâcon, in order to explain why her son was named Humbert and her grandson Leotold; Chaume, *Origines de Bourgogne*, I:533.

[79]Guichenon's family tree of the lords of Beaujeu is very different from mine; *His-*

The Lords of Beaujeu

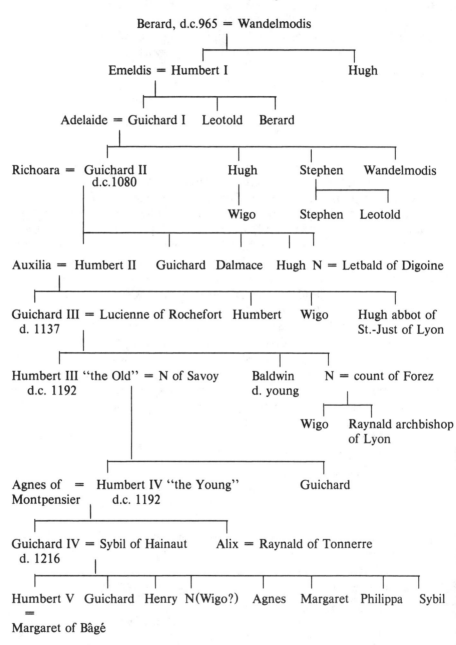

had three sons, Guichard I, Leotold, and Berard (Beaujeu a1 [pp. 35–36]; C 1218, 1774, 2269 [II:299; III:32–33, 400]). In a letter Pope Benedict VIII wrote to the Burgundian bishops in 1016, Guichard I appeared as someone who had appropriated a church from Cluny (Letter 16, PL CXXXIX:1602). Guichard I and his wife Adelaide and son Guichard II confirmed his father's gift to Cluny in 1020, by which time Humbert I must have died (C 2728 [III:751–52]). In addition to Guichard II, Guichard I and Adelaide had at least two other sons, Hugh and Stephen, and a daughter, Wandelmodis. The evidence is as follows. In 1076, when the papal legate dedicated the recently restored church of Beaujeu, first established over a century earlier, he recalled that Berard, Wandelmodis, and Humbert had founded the church, and that Lord Guichard, Hugh, and Stephen of Beaujeu, as well as Lord Guichard's sister Wandelmodis, had followed the example of their *parentes* in generosity, and that their "above mentioned *avus*" had given the church its relics (Beaujeu a2 [pp. 38–41]). It seems most likely that the word *parentes* in this context simply means "ancestors," and that the *avus* referred to was their grandfather Humbert I. The obituary of Notre-Dame of Beaujeu spoke of "Lord Hugh of Beaujeu who restored our church" (Obit. Lyon II:509).[80]

Guichard II married a woman named Richoara; they had sons Humbert II, Guichard, and Dalmace, recorded in charters dated between 1031 and 1060 (M 476, 483 [pp. 274–75, 279]). They also had a son named Hugh, who appeared in a charter with his brothers and mother in 1081, by which time Guichard II had doubtless died (Savigny 754 [pp. 390–91]). They also had a daughter, whose name is not known, who married Letbald, lord of Digoine, son of Joceran, and had a son named Letbald (C 3067, 3072, 3351 [IV:252–55, 447–49]). Because of her name, Richoara, and that of her son, Dalmace, a name not found before among the lords of Beaujeu, it is tempting to try to

---

toire de la souveraineté de Dombes, pp. 157–207. This book was originally written in the mid-seventeenth century. Guigue edited it (adding some notes of his own) and published it ten years after his own study of the lords of Beaujeu. In spite of some notes he made, it is not clear how much he agreed with Guichenon's family tree, in many ways different from his own version. Guichenon did not give references for this family tree, though Guigue added a few. Guichenon did not include Hugh among the children of Berard and Wandelmodis but instead gave them four other sons, Guichard, Stephen, Umfred, and Gui. Guigue, in his own genealogical discussion, explicitly omitted these four but did not include Hugh either. Méras treats Humbert I as an only child.

[80]Guichenon makes this whole group of people the children of Humbert I; hence he gives Humbert and Emeldis seven children, Hugh, Guichard, Leotold, Stephen, Berard, Elizabeth, and Wandelmodis. Guigue discusses the possibility of including Hugh, Stephen, and Wandelmodis among the children of Humbert I (rather than Guichard I) and ends up rejecting them entirely. Méras includes Hugh and Stephen but not Wandelmodis among the children of Guichard I.

attach Richoara to the family of the lords of Semur. However, she referred to her parents as Roclenus and Testa, which names would tend rather to attach her to the family of the lords of Brancion (C 3350 [IV:446−47]). (It is of course possible that she was related to both families, but whatever connection there was is not clear.)

The children of Guichard II sometimes acted with their cousins, the children of Hugh and Stephen. Around 1070 a man who called himself Stephen of Beaujeu, son of Stephen—most likely the brother of Guichard II—gave up a claim against Cluny with the consent of his cousins: Humbert, Guichard, and Dalmace, the sons of Guichard II; Wigo, son of Hugh; and a monk named Guichard, who may have been a son of Hugh or perhaps of Wandelmodis (C 3431 [IV:541−42]). Guichard II's son Dalmace may be identical with the Dalmace of Verneis who gave the church of Beaujeu two *curtiles* in 1090, when he was dying, with the consent of his *nepotes* Stephen and Wigo, who would have been his cousins (Beaujeu 20 [pp. 22−23]; cf. C 3278 [IV:394−85). Stephen, son of Stephen, is probably the same as the Stephen who gave the church of Beaujeu a gift for the soul of his late brother Leotold in 1090, with the consent of Lord Humbert II of Beaujeu (Beaujeu 24 [pp. 25−26]). Humbert II had appeared in a charter with cousins Stephen and Leotold a few years earlier (Marcigny 23 [pp. 21−22]).

Humbert II, successor of Guichard II, married a woman named Auxilia, who first appears in the documents with her husband in 1090 (Beaujeu 19, 21, 24 [pp. 22, 24−26]; Obit. Lyon II:509), after he had appeared in the documents without a wife in 1086 and 1087 (Savigny 826, 827 [pp. 438−40]).[81] Humbert and Auxilia had at least four sons, Guichard III, Humbert, Wigo, and Hugh, the last of whom became a canon of Mâcon and Lyon and abbot of the house St.-Just of Lyon. These four sons all appeared with their parents in a charter of 1094 (Hugh, naturally, was still only a boy, not yet abbot) (Beaujeu 21 [p. 24]). Hugh had taken office as abbot by 1117 (M 586 [pp. 352−53]).[82]

Guichard III married a woman named Lucienne (Obit. Lyon II:508). She was the daughter of Gui Rufus, count of Rochefort and lord of Montlhéry, and, while still a girl, had originally been engaged to Louis VI.[83] Toward the end of his life, Guichard retired to Cluny, where

[81]Guichenon rejects the idea that Auxilia was Humbert II's wife; rather, he has Humbert marry one Wandelmodis, whom he calls the daughter of Count Hugh II of Chalon. Both Guigue and Méras have Humbert II marry first an unnamed daughter of someone they call Hugh, brother of Count William I of Chalon, and then Auxilia, whom they call daughter of the count of Savoy.

[82]This charter calls him just "abbot," but his house is recorded in the necrology of the cathedral of Mâcon; Obit. Lyon II:381. See also Obit. Lyon I:76. Guichenon also gives Humbert II two daughters, named Elizabeth and Wandelmodis.

[83]Orderic Vitalis, *Historia ecclesiastica* 11.35, ed. Chibnall, VI:156. Suger, *Vita Ludovici*

he died in 1137 (Peter the Venerable, *Miracula* 1.27, PL
CLXXXIX:900; Obit. Lyon II:509). Guichard and Lucienne had two
sons, Humbert III, who succeeded, and Baldwin, who died young
(Obit. Lyon II:508), and a daughter, who married the count of Forez.
She was the mother of Wigo, count of Forez, and of Raynald, archbishop of Lyon (1192–1226).[84] Guichard III may also be the father
of Stephen, dean of the chapter of Mâcon in the mid-twelfth century,
who is called "of Beaujeu" (M 605 [p. 368]). The name Stephen
however suggests the cousins of the lords of Beaujeu rather than the
lords themselves.

Humbert III is often called "the Old"; he lived until nearly the end
of the twelfth century (M 599 [p. 362]; Savigny 944 [pp. 511–12]).
He went on Crusade around 1142 and returned safely. While in
Jerusalem he joined the Templars, but he gave up the order when he
returned to Burgundy.[85] Humbert III married the daughter of
Amadeus, Count of Savoy (Alberic de Trois-Fontaines, *Chronica*
1222, MGH SS XXIII:912; Beaujeu 8 [p. 14]).[86] Humbert III had two
sons, Humbert IV and Guichard, neither of whom survived their
father.[87] Humbert IV, often called "the Young" (Beaujeu a3 [pp.
41–43]; C 4332 [V:696]), had many quarrels with his father (Beaujeu
a3, a4 [pp. 41–44]). He married Agnes of Montpensier, who earlier
had married Raymund, son of Duke Hugh II of Burgundy (Alberic de
Trois-Fontaines, *Chronica* 1222, MGH SS XXIII:912) (see also above,
p. 260). He died on the Third Crusade while his father was still alive

---

8, ed. Waquet, p. 40. *Le cartulaire de Notre-Dame de Longpont* [ed. Jules Marion] (Lyon,
1879), pp. 235–36, no. 292.

[84]It may be presumed that Humbert III's sister was the mother of Count Wigo of
Forez, because Humbert called this count his *nepos*, and the count hoped to inherit
from Humbert, on his mother's account, after Humbert's sons had predeceased him;
Beaujeu 30 (p. 32); Georges Guichard, Comte de Neufbourg, Édouard Perroy, and J.-
E. Dufour, eds., *Chartes du Forez*, I (Mâcon, 1933), no. 13. Archbishop Raynald called
the count his *frater*; GC IV:25–26, no. 33. Humbert III's sister is usually called Sybil
by scholars, but only because they mistake "lady Sybil of Beaujeu, countess," the
daughter of the count of Hainaut and wife of Guichard IV (see below), for the countess
of Forez. Guichenon gives Guichard III and Lucienne three more sons, Guichard,
Martin, and Gontier, and two more daughters, Alix and Marie. Guigue also puts all
these, except Martin, in *his* family tree. There *is* a "Martin of Beaujeu" with a wife
named Guibors in the obituary of Notre-Dame of Beaujeu, but it is impossible to say
how he was related to the lords of Beaujeu, if at all; Obit. Lyon II:507.

[85]Peter the Venerable, Letters 172–73, *Letters*, I:407–13. See also Peter the Venerable, *Miracula* 1.27, PL CLXXXIX:903.

[86]Document number 8 of Beaujeu is misdated by the editor to the end of the
eleventh century. Therefore Guigue and Méras have *both* Humbert II and Humbert III
marry daughters of the count of Savoy; Guigue calls both these women Auxilia (the
name of Humbert II's wife), and Méras calls Humbert III's wife Alix.

[87]Guichard died in 1165, on 19 August; Guigue, ed., *Cartulaire Lyonnais*, I:53–58,
no. 39. Guigue adds another son, Hugh. Guichenon adds two more sons, Hugh and
Gui.

(Obit. Lyon II:508).[88] When Humbert III finally died, around 1192, he was succeeded by his grandson, Guichard IV, whose first known charter dates from this year (C 4361 [V:720—21]). Guichard IV had a sister, Alix, who married Raynald, count of Tonnerre (C 4334 [V:699]) (see below, p. 347). After his death, she became a nun at Fontevrault.[89]

Guichard IV married Sybil of Hainaut, who in one charter is called "countess" (Beaujeu a9 [pp. 52—53]). She was the daughter of Baldwin, count of Hainaut and Flanders, and sister of Isabelle of Hainaut, first wife of King Philip II (Alberic de Trois-Fontaines, *Chronica* 1191, MGH SS XXIII:868). Guichard's and Sybil's children are all known from his last testament, which he drew up in 1216 when he was dying.[90] (He died at Dover, fighting with the king's forces; C 4503 [VI:57—58].) He divided his property among his three oldest sons, leaving Beaujeu to Humbert V, Montpensier to Guichard, and Bugey to Henry. His fourth and youngest son—who is not named— he entrusted to his *consanguineus* Raynald, archbishop of Lyon (his first cousin once removed), to become a canon.[91] He also arranged the marriages of his daughters—or stated who would decide whom they married. Agnes, his oldest daughter, was to have a husband chosen by Louis, the royal heir, her *consanguineus* (cousin). She eventually married Theobold, count of Champagne, after he divorced his first wife (Alberic de Trois-Fontaines, *Chronica* 1222, MGH SS XXIII:912). Guichard engaged Margaret to Henry, son of Count William V of Mâcon (see above, p. 279). She does not however seem to have married him; she is recorded in the obituary of Notre-Dame of Beaujeu without a husband (Obit. Lyon II:509). Philippa he entrusted to his sister, the former countess of Tonnerre, now a nun at Fontevrault. He specified that his youngest daughter, Sybil, would be married to someone chosen by her mother and oldest brother. None of these children can have been much older than twenty, and some must have been very young. When Guichard IV had drawn up his first testament, apparently around 1195, shortly after he succeeded to Beaujeu, he had not had any wife or children. In that testament, he had said that, if he died without an heir, Beaujeu should go to his sister

[88]The editors of the obituary of Beaujeu identify the Humbert who died on Crusade as a thirteenth-century lord of Beaujeu, but Humbert IV seems more likely, as he is not explicitly called lord.
[89]See also Guigue, "Testament de Guichard de Beaujeu," pp. 161—67. Guichenon also gives them a brother, Peter, prior of La Charité.
[90]Guigue, "Testament de Guichard de Beaujeu," pp. 161—67.
[91]Guigue and Méras call him Louis. There is a Wigo of Beaujeu, canon both of Beaujeu and Lyon, in the obituary of Notre-Dame of Beaujeu, who may be he; Obit. Lyon II:509. The editors identify this Wigo as a canon of the end of the eleventh century, however.

and Bugey to Guichard, son of Lady Guicharda (Beaujeu a8 [pp. 50–52]). This lady, not otherwise attested, may have been a sister or an aunt.[92] Guichard's wife Sybil, who had her husband brought back from Dover to be buried at Cluny, chose to be buried there herself (C 4504 [VI:58]). Their son and heir, Humbert V, who went to Constantinople in 1239, also chose Cluny for his burial (C 4754 [VI:266]). He married Margaret of Bâgé.[93]

The Lords of Brancion and Uxelles

There were two separate families of lords of Brancion in the central Middle Ages, one that ruled Brancion in the tenth and eleventh centuries, and the better-known family, sometimes called the Grossi, who ruled Uxelles in the eleventh century and acquired Brancion in the twelfth. Only twice have the Grossi of Brancion and Uxelles been studied in any depth. J. Louis Bazin attempted to establish their family tree as part of his broad study of the village of Brancion. His work is flawed by a too hasty reading of the documents, especially those from before the year 1000; Bazin, *Brancion: Les seigneurs, la paroisse, la ville* (Paris, 1908), pp. 38–83. Georges Duby used the family as an example of the establishment of lineages of independent castellans in the Mâconnais; his work provides a useful corrective to Bazin for the early part of the family's history; Duby, *La société aux XIe et XIIe siècles dans la région mâconnaise*, 2nd ed. (Paris, 1971 [originally published 1952]), pp. 336–46. In addition, Ernest Petit gave a very brief survey of the family and attempted to construct a family tree; Petit IV:477–78. Martine Chauney has discussed the Grossi as an example of an ecclesiastical family, though she relies too much on secondary sources; "Le recrutement de l'épiscopat bourguignon aux XIe et XIIe siècles," *Annales de Bourgogne*, 47 (1975), 210–11. The recent discussion by Marguerite Rebouillat of the family's relations with Cluny in the twelfth and thirteenth centuries is based primarily on the secondary sources and collapses three eleventh-century generations into one; Rebouillat, "La lutte entre les seigneurs de Brancion et Cluny," in *La guerre et la paix: Frontières et violences au moyen âge*, Actes du 101e Congrès national des sociétés savantes (Paris, 1978), pp. 333–48. The details of the family's history come primarily from the charters of Cluny; unfortunately, very few of these charters are

---

[92]Guigue and Guichenon make her the daughter of Hugh, whom they made brother of Humbert the Young.
[93]Guichenon, *Histoire de Bresse*, preuves p. 10.

The Lords of Brancion and Neublans

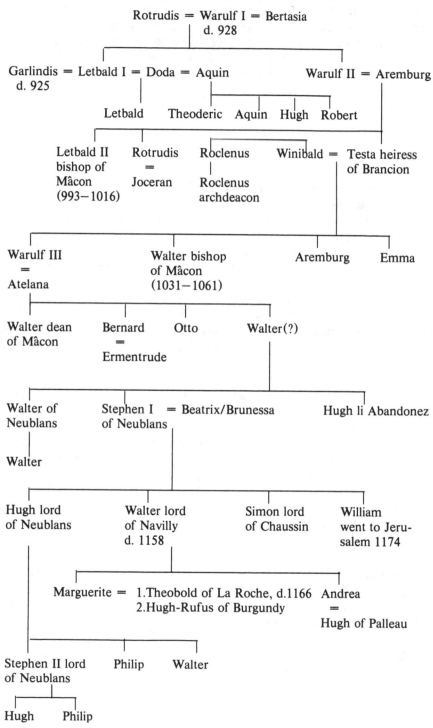

explicitly dated, and, of those that can be dated by internal evidence, the editor has given an incorrect date for many.

The lords of Brancion first appear at the beginning of the tenth century with Warulf, a *vir nobilis* who served Duke William I of Aquitaine and married a woman named Rotrudis (C 283, 387, 89 bis [I:278–79, 368–69; V:833–34]). His second wife was named Bertasia, also called noble. Warulf probably died in 928, when Bertasia made gifts for his soul (C 271, 359 [I:265–66, 336–38]).

Warulf I and Rotrudis had at least two sons, Letbald I and Warulf II (C 214, 283 [I:202–3, 278–79]; St.-Marcel 27 [pp. 28–29]). Letbald seems to have been the older. In a charter from 926 he called himself a *vassalus* of Duke William II (C 272 [I:267]). His first wife, Garlindis, died in 925, and he married his second wife, Doda, in 926 (C 214, 248, 254, 271, 272 [I:202–3, 239–40, 245–46, 265–67]). They had a son named Letbald (C 370, 802 [I:348, 754–56]), who soon disappears from the records. Letbald I last appeared in a dated charter in 930 (C 387 [I:368–69]). Doda outlived him by many years. After his death she married a man named Aquin, who called Giselbert, count of Burgundy, his lord. Doda and Aquin had sons named Theoderic, Aquin, Hugh, and Robert (C 721, 774, 798, 802, 856 [I:673–75, 728–29, 750, 754–56, 810–11]).[94]

Warulf II, younger son of Warulf I and Rotrudis, married a woman named Aremburg. The name Aremburg first appears in 960, but it is possible that the Alsoendis, wife of one Warulf, who appears in 951, is the same woman (C 818 [I:772–73]). In 960 Warulf and Aremburg had a "first-born son" named Letbald II (C 1088 [II:181–82]). Letbald seems to have joined the cathedral chapter of Mâcon around 970, when his *consanguineus* Odo, a canon there, received an abbey and three chapels from the bishop of Mâcon, with the stipulation that Letbald would hold them after his death (M 406, 478 [pp. 233–34, 275–76]).[95] Letbald II became bishop of Mâcon (993–1016) (Chron. St.-B., p. 175) (see also Appendix B, p. 398). Before he took this office, Maiolus, abbot of Cluny, gave him some land *in precaria* that his uncle Letbald I had given Cluny and some other land that Rudolph, who was probably another relative, had given Cluny (C 1460 [II:513–15]). This Rudolph is probably the same man as the one called a *consanguineus* of Maiolus Poudreux of Uxelles (C 941 [II:47]).

---

[94]Aquin became a monk at Cluny late in his life; see Joachim Wollasch, "Wer waren die Mönche von Cluny vom 10. bis zum 12. Jahrhundert?" in *Clio et son regard: Mélanges d'histoire, d'histoire de l'art et d'archéologie offerts à Jacques Stiennon* (Liège, 1982), p. 671.

[95]This Odo may be the same as, or closely related to, an Odo who gave Cluny some property at the very end of the tenth century, or an Odo who had a daughter named Testa; C 2351, 2508 (III:461, 585).

Since Letbald II took orders, Warulf II's daughter Testa eventually inherited the lordship of Brancion (C 2719 [III:741–43]). She married a man named Winibald (C 517, 2263, 2401 [I:502–3; III:394, 494–95]). (In addition to these two, Warulf and Aremburg also apparently had a daughter Rotrudis, wife of Joceran I of Uxelles; see below.) Winibald, husband of Testa, is probably the same Winibald who had a brother named Roclenus; when these two brothers gave Cluny a chapel in 994, the witnesses included Testa, Tetburgis (who may be Roclenus's wife), and Warulf (probably son of Winibald) (C 1969 [III:186]; see also C 2084 [III:279–80]). Winibald and Roclenus may be the sons of one Adalard, who appeared with a son named Roclenus about twenty-five years earlier (M 325 [p. 189]). Roclenus is doubtless the same Roclenus, father of archdeacon Roclenus, to whom Abbot Odilo of Cluny granted a vineyard at Brancion in 993. The archdeacon was called "Roclenus of Brancion" (C 1953 [III:170]; M 465 [p. 268]).[96]

Testa and Winibald had Warulf III, their heir; Walter, first provost and then bishop of Mâcon (1031–1061); Aremburg; and Emma (also known as Berna) (C 517, 2719, 2802, 2869, 2965 [I:502–3; III:741–43; IV:5–6, 66–67, 163]; the first charter is dated c. 940 by the editor, which is too early).[97] Warulf III may have married a woman named Atelana; there is at any rate a Warulf with a wife Atelana in the charters of Mâcon from the first decades of the eleventh century, which would be the right period (M 324, 465 [pp. 188–89, 267–68]). Warulf III was the father of Walter, who served as dean of Mâcon under his uncle Walter in the mid-eleventh century; Bernard of Brancion, who married a woman named Ermentrude; and Otto. Warulf III may indeed have had two sons named Walter, because he often appears with a secular son of that name, who seems to have

---

[96]Both Duby and Chauney call Winibald and Roclenus "of Neublans." Chauney erroneously makes the archdeacon Roclenus the uncle, rather than the nephew, of Winibald. She also gives Winibald and Roclenus a sister named Adelaide, the mother of Bishop Roclenus of Chalon (1072–1079), but apparently only to find a way to attach this bishop to the lords of Brancion; Duby, *La société mâconnaise*, p. 370, n. 97; Chauney, "Le recrutement de l'épiscopat," pp. 210–11.

[97]Aremburg, daughter of Testa and Winibald, may be the Aremburg who married a man named Bernard and had a son, also named Bernard, who gave Cluny some land that he had acquired from his *avunculus* Roclenus (who would be Winibald's brother); C 2973, 2974 (IV:168–70). This Aremburg also had a son named Letbald; C 2204 (III:352). Emma, Aremburg's sister, may be the same as the Emma who married a man named Odilo around the end of the tenth century and had sons named Richard, Leotold, and Walter; when Emma and her son Leotold made a gift to Cluny, a Warulf headed the witnesses; C 2651, 3065 (III:688; IV:250–51). A woman named Emma who called herself the "daughter of Odilard" may be the daughter of Emma of Brancion and Odilo. The younger Emma married a man named Bernard and had a son named Joceran and an adopted daughter named Letgardis, whom she married to a man named Walter; C 1547 (II:595).

predeceased his brothers (C 2869, 2965, 3746, 3747 [IV:66–67, 163; V:100–101]; M 475 [pp. 273–74]).

The original line of the lords of Brancion seems to have continued as lords of Neublans.[98] It is difficult, however, to trace family members in the second half of the eleventh century. A Walter of Neublans appears around 1080 (GC IV:232, no. 12; St.-Marcel 10 [p. 15]). He may be a son or grandson of Warulf III. After him, however, there is a relatively clear family tree of lords of Neublans in the twelfth century. A Stephen of Neublans, who had a brother named Hugh li Abandonez and a nephew Walter, went on the First Crusade (C 3737 [V:87–91]; St.-Marcel 45 [p. 49]). Hugh li Abandonez is doubtless the same as the Hugh of Brancion who appears in the late eleventh or early twelfth century (C 3920 [V:270–72]). He is probably the Hugh, nephew of Lord Ansedeus of Navilly, who inherited the castellany of Navilly around 1100 (St.-Marcel 36 [p. 41]). The nephew Walter is doubtless the Walter, son of Walter, who appears in a charter for Cluny about this time, acting with the lords of Neublans. One can assume his father Walter was identical with the Walter of Neublans who appears in a charter of St.-Marcel and was a brother of Stephen and Hugh (C 3716 [V:63]; St.-Marcel 45 [p. 49]). Stephen I of Neublans, apparently the same one who went on the First Crusade, went to Jerusalem again in 1120. At that time he left behind a wife named Beatrix (sometimes called Brunessa, La Ferté 233, 237 [pp. 188–89, 191]) and four sons, Hugh, Walter, Simon, and William (St.-Marcel 41 [pp. 45–47]). Stephen also came back successfully from this Crusading trip, for he appeared with his wife and sons in charters for the next twenty years or so.

His son Hugh succeeded him as lord of Neublans, and his son Simon became lord of Chaussin (La Ferté 264 [pp. 208–9]). In 1174 William of Neublans, brother of Lord Hugh, went to Jerusalem, saying that his *nepos* and heir was Stephen II of Neublans (Tournus, pp. 161–63; the original of this document is Arch. Saône-et-Loire, H 178, no. 5). Stephen I's son Walter is probably the Walter who became lord of Navilly and married Mathilda, the sister of Josbert of La Ferté, viscount of Dijon. Walter of Navilly witnessed Brunessa's gifts to La Ferté after the death of Stephen of Neublans (La Ferté 237 [p. 191]), a fact which suggests he was her son (though he might instead have been a nephew). When Walter of Navilly died in 1158, he left two

---

[98]This is Duby's conclusion, *La société mâconnaise*, p. 340, n. 97; he makes Walter of Neublans, mentioned below, the son of Warulf III. The lords of Neublans, whose castle was located east of the Saône, in the county of Burgundy, have been studied briefly by Jean Richard, "Lignées féodales et géographie des seigneuries dans le duché de Bourgogne," *Bulletin philologique et historique du comité des travaux historiques et scientifiques*, 1959, pp. 141–48.

daughters. Marguerite, who became lady of Navilly, married Theobold of La Roche, and Andrea married Hugh of Palleau (La Ferté
264–67 [pp. 208–11]). After Theobold of La Roche died in 1166,
Marguerite of Navilly married Hugh-Rufus, son of the duke of Burgundy (La Ferté 260, 263 [pp. 204, 205–6]) (see above, p. 259, and
below, p. 326). Although the document in which Hugh-Rufus appears
with Marguerite does not specifically name her, calling her simply the
daughter of Lord Walter of Navilly, she must be Marguerite, because
Marguerite and Andrea were their father's only two children (La Ferté
260 [p. 204]), and Andrea's husband was still alive in 1177 (La Ferté,
pp. 207–8), whereas Hugh-Rufus died in 1171, five years after
Marguerite's first husband.

Hugh, lord of Neublans, had sons Stephen II, who eventually succeeded as lord of Neublans, Philip, and Walter (La Ferté 249, 252,
264 [pp. 197, 199, 209]). Stephen II, lord of Neublans, had sons
Hugh and Philip (Cîteaux II, fols. 79r–v, no. 4).

Around the middle of the twelfth century this family was replaced
as lords of Brancion by a different family, the lords of Uxelles, who
were called the Grossi from the mid-eleventh century on. In the male
line the family begins with Joceran I, who lived in the final decades of
the tenth century. While it is tempting to see him as the Joceran, son
of Bernard, who appears in the documents from Cluny around 950 or
960, there is no positive evidence of his origins.[99] This Joceran
owned a large amount of allodial land northwest of Mâcon, including
the *villa* of Uxelles (Uxelles is eight kilometers west of Brancion). He
married Rotrudis, a daughter of Lord Warulf II of Brancion, before
980 (C 898, 1521, 1577 [II:13–14, 570–71, 622–23]).[100]

[99]In three documents this Joceran was called son of Bernard and Ava; C 376, 555,
966 (I:354, 538–39; II:62–63). In another he was son of a Bernard who was married to
one Emeltrude; C 947 (II:52). Emeltrude may be Bernard's second wife, or there may
be two different families here. Ava and Bernard buried a son named Aidoard at Cluny
in 947; C 709 (I:663–64). Joceran of Uxelles probably had a brother named Azelin,
who may be the same as this Aidoard; his sons referred to an *avunculus* of that name;
C 2617 (III:664–65). In addition, Joceran's son Bernard I referred to an *avunculus*
named Gui, probably another brother of Joceran; C 2959 (IV:157–58). Duby says,
rather vaguely, that Joceran came from the "clan des Evrard"; *La société mâconnaise*, p.
336.

[100]It is clear from the documents that Joceran's and Rotrudis's children were first
cousins with the next generation of lords of Brancion; see for example C 2827 (IV:31),
in which her son Maiolus referred to Letbald of Brancion as his *avunculus*. That Rotrudis rather than Joceran is the link is suggested strongly by the fact that a lady of
Brancion who would have been her grandmother is also named Rotrudis, while there is
no one named Joceran among the tenth-century lords of Brancion. Chauney incorrectly
makes the Grossi the lineal descendants of Warulf III, lord of Brancion (Rotrudis's
nephew), and omits Joceran I and his children from her family tree; "Le recrutement
de l'épiscopat," p. 210.

The Grossi of Brancion and Uxelles

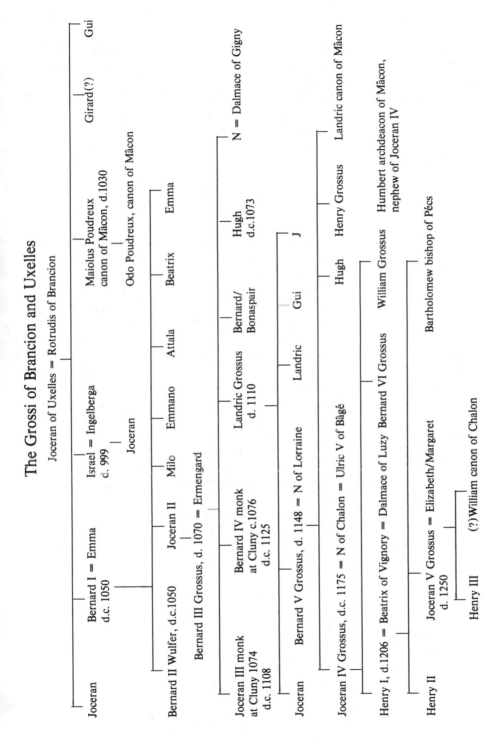

Joceran of Uxelles = Rotrudis of Brancion

Bernard I = Emma
d. 1050

Israel = Ingelberga
d. 999

Maiolus Poudreux
canon of Mâcon, d.1030

Girard(?)

Gui

Odo Poudreux, canon of Mâcon

Joceran

Joceran

Bernard II Wulfer, d.c.1050

Joceran II

Milo

Emmano

Attala

Beatrix

Emma

Bernard III Grossus, d. 1070 = Ermengard

Joceran III monk
at Cluny 1074
d.c. 1108

Bernard IV monk
at Cluny c.1076
d.c. 1125

Landric Grossus
d. 1110

Bernard/
Bonaspair

Hugh
d.c.1073

N = Dalmace of Gigny

Joceran

Bernard V Grossus, d. 1148 = N of Lorraine

Landric

Gui

J

Hugh

Henry Grossus

Landric canon of Mâcon

Joceran IV Grossus, d.c. 1175 = N of Chalon = Ulric V of Bâgé

William Grossus

Humbert archdeacon of Mâcon,
nephew of Joceran IV

Henry I, d.1206 = Beatrix of Vignory = Dalmace of Luzy Bernard VI Grossus

Bartholomew bishop of Pécs

Henry II

Joceran V Grossus = Elizabeth/Margaret
d. 1250

Henry III

(?)William canon of Chalon

Joceran and Rotrudis had six known sons, Joceran, Bernard I, Israel, Maiolus, Girard, and Gui. Their son Israel died in 999, when his brothers Bernard I, Maiolus (a cleric), and Joceran made gifts for his soul (C 2486, 2617 [III:568—69, 664—65]). Israel had married a woman named Ingelberga and had a son named Joceran (C 3132 [IV:297]). Israel's brother Joceran may be the same Joceran who made a gift to Cluny with a wife named Agia at the end of the tenth century; the first two witnesses were Maiolus and Bernard, who would have been his brothers (C 1761 [III:25]). This Joceran predeceased his brothers Bernard I and Maiolus (C 2904 [IV:103—4]). Joceran I's and Rotrudis's two other sons, Girard and Gui, are much less well documented.[101]

Their son Maiolus, also called Maiolus Poudreux, was a canon at Mâcon. He is probably not the same Maiolus as the provost of Mâcon of that name, however, as Provost Maiolus witnessed one charter in which Maiolus Poudreux was called only *clericus* (C 2406 [III:497—98]; see also M 49, 80 [pp. 38—39, 65]). Maiolus Poudreux had a son, Odo Poudreux, who also became a canon at Mâcon (C 1845, 3367 [III:88—89; IV:463]). Maiolus Poudreux, who took the habit at Cluny at the end of his life, probably died in 1030, when his son Odo gave up his claims to what his father had seized from Cluny (C 2827, 2828 [IV:31—32]).

Bernard I succeeded Joceran I. He is called both a *miles* and a *vir clarissimus* (C 2532 [III:603—4]), and at least once Bernard "Chapelle" (C 3334 [IV:425]). He married a woman named Emma. She was the daughter of a woman named Adelaide (C 2905 [IV:104—5]). Bernard and Emma first appear as a couple in a dated charter in 1001 (C 2532 [III:603—4]), though they were probably married before 999, the date of Bernard's brother Israel's death, since one of their (undated) charters has Maiolus and Israel as the first two witnesses (C 2351 [III:461]). They were still alive when Hugh the Great became abbot of Cluny in 1049. Their sons were Bernard II, Joceran II, Milo, and Emmano (also called Igmor), all of whom outlived their father (C 3007, 3334, 3407, 3436 [IV:202, 425—26, 513, 545—46]). Bernard II seems to have been the oldest, but he died before his brothers, apparently without heirs. He is sometimes called Bernard Wulfer or Golfer, perhaps after his Warulf relatives of Brancion (C 2908, 3407, 3435, 3436 [IV:108, 513, 544—46]). Milo, like Bernard II, predeceased his two brothers Joceran II and Emmano (C 3437

---

[101]Girard appears as son of Joceran and his wife Rotrudis only in a charter given—or reconfirmed—in 1033; C 2896 (IV:98—99). If this charter were actually given in 1033, the Joceran and Rotrudis in it cannot be the lord and lady of Brancion, who were dead by that date. Gui appears only in a 1042 charter of Bernard I, in which he is referred to as Bernard's late brother; C 2959 (IV:157—58). See also C 3176 (IV:325—26).

[IV:546—47]). Joceran II inherited part of the patrimony of Maiolus Poudreux, whom he called his *avunculus* (C 2445 [III:526—27]). Bernard I and Emma also had at least three daughters, named Attala, Beatrix, and Emma. Attala and Beatrix agreed, along with their brothers, to a gift to Cluny from their parents (C 3334 [IV:425—26]); and when Emma, wife of Bernard, made a gift to Cluny of some land for her burial, her children Joceran and Emma signed (C 2322 [III:442]).

Joceran II was the heir of Bernard I, but he does not seem to have outlived his father by many years. His wife's name is unknown. He was the father of Bernard III Grossus, the first to be given this *cognomen* (C 2881 [IV:75—76]; M 479 [p. 277]). Bernard III Grossus married a woman named Ermengard (C 3753 [V:106]). They had at least five sons, Joceran III, Bernard IV, Landric, Bonaspair (sometimes called Bernard), and Hugh. They also had a daughter who married Dalmace of Gigny (C 2994 [IV:192—93]; M 26 [p. 22]).[102] Bernard III died in 1070, on pilgrimage to Jerusalem (C 3066, 3077, 3428 [IV:251—52, 257, 539—40]).[103]

After his death, his sons, Joceran III Grossus and Bernard IV Grossus, both entered Cluny—even though Joceran seems to have been the oldest (M 26 [p. 22]; C 3474, 3475 [IV:582—84])—Joceran in 1074 and Bernard perhaps a few years later.[104] Landric Grossus then succeeded as lord of Uxelles. Joceran III became claustral prior of Cluny after having been prior of the Cluniac dependency of St.-Vivant of Vergy. Bernard IV became treasurer of Cluny, prior of the Cluniac house of St.-Marcel-lès-Chalon, then claustral prior of Cluny after the death of his brother (which occurred before 1110), an office he held until at least 1125, and was briefly abbot of St.-Martial of Limoges in 1114 (C 3077, 3104, 3440, 3472—75, 3685, 3754, 3896, 3909, 3926, 3972, 3983 [IV:257, 275, 550—51, 581—84; V:39—40, 107—8, 258—59, 278—79, 330, 339—40, 246—48]; M 26 [p. 22]; St.-Marcel 116 [pp. 95—96]).[105] Orderic Vitalis accused Bernard IV of

---

[102]Dalmace of Gigny was the brother of Fromoald, who had a son named Hugh. The three appear together in a charter for Cluny dating from the 1070s; C 3478 (IV:586—87). Dalmace had uncles named Robert and Wigo and a nephew named Oliver; C 2994, 2997 (IV:192—95).

[103]See also Peter the Venerable, *Miracula* 1.9, PL CLXXXIX:874—76. Petit erroneously leaves Bernard III out of his family tree, collapsing his father Joceran II and son Joceran III into one individual.

[104]Bernard IV Grossus appears in a charter as a layman, recalling his brother Joceran's conversion to Cluny and confirming what his father Bernard and grandfather Joceran had given Cluny; C 3473 (IV:582).

[105]See also Glauco M. Cantarella, "Due note cluniacensi," *Studi medievali*, 3rd ser., 16 (1975), 763—70; and, for Joceran's rule as prior of Vergy, the text edited by Richard, "Lignées féodales," p. 153. Joceran III is known to have died before his brother Landric, because Landric confirmed his burial gifts; C 3703 (IV:255—56). Landric probably died in 1110; see below.

being a chief instigator in the plot of 1122 to bring back Ponce as
abbot of Cluny, after Ponce's resignation, the brief rule of Abbot
Hugh II, and the election of Peter the Venerable.[106] Of their other
brothers, Hugh died young, before 1074, for when Joceran III and
Bernard IV gave Cluny a *mansus* for his soul, they acted as laymen
(C 2098 [III:291]). Landric and Bernard/Bonaspair, the only brothers
left in the world, called themselves "co-heirs" and recalled what they
had inherited from their father Bernard and grandfather Joceran
(C 3473, 3621 [IV:582, 786−87]).[107]

Landric Grossus, lord of Uxelles, married a woman whose name is
not known. His oldest son was named Joceran (C 3440, 3754
[IV:550−51; V:107−8]), but he must have died young, for he soon
disappears from the records.[108] Landric was succeeded by his son
Bernard V Grossus (C 3073 [IV:255−56]). Landric probably died in
1110, when Bernard V recalled the gifts to Cluny of his father Landric, grandfather Bernard, and great-grandfather. In this same charter
Bernard gave his brothers as Landric and Gui, the latter of whom was
still a *puer*. He also mentioned that he had a sister, with the initial J,
but that she was still unmarried (C 3896 [V:246−48]).[109] After a
journey to Jerusalem from which he returned in 1116, Bernard V
confirmed his ancestors' gifts again (C 3896, 3913 [V:246−48,
260−61]). Bernard V acquired Brancion; it is not quite clear how, but
he was the first of the Grossi to call himself lord of Brancion as well
as Uxelles (C 4131 [V:473−74]). When he gave up his claims against
Cluny's property before Abbot Ponce, he also specified that he had
settled claims arising from what Hugh of Brancion had had; Hugh of
Brancion had gone to the Holy Land (C 3920 [V:270−72]; GC
IV:242, nos. 27−28). It seems most likely that this Hugh of Brancion
is the same as Hugh li Abandonez of Neublans (see above, p. 299);
he had presumably left Neublans to his brother Stephen, but the
Grossi acquired Brancion, by inheritance or force. Bernard V married

---

[106]Orderic Vitalis, *Historia ecclesiastica* 12.30, ed. Chibnall, VI:312.

[107]Bernard/Bonaspair may be identical with the Bernard of Meley who was called the
uncle (*avunculus*) of the son of Landric Grossus; if so, he had a son named Robert
(C 3929, 4131 [V:282−83, 473−74]). Since Landric's son called Bernard, the prior of
Cluny and his paternal uncle, his *avunculus* in the same charter in which he called Bernard of Meley an *avunculus*, the term here may well have meant paternal uncle—or just
uncle in general. Bernard of Meley, however, might have been an uncle on the maternal side; the wife of Landric Grossus is not known, and a Humbert of Meley—whom it
would be hard to make a family member—and Bernard of Meley acted together;
C 3764 (V:116−17). Petit makes Bernard of Meley a maternal uncle.

[108]Chauney erroneously identifies him with Bishop Joceran of Langres (1113−1125);
"Le recrutement de l'épiscopat," pp. 210−11. Richard argues against this identification; "Lignées féodales," p. 153, n. 1.

[109]Petit gives Landric Grossus another son, named Hugh, apparently confusing
Landric's sons with his brothers.

the sister of Simon, duke of Lorraine (Alberic de Trois-Fontaines, *Chronica* 1193, MGH SS XXIII:871). He went to Jerusalem a second time, in 1147, on the Second Crusade, and died there. His son Joceran IV succeeded (C 4131 [V:473–74]).

In addition to Joceran IV Grossus, Bernard V had sons named Hugh and Henry Grossus, who appeared in charters from 1147 (M 602 [p. 364]; C 4106, 4127, 4131 [V:455–56, 469–71, 473–74]). Joceran IV also appears with a brother Landric, a canon at Mâcon (La Ferté 103 [pp. 102–3]). He also had "sisters," mentioned but not named by Alberic de Trois-Fontaines (*Chronica* 1193, MGH SS XXIII:871). Bernard V may also have been the father of Robert Grossus, elected to Cluny in 1157 and soon deposed (see Appendix C, p. 411). Robert is called a *cognatus* of the counts of Flanders (Robert of Mt.-St.-Michel, *Chronica* 1157, MGH SS VI:506), and the contemporary count of Flanders was the son of the duke of Lorraine and thus brother of Bernard V's wife.

Joceran IV Grossus was always distinguished in the documents from Joceran of Brancion, who had a nephew named Seguin; he was doubt-less a knight, named for his lord, and was not related in spite of the name similarities (M 625, 626 [pp. 378–79]).[110] Joceran IV married the daughter of the count of Chalon, who later married Lord Ulric V of Bâgé (Arch. Saône-et-Loire, H 25, no. 61; La Ferté 116 [pp. 110–11]; Alberic de Trois-Fontaines, *Chronica* 1193, MGH SS XXIII:871; C 4410 [V:785–87]) (see also above, pp. 287–89). Joceran IV had a nephew named Humbert, whom he persuaded Louis VII to make archdeacon of Mâcon in 1166; he was doubtless the same as the Humbert of Brancion who was found among the canons of Mâcon in 1152 and 1158 (M 613, 615 [pp. 373–74]). Humbert held the office until at least 1182 (RHGF XVI:134–35; M 508 [p. 296]).[111] Joceran last appears in 1174 (Tournus, pp. 161–63).

Joceran IV was the father of Henry I, who succeeded him as lord of Brancion (Alberic de Trois-Fontaines, *Chronica* 1193, MGH SS XXIII:871). Joceran IV's other sons were Bernard VI Grossus and William Grossus. In the first years of the thirteenth century, the lady of Brancion reached an agreement with the monks and burghers of Cluny after the monks had complained about her use of armed men;

---

[110]The knight Joceran of Brancion had a brother Humbert, a canon at Mâcon in 1172, and thus probably different from the Humbert, nephew of Joceran IV Grossus, who was archdeacon from 1166 or so (see below). Joceran of Brancion also had broth-ers named Seguin and Souffroy, monks at La Ferté; Arch. Saône-et-Loire, H 25, no. 17; summarized as La Ferté 18 (p. 34).

[111]Chauney incorrectly makes Humbert the brother, rather than the nephew, of Joceran IV. She also gives Joceran a brother named Geoffrey who she says was also a cathedral canon.

her sons Bernard VI Grossus and William Grossus agreed to the terms (C 4410 [V:785–87]).[112]

Henry I, lord of Brancion, married Beatrix of Vignory (C 4478, 4545 [VI:31, 94]) (see also below, p. 383). They had Henry II, Joceran V Grossus, Bartholomew, and a daughter, as indicated below. When Henry I died, he was buried at Cluny, as his son Bartholomew noted in 1234 when he elected burial there himself (C 4664 [VI:190–91]). Henry had died by 1207 when Beatrix married Dalmace, lord of Luzy (C 4428, 4482 [V:802; VI:35–38]; Vignory 105 [pp. 223–24]). She seems to have been widowed by Dalmace as well, for in 1225 she confirmed an agreement of her son Joceran in a charter in which she called herself "Beatrix Grossa, lady of Uxelles" (C 4545 [VI:94]); it is interesting that she took the *cognomen* of *Grossa*, even though she married into the family.

Joceran V first appears in a dated charter as lord of Brancion in 1208 (C 4447 [V:820]). Joceran V's brothers were Henry II and Bartholomew, bishop of Pécs (Fünfkirchen), an office he held by 1230 (C 4482, 4589, 4604, 4664, 4669 [VI:35–38, 131–32, 150–51, 190–93]). While Joceran took Brancion, his brother Henry II took Uxelles, and in the 1220s, when Joceran did homage to the abbot of Cluny, he said he did so "reserving the rights of my brother Henry" (C 4525, 4528 [VI:78–79, 81]). In addition, they had at least one sister, mentioned in a charter of 1214, although not named (C 4482 [VI:35–38]). Stephen, abbot of Cluny between 1230 and 1235, who is called "of Berzé" in at least one charter, was also referred to as Joceran's *consanguineus* in Joceran's charters. The exact relationship is not clear (C 4604, 4614, 4702 [VI:150–51, 156, 220–21]).[113]

Joceran V, who married a woman called either Margaret or Elizabeth,[114] was succeeded by his son Henry III (C 4711 [VI:230–34]; Plancher II.49 [p. xx]), and was also probably father of William of Brancion, a canon of Chalon who in 1250 arranged to be buried at La Ferté (Petit 2675 [IV:385–87]).[115] Joceran V went on Crusade with Louis IX, accompanied by his son Henry, and died in 1250 from

[112]William Grossus, called a *miles*, appears in other charters from 1195 and 1202; Arch. Saône-et-Loire, H 26, no. 3; Guigue, ed., *Cartulaire Lyonnais*, I:96–97, no. 69.

[113]See also M. Oursel-Quarré, "À propos du chartier de Cluny," *Annales de Bourgogne*, 50 (1978), 105–6.

[114]Duby says that Margaret was the daughter of Count William V of Mâcon; *La société mâconnaise*, p. 346, n. 128. However, the charter he cites as evidence, Arch. nat., J 259, no. 1, says only that Count John of Mâcon and his wife gave Joceran the right to an annual income of fifty pounds. Duby was perhaps confused by a reference to Margaret of Oyselles, third wife of Stephen III of Burgundy (although, even if he translated "Oysiarum" as Uxelles rather than Oyselles, he should have realized that Joceran was lord of Brancion, not Uxelles, which was held by his brother).

[115]Chauney erroneously puts William two generations earlier, making him the son of Joceran IV and thus equating him with the knight William Grossus.

wounds received at the battle of Mansourah.[116] Henry III sold both Brancion and Uxelles (which he inherited on the death of his uncle Henry) to the duke of Burgundy in 1259.[117]

The Counts of Chalon

Lambert was the first hereditary count of Chalon-sur-Saône. He first appears with this title in a charter from 960;[118] his father had probably just died at the time of this charter, for he and his parents all appear together in an act from 958 (Fleury 52 [pp. 130–32]). Lambert was the son of Robert, viscount of Dijon, and his wife Ingeltrude (Paray 2 [pp. 2–3]). Robert was a *fidelis* of Giselbert, count of Autun in the first half of the tenth century (St.-Étienne I.38 [pp. 58–60]; C 721 [I:673–75]). It is tempting to identify Lambert's father Robert as the Robert, brother of Rudolph, count of Dijon, who appeared with Rudolph in a charter for St.-Étienne in 952, recalling their mother and her husband Archimbald (apparently not their father) (St.-Étienne I.42 [pp. 63–64]). If so, this Count Rudolph (Lambert's uncle) may be the same Rudolph, count of Dijon, who in 958 abducted (and married) Letgardis, daughter of count Giselbert of Dijon; she had been married in 956 to Otto, brother of Hugh Capet.[119] Count Lambert had two younger brothers, Robert and Rudolph, both viscounts like their father, Robert of Chalon and Rudolph of Dijon (Paray 8 [p. 9]; Pérard, pp. 63–64). Robert married a woman named Elizabeth (St.-Marcel 8 [p. 14]). The chronicler of Bèze said that Viscount Rudolph, whom he called Rudolph Albus, became prior of Bèze (Chron. St.-B., pp. 288–89).

Lambert married a woman named Adelaide (C 1444 bis [II:755]). While there is no evidence of her origins in the sources, scholars have repeatedly tried to tie her to the family of Giselbert, count of Burgundy, both because Giselbert did have a daughter named Adelaide and because they feel a need to explain how Lambert could have

[116]Jean de Joinville, *Histoire de Saint Louis*, ed. Natalis de Wailly (Paris, 1867), pp. 182–84.

[117]Text in Bazin, *Brancion*, facing p. 82; and in Plancher II.59 [pp. xxiii–xxiv].

[118]D'Arbois de Jubainville, *Histoire de Champagne*, I (Paris, 1859), 452, no. 20.

[119]Rudolph stole Letgardis from his lord Otto, along with the castle of Beaune, according to the *Annales Nivernenses*, MGH SS XIII:89. See also Odorannus of Sens, "Chronica," in *Opera omnia*, ed. Robert-Henri Bautier and Monique Gilles (Paris, 1972), pp. 94–96. Maurice Chaume identifies this man rather vaguely as Count Raoul III of Dijon, last of the "Robertiens de Dijon," and a cousin of Count Lambert's; Chaume, *Origines de Bourgogne*, I:442, 447–48, 537. If Rudolph did marry Letgardis, he may be the father of Lambert, bishop of Langres (1016–1031) and of Lambert's sister Letgardis; Chron. St.-B., p. 195; see also Appendix B, p. 394.

The Counts of Chalon

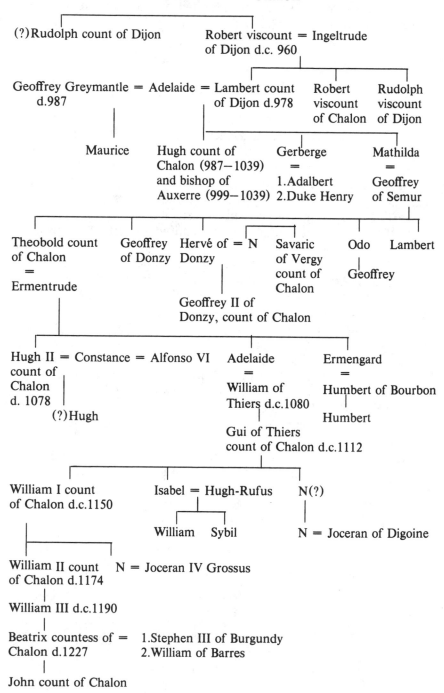

legitimately succeeded to Chalon.[120] I prefer to leave Adelaide's origins unknown; since Lambert's accession to Chalon was recognized by the king, he did not need a hereditary claim by his wife to legitimize his rule (Paray 2 [pp. 2–3]).

Lambert died in 978,[121] and his wife Adelaide quickly married Geoffrey Greymantle, count of Anjou. Geoffrey acted as count of Chalon from 979 until his own death in 987 (C 1474, 3341 [II:528–29; IV:429–31]). Adelaide and Geoffrey had one son, Maurice, known from the documents of his half brother, Hugh,[122] but Geoffrey's Angevin heirs were born to his first wife, Adela of Vermandois.[123] After Geoffrey died, Adelaide's and Lambert's son Hugh

[120]Ferdinand Lot and René Poupardin thought that Adelaide was a daughter of Giselbert, sister of a woman named Werra who married Robert, count of Troyes; Lot, *Les derniers Carolingiens*, pp. 323–34; Poupardin, *Le royaume de Bourgogne (888–1038): Étude sur les origines du royaume d'Arles* (Paris, 1907), pp. 206, 417. This suggestion, however, was questioned by Eugène Jarry, *Formation territoriale de la Bourgogne*, Provinces et pays de France 3 (Paris, 1948), p. 243. André Duchesne suggested in 1625 that Lambert's wife Adelaide was daughter of Robert, count of Troyes, and of his wife, the daughter of Giselbert, whom he called Adelaide-Werra; Duchesne, *Histoire de Vergy*, p. 46. He was followed by J. Louis Bazin, *Les comtes héréditaires de Chalon-sur-Saône (880–1234)*, Mémoires de la Société d'histoire et d'archéologie de Chalon-sur-Saône, n.s. 4 (Chalon, 1911); and by Vajay, "'Guerre de Bourgogne,'" p. 158. In 1619, however, Duchesne had suggested that Adelaide was a sister of Count William I of Arles; *Histoire des roys, ducs, et comtes de Bourgogne*, p. 387. Chaume suggested that Adelaide was either the daughter or the granddaughter of Charles-Constantine, count of Vienne in the first half of the tenth century; *Origines de Bourgogne*, I:447, n. 2. Ernst Sackur identified Adelaide with Attala/Tolana, daughter of Alberic I of Mâcon, in order to give Adelaide's grandson Otto-William a hereditary claim to Mâcon; Sackur, *Die Cluniacenser in ihrer kirchlichen und allgemeingeschictlichen Wirksamkeit bis zur Mitte des elften Jahrhunderts*, II (Halle an der Saale, 1894; rpt. Darmstadt, 1965), 469–71. He based this identification on a 944 charter of Attala's brother, Count Leotold, in which he referred to his sister and to his *consanguineus* Lambert; C 655 (I:609–10). Sackur incorrectly translated *consanguineus* as brother-in-law.

[121]Paray 4 (pp. 5–6) gives the year of Lambert's death as DCCCCLXXXVIII. However, his wife Adelaide was married to her second husband well before 988. It seems most likely that, when the cartulary of Paray was composed, the copyist added an extra X.

[122]C 1794 (III:49–50). Paray 180 (p. 90). Though Hugh refers to Maurice as his "brother," Hugh's biographer says that he was Lambert's only surviving son; *Gesta pontificum*, pp. 386–87. A charter from Anjou issued around the year 1000 speaks of Count Fulk and his brother Maurice and "their" (*eorum*) father Geoffrey; *Cartulaire noir de la cathédrale d'Angers*, ed. Ch. Urseau (Paris, 1908), pp. 56–58, no. 25. (Saint Maurice is the patron saint of Angers; Maurice was doubtless named for the saint and may have been intended for the church.) For Maurice, see also Bernard S. Bachrach, "Geoffrey Greymantle, Count of the Angevins, 960–987: A Study in French Politics," *Studies in Medieval and Renaissance History*, 17 (1985), 23–24. Although Bachrach speculates that Geoffrey arranged for Maurice to take the county of "Chalons" (as he erroneously refers to Chalon), in preference to Hugh, this seems unlikely, as the only charter for Burgundy in which Maurice is called *comes* (the ordinary title for a dead count's son) was one drawn up by Hugh, himself acting as *comes*; C 1794 (III:49–50). The fact that Hugh was in orders and indeed bishop of Auxerre for forty years did not keep him from being count of Chalon for over fifty years.

[123]For Adela of Vermandois, see the "Genealogiae comitum Andegavensium" 2, ed. Halphen and Poupardin, p. 248.

ruled Chalon until his own death in 1039; he continued to hold the office even after becoming bishop of Auxerre in 999 (*Gesta pontificum*, pp. 386–87).

It is clear that Hugh was son of Lambert and Adelaide because he called himself so in his own charters; he also named his sister Mathilda, who married Geoffrey of Semur (C 1474, 2722 [II:528–29; III:745–46]; Paray 180, 184 [pp. 90–92]). However, there has been much debate on Hugh's sister Gerberge. On the face of it, the evidence seems clear; Hugh's biography says that his *germana* was the wife of Henry, duke of Burgundy (brother of Hugh Capet) (*Gesta pontificum*, p. 387), and Henry is known to have married a woman named Gerberge (see above, p. 265). Some scholars, however, have translated *germana* as half sister,[124] even though *germana* is used here only a few lines from a use of *germanus frater* to mean full brother (saying that Hugh had no "full brother," although, as noted above, he did have a half brother). The only real difficulty with making Gerberge daughter of Lambert and Adelaide is in Adelaide's age. Gerberge, before marrying Henry, had married Adalbert, the last king of Italy, who was driven out of Italy in 962; at that time, she and her young son Otto-William had fled back to Burgundy (Raoul Glaber, *Historia* 3.2 [pp. 56–57]). Since Otto-William was married by 981 and had a grandson around the turn of the century, scholars have concluded his grandmother must have been too old to still be having children at the time of Otto-William's marriage. Therefore, since Adelaide had Maurice some time around 980, they have concluded that Otto-William's mother Gerberge must be daughter of someone other than Adelaide, perhaps an earlier wife of Lambert's.

But the real problem here lies with modern scholars trying to make generations at least twenty-five years long. If Adelaide were born around 935, she could have had her first child, Gerberge, around 948, and Gerberge would then have been in a position to have an infant son by 962, who would certainly be old enough to marry nineteen years later, and have *his* son marry twenty years after that. Adelaide would then have been forty-three when Lambert died and she married Geoffrey Greymantle, not too old to have a final child, even in the Middle Ages; Eleanor of Aquitaine after all had children well into her forties. While I would certainly not insist on these ages, it is thus possible that the sources are right in making Adelaide Gerberge's mother. These dates are quite tight, but they can be loosened somewhat if one assumes that Adalbert married Gerberge only *after* being

[124]For example, Chaume, *Origines de Bourgogne*, I:464, n. 3; and Jean Richard, "Origines féodales. Les Chalon, les Vergy et la Puisaye d'après une charte du XIe siècle," *Annales de Bourgogne*, 18 (1946), 119.

driven out of Italy. Though Raoul Glaber says that Gerberge had to
flee Italy in 962, it is hard to see how the daughter of the count of
Chalon would have met the Italian king; it makes more sense that
Adalbert married Gerberge only after seeking refuge in Burgundy.
Liudprand of Cremona says that Adalbert fled Italy in 962 and sought
refuge initially at Freinet in Provence (*Historia Ottonis* 4, MGH SS
III:340). An eleventh-century imperial chronicle says that Adalbert
fled to the region of Autun when driven out of Italy and lingered on
there for three years before he died (Benzo of Viviers, "Ad Henricum
IV imperatorem libri VII" 3.15, MGH SS XI:628). If Otto-William
then were born around 966, he would still have been old enough to
marry a highly desirable heiress in 981, and both his mother and his
grandmother could have been fifteen or sixteen when they had their
first children. There is after all at least as much reason to doubt
Raoul Glaber's account, since he wrote seventy years after the events
and with no personal knowledge of Italian politics, as to doubt Hugh
of Chalon's biographer, who had known his subject personally.

One other possibility has been suggested by Vajay.[125] He suggests
that Hugh's *germana* who married Duke Henry of Burgundy was not
Gerberge at all. It is quite clear from the documents that Otto-
William's mother Gerberge was the same Gerberge who married
Duke Henry, but Vajay has suggested that Henry also married another
woman (perhaps after Gerberge's death) and that *this* woman was
Hugh's sister. The chief appeal of this suggestion is that it reconciles
the sources, but the difficulty is *when* Henry could have married this
anonymous woman. He was certainly married to Gerberge by 980,
and I believe remained married to her until his death (see above, pp.
267–68).

One final point can be made about Hugh's generation. It has often
been assumed that the castles of Varzy and Cosne, which Hugh held
as bishop of Auxerre, came to him not from his see but from his
ancestors; Jean Richard has argued that these possessions in the
Puisaye may provide information on Adelaide's origins.[126] But this
conclusion is based on a misreading of the sources. Hugh's biography
states, "Apud castrum Varziacum, sue et antecessorum suorum
proprium ditioni . . . in Conada similiter castello sue matris sedis . . ."
("At the castle of Varzy, that belonged to his and his predecessors'
own dominium . . . at Cosne, a castle similarly belonging to his
mother see . . .") In quoting, Richard adds the word *matris* after the
first *sue*, in the phase describing Varzy, and omits *ditioni*; without

126Richard, "Origines féodales. Les Chalon," pp. 112–13. See also Yves Sassier,
Recherches sur le pouvoir comtal en Auxerrois du Xe au début du XIIIe siècle (Auxerre,
1980), p. 24.

ditioni, the *sue* does seem rather to hang, and he thus felt justified in adding the *matris*. He thus translates the passage as, "At the castle of Varzy, which was his mother's and his ancestors' own."[127] The term *antecessorum* however refers not to ancestors but to predecessors in the see of Auxerre, and the reference to Cosne explicitly refers to his *see*, not to his mother. Anyway, Cosne had belonged to the bishops of Auxerre long before Hugh became bishop.[128]

After Bishop Hugh's death in 1039 the county of Chalon passed to his nephew Theobold, son of Hugh's sister Mathilda and her husband Geoffrey, lord of Semur (Paray 7 [pp. 8−9]) (see below, pp. 359). Theobold was one of five sons; the other four were named Geoffrey, Hervé, Odo, and Lambert (C 2693 [III:721]). Theobold began appearing as count in charters with his uncle Hugh during the last years of Hugh's life (C 2846, 2909 [IV:46−47, 108−9]; Paray 140 [p. 68]). His brothers Geoffrey and Hervé became lords of Donzy (see below, pp. 327−29). Little is known of Odo and Lambert but their names. Odo did have a son named Geoffrey, mentioned in the chronicle of St.-Germain as having attacked the monastery.[129] Theobold, in a charter for St.-Marcel-lès-Chalon, referred to a *parens* named Ermensend, a nun, but it is not clear whether this was a sister, a cousin, or an aunt (St.-Marcel 30 [pp. 32−33]).

Theobold married a woman named Ermentrude (C 3341 [IV:429−31]). He died fighting in Spain, with many other Burgundian nobles, and was succeeded by his young son, Hugh II (Paray 10, 107 [pp. 10, 56−57]; St.-Marcel 30 [pp. 32−33]). Hugh II married Constance, daughter of Duke Robert I of Burgundy,[130] and may have had a son, also named Hugh, although in the one charter in which he is mentioned it is not completely clear whether the "S. Hugonis filii ejus" is Theobold's son Hugh II or Hugh II's own son (St.-Marcel 30 [pp. 32−33]). If the boy existed he seems to have predeceased his father, for on Hugh's death in 1078 the county of Chalon was shared by several of his relatives.

Hugh II had had two sisters. One, Ermengard, married Humbert of Bourbon, and had a son named Humbert who became a monk at Paray-le-monial (Paray 107 [pp. 56−57]; C 3602 [IV:760−62]). His other sister, Adelaide, married Lord William of Thiers (in the Auvergne) (C 3602 [IV:760−62]). He is probably the son of the

[127]*Gesta pontificum*, p. 391. Richard, "Origines féodales. Les Chalon," p. 113, n. 2.

[128]Constance Brittain Bouchard, *Spirituality and Administration: The Role of the Bishop in Twelfth-Century Auxerre*, Speculum Anniversary Monographs 5 (Cambridge, Mass., 1979), p. 19.

[129]"De gestibus abbatum S. Germani Autissiodoresis," ed. Philippe Labbe, *Novae bibliothecae manuscriptorum librorum*, I (Paris, 1657), 576.

[130]Falco, "Chronicon Trenorchiense" 49, ed. Giry and Poupardin, pp. 104−5. See also above, pp. 257−58.

William of Thiers who appeared with his parents, Lord Gui of Thiers and Riclendis, and his brothers, Theobold and Stephen, bishop of Le Puy, in charters from 1011 and 1016 (C 2682 [III:710–13]; GC II:75–77, no. 4; cf. C 3315 [IV:408–10]). He had probably died by 1080, when Adelaide and her son, called "W. of the Auvergne," appeared without him in the charter attesting to the election of a new bishop of Chalon; the charter commented that there was then "no territorial prince" at Chalon (GC IV:232, no. 12).

Adelaide and her husband William had a son, Gui, lord of Thiers and count of Chalon (Paray 87, 208 [pp. 46–47, pp. 107–8]). Gui was married by 1093, though his wife's name is not known (St.-Marcel 96 [p. 83]). But Gui was not the only count of Chalon. He shared the county with his cousin Geoffrey, son of Lord Hervé of Donzy.[131] Then, around 1100, as Geoffrey was leaving for Jerusalem, he sold his share of the county of Chalon to his uncle (*avunculus*) Savaric (GC IV:232–33, no. 13).[132] The exact relationship between Geoffrey of Donzy and Savaric is not clear. Because the sources call Savaric Geoffrey's uncle, most scholars have assumed that he was a younger brother of Geoffrey's father, Hervé of Donzy. Jean Richard, however, has suggested a somewhat more plausible hypothesis, that Savaric was the brother of Geoffrey's mother.[133]

By 1113 Gui of Thiers had died and been succeeded by his son, William I, as joint count of Chalon with Savaric (La Ferté 1 [pp. 41–42]). Savaric sold the duke of Burgundy Châtelet-Chalon some time after 1113 (La Ferté 82 [p. 90]), and apparently gave up his rights as count of Chalon at the same time, for his children did not inherit any share of the county, and Chalon went entirely to William I and his heirs. In addition to William I, Gui of Thiers had a daughter named Isabel, who married Hugh-Rufus, son of the duke of Burgundy and lord of Châtelet-Chalon. They had a son named William and a daughter Sybil (Petit 741 [III:265]). (For these, see also above, p. 259.) Isabel, or another sister, or perhaps a cousin, had a daughter

[131] Maurice Chaume has explored the question of exactly how the county of Chalon was divided, and he concluded it was held in *condominium* by the lords of Thiers, Donzy, and Semur; "Un problème de droit féodale: La succession de Chalon en 1080," *Mémoires de la Société pour l'histoire du droit et des institutions des anciens pays bourguignons, comtois et romands*, 2 (1935), 177–79. I would not follow him in including the lords of Semur in this *condominium*; they seem rather to have been intent on setting up an independent power center on the fringes of the county.

[132] The original of this charter is Arch. Saône-et-Loire, G 4. It is a cyrograph, apparently intended for the bishop of Chalon and Savaric to each have half, but it was never cut.

[133] Richard, "Origines féodales. Les Chalon," p. 115. Though *avunculus* was sometimes used to mean paternal uncle, its more usual meaning was maternal uncle.

who married Lord Joceran of Digoine; Joceran called his wife the *neptis* of Count William (La Ferté 229 [p. 185]).

William I was the father of William II. It is not entirely clear when William II succeeded his father, though William I was still alive in 1147 (La Ferté 20 [pp. 56–57]). Virtually nothing is known of William II except that he died in 1174 (Fleury 206 [II:57–59]). One of the Counts William of Chalon, perhaps he, died on 8 or 13 March (Obit. Sens I:429–30, 522). A woman of Chalon, apparently sister of William II, unnamed in the documents but usually called Alix by modern scholars, married Joceran IV Grossus, lord of Brancion and Uxelles (Alberic de Trois-Fontaines, *Chronica* 1193, MGH SS XXIII:871; La Ferté 116 [pp. 110–12]) (see also above, p. 305). William II's son William III succeeded (Arch. Saône-et-Loire, H 25, no. 16). He went to Jerusalem in 1189 and was the father of Beatrix, countess of Chalon (C 4396 [V:756–57]; Petit 799 [III:286–87]; Alberic de Trois-Fontaines, *Chronica* 1190, MGH SS XXIII:864).

Beatrix, who inherited Chalon after the death of William III, had a long and active career before retiring to Tournus in 1226, where she died the following year, on 7 April (Tournus, pp. 190–91; Beatrix 75 [p. 107]; Obit. Lyon II:582–83). She married Stephen III, count of Burgundy and Auxonne (Beatrix 24–26, 29 [pp. 65–66, 68]), though he later repudiated her (see above, p. 278). They were married by 1188 (Petit 799 [III:286–87]; Beatrix 52 [pp. 82–83]). After being divorced from Stephen, Beatrix married William of Barres, the king's seneschal (C 4396 [V:756–57]). In 1223 Beatrix did homage for Chalon to King Louis (Layettes 1600 [II:11]). She died in 1227, the year her son John first appears with the title of count of Chalon (C 4552, 4553 [VI:99–100]). In 1237, John gave the county of Chalon to the duke of Burgundy (Layettes 2559 [II:347]).

The Lords of Choiseul

H. de Faget de Casteljau has given an overview of this family and their branches in the twelfth and thirteenth centuries; "Recherches sur la maison de Choiseul," *Cahiers haut-marnais*, 102 (1970), 147–55; 105 (1971), 143–55; 107 (1971), 245–56; 110 (1972), 154–63. His work is marred by very imprecise references to the primary sources.

In 1084 there was a Rayner *miles*, lord of Choiseul, with a wife named Ermengard and children named Roger and Adelina. Rayner made gifts to Molesme for his wife's soul a few years later (Molesme 1.26, 27 [II:36–39]). When he was dying in 1102, Rayner gave pasture rights to Molesme, with the consent of his children, Roger and

The Lords of Choiseul

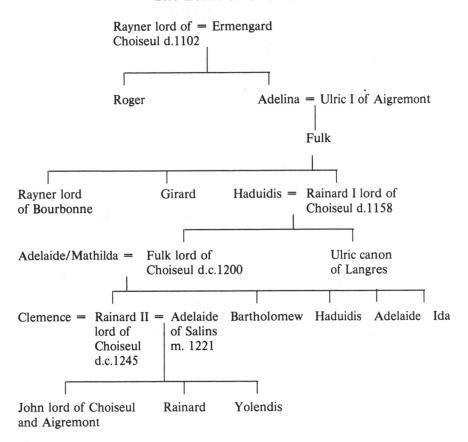

Adelina, and Adelina's husband, Ulric of Aigremont (Molesme 1.63, 2.370 [II:72–73, 390–91]). Roger outlived his father by several years, even making a successful trip to Jerusalem (Molesme 1.63 [II:72–73]), but he never seems to have married or had children. Choiseul seems to have gone with Adelina to the lord of Aigremont, for the next independent lord of Choiseul was Rainard, who lived in the middle of the twelfth century and was Ulric and Adelina's grandson, the son of their son Fulk (see above, p. 281).

Rainard I, lord of Choiseul, who died in 1158, mentioned in his last charters his wife Haduidis, son Fulk, and brother Rayner I of Bourbonne (Molesme 2.361, 362 [II:386–87]).[134] In addition to Fulk, Rainard also had a son named Ulric, who became a cathedral canon at Langres (Molesme 2.371 [II:391]). After his death, his wife married the lord of Beaucharmoy (Arch. Côte-d'Or, 7 H 7, fol. 74r; summarized as Molesme 2.377 [II:393]). Fulk, lord of Choiseul, married a woman named Adelaide (also called Mathilda in one document, Arch. Haute-Marne, 8 H 22)[135] and had children named Rainard II, Bartholomew, Haduidis, Adelaide, and Ida (Arch. Haute-Marne, 5 H 6, 8 H 10, 8 H 22, 8 H 23, 8 H 24, 8 H 50; Clairvaux I, p. 74, no. 8). He also had a nephew named Walter (Arch. Haute-Marne 5 H 6). In 1178 Lord Fulk of Choiseul spoke of the brothers Willenc and Louis—doubtless sons of Mileta of Aigremont—as his *cognati* (Arch. Haute-Marne, 8 H 23). Rainard II had married a woman named Clemence by 1192 (Clairvaux I, p. 74, no. 8; Arch. Haute-Marne, 8 H 24).[136]

In 1200 Rainard II was lord of Choiseul (Arch. Haute-Marne, 8 H 9). He was called a *cognatus* of Rayner, lord of Aigremont (Arch. Haute-Marne, 8 H 7). In 1221, apparently after being widowed, Rainard, lord of Choiseul, married Adelaide, lady of Salins, and gave her the castle of Choiseul in dowry (Arch. Haute-Marne, G 76, no. 1). In 1234 Rainard and Adelaide had sons named John and Rainard and a daughter named Yolendis (Arch. Côte-d'Or, 7 H 7, fol. 73r; summarized as Molesme 2.366 [II:388]). In 1245 John of Choiseul, lord of Aigremont, recalled his parents, Lord Rainard of Choiseul and Adelaide (Arch. Haute-Marne, 8 H 23).

[134]See also Faget de Casteljau, "La maison de Choiseul" [1971], p. 43.

[135]Faget de Casteljau quite convincingly suggests, on the basis of name similarities, that Adelaide/Mathilda was the daughter of Bartholomew of Vignory and his wife Eloise; ibid., p. 146.

[136]Faget de Casteljau calls Clemence the daughter of Gilbert, viscount of Vesoul, and of the family of the lords of Faucogny; ibid., p. 148.

The Lords of Clefmont

The lords of Clefmont-en-Bassigny, sometimes called counts, were among the more powerful castellans of northern Burgundy. The family of the lords of Clefmont has been briefly discussed by Hubert Flammarion, "Clefmont: Une maison comtale aux confins de la Bourgogne, de la Champagne et de la Lorraine (XIe–XIVe siècles)," *Annales de l'Est*, 5th ser., 27 (1975), 373–401. Since there were Carolingian counts of Bassigny in the area where the lord of Clefmont later held power, Flammarion has tried, without much success, to attach the counts of Clefmont to earlier lords. But there is not enough evidence to construct a family tree from any time before the twelfth century.

Simon I was count of Clefmont at the beginning of the twelfth century.[137] He seems to have been the grandson of a woman named Lancenna (GC XIII:486, no. 36). His wife was the daughter of Eblo II of Roucy and of his wife, Sybil of Sicily.[138] Simon married this woman after the death of her first husband, the lord of Ribemont (Alberic de Trois-Fontaines, *Chronica* 1119, MGH SS XXIII:823; "Genealogiae Fusniacenses," MGH SS XIII:254).[139] Simon's son and heir was named Robert Wicard.[140]

Robert Wicard, count of Clefmont, married a woman named Beatrix. Beatrix was the daughter of a couple named Gui and Adelaide, whom it is tempting to identify with Lord Gui V of Vignory and his wife Adelaide. This is especially so since Gui and Adelaide of Vignory appear in the same charter as Robert Wicard and Beatrix, making gifts to La Crête. Robert Wicard and Beatrix had at least two sons, Simon II, lord of Clefmont, and Robert Wicard II (Arch. Haute-Marne, 5 H 5, 5 H 7). They also had a daughter, Adelaide Wicheta, who married Lord Simon of Sexfontaines (Arch. Haute-Marne, 5 H 8, 8 H 107) (see below, p. 363).

Simon II was count of Clefmont for much of the second half of the twelfth century. His first wife, Auvys, appears with him in a charter

[137]Flammarion calls him Simon II, because he has put a "Simon I" in his eleventh-century family tree; therefore, in the following, his numbering of the Lords Simon is always one greater than mine.

[138]Sybil was the daughter of Robert Guiscard, duke of Sicily. It is interesting to note that Simon I of Clefmont named his heir for his wife's illustrious grandfather. William of Apulia, *Gesta Roberti Wiscardi* 4, MGH SS IX:279. Philipp Jaffé, ed., *Bibliotheca rerum Germanicarum*, II (Berlin, 1865; rpt. Aalen, 1964), 17, no. 1.7.

[139]The editor of Alberic's chronicle incorrectly identifies Clefmont-en-Bassigny as Chaumont. Flammarion calls this daughter of Eblo of Roucy "Agnes," though she is not named in the charters; "Clefmont," p. 379 and n. 1.

[140]Flammarion also gives them a son named Simon and two daughters who married lords of Beaujeu, one of whom had children named Hugh and Simon; "Clefmont," p. 379, n. 2, p. 382.

The Lords of Clefmont

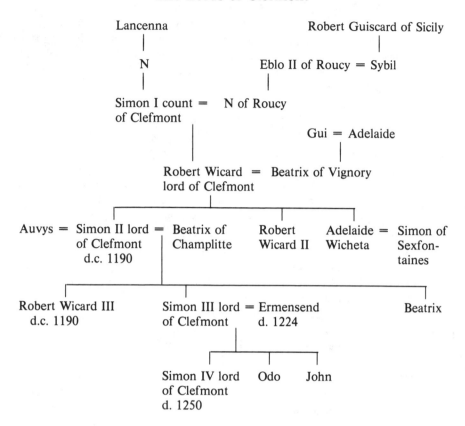

from 1167 (Petit 455 [II:320]). His second wife, Beatrix, was daughter of Odo of Champlitte (Arch. Haute-Marne, 1 H 72, no. 8). (For Odo of Champlitte, see above, pp. 275–77.) He appears with her before 1179. Lord Simon of Clefmont and his brother Wicard (as Robert Wicard II was usually called in the charters) settled their quarrel with the bishop of Langres in 1182 (Langres 150 [pp. 571–72]).[141] In 1188 Simon, lord of Clefmont, made gifts to Clairvaux with his wife Beatrix, son Robert Wicard III, infant son Simon III, and baby daughter Beatrix (Clairvaux I, p. 73, no. 2; Clairvaux II, pp. 12–13, no. 3).[142] The following year Simon II and his wife mentioned *two* daughters, but did not name them (Morment 50 [pp. 128–29]). Simon II was one of the Burgundian lords to die on the Third Crusade, killed with his son Robert Wicard III; his wife Beatrix and Simon, his surviving son, made gifts for their souls (Arch. Côte-d'Or, 7 H 7, fol. 135r; summarized as Molesme 2.685 [II:502]). Beatrix outlived her husband by many years. In 1207 she was married to Geoffrey, lord of Deuilly, and mentioned that her son Simon III was lord of Clefmont (Longué, fol. 118r).

In 1200 Simon III, lord of Clefmont, was married to Ermensend (Mores 48 [pp. 70–71]). She was probably the daughter of Lord Waleran of Breteuil and of Adelaide, daughter of Robert of Braine (himself son of Louis VI), whom Alberic de Trois-Fontaines says Simon of Clefmont married (*Chronica* 1162, MGH SS XXIII:845). Simon III and Ermensend had sons Simon IV and Odo by 1224 (Mores 84 [p. 85]), when Ermensend died. Simon IV, who succeeded, also spoke of another brother, named John, in a charter of 1235 (Mores 98 [p. 90]).[143] Simon IV became the liege man of Theobold, count of Champagne, in 1245 (Layettes 3354 [II:569–70]). He was buried at Morimond when he died in 1250.[144]

The Counts of Dijon and the Lords of Beaumont

The family of the lords of Beaumont has been briefly discussed by Jean Marilier as part of his study of the church of Losne, founded by a family member; Marilier, "Une réplique de Saint-Étienne de Vignory: Notre-Dame de Losne," in *Mélanges offerts à René Crozet*, ed. Pierre Gallais and Yves-Jean Riou (Poitiers, 1966), pp. 223–35. The

---

[141]Flammarion gives Wicard two sons, Wicard and Simon; "Clefmont," p. 383.

[142]Flammarion also gives Simon II a third son, Wicard, who died in infancy; "Clefmont," pp. 382, 385, n. 1.

[143]Flammarion makes John prior of Morimond; "Clefmont," p. 382.

[144]Epitaph in Louis Dubois, *Histoire de l'abbaye de Morimond* (Paris, 1851), p. 425.

family tree is on page 229, note 32. Petit also gives his version of the
family tree (I:93), without a discussion of the evidence; I disagree
with him on several points. The lords of Beaumont are known principally from the chronicles of St.-Bénigne and Bèze, houses to which
they made many gifts over the generations.

In a charter of the cleric Gibuin from the first half of the eleventh
century, inserted into the Chronicle of Bèze, Gibuin spoke of his
great-grandfather Gibuin, grandfather Hugh I, and father Hugh II,
lord of Beaumont and count of Atuyer. (Atuyer is the region between
Dijon and Langres, and Beaumont is the capital of this region.)
Gibuin and his niece Ermengard, who had married a man named
Fulk, made gifts for the soul of Gibuin's brother (Ermengard's
father) Hugh III. Gibuin added that he had a late brother Gui as well
(Chron. St.-B., pp. 333–35).

Gibuin's quick sketch of five generations of his family can be supplemented with other sources. The first Gibuin is doubtless the man
called the *germanus* of Duke Hugh the Black in 926 (C 256 [I:248]),
Hugh being son of Duke Richard le Justicier of Burgundy. It is not
clear whether *germanus* here means full brother or half brother
(perhaps illegitimate half brother, which would explain why Gibuin
rarely appears in the records, unlike the three well-known sons of
Richard le Justicier, Hugh the Black, Boso, and Raoul, king of
France). Gibuin was called a count in an early tenth-century charter
of his son, Hugh I.[145] Hugh I acted as count of Dijon and married a
woman named Alburgis. Hugh and Alburgis had four sons: Richard,
count of Dijon; Hugh II, count of Atuyer and Beaumont; Gibuin,
bishop of Châlons for most of the second half of the tenth century;
and Odo. Count Hugh I of Dijon died some time between 950 and
980. Hugh's wife, his sons Count Richard, Count Hugh II, and
Bishop Gibuin all made gifts to St.-Bénigne for his soul (Chron. St.-
B., pp. 127–28). At the beginning of the eleventh century Count
Richard acted at Dijon with his brothers Hugh II and Odo (Chron.
St.-B., p. 172). Count Richard married a woman named Addita, who
outlived both Richard and their son Leotold; she made gifts for their
souls in 1007 (Chron. St.-B., pp. 167–68). There were no more
counts of Dijon after Richard; Dijon was ruled by viscounts, directly
under the dukes of Burgundy. Both Richard's brother and his
nephew, however, called themselves counts of Atuyer. Richard's
brother Hugh II married a woman named Ermengard (St.-Étienne I.68
[pp. 89–90]); his family is described more fully below. One of the

[145]Alphonse Roserot, ed., "Chartes inédites des IXe et Xe siècles appartenant aux Archives de la Haute-Marne (851–973)," *Bulletin de la Société des sciences historiques et
naturelles de l'Yonne*, 51 (1897), 183–84, no. 12.

The Counts of Dijon and the Lords of Beaumont

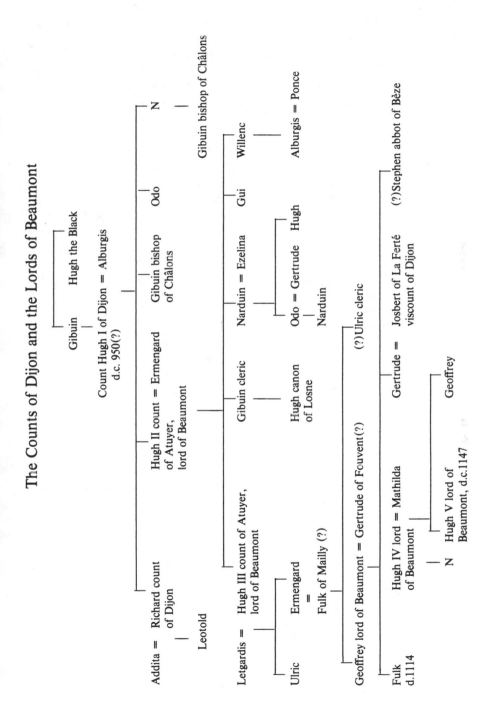

brothers in this generation—or perhaps an anonymous sister—had a son Gibuin, who succeeded his uncle Gibuin as bishop of Châlons at the very end of the tenth century.[146]

To return to the cleric Gibuin, son of Hugh II, who sketched his family's history in the eleventh century: Gibuin was one of a family of at least five brothers. His brother Hugh III was count of Atuyer and Beaumont; Hugh's wife was named Letgardis (Chron. St.-B., pp. 320–22, 326, 328). It is possible that this Letgardis is the same as the Letgardis *matrona* who was sister of Bishop Lambert of Langres (1016–1031) (Chron. St.-B., p. 195) (see Appendix B, p. 394). The cleric Gibuin appeared in other charters with his brother Narduin, who married a woman named Ezelina, and Narduin's children Odo and Hugh (St.-Étienne I.68 [pp. 89–90]; Chron. St.-B., pp. 315, 324–25). Narduin's son Odo, *optimus miles*, married a woman named Gertrude and had a son named Narduin, like his father (Chron. St.-B., pp. 320–22). In addition to the son of his brother Narduin, Gibuin had another nephew named Hugh (St.-Étienne I.68 [pp. 89–90]). As well as Gibuin, Hugh III, and Narduin, Hugh II and Ermengard had another son, named Gui, who predeceased his three brothers (Chron. St.-B., pp. 344–45); this is the same Gui whom Gibuin mentioned in recounting the history of his family. There seems also to have been a fifth son in this generation, Willenc; he is known only from a mention by his daughter Alburgis, the wife of one Ponce, who referred to her father Willenc as the brother of Hugh, lord of Beaumont, and who recalled her noble ancestor Gibuin (Chron. St.-B., pp. 332, 358).[147] The cleric Gibuin seems to have had a son himself, Hugh, a canon at Losne who was largely responsible for founding the church of Notre-Dame of Losne (Chron. St.-B., pp. 336–37, 353).[148]

Hugh III and his wife Letgardis had two children, Ulric and Ermengard, and Ermengard married Fulk, as mentioned above. However, Ulric does not seem to have married or had children, for Beaumont went to Ermengard and Fulk (Chron. St.-B., pp. 326–28). Fulk appeared in the charters of the duke of Burgundy as count of Beaumont in 1043 and 1053.[149] Fulk may have been of the family of the

---

[146]Gerbert of Reims, Letter 181, *Die Briefsammlung Gerberts von Reims*, ed. Fritz Weigle (Berlin: MGH, 1966), p. 211.

[147]Marilier does not include either Gui or Willenc in his family tree.

[148]Marilier, apparently believing a cleric could not have children, gives the cleric Gibuin a brother also named Gibuin, the father of this canon Hugh. He calls this Gibuin's wife a woman of Fouvent, although it is not clear on what grounds. The introduction of a second Gibuin into this generation seems unnecessary. The editors of GC and Petit both say that Gibuin was the same as the Gibuin who was archdeacon of Langres in 1068 (GC IV:145, no. 21) and who became archbishop of Lyon in 1076. This identification is quite possible, but there is no direct evidence for it.

[149]St.-B. II.324 (pp. 104–6). *Recueil des chartes de l'abbaye de Saint-Germain-des-Prés des origines au début du XIIIe siècle*, ed. René Poupardin, I (Paris, 1909), 95–97, no. 59.

lords of Mailly (as indicated below) and may have had a brother named William, for in 1114 his son spoke of an Uncle William (Chron. St.-B., pp. 438–39). In 1076 Fulk first appeared with his son Geoffrey (Chron. St.-B., pp. 377–78). It is possible that Fulk and his wife Ermengard also had a son named Ulric; an Ermengard, with a son Ulric *clericus*, is mentioned in the chronicle of Bèze (Chron. St.-B., p. 342).

Geoffrey succeeded his father as lord of Beaumont. He and his wife Gertrude and son Hugh gave Bèze some land in 1114 for the soul of his late son Fulk (Chron. St.-B., pp. 438–39). Geoffrey and Gertrude also had a daughter named Gertrude, who married Josbert de La Ferté, viscount of Dijon (Clairvaux/Waquet 13 [pp. 20–25]; see also below, p. 326). Geoffrey and Gertrude may also be the parents of Stephen, who became abbot of Bèze in 1088. A *vita* of Stephen said that his father was Geoffrey, that he was the heir of counts, and that his mother was the daughter of Arnulph, count of Reynel, and of a daughter of Count Girard of Fouvent (Chron. St.-B., pp. 380–82) (see also above, p. 286). If Abbot Stephen's father Geoffrey is the same as Geoffrey of Beaumont, then one knows Gertrude's family origins. This is an especially attractive hypothesis since Geoffrey appears at least once in the charters as lord of Fouvent, a title he would have acquired from his wife (Chron. St.-B., pp. 439–40). Girard, count of Fouvent, had been married to a woman named Gertrude (Chron. St.-B., pp. 310–11), a likely source for the name of Geoffrey's wife. Geoffrey also had a *nepos* Geoffrey Martel, apparently of Mailly, but it is not clear exactly what the connection was (Chron. St.-B., pp. 464–65, 500–503); most likely it was through the relatives of his father.

After Geoffrey of Beaumont's death, his son Hugh IV succeeded. He was called *princeps* of Beaumont castle (Theuley, fols. 2r–v). Hugh married a woman named Mathilda (Chron. St.-B., pp. 492–93). By 1134 they had two sons, named Hugh V and Geoffrey (Chron. St.-B., pp. 466–67; St.-Étienne II.65 [pp. 75–76]). Hugh IV also had a daughter by a concubine, according to his epitaph, though her name is not known (Chron. St.-B., pp. 478–81). Of these children, Geoffrey died in a tournament, predeceasing his father—who strove to lift the excommunication he had died under so that he might be buried (Chron. St.-B., pp. 483–85)—and Hugh V succeeded as lord of Beaumont (Petit 284 [II:234]). This is the last generation of lords of Beaumont known. Since young Hugh V is last seen leaving for Jerusalem (Chron. St.-B., pp. 492–93), the line may have ended with him. By the middle of the twelfth century Beaumont had come under the *potestas* of Gui, lord of Vergy (Theuley, fol. 2v) (see below, p. 378).

The Viscounts of Dijon

The father and brother of Lambert, count of Chalon, were viscounts of Dijon at the end of the tenth century (see above, p. 307).
It is not quite clear what (if any) relationship there was between
Lambert's family and that of Gui the Rich, whose descendants were
viscounts of Dijon in the eleventh and twelfth centuries. Gui was
perhaps a vassal of the count of Chalon.[150]

The line of descent from Gui the Rich, to his son Viscount Walter,
to his daughter who married Theobold of Beaune (he took the title of
viscount of Dijon), to their daughter who married Josbert of
Châtillon, is attested by a charter of St.-Bénigne from around 1100
(St.-B. II.375 [pp. 154—56]). Gui the Rich's wife is not known. He
had at least four sons, Walter, Warner, Hugh, and Gui. He may also
have had a son named Willenc; in one charter, Gui the Rich,
Viscount Walter, and "Walter's brother" Willenc were among the
witnesses, a phrasing suggesting that he may have been only the stepson of Gui the Rich (St.-B. II.324 [p. 105]).[151]

In 1043 Gui the Rich was called a "knight of Dijon," while his son
Walter was already viscount (St.-B. II.324 [p. 105]). Gui the Rich last
appears in a dated charter in 1054 (St.-B. II.338 [pp. 117—18]). When
he died, he made his testament before his sons Warner, the abbot of
St.-Étienne of Dijon, Walter, *proconsul*, and Hugh, with his sons'
nephew Gui (St.-Étienne I.75 [pp. 94—95]). This nephew Gui is
probably the son of their brother Gui, for whose soul Warner had
made pious gifts in 1017 (St.-Étienne I.62 [pp. 84—85]). Warner, who
had been provost of St.-Étienne of Dijon by 1017 and was later abbot
(St.-Étienne I.62 [pp. 84—85]; St.-B. II.323 [pp. 102—3]), died in 1050
at the age of seventy, according to an epitaph written a century later
(Pérard, p. 141). But this date must be in error, since he was still
alive when his father died, around 1055. A history of St.-Étienne calls
him the restorer of the house and says that his father, Gui the Rich,
was a *consanguineus* of Count Hugh of Beaumont (Pérard, pp. 124—
34). It is possible that Warner, canon of Langres, archdeacon for Bassigny and abbot of St.-Étienne between 1059 and about 1080 (St.-
Bénigne II.344 [pp. 123—32]; St.-Étienne I.80, 85 [pp. 99, 102—3]),
was related to the viscounts of Dijon, as was Warner, archdeacon of
Langres, who had been abbot of St.-Étienne of Dijon in the early

---

[150]G. Estournet made a not very convincing argument that Gui the Rich's mother
was a former concubine of Hugh the Great; "Origines des seigneurs de Nemours," *Annales de la Société historique et archéologique du Gâtinais*, 30 (1912), 57—61.

[151]In a charter of 1053 this Willenc, Walter's brother, is called Gui; this cannot be the
same as the Gui, son of Gui the Rich, who had died thirty-five years earlier; *Recueil des
chartes de Saint-Germain-des-Prés*, ed. Poupardin, I:95—97, no. 59.

The Viscounts of Dijon

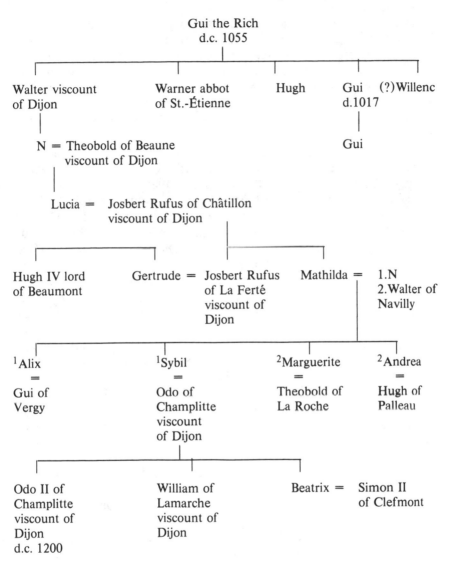

twelfth century, until it was reformed in 1113 (St.-Étienne II.22 [pp. 25–28]), and who died in 1126.[152]

Walter, viscount of Dijon, is known to have had only one child, his (unnamed) daughter, who married Theobold of Beaune and retired to the convent of Larrey (associated with St.-Bénigne) while her husband was still alive. It is possible that the wife of Otbert of Tilchâtel, said to be of her *progenia*, was this woman's sister or perhaps cousin (St.-B. II.375 [pp. 154–56]) (see also below, p. 366). Theobold's daughter inherited the office of viscount of Dijon and took it to her husband, Josbert of Châtillon.

Josbert of Châtillon is doubtless the same as the Josbert Rufus whose wife was named Lucia and who appeared in the early twelfth century. Their son Josbert Rufus, often called "of La Ferté," who appeared with his father in 1135 (Clairvaux/Waquet 6 [pp. 8–14]), was viscount of Dijon around 1147. He went to Jerusalem in 1145; at that time he called himself only "of La Ferté." He was then already married to Gertrude, sister of Hugh IV of Beaumont (Clairvaux/Waquet 10, 13 [pp. 16–17, 20–25]).

Josbert had a sister named Mathilda, who married Walter of Navilly. She had four daughters, named Alix, Marguerite, Andrea, and Sybil. Alix married Gui of Vergy, and Marguerite married Theobold of La Roche (Petit 409, 692 [II:295–99, 453]). Andrea married Hugh of Palleau, and Sybil married Odo of Champlitte, son of Count Hugh of Champagne and of Elizabeth, the daughter of Count Stephen I of Burgundy (Clairvaux/Waquet 119 [p. 127]; La Ferté 260 [p. 204]; Alberic de Trois-Fontaines, *Chronica* 1125, MGH SS XXIII:826; see also above, pp. 275–77). Since Walter is known to have had only two daughters, Marguerite and Andrea, Alix and Sybil must have been Mathilda's daughters by an earlier marriage.

Josbert and Gertrude do not seem to have had any children of their own, for Odo of Champlitte was acting as viscount of Dijon by 1170 (Petit 693 [II:456]). When Odo died, he was succeeded as viscount of Dijon first by his son Odo II, and then by his second son William, lord of Lamarche. Odo II and William had a sister named Beatrix who married the lord of Clefmont (see above, p. 319). Odo II died between 1196 and 1202; in the latter year, William left for Jerusalem.[153]

---

[152]See also Bernard of Clairvaux, Letter 59, *Opera*, VII (Rome, 1974), 152.
[153]Dumay, "Origines de Pontailler," pp. 230–31, 234–35, 243–44, nos. 13, 20, 34.

The Lords of Donzy

The lords of Donzy were a cadet branch of the counts of Chalon (see above, p. 312). Theobold I, count of Chalon, had two younger brothers, Geoffrey I and Hervé I, who in turn served as lords of Donzy. Geoffrey I died around 1038. Hervé I apparently married the sister of Savaric of Vergy; his son Geoffrey II referred to Savaric as his *avunculus* (GC IV:232–33, no. 13) (see below, p. 377). Hervé had four known sons, Raynald, Geoffrey II, Hervé, and Hugh, who all appeared with their father in a charter of 1055 (C 3348 [IV:444–46]). The second, Geoffrey II, was both lord of Donzy and count of Chalon after his cousin, Hugh II of Chalon, died without heirs. He appeared in a charter of 1086 as count of Chalon with sons named Raynald, William, and Hervé II and a *nepos* Raynald, son of Robert of Châtillon. This Raynald had a son named Narjod.[154] It seems most likely that Robert of Châtillon was a brother of Geoffrey II's unnamed wife, or perhaps a relative of Savaric of Vergy. In 1100 Geoffrey II sold his share of the county of Chalon as he was leaving for Jerusalem, and his heirs were lords only of Donzy. Geoffrey came back from the First Crusade and became a monk at the Cluniac priory of Donzy as he was dying; he died on 4 August (Obit. Sens III:238).

Hervé II, his son, succeeded. Hervé married the daughter of Hugh le Blanc of La Ferté; the next lord of Donzy, Geoffrey III, was her son (La Charité 58 [pp. 140–41]). In addition, Hervé had a daughter Agnes, who married Sulpice of Amboise and had four children, Hugh, Hervé, Denise, and Elizabeth; the chronicles of Amboise say Agnes was of "royal blood."[155] Geoffrey III seems to have married Clemence, daughter of Duke Hugh II of Burgundy.[156] They had two sons, Hervé III and Geoffrey, who appeared with their parents in documents from 1145 and 1151, although a charter of 1151 calls Geoffrey III's wife "B." (GC XII:119, no. 26; La Charité 58 [pp. 140–41]; Quantin I.328 [pp. 480–81]). Geoffrey III also had an unnamed daughter, who married first Anselm of Traînel, and then, after having been repudiated by him, Stephen, count of Sancerre, brother of Count Henry of Champagne (BN, Coll. Champagne 45, fol. 124; Suger, "Historia gloriosi regis Ludovici VII," RHGF XII:128). Geoffrey III died on 29 April (Fleury 264 [II:151–52]).

Hervé III, who succeeded, went on the Third Crusade. He was called lord of Gien as well as lord of Donzy (Lebeuf IV.16 bis [pp. 28–29]). He may have married a daughter of William Goet and of

---

[154]See the charter edited by Richard, "Origines féodales. Les Chalon," pp. 116–19.
[155]"Gesta Amboziensium dominorum," ed. Halphen and Poupardin, in *Chroniques des comtes d'Anjou*, pp. 114, 122.
[156]See the text quoted by Richard, "Sur les alliances familiales," p. 41, n. 4.

The Lords of Donzy

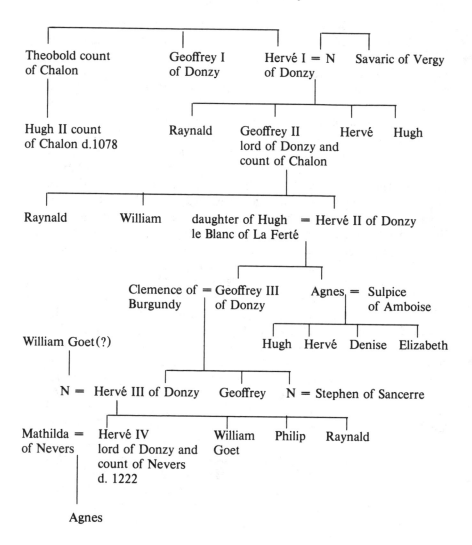

Elizabeth, daughter of Count Theobold of Champagne. Alberic de Trois-Fontaines says this anonymous woman was the mother of Geoffrey of Donzy, apparently meaning Geoffrey III (*Chronica* 1152, MGH SS XXIII:841), but Geoffrey III was born too early to be the great-grandson of Count Theobold. Alberic probably meant Hervé IV (the name William Goet among this woman's sons is indicative). Hervé III's wife precedeased him, dying on 22 January (Fleury 264 [II:151–52]). They had at least four sons, William Goet, Philip, Hervé IV, and Raynald. William Goet, the oldest, and Philip appeared in charters with their father in 1187 (Fleury 264 [II:151–52]; La Charité 76 [pp. 171–72]; Lebeuf IV.16 bis [pp. 28–29, mis-dated 1087 by the editor]), when he was leaving for Jerusalem. Raynald is called "of Montmirail" in his brother's charters (Nevers/St.-Étienne 23, p. 98; Layettes 502–3 [I:207]). Hervé III may have also been the father of Geoffrey, prior of the Cluniac house of La Charité.[157]

Hervé IV married Mathilda, heiress of Nevers, in 1199 and took the title of count of Nevers (see below, p. 350). They had one daughter, named Agnes.

The Lords of Fontaines-lès-Dijon

The following is a discussion of Bernard of Clairvaux's paternal relatives. The lords of Fontaines-lès-Dijon were not powerful lords by any means; their influence on Burgundian society was entirely through the church.

Bernard's father, Tescelin Sorus, lord of Fontaines, often appeared in the charters of the duke of Burgundy around the beginning of the twelfth century (Molesme 1.112 [II:115]; C 3531 [IV:653]; Autun/Église 1.12 [I:18–21]; St.-Marcel 34 [pp. 38–40]). Tescelin was one of the knights of the lord of Châtillon.[158] Alberic de Trois-Fontaines said that Tescelin was half brother, via his mother, of Gui of Aigremont, and that Gui's own half brother, via his father, was Ulric I of Aigremont (*Chronica* 1110, MGH SS XXIII:818; see above, pp. 279–81).

Tescelin and his wife, Aleth of Montbard (see below, p. 336), had six sons and a daughter, according to Bernard's *vitae*. All followed Bernard into the cloister. Bernard's oldest brother, Gui, was already

---

[157]Geoffrey was deposed and excommunicated in 1212; La Charité 19 (pp. 57–66). The editor suggests he was Hervé IV's brother.

[158]William of St.-Thierry, *Vita prima Sancti Bernardi* 1.1, PL CLXXXV:227. Godfrey of Clairvaux, *Vita tertia Sancti Bernardi* 1, PL CLXXXV:523–24.

The Lords of Fontaines-lès-Dijon

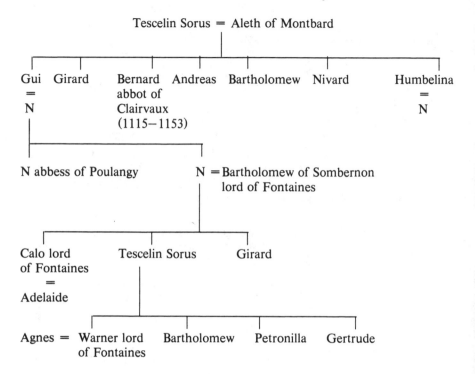

married, but his wife entered Larrey, a convent affiliated with St.-Bénigne, and went on to become abbess. The second son was named Girard. Bernard, the third son, had studied at Notre-Dame of Châtillon—then a house of secular canons though it adopted the Augustinian Rule not long thereafter—before entering Cîteaux. The fourth, fifth, and sixth sons were named Andreas, Bartholomew, and Nivard. The one daughter, Humbelina, became a nun at Jully, but only after she and her husband had had one child, a daughter.[159] Humbelina may be identical with the Humbelina who was wife of Anseric of Chacenay; this woman asked the brothers of Bernard of Clairvaux (who would have been her own brothers as well) to confirm her dying gifts to Jully (Jully, pp. 259—61).[160]

After this entire generation entered the church, the lordship of Fontaines seems to have gone to a daughter of Bernard's oldest brother Gui; she married Bartholomew, brother of Lord Warner of Sombernon. In a charter of 1154 Bartholomew is called both "of Fontaines" and "of Sombernon," after having been lord of Fontaines since about 1140 (Genus illustre, pp. 462—64, no. 22 [rpt. PL CLXXXV:1420—21]; Jobin, St. Bernard, pp. 584, 597—99, nos. 24, 33—34). Gui also had a second daughter, who became abbess of Poulangy; she is usually referred to by modern scholars as Adelina ("Chronicon Clarevallense" 1184, PL CLXXXV:1250). She may be the Adelina, niece of Agnes of La Roche, who in 1151 was a nun at Puits-d'Orbe, where Agnes was abbess (Arch. Côte-d'Or, 15 H 136, no. 1).

Bartholomew, lord of Fontaines, had sons named Calo, who inherited the lordship, Tescelin, and Girard. Calo, lord of Fontaines, seems to have died without heirs. In the gifts he made to St.-Bénigne when he died, he mentioned his wife Adelaide, his brothers Sorus (apparently the same as Tescelin) and Girard, and Sorus's sons Warner and Bartholomew (Genus illustre, pp. 463—64, no. 22 [rpt. PL CLXXXV:1420—21]; Arch. Côte-d'Or, 1 H 884). These sons inherited the lordship of Fontaines. In 1190 Lord Warner of Fontaines had a wife Agnes, brother Bartholomew, and sisters Petronilla and Gertrude (St.-Seine, pp. 258—59).

---

[159]William of St.-Thierry, Vita prima Sancti Bernardi 1.1, 1.3, PL CLXXXV:227, 233. Alain, Vita secunda Sancti Bernardi 7, PL CLXXXV:482. Godfrey of Clairvaux, Vita tertia Sancti Bernardi 2—4, 13, PL CLXXXV:525—26, 530. John the Hermit, Vita quarta Sancti Bernardi 1.3, PL CLXXXV:536.
[160]For the lords of Chacenay, see Theodore Evergates, Feudal Society in the Bailliage of Troyes under the Counts of Champagne, 1152—1284 (Baltimore, 1975), pp. 166—67.

The Lords of Grancey

The lords of Grancey are well documented in the twelfth century, but their appearances in the eleventh century are too scattered to establish a clear family tree for them. Gui of Grancey appeared in a charter for St.-Bénigne in 1038 (St.-B. II.323 [pp. 102–3]). In the mid-eleventh century Girard of Grancey gave up claims to the property of St.-Étienne of Dijon (St.-Étienne I.83 [p. 101]). Girard of Grancey witnessed the duke's gift to Molesme in 1077 (Molesme 1.11 [II:19]). Gui of Grancey was count of Saulx in the 1070s (St.-Étienne I.84 [p. 102]) and apparently until 1125 (see below, p. 351).

The family tree becomes much clearer when one reaches Raynald I. Raynald I was lord of Grancey from the 1080s to the first years of the twelfth century (Molesme 1.6 [II:12–13]; Langres 67 [p. 449]; St.-B. II.398 [pp. 173–77]).[161] He had brothers named Gui and Girard, a wife named Letuildis, and a son Raynald, still *parvulus* around the end of the eleventh century; this Raynald II succeeded his father (Molesme 1.70 [II:77–78]). Gui, brother of Raynald I, was called "of Lucenay" in Hugh of Flavigny's *Chronicon* entry for 1099 and was said to have an unnamed wife and daughters (MGH SS VIII:479).

In the 1120s Raynald II of Grancey was married to a woman named Agnes (Petit 259 [II:220]). They and their sons Raynald III and Odo assisted in the foundation of Auberive in 1135 (Auberive I, fols. 3r–4v, no. 1 [Auberive II, fols. 1r–4r, no. 1]; printed in GC IV:165, no. 42). She was called "Duchess"; this appellation (daughters of dukes were occasionally given the honorific "duchess") and the fact that her second son was named Odo make it tempting to consider Agnes a daughter of Duke Odo I of Burgundy. Raynald had a brother Giselbert, a canon (St.-Étienne II.82 [pp. 91–92]).

Raynald II was succeeded by Raynald III (*Genus illustre*, pp. 487–88, no. 48 [rpt. PL CLXXXV:1433–34]). He may have married a woman named Letuildis, since Raynald of Grancey and his wife Letuildis are recorded in a 1162 charter, which records several gifts to Clairvaux, although the charter may instead be referring to a previous gift from Raynald I and *his* wife (Clairvaux/Waquet 90 [p. 94]). Raynald III had sons Odo, his heir, and Robert, who became an ecclesiastical prior, perhaps at Auberive (Arch. Haute-Marne, 1 H 89, no. 15). Raynald's son Odo I was lord of Grancey by 1165 (Auberive I, fols. 8r–v, no. 15 [Auberive II, fol. 10r, no. 13]). After a long

---

[161]Orderic Vitalis said that Raynald was a *nepos* of the Norman magnate William of Breteuil and that he unsuccessfully tried to acquire William's inheritance when William died without a legitimate son; *Historia ecclesiastica* 11.4, ed. Chibnall, VI:40.

The Lords of Grancey

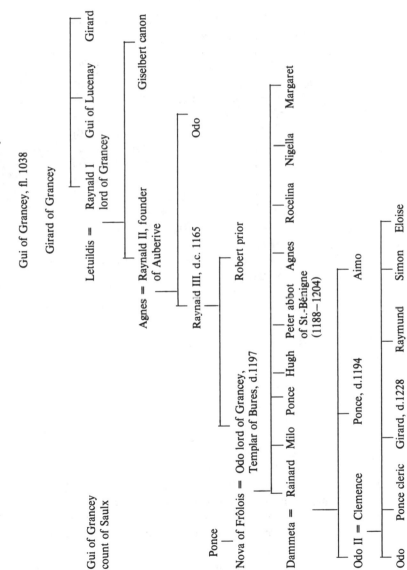

career, he became a Templar at Bures and lived until 1197 (Petit 881, 899 [III:321—23, 329]).

Odo I married the daughter of Ponce of Frôlois, a woman named Nova. He had sons named Rainard, Milo, Ponce, Hugh, and Peter, who became abbot of St.-Bénigne of Dijon (1188—1204). His son Hugh became lord of Colomme by marrying Aremburg, lady of Colomme. She had children named William, Peter, Hodierna, and Ameta in 1194 (apparently by her first marriage) (Arch. Haute-Marne, 1 H 104, no. 16). Odo I's daughter Agnes married Amadeus of Arceaux. His other daughters were named Rocelina, Nigella, and Margaret (Langres 121 [p. 527]; Petit 340, 881 [II:259—60; III:321—23]; Plancher I.113 [pp. lxii—lxiii]; Lugny, fol. 25r).

Odo I's son Rainard married a woman named Dammeta and had sons named Odo, Ponce, and Aimo (Arch. Haute-Marne, 1 H 89, no. 15; Auberive I, fol. 40v, no. 94 [Auberive II, fols. 95v—96r, no. 24]). Rainard's son Ponce died in 1194 (Auberive I, fol. 40v, no. 94 [Auberive II, fols. 95v—96r, no. 24]). Rainard predeceased his father Odo I, dying at the siege of Acre (Quantin II.405 [pp. 411—12]). While Odo was a Templar, his son Hugh of Colomme acted as lord of Grancey (Arch. Côte-d'Or, 111 H 1156). When Odo died in 1197, his grandson Odo II, lord of Grancey, made gifts for him and his other predecessors: his great-grandfather Raynald, his grandfather Odo (the Templar), his father Rainard, and his paternal uncles, Milo, Ponce, Hugh, and Peter, abbot of St.-Bénigne (Petit 881 [III:321—23]).

Odo II of Grancey married a woman named Clemence. They had at least six children, all of whom appeared with their parents in 1219: Odo, Ponce, who became a cleric, Girard, who died in 1228 while his parents were still alive, Raymund, Simon, and Eloise (Auberive I, fols. 40v—41r, nos. 95—96).

The Lords of Montbard

The lords of Montbard have been extensively discussed over the years because of interest in the family of Bernard of Clairvaux; his mother was a sister of the lord of Montbard. The most recent scholarly discussions are those of the Abbé Jobin, Ernest Petit, and Jacques Laurent: Jobin, *St. Bernard*, pp. xxi—xlvii; Petit, IV:455—76; Laurent, "Seigneurs de Montbard et seigneurs de Ricey," in *Mélanges Saint Bernard*, XXIVe Congrès de l'Association bourguignonne des Sociétés savantes (Dijon, 1953), pp. 9—18.

The first known lord of Montbard is Bernard I, who lived in the second half of the eleventh century (Molesme 1.6, 11 [II:12—13,

The Lords of Montbard

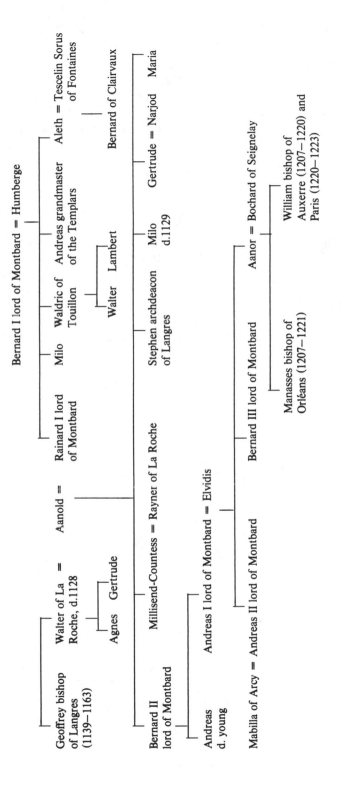

19]).[162] He married a woman named Humberge.[163] Bernard and Humberge first appear in the records in 1065, when they asked the abbot of St.-Pierre-le-Vif for the property Les Riceys and Pouilly.[164] Bernard I and Humberge had a large family. Their best-known child was Aleth, who married Tescelin Sorus of Fontaines and bore Bernard of Clairvaux (Geoffrey of Clairvaux, *Vita tertia Sancti Bernardi* 1, PL CLXXXV:524) (see also above, pp. 329–31).

In addition to Aleth, Bernard and Humberge had at least four sons. Rainard I succeeded as lord of Montbard; Milo became a *conversus* and helped found Fontenay (Molesme 1.242 [II:226–27]); and Waldric became a monk and also assisted in the foundation of Fontenay (Jobin, *St. Bernard*, pp. 641–42, no. 62). Waldric is identical with Waldric (or Gaudry), lord of Touillon, who appears in Fontenay's documents with sons Walter and Lambert, monks at Molesme, and at least two daughters who became nuns. The *Vita prima* of Bernard of Clairvaux said that his *avunculus*, Waldric, lord of Touillon, was among those who joined the Cistercian order with him.[165] Bernard I and Humberge also had a son named Andreas, for in 1129 Rainard I's son referred to an *avunculus* Andreas (Molesme 1.263 [II:244–45]). This Andreas is doubtless the same as the Andreas of Montbard who became grandmaster of the Templars after 1153, whom Bernard of Clairvaux called his uncle.[166]

---

[162]Laurent has suggested that Bernard was son of Otto, son of Count Rainard of Tonnerre. The only indications of this filiation are that the lords of Montbard wielded power in the old county of Tonnerre, and that one of Bernard of Clairvaux's biographers said, quite vaguely, that his maternal ancestors came from "ancient dukes of Burgundy"; Laurent, "Seigneurs de Montbard," pp. 11–13; John the Hermit, *Vita quarta Sancti Bernardi* 1, PL CLXXXV:535. Petit suggested that the lords of Montbard were a collateral branch of the counts of Bar (IV:456–57).

[163]Petit has suggested that Bernard married twice, his second wife being perhaps of the family of the lords of Maligny, or the lords of Noyers, or the lords of Grancey, but the records contain no evidence that Bernard had more than one wife; Petit, IV:458. Jobin calls Humberge "of Ricey." This identification was first made in the seventeenth century by the editors of GC, and seems based on a misreading of the Chronicle of St.-Pierre-le-Vif, cited below, in which Bernard and Humberge received Les Riceys from St.-Pierre. See Laurent, "Seigneurs de Montbard," pp. 9–10.

[164]*Chronique de Saint-Pierre-le-Vif de Sens, dite de Clarius*, ed. Robert-Henri Bautier and Monique Gilles (Paris, 1979), p. 126.

[165]William of St.-Thierry, *Vita prima Sancti Bernardi* 1.10, PL CLXXXV:232. See also Alain, *Vita secunda Sancti Bernardi* 12, PL CLXXXV:490. For Waldric of Touillon and his children, see Molesme 1.218 (II:200–202).

[166]Bernard of Clairvaux, Letters 288, 289, *Opera*, VIII (Rome, 1977), 203–6. *Vita prima Sancti Bernardi* 3.4, PL CLXXXV:309–10. Jobin, *St. Bernard*, pp. 606–11, nos. 41–43. For Andreas, see also Marie Luise Bulst-Thiele, *Sacrae domus militiae templi Hierosolymitani magistri*, Abhandlungen der Akademie der Wissenschaften in Göttingen, Philologisch-historische klasse, 3rd. ser. 86 (Göttingen, 1974), pp. 57–61. Jobin gives Bernard and Humberge another daughter, Diane, who he says married Otto of Châtillon.

Lord Rainard I married a woman named Aanold or Aanor (Molesme 1.250 [II:233–34]). After his death, she married Walter of La Roche, constable of the duke of Burgundy. When he too died, she retired to Jully (Jully, pp. 257–58). Walter's young daughters Gertrude and Agnes agreed to Aanold's entry gift to Jully; it seems most likely that they were her daughters as well, though the charter only calls them Walter's. Walter of La Roche, a castellan from the region of Fontenay, was of a family of four brothers: besides Walter, they were Rayner of La Roche, Nivard, and Geoffrey, bishop of Langres (1139–1163) (for Bishop Geoffrey's connection to this family, see Appendix B, p. 396). Rayner assisted in the foundation of Auberive in 1135 (Auberive I, fols. 3r–4v, no. 1 [Auberive II, fols. 1r–4r, no. 1]), was among the early donors to Longué, to which he made gifts for the souls of his brothers Walter and Nivard (Petit 245 [II:214]), and went on to be the duke's seneschal in the 1140s (Langres 306 [p. 770]). In addition, these four brothers had a sister Agnes, first abbess of Puits-d'Orbe (Jobin, *St. Bernard*, p. 635, no. 62). Agnes had a niece named Adelina (Arch. Côte-d'Or, 15 H 136, no. 1).

Rainard I and Aanold had at least three sons and a daughter: Bernard II, who succeeded; Millisend-Countess, who married Rayner of La Roche, her stepfather's brother (Molesme 1.263 [II:244–45]); the cleric Stephen (Molesme 1.264 [II:245]), who seems identical with Stephen of Montbard, archdeacon of Langres in the 1140s (Quantin I.273 [pp. 423–24]), and Milo, who died young and was buried at the nunnery of Puits-d'Orbe in 1129 (GC IV:161, no. 38). A list of early donors to Fontenay, drawn up in 1273, says that Rainard and his wife Aanold made pious gifts with their daughters Gertrude and Maria and Gertrude's husband Narjod, a knight (Plancher I.58 [p. xl]).

Bernard II had two sons, both named Andreas, by an unknown woman. The first died young (Molesme 1.228 [II:212–13]), and the second succeeded as Lord Andreas I.[167] Andreas married a woman named Elvidis.[168] They had at least three children, Andreas II, who succeeded (Petit 457 [II:320–21]); Bernard III, usually called "of Époisses" by modern scholars; and Aanor, who married Bochard, lord of Seignelay (*Gesta pontificum*, pp. 451, 463–64; see also below, p. 356).[169] Andreas II married Mabilla, daughter of Geoffrey, lord of Arcy-sur-Cure (Quantin II.304 [pp. 324–25]; Jobin, *St. Bernard*, pp. 622–23, no. 53). Andreas and Mabilla may have had a daughter but had no sons. After Andreas's death, which had taken place by 1196, Mabilla married Bartholomew of Pouilly (Reomaus, pp. 230–31), and

---

[167]Petit suggests that Bernard, abbot of Fontenay, was also a son of Bernard II.
[168]Petit calls her the daughter of Anseric of Montréal. Jobin calls her "of Époisses."
[169]Petit adds another son, John, whom he calls a monk at Fontenay.

the lordship of Montbard passed to Andreas's younger brother Bernard III, the ancestor of the thirteenth-century lords of Montbard (Quantin II.474 [pp. 481–82]).

The Lords of Montréal

H.-P.-C. de Chastellux included a discussion of the twelfth-century lords of Montréal in his work on the lords of Chastellux and printed a number of their charters; *Histoire de Chastellux*. Petit gives a very brief discussion of the lords of Montréal and a family tree (V:496–97). He includes more relatives in his tree than I have found in the charters.

Hugh was lord of Montréal in the first part of the twelfth century.[170] His sister Richardis married a castellan named Artald (Arch. Saône-et-Loire, H 142). Hugh married a woman named Aluisa or Elvidis.[171] He had died by 1129, when his widow Aluisa confirmed his pious gifts (Arch. Yonne, H 1562; Jully, p. 258).

Hugh was succeeded by his son, Anseric I. He first appears in a charter in 1129, called simply the son of Elvidis, lady of Montréal (Jully, p. 258). He seems not to have succeeded immediately, probably because he was too young, for in the early 1130s a man named Gui, perhaps an uncle or even his mother's second husband, was lord of Montréal.[172] Anseric was married by 1145, although the charter in which his wife is mentioned does not give her name (Pontigny 42 [pp. 115–16]). He went on Crusade in 1147 (Quantin I.278 [p. 429]) and only appears in the charters with a named wife, Adelaide, after his return from Crusade (Quantin I.357 [pp. 515–16]). She was the daughter of Manasses of Pleurs and the widow of the lord of Montmirail (Pontigny 49 [p. 122]; "Genealogiae Fusniacenses," MGH SS XIII:254).[173] Anseric I and Adelaide appeared in a charter of 1164 with sons Anseric II, their heir, and John, and daughter Aluisa (Quantin II.157 [pp. 174–75]). Their daughter Aluisa may be

---

[170]Duchesne, *Histoire de Vergy*, p. 112. Petit calls Hugh son of Lord Milo of Chacenay. Chastellux made Hugh the descendant of a series of Lords Anseric of the tenth and eleventh centuries, though recognizing that there is no evidence for this lineage.

[171]Petit calls her "de Baudemont."

[172]Chastellux, ed., *Histoire de Chastellux*, p. 249, no. 5. In his family tree (facing p. 258) Chastellux calls Gui Anseric I's older brother.

[173]Chastellux calls her "of Ménessaire." He makes Anseric I into two people (whom he calls Anseric IV and Anseric V). Manasses of Pleurs, whom the "Genealogiae Fusniacenses" erroneously calls brother rather than father of Adelaide, was the son of a daughter of Andreas of Ramerupt. Alberic de Trois-Fontaines calls this woman the ancestress of the lords of Pleurs, Montmirail, Montréal, and Arcis-sur-Aube; *Chronica* 1110, MGH SS XXIII:818.

The Lords of Montréal

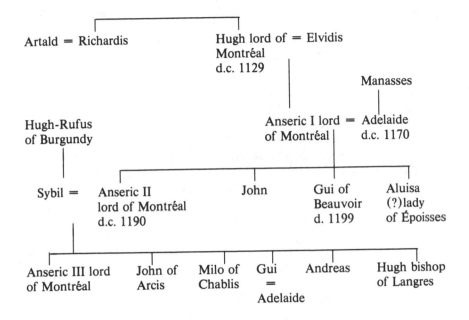

the "Elvys of Montréal" who became lady of Époisses and is recorded in the obituary of the collegial chapter of Montréal.[174] Anseric I and Adelaide were also the parents of Gui of Beauvoir, who died in 1199, according to the same obituary (Petit V:415).[175] Anseric outlived Adelaide; he made gifts for her soul in 1170 (Quantin II.206 [pp. 223–25]). He was referred to as Anseric of Montmirail by his son Anseric II (Petit 677 [II:415–16]).

Anseric II, lord of Montréal, acted as the duke's seneschal (Pontigny 48 [pp. 121–22]; Petit 784 [III:279–80]). He married Sybil, daughter of Hugh-Rufus, brother of the duke of Burgundy.[176] They had sons Anseric III, their heir; John, who became lord of Arcis-sur-Aube;[177] Milo, who became lord of Chablis (Layettes 908 [I:344]); and Gui, who became lord of Beauvoir. Their son Andreas died young (Petit 677, 751, 809 [II:415–16; III:267–68, 290–91]; Quantin III.181 [p. 82]; Pontigny 356 [pp. 352–53]; Arch. Yonne, G 2276). They were also the parents of the Hugh of Montréal who became bishop of Langres in 1219 (Petit V:412; Alberic de Trois-Fontaines, *Chronica* 1219, MGH SS XXIII:909).[178]

Anseric II may have died on the Third Crusade, on which he left in 1189 (Petit 809 [III:290–91]; Alberic de Trois-Fontaines, *Chronica* 1189, MGH SS XXIII:864). It is not clear whether the Anseric, lord of Montréal, who appeared in a charter of the countess of Nevers in 1195, was Anseric II or his son (Quantin II.458 [pp. 467–68]). Sybil outlived her husband; she was a widow in 1197 (Quantin II.474 [pp. 481–82]).

The Counts of Nevers, Auxerre, and Tonnerre

The history of the family of the counts of Nevers is summarized in the twelfth-century "Origo brevis Nivernensium comitum," written by Hugh of Poitiers (Vézelay, pp. 235–39). The counts of Nevers were studied extensively by René de Lespinasse as part of his broader history of the region; *Le Nivernais et les comtes de Nevers*, 2 vols.

---

[174]Petit identifies her rather with the wife of Andreas I of Montbard.

[175]See also Chastellux, ed., *Histoire de Chastellux*, p. 275, no. 42.

[176]Alberic de Trois-Fontaines, *Chronica* 1161, MGH SS XXIII:845; Petit 557, 755 (II:362–63; III:269); Chastellux, ed., *Histoire de Chastellux*, pp. 280–81, no. 50. See above, p. 259.

[177]For the descendants of John of Arcis, see Evergates, *Feudal Society in the Bailliage of Troyes*, pp. 158–59.

[178]Petit and Chastellux give them another son named Anseric, lord of Marmeaux. Chastellux gives them two daughters, Elizabeth and Adelaide.

(Paris, 1909–1911). Though this work is flawed by many slips and inconsistencies, it remains the only modern work on the family.

According to the "Origo," the family began with Adalgar, bishop of Autun, a Poitevin who had served in the royal court, and his nephew Landric.[179] Adalgar and Landric, the "Origo" continued, were present at the siege of the little castle of Metz, in the Nivernais, at which Landric so distinguished himself that he was given the castle to keep. This Landric married a wife from Anjou and had a son named Bodo.[180] Bodo, who built the castle of Monceaux, had a son named Landric, the first count of Nevers, according to the "Origo." Landric in turn was succeeded by his son Raynald. Raynald was killed fighting the duke of Burgundy and left the counties of Nevers and Auxerre (which he had acquired when he married the sister of King Robert II) to his son William I. William had two sons, William and Raynald, who predeceased him, but Raynald left a son, William II, who in turn had two sons, William and Raynald, who went on the Second Crusade with Louis VII while William II retired to La Grande Chartreuse.

This genealogy can be supplemented by other sources, the earliest dating from the time of Landric, first count of Nevers. Landric was a vassal of Duke Henry of Burgundy, Otto-William's stepfather, and appeared in his charters around 987 with the designation *gloriosus miles* (Nevers/St.-Cyr 23 [pp. 49–50]; Autun/St.-Symphorien 16 [pp. 39–42]). According to Hugh of Flavigny, Landric had a *propinquus* Robert, who was expelled as abbot of Flavigny and set himself up as abbot of Corbigny instead, sometime around the year 980 ("Series abbatum Flaviniacensium," MGH SS VIII:503) (see also Appendix C, p. 414). Landric seems to have become count of Nevers in 991 or 992 (*Annales Nivernenses* 991, MGH SS XIII:90; Plancher I.30 [p. xxiv]). In the late 980s Otto-William had held the county of Nevers (St.-Cyr 23 [p. 50]) (for Otto-William, see above, p. 265). Landric

[179]The exact relationship between Bishop Adalgar and Landric is not clear. There is a Landric, a *fidelis* of Charles the Bald, to whom the king gave the chapel of St.-Aubin in the Mâconnais in 842; this Landric and his wife Hildesendis gave the chapel to the cathedral of Mâcon shortly afterward; *Recueil des actes de Charles II le Chauve, roi de France*, I, ed. Arthur Giry, Maurice Prou, and Georges Tessier (Paris, 1943), 25–27, no. 10; M 60 (pp. 48–49). It is possible that Landric and Hildesendis are the parents of Landric, ancestor of the counts of Nevers, and that Hildesendis (more likely than her husband to be a stranger to Burgundy) might be the sister of Adalgar. Lespinasse argues not that Hildesendis was Adalgar's sister but that her husband was Adalgar's brother; *Le Nivernais*, I:192. The same identification was made by Léon Mirot, "Les origines des premiers comtes héréditaires de Nevers," *Annales de Bourgogne*, 17 (1945), 9.

[180]This Bodo may be the same Bodo who issued a charter for Cluny in 950 (C 783 [I:737]). Claude Hohl makes this identification, "Le comte Landri de Nevers," p. 782. The Bodo of this charter had a *cognatus* Raynald. One Landric witnessed the charter; this might be his father or possibly a brother. Mirot says he is Bodo's brother; "Les origines des comtes de Nevers," p. 11.

The Counts of Nevers, Auxerre, and Tonnerre

Adalgar   N (? Hildesendis) = Landric
bishop of Autun
d. 894 |
                           Landric of Metz
                                    |
                                  Bodo   Otto-William
                                    | |
                           Landric count of Nevers, d. 1028 = Mathilda

Bodo   Landric   Raynald count of = Hadwidis/Adelaide Gui Robert
                   Nevers, d. 1040 | of France

Ermengard = William I count   Gui monk at   Robert the   Henry
countess of of Nevers and   Chaise-Dieu   Burgundian
Tonnerre   Auxerre, d.1098

Raynald of = Agnes of William of   Robert bishop Ermengard Eloise
Nevers   Beaugency Tonnerre   of Auxerre   =   =
d.c. 1090   (1076–1092)   Hubert   William
                                | of Maine of Évreux
                           N = Aimo of Bourbon

William II count of Nevers,   = Adelaide   Robert
Auxerre, and Tonnerre, d.1149

William III count of Nevers = Ida   Raynald count of   Robert
and Auxerre, d.1161 | Tonnerre, d.1148

William IV count   2.Gui count = Mathilda Raynald   Adelaide Ermengard
of Nevers, d.1168   of Nevers   =   =   =
   =   d.1176   1.Odo of   Adelaide Raynald
Aanor of Vermandois   Issoudun   of Beaujeu of Joigny
                                3.Peter of
                                Flanders
                                4.Robert II of Dreux

William V   Agnes = Peter of Courtenay, count = Yolendis
   d. 1181   d.1193   of Nevers and Auxerre
                                |

1.Hervé IV of Donzy, = Mathilda = 2.Wigo of Forez
count of Nevers, d.1222 d.c.1257   d. 1241
                      |

              Agnes, d.1226 = Gui of St.-Paul, d.1226
                             |
                   Yolendis countess of Nevers

married Otto-William's daughter, a woman named Mathilda (Raoul Glaber, *Historia* 3.2 [pp. 56–57]; C 2811 [IV:13–14]). It is possible that Landric's marriage to Mathilda took place in 991 or 992, the year he first appears as count of Nevers—or rather that they were engaged in that year. Since Otto-William had married only around 981, Mathilda could not have been older than ten in 992. Landric's first two sons, Bodo and Landric, began to appear with him in his charters ten years later (Nevers/St.-Cyr 47 [pp. 88–89]; Quantin I.83 [pp. 159–60]),[181] but it is possible that they were sons of another woman, because they seem to have had no claim to Nevers. Count Landric had three more sons—these three at least born to Mathilda—named Raynald, Gui, and Robert. Raynald and Gui named their parents in a charter they gave Cluny after Landric's death (C 2811 [IV:13–14]). Gui may be the same Gui who appears with Count Landric in a charter of 1023; if so, he had a wife named Acherada (C 2781 [III: 805–7]). Robert appears in only one charter ("Ex gestis abbatum S. Germani Autissiodorensis," RHGF XI:648), but, according to the *Miracula* of St.-Benoît-sur-Loire, as an infant he was engaged to Mathilda, daughter and heiress of Gimo of St.-Satur (near Sancerre). The marriage was never consummated, however, and Mathilda became a nun, founding a house of canons at St.-Satur.[182]

Landric had a rather tumultuous relationship with King Robert. According to a contemporary satirical poem, Landric helped Robert remain married to—or at least "in his little bed" with—the king's cousin Bertha.[183] But Landric rebelled against King Robert in the Burgundian wars that broke out after the death of Duke Henry in 1002. In the aftermath of the wars, however, the king allowed Landric to take the county of Auxerre and marry his son to the king's sister. Landric died in 1028, on 11 May ("Annales Vizeliacenses" 1028, Vézelay, p. 220; Obit. Sens III:235).

There has been a great deal of debate about Hadwidis (or Adelaide), wife of Landric's son Raynald. On the one hand, the "Origo" and the "Annales Vizeliacenses" call her the sister of Robert II (Vézelay, pp. 218, 238). On the other hand, Raoul Glaber calls her Robert's daughter (*Historia* 4.9 [p. 113]). Most scholars prefer to follow Raoul Glaber.[184] It is not even clear whether her name was

[181]Bodo may be the same Bodo who married Adela, daughter of Fulk Nerra of Anjou, and had Bochard, count of Vendôme. See Olivier Guillot, *Le comte d'Anjou et son entourage au XIe siècle* (Paris, 1972), p. 27 and n. 139. Lespinasse says that Bodo became count of Vendôme and Landric lord of Monceaux; *Le Nivernais*, I:212.

[182]André of Fleury, *Miracula Sancti Benedicti* 5.16, ed. E. de Certain, *Les miracles de Saint Benoît* (Paris, 1858), pp. 213–14. For Mathilda's later foundation of a house at St.-Satur, see GC II:51–52, no. 58.

[183]Adalbero of Laon, *Rythmus satyricus* 24, ed. Hohl, "Le comte Landri de Nevers," p. 795. See also Bouchard, "Origins of the Nobility," p. 519.

[184]See, for example, Sassier, *Le pouvoir comtal en Auxerrois*, pp. 33–35; Lewis, *Royal*

Adelaide, the name given her by a later addition to the "Annales Vizeliacenses" (1031, Vézelay, p. 220), or Hadwidis, the name by which she signed one charter (C 2811 [IV:13−14]). I prefer to follow the original author of the chronicles of Vézelay, rather than the quite unreliable genealogies of Raoul Glaber,[185] for the following reasons.

Although the "Annales" of Vézelay mention Raynald's marriage in 1002, Raynald and his wife Hadwidis (or Adelaide) do not appear in a charter together until around the time of Landric's death (C 2811 [IV:13−14]). Raynald at any rate could not have been more than five or six years old in 1002, because his mother Mathilda was not born before 982 or so. Hadwidis (or Adelaide), if she were *daughter* of Robert II, could not even have been born in 1002, since Robert did not marry Constance, by whom he had all his children, until about 1006. Alternately, if Hadwidis were a *sister* of Robert II, she may have been older than her husband. At any rate, any "marriage" that might have taken place in 1002 would have been a promise to marry rather than an actual wedding. It has been argued that a marriage between Raynald and a royal girl, with the county of Auxerre as dowry, could not have taken place in 1002, the date given by the Vézelay sources, because in that year Landric rebelled against the king and fought doggedly against the bishop of Auxerre for control of that city, which would not have been necessary if Auxerre had already been his.[186] But it is also possible that Landric believed that the king had promised him Auxerre after the death of Duke Henry in 1002, and that the king's attempt to take control of Burgundy was a betrayal of this promise; such a betrayal would explain Landric's rebellion after his earlier close ties with the king.

Raynald was killed in 1040, on 29 May, at Seignelay (northeast of Auxerre), in a battle with the duke of Burgundy ("Annales Vizeliacenses" 1040, Vézelay, pp. 220−21; Raoul Glaber, *Historia* 4.9 [p. 113]; *Annales Nivernenses* 1040, MGH SS XIII:90; Obit. Sens

---

Succession in Capetian France, p. 24 and n. 74; and Lespinasse, *Le Nivernais*, I:214. Sassier argues that, because a chronicle calls Raynald's son the *nepos* of King Henry, Raynald's wife must have been King Henry's sister. However, *nepos* was also frequently used in the Middle Ages to mean first cousin; Sassier, *Le pouvoir comtal en Auxerrois*, p. 34; *Gesta pontificum*, p. 398. Lewis cites as "proof" a charter in which Duke Robert of Burgundy (son of Robert II) leads the witnesses, followed, after some other signatories, by "S. Raynaldi Autissiodorensis comitis et fratris ejus"; Lewis, *Royal Succession in Capetian France*, p. 24, n. 74; St.-B. II.315 (pp. 95−97). But this charter does not mean that Raynald was the duke's brother-in-law; rather, it indicates that one of Raynald's four brothers signed the charter as well as Raynald.

[185] Raoul Glaber also erroneously made Queen Constance the daughter of Duke William of Aquitaine, rather than Count William of Provence, and said that Constance was the *cognata* of Count Hugh of Chalon, whereas they were only tangentially related: her mother was the sister of Hugh's mother's second husband.

[186] Sassier, *Le pouvoir comtal en Auxerrois*, p. 23.

III:263).[187] Raynald had at least two sons, William I, who succeeded him as count, and Gui, a monk at Chaise-Dieu, known only from one mention in a charter for Cluny (C 3580 [IV:716]).[188] He was probably also the father of Robert the Burgundian, a powerful noble who fought for the count of Anjou in the middle years of the eleventh century.[189] Orderic Vitalis refers to the wife of Hubert, viscount of Maine, as the *neptis* of Robert the Burgundian;[190] since this woman was the daughter of Count Raynald's son William I, as indicated below, Robert the Burgundian may well be William's brother. Robert the Burgundian had brothers named Henry and Gui—if Henry is a son of Count Raynald of Nevers, he is otherwise unattested.[191] Robert the Burgundian had a son, Raynald the Burgundian, who was lord of Craon by 1080.[192] In addition to these sons, Count Raynald of Nevers may have had a daughter named Adelaide; Geoffrey II of Semur was said to have married an Adelaide, daughter of "Count Raynald"; the contemporary count of Burgundy however was also named Raynald, so he may be meant instead (Marcigny 1 [p.1]) (see above, p. 272, and below, p. 360).

Though the "Origo" says that William I was count for fifty years, it was actually closer to sixty, from his father's death until his own death in 1098 (*Annales Nivernenses* 1098, MGH SS XIII:91). He married Ermengard, heiress of Tonnerre (*Gesta pontificum*, pp. 398–402; see also below, p. 371). He had three sons, Raynald, William, and Robert, who appeared with their father in charters of 1063 and 1083, and who all predeceased him, Raynald dying around 1089, Robert in 1092, and William about the same time (GC XII:328, no. 36; Nevers/St.-Cyr 79 [p. 136]; (Molesme 1.28, 56 [II:40–43, 67]; Nevers/St.-Étienne 2 [pp. 76–78]). He also had a daughter Ermengard, who married Hubert, viscount of Maine, in 1069/70, and a

[187]Lespinasse locates this battle at Ste.-Vertu, near Noyers, rather than Seignelay, though the chroniclers seem quite specific that it was Seignelay; *Le Nivernais*, I:226, n. 1. According to the "Origo," this battle was fought over control of Auxerre (Vézelay, p. 238), a statement that lends credence to the hypothesis that the king gave Landric Auxerre in 1002 and that Landric's rebellion stemmed from the king's attempt to regain it.

[188]This is probably the Gui, brother of the count of Nevers, whose death is recorded on 26 January in the necrology of the Cluniac priory of St.-Martin-des-Champs; Obit. Sens I:242. The editor is mistaken in identifying this Gui as the Count Gui who died in 1176.

[189]*Cartulaire de l'abbaye de Saint-Aubin d'Angers*, ed. Bertrand de Broussillon, 3 vols. (Paris, 1903), I:440–41, no. 381. See also M. Prou, ed., *Recueil des actes de Philippe Ier, roi de France (1059–1108)* (Paris, 1908), pp. 99–100, 396, nos. 33, 158. Note the repeated ties between Nevers and Anjou.

[190]Orderic Vitalis, *Historia ecclesiastica* 7.10, ed. Chibnall, IV:48.

[191]*Cartulaire de Saint-Aubin*, ed. Bertrand de Broussillon, II:171–74, no. 676.

[192]Ibid., I:189–91, 440–41, nos. 165, 381. Raynald the Burgundian seems to have been the father of Robert, second grandmaster of the Templars (1136/7–1149); see Bulst-Thiele, *Sacrae domus militiae templi Hierosolymitani magistri*, pp. 30–40.

daughter, Eloise, who married Count William of Évreux.[193] Raynald
was titular count of Nevers under his father,[194] while his brother William was count of Tonnerre (Molesme 1.28 [II:40–43]). Robert was
simultaneously count of Auxerre and bishop of Auxerre (*Gesta
pontificum*, p. 401; La Charité 23 [pp. 76–77]) (see also Appendix B,
pp. 388–89). This division of the three counties among sons was
very common in this family of counts in the twelfth century—as was
the subsequent reunion of the counties in the next generation when
only one brother had heirs of his own.

Though none of these three sons survived their father, Raynald,
whom the "Origo" calls lord of Mailly and Hubans, had a son, William II, who, like his grandfather, ruled for an exceptionally long
time, fifty years. William of Tonnerre, second son of William I, had
only a daughter, according to the "Origo," who married Aimo of
Bourbon; interestingly, one of William II's first acts after succeeding
his grandfather was to go to war against Aimo of Bourbon, his
cousin's husband (*Annales Nivernenses* 1099, MGH SS XIII:91). William II was born to Raynald's second wife, the daughter of Lancelin of
Beaugency according to the "Origo," named Agnes according to a
charter of her son (Molesme 1.217 [II:198–200]). In this charter
William II also recalled his grandfather, William I; his father, Raynald;
and his uncles, William of Tonnerre and Bishop Robert of Auxerre.
William II also had a half sister, whom the "Origo" said was born to
Raynald's first wife, the daughter of the count of Forez, and who married Milo of Courtenay. She may be the mother of Hugh, who is
called *nepos* of William II in a charter of 1144 (Lebeuf IV.35 [p. 38]).

William II's long and active career included a journey to join the
victorious Crusaders after the fall of Jerusalem in 1101 (Molesme I.28
[II:40–43]). He was accompanied by his brother Robert, who is
known only from the historians of the Crusades.[195] Since Robert
does not appear again in the records, one can presume he was killed
on Crusade with so many other nobles. William II married a woman
named Adelaide (Autun/Église 2.6 [I:91–92]; Quantin I.102 [p.
198]).[196] William and Adelaide had sons William III and Raynald,

---

[193]Prou, *Recueil des actes de Philippe Ier*, p. 137, no. 50. Orderic Vitalis, *Historia ecclesiastica* 7.10, 11.33, ed. Chibnall, IV:46, VI:148. Lespinasse mistakenly adds another
daughter, Sybil, who he says married Duke Hugh I of Burgundy; *Le Nivernais*, I:250,
259. He seems to have compounded the common error of making Sybil, wife of Duke
Odo I, the wife of Odo's brother Hugh instead, by making Sybil the daughter of Count
William of Nevers rather than Count William of Burgundy. This error originated with
the editor of the Cluny documents; C 3516 (IV:632, n. 2).

[194]Prou, *Recueil des actes de Philippe Ier*, pp. 113, 248, nos. 39, 95.

[195]Alberic of Aix, *Historia Hierosolymitanae expeditionis* 8.30, PL CLXVI:620.

[196]Lespinasse assigns this second charter to William I rather than William II and thus
mistakenly gives William I a second wife named Adelaide; *Le Nivernais*, I:256, n. 2.
The correct identification of the count of this charter as William II comes from the *Gesta pontificum*, p. 405.

discussed below. They may have also had a son named Robert. This Robert is mentioned only in an 1134 charter from St.-Michel of Tonnerre (of slightly dubious authenticity) (Quantin I.174 [pp. 296–99]). William II abdicated as count in favor of his sons in 1146 and retired to La Grande Chartreuse in 1147, at the urging of the abbots of Clairvaux and Pontigny. He died there in 1149.[197]

His sons, William III of Nevers and Raynald of Tonnerre, went on the Second Crusade with Louis VII. Raynald died in the Holy Land as a captive. Hugh of Poitiers, the chronicler of Vézelay, considered Raynald's death a judgment for his father's injuries to the church of Vézelay.[198] William III, however, returned, escaping shipwreck on the return voyage (Vézelay, pp. 423–24). He died in 1161 and was buried at St.-Germain of Auxerre (*Annales Nivernenses* 1161, MGH SS XIII:91; Nevers/St.-Étienne 9 [pp. 86–88]).

William III had married Ida, sister of the countess of Champagne.[199] She first appears in a charter with him in 1142, while his father was still alive (M 601 [p. 363]). She acted as regent for her husband while he was in the Holy Land (RHGF XV:491, no. 21). They had three sons and two daughters. Their sons were William IV, Gui, and Raynald (Nevers/St.-Étienne 12 [pp. 89–91]); the two oldest succeeded each other as counts of Nevers, as indicated below. Raynald, who took the title of lord of Decize, seems to have died on the Third Crusade, for he left for Jerusalem in 1190 (C 4341 [V:705–6]), does not appear in the records again, and is recorded in the obituary of the cathedral of Auxerre as being killed on 5 August (Obit. Sens III:238).[200] He married Adelaide of Beaujeu, who took the title of Countess of Tonnerre during his life and retired to Fontevraud after his death (see above, p. 294).[201] Of the daughters of William III and Ida, Adelaide married Raynald, count of Joigny (Quantin II.121 [pp. 130–31]), but there is no record of whom, if anyone,

---

[197]*Annales Nivernenses* 1149, MGH SS XIII:91; La Charité 55 [pp. 134–36]; Robert of St.-Marien, *Chronicon* 1136, 1147, MGH SS XXVI:233, 236. Bernard of Clairvaux, Letters 496, 515, *Opera*, VIII:453, 474.

[198]William and Raynald seem to have become separated in the Holy Land; as late as 1153, long after he was back in Burgundy, William was still speaking of the possible return of his brother, though other sources indicate he had died by then; Pontigny 50 (pp. 122–24). See the 1148 letter of Louis VII to Suger, announcing the death of many lords, including Raynald of Tonnerre, at Laodicea; RHGF XV:496, no. 36.

[199]William, archbishop of Sens, son of the count of Champagne, called Ida his maternal aunt, *matertera*; Pontigny 8 [pp. 89–90]). Countess Mathilda of Champagne was daughter of Duke Engelbert of Carinthia; Orderic Vitalis, *Historia ecclesiastica* 11.5, ed. Chibnall, VI:42.

[200]Lespinasse says that he was among those killed at Acre; *Le Nivernais*, I:419.

[201]C 4334, 4341 (V:699, 705–6); La Charité 79 (pp. 175–76). Guigue, ed., "Testament de Guichard III de Beaujeu," pp. 161–67.

Ermengard married; she is mentioned only in a charter from Molesme
(Molesme 2.44 [II:278]).[202]

Countess Ida outlived her husband William III; when she died, on
either 5 or 25 May, she was buried at St.-Germain (Obit. Sens III:362,
465). William III's sons seem to have been quite young when he
died. William IV was knighted only in 1159 (Quantin II.89 [pp.
96—97]), two years before his father died. The second son, Gui, was
mentioned with his father in 1158, but in 1164, when he appeared in a
charter of his older brother, the charter indicated that he had not yet
come of age (Autun/Église 2.11 [I:96—97]; Nevers/St.-Étienne 9 [pp.
86—88]). By 1166 William IV had married a woman named Aanor
(La Charité 65 [pp. 154—56]; Pontigny 117 [p. 184]). According to
Robert of Mt.-St.-Michel, she was the daughter of Raoul, count of
Vermandois, and the sister of the countess of Flanders (*Chronica*
1170, MGH SS VI:519). Like their father and uncle, William IV and
Gui went to the Holy Land, where William died in 1168; he was
buried at Bethlehem (Nevers/St.-Cyr 102 [pp. 169—79]; Robert of
St.-Marien, *Chronicon* 1168, MGH SS XXVI:239; Jully, p. 268). Wil-
liam IV did not leave any heirs; his widow, Aanor, married Count
Matthew of Boulogne after his death (Robert of Mt.-St.-Michel,
Chronica 1170, MGH SS VI:519). When Matthew died as well, by
1175, she married the count of Beaumont (Quantin II.249 [pp.
267—68]).

William's brother Gui succeeded him as count of Nevers, Auxerre,
and Tonnerre (C 4239 [V:592—93]; Nevers/St.-Étienne 12 [pp.
89—91]). He married Mathilda, a cousin of the duke of Burgundy;
she was daughter of Raymund, son of Duke Hugh II (Petit 599
[II:383]; see also above, p. 260). She had earlier been married to Odo
of Issoudun during the mid-1160s (GC IV:92, no. 58; *Genus illustre*, p.
556, no. 96 [rpt. PL CLXXXV:1469—70]). From Odo of Issoudun
she had a son named Odo, who inherited that lordship and went on
the Third Crusade (Layettes 380 [I:164—65]).

The marriage between Mathilda and Gui apparently took place
shortly before Gui left for the Holy Land. Mathilda appears in a charter in 1169, recalling her late brother-in-law William's gifts to Fontenay, and appears alone, suggesting that she had heard of William's
death but that Gui had not yet returned (Petit 491 [II:336]). Mathilda
and Gui first appear in a charter together in 1170, and he had no sons
yet in 1171 (C 4239 [V:592—93]; Jully, p. 268). Gui and Mathilda
eventually had two children, William V and Agnes, both very young

---

[202]Lespinasse does not mention either of these daughters; rather, he gives William III
and Ida only one daughter, Agnes, wife of Erard II, count of Brienne, though it is not
clear on what grounds; Lespinasse, *Le Nivernais*, I:340 n. 1.

when Gui died in 1176, on 19 October (*Gesta pontificum*, pp. 422–24; GC XII:135–36, no. 51; Obit. Sens III:465). They may also have had a second daughter, Ida, who appears in a charter with her mother in 1179 (Cîteaux/Marilier 237 [p. 187]). Though Ida could have been the daughter of any of the three men Mathilda had been married to by that time, the name Ida, that of Gui's mother, suggests she was Gui's daughter.

Mathilda acted as regent for her children. Immediately after Gui's death she married Peter, brother of the count of Flanders (GC IV:92, no. 58; Alberic de Trois-Fontaines, *Chronica* 1175, MGH SS XXIII:855). They had a daughter named Sybil (Robert of Mt.-St.-Michel, *Chronica* 1177, MGH SS VI:525; Cîteaux/Marilier 248 [pp. 196–97]). After Peter too died, Mathilda married Robert II of Dreux, but she was forced to separate from him on grounds of consanguinity (Robert of St.-Marien, *Chronicon* 1181, MGH SS XXVI:244; Robert of Mt.-St.-Michel, *Chronica* 1177, MGH SS VI:525).[203] The heir, William V, died while still a child in 1181 (Quantin II.309 [pp. 328–29]; Robert of St.-Marien, *Chronicon* 1181, MGH SS XXVI:244). The male line of counts of Nevers thus came to an end; for the next several generations the counties of Nevers, Auxerre, and Tonnerre were held by heiresses.

William V's sister Agnes was the heiress of the three counties in 1181. She married Oliver Albus, lord of Grignon. Though he soon died (Fontenay I, fol. 101v, no. 14), the countesses of Nevers retained Grignon. Next, Agnes married Peter of Courtenay, the king's cousin, in 1184 (Robert of St.-Marien, *Chronicon* 1184, MGH SS XXVI:247; *Gesta pontificum*, pp. 440–41; C 4297 [V:660–62]; Nevers/St.-Étienne 16 [pp. 93–95]). Peter became count of Auxerre and Nevers, and he and Agnes bought Tonnerre from her mother Mathilda in 1192 (Petit 876 [III:318–19]). Mathilda retired to Fontevraud, where she was still living as a nun in 1210 (Quantin III.97 [pp. 43–44]). Her death took place on 17 December (Obit. Sens III:269). Peter and Agnes had only one child, a girl named Mathilda like her grandmother, before Agnes died in 1193, on 5 or 6 February (La Charité 80 [pp. 176–78]; Nevers/St.-Étienne 23 [p. 98]; Obit. Sens III:250, 464). Peter then married Yolendis, daughter of Baldwin, count of Hainaut and Flanders. Peter took the title of marquis of Namur (Quantin III.135 [p. 62]). He and Yolendis had four sons and five daughters, but they all attempted to establish their rule in Flanders, in Constantinople, or in the Holy Land, so I shall not follow

[203]Mathilda and Robert were both descended from King Robert II. They were related within five degrees on his side and six on hers.

them here (Alberic de Trois-Fontaines, *Chronica* 1191, 1218, MGH SS XXIII:868, 906).

In 1199 Countess Mathilda married Hervé IV, lord of Donzy, who acted as count of Nevers, while Peter of Courtenay retained the counties of Auxerre and Tonnerre (Robert of St.-Marien, *Chronicon* 1199, MGH SS XXVI:259; Layettes 502 [I:207]). Hervé and Mathilda were related within four degrees, too closely by the canonical definition of consanguinity, but the pope issued them a special dispensation to allow them to remain married (Innocent III, Letters 8.112, 16.151, PL CCXV:679–80; CCXVI:943–44).[204] They had one daughter, named Agnes.[205] Hervé and Mathilda left on Crusade together in 1218 (Quantin III.215 [pp. 95–96]). Mathilda outlived Hervé, who died in 1222, on 23 January (Obit. Sens III:464). In that year she confirmed his gifts to Pontigny (Lebeuf IV.146 [pp. 87–88]), promised the king she would not marry again without his permission, and received homage as countess of Nevers (Quantin III.274, 276 [pp. 120–21]). She married Wigo (or Gui), count of Forez, a few years later (Alberic de Trois-Fontaines, *Chronica* 1218, MGH SS XXIII:906; C 4694 [VI:212–13]; Lebeuf IV.154 [p. 92]; Quantin III.368 [p. 165]). In 1239 Wigo left for the Holy Land, where he died in 1241, on 31 July (Quantin III.451 [pp. 204–5]; Alberic de Trois-Fontaines, *Chronica* 1241, MGH SS XXIII:949; Obit. Sens III:260). In 1242 his son and heir Gui, born to his first wife, agreed to let Mathilda have her dotal property in Forez and gave up any claim to his father's acquisitions in the Nivernais (Layettes 3004 [II:485–86]; Quantin III.484 [p. 221]). Mathilda outlived her second husband by many years; she made her testament in 1257 (Lebeuf IV.191 [pp. 110–11]).

After Peter of Courtenay and Hervé had died (both shortly after 1220), the three counties of Nevers, Auxerre, and Tonnerre had passed to Agnes, daughter of Hervé and Mathilda, and the third heiress in a row. She had been engaged in 1214 to Philip, oldest son of Louis VIII, and seems to have actually married him in 1218; he lived only a short time (Quantin III.212 [p. 94]). She next married Gui, lord of St.-Paul and of Châtillon-sur-Marne, in 1221. Gui was son of Gaucher of St.-Paul and Châtillon (Nevers/St.-Étienne 27 [pp.

[204]Their great-grandmothers were sisters: Ida, countess of Nevers, and Mathilda, countess of Champagne. For Hervé's descent from the counts of Champagne, see above, p. 329, and Lespinasse, *Le Nivernais*, II:23, n. 1. They may have even been related within three degrees, as Hervé's grandmother Clemence was probably daughter of Duke Hugh II and hence a sister of Raymund, the father of Countess Mathilda of Nevers.

[205]Lespinasse erroneously gives Hervé and Mathilda a son named William. This error is based on Petit's summary of a charter; Petit 1152 (III:411). The charter in question refers to a Count William who was one of Mathilda's ancestors, but Petit mistakenly calls him her son.

101–3]; Alberic de Trois-Fontaines, *Chronica* 1214, MGH SS XXIII:902; RHGF XVIII:783–85; Layettes 1302, 1447 [I:467–68, 516]). Both Agnes and Gui of St.-Paul died in 1226; this may be why her mother Mathilda remarried shortly thereafter (Lebeuf IV.154–56 [pp. 92–93]). Gui and Agnes too had only a daughter who reached maturity, Yolendis. She inherited Nevers.

The Lords of Saulx

The lords of Saulx held the county of Langres until 1178 and consequently were sometimes called counts of Saulx. Count Gui I of Saulx appeared with the duke in 1053.[206] In 1057 Count Gui quarreled with St.-Bénigne (St.-B. II.340 [pp. 119–21]). The count of Saulx from the 1070s to the first decades of the twelfth century was Gui II, also called of Grancey (St.-Étienne I.84 [p. 102]; Molesme 1.70 [II:77–78]). He may have been the son of the Count Gui of the 1050s and the brother of Raynald I of Grancey, who is known to have had a brother Gui (see above, p. 332). Count Gui II of Saulx, who made gifts to the monastery of Couches in 1086, had these gifts confirmed by his wife, the Countess Letgardis, and his son Eblo in 1110 (Plancher II.1–2 [pp. i–ii]). Letgardis was daughter of Geoffrey of Rumigny and of Haduidis, daughter of Eblo I of Roucy ("Genealogiae Fusniacenses," MGH SS XIII:254). Gui of Saulx appears in Cîteaux's early charters from around 1100 and 1110 (Cîteaux/Marilier 26, 41 [pp. 52–53, 63–65]). Gui, called *nobilis vir*, established secular canons in the church of Saulx in the 1120s (Pérard, p. 225). His son Eblo succeeded him after Gui had ruled as count of Saulx for a good fifty years.

Eblo, count of Saulx, had a brother William. Eblo married a woman named Regina and had sons Gui (the oldest and the heir) and Girard around 1135 (*Genus illustre*, p. 486, no. 47 [rpt. PL CLXXXV:45]; Langres 280 (p. 735); St.-Étienne II.37 [pp. 45–46]; GC IV:165, no. 42). Eblo and Regina went on to have at least three more sons, named Eblo, William, and Milo. Regina's charters mention Eblo and William (St.-Étienne III.13 [pp. 15–16]), and their son Gui mentioned his brother Milo in his own charters, as indicated below.

Gui III was lord of Saulx in the mid- to late twelfth century. He may also have briefly acquired Tilchâtel, according to a charter for St.-Étienne of Dijon (St.-Étienne III.13 [pp. 15–16]). Gui had acted

[206]*Recueil des chartes de Saint-Germain-des-Prés*, ed. Poupardin, I:97, no. 59.

The Lords of Saulx

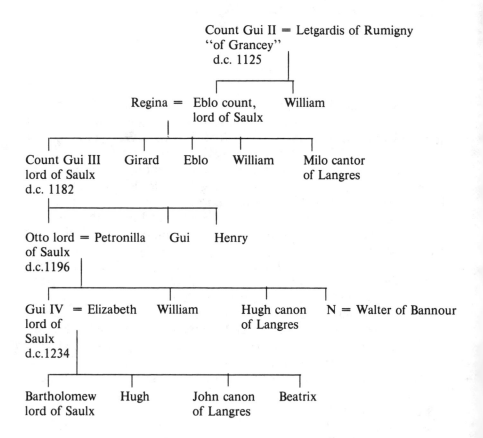

Count Gui I
fl. 1053, 1057

Count Gui II = Letgardis of Rumigny
"of Grancey"
d.c. 1125

Regina = Eblo count,   William
         lord of Saulx

Count Gui III   Girard   Eblo   William   Milo cantor
lord of Saulx   of Langres
d.c. 1182

Otto lord = Petronilla   Gui   Henry
of Saulx
d.c.1196

Gui IV = Elizabeth   William   Hugh canon   N = Walter of Bannour
lord of   of Langres
Saulx
d.c.1234

Bartholomew   Hugh   John canon   Beatrix
lord of Saulx   of Langres

as count of Langres, but in 1178 the duke of Burgundy bought the county from him and gave it to the bishop of Langres (GC IV:187—88, no. 71). Gui appears in the charters with brothers Girard and Eblo, knights, and Milo, cantor of Langres, and sons Gui and Henry as well as Otto, his heir (Petit 490, 531 [II:335—36, 352]). Milo had joined the chapter at Langres by 1164 at the latest (Clairvaux/Waquet 122 [p. 134]). Gui III's son Henry married the lady of "Salvia" (Arch. Haute-Marne, 1 H 89, no. 8). Gui III was also probably the father of the lady of Mt.-St.-Jean, who called herself the daughter of Gui, *vir militaris* of Saulx castle (Petit 335 [II:257—59]). Gui's son and successor, Otto, remembered Gui in 1182 (GC IV:191, no. 76). In this charter Girard, dean of Langres, Milo, the cantor, and Peter, dean of Bar, all witnessed as his *avunculi*. (Milo was his paternal uncle, Girard must have been a maternal uncle or perhaps a great-uncle, and it is not clear how Peter was related.) Gui III had presumably died in this year.

Gui's son and heir Otto was called simply lord of Saulx, rather than count, now that his family no longer held the county of Langres. He married a woman named Petronilla and had a son Gui while his father was still alive (Petit 490 [II:335—36]). In 1188/9 Otto was lord of Saulx, with wife Willelma (which may be a variation of Petronilla) and sons Gui (the oldest), William, and Hugh. Otto's son-in-law (*gener*) was Walter of Bannour (St.-Seine, p. 259; Plancher I.114 [p. lxiii]; *Genus illustre*, pp. 613—14, no. 142 [rpt. PL CLXXXV:1501—2]). His son Hugh went on to become a canon at Langres; he died in 1222 (*Genus illustre*, p. 496, no. 60 [rpt. PL CLXXXV:1438]).

Otto's son Gui IV, who had succeeded him by 1196 (GC IV:25, no. 31), married a woman named Elizabeth. That she named one of her sons Bartholomew makes it tempting to think that she is identical with Bartholomew of Vignory's daughter Elizabeth (see below, p. 383). In 1197 he already had sons named Hugh and Bartholomew (Chalon, p. 965; Petit 869 [III:315—16]; Pérard, pp. 233—34; this last charter is misdated 1147 by the editor). Gui and Elizabeth appeared with children named Bartholomew and Beatrix in 1203 (*Genus illustre*, p. 487, no. 48 [rpt. PL CLXXXV:1433—34]). Gui was still alive in 1230, when he appears in a charter for St.-Seine with his son Bartholomew. Bartholomew acted as sole lord of Saulx in 1234 (Plancher I.183, 188 [pp. cii, civ]). In that year Bartholomew's brother John, another son of Gui IV, was a canon of Langres (GC IV:205—6, no. 103).

The Lords of Seignelay

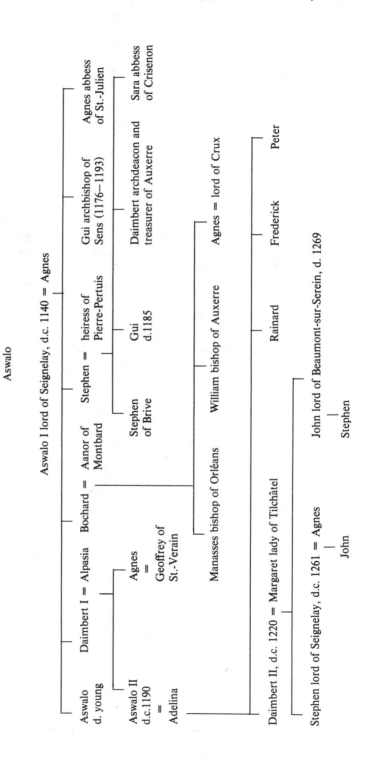

The Lords of Seignelay

Elsewhere I have discussed this particular family as an example of the way noble families viewed themselves in the twelfth century; Constance B. Bouchard, "The Structure of a Twelfth-Century French Family: The Lords of Seignelay," *Viator*, 10 (1979), 39—56. Yves Sassier has also briefly discussed the family as an example of the lords who held power in the Auxerrois; Sassier, *Le pouvoir comtal en Auxerrois*, pp. 104—8. Waast-Barthélemy Henry wrote a rather unreliable history of Seignelay a century ago; *Mémoires historiques sur la ville de Seignelay*, 2 vols. (Avallon, 1833—1853).

The first mention of the lords of Seignelay is by Raoul Glaber, who spoke of Bovo and his son Aswalo, of the "sacrilegious" castle of Seignelay (Raoul Glaber, *Historia* 5.1 [pp. 119—20]). It is tempting to see these men as the ancestors of the later lords of Seignelay. Several men named Aswalo who may be lords of Seignelay appear in the charters of the Auxerrois in the eleventh century; for example, an Aswalo excommunicated by Abbot Heldric of St.-Germain at the very beginning of the eleventh century tried to get the sentence lifted so he could be buried there;[207] and an Aswalo witnessed an episcopal charter in 1055 (C 3348 [IV:444—46]).

Aswalo I, the first lord of Seignelay to be fully documented, lived in the early twelfth century. A document in which he appeared in 1106, a settlement of his quarrels with St.-Germain, has as a witness Jolduin, viscount of Sens, called *frater suus*, but since the document is badly preserved it is not entirely clear if Aswalo's brother or another of the witnesses is meant.[208] Aswalo I married a woman named Agnes. They had at least five sons, Aswalo, who died young (Molesme 1.160 [II:153]), Daimbert I, who succeeded, Bochard, Stephen, who became lord of Pierre-Pertuis, and Gui, who became archbishop of Sens (1176—1193). They also had a daughter Agnes, abbess of St.-Julien of Auxerre (Pontigny 153 [pp. 209—10]; *Gesta pontificum*, pp. 451, 453; Arch. Yonne, H 1743). Before Gui became archbishop he had been a canon at Auxerre (GC XII:55, no. 64). The obituary of Auxerre cathedral calls him "of Noyers," apparently because he was the uncle of Hugh of Noyers, bishop of Auxerre (1183—1206) (*Gesta pontificum*, p. 447), and says that Archbishop Gui

---

[207]Edmund Martène and Ursin Durands, eds., *Thesaurus novus anecdotorum*, I (Paris, 1717; rpt. New York, 1968), 106—7.

[208]Maximilien Quantin, ed., "Une sentence de Guillaume Ier, comte de Nevers, de l'an 1106," *Bulletin de la Société des sciences historiques et naturelles de l'Yonne*, 40 (1886), 231—34. In 1032 the viscount of Sens was named Daimbert, a name that reappears among the twelfth-century lords of Seignelay. This Daimbert was son of a man named Mainard and brother of another Mainard, later archbishop of Sens; *Chronique de Saint-Pierre-le-Vif*, ed. Bautier and Gilles, pp. 118, 126.

was provost of Auxerre before his election. He died on 22 December (Obit. Sens III:269).

Aswalo and his wife Agnes last appear in dated charters in 1139 and 1140, along with their sons Daimbert, Bochard, and Stephen (Pontigny 130 [p. 192]; Quantin I.140 [pp. 258–59]). In 1143 and 1146 Daimbert I of Seignelay appeared in charters with his brothers Bochard and Stephen (Pontigny 88, 138 [pp. 160, 198]). By 1147 Daimbert had married a woman named Alpasia (Pontigny 140, 145 [pp. 200, 204]). When Daimbert died relatively young, his brother Bochard married Aanor of Montbard (see above, p. 337), and Stephen apparently married the heiress of Pierre-Pertuis, for he appeared in later charters as lord of Pierre-Pertuis (Nevers/St.-Cyr 101 [p. 168]). Bochard acted as lord of Seignelay while Daimbert I's children were young (Quantin II.250 [pp. 268–69]).

Bochard and Aanor had two sons, Manasses and William, who became archdeacon and treasurer of Sens under their uncle Gui, archbishop of Sens, and in 1207 bishops of respectively Orléans and Auxerre (Gesta pontificum, pp. 451, 463–64; Quantin III.57 [pp. 27–28]). William went on to become bishop of Paris in 1220. He died in 1223, on 23 November (Gesta pontificum, p. 481; Obit. Sens I:13).[209] William had a nephew named Andreas who served in the chapter of Auxerre under him and who became archdeacon (Obit. Sens III:261). Bochard and Aanor also had a daughter named Agnes. She married the lord of Crux, bore him Hugh, lord of Crux, and died in 1202 (Quantin III.10 [p. 5]).

Stephen of Pierre-Pertuis had sons Daimbert, archdeacon and treasurer of Auxerre in 1184 and 1185, and Stephen of Brive, miles. Daimbert also served as sacristan of Nevers (Obit. Sens III:256). Stephen of Pierre-Pertuis also had a son Gui, who died in 1185 (Quantin II.345, 346, 410 [pp. 358–60, 415–16]; Pontigny 122 [p. 187]), and a daughter Sara, who became a nun at Crisenon (Crisenon 161 [fol. 78v]), probably identical with the Abbess Sara who held office around the beginning of the thirteenth century.

Daimbert I and Alpasia had at least two children, Aswalo II and Agnes, and by the 1160s Aswalo was old enough to act as lord of Seignelay—though Bochard also acted as lord of Seignelay as late as 1175 (Quantin II.250 [pp. 268–69]). In 1167 Aswalo II, lord of Seignelay, appeared in the documents with a wife named Eluidis (or Adelina) and a sister Agnes (Pontigny 129 [pp. 190–91]). Agnes married Geoffrey, lord of St.-Verain, by 1186 (Quantin II.390 [p. 397];

---

[209]See also Constance Brittain Bouchard, Spirituality and Administration: The Role of the Bishop in Twelfth-Century Auxerre, Speculum Anniversary Monographs 5 (Cambridge, Mass., 1979), pp. 121–40.

Pontigny 340 [p. 343]). Aswalo II and Adelina had sons named Daimbert, Rainard, Frederick, and Peter (Quantin II.377 [pp. 387–88]; Pontigny 149, 153, 154 [pp. 206–7, 210–11]). Aswalo went on the Third Crusade (Quantin II.410 [pp. 415–16]).

Aswalo II probably died in the Holy Land with his three youngest sons, but his son Daimbert II continued the lineage. In 1203 Daimbert II appeared in the documents with his wife Margaret and son Stephen (Quantin III.20 [pp. 8–9]). Margaret was lady of Tilchâtel (Vergy, p. 50), having been earlier married to the lord of Tilchâtel (see below, p. 368). Daimbert II had died by 1220, and his son Stephen succeeded as lord of Seignelay. Margaret too had died by 1224. Stephen, who had a brother named John, had married a woman named Agnes by 1224 (Quantin III.258, 303, 309 [pp. 113–14, 132, 135]; Pontigny 232 [p. 266]).

The Lords of Semur

The lords of Semur are recorded in a mid-twelfth-century genealogy that was preserved in the cartulary of Marcigny, a house of nuns founded by members of the family (Marcigny 1 [p. 1]). Family members are also often found in the charters of Cluny and Savigny. The family has been studied most recently by Jean Richard, in connection with his edition of the cartulary of Marcigny. Richard follows the family down to the 1140s. My reconstruction of the family tree differs only slightly from his.

The first known lord of Semur was a man named Freelan, who lived in the tenth century (Marcigny 1 [p. 1]). His son Joceran, who died by 1000 (Savigny 435 [p. 236]), succeeded him as lord of Semur. This Joceran may be the same person as the *miles nobilis* Joceran Bers of Semur whom the abbot of Savigny recalled around 1128 as having been generous to his house; this Joceran Bers however had been succeeded by Dalmace, according to the charter of 1128 (Savigny 915 [pp. 490–91]), while Joceran had no sons by that name (though the charter might be referring to his grandson Dalmace). Joceran had at least three brothers, Freelan, Robold, and Hugh, abbot of Savigny, an office he took in 984 (Savigny 435, 527, 645 [pp. 236, 268, 324–25]).[210] He also had a sister, Adelina, abbess of Pélages

---

[210]See also Schieffer, ed., *Die Urkunden der Rudolfinger*, p. 212, no. 70. The genealogy of Marcigny does not mention Hugh and calls Freelan an abbot; it is likely that either in transcribing or in translating (the only existing version of this genealogy is an eighteenth-century French translation) "Freelan" and "Hugh, abbot" were conflated; Marcigny 1 (p. 1).

The Lords of Semur

Freelan lord of Semur

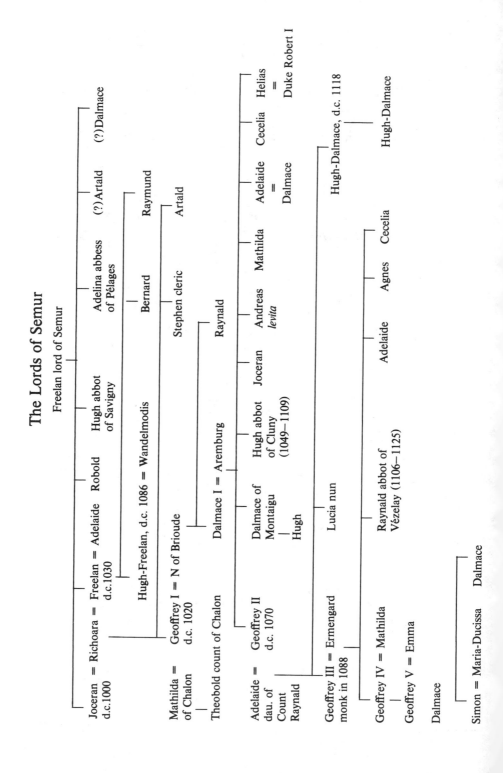

(Savigny 645, 646 [pp. 324–26]). The genealogy of this family adds two more brothers, Artald and Dalmace (Marcigny 1 [p. 1]). They are unattested in other sources, however, and the name Dalmace may be an error, because that name seems to have entered the family only with the marriage of Joceran's son to the daughter of a Dalmace, as indicated below.

Joceran married a woman named Richoara (Savigny 527, 716 [pp. 268, 369–70]), who apparently married his brother Freelan after his death (Savigny 435 [p. 236]). Freelan, who died by 1030, had three sons, Hugh-Freelan, Bernard, and Raymund (Savigny 644, 645, 756 [pp. 323–25, 392–93]), though it is not clear whether these were all by Richoara. A Freelan with a wife named Adelaide and son Bernard made a gift to Cluny at some point in the early eleventh century (C 2471 [III:550–51]).[211] Hugh-Freelan, who died around 1086, married a woman named Wandelmodis or Tadalmodis and had a son named Bernard (Savigny 756, 770 [pp. 392–93, 405–6]).

In the meantime, Joceran's son, Geoffrey I, succeeded his father as lord of Semur. He had two brothers, Stephen (a cleric) and Artald (Savigny 527, 716 [pp. 268, 369–70]). Geoffrey, who died around 1020, married twice. His first wife was Mathilda, daughter of Count Lambert of Chalon; from them descended the eleventh-century counts of Chalon (see above, p. 312). His second wife is called the daughter of Dalmace, viscount of Brioude (in the Auvergne), in the family's twelfth-century genealogy (Marcigny 1 [p. 1]).[212] Their descendants were the eleventh- and twelfth-century lords of Semur.

Geoffrey I and his second wife had two sons, Dalmace I, lord of Semur, and his brother Raynald. Dalmace married a woman named Aremburg, described in the twelfth-century genealogy as a "sister of Count Theobold" (Marcigny 1 [p. 1]). This would seem to be Theobold, count of Chalon. But Theobold and Dalmace were half brothers, both sons of Geoffrey I of Semur. It is most likely that the genealogy is simply mistaken and that the monk who drew it up wanted to explain why Dalmace's and Aremburg's children referred to an "uncle Theobold," not realizing that Dalmace was Theobold's half brother. He therefore assumed Aremburg must have had a brother of that name.[213]

[211]Richard makes all of Freelan's sons the children of Adelaide.

[212]The cartulary of St.-Julien of Brioude lists viscounts of Brioude named Dalmace from the early years of the tenth century; Henry Doniol, ed., *Cartulaire de Brioude* (Clermont, 1863), pp. 51–54, 83–84, nos. 28, 30, 63.

[213]In an attempt to make Aremburg a sister of Count Theobold, Richard has suggested that perhaps Mathilda of Chalon had been married before she married Geoffrey, and that Aremburg was a child of this marriage. Vajay has argued—not particularly convincingly—that Mathilda had married Henry, duke of Burgundy, and that Aremburg was their daughter; "'Guerre de Bourgogne,'" pp. 164–65. It seems unwise to build family trees on a statement that is probably a simple mistake.

Dalmace I and his wife had a large family, five known sons and four or five daughters. The sons were Geoffrey II, lord of Semur; Dalmace, lord of Montaigu; Hugh, abbot of Cluny (1049–1109); Joceran; and Andreas, who is called *levita* in the genealogy, and hence was also a monk (C 3347 [IV:443–44]; Marcigny 1, 2 [pp. 1–3]; see also Raynald of Vézelay's *Vita* of Abbot Hugh, Vézelay suppl., p. 39). Richard hesitates about including Dalmace, lord of Montaigu, but he is clearly attested in the documents; Geoffrey II is known to have had a brother Dalmace (C 2940, 3346, 3347 [IV:141–42, 442–44]), and the biographer of Hugh, abbot of St.-Germain (1100–1115) and bishop of Auxerre (1115–1136), states explicitly that Hugh was son of Dalmace, lord of Montaigu, and nephew of Hugh, abbot of Cluny (*Gesta pontificum*, p. 410). The daughters included Helias, wife of Duke Robert I of Burgundy (see above, p. 257), as well four girls mentioned in the foundation charter of Marcigny: Mathilda, Adelaide, Cecelia, and Evella (Marcigny 2 [pp. 1–3]). Evella may just be another form of the name Helias. Adelaide married Dalmace of Châtel-Montagne and retired to Marcigny after his death (Marcigny 3, 280 [pp. 3–5, 159–60]). One of her sisters—Mathilda, according to Richard—married Guichard, lord of Bourbon-Lancy, for Guichard's son Dalmace referred to Abbot Hugh of Cluny as his uncle (Marcigny 19, 285 [pp. 19–20, 163–64]). This woman, like Adelaide, retired to Marcigny (Marcigny 24 [pp. 22–23]).

Geoffrey II married a woman named Adelaide, called daughter of "Count Raynald" in the genealogy; she might be either daughter of Count Raynald of Burgundy or of Count Raynald of Nevers (Marcigny 1 [p. 1]). Geoffrey and Adelaide, together with Geoffrey's brother Abbot Hugh, founded the house of Marcigny, a nunnery dependent on Cluny, in 1054 (C 3346 [IV:442–43]; Marcigny 2 [pp. 1–3]). Geoffrey's brother Dalmace assisted in this foundation. Geoffrey and Dalmace made the gift of the church in which the nunnery was established for the souls of their father Dalmace and grandfather Geoffrey. The foundation was witnessed by their uncle, Count Theobold.[214] Geoffrey II retired to Cluny after his wife died and was buried at Marcigny (Marcigny 9, 10 [pp. 10–11]), probably around 1070. Geoffrey and Adelaide had had two known sons, Geoffrey III, lord of Semur, and Hugh-Dalmace (Marcigny 1, 3, 5 [pp. 1, 3–8]). They also had a daughter, Lucia, who became a nun at Marcigny while her father was still in the world (Marcigny 6, 16 [pp. 8, 17]). Hugh-Dalmace went to Jerusalem in 1118 and seems to have died on his journey (Marcigny 161 [pp. 95–96]; cf. Savigny 884 [pp. 465–66]). He had a son,

---

[214]The charter C 3346 may be the source of the confusion that made the twelfth-century genealogist give Aremburg a brother Theobold.

named Hugh-Dalmace like his father, who confirmed his father's gifts to Marcigny in the 1130s (Marcigny 301 [p. 179]).

Geoffrey III and his wife Ermengard retired to Marcigny in 1088. They took with them their son Raynald and three daughters, named Adelaide, Agnes, and Cecilia in a restrospective charter (Marcigny 15 [p. 16, n. 2]); their son Geoffrey IV however remained in the world as lord of Semur (Marcigny 155 [pp. 94–95]). Geoffrey III became prior of Marcigny, a position he held until his death in 1123 (Marcigny 291 [pp. 172–73]). Raynald was later abbot of Vézelay (1106–1125) and archbishop of Lyon (1125–1128) (Marcigny 111 [pp. 81–82]; Peter the Venerable, *Miracula* 1.26, PL CLXXXIX:898–900; see also Appendix C, p. 431).

Geoffrey IV married a woman named Mathilda, called "countess" in the genealogy, and had one known son, Geoffrey V, who married a woman named Emma (Marcigny 1, 111 [pp. 1, 81–82]). The Marcigny genealogy goes no further than this, but there continued to be lords of Semur throughout the twelfth century. Geoffrey V was probably the father of a Dalmace of Semur who appears in the records around 1168 (La Charité 33 [pp. 93–96]). In 1190 Simon, *nobilis vir*, called lord of the castle of Semur, recognized that what "Geoffrey-Dalmace" had held from the abbey of St.-Martin had been held in fief, not as his own property. This Geoffrey-Dalmace may be the same person as the Dalmace who appeared in 1168, or the name Geoffrey-Dalmace may actually mean Geoffrey, son of Dalmace (the "Dalmace" is in the genitive), in which case this Geoffrey may be a son of the Dalmace of 1168. In the document of 1190 Lord Simon appeared with a wife called Ducissa and a brother Dalmace (Autun/St.-Martin 23 [pp. 49–50]). Ducissa was a nickname; his wife Maria was so called because she was the daughter of Duke Hugh III of Burgundy (Arch. Allier, H 140; see also above, p. 261). Simon went on the Third Crusade (Petit 845 [III:304]) but returned alive. He died in 1219. Simon and Maria-Ducissa had a son named Dalmace.[215]

The Lords of Sexfontaines

It is possible that the lords of Sexfontaines were descended from the counts of Auxois, who wielded authority at Sexfontaines at the beginning of the eleventh century (see above, pp. 284–86). Raynald was lord of Sexfontaines in the 1070s (Molesme 1.197, 256 [II:177,

---

[215]Guichard et al., eds., *Chartes du Forez*, vol. I, no. 41.

The Lords of Sexfontaines

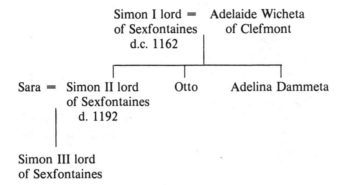

Raynald of Sexfontaines

Simon I lord = Adelaide Wicheta
of Sexfontaines   of Clefmont
d.c. 1162

Sara = Simon II lord   Otto   Adelina Dammeta
of Sexfontaines
d. 1192

Simon III lord
of Sexfontaines

239]), and the same or a different Raynald was lord of Sexfontaines around 1100 (Molesme 1.15 [II:22]). In the 1140s Raynald, a *miles* of Sexfontaines, recalled his grandfather, Lord Raynald (Molesme 1.258 [II:240]).

A clear family tree for the lords of Sexfontaines emerges only with Lord Simon I. Simon I, lord of Sexfontaines, was one of the early donors to the abbey of La Crête, apparently in the 1140s or 1150s (Arch. Saône-et-Loire, 5 H 5). Simon gave up quarrels with the bishop of Langres in 1159 (Langres 143 [p. 561]). In 1162 Lord Simon was married to Adelaide Wicheta of Clefmont (daughter of Lord Robert Wicard; see above, p. 317). He went to Jerusalem in this year and does not appear in the documents again (Arch. Haute-Marne, 5 H 8). Adelaide Wicheta and Simon had children named Otto and Adelina Dammeta, mentioned in 1165, by which time Simon I was probably dead (Arch. Haute-Marne, 8 H 107).[216] They were also the parents of Simon II of Sexfontaines (Arch. Haute-Marne, 8 H 67, no. 13). After Simon I's death, Adelaide married a man named Egidius, or Giles (Arch. Haute-Marne, 5 H 6).[217]

Lord Simon II of Sexfontaines married a woman named Sara (Clairvaux II, pp. 63–64, no. 46). In 1192 Simon died at Toul. He was called *illustris vir* in the charter the bishop of Langres issued to attest to his burial gifts. His wife and oldest son Simon III confirmed his gifts to Clairvaux (Clairvaux I, pp. 80–81, nos. 33, 35). Simon III was lord of Sexfontaines in 1218 and 1220 (Layettes 1275, 1404 [I:457, 501–2]).[218]

The Lords of Sombernon

The first known lord of Sombernon is Warner, who lived in the first decades of the eleventh century, and had a brother Aldo, perhaps identical with Aldo I of Tilchâtel (see below, p. 366) (St.-B. II.229 [pp. 25–26]). It is tempting to see Warner and Aldo as the children of the noble couple Warner and Alda, who lived around the year 1000 (Chron. St.-B., pp. 170–72). According to a donation charter by which Warner gave land at Salmaise to St.-Bénigne in 1020, he had a wife named Istiburgis and daughters named Anna and Addilla (St.-B. II.272 [pp. 63–64]). This Addilla may be the same as the Oddilla

---

[216]Hubert Flammarion suggests—on what evidence is unclear—that Otto "probably" became abbot of Luxeuil, and says that Adelina Dammeta married Walter of Épinal; Flammarion, "Clefmont," p. 380, n. 2.

[217]Flammarion calls him "of Gondecourt."

[218]In this second charter the editor incorrectly calls Simon "de Ceffonds."

The Lords of Sombernon

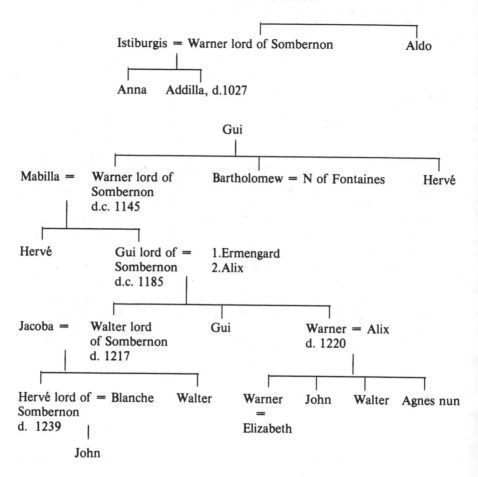

who gave St.-Bénigne more land at Salmaise for her burial in 1027, with the confirmation of her mother, here called Engelberga (Petit 1491 [III:492]). It is not clear what, if any, connection there was between Warner of Sombernon and the contemporary Walo of Salmaise, son of Aimo I of Auxois (see above, p. 284).

After 1027 there is a gap in the family tree of the lords of Sombernon until the 1070s, when Gui of Sombernon appeared in the records (St.-Marcel 33 [pp. 36–38]). Gui was the uncle of the brothers Gui and Hugh of Molay (St.-Marcel 33 [pp. 36–38]). In the first decades of the twelfth century Gui's son Warner was lord of Sombernon (Petit 1492 [III:496–97]). Warner had a brother named Hervé (Arch. Côte-d'Or, 111 H 1169). In the 1120s Lord Warner of Sombernon appeared with a wife named Mabilla and a son named Hervé (Cîteaux/Marilier 55, 77 [pp. 71, 84–85]). This Warner and his son Hervé founded the Cistercian house of La Bussière in 1131 (Cîteaux/Marilier 85 [p. 90]). In the 1140s Warner, lord of Sombernon, appeared in the records with a brother named Bartholomew and sons Hervé and Gui (Jobin, *St. Bernard*, p. 597, no. 33; Petit 1492 [III:496–98]). Bartholomew, Lord Warner's brother, seems to have become lord of Fontaines by marrying a daughter of Bernard of Clairvaux's oldest brother (see above, p. 331).

Hervé, the oldest son of Lord Warner (Petit 1492 [III:496–97]), seems to have died young, for Gui inherited Sombernon. He married a woman named Ermengard and had a *nepos* Odo of Mirebeau in 1148 (Jobin, *St. Bernard*, pp. 598–99, no. 34). He appears in another charter with a wife named Alix (Cîteaux/Marilier 170 [p. 135]).

Gui had sons Walter, who succeeded by 1187, Gui, and Warner (Petit 773 [III:276]; Cîteaux II, fol. 54r, no. 9; Arch. Côte-d'Or, 111 H 1169). Walter, lord of Sombernon, was present at the siege of Acre in 1191 (Petit 867 [III:314–15]). He was one of the few Burgundians to come home alive and, apparently soon after his return, married a woman named Jacoba. Walter and Jacoba did not yet have children old enough to witness their parents' charters in 1196 (Petit 912, 929 [III:332–33, 339]), though by 1200 Walter and Jacoba appeared with sons named Hervé and Walter (St.-Seine, pp. 263–64; edited as Plancher I.156 [pp. lxxxxii–lxxxxiii]). In 1208 Walter, lord of Sombernon, recalled his relatives, his grandfather Warner, father Gui, and uncle Hervé. He acted with his wife Jacoba and sons Hervé and Walter. Walter died and was buried at La Bussière in 1217 (*Genus illustre*, pp. 466, 468–69, nos. 25, 28 [rpt. PL CLXXXV:1422–24]). Walter's younger brother Warner died in 1220. He had married a woman named Alix and had three known sons, Warner, John, and Walter. He also had a daughter Agnes, who became a nun at Prâlon. Warner's son Warner had married a woman named Elizabeth by 1220 (*Genus illustre*, p. 469, no. 29 [rpt. PL CLXXXV:1424]).

Walter's son Hervé succeeded as lord of Sombernon. He did homage to the countess of Champagne in 1219 (Layettes 1351 [I:482]). He had a wife named Blanche and a son John when he died and was buried at La Bussière in 1239 (*Genus illustre*, pp. 469, 474–75, nos. 29, 35 [rpt. PL CLXXXV:1424, 1427]).

The Lords of Tilchâtel

The lords of Tilchâtel have been briefly studied by Henri de Faget de Casteljau, "Les sires de Til-châtel: Feaux de Langres aux marchés des deux Bourgognes, X^e–XVe siècles," *Les cahiers haut-marnais*, 143 (1980), 145–59. I do not always agree with his reconstruction.

The first known lord of Til was a man named Aldo I. This Aldo may be identical with the Aldo who was brother of Lord Warner of Sombernon (St.-B. II.229 [pp. 25–26]) (see above, p. 363).[219] Aldo was the father of Lord Aimo I, who, with his wife Hildegard and brother Otbert, helped establish the house of canons at St.-Florent of Til as a dependency of St.-Étienne of Dijon in 1033 (St.-Étienne I.64 [pp. 86–87]; Petit 17 [I:358]).[220] Aimo I's son Aldo II, who married a woman named Elizabeth, made additional gifts to the house (St.-Étienne I.66 [pp. 88–89]).

In 1066 Aldo II of Tilchâtel witnessed a confirmation of the possessions of St.-Bénigne by the ducal council (St.-B. II.344 [pp. 123–25]; Petit 40 [I:383–85]). His son Otbert succeeded some time after 1076 (St.-Étienne II.2 bis [pp. 3-4]; Chron. St.-B., pp. 377–78). Otbert of Tilchâtel married a woman of the family of the viscounts of Dijon (St.-B. II.375 [pp. 154–56]) (see above, p. 326). Otbert's brother Aldo III called himself son of Aldo, son of Aimo; his wife was named Florida (St.-Étienne II.3 [pp. 4–5]).

The next lord of Tilchâtel, Aimo II, was doubtless son of Otbert, for Aimo II and his brother Gui referred to what their paternal uncle Aldo III had given St.-Florent (St.-Étienne II.28 [pp. 37–38]). In the early twelfth century Aimo II, lord of Tilchâtel, appeared in the charters of St.-Bénigne and St.-Florent (St.-B. II.452 [pp. 222–23]; St.-

[219]Faget de Casteljau makes Aldo and Warner sons of a man named Aldo; "Les sires de Til," p. 148.

[220]Faget de Casteljau calls Otbert "de Spoy" and gives him a son named Humbert, father in turn of Otbert II "de Spoy"; ibid., p. 149. There was an Otbert of Tilchâtel, lord of Spoy, who became a monk at Bèze in the 1080s and had sons named Humbert, Aimo, and Gui, the last of whom was a cleric; Chron. St.-B., p. 447.

The Lords of Tilchâtel

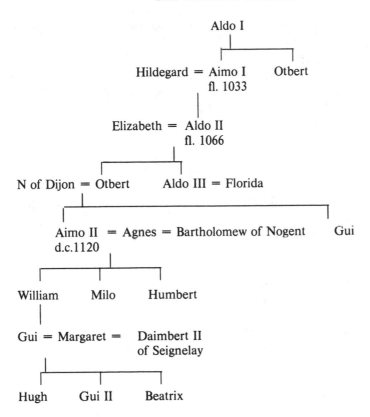

Étienne II.42 [p. 50]). He married a woman named Agnes, who made gifts to Bèze for his soul after his death, which took place around 1120 (Chron. St.-B., pp. 467–68). Agnes is doubtless identical with the Agnes who married Lord Bartholomew I of Nogent as her second husband (Arch. Haute-Marne, 10 H 12).

In the 1120s William of Til appeared with brothers named Milo and Humbert (St.-Étienne II.29 [pp. 38–39]).[221] Around this time he made one of his sons an Augustinian canon at St.-Étienne of Dijon (St.-Étienne II.29 [pp. 38–39]). In 1169 William was lord of Tilchâtel (GC IV:183, no. 66; see also Chron. St.-B., p. 497; and St.-Étienne III.22 [pp. 27–28]). He died at the castle of Nogent and had his dying gifts confirmed by his half brother Bartholomew II of Nogent (St.-Étienne IV.9 [p. 30]). The next lord of Til, Lord Gui, seems to have been William's son,[222] though a charter of St.-Étienne from the mid-twelfth century says that Til was acquired about this time by Gui, oldest son of Count Eblo of Saulx (St.-Étienne III.13 [pp. 15–16]). Gui of Saulx and Gui of Til seem to have been different people, however.

Gui, lord of Tilchâtel, confirmed his predecessors' gifts to St.-Florent around 1180 (St.-Étienne IV.74 [pp. 85–86]). In 1184 he obtained the duke's permission to add to the fortifications of Tilchâtel (Pérard, pp. 259–60). In 1186 he had a wife named Margaret and a son Hugh (St.-Étienne IV.93–94 [pp. 107–8]).[223] Lord Gui and his wife Margaret appear with children named Hugh and Beatrix in 1189; at that time they said that they had other daughters who, however, were not yet old enough to confirm (Arch. Haute-Marne, 1 H 104, no. 15). Gui and Margaret went on to have a second son, Gui II (see below). Either Gui I or his wife had a brother Robert, first dean and then bishop of Langres in 1204, for Gui's son Hugh called Dean Robert his uncle (Arch. Haute-Saône, H 406). After Gui's death Lady Margaret of Tilchâtel married Daimbert II, lord of Seignelay (Vergy, p. 50; see above, p. 357). Gui was succeeded first by his son

---

[221]Faget de Casteljau, instead of giving William these brothers, gives him brothers named Aimo and Aldo; "Les sires de Til," pp. 151–52. There was an Aldo of Til, who acted with William of Til, who appears in the records after Aimo II's death; St.-Étienne II.108 (pp. 121–22).

[222]Faget de Casteljau says that Lord Gui was born to William and to Beatrix of Vignory, widow of Robert Wicard of Clefmont, but the evidence does not support his statement, and the name of William's wife is not known; "Les sires de Til," pp. 152–53.

[223]Faget de Casteljau calls Margaret the daughter of Hugh of Mt.-St.-Jean and gives Gui and Margaret another son, William, and other daughters, named Felicity and Gillette; ibid., pp. 154–55.

Hugh and then by his son Gui II. In 1218/9 and 1226 Gui II was lord of Tilchâtel (Layettes 1305, 1341 [I:468–69, 478]; Arch. Haute-Marne 15 H 4).

The Counts of Tonnerre

The family tree of the tenth- and eleventh-century counts of Tonnerre is complicated because the genealogical evidence in the charters does not at first glance seem to fit together. The first explicit mention of the hereditary counts of Tonnerre appears in 980, when Count Milo and his wife Ingeltrude restored the monastery of St.-Michel of Tonnerre to a regular life. A few years later Milo himself became a monk at St.-Michel (Quantin I.76, 79 [pp. 146–47, 152–54]). He is doubtless the Count Milo whose mother Adela appeared in a charter in 975 (Fleury 61 [pp. 148–53]). It is possible to identify his mother Adela as the Countess Adela, daughter of Humbert I of Salins, who was the mother of Wandelmodis and grandmother of Ingelbert, count of Brienne.[224]

Another charter from the counts of Tonnerre was issued in 1046, by a Count Milo whom I have called Milo III. In this charter Milo recalled his *pater* Milo, his *proavus* Gui, and his *atavus* Milo, the *fundator* of St.-Michel. He mentioned his late brother Gui and his late son Gui, for whom he was making a gift to the monastery, approved by his wife Azeca and sons Warner, Geoffrey, and Hugh-Rainard (Quantin I.94 [pp. 180–82]). It seems easiest to translate *pater*, *proavus*, and *atavus* as father, grandfather, and great-grandfather, making Milo III the great-grandson of the restorer (*fundator*) of St.-Michel. Maurice Chaume, however, insisting on exact Latin terminology, has introduced an *avus* between *pater* and *proavus* and an *abavus* between *proavus* and *atavus*, making the *atavus* Milo an original founder of St.-Michel in the ninth century. His schema seems unnecessarily complicated, especially since there is no evidence in the records of any counts of Tonnerre before the man who restored St.-Michel in 980.[225]

[224]"Genealogiae comitum Andegavensium" 5, ed. Halphen and Poupardin, p. 249. See also above, pp. 262–64.

[225]Maurice Chaume, "Notes sur quelques familles comtales Champenoises (Xᵉ–XIᵉ siècles)," *Recherches d'histoire chrétienne et médiévale* (Dijon, 1947), pp. 278–83. The closest thing to evidence of a ninth-century Count Milo of Tonnerre is the characterization by Charles the Bald in 853 of the counties of Autun, Mâcon, Dijon, Chalon, Atuyer, Tonnerre, Beaune, and Duesme as "the counties of Milo and of Isembard"; MGH Capitularia II:276. Charles made Count Isembard, two bishops, and an abbot his *missi* for these counties; Milo, whoever he was, did not seem to be in the picture.

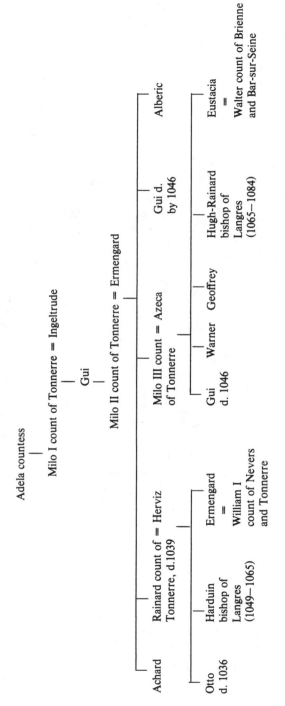

The Counts of Tonnerre

A Count Milo of Tonnerre does appear in the documents around the beginning of the eleventh century. It seems likely that he is the *Milo pater* (Milo II) mentioned by Milo III, but he gives his sons as Achard, Rainard, and Alberic—no Milo is mentioned. His wife was Ermengard (Quantin I.81 [pp. 156—57]). Rainard, son of Ermengard, appears as count in the documents in 1036 and again in 1039, when he died. Rainard had a son Otto, who died in 1036, children Harduin and Ermengard who survived him, and a wife named Herviz (Quantin I.90, 92 [pp. 171—73, 177—78]). It is somewhat difficult to reconcile these charters, but the most likely explanation is that Counts Milo III and Rainard were brothers and succeeded each other as counts of Tonnerre. There is indeed an undated document from St.-Michel which gives both a Count Milo and a Count Rainard among the witnesses (Quantin I.80 [pp. 154—55]). Achard and Alberic, presumably their other brothers, also appear among the witnesses of this charter.

The fates of these two brothers' numerous children are not entirely clear. Many, like Rainard's son Otto or Milo III's son Gui, may have died young. Hugh-Rainard, son of Milo III, succeeded his father as count (Quantin I.94 [p. 181]) and became bishop of Langres in 1065. His sister Eustacia married Walter, count of Brienne.[226] Their cousin Harduin seems identical with the Harduin who preceded Hugh-Rainard in the see of Langres (1049—1065) (see also Appendix B, p. 395). Ermengard, Harduin's sister, succeeded to the county when her cousin Hugh-Rainard became bishop, and she took Tonnerre with her when she married William I, count of Auxerre and Nevers (*Gesta pontificum*, pp. 398—402) (see also above, p. 345).

Since Walter received the county of Bar-sur-Seine when he married Hugh-Rainard's sister, and since Hugh-Rainard said in 1068 that the chapel in the castle of Bar had been founded by his ancestors ("Historia translatio reliquorum S. Mamantis," RHGF XI:482; Quantin I.99 [pp. 190—92]), it seems most logical to assume (as most scholars have done) that the tenth-century counts of Tonnerre were also counts of Bar. Ernest Petit however maintained that Milo II's wife Ermengard was the daughter and heiress of one Rainard, whom he called count of Bar (Petit II:430). His reasoning here seems rather tenuous. There is a *Rainardus comes* who appears in two charters that Petit dated 992 and 997 (Quantin I.80, 88 [pp. 154—55, 167—69]; the editor dated the first one only approximately and the second as 1035). Since his dates seem too early for the Count Rainard of Tonnerre who died in 1039

---

[226]Abbé Lalore, ed., *Collection des principaux cartulaires du diocèse de Troyes*, IV (Paris, 1878), 173—74, no. 48. For Eustacia and Walter's descendants, the counts of Brienne and Bar-sur-Seine, see Evergates, *Feudal Society in the Bailliage of Troyes*, pp. 159—61, 164—65.

(and indeed since *Milo comes* also appears in one of the charters), Petit hypothesized that this count was the count of Bar and must have been Ermengard's father, since she named her own son Rainard. Finally, he assumed that this Count Rainard must be identical with the Rainard, son of the *miles* Raoul of Bar, mentioned in the Chronicle of St.-Bénigne (p. 161), and he believed that an independent line of hereditary counts of Bar had been proven. It seems most reasonable, however, to identify Count Rainard either with the contemporary Count Rainard of Sens—especially since in one of the charters Petit cited (Quantin I.88) he was involved in a dispute with St.-Pierre-le-Vif of Sens—or with the count of Tonnerre named Rainard. (Count Rainard of Sens did not take the county until the first decades of the eleventh century, but as the dating of these charters is only approximate, the dates do not preclude the possibility that either this Count Rainard or Milo III's brother was the Rainard in question.)

Petit also identified Milo II's wife Ermengard with the contemporary Ermengard, wife of Humbert of Vermandois, saying that Ermengard married Humbert after Milo's death (Petit II:425). But the identity of name here does not seem enough to establish identity of person. Petit argued that Count Rainard of Tonnerre, who witnessed a charter of Countess Ermengard of Vermandois (GC IV:139–41, no. 15), would have done so only if he was her son, but Rainard could be expected to witness any foundation of a house within his county, such as that which Ermengard of Vermandois established.[227]

The Lords of Toucy

The lords of Toucy produced an exceptionally large number of Crusaders in the twelfth and early thirteenth centuries. Yves Sassier has briefly discussed their family in the context of comital power in the Auxerrois; Sassier, *Le pouvoir comtal en Auxerrois*, pp. 90–101.

The family first appears in the records around the end of the eleventh century; although some people with the same names as the twelfth-century lords appear around Toucy in the eleventh century, it is impossible to create a family tree for them. A *miles* named Itier acted with Count Landric of Nevers in 1001 and 1002, and an Itier called himself *miles* of St.-Cyr in 1046 (Nevers/St.-Cyr 47, 64 [pp. 88–89, 110]; Quantin I.83 [pp. 159–60]). According to a brief

---

[227]In spite of these and a few other minor disagreements with Petit, I would agree with his reconstruction of the family tree of the counts of Tonnerre (Petit II:419–41) much more than with Chaume's.

The Lords of Toucy

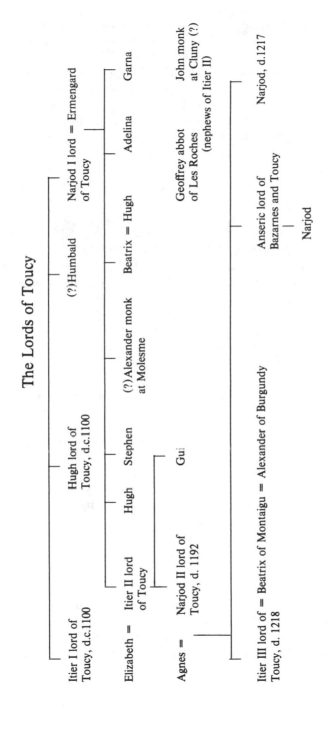

chronicle of Auxerre, a war between a certain Itier and a certain Agano, in which the count of Troyes intervened, led to the burning of the castle of Toucy in 1060 ("Chronicon brevis Autissiodorensis," RHGF XI:292; the editor gives "Crociacum" for "Tociacum").

The brothers Itier of Toucy and Hugh appear in a charter of 1086, along with Humbald *enfans* of Toucy, who may be another brother.[228] Itier I, the oldest brother, died on the way to Jerusalem. Hugh also died on Crusade, and their brother Narjod I succeeded as lord of Toucy. Narjod had a wife named Ermengard and daughters named Beatrix and Adelina, as well as other children referred to but not named (probably because they were underage), at the time Narjod was preparing for his trip to the Holy Land. It is also possible that the "Alexander filius Norgaudi" who witnessed a charter of Narjod on behalf of the abbot of Molesme was also this Narjod's son and a monk at Molesme (Molesme 1.53, 54, 78, 101, 139 [II:63–65, 83–84, 105–6, 136–37]). Narjod too finally went to Jerusalem. His daughter Beatrix married Hugh Manceau of Cosne, who acted as lord of Toucy while his father-in-law was in Jerusalem (Fleury 107, 164 [I:267–69, 351–56]; Lebeuf IV.27 [p. 34]).[229]

Itier II succeeded his father Narjod as lord of Toucy. The pope called him *nobilis vir* in a bull of 1147 (Fleury 164 [I:351–56]). In 1134 he and his brother Stephen confirmed their father's gifts, with the consent of their mother Ermengard, and recalled their late brother Hugh, who had, like their father and uncles, died going to Jerusalem (Crisenon 7 [fols. 4v–5r]; Quantin I.176 [p. 301]). Itier had a sister Garna, called *nobilis matrona* in a charter recalling her in 1178 (Quantin II.279 [pp. 298–99]). Itier II's wife was named Elizabeth. His nephew Geoffrey was the first abbot of the Cistercian house of Les Roches (Pontigny 69 [pp. 140–41]; Quantin I.267, 268 [pp. 418–20]). Abbot Geoffrey of Les Roches had a brother named John, who seems to have been a Cluniac monk, since Abbot Peter the Venerable of Cluny referred to him as *filius noster* (Peter the Venerable, Letter 136, *Letters*, I:341–43). Stephen, the first abbot of Reigny (1134–1162) and before that abbot of Fontemois, seems to have been attached to this family, as he is called "of Toucy" in his obituary (Quantin I.175 [pp. 299–300]). However, he is probably not the Stephen, brother of Lord Itier II, mentioned in 1134, because the charter does not refer to the brother as an abbot. While Stephen was abbot of Fontemois, a certain Hervé of Toucy, perhaps another relative or perhaps a relative of the *Narbonnia* of Toucy (see Appendix B, p. 390), was a monk at Pontigny (Crisenon 52 [fols. 21r–v]).

---

[228]This charter was edited by Richard, "Origines féodales. Les Chalon," pp. 116–19.
[229]See also Sassier, *Le pouvoir comtal en Auxerrois*, p. 75, n. 75.

Itier II was succeeded as lord of Toucy by his son Narjod II, who had a brother named Gui (Fleury 173, 177, 189, 207 [I:399; II:4—6, 21—22, 59—62]; Lebeuf IV.53 [p. 45]; Crisenon 10 [fol. 6r]). Like many of his predecessors, Narjod II died on Crusade. He was present at the disastrous siege of Acre and died in 1192. He was succeeded by his son Itier III, born to his wife Agnes (Crisenon 38, 41 [fols. 14r—15v]).

Itier III also initially acted as lord of Bazarnes (Crisenon 32 [fol. 13r]; Arch. Yonne, H 1562, p. 5, no. 6; Quantin III.5 [p. 3]). Itier's brothers were Anseric, called lord of Bazarnes by 1210, and Narjod (Quantin III. 5, 90, 104 [pp. 3, 41, 47]). His brother Narjod died in 1217 (Quantin III.735 [pp. 385—86]). By 1210 Lord Itier was married to Beatrix, lady of Montaigu (Petit 1468 [III:484]). She had earlier been married to Alexander, son of Duke Hugh III (see above, p. 261). Itier III and his brother Anseric went on Crusade in 1218, and Itier apparently died on the expedition, for his wife was a widow in 1219 (Robert of St.-Marien, *Chronicon* 1217, MGH SS XXVI:277; Fleury 364 [II:250—51]). Itier III's brother Anseric became the next lord of Toucy. He had a son named Narjod (Lebeuf IV.154 [p. 92]).

The Lords of Vergy

The discussion of the lords of Vergy has been thoroughly confused since the seventeenth century, when André Duchesne tried to make the ninth- and tenth-century counts of Autun, the counts of Chalon, and the lords of Donzy all part of one patrilineal family, which he called the lords of Vergy; Duchesne, *Histoire de Vergy*.

The first known generation of lords of Vergy was that of Humbert (or Enzelin), lord of Vergy and archdeacon of Langres in 1023, and eventually bishop of Paris (Petit 19, 23, 29 [I:360—61, 363—64, 371—72]; St.-B. II.275 [p. 67]; Chron. St.-B., p. 174). However, there must have been at least one generation of lords before him, for in 1033 (after he had become bishop of Paris) he said that he was lord of Vergy *paterno et haereditario jure* (GC IV:77, no. 41). His sister Elizabeth was countess of Mâcon, having married Count Otto by 1016 or so (M 268, 464 [pp. 161, 266—67]; C 2713 [III:736]; see also above, p. 271). Humbert and Elizabeth had an uncle Berald, archdeacon of Langres before Humbert, who died in 1022. They also had a nephew Gibald (C 2776 [III:798—800; Chron. St.-B., p. 161). It is not completely clear how either the uncle or nephew were related to them. Archdeacon Berald was the nephew of Bishop Fulk of Soissons (Flavigny 41 [pp. 84—85; summarized Collenot, pp. 85—86]), and both he

The Lords of Vergy

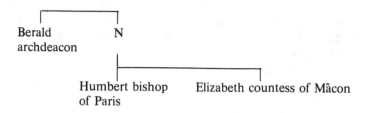

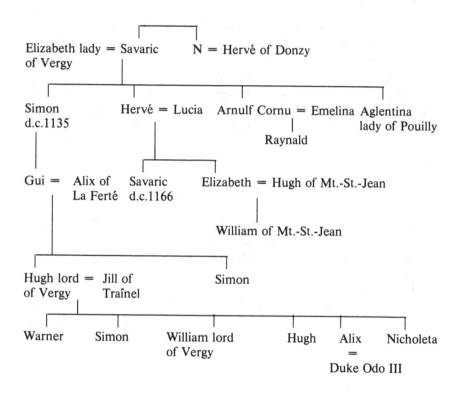

and Bishop Fulk were brothers of counts of Soissons. Gibald may be identical with the Gerald or Berald, nephew of Bishop Fulk, who became bishop of Soissons in the 1020s (GC IV:77, no. 40). It seems most likely that Humbert's and Elizabeth's mother was a relative of the count of Soissons.

There is then a gap in the known family tree of the lords of Vergy until late in the eleventh century, when Elizabeth was lady of Vergy and her husband Savaric called himself lord (Cîteaux/Marilier 26 [pp. 52–53]). It is possible that the Sivin *miles* of Vergy who appeared with the duke in 1053 was a relative, but this is far from clear.[230] Savaric's own family background is not known for certain. His sister doubtless married Hervé I, lord of Donzy, for Hervé's son called Savaric his *avunculus* (St.-Étienne II.51 [pp. 59–61]; GC IV:232–33, no. 13; see also above, p. 327). Savaric was apparently lord of Châtel-Censoir, since the Chronicle of Vézelay called both him and his brother-in-law Hervé of Donzy lords of Châtel-Censoir, and one might assume that Hervé had been given a share in the lordship when he married Savaric's sister (*Chronique* 2, Vézelay, p. 421). Scholars have long considered Savaric a brother rather than a brother-in-law of Hervé I of Donzy; however, since the lords of Donzy had inherited neither Châtel-Censoir nor Vergy, it seems more likely that the tie between Savaric and the lords of Donzy was through marriage.[231]

Savaric and Elizabeth had at least three sons and a daughter. Savaric acted with his sons Simon and Hervé in 1096, when he bought a share of the county of Chalon from his nephew (GC IV:233, no. 13). Savaric and Elizabeth made gifts to Cîteaux with their sons Arnulf Cornu, Simon, and Hervé soon after the foundation of the New Monastery (Cîteaux/Marilier 41, 51 [pp. 63–65, 68–70]). Their son Arnulf Cornu (probably the youngest) married a woman named Emelina and had a son Raynald and a daughter whose name is not known. Arnulf and Emelina founded the nunnery of Tart in 1132 and were buried there (St.-Étienne II.36 [pp. 44–45]; Cîteaux/Marilier 41 [pp. 63–65]; Arch. Côte-d'Or, 78 H 1042). Simon and Hervé acted as joint lords of Vergy around 1131; Simon seems to have predeceased his brother (Cîteaux/Marilier 89 [p. 91]). Their sister Aglentina was lady of Pouilly (St.-Étienne II.51 [pp. 59–61]). Elizabeth, lady of Vergy, had at least two other sons, perhaps born to someone other than Savaric: Rudolph Crassus and Grival. The latter was provost of St.-Étienne of Dijon (St.-Étienne II.44 [p. 52]).

[230]*Recueil des chartes de Saint-Germain-des-Prés*, ed. Poupardin, I:95–97, no. 59.

[231]Recently, Yves Sassier has tried to suggest that Savaric was a cousin rather than an uncle, but this seems an unnecessary complication, as at the time *avunculus* (unlike *nepos*) generally specified an uncle-nephew relationship; see Sassier, *Le pouvoir comtal en Auxerrois*, pp. 86–87, n. 138.

Hervé, lord of Vergy, married a woman named Lucia (La Bussière 7.1 [fols. 64v–65r]). He had two known children, Savaric and Elizabeth, named for his parents (St.-Étienne II.51 [pp. 59–61]). He also had a *nepos* Hervé, abbot of St.-Étienne of Dijon in 1171, though it is not entirely clear how the two Hervés were related (Cîteaux/Marilier 200 [pp. 160–61]). Lord Hervé's daughter Elizabeth married Hugh of Mt.-St.-Jean. Hervé designated Hugh as his heir for Vergy by 1167 (Cîteaux/Marilier 178 [pp. 145–46]), though he himself was still alive in 1171 (Cîteaux/Marilier 200 [pp. 160–61]). The designation of Hugh as his heir probably took place upon the death of his son Savaric, who disappears from the records after the mid-1160s (Cîteaux/Marilier 166 [pp. 131–32]).

The lordship of Vergy however went to Gui, son of Lord Hervé's brother Simon (La Bussière 7.1 [fols. 64v–65r]). He called himself the *cognatus* of Hervé's son Savaric (Cîteaux/Marilier 166 [pp. 131–32]). Gui had already been acting as lord during Hervé's lifetime (Cîteaux/Marilier 170 [p. 135]). Indeed, Hervé, Gui, and someone named Philip were called co-lords of Vergy in the 1140s (Petit 283 [II:232–33]; Arch. Côte-d'Or, 20 H 674). Though Gui rather than the lord of Mt.-St.-Jean called himself lord of Vergy, Lord William of Mt.-St.-Jean (grandson of Hervé of Vergy) claimed half of Vergy in the duke's court at the end of the century, calling himself *consanguineus* of Gui's son Hugh (Arch. Côte-d'Or, B 10470).

Gui, lord of Vergy, married Alix, daughter of Mathilda of La Ferté, the sister of the viscount of Dijon. Apparently through this marriage he also became lord of Beaumont (Arch. Haute-Saône, H 422; Cîteaux I, fols. 104r–v, no. 10; see also above, pp. 323 and 326). Gui was present at the siege of Acre in 1191 and apparently died there (Petit 867 [III:314–15]). Gui and his wife Alix had appeared in the documents with two sons, Hugh and Simon (Cîteaux/Marilier 190 [pp. 153–54]; La Bussière 7.1 [fols. 64v–65r]). Hugh acted as lord of Vergy in 1187, when he was already married to Jill, and named his brother as Simon (C 4314 [V:673–75]). Jill was the daughter of Warner II of Traînel and was called lady of Autrey in a charter of her sons (Robert of St.-Marien, *Chronica* 1183, MGH SS XXVI:247; Mores 70 [p. 80]).[232] In 1189 Hugh had a brother Simon, wife Jill, and son Warner (Cîteaux II, fols. 54r, 57r–v, nos. 9, 16). In addition to Warner, his oldest, he also had a son named Simon born before his father left on Crusade (Vergy, pp. 9–10).

Hugh and Jill went on to have a large family, even though both Warner and Simon seem to have predeceased their parents. Their other children included William, lord of Vergy, who succeeded his

---

[232]See also Duchesne, *Histoire de Vergy*, p. 145.

father (Cîteaux I, fol. 10v, no. 11); Hugh (Mores 70 [p. 80]); Alix, who married Duke Odo III and became duchess of Burgundy (Obit. Lyon II:621; see also above, p. 261); a daughter named Nicholeta (Arch. Côte-d'Or, 111 H 1169); and possibly Margarita, lady of Nesles through her marriage with André of Nesles.

The Lords of Vignory

The lords of Vignory (a castle located north of Langres) are known primarily from their gifts to the priory of St.-Étienne of Vignory and to St.-Bénigne of Dijon. Their family tree has been studied twice before, by J. d'Arbaumont, who also edited a number of the documents in which they appear (Vignory, pp. lxviii—ciii), and by Ernest Petit (Petit I:304; II:430—38). These two authors, apparently unaware of each other's work, differ slightly in their interpretations, and I in turn disagree to some extent with them (their works did correct many factual errors of earlier scholars).

The earliest known ancestor of this family is a tenth-century Norman, one Raoul Barbeta. His existence is known only from a genealogy of the lords of Vignory drawn up in the twelfth century, where the list begins, "Rodulphus Barbeta, Normannus."[233] It seems likely, though not necessary, that he was the father of Gui I, the first lord of Vignory attested by contemporary documents. After Raoul Barbeta, the twelfth-century genealogy lists lords Gui and Roger, who were definitely father and son. Gui founded a college of canons at Vignory in 1032 (St.-B. II.311 [pp. 89—90]). The chronicle of St.-Bénigne states that Roger, lord of the castle of Vignory, decided to put monks from St.-Bénigne in the church of St.-Étienne of Vignory in place of the secular canons who had lived there since his father Gui built the church (Chron. St.-B., pp. 194—95). In his donation charter Roger gave several genealogical details on his family: he had a brother Girard, archdeacon of Langres, a wife named Mathilda, and three sons, Gui, Girard, and Roger, the last of whom was a cathedral canon at Langres (St.-B. II.332 [pp. 111—13]; see also St.-B. II.316 [p. 97]). Roger seems to have died around 1050 or 1055, when he disappeared from the records.[234]

---

[233]Quoted in Petit II:434, n. 2. D'Arbaumont was unfamiliar with this list and did not mention Raoul Barbeta.

[234]D'Arbaumont gave Roger another brother, Bruno, abbot of Der, but I have found no evidence of this relationship. Abbot Bruno of Montier-en-Der, who was known as Wandelger before he became abbot, held that office from about 1050 to about 1085; see Lalore, ed., *Collection des cartulaires de Troyes*, IV:162, no. 33. D'Arbaumont also suggested (p. lxx, n. 4) that several knights found in the documents and qualified as "de

The Lords of Vignory

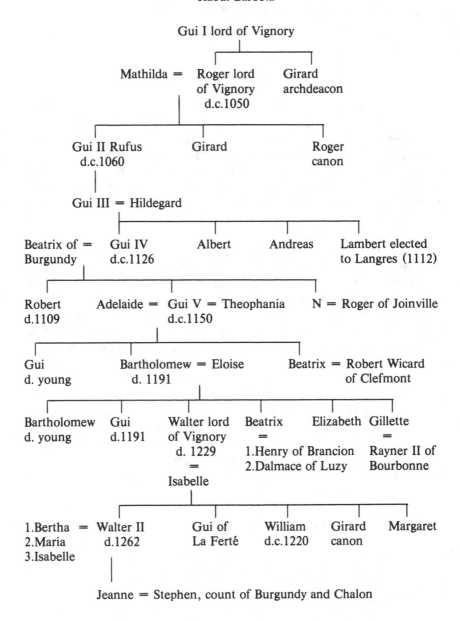

Petit has attempted to attach the lords of Vignory to the families of the counts of Tonnerre and of Lambert, bishop of Langres (1016– 1031). A certain Countess Letgardis made a gift to St.-Michel of Tonnerre early in the eleventh century for the soul of her son Roger (Petit 687 [II:430–31]), whom Petit identified with Roger of Vignory—even though Roger of Vignory was still alive thirty or forty years later, and though it is not at all clear why the lady of Vignory should have been called a countess. He further identified this Letgardis as of the family of the counts of Tonnerre—because of where she made her gift—and equated her with the Letgardis who is said by the chronicle of St.-Bénigne to have been the sister (*soror*, which he translated as sister-in-law) of Bishop Lambert (Chron. St.-B., p. 195), whom he already considered a brother of the lord of Vignory. The charter was witnessed by a Count Roger, who may have been her husband, which makes it even more unlikely that she was Lord Gui of Vignory's wife.

After Roger the twelfth-century genealogy of the lords of Vignory lists four named Gui, that is Gui II, III, IV, and V. Gui II is also called "Rufus" in this genealogy. He is doubtless the same as the eldest son of Roger, mentioned above. He may have died young, not long after his father; a charter from 1057 lists Girard of Vignory and his nephew (*nepos*) Gui, whom one might identify as respectively the brother and son of Gui II (St.-B. II.340 [pp. 119–21]). If so, then Gui II's younger brother may have acted as regent for his nephew.[235] However, the brothers Girard and Gui II appear together again in a charter tentatively dated 1059; if this date is accurate, Gui II may not have witnessed the charter for St.-Bénigne in 1057 simply because he was away, not because he was dead (Vignory 2.3 [pp. 171–72]).

Gui II's wife's name is not known, and Gui III is his only known child. Gui III was lord of Vignory in his own right in 1081 at the latest, when he confirmed his predecessors' gifts to St.-Bénigne (St.-B. II.355 [pp. 134–35]). In this charter he gave his wife as Hildegard and his son as Gui *infans*.[236] In addition to his infant son Gui (Gui

---

Vangionis rivi castello" must somehow be related to the lords of Vignory; but I feel it more likely that these were household knights, living with their lord at the castle, rather than cousins.

[235]D'Arbaumont attributes this charter to Roger's brother Girard and his own son Gui II, but as the Girard here is not identified as the archdeacon of Langres—an oversight that would be most unusual—I think it better to identify this Girard as Roger's son of that name.

[236]Both Petit and d'Arbaumont collapse Gui II and Gui III into one person, ignoring the testimony of the twelfth-century genealogy that four men named Gui succeeded each other. D'Arbaumont cited a charter in which the lord of Vignory signed, "Ego Vuido Vuangionis rivi senior," and translated *senior* as "the Ancient," adding that Gui II was lord for forty-five years. The word *senior*, however, was often used simply as a synonym for *dominus*. That Gui II had a son Gui old enough to be a competent witness

IV), Gui III had at least three other sons, Albert and Andreas, *pueri* in 1081 (St.-B. II.355 [pp. 134—35]; Vignory 2.4 [p. 172]), and Lambert, archdeacon of Langres (St.-B. II.424 [pp. 200—201]). Lambert was elected bishop of Langres in 1112 but was never consecrated (Molesme 1.217B [II:199]) (see also Appendix B, p. 395).[237]

Gui IV had succeeded his father as lord of Vignory by 1100 (St.-B. II.394 [pp. 171—72]). He married Beatrix, sister of Duke Odo I of Burgundy (see above, p. 258). Gui and Beatrix had two sons, Robert (sometimes called Josbert) and Gui V. Both were already born by 1100. Robert, the oldest, died around 1109 (Molesme 1.220, 252 [II:204, 235]; St.-B. II.356, 394, 424 [pp. 135—36, 171—72, 200—201]; C 3879 [V:231—32]). The younger son, Gui V, succeeded his father as lord of Vignory, apparently around 1126 (Vignory 2.23 [pp. 180—81]). Gui and Beatrix also had a daughter who married Roger, son of Lord Geoffrey II of Joinville (Alberic de Trois-Fontaines, *Chronica* 1110, MGH SS XXIII:818).

Gui V apparently married twice. He had a wife named Adelaide while his father was still alive (Vignory 2.23 [pp. 180—81]), and a pancarte of gifts to Clairvaux, issued around 1147, mentions the donations of Lord Gui of Vignory and his wife Adelaide, as does a contemporary pancarte of La Crête (Clairvaux/Waquet 6, 17, [pp. 9, 36]; Arch. Haute-Marne, 5 H 5). But another pancarte from Clairvaux, drawn up at about the same time, lists, among the witnesses to a gift, Gui, lord of Vignory, and his wife Theophania (Clairvaux/Waquet 18 [p. 40]).

Gui V and Adelaide had a son, Gui, mentioned in a charter with his parents (Vignory 2.28 [pp. 183—84]).[238] He did not succeed his father, however. Rather, Vignory went to his brother Bartholomew, the next lord of Vignory, called son of Gui V of Vignory in a charter of Clairvaux (Clairvaux/Waquet 32 [p. 56]). He is the last lord of Vignory mentioned in the twelfth-century genealogy. Gui V and Adelaide are probably identical with the Gui and Adelaide who were the

---

in 1057, while Gui III's son Gui was still underage (*infans*) fourteen years later, in 1081, also indicates that these were two different men.

[237]The name Lambert here lends some credence to the idea that Lambert, bishop of Langres at the beginning of the eleventh century, was related to this family; parents often named their children who were destined for the church after older relatives already in the church. Both d'Arbaumont and Petit give Gui III (their Gui II) a fifth son, Roger, abbot of Der. The apparent evidence for this attribution is a rubric of a charter, concerning Gui IV of Vignory, copied into the cartulary of Der. The rubric reads, "De Guidone Wangionis rivi, fratris Rogerii abbatis" (Vignory, pp. lxxiv, 181, n. 2). To mean that Gui and the abbot were brothers, the rubric would have to read *fratre* rather than *fratris*—cartulary rubrics are at any rate not wholly reliable, as they were usually copied from identifying words written somewhat later on the back (outside) of a document. Abbot Roger appears in the documents between about 1114 and 1129.

[238]This is the Gui whom Petit and d'Arbaumont call Gui V.

parents of Beatrix, who married Robert Wicard of Clefmont (Arch. Haute-Marne, 5 H 7) (see also above, p. 317).

Around 1150 Bartholomew appeared in the documents as lord of Vignory with a wife named Eloise or Elizabeth (Arch. Haute-Marne, 5 H 10; Vignory 2.30 [pp. 184–85]).[239] Bartholomew and Eloise had at least five children, Bartholomew, Gui, Walter, Beatrix, and Elizabeth. Their son Bartholomew must have died young, since he is found only in a charter of 1166 (Arch. Haute-Marne, 5 H 10). Walter succeeded his father as lord of Vignory in 1191, after Lord Bartholomew and Gui, the oldest surviving son, died at the siege of Acre (Vignory 2.46, 60 [pp. 192, 200–201]; Alberic de Trois-Fontaines, *Chronica* 1191, MGH SS XXIII:868; Clairvaux I, p. 106, no. 8). Beatrix married successively Lord Henry I of Brancion (see above, p. 306) (C 4478, 4545 [VI:31, 94]) and Dalmace, lord of Luzy (C 4428 [V:802]). Elizabeth appears only in a charter of 1179, in which she is identified as the daughter of Lord Bartholomew of Vignory (Auberive I, fol. 6v, no. 7 [Auberive II, fols. 13r–v, no. 22]). It is possible that she is identical with the Elizabeth who married Gui IV of Saulx (see above, p. 353). Bartholomew and Eloise were also probably the parents of Gillette, the wife of Rayner II of Bourbonne (see above, p. 284); when Lord Walter of Vignory made a gift to Clairvaux around the beginning of the thirteenth century, Gillette had to agree, "as it concerned her inheritance" (Clairvaux II, p. 396, no. 24).[240]

Walter ruled as lord of Vignory until 1229. He and his wife, who was called both Isabelle and Elizabeth in the documents, had at least four sons and a daughter, all named with their parents in a charter of 1213: Walter II, Gui, William, Girard, and Margaret (Vignory 2.79 [pp. 208–9]). All these children except Girard had already appeared in a charter with their parents in 1205 (Clairvaux I, p. 112, no. 18). Gui became lord of La Ferté-sur-Amance by 1231 (Vignory 2.112 [p. 227]; Molesme 2.375 [II:392–93]). William seems to have died before his parents, for he disappeared from the documents around 1220. Girard became a canon at Langres, according to a charter of his brother Walter (Vignory 2.140 [pp. 244–45]).

Walter II became lord of Vignory in 1229. He married Bertha, widow of the count of Kibourg. She may be identical with the woman known as Alix who, like Bertha, was a sister of Duke Matthew of

---

[239]H. de Faget de Casteljau says that Eloise was the sister of Erard of Brienne; "La maison de Choiseul" [1971], p. 146. This claim is based on a document in which Erard referred to his sister's husband as Bartholomew, though he did not name his sister or refer to this Bartholomew as lord of Vignory; Quantin II.181 (pp. 198–99).

[240]Bartholomew and Eloise may also have been the parents of Adelaide/Mathilda, wife of Lord Fulk of Choiseul; see above, p. 316.

Lorraine and had been widowed by the count of Kibourg by 1229.[241]
Bertha died in 1242, when Walter founded her anniversary at Clairvaux (Vignory 2.152 [p. 250]). He married twice more, apparently in
an attempt to gain a male heir, since he had no sons. Between 1252
and 1254 the documents give him a wife named Maria (Vignory
2.162, 164 [pp. 255–57]). His third wife was Isabelle, daughter of the
count of Sancerre, widowed when he died in 1262 (Vignory 2.168 [p.
259]). Walter II left only one child, Jeanne, who married Stephen,
son of Count John of Burgundy and Chalon (see above, p. 278), and
took the lordship of Vignory to him (Vignory 2.171 [pp. 260–62]).

[241]Vignory 2.140 (pp. 244–45). Augustin Calmet, ed., *Histoire ecclésiastique et civile de
Lorraine*, II (Nancy, 1728), preuves col. ccccxli.

APPENDIX B

The Burgundian Bishops

The following lists of Burgundian bishops cover those who held office between 980 and 1198. For each bishop, I give a paragraph on his family, his ecclesiastical background, his election, and his resignation or deposition, if any. The bishoprics are arranged alphabetically. In most cases I have not bothered to draw an explicit contrast with the lists as given in *Gallia Christiana*; those lists were usually based on less evidence than is presently available. While in many cases I cite the lists of bishops given in DHGE, I also do not always agree with the dates given there, as a comparison will indicate. Since the editors of DHGE rarely state their reasons for a particular date, however, I have usually not drawn an explicit contrast with their lists either. Although the years in which most bishops held office can be determined with reasonable accuracy, their exact death dates are given variously in different obituaries.

The bishops of five of the Burgundian sees (all but Nevers) were studied briefly by Martine Chauney, "Le recrutement de l'épiscopat bourguignon aux XIe et XIIe siècles," *Annales de Bourgogne*, 47 (1975), 193–212. She and I differ on many details, however; her work is flawed by a reliance on secondary authors rather than the sources. My listing of bishops more or less follows the style of the so-called "new Gams," the *Series episcoporum ecclesiae Catholicae occidentalis ab initio usque ad annum MCXCVIII*, a series of volumes projected to cover all the bishops of western Europe before 1198. Though none of the French volumes of this new series have yet appeared, the German volumes have just begun coming out. (I do not, however, follow the style of this series in giving a separate list of "literature" on each bishop.)

Autun

There is a brief list of the bishops of Autun in DHGE V:907–10.

Walter I, 978–1018

The date of his succession is given by Hugh of Flavigny's "Series" of the abbots of Flavigny (MGH SS VIII:503). His last dated document is from February, 1018 (Petit 9 [I:349–50]). The editors of GC misread the date, MXVIII, as MXXIII and thus erroneously dated his death to 1023 (GC IV, col. 378). He died on 29 September (Obit. Lyon II:401; Obit. Sens III:241).

Helmuin, 1018–1055

Helmuin succeeded Walter in 1018, as indicated by the fact that both bishops appear in charters dated in the thirtieth year of Robert as king (dating from his original coronation in 988), one of which was also dated MXVIII (as noted above) (Petit 7, 9, 10 [I:348–53]).

Agano of Mt.-St.-Jean, 1055–1098

Brother of Rainard, lord of Mt.-St.-Jean (Autun/Église 1.27, 40 [I:44–46, 62–66]), and of Waldric of Couches, who died at Flavigny as a monk ("Necrologium Flaviniacensis," MGH SS VIII:285). Had been provost (Flavigny 48 [pp. 97–99; summarized Collenot, p. 94]).

Narjod, 1098–1112

Often called "of Toucy," but there is no evidence of his family; the designation of Toucy seems based only on his name. Had been precantor of Autun (Hugh of Flavigny, *Chronicon*, MGH SS VIII:477) and a canon of Auxerre, according to the obituary of Auxerre cathedral, which recorded his death on 2 May (Obit. Sens III:234).

Stephen I, 1112–1139

Often called "of Bâgé."[1] He had been cantor of the cathedral of Autun (Autun/St.-Symphorien 20 [p. 52]). The canons of Notre-Dame of Beaune called him their abbot (Cîteaux/Marilier 58 [p. 73]). His nephew Humbert was archdeacon under him. Retired to Cluny (Peter the Venerable, Letter 143, *Letters*, I:353). Died on 24 May (Obit. Sens III:465).

Robert of Burgundy, 1140

Brother of Duke Odo II of Burgundy (see Appendix A, p. 260). He had been dean of Langres.[2]

---

[1]Chauney calls both him and his successor Humbert "of Bâgé"; "Le recrutement de l'épiscopat," p. 199.

[2]A charter of 1141 mentions that the office of dean of Langres was vacant because Dean Robert had been promoted to the bishopric of Autun; Quantin I.124 (p. 233). This charter is dated MCXLI, mistakenly given as MCXVI by the editor. Giles Con-

Humbert, 1140–1148

It is possible that he and his predecessor Stephen are of the family of the lords of Bâgé, as he attended the funeral of Lord Raynald of Bâgé in 1169 (M 622 [p. 377]). In this case he may be related to Bishop Stephen of Mâcon, who also attended. Humbert was nephew of his predecessor Stephen, under whom he was archdeacon (Cîteaux/Marilier 97 [p. 96]); see above. He was translated to the archdiocese of Lyon (1148–1153) (Petit 445 [II:314–15]); he retired to La Grande Chartreuse, where he lived at least another sixteen years (Obit. Lyon I:118; M 622 [p. 377]).

Henry of Burgundy, 1148–1170

Brother of his predecessor Robert and of Duke Odo II of Burgundy (see Appendix A, p. 260). He had been archdeacon since at least 1140 (Arch. Côte-d'Or, 20 H 674; Suger, Letter 10, RHGF XV:487; Plancher I.66 [p. xliv]). Died on 5 March (Obit. Lyon II:614).[3]

Stephen II, 1170–1189

He may be the Stephen who was provost of Autun in 1166 (Petit 445 [II:314–15]).[4] Died on 3 November (Obit. Lyon II:107).

Walter II, 1189–1223

He was buried at St.-Symphorien of Autun (Autun/Église, I:333).

Auxerre

For the bishops of Auxerre, see especially the *Gesta pontificum*, the biographies written shortly after each bishop's death. See also Constance Brittain Bouchard, *Spirituality and Administration: The Role of the Bishop in Twelfth-Century Auxerre*, Speculum Anniversary Monographs 5 (Cambridge, Mass., 1979); and Bouchard, "The Geographical, Social and Ecclesiastical Origins of the Bishops of Auxerre and

---

stable has cast some doubt on the accuracy of this charter; "The Disputed Election at Langres in 1138," *Traditio*, 13 (1957), 127, 151–52. But as he notes, the comment about Dean Robert may be accurate even if the rest of the charter has been altered. In describing the disputed election, Bernard of Clairvaux said that Dean Robert was one of the group going to Rome in 1138 to ask for the *licentia eligendi* for Langres, and Peter the Venerable sent a letter with this group formally introducing the "duke's son" to the pope. He was most likely referring to Robert; Bernard of Clairvaux, Letter 164, *Opera*, VII (Rome, 1974), 372; Peter the Venerable, Letter 72, *Letters*, I:206.

[3]Chauney erroneously says that he retired to Cîteaux, probably because he is recorded in Cîteaux's obituary, along with many other friends of the abbey; "Le recrutement de l'épiscopat," p. 205.

[4]The editors of GC identify him with the Stephen, cantor of the cathedral of Auxerre in 1166, who acted as prior of St.-Loup of Auxerre; Quantin II.166 (pp. 184–85).

Sens in the Central Middle Ages," *Church History* 46 (1977), 277—95.
There are a few different dates in the list in DHGE V:945—46.

Heribert I, 971—996
Illegitimate son of Hugh Capet and his concubine, Raingardis (*Gesta pontificum*, pp. 382—83). Died on 23 August (Obit. Sens III:240).

John, 996—999
Said to be of "middle" or "mediocre" origins. Son of a couple named Ansald and Raingardis. May be the half brother of his predecessor; his mother has the same name (and may thus be the same person) as Hugh Capet's concubine who bore Heribert. At any rate, he was put into office by the king in return for service at court, over the candidate Duke Henry proposed.[5]

Hugh I of Chalon, 999—1039
Son of Lambert, count of Chalon, and his wife Adelaide (*Gesta pontificum*, pp. 386—87; see also Appendix A, pp. 309—10). Put into office "at the request of King Robert," according to his biography at Auxerre. He acted as both count of Chalon and bishop of Auxerre (St.-B. II.296 [pp. 79—81]). He took the monastic habit at St.-Germain as he was dying (*Gesta pontificum*, p. 392). He died on 3 or 4 November (Obit. Sens III:239; Lebeuf IV:19).

Heribert II, 1039—1052
A native of Auxerre, whose parents were named Walter and Emma. Chosen by Hugh of Chalon to succeed him. He was however driven out of office by Duke Robert, according to his biographer, and became a monk at St.-Sauveur in the Senonais. He died on 26 January (*Gesta pontificum*, pp. 392—93; Obit. Sens III:227).

Geoffrey of Champallemand, 1052—1076
Of the family of the viscounts of Nevers, son of Viscount Hugh and of Ermentrude (Nevers/St.-Cyr 9 [pp. 22—23]; *Gesta pontificum*, p. 393). Nephew of Bishop Hugh I of Nevers and uncle (*patruus*) of Bishop Hugh II, who was provost under him (see below, p. 400). Made bishop by King Henry, whom he had served as a cleric at court (*Gesta pontificum*, pp. 393—98). Died on 16 September (Obit. Sens III:241, 468).

Robert of Nevers, 1076—1092
Son of Count William I of Nevers, Auxerre, and Tonnerre, and count of Auxerre in his own right (*Gesta pontificum*, p. 401; La

---

[5]*Gesta pontificum*, p. 384. See also G. Estournet, "Origines des seigneurs de Nemours," *Annales de la Société historique et archéologique du Gâtinais*, 30 (1912), 57—58.

Charité 23 [pp. 76–77]; see also Appendix A, pp. 345–46). Investigated at the 1077 Council of Autun by the papal legate and censured for having been ordained too young, though he was freed of the accusation of having received investiture from the king (Mansi XX:488; Hefele-Leclercq V, i:224). He took the monastic habit as he died; his death took place on 12 February. He was buried at St.-Étienne of Nevers (*Gesta pontificum*, p. 401; Obit. Sens III:228).

Humbald, 1092–1114
Son of the noble parents Humbald and Adela, according to his biographer (*Gesta pontificum*, p. 402). Had been a canon at the cathedral since at least 1052 and had been serving as dean when elected bishop (Lebeuf IV.14 [pp. 26–27]). Consecrated by Pope Urban II in Milan in 1095 (*Gesta pontificum*, p. 402; Obit. Sens III:234).[6] He made his nephew Ulger provost under him, and Ulger tried (unsuccessfully) to have himself elected bishop to succeed Humbald (Obit. Sens III:234; *Gesta pontificum*, pp. 410–11). Humbald died on 20 October (Obit. Sens III:242).

Hugh II of Montaigu, 1115–1136
Son of Dalmace of Montaigu, the brother of Lord Geoffrey II of Semur, and hence nephew of Hugh, abbot of Cluny (1049–1109) (see Appendix A, p. 360). Became a monk at Cluny under his uncle, and became the first Cluniac abbot of St.-Germain of Auxerre in 1100 (see Appendix C, p. 428). His election was disputed and only settled when appealed to Rome (*Gesta pontificum*, pp. 410–11). His cousin Raynald was abbot of Vézelay (1106–1125) and archbishop of Lyon (1125–1128), and his cousin Gervais succeeded him as abbot of St.-Germain in 1115. He died on 10 or 11 August (*Gesta pontificum*, p. 416; Obit. Sens I:450, 526; Obit. Sens III:329).

Hugh III of Mâcon, 1136–1151
Of a knightly family of Mâcon. He came to Cîteaux with St. Bernard.[7] Hugh became first abbot of Pontigny (1114–1136), before his election to Auxerre (Pontigny 108, 109 [pp. 176–78]) (see Appendix C, p. 422). He died at Pontigny on 12 October (Obit. Sens III:242).

Alain, 1152–1167
From Flanders. Originally a monk of Clairvaux. Had been first abbot of the Cistercian house of Larrivour, taking office in 1140 (*Gesta pontificum*, pp. 420–21; Robert of St.-Marien, *Chronicon* 1151, MGH SS XXVI:236; GC XII:260–61, no. 21). His election was

[6]For the date of his election, see Bouchard, *Spirituality and Administration*, p. 18.
[7]*Gesta pontificum*, p. 417. *Vita prima Sancti Bernardi* 1.13–14, PL CLXXXV:235. See also Bouchard, *Spirituality and Administration*, p. 52, on the long-standing scholarly confusion over Hugh's family.

disputed; the cathedral chapter became deadlocked over three separate candidates. The election was settled only when Pope Eugenius III asked Bernard of Clairvaux to choose a bishop. In one letter Bernard refers to Alain as "Regniacensis," which may refer to a birthplace in Regny, in Picardy. "Regniacensis," however, was also the Latin for the Cistercian monastery of Reigny in the Auxerrois. But Alain is not known to have had any association with Reigny before becoming bishop of Auxerre.[8] He had at least one brother, whose anniversary he established at the collegial church of Varzy, along with that of his mother, but their names are not known (Obit. Sens III:416, 418). Alain resigned and returned to Clairvaux (Alexander III, Letter 468, PL CC:466). Died in 1178, according to the chronicle of Clairvaux, although his testament is dated 1182 ("Chronicon Clarevallense" 1165, 1178, PL CLXXXV:1248–49; GC XII:136–37, no. 53). He died on 11 or 14 October and was buried at Clairvaux (Obit. Sens III:265; "Liber sepulcrorum Clarevallensium," PL CLXXXII: 485–86).

William of Toucy, 1167–1181

Of the noble *Narbonnia* family of Toucy (not the same as the lords of Toucy), son of Girard, a *vir nobilis* according to William's biographer, and of Agnes (*Gesta pontificum*, pp. 421–22). Younger brother of Archbishop Hugh of Sens (1143–1168) (*Gesta pontificum*, p. 428; Quantin II.286 [p. 306]). William joined the chapter of Sens by 1141 (Pontigny 58 [pp. 130–31]). He and his younger brother Hervé served under their brother in the chapter of Sens from at least 1146, as archdeacon and provost respectively (Pontigny 65 [p. 138]; Quantin I.263 [p. 416]). After Hervé's death William filled both offices, from around 1160 to his election to Auxerre (*Gesta pontificum*, p. 421; Quantin II.155 [pp. 170–71]; GC XII:360, no. 3). He also acted as treasurer of Auxerre for one year before his election (Robert of St.-Marien, *Chronicon* 1166, 1167, MGH SS XXVI:239). He is called *electus* in a charter of 1167 (Pontigny 73 [pp. 143–44]). After his election to Auxerre, his nephew, Hugh, succeeded him as archdeacon of Sens (*Gesta pontificum*, p. 431); young Hugh also became cantor of Auxerre under his uncle (Arch. Yonne, H 1627, no. 98). William died on 26 or 28 February (Obit. Sens III:251, 417).

Hugh IV of Noyers, 1183–1206

Son of Lord Milo of Noyers and of Adelina of Chappes, brother of Lord Clarembald of Noyers (Pontigny 46 [pp. 118–20]; Petit 852

[8]Bernard of Clairvaux, Letters 274–76, 280, 282, *Opera*, VIII (Rome, 1974), 185–88, 192–94, 196–97; idem., *De Consideratione* 3.2.11, in *Opera*, III (Rome, 1963), 438–39. For this election, see also Bouchard, *Spirituality and Administration*, pp. 69–71.

[III:306–7]; *Gesta pontificum*, pp. 431, 436). His uncle Gui was archbishop of Sens (1176–1193) (*Gesta pontificum*, p. 447). Had been treasurer of Auxerre for at least five years before his election (Pontigny 46 [pp. 118–20]; Quantin II.278 [p. 298]; Robert of St.-Marien, *Chronicon* 1183, MGH SS XXVI:247). His election was disputed and was settled only when the other candidate (Garmund Clement, abbot of Pontigny) died at Rome (Robert of St.-Marien, *Chronicon* 1182, MGH SS XXVI:246). His *consanguineus* Gui served as archdeacon under him until Gui died, around 1186 (GC XII:139, no. 56). Another *cognatus*, Daimbert (probably son of Stephen of Pierre-Pertuis), was archdeacon of Auxerre and sacristan of Nevers (Obit. Sens III:256; see also Appendix A, p. 356). Hugh was elected to the archbishopric of Sens in 1199, but the pope refused to recognize his candidacy (Robert of St.-Marien, *Chronicon* 1199, MGH SS XXVI:259–60). He died in Rome, on 6 or 8 December (Robert of St.-Marien, *Chronicon* 1206, MGH SS XXVI:270; Obit. Sens I:14; Obit. Sens III:268).

Chalon

The history of the bishops of Chalon has been studied by J. Louis Bazin, *Histoire des évêques de Chalon-sur-Saône*, Mémoires de la Société d'histoire et d'archéologie de Chalon-sur-Saône, n.s. 6 (Chalon, 1914). See also DHGE XII:298–300, for a listing of the bishops.

Rudolph, 977–994
Sometimes said to be identical with Rudolph, brother of Count Lambert of Chalon, but there seems to be no evidence for this other than their names.

Lambert, 994–1015
As in the case of his predecessor, attempts are sometimes made to link him with the counts of Chalon. He was probably the Lambert *clericus* found in a 980 charter of his predecessor (GC IV:227, no. 7).

Geoffrey, 1015–1039
The date of his election is given by the chronicle of St.-Bénigne (pp. 180–81).[9]

---

[9]Bazin however says that he assumed office before 1015; *Histoire des évêques*, pp. 117–22. Chauney incorrectly dates his rule 999–1039 (probably on the basis of the faulty list in DHGE) and on the basis of the name "Geoffrey" calls him "of Semur"; "Le recrutement de l'épiscopat," p. 200.

Gui, 1044–1058

Achard, 1059–1070[10]

Roclenus, 1072–1079

Of a noble family, son of a woman named Adelaide whose daughters were Gertrude, Ingeltrude, and Marie (it is not clear if these are his full sisters). He had brothers Humbert and Landric; the latter died in 1063, when Roclenus gave Cluny a church at Charmée for his soul (C 3391 [IV:492–95]). It is tempting to consider him a relative of Bishop Roclenus of Nevers, but there is no evidence other than their names. He had been dean and provost since 1063 (GC IV:229, no. 10; C 3391, 3403 [IV:492–95, 506]).[11] Sometimes a "Bishop Frotgar" is added to the list of bishops of Chalon between 1077 and 1079, because Frotgar of Châlons, who often appeared with King Philip I, is confused with the bishop of Chalon.[12]

Walter I of Couches, 1080–1123

Of the noble family of the lords of Couches (La Ferté 33 [p. 67]). Had been archdeacon of Chalon (GC IV:231, no. 12). Elected over the candidate to whom the king had given lay investiture (Hugh of Flavigny, *Chronicon*, MGH SS VIII:421). Though the date of his death is often given as 1120, he was still alive in March, 1122 (GC XV:22, no. 19). He died on 12 January (Obit. Lyon II:485).

Jotsald, 1123–1126

Had been dean (St.-Marcel 52, 75 [pp. 56, 72]). He died on 27 June (Obit. Lyon II:493).

Walter II of Sercy, 1126–1158

Brother of Gui of Sercy (La Ferté 158, 163 [pp. 137, 139]; Arch. Saône-et-Loire, H 54, no. 20; Sercy is twenty-four kilometers southwest of Chalon). Had been archdeacon (Vignory ii [p. 31]; Arch. Haute-Marne, 24 H 1). His nephew, Walter of Sercy, was archdeacon under his successors, Peter and Engelbert (Chalon, p. 77; Cîteaux/Marilier 210 [p. 169]; St.-Étienne IV.75 [pp. 86–87), and eventually dean (La Ferté 152 [p. 134]). Another Walter of Sercy, perhaps another nephew, was a canon at Mâcon (Obit. Lyon II:402) and eventually dean (GC IV:243, nos. 28, 29). At the end of his life,

---

[10]Bazin says that he had been dean of Chalon; *Histoire des évêques*, pp. 123–27. He is erroneously omitted from DHGE.

[11]Chauney calls him "of Brancion"; "Le recrutement de l'épiscopat," p. 199. Bazin rejects this possibility; *Histoire des évêques*, pp. 128–34. The names of his brothers and mother are not those of the lords of Brancion; therefore I too do not accept this identification.

[12]*Recueil des actes de Philippe Ier, roi de France (1059–1108)*, ed. M. Prou (Paris, 1908), pp. 224–26, no. 86.

Bishop Walter became a Carthusian; he died on 27, 28, or 29 July (Obit. Lyon II:384; Obit Sens I:449, 525; Obit. Sens IV:345).[13]

Peter of St.-Marcel, 1158–1178
Son of Salicher, a knight of St.-Marcel; he had brothers named Odo, Hugh, and Girard (St.-Marcel 119 [p. 97]). He had a nephew Peter in the chapter (Chalon, p. 52), and Hugh of St.-Marcel, archdeacon of the chapter after 1178, may have been another nephew (Arch. Saône-et-Loire, H 25, no. 31). Peter had been a member of the cathedral chapter since at least 1136 (Chalon, p. 111). He had been archdeacon and dean (La Ferté 56, 175 [pp. 77, 146]). (He is sometimes erroneously called a Cistercian, probably because he is remembered in Cîteaux's necrology, but many non-Cistercian bishops were recorded there.) He died on 6 or 8 November (Obit. Lyon II:603, 619).

Engelbert, 1178–1180
Had been abbot of Molesme (1177–1178) (Molesme II:546) (see Appendix C, p. 420). Resigned in 1180, after three years as bishop, according to Alberic de Trois-Fontaines (*Chronica* 1177, MGH SS XXIII:855), who said that Engelbert continued to ordain priests after his resignation.[14]

Robert, 1180–1215
His first known charter is dated 1180 (Arch. Côte-d'Or, 16 H 135). He died on 12 January (Obit. Lyon II:572).

Langres

There is an early thirteenth-century list of bishops of Langres, "Series episcoporum Lingonensium," MGH SS XIII:379–80. This was compiled at St.-Étienne of Dijon and gives only the bishops' names. A good deal of information on the bishops of Langres—at least their dates of election and death—appears in the "Annales S. Benigni Divionensis," MGH SS V:38–50.

Bruno, 980–1016
Son of Alberada and a man whom scholars usually call Raynald of Roucy, without primary evidence. Alberada was the daughter of Duke Giselbert of Lorraine and of Gerberge, daughter of Henry the

---

[13]Bazin thinks that the lords of Sercy were a cadet branch of the lords of Brancion, because their coats of arms were similar; *Histoire des évêques*, pp. 148–57.

[14]Bazin says that he became a Carthusian after his resignation; *Histoire des évêques*, pp. 167–69. Chauney says that he became a Premonstratensian; "Le recrutement de l'épiscopat," p. 205.

Fowler. Bruno was hence great-nephew of Bruno, bishop of Cologne. He was made bishop by King Lothair, his uncle, after having been a cleric of Reims. (For Alberada, see Appendix A, p. 269.) Bruno was made bishop at the uncanonically youthful age of twenty-four (Chron. St.-B., pp. 128—30). He died on 29 January (BN, Coll. Bourgogne 9, fol. 98r). He had a nephew Bruno, archdeacon under him, who held that office until at least 1032 (St.-B. II.311 [pp. 89—90]; Chron. St.-B., p. 295); this Bruno went on to become treasurer of Langres in the 1030s (Arch. Haute-Marne, 12 H 3).

Lambert I, 1016—1031
Usually called "of Vignory," without evidence (probably because there was a Lambert of Vignory who was bishop of Langres a century later). Had been provost under Bruno (Chron. St.-B., p. 295; Quantin I.74 [pp. 143—44]). His sister was Letgardis *matrona* (Chron. St.-B., p. 195). This woman may be the Countess Letgardis who made a gift to St.-Michel of Tonnerre for the soul of her late son Roger at the beginning of the eleventh century, with the confirmation of the bishop and canons of Langres, including Lambert (who was still provost) (Petit 687 [II:430—31]). (One possibility, though based on nothing more than name similarities, is that Bishop Lambert and Countess Letgardis were the children of Letgardis, the daughter of Count Gisel-bert of Burgundy, and of her second husband, Rudolph of Dijon, uncle of Count Lambert of Chalon; see Appendix A, p. 307.)

Richard, 1031
A cleric put in by the king "against the will of clergy and people"; driven out of the see and poisoned within five months, according to the chronicle of St.-Bénigne (p. 178). The "Annales S. Benigni Divi-onensis" say that Girard, the archdeacon, drove Richard out of office and that he died in Flanders (MGH SS V:41).

Hugh of Verdun, 1031—1049
Often called "of Breteuil." His brother Waleran was abbot of Ver-dun ("Annales S. Benigni Divionensis" 1046, MGH SS V:41); Hugh and Waleran were sons of Count Gilduin of Verdun, whom Waleran succeeded as count (Hugh of Flavigny, *Chronicon*, MGH SS VIII:406). He had been a cleric of Chartres and was put into office by the king. He was deposed by the council of Reims for simony, tyranny, and homicide (Anselm of St.-Remi, "Historia dedicationis ecclesiae Sancti Remigii," PL CXLII:1454; Chron. St.-B., p. 179).[15]

---

[15] A sympathetic biography of Hugh has been written by Jean-Charles Didier, "Hughes de Breteuil, évêque de Langres († 1050)," *Recherches augustiniennes*, 16 (1981), 289—98.

Harduin of Tonnerre, 1049—1065
Put in to replace Hugh (Chron. St.-B., pp. 179, 337). He was son of Count Rainard of Tonnerre and the cousin of his successor (see Appendix A, p. 371).

Hugh-Rainard of Tonnerre, 1065—1084
Called either Hugh or Rainard or sometimes both. Son of Count Milo III of Tonnerre (Quantin I.94 [pp. 180—82]). Acted as count of Tonnerre and Bar-sur-Seine, theoretically as regent for his ·nephews ("Historia translatio reliquorum S. Mamantis," RHGF XI:482). A cousin of his predecessor Harduin. A later addition in the "Annales S. Benigni Divionensis" says that he died in 1077 (MGH SS V:42), but he was still active in 1084 (Molesme 1.26 [II:36—39]).

Robert of Burgundy, 1084—1111
Brother of Duke Hugh I of Burgundy (Molesme 1.29 [II:44]; see also Appendix A, p. 258). Had been archdeacon of Langres before his election (Molesme 1.3, 6 [II:7, 12]). Retired to Molesme and took the habit there as he was dying (Molesme 1.220 [II:204]). Recorded in Cîteaux's necrology on 20 March (Obit. Lyon II:614).

Lambert II, 1112
Of the family of the lords of Vignory (see Appendix A, p. 382). Claimed the office and signed charters as *electus* for a short time (Molesme 1.217B [II:198—200]; St.-B. II.433 [pp. 209—10]), but was never consecrated. Had been archdeacon and treasurer of Langres, to which offices he returned (Quantin I.107, 113, 145 [pp. 206, 215—16, 264]; Molesme 1.5, 2.7B [II:10, 264—65]). He lived until at least 1129 (GC IV:161—63, nos. 38, 39). Not included in the "Series" of bishops of Langres, or in the bishops listed in the "Annales S. Benigni."

Joceran, 1113—1125
Often called "of Brancion," but without evidence.[16] Had been archdeacon of Langres (GC IV:154, no. 29). Resigned ("Annales S. Benigni Divionensis" 1125, MGH SS V:44; Petit 252 [II:220]). Died on 18 April (Obit. Lyon II:370).

Willenc of Aigremont, 1125—1136
Sometimes erroneously called "of Saulx." Son of Fulk, lord of Aigremont, and brother of Lord Ulric (GC IV:168, no. 43; see also Appendix A, p. 281). Had been dean and archdeacon since 1111 at

[16]Chauney calls Joceran the brother of Bernard V Grossus of Brancion, apparently only on the basis of name similarities. Elsewhere she confuses him with his successor, Willenc, and calls him "of Aigremont"; "Le recrutement de l'épiscopat," pp. 198, 210—11.

the latest (St.-Étienne II.22 [pp. 25–28]; GC IV:155, 157, nos. 30, 33; Molesme 1.220 [II:204]), apparently after having been archdeacon in 1106–1108 (Quantin I.110, 113 [pp. 210–11, 215–16]), or even as early as 1098 (St.-Étienne I.98 [pp. 115–16]). He had nephews Ulric, Werric (unless these two are the same), and Fulk, the last of whom stayed with his uncle in the cathedral chapter in spite of the pleadings of Bernard of Clairvaux.[17] Ulric became archdeacon of the chapter and provost of Sts.-Géosmes (Quantin I.297 [pp. 451–52]), and Fulk became archdeacon (GC IV:161, no. 38).

William of Sabran, 1138

A Cluniac monk of the family of the lords of Sabran (which is located on the lower Rhône) ("Annales S. Benigni Divionensis" 1136, MGH SS V:44). Deposed shortly after his election, at the instigation of Bernard of Clairvaux.[18] William died as a prior at the Cluniac house of St.-Saturnin.

Geoffrey of La Roche, 1139–1163

Of the castellan family of the lords of La Roche, near Fontenay.[19] The evidence for this family connection is as follows. Geoffrey is known to have had a brother Rayner (*Genus illustre*, p. 461, no. 20 [rpt. PL CLXXXV:1419]), doubtless the same as the Rayner de La Roche who frequently appeared in Fontenay's charters, for another charter refers to a Geoffrey, monk of Clairvaux, who was brother of the lord of La Roche (Molesme 1.263 [II:244–45]). This connection would explain why the biographers of Bernard of Clairvaux said Bernard was related to Bishop Geoffrey (William of St.-Thierry, *Vita prima Sancti Bernardi* 1.9, 2.5, PL CLXXXV:253, 284; Alain, *Vita tertia Sancti Bernardi* 11, PL CLXXXV:489): Geoffrey was Bernard's aunt's brother-in-law, and also the brother-in-law of Bernard's cousin Millisend (see Appendix A, p. 337). Geoffrey's sister Agnes was the first abbess of Puits-d'Orbe (Jobin, *St. Bernard*, p. 635, no. 62). He had been a monk of Clairvaux ("Annales S. Benigni Divionensis" 1136, MGH SS V:44) and prior (Ernald, *Vita prima Sancti Bernardi* 2.5, PL CLXXXV:284). According to his epitaph, he was the first abbot of Fontenay before becoming prior of Clairvaux (quoted in GC IV, col. 492). He went to Jerusalem with Louis VII in 1147, and Bernard of Clairvaux acted as bishop in his absence (Petit 297 [II:239–40]). Resigned ("Annales S. Benigni Divionensis" 1163,

---

[17]Bernard of Clairvaux, Letter 2, *Opera*, VII:12–22.

[18]The controversial election and deposition of William of Sabran have been discussed most thoroughly by Constable, "The Disputed Election at Langres," pp. 119–52. The principal sources are the letters of Peter the Venerable, nos. 29, 64, 72, *Letters*, I:101–4, 193–94, 206; and of Bernard of Clairvaux, nos. 164–70, *Opera*, VII:372–85.

[19]This identification was first made by Jobin, *St. Bernard*, pp. xliii–xlv.

MGH SS V:45; Molesme 2.158 [II:316]) and retired to Clairvaux, where he died in 1164 ("Chronicon Clarevallense" 1161, 1164, PL CLXXXV:1247–48).

Walter, 1163–1179
Son of Duke Hugh II of Burgundy ("Annales S. Benigni Divionensis" 1163, MGH SS V:45; see also Appendix A, p. 260). Had been archdeacon of Langres, from 1154 at the latest (Plancher I.79 [p. li]; Petit 340 [II:259–60]). Had been archbishop of Besançon (1162–1163) (Alberic de Trois-Fontaines, *Chronica* 1161, MGH SS XXIII:845). Died on 6 January (BN, Coll. Bourgogne 9, fol. 97r).[20]

Manasses of Bar, 1179–1193
Son of Count Gui of Bar-sur-Seine; brother of Count Milo and of Isabelle, wife first of Anselm of Traînel and then of Count Theobold of Bar-le-Duc (Arch. Yonne, H 2142; Alberic de Trois-Fontaines, *Chronica* 1214, MGH SS XXIII:899).[21] Manasses also had a brother Theobold whose wife was named Margaret (St.-Étienne IV.67 [pp. 79–80]). Wiard of Reynel was his *consanguineus* (Langres 167 [p. 592]). He was nephew of Abbot Raynald of Cîteaux (1134–1150), who was also of the family of the counts of Bar. Manasses had been dean (GC IV:181, no. 63; Jully, p. 269), an office he held from at least 1166 (Arch. Haute-Marne, 2 H 1). He is called "electus" in a charter of 1179 (Langres 21 [p. 384]). He went on the Third Crusade ("Chronicon Clarevallense" 1192, PL CLXXXV:1252). While he was gone, Peter III, abbot of St.-Bénigne, was acting bishop of Langres (Châtillon, fols. 25v–26r). Manasses died on 19 August (Obit. Sens IV:338).

Warner of Rochefort, 1193–1200
Nephew of Simon, lord of Rochefort (Auberive I, fol. 159v, no. 11). Had been abbot of Clairvaux (1186–1193) ("Annales S. Benigni Divionensis" 1195, MGH SS V:46), and before that of Auberive. Deposed by Innocent III, according to the "Annales S. Benigni Divionensis" (1200, MGH SS V:47); resigned in order to write religious treatises, according to Alberic de Trois-Fontaines, who added that the pope let him retain the right to ordain priests and consecrate churches (*Chronica* 1200, MGH SS XXIII:878).

---

[20]Chauney erroneously says that he resigned to become a Carthusian, doubtless owing to a confusion with Bishop Walter II of Chalon; "Le recrutement de l'épiscopat," p. 205.

[21]Theodore Evergates makes Manasses the acting count of Bar between 1151 and 1168, although the Manasses who was count then called himself son, rather than brother, of Count Milo; Mores 11 (p. 54); Evergates, *Feudal Society in the Bailliage of Troyes under the Counts of Champagne, 1152–1284* (Baltimore, 1975), p. 160.

Mâcon

There is an early thirteenth-century list of bishops of Mâcon in the cathedral's cartulary, which gives only their names; M 51 (p. 40). M.-C. Ragut gives a brief list of the bishops of Mâcon in the introduction to the cathedral's cartulary; M, pp. ccxciii–ccxcv. His dates and family connections for these bishops do not always agree with mine.

Milo, 981–993
Had been abbot of Bèze (Chron. St.-B., p. 285).[22] He is probably the "Milo, monk and bishop" recorded in the necrology of Moûtier-St.-Jean as dying on 14 January (BN, Coll. Bourgogne 9, fol. 97v).

Letbald of Brancion, 993–1016
Son of Aremburg, a *femina nobilis*, and her husband, Warulf II of Brancion (see Appendix A, p. 297). Letbald had an older relative, named Odo, in the cathedral chapter of Mâcon (Chron. St.-B., p. 175; M 406 [pp. 233–34]; C 1088 [II:181–82]). Uncle of Bishop Walter and of Warulf of Brancion.[23]

Jocelin, 1016–1031
Resigned to become a canon regular at St.-Pierre of Mâcon, which he had restored. He died on 8 July (Obit. Sens I:446; Obit. Lyon II:493).[24]

Walter of Brancion, 1031–1061
His mother was Testa and his brother Warulf of Brancion (C 2869 [IV:66]; see Appendix A, p. 298).[25] He served in the chapter of Mâcon under his uncle, Bishop Letbald (M 347 [pp. 200–201]). Had been archdeacon and provost (M 43, 53, 198 [pp. 35, 40–41, 127]). His nephew Walter was dean under him (M 475 [pp. 273–74]). He retired to Cluny, apparently in 1061, when his successor took office, and was murdered in 1064, on 29 July (Obit. Lyon II:384; M 33 [pp. 27–28]).

Drogo, 1061–1072
The *stultus* bishop whom Nicholas II accused the king of putting into office (Letter 26, PL CXLIII:1348). Died in 1072 (M 5 [pp. 3–4]), on 6 or 7 March. Buried at Orléans (Obit. Lyon II:483, 488).

---

[22]Chauney suggests, without evidence, that he might be related to Aremburg, mother of his successor Letbald; "Le recrutement de l'épiscopat," p. 200.

[23]Benedict VIII, Letter 16, PL CXXXIX:1602. In the pope's letter, written in 1016, the reference to Letbald implies he had died.

[24]Ragut calls him "of Vienne," as does Chauney; "Le recrutement de l'épiscopat," p. 199.

[25]Ragut erroneously calls him "of Beaujeu."

Landric of Berzé, 1074–1096
Brother of Hugh of Berzé, canon of Autun (C 3565, 3667, 3674 [IV:702–3; V:16–17, 27–28]). He gave the church of Berzé to the cathedral of Mâcon (Obit. Lyon II:388). Had been archdeacon of Autun. Invested by Gregory VII over the objections of the king.[26] He died on 25 August (Obit. Lyon II:388).

Berard of Châtillon, 1096–1122
Son of Milo, lord of Châtillon-en-Dombs, who later became a monk. He had a brother named Stephen, a *miles* (Obit. Lyon II:390, 392); a brother Humbert, with whom he went to Jerusalem (GC IV:284, no. 30); and a sister Humbergia (Obit. Lyon II:367). Had been archdeacon of Lyon (GC IV:284, no. 30). He is known to have assumed office in 1096 because a charter explicitly dated 1106 is said to be in the eleventh year of his episcopate (M 547 [pp. 321–22]). He died on 20 July (Obit. Lyon II:494, 508).

Joceran, 1122–1143
Had been archdeacon (M 3–4 [pp. 2–3]) and later dean (M 577, 586 [pp. 344–45, 352–53]; C 3928 [V:282]). He died on 17 September (Obit. Lyon II:398, 509).

Ponce I, 1144–1166
Both he and Ponce II (1199–1220) have been variously called "of Villars" or "of Rochebaron," but without evidence.[27] The see was vacant for a year after his death (Tournus, pp. 168–69).

Stephen, 1167–1182
Perhaps from the family of the lords of Bâgé, as he attended the funeral of Lord Raynald of Bâgé (M 622 [p. 377]). If so, he may have been related to Bishops Stephen I and Humbert of Autun (see above, pp. 386–87). He had been archdeacon (Obit. Lyon II:415; M 601 [p. 363]). He died on 15 December (Obit. Lyon II:565).

Raynald of Vergy, 1182–1198
Called "of Vergy" (M 558 [p. 331]).[28] Had been cantor of the cathedral (M 508 [p. 296]). He was "electus" in 1182 (Autun/ Évêché 1.140 [p. 148]). Died on 6 September (Obit. Lyon II:393).

[26]Erich Caspar, ed., *Das Register Gregors VII*, MGH Epp. II, i:53–58, nos. 1.35, 36. See also M 15–16 (pp. 13–15).
[27]Ragut calls him "of Rochebaron." Chauney calls him "of Villars." The Ponce who died on October 18 is called "of Villars" by the editors of the obituary of Mâcon; Obit. Lyon II:406. The Ponce who died on 30 April (or 28 April, Obit. Lyon II:508), called of "Rochebaron" by the editors of the obituary of the cathedral of Lyon, had been precantor of Lyon; Obit. Lyon I:76.
[28]The editors of the obituary of Mâcon however say that his family was not that of the lords of Vergy but rather that of the lords of Vergyé in the Mâconnais; Obit. Lyon II:393, n. 2.

Nevers

The "Annales Nivernenses" give the dates of most of these bishops (MGH SS XIII:88–92).

Roclenus, 978–1011
Had a nephew Evrard, a canon under him at Nevers (Nevers/St.-Cyr 47 [pp. 88–89]).

Girard, 1015
Died almost immediately ("Annales Nivernenses" 1015, MGH SS XIII:90).

Hugh I of Nevers, 1016–1069
Son of Viscount Hugh of Nevers and his wife Elizabeth (Nevers/St.-Cyr 5 [pp. 13–15]). Brother of the viscount of Nevers, also called Hugh, and of men named Leo and Raynald (C 3388 [IV:489]). His nephew Geoffrey was bishop of Auxerre (*Gesta pontificum*, p. 393), and his great-nephew Hugh became bishop of Nevers in 1074, having served under this Hugh as dean (C 3388 [IV:489]). (Charters of St.-Cyr of Nevers refer to Hugh I's nephew, Hugh II, as Hugh *tertius*, Nevers/St.-Cyr 77, 79 [pp. 129–33, 136], and to this Hugh as Hugh II, but it is then not known who is meant by Hugh I. Some charters called the Hugh who became bishop in 1110 Hugh *tertius*, others *quartus*; Lebeuf IV.37 [pp. 39–40]; BN, MS nouv. acq. lat. 2298, no. 1.) Hugh I did penance at the 1049 Council of Reims for simony because his parents had bought the see for him, though he said he had not known they had done so (PL CXLII:1435). He died on 23 November (Obit. Sens I:470; Obit. Sens III:467).

Malguin, 1069–1074
Probably the same Malguin who was a longtime member of the cathedral chapter of Nevers; he was a deacon in 1029 and held the office of archdeacon between 1045 and 1063 (GC XII:324–25, 328, nos. 33, 34, 36). He confirmed the gift of St.-Étienne of Nevers to Cluny just after taking office (GC XII:329, no. 37). Not in the "Annales Nivernenses." He is however in the obituary of Nevers cathedral, where his death is recorded on 1 June (Obit. Sens III:467).

Hugh II of Nevers, 1074–1096
Great-nephew of his predecessor Hugh and nephew of Geoffrey, bishop of Auxerre (Nevers/St.-Cyr 9, 77 [pp. 22–23, 129–33]). His uncle Geoffrey made him provost of Auxerre under him (*Gesta pontificum*, pp. 393–98). He became dean of Nevers (C 3724 [V:67–74]). He was elected canonically "by clergy and people" according to his necrology (Nevers/St.-Cyr 77 [pp. 129–33]). He died on 7 or 8 May (Obit. Sens III:234, 465).

Gui, 1097–1099

Hervé, 1099–1110
Became bishop after the Council of Étampes settled his disputed election (Ivo of Chartres, Letter 76, PL CLXII:97–98; Hefele-Leclercq V, i:466). Died on 8 August (Obit. Sens III:239, 465).

Hugh III, 1110–1119
Died on 25 February (Obit. Sens III:464).

Fromond, 1119–1145
Originally dean of the cathedral of Nevers, but after restoring the house of St.-Martin of Nevers in 1110 and setting Augustinian canons in it, took the habit there himself and was buried there when he died on 29 or 30 November (Obit. Sens I:521; Obit. Sens III:466, 477; Arch. nat., L 1000, no. 4, p. 1).

Geoffrey, 1146–1159
Died on 14 or 20 February (Obit. Sens I:521; Obit. Sens III:464).

Bernard of St.-Saulge, 1159–1176
The obituary of the cathedral chapter of Nevers calls him "of St.-Saulge" but says that his parents, for whom he established an anniversary, were Josbert "of Trolio" and Alpasia (Obit. Sens III:464). Had been a member of the cathedral chapter and dean (GC XII:342, no. 51; BN, MS nouv. acq. lat. 2298, no. 2). He died on 15 January (Obit. Sens III:464).

Theobold, 1176–1188
Had been dean ("Annales Nivernenses" 1176, MGH SS XIII:91; C 4239 [V:593]; Quantin II.233 [pp. 249–51]). His nephew Theobold was treasurer of the cathedral chapter under him (Nevers/St.-Cyr 113 [p. 191]). He died on 25 April (Obit. Sens III:464).

John, 1190–1196
Had been dean (GC XII:345, no. 54).

Walter of Pougy, 1196–1202
Brother of Raynald, lord of Pougy. Had been archdeacon of Troyes under his uncle Manasses, bishop of Troyes (1181–1190).[29] He was thus a cousin of Hervé of Chitry, dean of Auxerre at the end of the twelfth century, who was also nephew of Bishop Manasses (Obit. Sens III:253). He died on 30 December (Obit. Sens III:464).

---

[29] Abbé Lalore, ed., *Collection des principaux cartulaires du diocèse de Troyes*, I (Paris, 1875), 115–16, no. 81; V (Paris, 1880), 89–90, no. 81. For the lords of Pougy, see Evergates, *Feudal Society in the Bailliage of Troyes*, pp. 193–95.

APPENDIX C

The Burgundian Abbots

The following lists of abbots of the major Burgundian houses are organized in the same manner as the lists of bishops. I made a preliminary study of some of these abbots; Constance B. Bouchard, "Changing Abbatial Tenure Patterns in Burgundian Monasteries during the Twelfth Century," *Revue Bénédictine*, 90 (1980), 257–62. Since many abbots appeared only in the charters of their own houses—unlike the bishops who appeared in charters and chronicles from all the houses in their dioceses—the abbots are much less well documented than the bishops.

Auberive

A list of abbots of Auberive is given in DHGE V:218–19.

Raimbald
The first abbot of the house when it was founded in 1135. He was abbot in 1138 and sometime after 1139 (GC IV:169, no. 45; Arch. Haute-Marne, 1 H 53). He is probably the same as the Abbot Raynald of Auberive who appears in 1147 (Reomaus, pp. 197–200).

Rayner
His "year 1" was 1158 (Arch. Haute-Marne, 1 H 21, no. 1). He was abbot in 1162 and 1163 (Auberive I, fols. 7r–v, no. 10; Arch. Haute-Marne, 5 H 6). He resigned by 1165 (Auberive I, fols. 8r–v, no. 15 [Auberive II, fol. 10r, no. 13]).

William
Abbot in 1165 and 1179 (Mores 7 [pp. 51–52]; Arch. Haute-Marne, 2 H 3, 2 H 4).

Warner of Rochefort, 1180—1185
Nephew of Simon, lord of Rochefort (Auberive I, fol. 159v, no.
11). Went on to become abbot of Clairvaux (1186—1193) and bishop
of Langres (1193—1200).

Simon
Abbot in 1185 and 1188 (Lugny, fols. 7v—8r; Clairvaux I, p. 73,
no. 2).

Bénigne
Abbot in 1197 (Lugny, fols. 11v—12r).

Beaulieu

John I
Probably the first abbot when the house was founded in 1166; abbot
in 1169 (Clairvaux/Waquet 134 [p. 146]).

Gui I
Abbot in 1178 (Petit 628 [II:397]).

Hugh
Abbot in 1182 and 1184 (Auberive II, fols. 48v—49r, no. 7; Arch.
Haute-Marne, 2 H 6).

John II
Brother of Erard, count of Brienne. Abbot in 1185 and 1191.[1]

Gui II
Abbot in 1197 (Arch. Haute-Marne, 2 H 4).

Bèze

A list of abbots of Bèze is given in DHGE VIII:1344.

Milo
Was also bishop of Mâcon (981—993) (see Appendix B, p. 398).

William, c. 995—1031
Simultaneously abbot of St.-Bénigne of Dijon (see below, p. 424).

---

[1]Langres 275 (p. 727). M.-C. Guigue, ed., *Cartulaire Lyonnais*, I (Lyon, 1885), 81,
no. 56. The editor incorrectly calls Erard of Brienne (Brenensis) the count of Braine.

Ulger
Had been prior under William, whom he succeeded. Abbot in 1052 (Chron. St.-B., pp. 316–18, 338).

Odo
Had a brother named Hugh, with a son Odo. Abbot Odo died in the 1060s (Chron. St.-B., pp. 339, 373, 435).

Gui I
Had been a monk at Montiéramey. Resigned and returned there after a few years as abbot (Chron. St.-B., pp. 373–74).

Gausbert
Had been prior of St.-Bénigne. Abbot in 1080. Resigned to become a monk at Cluny (Chron. St.-B., pp. 374, 380).

Stephen
Son of Count Geoffrey (probably of Beaumont, see Appendix A, p. 323) and of the daughter of Count Arnulph of Reynel. Originally a monk for ten years at St.-Oyen-de-Joux, in the Jura, then monk for a year at Cluny, where his *avunculus* Gui was prior, then head of a cell, dependent on St.-Oyen, located at Bar-sur-Aube. Made abbot of Bèze by Bishop Robert of Langres in 1088. Still abbot in 1119 (Chron. St.-B., pp. 380–83, 453).

Girard
Abbot in 1127 and 1139 (Tonnerre, Bibliothèque municipale, MS 32 [on microfilm at the Arch. Yonne, 1 Mi 389]; Chron. St.-B., p. 467).

Widric
Uncle of Stephen of Bigorne (Theuley, fol. 4v). Resigned.

Geoffrey

Hugh
Contemporary with Bishop Walter of Langres (1163–1179) (Arch. Haute-Saône, H 422).

Gui II
Resigned, became prior of Fouvent (Arch. Côte-d'Or, 3 H 1, pp. 5–6).

Peter
Abbot in 1174 and 1176 (Arch. Haute-Saône, H 409; Arch. Côte-d'Or, 3 H 1, pp. 5–6).

Albert

La Bussière

A list of abbots of La Bussière is given in DHGE X:1427.

William
First abbot when the house was founded in 1131 (La Bussière 7.1 [fols. 64v–65r]).

Peter
Abbot in 1145 (La Bussière 2.8 [fols. 14r–v]).

Hugh
Abbot in 1154 (*Chronique* 1, Vézelay, p. 410).

Galo
Called "of Montréal" (La Bussière 3.2 [fols. 24r–v]). Abbot in 1162 (La Bussière 2.16 [fols. 17v–18r]). His nephew, also named Galo, was a monk, apparently at Cîteaux (Cîteaux/Marilier 170 [p. 135]). Resigned in 1173 (La Bussière 6.3 [fols. 42v–43r]; Cîteaux/ Marilier 220 [p. 177]).

Robert
Abbot in 1175 and 1176 (Cîteaux/Marilier 226 [p. 180]; La Bussière 16.6 [fol. 141v]).

Constantine
Abbot in 1180 and 1184 (Autun/St.-Symphorien 34 [p. 75]; Cîteaux II, fols. 53r–v, no. 7).

Anseric
Abbot in 1185 and 1188 (La Bussière 1.4, 1.6, 2.9, 7.2 [fols. 3v–4v, 14v–15r, 65r–v]).

Gui
Abbot in 1190 and 1194 (Arch. Côte-d'Or, 16 H 138; La Bussière 2.17 [fol. 18r]).

Herbert
Abbot in 1196 and 1197 (La Bussière 6.16, 8.2 [fols. 45v, 80v–81r]; Lugny, fols. 11v–12r).

Cîteaux

There is an early thirteenth-century list of the abbots whom the Cistercians commemorated (which, however, did not include everyone who had held the office of abbot of Cîteaux, but apparently only those who died there); Obit. Lyon II:612. The twelfth-century abbots of

Cîteaux have been studied closely by Jean Marilier, "Catalogue des abbés de Cîteaux pour le XIIᵉ siècle. Addition et rectification à la Gallia Christiana," *Cistercienser-Chronik* 55 (1948), 1–11.

Robert, 1098–1099
Had been abbot of Molesme, to which he returned in 1099.[2]

Alberic, 1099–1108
Had been prior of Molesme.[3] Called first abbot of Cîteaux in the thirteenth-century obituary, which added that he died on 26 January (Obit. Lyon II:613).

Stephen Harding, 1108–1133
English by origin. One of the original group of brothers from Molesme.[4] Had been prior. Called second abbot in the obituary. Resigned. Died 1134, on 28 March (Obit. Lyon II:615; Canivez, *Statuta*, I:11).

Gui, 1133–1134
Had been abbot of Trois-Fontaines (1128–1133). Resigned because of what Orderic Vitalis called disgrace and folly.[5] He is not in the thirteenth-century Cistercian list of abbots.

Raynald of Bar, 1134–1150
Son of Milo, count of Bar-sur-Seine.[6] Had been a monk of Chaise-Dieu before joining the Cistercian order ("Ex Vita B. Stephani Obazinensis abbatis," RHGF XIV:332). Bernard refers to him as his "son," which suggests he had been a monk at Clairvaux.[7] Called third abbot. Died on 16 December (Obit. Lyon II:621).

Goswin, 1150–1155
Had been abbot of Bonnevaux (1141–1151).[8] Called fourth abbot in the obituary, which adds that he died on 31 March (Obit. Lyon II:615).

Lambert, 1155–1161
Had been abbot of Clairefontaine (1133–1154) and Morimond

---

[2]Orderic Vitalis, *Historia ecclesiastica* 8.26, ed. Marjorie Chibnall, IV (Oxford, 1973), 324.

[3]"Exordium parvum" 9, ed. Bouton and Van Damme, *Textes*, p. 69. Molesme 1.4 (II:8).

[4]"Exordium parvum" 17, ed. Bouton and Van Damme, *Textes*, p. 81. Orderic Vitalis, *Historia ecclesiastica* 8.26, ed. Chibnall, IV:324.

[5]Orderic Vitalis, *Historia ecclesiastica* 8.26, ed. Chibnall, IV:324.

[6]Ibid.

[7]Bernard of Clairvaux, Letter 280, *Opera*, VIII (Rome, 1977), 180.

[8]Ibid.

(1154—1155). Resigned; still alive in 1172 (Arch. Haute-Marne, 8 H 103, no. 1). Not in the thirteenth-century list of abbots.

Fastrède, 1161—1163
Had been abbot of Cambron (1148—1157) and Clairvaux (1157—1161) ("Chronicon Clarevallense" 1157, 1162, PL CLXXXV:1247; Clairvaux/Waquet 92 [p. 97]). Called fifth abbot in the Cistercian obituary, which adds that he died on 21 April (Obit. Lyon II:615).

Gilbert, 1163—1168
Had been abbot of Ourscamp (1129—1163). Called sixth abbot in the Cistercian obituary, which adds that he died on 17 October (Obit. Lyon II:619).

Alexander, 1168—1178
Had been abbot of Grandselve (1150—1168), the second abbot after the house was associated with the Cistercian order. Called seventh abbot in the Cistercian obituary, which adds that he died on 29 July (Obit. Lyon II:617).

William, 1178—1180
Had been abbot of Savigny (1177—1178). Called "of Toulouse."[9] Sometimes incorrectly said to have been abbot of La Ferté. Called eighth abbot. Died on 11 January (Obit. Lyon II:612).

Peter, 1180—1184
Had been abbot of Pontigny (1177—1180). Became bishop of Arras (1184—1203) (Robert of Mt.-St.-Michel, *Chronica* 1185, MGH SS VI:534). Not in the thirteenth-century list of abbots.

Bernard, 1184—1186
Had been abbot of Fontenay.[10] Called ninth abbot. Died 1 January (Obit. Lyon II:612).

William II, 1186—1189
Had been abbot of La Prée.[11] It was either he or William III who was called tenth abbot in the obituary. The "tenth abbot" died on 28 November (Obit. Lyon II:612, 621). Another Abbot William, called sixteenth abbot—or tenth abbot in one manuscript—died on 12 February (Obit. Lyon II:613).

[9]"Indiculus abbatum Savigniacensis," RHGF XIV:519. "Ex historia praelatorum B. Mariae de Fontanis," ibid., p. 497.
[10]*Annales monasterii de Waverleia*, ed. Henry Richard Luard, Rerum Brittanicarum medii aevi scriptores 36, 2 (London, 1865), p. 243.
[11]Ibid., p. 244.

Theobold, 1189–1190
  Not in the thirteenth-century list of abbots.

William III, 1190–1194
  Neither he nor William II appears in the thirteenth-century list of abbots.

Peter II, 1194
  Called the eleventh abbot. Died on 27 March (Obit. Lyon II:614).

Gui II, 1194–1200
  Had been abbot of Notre-Dame du Val. Became a cardinal (Obit. Lyon II:616).

Clairvaux

There is a "Chronicon Clarevallense," apparently written at the end of the twelfth century, which gives much of the information on the abbots of Clairvaux; PL CLXXXV:1247–52.

Bernard, 1115–1153
  Son of the lord of Fontaines-lès-Dijon. (For his family, see Appendix A, pp. 329–31, 334–36.)

Robert, 1153–1157
  Had been abbot of Dunes (1137–1153).[12]

Fastrède, 1157–1161
  Had been abbot of Cambron (1148–1157) and became abbot of Cîteaux (1161–1163) ("Chronicon Clarevallense" 1157, 1162, PL CLXXXV:1247; Clairvaux/Waquet 92 [p. 97]).

Geoffrey, 1162–1165
  Had been Bernard's secretary. Had been abbot of Igny ("Chronicon Clarevallense" 1162, PL CLXXXV:1247). Deposed by Alexander III for his "reprehensible life" (Canivez, Statuta, I:75–76). Became abbot of Fossa Nova in 1170, when Abbot Girard was promoted to Clairvaux, and of Hautecombe in 1176, when Abbot Henry was promoted to Clairvaux ("Chronicon Clarevallense" 1176, PL CLXXXV: 1249).

[12]Ibid., p. 235.

Ponce, 1165—1170

From the Auvergne. Had been abbot of Grandselve. Became bishop of Clermont (1170—1189) ("Chronicon Clarevallense" 1165, 1170, PL CLXXXV:1248).

Girard, 1170—1175

Like his predecessor, from the Auvergne. Had been abbot of Fossa Nova ("Chronicon Clarevallense" 1170, PL CLXXXV:1248). A charter of 1171 was given in "the first year that Girard was abbot" (Clairvaux/Waquet 142 [p. 153]). Killed by a "demoniac monk" at Igny, "martyred" according to the "Chronicon Clarevallense" (1175, PL CLXXXV:1248—49; see also Robert of Mt.-St.-Michel, *Chronica* 1175, MGH SS VI:524).

Henry of Merzé, 1176—1179

From Merzé, in the region of Cluny; when his brother Geoffrey died, Henry gave property at Merzé to Cluny for Geoffrey's burial and in memory of his parents and his other brothers and sisters, who were also buried there (C 4248 [V:604—5]).[13] Henry had been abbot of Hautecombe before taking office at Clairvaux. After refusing election to Toulouse, he became a cardinal; he died in 1189 ("Chronicon Clarevallense" 1176, 1179, 1187, PL CLXXXV:1249, 1252; Letter 25 to Alexander III, PL CC:1383).

Peter Monocule, 1179—1186.

Italian, born of *excelsis parentibus*, according to a *vita* written around 1200. Had been abbot of Val-Roi and of Igny (*Acta Sanctorum* October XIII:70, 80).

Warner of Rochefort, 1186—1193

Nephew of Simon, lord of Rochefort (Auberive I, fol. 159v, no. 11). Had been abbot of Auberive (1180—1185). Became bishop of Langres (1193—1200) ("Chronicon Clarevallense" 1186, 1192, PL CLXXXV:1250—52; "Annales S. Benigni Divionensis" 1195, MGH SS V:46).

Gui, 1195—1213

Had been abbot of Ourscamp. Refused election to Reims in 1204.[14] Resigned.

---

[13]This connection with Merzé was originally noted by M. Oursel-Quarré, "À propos du chartier de Cluny," *Annales de Bourgogne*, 50 (1978), 105; she cited the wrong charter, however.

[14]Étienne Baluze, ed., *Miscellaneorum*, II (Paris, 1679), 245—47.

Cluny

Maiolus, 948–994

Of a noble family of Avignon. His parents were Fulcher, son of Fulcher, and Raimodis, daughter of Maiolus and Landrada (C 105, 843, 1071 [I:117–19, 798–99; II:164–66]).[15] According to his biographer, Maiolus came to Mâcon as a youth, fleeing the Saracens, and originally began his studies with the intention of joining the cathedral chapter of Mâcon, but instead, after refusing election to Besançon, he became a monk at Cluny (Syro, *Vita Sancti Maioli* 1, PL CXXXXVII:745–51). He died on 11 May (Obit. Lyon II:484).

Odilo, 994–1049

From a noble family of the Auvergne, son of Berald, son of Itier. His mother was named Gerberge. Odilo was one of a family of at least eight brothers. Of these brothers, Stephen succeeded their father as lord, Berald became provost of Le Puy, Itier died before Odilo became abbot, and the others were named Bertran, Eblo, William, and Giles (C 1838, 2788 [III:82–83, 811–15]). Odilo had been prior.

Hugh the Great, 1049–1109

Of the family of the lords of Semur (see Appendix A, p. 360). His parents originally put him in the cathedral school of Auxerre, where his great-uncle Hugh was bishop, but he left it at age fifteen for Cluny, *patre nesciente* (Gilo, "Vita Sancti Hugonis" 1.2–3, ed. Cowdrey, "Studies," pp. 49–50). Hugh had been prior (C 2950 [IV:150]; see also Raynald of Vézelay's *Vita* of Hugh, Vézelay suppl., p. 40). He died on 29 April (Obit. Lyon II:372).

Ponce of Melgueil, 1109–1122

Son of the count of Melgueil (Robert of Mt.-St.-Michel, *Chronica* 1117, MGH SS VI:485). Hugh the Great had approved the choice of Ponce as his successor. Ponce resigned but attempted unsuccessfully to return to Cluny, in what the pope referred to as a "scandal."[16] He died on 29 December (Obit. Sens I:475).

Hugh II, 1122

His father was from Besançon, his mother from Lyon. Had been

---

[15]See also Jean Barruol, "L'influence de Saint Mayeul et de sa famille dans la renaissance méridionale du XIe siècle, d'après une documentation nouvelle du Cartulaire d'Apt," in *Cartulaire de l'église d'Apt (835–1130?)*, ed. Noël Didier (Paris, 1967), pp. 67–83.

[16]Peter the Venerable, *Miracula* 2.12–13, PL CLXXXIX:922–36. Orderic Vitalis, *Historia ecclesiastica* 11.39, 12.30, ed. Chibnall, VI (Oxford, 1978), 170, 310–16. Calixtus II, Letter 190, PL CLXIII:1256–57.

prior of Marcigny. Ruled for three months.[17] He died on 9 July (Obit. Sens I:446).

Peter the Venerable, 1122–1156

Of Montboissier, of a noble castellan family of the Auvergne. His parents were named Maurice and Raingardis. He was one of eight sons, seven of whom reached maturity.[18] His brother Jordan was abbot of Chaise-Dieu (*Chronique* 1, Vézelay, p. 396). His brother Ponce was abbot of Vézelay (1138–1161) ("Annales Vizeliàcenses" 1138, Vézelay, p. 226). His brother Herman was prior of Cluny under Peter and later abbot of Manglieu, in the Auvergne (Geoffrey of Vigeois, *Chronicon*, RHGF XII:432). His brother Heracleus was archbishop of Lyon (1153–1163). He also had two secular brothers, Hugh and Eustace (Peter the Venerable, Letters 160, 185, *Letters*, I:385–87, 427–34). Peter had been prior of Vézelay. He was buried on 25 December (Obit. Sens I:475, 528).

Robert Grossus, 1157

A relative of the counts of Flanders. Called a *semi-laicus* by Robert of Mont-St.-Michel, who said that he was elected because of his relatives, not his own merits, in a "tumultuous" election (*Chronica* 1157, MGH SS VI:506).[19] Deposed and excommunicated by the pope (C 4193 [V:540]).

Hugh III, 1158–1161

Called "of Frisia" in a fragmentary chronicle of St.-Étienne of Nevers.[20] Had been claustral prior (Robert of Mt.-St.-Michel, *Chronica* 1157, MGH SS VI:506). His election put an end to the tumult over the election and deposition of Robert Grossus as abbot (Peter of Celle, Letter 1.26, PL CCII:432).

---

[17]Peter the Venerable, *Miracula* 2.12, PL CLXXXIX:923. Robert of Mt.-St.-Michel, *Chronica* 1117, MGH SS VI:485. Orderic Vitalis, *Historia ecclesiastica* 12.30, ed. Chibnall, VI:312.

[18]Radulf, "Vita Petri Venerabilis" 1, PL CLXXXIX:17. Peter of Poitiers, "Panegyricus Petro Venerabili," PL CLXXXIX:55–56. For Peter's family, see also the "Cartulaire de Sauxillanges," ed. Henry Doniol, *Mémoires de l'Académie des sciences, belles-lettres et arts de Clermont-Ferrand*, 3 (1861), 1024–25, nos. 795, 796.

[19]Nicolas Huyghebaert argues convincingly that Robert was a member of the Grossi family, the lords of Brancion and Uxelles; the contemporary count of Flanders was brother of a woman who married Bernard V of Brancion. If Robert were son of Bernard V, he would have entered Cluny under his great-uncles, who were prior and chamberlain. Robert seems to have been briefly prior of St.-Pierre-St.-Paul of Abbeville and probably Ste.-Geneviève of Paris in the 1140s; Huyghebaert, "Une crise à Cluny en 1157: L'élection de Robert le Gros, successeur de Pierre le vénérable," *Revue bénédictine*, 93 (1983), 337–53.

[20]"Fragmentum chronici Cluniacensis," ed. Edmund Martène and Ursin Durand, *Thesaurus novus anecdotorum*, III (Paris, 1717; rpt. New York, 1968), col. 1387.

Stephen, 1161–1173

Had been prior of St.-Marcel-lès-Chalon. Resigned, according to the fifteenth-century "Chronicon Cluniacense," which adds that he died the following year.[21] He was buried on 12 August (Obit. Sens I:450, 526).

Rudolph, 1173–1176.

Had been prior of La Charité-sur-Loire (Robert of Mt.-St.-Michel, *Chronica* 1173, 1177, MGH SS VI:522, 525). Of Sully; a nephew of Henry, bishop of Winchester, according to the "Chronicon Cluniacense."[22] Robert of Mt.-St.-Michel calls him a cousin of Count Theobold of Blois (*Chronicon* 1173, 1177, MGH SS VI:522, 525). Resigned, according to the chronicle of St.-Étienne; deposed, according to Robert of Mt.-St.-Michel, who said he again became prior of La Charité.[23]

Walter, 1176–1177

Had been prior of St.-Martin-des-Champs (1161–1176). The necrology of St.-Martin, recording his death on 6 September, said he was of "Chaelons," probably Châlons-sur-Marne.[24]

William, 1177–1179

Had been prior of St.-Martin-des-Champs (1158–1161) and abbot of Ramsay (1161–1177) (Robert of Mt.-St.-Michel, *Chronica* 1161, 1180, MGH SS VI:511, 529).[25] He died on 11 January (Obit. Sens I:422, 520).

Theobold, 1179–1183

Had been prior of St.-Crispian (Robert of Mt.-St.-Michel, *Chronica* 1181, MGH SS VI:529). Had been abbot of St.-Basle, according to the "Chronicon Cluniacense."[26] Became the cardinal bishop of Ostia (Urban III, Letter 27, PL CCII:1377; Robert of Mt.-St.-Michel, *Chronica* 1185, MGH SS VI:534).

Hugh IV of Clermont, 1183–1199

Son of Raynald II of Clermont. Had been abbot of St.-Lucien of Beauvais, according to the "Chronicon Cluniacense." His epitaph and

---

[21]*Bibliotheca Cluniacensis*, ed. Martin Marrier and André Quercetanus [Duchesne] (1614; rpt. Mâcon, 1915), col. 1660.

[22]Ibid., cols. 1660–61.

[23]"Fragmentum chronici Cluniacensis," ed. Martène and Durand, col. 1387. Robert of Mt.-St.-Michel, *Chronica* 1177, MGH SS VI:525.

[24]See also Joachim Mehne, ed., "Eine Totenliste aus Saint-Martin-des-Champs," *Frühmittelalterliche Studien*, 10 (1976), 232; and Robert of Mt.-St.-Michel, *Chronica* 1177, MGH SS VI:525.

[25]See also David Knowles, C. N. L. Brooke, and Vera C. M. London, *The Heads of Religious Houses: England and Wales, 940–1216* (Cambridge, England, 1972), p. 62.

[26]*Bibliotheca Cluniacensis*, col. 1662.

the fragmentary chronicle of St.-Étienne said that he was from Clermont.[27] Robert of Mt.-St.-Michel calls him the son of the count of Clermont and says that he had once been abbot of a Cistercian house, then became abbot of Flavigny, and finally abbot of St.-Lucien of Beauvais before becoming abbot of Cluny (*Chronica* 1185, MGH SS VI:534). He died on 7 April (Obit. Sens I:433).

La Crête

A list of abbots of La Crête is given in DHGE XIII:1033.

Baldwin
He was first abbot of the house when it was founded in 1121 (Arch. Haute-Marne, 5 H 5, 5 H 10).

Milo
He may have been the second abbot. He was abbot in 1152 and 1160 (GC XIII:509, no. 58; Arch. Haute-Marne, 5 H 10).

Bernard
Abbot in 1160 (Arch. Haute-Marne, 5 H 9).

Peter
Abbot in 1164 and 1168 (Arch. Haute-Marne, 5 H 7; 10 H 4).

Theobold
Abbot in 1172 and 1175 (Arch. Haute-Marne, 10 H 5; 5 H 6).

Warner

Gemmo
Abbot in 1181 (Arch. Haute-Marne, 10 H 9).

William
Abbot in 1183 and 1188 (Arch. Haute-Marne, 8 H 7, no. 3; 8 H 77, no. 3).

Galo
Abbot in 1197 (Arch. Haute-Marne, 5 H 10).

---

[27]Ibid., col. 1663. "Fragmentum chronici Cluniacensis," ed. Martène and Durand, col. 1387.

La Ferté-sur-Grosne

A list of abbots of La Ferté is given in DHGE XVI:1307.

Philibert/Bertaud, 1113—1120

Opizon, 1120—1121

Peter, 1121—1126
Became archbishop of Tarentaise (1126—1132) (GC IV:238, no. 21).

Bartholomew, 1124—1161
Uncle of Joceran of Charolles (La Ferté 215 [p. 177]). Sometimes said to be identical with Bartholomew, brother of Bernard of Clairvaux, although there is no evidence for this claim.

William I, 1162—1186
Had been prior (La Ferté 163 [p. 140]).

Berno, 1186—1194

William II, 1194—1199

Flavigny

Hugh of Flavigny gave a brief "Series" of the abbots of Flavigny, to the end of the eleventh century, at the end of his *Chronicon*, and included a copy of the necrology; MGH SS VIII:285—87, 502—3. A list of the abbots is given in DHGE XVII:404—5.

Robert
A relative of Count Landric of Nevers, considered a destroyer of the house by the monks of Flavigny (see Appendix A, p. 341). When driven out, Robert fled to Corbigny, a dependency of Flavigny, and tried to make himself independent abbot there ("Series," MGH SS VIII:503).

Heldric, c. 986—1009
He was a monk of Cluny invited to be abbot of Flavigny after the monks had driven out Robert ("Series," MGH SS VIII:503). In 992 Bishop Walter of Autun confirmed the brothers' life under the Rule of St. Benedict (Plancher I.30 [pp. xxiv—xxv]). Heldric was at the same time abbot of St.-Germain and of Moûtier-St.-Jean (Reomaus, p. 174). He died on 14 December (MGH SS VIII:287).

Amadeus
Succeeded in 1010 (MGH SS VIII:503). Abbot in 1026 and 1034 (GC IV:77—78, nos. 40, 42). Died on 19 March (MGH SS VIII:286; Obit. Sens I:431, 522).

Aimo
Forced to resign as abbot when accused of simony by Leo IX in 1049 ("Series," MGH SS VIII:503). Died on 26 December (MGH SS VIII:287).

Odo I, 1049—1051
Had been abbot of Montiéramey, near Troyes. Resigned ("Series," MGH SS VIII:503). Died on 26 August (MGH SS VIII:286).

Odo II, 1051—1084
Apparently the same as the Aldo who was abbot in 1066 (Petit 40 [I:383—85]). Died on 9 August (MGH SS VIII:286).

Raynald, 1084—1090
Brother of Duke Odo I of Burgundy ("Series," MGH SS VIII:503). King Philip said in 1085 that Raynald "was joined to him in the flesh."[28] Raynald died on 10 February (MGH SS VIII:285). Hugh of Flavigny said that after Raynald's premature death, the house lacked an abbot for seven years, except for two months when one Elmuin was abbot ("Series," MGH SS VIII:503).

Hugh, 1097—1100
The author of the *Chronicon* of Flavigny, he began to rule in 1097 (*Chronicon*, MGH SS VIII:475). He said that his mother, Lady Dada of Montfaucon, was the daughter of Chlotildis, a daughter of the emperor Otto III (MGH SS VIII:287). He had been a monk at St.-Bénigne before becoming abbot of Flavigny, at the urging of Archbishop Hugh of Lyon and Bishop Agano of Autun. Expelled from Flavigny in 1100 (*Chronicon*, MGH SS VIII:475—76, 488).

Girard
Had been prior (Hugh of Flavigny, *Chronicon*, MGH SS VIII:488). He was abbot in 1107 and 1113 (Autun/Église 1.32 [I:53—54]; Flavigny 21 [pp. 47—48; summarized Collenot, pp. 96—98]).

Rudolph

Agano
Abbot in 1142 (Arch. Côte-d'Or, 15 H 257, no. 1).

---

[28] *Recueil des actes de Philippe Ier, roi de France (1059—1108)*, ed. M. Prou (Paris, 1908), pp. 284—85, no. 112.

Hugh of Clermont
According to Robert of Mt.-St.-Michel, he was son of the count of
Clermont, had started his ecclesiastical career as abbot of a Cistercian
house, then became abbot of Flavigny, from which office he was
driven out, then abbot of St.-Lucien of Beauvais, and finally abbot of
Cluny (1183–1199) (*Chronica* 1185, MGH SS VI:534; see also above,
pp. 412–13).

Raynald II
Sometimes called "of Bille." Abbot in 1149 and 1160 (Arch.
Côte-d'Or, 1 F 213, pp. 342–44; Plancher I.74, 78 [pp. xlix–li]).[29]
Deposed by Bishop Stephen of Autun, around 1171 or 1172, for
refusing to recognize the bishop of Autun's suzerainty over Flavigny
(Arch. Saône-et-Loire, G 537, 2 G 355 [2]).

Galcher
He had been a monk of Cluny. He appeared as abbot between 1173
and 1181 (Reomaus, p. 215; Arch. Côte-d'Or, 15 H 120; Plancher I.98
[pp. lviii–lix]). He became abbot of St.-Médard of Soissons in 1185
and died within ten months ("Ex Chronico S. Medardi Suessionensis"
1185, RHGF XVIII:720).

Raynald III, 1186–1197
Deposed by Pope Celestine III (Innocent III, Letter 1.299, PL
CCXIV:257–60).

Gilbert, 1198–1199
A regular canon, who succeeded after a hotly disputed election
(Innocent III, Letter 1.299, PL CCXXIV:257). His successor, Aimo
(Arch. Côte-d'Or, 15 H 199), seems to have been the "A.," prior of
Semur-en-Auxois, who was his principal rival.

Fontenay

A list of abbots of Fontenay is given in DHGE XVII:904.

Geoffrey I of La Roche, 1119–1131
He was the first abbot of Fontenay and went on to be prior of Clairvaux (Ernald, *Vita prima Sancti Bernardi* 2.5, PL CLXXV:284). He
was later bishop of Langres (1139–1163), according to his epitaph
(quoted in GC IV, col. 492) (see above, Appendix B, p. 396.)

---

[29]The editors of DHGE call Raynald III, rather than Raynald II, "of Billey."

William
Abbot in 1131 and 1154 (PU Burgund, pp. 20—21, no. 2; Fontenay I, fols. 101r—v, no. 13).[30]

Arnold
Abbot in 1157 and 1162 (Plancher I.75 [p. 1]; Arch. Côte-d'Or, 15 H 243).

Rudolph
Abbot in 1163 (Lebeuf IV.52 [p. 45]).

Hugh
Abbot in 1165 (Fontenay I, fols. 96r—97r, no. 1).

Geoffrey II
Contemporary with Walter, bishop of Langres (1162—1179) (Arch. Haute-Marne, 1 H 85, no. 1).[31]

Bernard
Abbot in 1169 and 1183 (Pérard, p. 399—400; PU Burgund, pp. 80—81, no. 56). He became abbot of Cîteaux (1184—1186) (see above, p. 407).

Josbert
He had a brother named Odo (St.-Étienne IV.96 [pp. 109—10]). Abbot in 1186 and 1189 (C 4309 [V:669]; Arch. Côte-d'Or, 15 H 249, no. 3). Resigned; he was called "former abbot" in 1195 (Arch. Haute-Marne, 1 H 49, no. 1).

Hubert
Abbot in 1195 and 1198 (Fontenay I, fols. 92r—v, no. 7; Fontenay II, fols. 34v—35r, no. 29). He resigned, for he was called "former abbot" in 1199, at which time Bernard II was abbot (Fontenay I, fol. 111r, no. 37).

Longué

Gui, 1153—1160
Son of Hugh, viscount of La Ferté (Arch. Haute-Marne, 5 H 10). He was the first abbot of the house when it became Cistercian (Longué, fol. 88v).

---

[30]The editors of DHGE call him "of Spiri."
[31]The editors of DHGE omit Geoffrey, instead making one "William II of Montbard" abbot between 1167 and 1169.

Rudolph, 1160—1194

Brother of Baldwin, a *miles* of Bricon, and of Lord Simon of Bricon (Arch. Haute-Marne, 5 H 10; Longué, fol. 20r, no. 1). He was hence a nephew of his predecessor Gui.[32] His first dated charter is from 1160 (Arch. Haute-Marne, 1 H 96, no. 1). He resigned, for he was called "former abbot" in 1195 (Arch. Haute-Marne, 1 H 49, no. 1; Longué, fol. 20r, no. 1). He was still alive in 1198 (Clairvaux I, pp. 267—68, no. 5).

Arnold, 1194—1215

Abbot in 1195 and 1198 (Clairvaux I, p. 264, no. 2; Longué, fols. 136v—137r).

Maizières

Angelicus

He was the first abbot when the house was founded in 1132 (GC IV:241, no. 24).

William

Abbot in 1151 and 1154 (Cîteaux/Marilier 139 [pp. 117—18]; Petit 342 [II:260]).

Richard

Abbot in 1164 (Cîteaux/Marilier 167 [pp. 132—33]).

William

Abbot in 1166 and 1173 (La Ferté 260 [p. 204]; Arch. Saône-et-Loire, 20 H 17 suppl.).

Zacharias

Artald

Abbot in 1179/80 (Arch. Saône-et-Loire, H 25, no. 34).

Gui

Had been prior. Abbot in 1190 and 1197 (Arch. Saône-et-Loire, H 54, nos. 3, 12, 23).

[32]See Jean-Marc Roger, "Les Morhier Champenois," *Bulletin philologique et historique du Comité des travaux historiques et scientifiques*, 1978, pp. 77—130.

Molesme

There is a thirteenth-century "Chronicon" of the abbots of Molesme, from which much of the following chronological information is drawn (Molesme II:546—47). Laurent discussed the abbots in the introduction to his edition of the abbey's cartularies (Molesme I:157—78). There is also a thirteenth-century obituary of Molesme (Petit V:383—95), which includes many of the abbots.

Robert, 1075—1111
The first abbot of Cîteaux (1098—1099), but returned to Molesme. During his absence, one Geoffrey acted as abbot but stepped down when Robert returned.[33] Robert died on 30 April (Obit. Lyon II:615).

Gui of Châtel-Censoir, 1111—1132
Of the noble family of Châtel-Censoir, brother of Ascelin, son of Wibert and Regina. His brother Hugh also became a monk (Molesme 1.238 [II:222]). Had been prior (Molesme 1.30 [II:45]).

Evrard, 1132—1140

Girard, 1140—1148

Stephen I, 1148—1156
Called the fifth abbot in the obituary (Petit V:392).

Willenc, 1156—1163
Had been prior (Mores 2 [p. 49]). Resigned (Molesme 2.304 [II:368]; Petit V:386). He was still alive in 1185 (Arch. Haute-Marne, 2 H 5).[34]

Nivelon, 1163—1166
Uncle of Haycus of Plancey (Arch. Côte-d'Or, 7 H 750).[35] Resigned (Molesme II:546; Petit V:385).

Theobold, 1166—1171
Had been prior of Cluny and died on pilgrimage, according to the thirteenth-century list of abbots (Molesme II:546). He seems to have been a Carthusian at some point before becoming abbot, according to a letter of Peter of Celle (Letter 2.140, PL CCII:583). The obituary

---

[33]"Exordium parvum" 1, 5, ed. Bouton and Van Damme, *Textes*, pp. 56—57, 62—63. "Chronicon," Molesme II:546. Orderic Vitalis, *Historia ecclesiastica* 8.26, ed. Chibnall, IV:324. Petit V:386.

[34]Laurent calls him "of Choiseul"; Molesme I:164. There does not seem to be any evidence for this, however. Laurent dates the beginning of the "decadence" of the abbey to Willenc's rule.

[35]Laurent calls him "of Bazoches," without evidence; Molesme I:165—66.

of Molesme called Theobold the sixth abbot and said he died on pilgrimage (Petit V:384).[36]

Thomas, 1171—1177
Sometimes called of the family of the lords of Chacenay.[37] Had been prior (Molesme 2.440 [II:412]). Resigned (Molesme II:546; Petit V:384).[38]

Engelbert, 1177—1178
Became bishop of Chalon-sur-Saône (1178—1180) (see Appendix B, p. 393). The thirteenth-century "Chronicon" says that he was "electus in episcopum" (Molesme II:546), and the bishop of Chalon is the only contemporary Engelbert.

Stephen II, 1178—1181
Resigned (Molesme II:546; Petit V:385).

William, 1181
Known only from a bull of Alexander III, in which the pope confirmed Molesme's possessions (Pflugk-Harttung, I:283—84, no. 320).

Raynald, 1182—1187
Had been prior (Molesme II:540—41 [documents 9 and 10 of Appendix II]).[39]

Galcher of Méry, 1187—1191
A *consanguineus* of Warin, lord of Méry-sur-Seine.[40] Resigned (Molesme II:546). Became abbot again, 1198—1209.

Bruno, 1191—1193
Resigned (Molesme II:547; Petit V:384).

Stephen II, 1193—1195
The same as the abbot of 1178—1181; see above. Resigned again (Molesme II:547).

Odo, 1195—1198

[36]Laurent calls him "de Châtillon de Bazoches," without evidence; Molesme I:166.

[37]Theodore Evergates, in his discussion of the lords of Chacenay, mistakenly makes a Thomas of Chacenay abbot of *Clairvaux* between 1171 and 1175; Evergates, *Feudal Society in the Bailliage of Troyes under the Counts of Champagne, 1152—1284* (Baltimore, 1975), p. 167.

[38]Laurent adds a Stephen II, abbot in 1175; Molesme I:169. He is not in the thirteenth-century list of abbots, only in one charter for St.-Gervais of Auxerre (Arch. Côte-d'Or, 7 H 1072). It seems more likely that this is Stephen I, who had resigned and yet still occasionally witnessed charters.

[39]Laurent says that he resigned; Molesme I:170.

[40]Abbé Lalore, ed., *Collection des principaux cartulaires du diocèse de Troyes*, V (Paris, 1880), 108, no. 104.

Morimond

There is an old history of Morimond by Louis Dubois, *Histoire de l'abbaye de Morimond* (Paris, 1851); the list of twelfth-century abbots is on pp. 413—14.

Arnold, 1115—1125
Resigned.[41]

Walter I, 1126—1131
Had been prior.

Otto of Freising, 1131—1138
Grandson of Henry IV and uncle of Frederick Barbarossa. Became bishop of Freising (1138—1158). Died and was buried at Morimond (Rahewin, *Gesta Friderici imperatoris* 4.11, MGH SS XX:451—52).

Raynald, 1139—1154
Resigned; there was a Raynald, former abbot of Morimond, in 1172 (Arch. Haute-Marne, 8 H 103).[42]

Lambert, 1154—1155
Had been abbot of Clairefontaine (1133—1154). Became abbot of Cîteaux (1155—1161).

Henry I, 1156—1157

Aliprand I, 1157—1159

Odo, 1160—1161
Had been prior of Morimond and abbot of Beaupré.

Walter II, 1161—1162[43]

Aliprand II, 1162—1168
Had been abbot of Morimonte.

Gilbert, 1168—1169.

Henry II, 1170—1182

---

[41]Bernard of Clairvaux, Letters 4—6, 359, *Opera*, VII (Rome, 1974), pp. 24—30; VIII:304—5. See also Canivez, *Statuta*, I:4—5. Dubois says that he was of a noble German family and that his brother Frederick was archbishop of Cologne; *Morimond*, p. 20.

[42]Dubois calls him brother of Frederick, count of Toul, who married Helvidis, sister of Duke Matthew of Lorraine.

[43]Dubois says that he was translated to Cîteaux. There is no twelfth-century Abbot Walter of Cîteaux, however.

Peter, 1183—1193
  Resigned.

Henry III, 1193—1195

Bartholomew, 1195—1196

Peter, 1196—1198
  The same as the abbot of 1183—1193; see above.

Pontigny

A history of Pontigny was written by V.-B. Henry, *Histoire de l'abbaye de Pontigny* (Avallon, 1882). I disagree with him on several points, as indicated below.

Hugh of Mâcon, 1114—1136
  A knight from the region of Mâcon. Became bishop of Auxerre (1136—1151) (see Appendix B, p. 389).

Guichard, 1136—1165
  Became archbishop of Lyon after a disputed election (1165—1180), and apostolic legate ("Chronicon Clarevallense" 1174, PL CLXXXV: 1248; GC IV:19—20, nos. 23—25).[44]

Warin, 1166—1174
  Robert of Mt.-St.-Michel calls him both "de Gelardum" and "de Girardo" (*Chronica* 1175, 1181, MGH SS VI:524, 529). These epithets perhaps indicate that he was from Guelders. Robert of St.-Marien says that his family was noble (*clarus*). He may be the same Warin who was abbot of Quincy in 1166 (see below, p. 423).[45] Warin became archbishop of Bourges (1174—1180) (Robert of St.-Marien, *Chronicon* 1174, MGH SS XXVI:241).

William, 1174—1176[46]

Peter, 1177—1180
  Became abbot of Cîteaux (1180—1184) and bishop of Arras (1184—1203).[47]

---

[44]Henry says that Guichard was of the family of the lords of Beaujeu, a comment apparently based only on his name. This seems very unlikely, since Lord Humbert III of Beaujeu vigorously opposed his election to Lyon; see Matthieu Méras, *Le Beaujolais au moyen âge*, 2nd ed. (Villefranche-en-Beaujolais, 1979), pp. 35—36.

[45]Tonnerre, Bibliothèque municipale, MS 39, fol. 4v (on microfilm at the Arch. Yonne, 1 Mi 394).

[46]Henry erroneously puts William before rather than after Warin in the list of abbots.

[47]Henry says that he was bishop of Arras in 1180—1203; he leaves out Peter's rule as abbot of Cîteaux.

Garmund Clement, 1181–1183
Brother of Robert and Giles Clement, important figures at the royal
court. Elected to Auxerre in a disputed election, but died at Rome
before he was consecrated (Robert of St.-Marien, *Chronicon* 1182,
MGH SS XXVI:246). He may be the same Garmund who was abbot
of Quincy in the late 1170s (Pontigny 11 [p. 92]; Quantin II.275 [pp.
244–45]).

Mainard, 1184–1195

John, 1195

Girard, 1196–1202
Became a cardinal (Obit. Sens III:453).

Quincy

Alberic
Abbot in 1135 (GC IV:164, no. 41).

Urban
Abbot in 1145 and 1146 (Quantin II.63 [pp. 66–67]; Arch. Côte-
d'Or, 17 H 620).

Hugh
Abbot in 1154 (PU Berry, pp. 58–59, no. 28).

Warin
Abbot in 1163 (PU Berry, pp. 77–78, no. 44). He may be the
Warin who became abbot of Pontigny (1166–1174).

Walter
Abbot in 1172 (Arch. Yonne, H 2150).

Garmund
Abbot in 1178 (Quantin II.275 [pp. 244–45]). He may be the Garmund Clement who became abbot of Pontigny (1181–1183).

Milo
Abbot in 1192 and 1194 (Auxerre, Bibliothèque municipale, MS
161, fols. 62r–v; Tonnerre, Bibliothèque municipale, MS 40 [on
microfilm at the Arch. Yonne, 1 Mi 395]).

John
Abbot in 1198 (Quantin II.482 [pp. 489–92]).

Reigny

A list of the abbots of Reigny is given in DHGE V:951.

Stephen, 1134–1162
First abbot of Reigny. Before the monks established Reigny they had been at Fontemois, originally a hermitage that in 1127 had become an abbey, under Stephen. Stephen's obituary said that he died at the age of sixty-two. This same source called him "of Toucy" (Quantin I.175 [pp. 299–300]).

Ascelin, 1162–1175
Resigned and became a monk at Pontigny, by 1175 at the latest (Quantin II.251 [pp. 269–70]).

Galo, 1175–1190
Abbot in 1182 and c. 1190 (Quantin II.317 [pp. 335–36]; Arch. Yonne, H 1627).

Helias
Abbot in 1191 and 1200 (Quantin II.427 [p. 431]; Autun/Évêqué 1.133 [p. 137]).

St.-Bénigne of Dijon

The eleventh-century abbots of St.-Bénigne are described by the chronicle of that house, and both the eleventh- and twelfth-century abbots by the briefer "Annales" ("Annales S. Benigni Divionensis," MGH SS V:38–50).

Manasses, 955–987
A terrible abbot according to the chronicle of St.-Bénigne, deposed by Bishop Bruno of Langres (Chron. St.-B., pp. 127, 129).

Azo, 987–989
Originally from Aquitaine. Had been a monk of Montier-en-Der, put into office by Bishop Bruno of Langres. Resigned after two years (Chron. St.-B., p. 130). He died on 1 December (Obit. Sens I:471, 528). He is not mentioned in the thirteenth-century list of abbots of the house (Dijon, Bibliothèque municipale, MS 634, fol. 126r).

William, 990–1031
From Italy. His parents were Robert, the son of the Swabian Vibo, and Perinza, a noble woman of Lombardy (Vita Willelmi 2, p. 463). He had two brothers, Count Nitard and Geoffrey (Chron. St.-B., pp.

154—55). A cousin of Otto-William, count of Burgundy (*Vita Willelmi* 12, p. 471). Had been a monk of Cluny, sent to St.-Bénigne to reform it (Chron. St.-B., pp. 130—49). He died on 1 January (Obit. Sens I:421, 519).

Halinard, 1031—1052
Of a noble family; his father was of the region of Langres and his mother from Autun.[48] A godson of Bishop Walter of Autun. Studied at the Langres cathedral school, before becoming a monk against his parents' wishes. Became prior of St.-Bénigne. Chosen to succeed as abbot by his predecessor William (Chron. St.-B., pp. 178, 182—84). Became archbishop of Lyon while still abbot (1046—1052) (Chron. St.-B., pp. 186—92). Died in Rome on 29 July ("Annales S. Benigni Divionensis" 1052, MGH SS V:42; Obit. Sens I:449).

John, 1052—1054
Had been a monk of St.-Bénigne and abbot of Fécamp (a house reformed by Abbot William). Resigned ("Annales S. Benigni Divionensis," MGH SS V:42).

Adalbero, 1056—1076

Jarenton, 1076—1113
From the region of Vienne. His father Arnold was a knight and his mother Agnes became a nun in her later years. He had studied under Hugh the Great at Cluny. His nephew Itier is remembered in the obituary of St.-Bénigne, as are his parents.[49] Had been prior of Chaise-Dieu. He was selected to succeed Adalbero at the Council of Autun (1076), at the urging of Bishop Hugh-Rainard of Langres and Duke Hugh I of Burgundy (Hugh of Flavigny, *Chronicon*, MGH SS VIII:413, 415; "Annales S. Benigni Divionensis" 1077, MGH SS V:42). He died on 10 February (Obit. Sens I:426, 520).

Ademar, 1113—1116
Perhaps the Abbot Ademar who died on 22 September (Obit. Sens I:458).

Henry, 1116—1122
Resigned ("Annales S. Benigni Divionensis" 1123, MGH SS V:43).

---

[48]Henri de Faget de Casteljau says that he was the son of Warner of Sombernon and his wife Istiburgis, but without evidence; "Les sires de Til-châtel: Feaux de Langres aux marchés des deux Bourgognes, X^e—XVe siècles," *Les cahiers haut-marnais*, 143 (1980), 148.

[49]Dijon, Bibliothèque municipale, MS 632, fols. 129v, 136v, 141r.

Hugh, 1122—1129

His parents were Hugh Berold and Amelia, his brothers Geoffrey and Richard Berold, and his nephews Hugh and Peter Berold. His family seems to have been dependent vassals of the Grossi (the lords of Uxelles) (C 3060, 3574, 3966 [IV:246—47, 768—69; V:326]). Probably related to or identical with the Hugh Berold who was prior of St.-Marcel-lès-Chalon in 1114 (St.-Marcel 75 [pp. 71—72]). Had been a monk of Cluny. Resigned ("Annales S. Benigni" 1123, 1129, MGH SS V:43—44).

Peter I, 1129—1142

From the region of Geneva ("Annales S. Benigni Divionensis" 1129, MGH SS V:44). Went to Santiago with Duke Hugh II of Burgundy (Pérard, p. 222). Resigned ("Annales S. Benigni Divionensis" 1142, MGH SS V:44).

Peter II, 1142—1145

Apparently had been a monk of St.-Étienne of Beaune, which was a dependency of St.-Bénigne, for the "Annales" of St.-Bénigne call him "Belnensis." Resigned ("Annales S. Benigni Divionensis" 1142, 1145, MGH SS V:44).

Philip, 1145—1175

Resigned ("Annales S. Benigni Divionensis" 1175, MGH SS V:45).

John, 1175—1182

A Lombard, who had been a monk at Fruttuaria, a house reformed by St.-Bénigne early in the eleventh century. Resigned ("Annales S. Benigni Divionensis" 1182, MGH SS V:46).

Aimo, 1182—1188

Had been abbot of St.-Seine (1166—1182) ("Annales S. Benigni Divionensis" 1182, MGH SS V:46).

Peter III of Grancey, 1188—1204

Son of Lord Odo I of Grancey, who died as a Templar of Bures, and uncle of Lord Odo II (Petit 881 [III:321-23]; see Appendix A, p. 334). Resigned ("Annales S. Benigni Divionensis" 1204, MGH SS V:47).

St.-Germain of Auxerre

There is a thirteenth-century history of the abbots of St.-Germain which contains some information on the abbots available nowhere else; it is possible that this history incorporates now lost sources from the earlier period. It has not been reedited since the seventeenth century; "De gestibus abbatum S. Germani Autissiodorensis," ed.

Philippe Labbe, *Novae bibliothecae manuscriptorum librorum*, I (Paris, 1657), 570—93. Selections however have been reprinted in RHGF: "Ex gestis abbatum S. Germani Autissiodorensis," RHGF X:296; XI:377; XII:306—7. Waast-Barthélemy Henry wrote a history of the abbey, including its abbots, which contains a number of unfounded statements; *Histoire de l'abbaye de Saint-Germain d'Auxerre* (Auxerre, 1853).

Heldric, 986—1009

A Cluniac monk under Abbot Maiolus, became abbot of St.-Germain when Duke Henry of Burgundy, who had been lay abbot, gave St.-Germain to Cluny to reform (*Gesta pontificum*, pp. 382—83; Quantin I.82 [p. 158]). His biographer said he first held office under Louis V, which would mean in 986 ("Ex gestis abbatum," RHGF X:296). He was at the same time abbot of Flavigny and Moûtier-St.-Jean (Reomaus, p. 174).

Achard, 1010—1020[50]

Theobold, 1020—1032

A monk of St.-Germain before his election (*Gesta pontificum*, p. 389).[51]

Odo, 1032—1052

He was put into office by King Henry, with the consent of Henry's mother, Henry's brother Duke Robert, and their uncle Count Raynald of Nevers ("Ex gestis abbatum," RHGF XI:377).

Boso, 1052—1064

Prior; acted as abbot but never consecrated.

Walter, 1064—1074

Had been a monk of Fleury ("Ex gestis abbatum," RHGF XI:377).[52]

Roland, 1075—1085

Guibert, 1085—1096

Of a noble family, a monk at St.-Germain from boyhood ("Ex gestis abbatum," RHGF XI:377; XII:306). Deposed at the instigation of Bishop Humbald of Auxerre (*Gesta pontificum*, p. 406; "Ex gestis abbatum," RHGF XII:306).[53]

[50]Had been prior according to Henry.
[51]Henry says that he had been prior of Moûtier-St.-Jean.
[52]Henry says that he had been prior of Précy.
[53]For Guibert's deposition and the brief rule of Robert, see also Constance Brittain Bouchard, *Spirituality and Administration: The Role of the Bishop in Twelfth-Century Auxerre*, Speculum Anniversary Monographs 5 (Cambridge, Mass., 1979), pp. 26—28.

Robert, 1096–1100
A somewhat shadowy figure, perhaps the prior of Cluny sent to St.-Germain when the bishop of Auxerre asked for someone to reform the house.

Hugh of Montaigu, 1100–1115
Son of Lord Dalmace of Montaigu, who was a brother of the lord of Semur. A nephew of Hugh the Great, abbot of Cluny, under whom he had been a monk before he became abbot of St.-Germain ("Ex gestis abbatum," RHGF XII:306). Became bishop of Auxerre (1115–1136) (see Appendix B, p. 389).

Gervais, 1115–1148
Of a noble family, according to his biographer. Like his predecessor Hugh, he was a nephew of Hugh the Great, abbot of Cluny, under whom he had first become a monk ("Ex gestis abbatum," RHGF XII:306).

Harduin, 1148–1174
A relative of his predecessor Gervais (*consanguineus*). Of a noble Burgundian family ("Ex gestis abbatum," RHGF XII:307). He died on 11 January (Obit. Sens I:520).

Humbert, 1174–1188
From the region of the Charrolais in Burgundy. Resigned ("Ex gestis abbatum," RHGF XII:307).

Ruldolph, 1188–1208

St.-Seine

Helmuin
Abbot in 1066 (St.-B. II.344 [pp. 123–25]).

Gregory
Abbot in 1093 (Plancher I.43 [pp. xxxi–xxxii]; summarized as Petit 81 [I:408]).

Henry
Abbot in 1107 and 1110 (Chron. St.-B., p. 423; Petit 152 [I:446–47]). He had been a monk at Bèze (Chron. St.-B., p. 383). He may be the same Henry who became abbot of St.-Bénigne (1116–1122).

Warner
Abbot in 1127 (GC IV:160, no. 37).

Herbert
  Abbot in 1134 and 1140 (GC IV:89–90, no. 55; 170, no. 47).

Richard
  Abbot in 1152 and 1155 (Petit 335 [II:257–59]; Arch. Haute-
Marne, 10 H 8).

Ayrad
  Abbot in 1163 (Petit 401 [II:292]).

Aimo, 1166–1182
  Became abbot of St.-Bénigne of Dijon (1182–1188), where he had
originally been a monk ("Annales Sancti Benigni Divionensis" 1182,
MGH SS V:46).

Nivard, 1182–1204
  Both Pérard (p. 265) and the editors of GC added another abbot,
named Halinard or Monard, as abbot after 1186, but this is because
they misread the thirteenth-century cartulary of St.-Seine, in which
the initial N is written almost like an M or H. Nivard was still abbot
between 1194 and 1200 (St.-Seine, p. 266; Plancher I.156 [pp.
lxxxxii–lxxxxiii]). He became abbot of St.-Bénigne in 1204 (Dijon,
Bibliothèque municipale, MS 591, fol. 137; "Annales S. Benigni
Divionensis" 1204, MGH SS V:47).

Tournus

Odo
  Abbot in 989 (Tournus, p. 120)

Wago

Berno

Ardagnus
  Abbot in 1037 (Tournus, p. 125)

William

Gerald
  Abbot in 1064 (GC XII:328, no. 36).

Peter I
  Abbot in 1075 and 1097 (Tournus, pp. 130–31; C 3726
[V:75–77]). Died in 1108 (Tournus, pp. 139–40).

William
   Abbot in 1108 (C 3869 [V:220–23]).

Franco

Theoderic

Peter II
   Uncle of Hugh of Beaufort (Tournus, pp. 161–63). Abbot in 1132
(PU Burgund, pp. 23–26, no. 4) and 1152 (Cartulary no. 44,
Chronique 1, Vézelay, pp. 343, 408).

Letbald
   Abbot in 1171 (Tournus, p. 169). Died on 8 March (Obit. Sens
I:429, 521).

Robert
   Resigned.[54]

Girard
   Abbot in 1179 (Alexander III, Letter 1411, PL CC:1225).

Joceran

P.
   Abbot in 1193 (La Bussière 3.5 [fols. 25r–v]).

Vézelay

   The dates of the abbots of Vézelay are known primarily from the
"Annales Vizeliacenses" (Vézelay, pp. 195–233).

Eldrad, 956–998

Robert, 999–1008

Evrard, 1008–1011

Herman, 1011–1037

Geoffrey, 1037–1068

Boniface, 1068–1075
   He died on 12 September (Obit. Sens I:526).

---

[54]Stanley Chodorow and Charles Duggan, eds., *Decretales ineditae saeculi XII*, Monumenta iuris canonici, ser. B, 4 (Vatican City, 1982), p. 4, no. 3.

Berno, 1075–1083
He died on 19 July (Obit. Sens I:447, 525).

Stephen, 1083–1088

Joceran, 1088–1096

Artald, 1096–1106
Murdered (Cartulary no. 19, Vézelay, p. 302).

Raynald of Semur, 1106–1125
Son of Geoffrey III of Semur. He entered Cluny with his parents
and sisters in 1088 (Marcigny 15, 111 [pp. 16, 81–82]; see also
Appendix A, p. 361). Became archbishop of Lyon (1125–1128)
(*Chronique* 2, Vézelay, p. 421; Peter the Venerable, *Miracula* 1.26, PL
CLXXXIX:898–900).

Baldwin, 1125–1129

Girard, 1130

Alberic, 1131–1138
Had been sub-prior of Cluny, put into office at Vézelay by the pope
(Cartulary no. 20, Vézelay, p. 304). Became cardinal bishop of Ostia
and papal legate ("Annales Vizeliacenses" 1138, Cartulary no. 34;
Vézelay, pp. 226, 327).

Ponce, 1138–1161
Sometimes called "the Venerable." Brother of Peter the Venerable
of Cluny and of Jordan, abbot of Chaise-Dieu ("Annales Vizeliacenses" 1138, *Chronique* 1, Vézelay, pp. 226, 396). (For more
detail, see above, p. 411.) Joined by *cognationis affinitate* to William
III, count of Nevers (*Chronique* 2, Vézelay, p. 424).

William of Mello, 1161–1171
Of the noble family of the lords of Mello, uncle of William and
Raynald (*Chronique* 4, Vézelay, p. 582). Had been abbot of St.-Martin
of Pontoise (*Chronique* 3, Vézelay, p. 514).

Girard of Arcy, 1171–1198
Brother of Geoffrey, lord of Arcy (Quantin II.304 [pp. 324–25]).
A *consanguineus* of William of Toucy, bishop of Auxerre (1167–1181)
(*Gesta pontificum*, p. 428).

Printed Sources

The following list of printed sources is normally arranged by title rather than editor, in the case of a cartulary, and medieval author rather than modern editor, in the case of a chronicle. An exception is made, however, in cases where an editor compiled his material from diverse sources. A few secondary sources useful primarily for the charters printed in them are also included. I have not repeated the titles of the monumental collections given in the Abbreviations, or the manuscript sources listed there. As in the Selected Bibliography, I have omitted a few sources that I cited only once and which are only tangential to the themes of this book.

Adalbero of Laon. "Carmen ad Rotbertum regem." Edited by Claude Carozzi. *Poème au roi Robert.* Classiques de l'histoire de France au moyen âge 32. Paris, 1979.
———. *Rhythmus satyricus.* Edited by Claude Hohl. "Le comtc Landri de Nevers dans l'histoire et dans la Geste de *Girart de Roussillon.*" In *La chanson de geste et le mythe carolingien. Mélanges René Louis.* St.-Père-sous-Vézelay, 1982.
Alain. *Epistolae.* PL CCI:1383—86.
———. *Vita secunda Sancti Bernardi.* PL CLXXXV:469—524.
Alberic of Aix. *Historia Hierosolymitanae expeditionis.* PL CLXVI:389—716.
Alberic de Trois-Fontaines. *Chronica.* MGH SS XXIII:674—950.
Annales monasterii de Waverleia. Edited by Henry Richard Luard. Rerum Brittanicarum medii aevi scriptores 36, 2. London, 1865.
"Annales Nivernenses." MGH SS XIII:88—92.
"Annales S. Benigni Divionensis." MGH SS V:38—50.
Anselm of St.-Remi. "Historia dedicationis ecclesiae Sancti Remigii." PL CXLII:1415—40.
Bazin, J. Louis. *Brancion: Les seigneurs, la paroisse, la ville.* Paris, 1908.
Benedict VIII. *Epistolae.* PL CXXXIX:1579—1658.
Bernard of Clairvaux. *Opera.* Edited by Jean Leclercq and Henri Rochais. Rome, 1957—.

La "Bible" au seigneur de Berzé. Edited by Félix Lecoy. Paris, 1938.

Bibliotheca Cluniacensis. Edited by Martin Marrier and André Quercetanus [Duchesne]. 1614; reprint Mâcon, 1915.

Bouton, Jean de la Croix; and Van Damme, Jean Baptiste, eds. *Les plus anciens textes de Cîteaux.* Commentarii Cistercienses, Studia et Documenta 2. Achel, 1974.

Bulliot, J.-Gabriel, ed. *Essai historique sur l'abbaye de Saint-Martin d'Autun.* Vol. II, *Chartes et pièces justificatives.* Autun, 1849.

Calixtus II. *Epistolae.* PL CLXIII:1093–1338.

Canivez, Josephus-Maria, ed. *Statuta capitulorum generalium ordinis Cisterciensis.* Vol. I. Bibliothèque de la Revue d'histoire ecclésiastique 9. Louvain, 1933.

Cartulaire de Brioude. Edited by Henry Doniol. Clermont, 1863.

Cartulaire de l'abbaye de Saint-André-le-Bas de Vienne. Edited by C.-U.-J. Chevalier. Vienne and Lyon, 1869.

Cartulaire de l'abbaye de Savigny. Edited by Auguste Bernard. Paris, 1853.

Cartulaire de l'église collégiale Notre-Dame de Beaujeu, suivi d'un appendice et d'un tableau généalogique de la maison de Beaujeu. Edited by M.-C. Guigue. Lyon, 1864.

Cartulaire de l'église d'Apt (835–1130?). Edited by Noël Didier. Paris, 1967.

Cartulaire de l'église d'Autun. Edited by Anatole de Charmasse. 2 vols. Paris, 1865–1900.

Cartulaire de l'évêché d'Autun. Edited by Anatole de Charmasse. Autun, 1880.

Le cartulaire de Marcigny-sur-Loire (1045–1144). Essai de reconstitution d'un manuscrit disparu. Edited by Jean Richard. Dijon, 1957.

Cartulaire de Saint-Cyr de Nevers. Edited by René de Lespinasse. Nevers, 1916.

Cartulaire de Saint-Vincent de Mâcon. Edited by M.-C. Ragut. Mâcon, 1864.

Cartulaire des comtes de Bourgogne (1166–1321). Edited by M.-J. Gauthier. Mémoires et documents inédits pour servir à l'histoire de la Franche-Comté 8. Besançon, 1908.

"Cartulaire du prieuré de Jully-les-Nonnains." Edited by Ernest Petit. *Bulletin de la Société des sciences historiques et naturelles de l'Yonne,* 34 (1880), 249–302.

Cartulaire du prieuré de La Charité-sur-Loire. Edited by René de Lespinasse. Nevers, 1887.

Cartulaire du prieuré de Paray-le-monial. Edited by Ulysse Chevalier. Paris, 1890.

Cartulaire du prieuré de Saint-Marcel-lès-Chalon. Edited by Marcel and Paul Canat de Chizy. Chalon, 1894.

Cartulaire du prieuré de Vignory. Edited by J. d'Arbaumont. Langres, 1882.

Cartulaire noir de la cathédrale d'Angers. Edited by Ch. Urseau. Paris, 1908.

Cartulaires de l'abbaye de Molesme. Edited by Jacques Laurent. 2 vols. Paris, 1907–1911.

"Catalogue des actes de l'hôpital de Morment (1121–1302)." Edited by Odile Grandmottet. *Cahiers haut-marnais,* 62/63 (1960), 99–175.

"Chartes de l'abbaye de Corbigny." Edited by Anatole de Charmasse. *Mémoires de la Société Eduenne,* n.s. 17 (1889), 1–39.

"Chartes de l'abbaye de Mores." Edited by Charles Lalore. *Mémoires de la Société académique d'agriculture, des sciences, arts et belles-lettres du département de l'Aube*, 37 (1873), 5–107.

Chartes de l'abbaye de Saint-Étienne de Dijon (VIIIᵉ, IXᵉ, Xᵉ et XIᵉ siècles). Edited by J. Courtois. Paris and Dijon, 1908.

Chartes de l'abbaye de Saint-Étienne de Dijon de 1098 à 1140. Edited by Adrien Bièvre Poulalier. Dijon, 1912.

Chartes de l'abbaye de Saint-Étienne de Dijon de 1140 à 1155. Edited by M. Bourrier. Paris and Dijon, 1912.

Chartes de l'abbaye de Saint-Étienne de Dijon de 1155 à 1200. Edited by Georges Valat. Paris and Dijon, 1907.

"Chartes de l'église Saint-Pierre de Tonnerre." Edited by M. Jolivot. *Bulletin de la Société des sciences historiques et naturelles de l'Yonne*, 36 (1882), 191–94.

"Les chartes de Saint-Étienne de Nevers." Edited by René de Lespinasse. *Bulletin de la Société nivernaise des lettres, sciences et arts*, 3rd ser., 12 (1908), 76–130.

Chartes et documents concernant l'abbaye de Cîteaux, 1098–1182. Edited by J. Marilier. Rome, 1961.

Chartes et documents de Saint-Bénigne de Dijon (990–1124). Edited by Georges Chevrier and Maurice Chaume. Dijon, 1943.

Chastellux, H.-P.-C. de, ed. *Histoire généalogique de la maison de Chastellux*. Auxerre, 1869.

Chifflet, Pierre-François, ed. *Lettre touchant Beatrix, comtesse de Chalon*. Dijon, 1656.

——, ed. *S. Bernardi Clarevallensis abbatis genus illustre assertum*. Dijon, 1660.

"Chronicon Clarevallense." PL CLXXXV:1247–52.

Chronique de l'abbaye de Saint-Bénigne de Dijon, suivie de la Chronique de Saint-Pierre de Bèze. Edited by E. Bougaud and Joseph Garnier. Analecta Divionensia 9. Dijon, 1875.

La chronique de Saint-Maixent, 751–1140. Edited by Jean Verdon. Les classiques de l'histoire de France au moyen âge 33. Paris, 1979.

Chronique de Saint-Pierre-le-Vif de Sens, dite de Clarius. Edited by Robert-Henri Bautier and Monique Gilles. Paris, 1979.

Chroniques des comtes d'Anjou et des seigneurs d'Amboise. Edited by Louis Halphen and René Poupardin. Paris, 1913.

Consuetudines Cluniacensium antiquiores cum redactionibus derivatis. Edited by Kassius Hallinger. Corpus consuetudinum monasticarum 7, 2. Sieburg, 1983.

Cowdrey, H. E. J. "Two Studies in Cluniac History, 1049–1126." *Studi Gregoriani*, 11 (1978), 1–297.

D'Arbois de Jubainville, H. *Histoire des ducs et des comtes de Champagne*. 6 vols. Paris, 1859–1886.

"De gestibus abbatum S. Germani Autissiodorensis." Edited by Philippe Labbe. In *Novae bibliothecae manuscriptorum librorum*. Vol. I. Paris, 1657.

Dubois, Louis. *Histoire de l'abbaye de Morimond*. Paris, 1851.

Duchesne, André. *Histoire généalogique de la maison de Vergy*. Paris, 1625.

Dumay, Gabriel. "Les origines de la maison de Pontailler. Les sires de

Talmay (1125–1385). Documents et pieces justificatives." *Mémoires de la Société bourguignonne de géographie et d'histoire*, 26 (1910), 221–352.

Eugenius III. *Epistolae.* PL CLXXX:1013–1614.

"Ex historia praelatorum B. Mariae de Fontanis." RHGF XIV:494–98.

"Ex Vita B. Stephani Obazinensis abbatis." RHGF XIV:332–33.

Flodoard. *Annales.* Edited by Ph. Lauer. Paris, 1905.

Fulcher of Chartres. *Historia Hierosolymitana (1095–1127).* Edited by Heinrich Hagenmeyer. Heidelberg, 1913.

Garnier, Joseph, ed. "Chartes bourguignonnes inédits des IXe, X^e et XIe siècles." *Mémoires présentés par divers savants à l'Académie des inscriptions et belles-lettres de l'Institut national de France*, 2nd ser., 2 (1849), 1–168.

"Genealogiae Fusniacenses." MGH SS XIII:251–56.

Geoffrey of Clairvaux. *Vita tertia S. Bernardi.* PL CLXXXV:523–30.

Geoffrey of Vigeois. *Chronicon.* RHGF XII:421–51.

Gesta pontificum Autissiodorensium. Edited by L.-M. Duru. In *Bibliothèque historique de l'Yonne.* Vol. I. Auxerre, 1850.

Le grand cartulaire du chapitre cathédral de Langres. Edited by Hubert Flammarion. 2 vols. Diss., Université de Nancy II, 1980.

Guichard, Georges; Comte de Neufbourg; Perroy, Édouard; and Dufour, J.-E., eds. *Chartes du Forez.* Vol. I. Mâcon, 1933.

Guigue, M.-C., ed. *Cartulaire Lyonnais.* Vol. I. Lyon, 1885.

Hermann. "Liber de restauratione S. Martini Tornacensio." MGH SS XIV:274–317.

Hildebert of Le Mans. "Vita Hugonis abbatis." PL CLIX:857–94.

"Historia translatio reliquorum S. Mamantis." RHGF XI:482–83.

Hlawitschka, Eduard. *Studien zur Äbtissinnenreihe von Remiremont (7.–13. Jh.).* Saarbrücken, 1963.

Hugh of Flavigny. *Chronicon.* MGH SS VIII:280–502.

——. "Series abbatum Flaviniacensium." MGH SS VIII:502–3.

Innocent III. *Regesta sive epistolae.* PL CCXIV–CCXVI.

Ivo of Chartres. *Epistolae.* PL CLXII:11–288.

Jobin, Abbé. *Saint Bernard et sa famille.* Paris, 1891.

John the Hermit. *Vita quarta Sancti Bernardi.* PL CLXXXV:531–50.

Lalore, Abbé Ch., ed. *Collection des principaux cartulaires du diocèse de Troyes.* 7 vols. Paris, 1875–1890.

Lebeuf, Abbé. *Mémoires concernant l'histoire civile et ecclésiastique d'Auxerre et de son ancien diocèse.* New edition by M. Challe and Maximilien Quantin. 4 vols. Auxerre, 1848–1855.

Louis VI. *Epistolae.* RHGF XV:338–44.

Louis VII. *Epistolae.* RHGF XVI:1–170.

Marion, Jules. "Notice sur l'abbaye de La Bussière." *Bibliothèque de l'École des chartes*, 4 (1842/43), 549–63.

Mehne, Joachim. "Eine Totenliste aus Saint-Martin-des-Champs." *Frühmittelalterliche Studien*, 10 (1976), 212–47.

Meinert, Hermann, ed. *Papsturkunden in Frankreich, neue Folge.* Vol. I, *Champagne und Lothringen.* 2 vols. Abhandlungen der Akademie der Wissenschaften in Göttingen, Philogisch-historische Klasse, 3rd ser., 3–4. Göttingen, 1932–33; reprint 1972.

Les miracles de Saint Benoît. Edited by E. de Certain. Paris, 1858.

Monumenta Vizeliacensia. Textes relatifs à l'histoire de l'abbaye de Vézelay. Edited by R. B. C. Huygens. Corpus Christianorum continuatio mediaevalis 42. Turnhout, 1976.

Monuments de l'histoire des abbayes de Saint-Philibert (Noirmoutier, Grandlieu, Tournus). Edited by Arthur Giry and René Poupardin. Paris, 1905.

Nouvelle histoire de l'abbaie de Saint-Filibert et de la ville de Tournus. Vol. II, *Preuves.* Edited by Pierre Juénin. Dijon, 1733.

Obituaires de la province de Lyon. Vol. I, *Diocèse de Lyon, première partie.* Edited by Georges Guigue and Jacques Laurent. Paris, 1933.

Obituaires de la province de Lyon. Vol. II, *Diocèse de Lyon, deuxième partie, diocèses de Mâcon et de Chalon-sur-Saône.* Edited by Jacques Laurent and Pierre Gras. Paris, 1965.

Obituaires de la province de Sens. Vol. I, *Diocèses de Sens et de Paris.* Edited by Auguste Molinier. Paris, 1902.

Obituaires de la province de Sens. Vol. III, *Diocèses d'Orléans, d'Auxerre, et de Nevers.* Edited by Alexandre Vidier and Léon Mirot. Paris, 1909.

Obituaires de la province de Sens. Vol. IV, *Diocèses de Meaux et de Troyes.* Edited by M. Boutillier du Retail and M. Piétresson de Saint-Aubin. Paris, 1923.

Odo of Deuil. *De profectione Ludovici VII in Orientem.* Edited by Virginia Gingerick Berry. New York, 1948.

Odorannus of Sens. *Opera omnia.* Edited by Robert-Henri Bautier and Monique Gilles. Paris, 1972.

Orderic Vitalis. *Historia ecclesiastica.* Edited by Marjorie Chibnall. 6 vols. Oxford, 1969–1980.

Pérard, Estienne, ed. *Recueil de plusieurs pièces curieuses servant à l'histoire de Bourgogne.* Paris, 1664.

Peter of Celle. *Epistolae.* PL CCII:405–630.

Peter of Poitiers. "Panegyricus Petro Venerabili." PL CLXXXIX:47–58.

Peter the Venerable. *The Letters of Peter the Venerable.* Edited by Giles Constable. Harvard Historical Series 78. Cambridge, Mass., 1967.

———. *Miracula.* PL CLXXXIX:851–954.

———. *Statuta.* PL CLXXXIX:1025–48.

Petit, Ernest, ed. *Histoire des ducs de Bourgogne de la race capétienne.* 6 vols. Paris and Dijon, 1885–1898.

Pflugk-Harttung, J. v., ed. *Acta pontificum Romanorum inedita.* 3 vols. Tübingen, 1881–1886; reprint Graz, 1958.

Plancher, Urbain, ed. *Histoire générale et particulière de Bourgogne.* 4 vols. Dijon, 1739–1781; reprint Farnborough, England, 1968.

Le premier cartulaire de l'abbaye cistercienne de Pontigny (XIIe–XIIIe siècles). Edited by Martine Garrigues. Collection de documents inédits sur l'histoire de France 14. Paris, 1981.

Quantin, Maximilien, ed. *Cartulaire général de l'Yonne.* 2 vols. Auxerre, 1854–1860.

———, ed. *Recueil de pièces pour faire suite au Cartulaire général de l'Yonne.* Auxerre, 1873.

———, ed. "Une sentence de Guillaume Ier, comte de Nevers, de l'an 1106." *Bulletin de la Société des sciences historiques et naturelles de l'Yonne,* 40 (1886), 231–34.

Radulf. "Vita Petri Venerabilis." PL CLXXXIX:15—28.

Raoul Glaber. *Historia*. Edited by Maurice Prou. Paris, 1886.

——. *Vita Willelmi*. Edited by Niethard Bulst. "Rodulphus Glabers Vita domni Willemi abbatis. Neue Edition." *Deutsches Archiv für Erforschung des Mittelalters*, 30 (1974), 462—87.

Recueil des actes de Philippe Ier, roi de France (1059—1108). Edited by M. Prou. Paris, 1908.

Recueil des actes du prieuré de Saint-Symphorien d'Autun de 696 à 1300. Edited by André Déléage. Autun, 1936.

Recueil des chartes de l'abbaye de Clairvaux, XIIe siècle. Fascicule I. Edited by Jean Waquet. [Troyes, 1950].

Recueil des chartes de l'abbaye de Clairvaux, XIIe siècle. Fascicule II. Edited by Jean Waquet, Jean-Marc Roger, and Philippe Grand. Troyes, 1982.

Recueil des chartes de l'abbaye de Cluny. Edited by Auguste Bernard and Alexandre Bruel. 6 vols. Paris, 1876—1903.

Recueil des chartes de l'abbaye de Saint-Benoît-sur-Loire. Edited by Maurice Prou and Alexandre Vidier. 2 vols. Paris, 1900—1937.

Recueil des chartes de l'abbaye de Saint-Germain-des-Prés des origines au début du XIIIe siècle. Edited by René Poupardin. 2 vols. Paris, 1909—1930.

Recueil des pancartes de l'abbaye de La Ferté-sur-Grosne, 1113—1178. Edited by Georges Duby. Paris, 1953.

Robert of Mont-St.-Michel. *Chronica*. MGH SS VI:475—535.

Robert of St.-Marien. *Chronicon*. MGH SS XXVI:226—87.

Roger, Jean-Marc. "Trois actes d'Hughes I Morhier pour l'abbaye de Clairvaux (1199—1206, v. st.)." *Cahiers haut-marnais*, 109 (1972), 57—64.

Roverius, Petrus, ed. *Reomaus, seu Historia Monasterii S. Joannis Reomaensis*. Paris, 1637.

Schieffer, Theodor, ed. *Die Urkunden der burgundischen Rudolfinger*. Munich: MGH, 1977.

Simon. "Gesta abbatum Sancti Bertini Sithiensium." MGH SS XIII:635—63.

Soultrait, Cte. de, ed. *Inventaire des titres de Nevers*. Nevers, 1873.

Suger. *Epistolae*. RHGF XV:483—532.

——. *Vita Ludovici Grossi regis*. Edited by Henri Waquet. Paris, 1929.

Syro. *Vita Sancti Maioli*. PL CXXXVII:745—78.

"Testament de Guichard III de Beaujeu." Edited by M.-C. Guigue. *Bibliothèque de l'École des chartes*, 18 (1856/7), 161—67.

Urban II. "Sermones." PL CLI:561—82.

Urban III. *Epistolae*. PL CCII:1331—1534.

Vizeliacensia II. Textes relatifs à l'histoire de l'abbaye de Vézelay. Edited by R. B. C. Huygens. Corpus Christianorum continuatio mediaevalis 42 supplementum. Turnhout, 1980.

Wiederhold, Wilhelm, ed. *Papsturkunden in Frankreich*. Vol. I, *Franche-Comté*. Nachrichten von der Königlichen Gesellschaft der Wissenschaften zu Göttingen, Philologisch-historische Klasse. Göttingen, 1906; reprint 1967.

——, ed. *Papsturkunden in Frankreich*. Vol. II, *Burgund mit Bresse und Bugey*. Nachrichten von der Königlichen Gesellschaft der Wissenschaften zu Göttingen, Philologisch-historische Klasse. Göttingen, 1906; reprint 1967.

——, ed. *Papsturkunden in Frankreich*. Vol. V, *Berry, Bourbonnais, Nivernais und Auxerrois*. Nachrichten von der Königlichen Gesellschaft der Wissenschaften zu Göttingen, Philologisch-historische Klasse. Berlin, 1910.

William of Jumièges. *Gesta normannorum ducum*. Edited by Jean Marx. Paris, 1914.

William of St.-Thierry. *Vita prima Sancti Bernardi*. PL CLXXXV:226–477.

Selected Bibliography

The following bibliography contains only books and articles directly pertinent to the themes of this book; I have not included works that I cited only once and which treat the issues of eleventh- and twelfth-century Burgundy, nobility, and monasticism only peripherally. If I cited several articles out of a book of collected articles, I here give the title of the volume but not of the individual articles; individual titles will be found in the footnotes.

Amargier, P.-A. "La capture de Saint Maieul de Cluny et l'expulsion des Sarrasins de Provence." *Revue Bénédictine*, 73 (1963), 316–23.

Atsma, Hartmut. "Les monastères urbaines du nord de la Gaule." *Revue d'histoire de l'Église de France*, 62 (1976), 163–87.

Bazin, J. Louis. *Les comtes héréditaires de Chalon-sur-Saône (880–1234)*. Mémoires de la Société d'histoire et d'archéologie de Chalon-sur-Saône, n.s. 4. Chalon, 1911.

———. *Histoire des évêques de Chalon-sur-Saône*. Mémoires de la Société d'histoire et d'archéologie de Chalon-sur-Saône, n.s. 6. Chalon, 1914.

Beech, George T. *A Rural Society in Medieval France: The Gâtine of Poitou in the Eleventh and Twelfth Centuries*. Baltimore, 1964.

Benedictine Culture, 750–1050. Edited by W. Lourdaux and D. Verhelst. Mediaevalia Lovaniensia, Studia 11. Louvain, 1983.

Benson, Robert L. *The Bishop-Elect*. Princeton, 1968.

Berlow, Rosalind Kent. "Spiritual Immunity at Vézelay (Ninth to Twelfth Centuries)." *Catholic Historical Review*, 62 (1976), 573–88.

Berman, Constance H. "Cistercian Development and the Order's Acquisition of Churches and Tithes in Southwestern France." *Revue Bénédictine*, 91 (1981), 193–203.

———. "Land Acquisition and the Use of Mortgage Contract by the Cistercians of Berdoues." *Speculum*, 57 (1982), 250–66.

Bernard de Clairvaux. Edited by the Commission d'histoire de l'ordre de Cîteaux. Paris, 1953.

Bienvenu, Jean-Marc. "Robert d'Arbrissel et la fondation de Fontevraud (1101)." *Cahiers d'histoire*, 20 (1975), 227–43.

Bligny, Bernard. "L'Église et le siècle de l'an mil au début du XIIe siècle." *Cahiers de civilisation médiévale*, 27 (1984), 5–33.

_____. *L'Église et les ordres religieux dans le royaume de Bourgogne aux XIe et XIIe siècles.* Paris, 1960.

_____. "Le royaume de Bourgogne." In *Karl der Grosse, Lebenswerk und Nachleben.* Vol. I. Edited by Wolfgang Braunfels. Düsseldorf, 1965.

Boissard, Jean-Marc. "Structures et attributions du chapitre cathédral de Chalon-sur-Saône du milieu du XIIe au milieu du XIVe siècle." *Mémoires de la Société d'histoire et d'archéologie de Chalon-sur-Saône*, 42 (1970/71), 89–140.

Bolton, Brenda M. "Paupertas Christi: Old Wealth and New Poverty in the Twelfth Century." In *Renaissance and Renewal in Christian History.* Edited by Derek Baker. Studies in Church History 14. Oxford, 1977.

Bouchard, Constance B. "Changing Abbatial Tenure Patterns in Burgundian Monasteries during the Twelfth Century." *Revue Bénédictine*, 90 (1980), 249–62.

_____. "Consanguinity and Noble Marriages in the Tenth and Eleventh Centuries." *Speculum*, 56 (1981), 268–87.

_____. "The Geographical, Social and Ecclesiastical Origins of the Bishops of Auxerre and Sens in the Central Middle Ages." *Church History*, 46 (1977), 277–95.

_____. "Laymen and Church Reform around the Year 1000: The Case of Otto-William, Count of Burgundy." *Journal of Medieval History*, 5 (1979), 1–10.

_____. "Noble Piety and Reformed Monasticism: The Dukes of Burgundy in the Twelfth Century." In *Noble Piety and Reformed Monasticism: Studies in Medieval Cistercian History VII.* Edited by E. Rozanne Elder. Kalamazoo, Mich., 1981.

_____. "The Origins of the French Nobility: A Reassessment." *American Historical Review*, 86 (1981), 501–32.

_____. "Property Transactions and the Twelfth-Century Cistercians." In *Proceedings of the Eleventh Annual Meeting of the Western Society for French History.* Edited by John F. Sweets. Lawrence, Kans., 1984.

_____. *Spirituality and Administration: The Role of the Bishop in Twelfth-Century Auxerre.* Speculum Anniversary Monographs 5. Cambridge, Mass., 1979.

_____. "The Structure of a Twelfth-Century French Family: The Lords of Seignelay." *Viator*, 10 (1979), 39–56.

Boussard, Jacques. "Les évêques en Neustrie avant la réforme grégorienne (950–1050 environ)." *Journal des savants*, 1970, pp. 161–96.

Brooke, C. N. L. "Gregorian Reform in Action: Clerical Marriage in England, 1050–1200." *Cambridge Historical Journal*, 12 (1956), 1–21.

Bulst, Niethard. *Untersuchungen zu den Klosterreform Wilhelms von Dijon (962–1031).* Pariser historische Studien 11. Bonn, 1973.

Bumke, Joachim. *The Concept of Knighthood in the Middle Ages.* Translated by W. T. H. and Erika Jackson. New York, 1982.

Bynum, Caroline Walker. "Did the Twelfth Century Discover the Individual?" *Journal of Ecclesiastical History*, 31 (1980), 1–17.

———. *Docere verbo et exemplo: An Aspect of Twelfth-Century Spirituality.* Harvard Theological Studies 31. Missoula, Mont., 1979.

———. "The Spirituality of Regular Canons in the Twelfth Century: A New Approach." *Medievalia et Humanistica,* n.s., 4 (1973), 3—24.

Cantarella, Glauco M. "Due note cluniacensi." *Studi medievali,* 3rd ser., 16 (1975), 763—80.

Carozzi, Claude. "Les fondements de la tripartition sociale chez Adalbéron de Laon." *Annales: Économies, Sociétés, Civilisations,* 33 (1978), 683—702.

Chandler, Victoria. "Politics and Piety: Influences on Charitable Donations during the Anglo-Norman Period." *Revue Bénédictine,* 90 (1980), 63—71.

Chaume, Maurice. "Observations sur la chronologie des chartes de l'abbaye de Cluny." *Revue Mabillon,* 16 (1926), 44—48; 29 (1939), 81—89, 133—42; 31 (1941), 14—29, 42—45, 69—82; 32 (1942), 15—20, 133—36; 38 (1948), 1—6; 39 (1949), 41—43; 42 (1952), 1—4.

———. *Les origines du duché de Bourgogne.* 2 vols. Dijon, 1925—1931; reprint 1977.

———. "Un problème de droit féodale: La succession de Chalon en 1080." *Mémoires de la Société pour l'histoire du droit et des institutions des anciens pays bourguignons, comtois et romands,* 2 (1935), 177—79.

———. *Recherches d'histoire chrétienne et médiévale.* Dijon, 1947.

Chauney, Martine. "Deux évêques bourguignons de l'an mil: Brunon de Langres et Hughes Ier d'Auxerre." *Cahiers de civilisation médiévale,* 21 (1978), 385—93.

———. "Les origines du prieuré clunisien de Saint-Marcel-lès-Chalon." In *Mélanges d'histoire et d'archéologie offerts au professeur Kenneth John Conant.* Mâcon, 1977.

———. "Le recrutement de l'épiscopat bourguignon aux XIe et XIIe siècles." *Annales de Bourgogne,* 47 (1975), 193—212.

Chenu, M.-D. *Nature, Man, and Society in the Twelfth Century.* Edited and translated by Jerome Taylor and Lester K. Little. Chicago, 1968.

Chevalier, Bernard. "Les restitutions d'églises dans le diocèse de Tours du Xe au XIIe siècle." In *Études de civilisation médiévale (IXe—XIIe siècle): Mélanges offerts à Edmond-René Labande.* Poitiers, 1974.

Cheyette, Fredric L. "Suum cuique tribuere." *French Historical Studies,* 6 (1970), 287—99.

Cistercian Ideals and Reality. Edited by John R. Sommerfeldt. Cistercian Studies Series 60. Kalamazoo, Mich., 1978.

Cluniac Monasticism in the Central Middle Ages. Edited by Noreen Hunt. London, 1971.

Constable, Giles. "Cluniac Administration and Administrators in the Twelfth Century." In *Order and Innovation in the Middle Ages: Essays in Honor of Joseph R. Strayer.* Edited by William C. Jordan, Bruce McNab, and Teofilo F. Ruiz. Princeton, 1976.

———. "The Disputed Election at Langres in 1138." *Traditio,* 13 (1957), 119—52.

———. "Monastic Possession of Churches and 'Spiritualia' in the Age of Reform." In *Il monachesimo e la riforma ecclesiastica (1049—1122).* Miscellanea del Centro di studi medioevali 6. Milan, 1971.

_____. *Monastic Tithes from Their Origins to the Twelfth Century.* Cambridge, England, 1964.

_____. "The Study of Monastic History Today." In *Essays on the Reconstruction of Medieval History.* Edited by Vaclav Mudroch and G. S. Couse. Montreal, 1974.

_____. "Twelfth-Century Spirituality and the Late Middle Ages." *Medieval and Renaissance Studies*, 5 (1969), 27–60.

Coolidge, Robert T. "Adalbero, Bishop of Laon." *Studies in Medieval and Renaissance History*, 2 (1965), 1–114.

Cowdrey, H. E. J. *The Cluniacs and the Gregorian Reform.* Oxford, 1970.

_____. "The Peace and the Truce of God in the Eleventh Century." *Past and Present*, 46 (1970), 42–67.

Dalarun, Jacques. *L'impossible sainteté: La vie retrouvée de Robert d'Arbrissel (v. 1045–1116), fondateur de Fontevraud.* Paris, 1985.

Défourneaux, Marcelin. *Les français en Espagne aux XIe et XIIe siècles.* Paris, 1949.

Devailly, Guy. "Les grandes familles et l'épiscopat dans l'ouest de la France et les Pays de la Loire." *Cahiers de civilisation médiévale*, 27 (1984), 49–55.

Didier, Jean-Charles. "Hughes de Breteuil, évêque de Langres († 1050)." *Recherches augustiniennes*, 16 (1981), 289–331.

Dormeier, Heinrich. *Montecassino und die Laien im 11. und 12. Jahrhundert.* Schriften der Monumenta Germaniae historica 27. Stuttgart, 1979.

Duby, Georges. "Les chanoines réguliers et la vie économique des XIe et XIIe siècles." In *La vita comune del clero nei secoli XI e XII.* Miscellanea del Centro di studi medioevali 3. Milan, 1962.

_____. *The Chivalrous Society.* Translated by Cynthia Postan. Berkeley and Los Angeles, 1977.

_____. *The Early Growth of the European Economy: Warriors and Peasants from the Seventh to the Twelfth Century.* Translated by Howard B. Clarke. Ithaca, 1974.

_____. *The Knight, the Lady and the Priest: The Making of Modern Marriage in Medieval France.* Translated by Barbara Bray. New York, 1983.

_____. *La société aux XIe et XIIe siècles dans la région mâconnaise.* 2nd ed. Paris, 1971.

_____. *The Three Orders: Feudal Society Imagined.* Translated by Arthur Goldhammer. Chicago, 1980.

Duchesne, André. *Histoire des roys, ducs, et comtes de Bourgogne et d'Arles.* Paris, 1619.

Evergates, Theodore. *Feudal Society in the Bailliage of Troyes under the Counts of Champagne, 1152–1284.* Baltimore, 1975.

Faget de Casteljau, H. de. "Recherches sur la maison de Choiseul." *Cahiers haut-marnais*, 102 (1970), 147–55; 105 (1971), 143–55; 107 (1971), 245–56; 110 (1972), 154–63.

_____. "Les sires de Til-châtel: Feaux de Langres aux marchés des deux Bourgognes, Xe–XVe siècles." *Les cahiers haut-marnais*, 143 (1980), 145–59.

Fechter, Johannes. *Cluny, Adel und Volk.* Diss., University of Tübingen, 1966.

Flammarion, Hubert. "Clefmont: Une maison comtale aux confins de la

Bourgogne, de la Champagne et de la Lorraine (XIe–XIVe siècles)."
    Annales de l'Est, 5th ser., 27 (1975), 373–401.
Fletcher, R. A. *The Episcopate in the Kingdom of León in the Twelfth Century.*
    Oxford, 1978.
Freed, John B. "The Formation of the Salzburg Ministerialage in the Tenth
    and Eleventh Centuries: An Example of Upward Social Mobility in the
    Central Middle Ages." *Viator*, 9 (1978), 67–102.
Gaudemet, Jean. *Le gouvernement de l'Église à l'époque classique.* Part II, *Le
    gouvernement local.* Histoire du droit et des institutions de l'Église en
    Occident 8. Paris, 1979.
———. "Recherches sur l'épiscopat médiévale en France." In *Proceedings of
    the Second International Congress of Medieval Canon Law.* Edited by
    Stephan Kuttner and J. Joseph Ryan. Vatican City, 1965.
Geary, Patrick. "L'humiliation des saints." *Annales: Économies, Sociétés,
    Civilisations*, 34 (1979), 27–42.
Genicot, Léopold. *Les généalogies.* Typologie des sources du moyen âge 15.
    Turnhout, 1975.
———. "Haute clergé et noblesse dans le diocèse de Liège du XIe au XIVe
    siècle." In *Adel und Kirche.* Edited by Josef Fleckenstein and Karl Schmid.
    Freiburg, 1968.
Gold, Penny Schine. *The Lady & the Virgin: Image, Attitude, and Experience
    in Twelfth-Century France.* Chicago, 1985.
Grundmann, Herbert. *Religiöse Bewegungen im Mittelalter.* New edition. Hil-
    desheim, 1961.
Guerreau-Jalabert, Anita. "Sur les structures de parenté dans l'Europe
    médiévale." *Annales: Économies, Sociétés, Civilisations*, 36 (1981),
    1028–49.
Guichenon, Samuel. *Histoire de la souveraineté de Dombes.* Edited by M.-C.
    Guigue. Lyon, 1874.
Guillemain, Bernard. "Les origines des évêques en France aux XIe et XIIe
    siècles." In *Le istituzioni ecclesiastiche della "Societas Christiana" dei secoli
    XI–XII: Papato, cardinalato ed episcopato*, Miscellanea del Centro di studi
    medioevali 7. Milan, 1974.
Hallinger, Kassius. *Gorze—Kluny: Studien zu den monastischen Lebensformen
    und Gegensätzen im Hochmittelalter.* Studia Anselmiana. Rome, 1950.
Hartigan, Francis X. "Reform of the Collegiate Clergy in the Eleventh Cen-
    tury: The Case of Saint-Nicholas of Poitou." *Studies in Medieval Culture*,
    6/7 (1976), 52–62.
Henry, V.-B. *Histoire de l'abbaye de Pontigny.* Avallon, 1882.
———. *Histoire de l'abbaye de Saint-Germain d'Auxerre.* Auxerre, 1853.
———. *Mémoires historiques sur la ville de Seignelay.* 2 vols. Avallon,
    1833–1853.
Hill, Bennett D. *English Cistercian Monasteries and Their Patrons in the
    Twelfth Century.* Urbana, Ill., 1968.
Hourlier, Jacques. *L'âge classique, 1140–1378: Les religieux.* Histoire du
    droit et des institutions de l'Église en Occident 10. Paris, 1971.
———. "Cluny et la notion d'ordre religieux." *À Cluny: Congrès scientifique,
    9–11 juillet 1949.* Dijon, 1950.
Hunt, Noreen. *Cluny under Saint Hugh, 1049–1109.* London, 1967.

Huyghebaert, Nicolas. "Une crise à Cluny en 1157: L'élection de Robert le Gros, successeur de Pierre le vénérable." *Revue bénédictine*, 93 (1983), 337–53.

Institutions ecclésiastiques. Edited by Ferdinand Lot and Robert Fawtier. Histoire des institutions françaises au moyen âge 3. Paris, 1962.

Institutions seigneuriales. Edited by Ferdinand Lot and Robert Fawtier. Histoire des institutions françaises au moyen âge 1. Paris, 1957.

Istituzioni monastiche e istituzioni canonicali in Occidente (1123–1215). Miscellanea del Centro di studi medioevali 9. Milan, 1980.

Janauschek, Leopold. *Originum Cisterciensium*. Vienna, 1877; reprint Ridgewood, N. J., 1964.

Jarry, Eugène. *Formation territoriale de la Bourgogne*. Provinces et pays de France 3. Paris, 1948.

Johnson, Penelope. "Pious Legends and Historical Realities: The Foundations of la Trinité de Vendôme, Bonport and Holyrood." *Revue Bénédictine*, 91 (1981), 184–93.

――――. *Prayer, Patronage, and Power: The Abbey of la Trinité, Vendôme, 1032–1187*. New York, 1981.

Kaiser, Reinhold. *Bischofsherrschaft zwischen Königtum und Fürstenmacht. Studien zur bischöflichen Stadtherrschaft im Westfränkisch-französischen Reich im frühen und hohen Mittelalter*. Pariser historische Studien 17. Bonn, 1981.

Kemp, B. R. "Monastic Possession of Parish Churches in England in the Twelfth Century." *Journal of Ecclesiastical History*, 31 (1980), 133–60.

Kempf, Jean-Pierre. *L'abbaye de Cherlieu, XIIe–XIIIe siècles: Économie et société*. Vesoul, 1976.

Kinder, Terryl N. "Some Observations on the Origins of Pontigny and Its First Church." *Cîteaux*, 31 (1980), 9–19.

Knowles, David; Brooke, C. N. L.; and London, Vera C. M. *The Heads of Religious Houses: England and Wales, 940–1216*. Cambridge, England, 1972.

Lackner, Bede K. *The Eleventh-Century Background of Cîteaux*. Cistercian Studies Series 8. Washington, D.C., 1972.

Laharie, Muriel. "Évêques et société en Périgord du Xe au milieu du XIIe siècle." *Annales du Midi*, 94 (1982), 343–36.

Laurent, Jacques; and Claudon, Ferdinand. *Abbayes et prieurés de l'ancienne France*. Vol. XII, iii, *Diocèses de Langres et de Dijon*. Archives de la France monastique 45. Paris, 1941.

LeBras, Gabriel. *Institutions ecclésiastiques de la Chrétienté médiévale*. Histoire de l'Église depuis les origines jusqu'à nos jours 12. Paris, 1959–1964.

Leclercq, Jean; Vandenbroucke, François; and Bouyer, Louis. *The Spirituality of the Middle Ages*. A History of Christian Spirituality 2. New York, 1968.

Lekai, Louis J. *The Cistercians: Ideals and Reality*. Kent, Ohio, 1977.

Lemarignier, Jean-François. "Le monachisme et l'encadrement religieux des campagnes du royaume de France situées au nord de la Loire, de la fin du Xe à la fin du XIe siècle." In *Le istituzioni ecclesiastiche della "Societas Christiana" dei secoli XI–XII: Diocesi, pievi e parrocchie*. Miscellanea del Centro di studi medioevali 8. Milan, 1977.

――――. "Structures monastiques et structures politiques dans la France de la fin du Xe et les débuts du XIe siècle." In *Il monachesimo nell'alto medioevo e la formazione della civiltà occidentale*. Settimane di studio del Centro di studi sull'alto medioevo 4. Spoleto, 1957.

Lespinasse, René de. *Le Nivernais et les comtes de Nevers*. 2 vols. Paris, 1909–1911.

Lewis, Andrew W. *Royal Succession in Capetian France: Studies on Familial Order and the State*. Cambridge, Mass., 1981.

Lewis, Patricia A. "Mortgages in the Bordelais and Bazadais." *Viator*, 10 (1979), 23–38.

Leyser, Henrietta. *Hermits and the New Monasticism: A Study of Religious Communities in Western Europe, 1000–1150*. London, 1984.

Lipkin, Joel. "The Entrance of the Cistercians into the Church Hierarchy, 1098–1227: The Bernardine Influence." In *The Chimaera of His Age: Studies on Bernard of Clairvaux*. Edited by E. Rozanne Elder and John R. Sommerfeldt. Studies in Medieval Cistercian History 5. Kalamazoo, Mich., 1980.

Little, Lester K. "La morphologie des maledictions monastiques." *Annales: Économies, Sociétés, Civilisations*, 34 (1979), 43–60.

——. *Religious Poverty and the Profit Economy in Medieval Europe*. Ithaca, 1978.

Locatelli, René. "L'implantation cistercienne dans le comté de Bourgogne jusqu'au milieu du XVIe siècle." *Cahiers d'histoire*, 20 (1975), 167–220.

Lohrmann, Dietrich. *Kirchengut im nordlichen Frankreich: Besitz, Verfassung und Wirtschaft im Spiegel der Paptstprivilegien des 11.–12. Jahrhunderts*. Bonn, 1983.

Lot, Ferdinand. *Les derniers Carolingiens*. Paris, 1891.

Luchaire, Achille. *Études sur les actes de Louis VII*. Paris, 1885; reprint Brussels, 1964.

Lynch, Joseph H. "Monastic Recruitment in the Eleventh and Twelfth Centuries: Some Social and Economic Considerations." *American Benedictine Review*, 26 (1975), 425–47.

——. *Simoniacal Entry into Religious Life from 1000 to 1260*. Columbus, Ohio, 1976.

McGinn, Bernard. "*Iter Sancti Sepulchri*: The Piety of the First Crusaders." In *Essays on Medieval Civilization*. Edited by Bede Karl Lackner and Kenneth Roy Philip. The Walter Prescott Webb Memorial Lectures 12. Austin, Texas, 1978.

Marilier, Jean. "Catalogue des abbés de Cîteaux pour le XIIe siècle. Addition et rectification à la Gallia Christiana." *Cistercienser-Chronik*, 55 (1948), 1–11.

——. "Une réplique de Saint-Étienne de Vignory: Notre-Dame de Losne." In *Mélanges offerts à René Crozet*. Edited by Pierre Gallais and Yves-Jean Riou. Poitiers, 1966.

Mariotte, Jean-Yves. *Le comté de Bourgogne sous les Hohenstaufen, 1156–1208*. Cahiers d'Études Comtoises 4. Paris, 1963.

Martindale, Jane. "The French Aristocracy in the Early Middle Ages: A Reappraisal." *Past and Present*, 75 (1977), 5–45.

Medieval Women. Edited by Derek Baker. Studies in Church History, Subsidia 2. Oxford, 1978.

Mehne, Joachim. "Cluniacenserbischöfe." *Frühmittelalterliche Studien*, 11 (1977), 241–87.

Meisel, Janet. *Barons of the Welsh Frontier: The Corbet, Pantulf, and Fitz Warin Families, 1066–1272*. Lincoln, Nebr., 1980.

Mélanges Saint Bernard. XXIVe Congrès de l'Association bourguignonne des sociétés savantes. Dijon, 1954.

Méras, Matthieu. *Le Beaujolais au moyen âge*. 2nd ed. Villefranche-en-Beaujolais, 1979.

Mirot, Léon. "Les origines des premiers comtes héréditaires de Nevers." *Annales de Bourgogne*, 17 (1945), 7–15.

Murray, Alexander. *Reason and Society in the Middle Ages*. Oxford, 1978.

Neue Forschungen über Cluny und die Cluniacenser. Edited by Gerd Tellenbach. Freiburg, 1959.

Newman, William Mendel. *Les seigneurs de Nesle en Picardie (XIIe–XIIIe siècle)*. 2 vols. Paris and Philadelphia, 1971.

Olsen, Glenn. "The Idea of the *Ecclesia Primitiva*, in the Writings of the Twelfth-Century Canonists." *Traditio*, 25 (1969), 61–86.

Oursel-Quarré, M. "À propos du chartrier de Cluny." *Annales de Bourgogne*, 50 (1978), 103–7.

Pacaut, Marcel. "Structures monastiques, société et Église en Occident aux XIe et XIIe siècles." *Cahiers d'histoire*, 20 (1975), 119–31.

Parisse, Michel. "L'évêque et l'Empire au XIe siècle. L'exemple lorrain." *Cahiers de civilisation médiévale*, 27 (1984), 95–105.

———. "La noblesse Lorraine, XIe–XIIe s." Diss., Université de Nancy II, 1975.

Poeck, Dietrich. "Laienbegräbnisse in Cluny." *Frühmittelalterliche Studien*, 15 (1981), 68–179.

Poly, Jean-Pierre. *La Provence et la société féodale, 879–1166*. Paris, 1976.

Poly, Jean-Pierre; and Bournazel, Éric. *La mutation féodale, X^e–XIIe siècles*. Paris, 1980.

Poupardin, René. *Le royaume de Bourgogne (888–1038): Étude sur les origines du royaume d'Arles*. Paris, 1907.

Procter, Evelyn S. *Curia and Cortes in León and Castile, 1072–1295*. Cambridge, England, 1980.

Pycke, Jacques. *Le chapitre cathédral Notre-Dame de Tournai de la fin du XIe à la fin du XIIIe siècle: Son organisation, sa vie, ses membres*. Louvain, 1986.

Racinet, Philippe. "Implantation et expansion clunisiennes au nord-est de Paris (XIe–XIIe siècles)." *Le moyen âge*, 90 (1984), 5–37.

Rameau, Mgr. "Les comtes héréditaires de Mâcon." *Annales de l'Académie de Mâcon*, 3rd ser., 6 (1901), 121–209.

Rebouillat, Marguerite. "La lutte entre les seigneurs de Brancion et Cluny." In *La guerre et la paix: Frontières et violences au moyen âge*. Actes du 101e Congrès national des sociétés savantes. Paris, 1978.

Reilly, Bernard F. *The Kingdom of León-Castilla under Queen Urraca, 1109–1126*. Princeton, 1982.

———. "Santiago and Saint Denis: The French Presence in Eleventh-Century Spain." *Catholic Historical Review*, 54 (1968), 467–83.

Religious Motivation: Biographical and Sociological Problems for the Church His-

torian. Edited by Derek Baker. Studies in Church History 15. Oxford, 1978.

Renardy, Chr. "Recherches sur la restitution ou la cession de dîmes aux églises dans le diocèse de Liège du XIe au début du XIVe siècle." *Le moyen âge,* 76 (1970), 205–61.

Reuter, Timothy. "The 'Imperial Church System' of the Ottonian and Salian Rulers: A Reconsideration." *Journal of Ecclesiastical History,* 33 (1982), 347–74.

Richard, Jean. *Les ducs de Bourgogne et la formation du duché du XIe au XIVe siècle.* Paris, 1954.

––––. "Lignées féodales et géographie des seigneuries dans le duché de Bourgogne." *Bulletin philologique et historique du comité des travaux historiques et scientifiques,* 1959, pp. 137–54.

––––. "Origines féodales. Les Chalon, les Vergy, et la Puisaye d'après une charte du XIe siècle." *Annales de Bourgogne,* 18 (1946), 112–19.

––––. "Sur les alliances familiales des ducs de Bourgogne aux XIIe et XIIIe siècles." *Annales de Bourgogne,* 30 (1958), 34–46, 232.

Roehl, Richard. "Plan and Reality in a Medieval Monastic Economy: The Cistercians." *Studies in Medieval and Renaissance History,* 9 (1972), 81–113.

Roger, Jean-Marc. "Les Morhier Champenois." *Bulletin philologique et historique du Comité des travaux historiques et scientifiques,* 1978, pp. 77–130.

Rosenthal, Joel T. *The Purchase of Paradise: Gift Giving and the Aristocracy, 1307–1485.* London, 1972.

Rosenwein, Barbara H. "Feudal War and Monastic Peace: Cluniac Liturgy as Ritual Aggression." *Viator,* 2 (1971), 129–57.

––––. *Rhinoceros Bound: Cluny in the Tenth Century.* Philadelphia, 1982.

––––. "Rules and the 'Rule' at Tenth-Century Cluny." *Studia monastica,* 19 (1977), 307–20.

Rosenwein, Barbara H.; and Little, Lester K. "Social Meaning in the Monastic and Mendicant Spiritualities." *Past and Present,* 63 (1974), 4–32.

Sackur, Ernst. *Die Cluniacenser in ihrer kirchlichen und allgemeingeschichtlichen Wirksamkeit bis zur Mitte des elften Jahrhunderts.* 2 vols. Halle an der Saale, 1892–1894; reprint Darmstadt, 1965.

Sassier, Yves. "Quelques remarques sur les diplômes d'immunité octroyés par les Carolingiens à l'abbaye de Saint-Germain d'Auxerre." *Bibliothèque de l'École des chartes,* 139 (1981), 37–54.

––––. *Recherches sur le pouvoir comtal en Auxerrois du Xe au début du XIIIe siècle.* Auxerre, 1980.

Schmid, Karl; and Wollasch, Joachim. "Die Gemeinschaft der Lebenden und Verstorbenen in Zeugnissen des Mittelalters." *Frühmittelalterliche Studien,* 1 (1967), 365–405.

Schulte, Aloys. *Der Adel und die deutsche Kirche im Mittelalter.* Stuttgart, 1910.

Segl, Peter. *Königtum und Klosterreform in Spanien: Untersuchungen über die Cluniacenserklöster in Kastilien-León von Beginn des 11. bis zur Mitte des 12. Jahrhunderts.* Kallmünz, 1974.

Southern, R. W. *Western Society and the Church in the Middle Ages.* Harmondsworth, England, 1970.

Stroll, Mary. "New Perspectives on the Struggle between Gui of Vienne and Henry V." *Archivum historiae pontificiae*, 18 (1980), 97–115.

Sutherland, Jon N. "The Recovery of Land in the Diocese of Grenoble during the Gregorian Reform Epoch." *Catholic Historical Review*, 64 (1978), 377–97.

Tellenbach, Gerd. "Il monachesimo riformato ed i laici nei secoli XI e XII." In *I laici nella "Societas christiana" dei secoli XI e XII*. Miscellanea del Centro di studi medioevali 5. Milan, 1968.

Teske, Wolfgang. "Laien, Laienmönche und Laienbrüder in der Abtei Cluny. Ein Beitrag zum 'Konversen-Problem.'" *Frühmittelalterliche Studien*, 10 (1976), 248–322; 11 (1977), 288–339.

Vajay, S. de. "À propos de la 'Guerre de Bourgogne': Note sur les successions de Bourgogne et de Mâcon aux Xe et XIe siècles." *Annales de Bourgogne*, 34 (1962), 153–69.

――――. "Bourgogne, Lorraine et Espagne au XIe siècle: Étiennette, dite de Vienne, comtesse de Bourgogne." *Annales de Bourgogne*, 32 (1960), 233–61.

Valous, Guy de. "Le domaine de l'abbaye de Cluny aux Xe et XI^c siècles." *Annales de l'Académie de Mâcon*, 3rd ser., 22 (1920–1921), 299–481.

――――. *Le temporel et la situation financière des établissements de l'ordre de Cluny du XIIe au XIVe siècle*. Archives de la France monastique 41. Paris, 1935.

van den Eynde, D. "Remarques chronologiques sur le cartulaire de Cluny." *Antonianum*, 43 (1968), 216–59.

Van Engen, John. "The 'Crisis of Cenobitism' Reconsidered: Benedictine Monasticism in the Years 1050–1150." *Speculum*, 61 (1986), 269–304.

Vauchez, André. *La spiritualité du moyen âge occidental, VIIIe–XIIe siècles*. Paris, 1975.

Vaughn, Sally N. *The Abbey of Bec and the Anglo-Norman State, 1034–1136*. Woodbridge, England, 1981.

Verdon, Jean. "Les moniales dans la France de l'Ouest aux XIe et XII^c siècles: Étude d'histoire sociale." *Cahiers de civilisation médiévale*, 19 (1976), 247–64.

Vicaire, M.-H. *The Apostolic Life*. Translated by William E. De Naple. Chicago, 1966.

Walker, David. "The Organization of Material in Medieval Cartularies." In *The Study of Medieval Records: Essays in Honour of Kathleen Major*. Edited by D. A. Bullough and R. L. Storey. Oxford, 1971.

Ward, J. C. "Fashions in Monastic Endowment: The Foundations of the Clare Family, 1066–1314." *Journal of Ecclesiastical History*, 32 (1981), 427–51.

Weinberger, Stephen. "Cours judiciares, justice et responsabilité sociale dans la Provence médiévale: IXe–XIe siècle." *Revue historique*, 542 (1982), 273–88.

――――. "Nobles et noblesse dans la Provence médiévale (ca. 850–1100)." *Annales: Économies, Sociétés, Civilisations*, 36 (1981), 913–21.

Weinfurter, Stefan; and Engels, Odilo. *Series episcoporum ecclesiae Catholicae occidentalis ab initio usque ad annum MCXCVIII*, 5th ser., 1. Stuttgart, 1982.

White, Stephen D. "*Pactum . . . Legem Vincit et Amor Judicium*: The

Settlement of Disputes by Compromise in Eleventh-Century Western France." *American Journal of Legal History*, 22 (1978), 281–308.

Wollasch, Joachim. *Mönchtum des Mittelalters zwischen Kirche und Welt*. Munich, 1973.

——. "Parenté noble et monachisme réformateur. Observations sur les 'conversions' à la vie monastique aux XIe et XIIe siècles." *Revue historique*, 535 (1980), 3–24.

——. "Reform und Adel in Burgund." In *Investiturstreit und Reichsverfassung*. Edited by Josef Fleckenstein. Munich, 1973.

——. "Wer waren die Mönche von Cluny vom 10. bis zum 12. Jahrhundert?" In *Clio et son regard: Mélanges d'histoire, d'histoire de l'art et d'archéologie offerts à Jacques Stiennon*. Liège, 1982.

Index

This index does not include the individuals mentioned in the appendixes unless they are also discussed in the text. For example, Wandelmodis, daughter of Guichard I of Beaujeu, is mentioned only in Appendix A, under the lords of Beaujeu, and therefore can be found by looking in the index for the appendix pages referring to the lords of Beaujeu in general. When there are a great many individuals with the same name, I have placed the ecclesiastics before the laymen, and the bishops before the abbots, alphabetizing by name of diocese or castle as appropriate.

Aanold, aunt of Bernard of Clairvaux, 58, 337

Abbots, social origins of, 76–78. *See also* Lay abbots *and names of individual monasteries*

Acey, monastery, 157

Acre, siege of, 198–99, 334, 375

Adalbero of Laon, 23

Adalbert, last king of Italy, 33, 265, 310–11

Adalgar, bishop of Autun (d. 894), 67, 341

Adam of Savoisy, 223

Adela, countess of Blois, 57–58

Adelaide of Chalon, mother of Gui of Thiers, 143, 312–13

Adelaide Wicheta, lady of Sexfontaines, 141–42, 363

Advocates, monastic, 125–30

Agano of Mt.-St.-Jean, bishop of Autun (1055–1098), 70, 415, 386

Agano of Bar, knight, 53

Age of consent, 211

Agnes, empress, 143

Agnes, daughter of Otto-William, duchess of Aquitaine, 98, 142, 269–70

Ahuy, 199

Aigremont, lords of, 120, 147, 176, 185, 187, 279–84, 395. *See also* Fulk *and* Ulric I

Aimo I, count of Auxois, 179, 193, 284, 365

Aimo, lord of Marigny, 219

Aimo of Marmagne, 136–37

Aimo I, lord of Tilchâtel, 127, 366

Aimo Pilo, 193

Aix, Rule of (816), 47, 48 n. 4

Alain, bishop of Auxerre (1152–1167), 57, 75–76, 182, 215, 389–90

Alberic II, count of Mâcon (962–980), 95, 262–65

Alberic of Reynel, 233

Albuin, canon of Autun (d. 1109), 79

Aldo III, lord of Tilchâtel, 127, 366

Alexander II, pope (1061–1073), 143

Alfonso VI, king of Castile, 143–45, 258, 274

Allodial land, 163, 196, 231

Andreas, archdeacon of Auxerre, 81

Andreas of Savoisy, 223

Anna, daughter of Richard of La Douze, 59

Anniversaries, 190–91, 195–97

Annual incomes, as type of gift, 183–86

Ansius-Hildebert, founder of Pontigny, 119

"Apostolic life" in the twelfth century, 55, 88, 124; preaching, 111–12

Arc, lord of, 115

Archimbald, viscount of Mâcon, 210

Arnoncourt, 185

Arnulf Cornu of Vergy, 123, 377

Artald, lord of Château Loup, 235, 338

Ascelin, lord of Châtel-Censoir, 221, 234

Aubepierre, 115

Auberive, monastery, 37, 84, 121, 138, 151, 200, 206, 209; abbots of, 402–3

Augustinian Rule, 48, 112, 114, 249

Autun: bishopric of, 31–32, 68, 70–71, 73 n. 16, 75, 85, 152, 192, 204; bishops of, 386–87 (see also Adalgar, Agano of Mt.-St.-Jean, Henry of Burgundy, Humbert, Robert of Burgundy, Stephen I, Stephen II, Walter); cathedral chapter of, 50; Council of (1076/7), 70, 425

Auxerre: bishopric of, 31–32, 67–71, 75–76, 80, 85, 113, 206; bishops of, 387–91 (see also Alain, Geoffrey of Champallemand, Heribert, Hugh of Chalon, Hugh of Mâcon, Hugh of Montaigu, Hugh of Noyers, Humbald, John, Robert of Nevers, William of Seignelay, William of Toucy)

Auxois, counts of, 284–86. See also Aimo I

Avalleur, knights of, 58, 216

Avallon, viscounts of, 54 n. 23

Bâgé, lords of, 34, 287–89. See also Ulric III

Bannum, Cluny's, 202

Bar-sur-Aube, 58, 85

Bar-sur-Seine, counts of, 34, 76, 85, 134, 239, 371–72, 397, 406

Bartholomew, bishop of Pécs, 167, 306

Bartholomew of Châtillon, 136

Bartholomew de Mur, 234–35

Bassigny, viscounts of, 51 n. 15

Baume, monastery, 158

Beatrix, heiress of Burgundy (1156), 33, 153, 157–58, 277

Beatrix of Burgundy, lady of Vignory, 151, 258, 382

Beatrix of Vignory, lady of Clefmont, 139, 317, 383

Beaujeu, lords of, 34, 60, 130, 279, 289–95, 347. See also Guichard IV, Humbert II, Humbert III, Humbert IV

Beaulieu, monastery, 37, 187; abbots of, 403

Beaumont, 206; lords of, 34, 319–23 (see also Gibuin and Hugh III)

Beaune: priory of, 231; viscounts of, 123, 186, 202, 231 (see also Raynald). See also Notre-Dame of Beaune

Belfays, nunnery, 187

Belleville, 197

Benedict of Aniane, 90

Benedictine Rule, 48, 88, 117, 180, 230, 239, 249; observance in 9th- and 10th-century Burgundy, 90, 93, 104

Berard of Châtillon, bishop of Mâcon (1096–1122), 156, 180, 399

Bernard, abbot of Clairvaux (1115–1153), 54, 73, 76, 114, 120, 146, 215, 390, 396, 408; arrival at Cîteaux, 118–19, 389; family of, 58, 61, 78, 134, 237–38, 329, 336, 346 (see also Aanold; Fontaines-lès-Dijon, lords of; Tescelin Sorus); relations with Peter the Venerable, 119; views on "church and state," 128–30; views on conversion and novices, 52, 55–56, 85; views on pious gifts, 181, 184–85, 189, 228, 243

Bernard of Verdun, archdeacon of Chalon, 74

Bernard of Meix, knight, 116

Bernard of Segni, 66

Bernard I, lord of Uxelles, 161, 167, 216, 302–3

Bernard III Grossus, lord of Uxelles, 163–64, 303

Bernard V Grossus, lord of Uxelles, 164–66, 168, 187, 304–5

Berzé, lords of, 68, 74, 229, 399

Besançon, 33, 131, 155–57, 273–74, 283, 397

Bèze, monastery, 72, 138, 200; abbots of, 403–4 (see also Milo, Stephen of Beaumont, William)

"Bible" of the lord of Berzé, 229

Bishops, social origins of, 67–76. See also the names of individual dioceses

Bochard, lord of Seignelay, 61–62, 337, 356

Bochard Borseron, 121

Bonnevaux, monastery, 157

Bordeaux, 71

Bosonids, 91 n. 4, 96–97, 104

Bouilly, 175

Bourberain, 194

Bourbon, 85, 107, 111, 143, 192, 312, 346

Bourbonne, lords of, 279–84, 316

Bourras, monastery, 41, 200, 214

Boye, 100

Bragny, 176

Brancion, lords of, 34, 68, 74, 80, 99–100, 160–68, 176, 295–307, 398. See also Doda; Letbald, bishop of

Mâcon; Letbald I; Testa; Walter,
bishop of Mâcon; Warulf II; *and*
Uxelles, lords of
Bray, 164
Brétigny, 202
Bricon, lords of, 61, 74, 205, 418
Brienne, counts of, 184 n. 38, 264, 348
 n. 202, 371, 403
Brionnais, 122
Bruno, archbishop of Cologne, 62, 394
Bruno, bishop of Langres (980–1016),
 35, 62, 68, 72, 81, 84, 110, 236, 269,
 393–94
Bruno, nephew of Bishop Bruno of
 Langres, 62, 81, 269–70,
 394
Burgundy: duchy of, 31–32, 35; dukes
 of, 33, 50, 61, 75–76, 81, 84, 123,
 150–52, 167, 194, 202, 221, 247–48,
 256–61 (*see also* Henry, Hugh the
 Black, Hugh the Great, Hugh I, Hugh
 II, Hugh III, Odo I, Odo II, Odo III,
 Richard le Justicier, Robert I); king-
 dom and county of ("trans-Saône"
 Burgundy), 31, 33, 104, 153, 155–56,
 158, 238, 261–79
Burgundy and Mâcon, counts of, 33, 96,
 152–60, 212, 261–79 (*see also* Girard,
 Gui II, Otto, Otto-William, Raynald I,
 Raynald II, Raynald III, Stephen I,
 Stephen II, Stephen III, William Tête-
 Hardi, William II, William III, William
 IV, William V)
La Bussière, monastery, 37, 40, 53, 123,
 131, 185, 190, 194 n. 22, 196, 218,
 259; abbots of, 405
Bussières, 167
Bussières-lès-Belmont, 187, 199
Bussy, 207
Buxerolles, 206

Calixtus II, pope (1119–1124), 113,
 155–57, 273–74
Calo of Lucenay, 214
Canons: regular, 47–49, 112–16; secu-
 lar, 47–48
Carthusians, 111, 124, 195, 229
Cartularies, composition of, 37, 39–42
Castellans, rise of, 27, 148, 250. *See also*
 names of individual castellanies
Cathedral chapters: election by, 73–75,
 88–89; entry into, 47, 49–50, 59–60,
 74–75; organization of, 47–48, 85
Cérilly, knights of, 147
Chacenay, lords of, 198 n. 35, 227–28,
 331, 420
Chalon-sur-Saône: bishopric of, 31–32,
 68, 70–71, 73, 76, 212; bishops of,
 391–93 (*see also* Engelbert, Peter of

St.-Marcel, Roclenus, Walter of
 Couches, Walter of Sercy); cathedral
 chapter of, 183, 190; counts of, 33, 60,
 97, 111, 126, 143, 176, 187, 198 n. 35,
 212, 287, 307–14, 388, 391 (*see also*
 Geoffrey II of Donzy, Geoffrey Grey-
 mantle, Gerberge, Gui of Thiers,
 Hugh I, Hugh II, Lambert, Savaric,
 Theobold, William I, William II)
Champigny, 206
Chanceaux, 179
La Charité, Cistercian monastery, 157
La Charité-sur-Loire, Cluniac priory, 84,
 93–94, 130, 176, 226, 235
Charles-Constantine, count of Vienne,
 97
Chartres, 72
Château-Chalon, nunnery, 157
Châtel-Censoir, lords of, 78, 175 n. 5,
 210 n. 5, 221, 234, 419
Châtillon, castle of, 85, 115, 136,
 237–38. See also Notre-Dame of
 Châtillon
Chaublanc, 202
Chaudenay, 187
Chaume, 206
Cherlieu, monastery, 157
Choiseul, lords of, 176, 279, 281–82,
 314–16. See also Fulk, Rayner
Church, entry into, 46–64, 219; entry
 gifts, 52–54. See also Monasteries,
 entry into; Nunneries, entry into;
 Oblates
Church leaders, origins of, 46, 62–78.
 See also Dynasties, ecclesiastical
Churches, gifts of, 99, 177–81, 226
Cirfontaines, 206
Cistercian chapter general, 49, 55, 131,
 184, 188, 194, 197, 207, 223
Cistercian order, 31, 34–35, 39–40, 83,
 85, 230 n. 18, 232, 248–49, 251–52;
 acquisitions of property by, 171, 174,
 191, 201, 221; bishops from, 75; burial
 of nobles by, 194; conversion to,
 54–55, 58; foundation and early
 growth of, 115–24; knights as patrons
 of, 131–33, 137–38, 148–49; masses
 for Crusaders in, 198; oblates in, 49;
 pasture rights sought by, 188; and the
 pawning of property, 223; possession
 of annual incomes by, 184–86; possession of churches by, 180–83; quarrels with laymen, 214–15; relations
 with the counts of Burgundy, 155,
 157, 159; relations with the dukes of
 Burgundy, 151–52; spread into Spain,
 143, 146
Cîteaux, monastery, 34, 37, 84, 111 n.
 13, 123, 129, 146, 173, 194, 198, 219,

Cîteaux (*cont.*)
241, 252–53; abbots of, 405–8 (*see
also* Robert, Stephen Harding); and
the counts of Burgundy, 157–58; and
the dukes of Burgundy, 151, 190;
foundation of (1098), 116, 118–19;
early acquisitions of, 186, 202–4, 221,
231
Civry, 133, 221
Clairvaux, monastery, 34, 37, 53, 57, 75,
78, 121, 151, 184, 187, 200, 215;
abbots of, 408–9 (*see also* Bernard,
Warner); foundation of (1115), 119,
237–38; early acquisitions of, 204–6;
and the lords of Clefmont, 139–41
Clarembald, lord of Chappes, 122
Clarembald, lord of Noyers, 199, 390
Clefmont, 176; lords of, 139–41,
317–19, 326 (*see also* Robert Wicard
I, Robert Wicard II, Simon I, Simon
II)
Clemence of Burgundy, countess of
Flanders, 146, 273–75
Clermont, Council of (1095), 180
Cluniac order, 31, 75, 83–85, 110, 119,
179, 229; early development of, 90–
101; oblates in, 49; spread into Flanders, 146; spread into Spain, 143–45
Cluny, monastery, 34, 40–42, 49–52,
58, 77, 88, 107, 132, 138, 142–43, 151
n. 6, 168, 174–77, 187, 190, 196–97,
199–202, 209, 210 n. 5, 220–23,
226–28, 232–33, 240, 249, 252–53,
258, 271; abbots of, 410–13 (*see also*
Hugh the Great, Maiolus, Odilo, Peter
the Venerable, Ponce, Robert
Grossus); advocates of, 96, 126; burial
of laymen at, 192–94; charters of,
41–42; and the counts of Burgundy,
153–55, 158–60; foundation of (909),
90–91; in the 10th century, 90–101;
and the Grossi of Uxelles, 160–67;
and the kings of Spain, 143–46; and
Louis VI, 129; quarrels with laymen,
211–14; relations with the lords of
Semur, 50–51, 83; scholarship on, 25,
41 n. 33
Comital courts, 212
Conflict settlement, 126–27, 210–17
Conrad III, German emperor, 128, 156
Constance, wife of Hugh II of Chalon
and of Alfonso VI, 143–45, 257–58,
312
Conversi, 54–55
Conversion, motives for, 59–64. *See
also* Church, entry into
Coulanges, 100
Counts, origins of, 27. *See also names of
individual counties*

La Crête, monastery, 37, 139–42, 206,
218, 233; abbots of, 413
Crisenon, nunnery, 37, 123, 182, 183 n.
34, 196, 198–99, 222, 235
Crusades: as time of gifts, 197–99;
money-raising for, 221–23, 251; First
Crusade, 107, 155, 197, 199, 221–22,
251; Second Crusade, 198, 217, 235,
243, 338; Third Crusade, 198,
260–61, 293, 319, 327. *See also* Acre,
siege of

Dalmace of Gigny, 210 n. 5
Dalmace of Vernay, 211
Dijon, 153, 202; counts of, 319–23;
viscounts of, 236, 277, 307, 323–26
(*see also* Gui the Rich)
Doda, lady of Brancion, 99–100, 297
Dominicans, 112
Dommartin, 175
Donations. *See* Gifts
Donors, social origins of, 95–101,
131–38, 191–92. *See also* Women
Donzy, lords of, 34, 198 n. 35, 327–29
(*see also* Geoffrey II, Geoffrey III,
Hervé IV)
Dynasties, ecclesiastical, 79–84 (*see also*
Gregorian reform, impact on
ecclesiastical dynasties); significance of
uncle-nephew relationships, 29, 50,
79–83

Eblo, count of Saulx, 121, 351, 368
Ecclesiastical leaders. *See* Church
leaders
Elizabeth of Marmagne, 136–37, 142
Elizabeth of Vergy, countess of Mâcon,
153, 192, 271, 375–77
Emma, lady of Uxelles, 161, 302–3
Engelbert, abbot of Molesme and bishop
of Chalon (1178–1180), 75, 393, 420
Ermengard, lady of Bourbon, 107, 143,
312
Ermensend of Venarey, 136
Ermentrude of Burgundy, countess of
Montbéliard, 146, 273, 275
Escharlis, monastery, 130
Eugenius III, pope (1145–1153), 223
Everard of Bricon, dean of Langres, 74
Everard of Bricon, canon of Langres, 74
Exchanges of property, 221

Fain, 147
Family, defined, 29. *See also* Dynasties,
ecclesiastical *and* Nobility
Faverolles, 206, 216 n. 30
La Ferté-sur-Aube, lords of, 119, 184 n.
38, 206, 237, 327, 417
La Ferté-sur-Grosne, monastery, 34,

120, 159–60, 166, 176, 212, 219;
    abbots of, 414 (see also Peter); foun-
    dation of (1113), 119, 187
Feudal and "anti-feudal," meaning of,
    25–26, 252–53
Fidejussores, 211
Flacey, 53, 147
Flavigny, monastery, 34, 37, 50, 93, 137,
    179, 193, 206 n. 55, 207, 214; abbots
    of, 414–15 (see also Heldric, Raynald
    of Burgundy)
Fleury-la-Vallée, 179
Fontaines-lès Dijon, lords of, 78,
    279–81, 329–31. See also Tescelin
    Sorus
Fontaines-lès-Sèches, 134, 207
Fontemois, hermitage, 121
Fontenay, monastery, 37, 40, 53–54,
    75, 191, 194 n. 22, 200, 207–8, 214,
    218, 223, 234, 243; abbots of, 416–17
    (see also Geoffrey of La Roche); rela-
    tions with local knights, 133–37, 147
Fontevraud, nunnery, 57, 294, 347, 349
Forcey, 139
Forez, 111, 279, 293
Fouvent, 85, 286, 323
Franciscans, 112
Frederick Barbarossa, 33, 153, 157, 261
Fresne, 136
Friars, 112, 252–54
Fulk, nephew of Willenc of Aigremont,
    archdeacon of Langres, 81, 396
Fulk, lord of Aigremont, 147, 281, 395
Fulk, lord of Choiseul, 187, 316
Fulk of Mailly, 194, 322–23
Fulk of Rahon, 120

Galcher, lord of Salins, 196
Gaudin of Brémur, 243
Gaudin, lord of Duesme, 113
Gémigny, 202
Geoffrey of Champallemand, bishop of
    Auxerre (1052–1076), 70, 80, 388,
    400
Geoffrey of La Roche, abbot of Fon-
    tenay (1119–1131) and bishop of
    Langres (1139–1163), 75, 122, 215,
    396–97, 416
Geoffrey Greymantle, count of Anjou
    and Chalon (d. 987), 106–7, 110, 270,
    309
Geoffrey II, lord of Donzy and count of
    Chalon, 126, 313, 329
Geoffrey III, lord of Donzy, 121, 210 n.
    5, 260, 327
Geoffrey of Menou, 63
Gerberge of Chalon, mother of Otto-
    William, 33, 267–68, 310–11
Gersendis of Courteron, 227–28

Gervais, abbot of St.-Germain
    (1115–1148), 50, 428
Gessey-le-Franc, 199
Gibuin I, bishop of Châlons, 62, 320–22
Gibuin II, bishop of Châlons, 62, 322
Gibuin of Beaumont, canon, 62, 320–22
Gifts: at time of death, 190–92; claims
    against, 209–18; counter-gifts,
    217–20; entry gifts, 52–54; forms for,
    37–39; location of, 200–208; motiva-
    tions for, see Motivations for noble
    generosity; types of, 173–89 (see also
    Annual incomes, Churches, Land,
    Mills, Ovens, Pasture and forest
    rights, Peasants, Tithes). See also
    Laudatio
Gigny, 243
Gilly, 202, 219
Gimo of Châtel-Censoir, 210 n. 5
Girard, bishop of Nevers (1015), 71, 400
Girard of Montsaugeon, archdeacon of
    Langres, 74
Girard of Bourmont, 147, 282
Girard, count of Mâcon and Salins,
    158–59, 277–78
Girard of Rahon, 190–91, 195
Girard of Semur, 221
Girard "the Hairy," 147
Giselbert, count of Autun and duke of
    Burgundy (d. 956), 33, 92, 307, 394
Giselbert of Marmagne, 136
Grâce-Dieu, 157
Grancey, lords of, 78, 85, 121, 138, 198
    n. 35, 332–34, 351, 426. See also Rai-
    nard, Raynald II
Grandmont, 197
Grandrupt, 139, 206
Gregorian reform, 88, 128, 173, 179,
    189, 232 n. 25, 247; impact on
    ecclesiastical dynasties, 72–73, 77–79,
    83, 86. See also Investiture Contro-
    versy
Gregory VII, pope (1073–1085), 56 n.
    31, 72, 88, 128, 179–82, 273
Grignon, 136, 203, 349
Grossi, family of, 160–68, 300–307.
    See also Uxelles
Gui, bishop of Nevers (1097–1099), 71,
    401
Gui, archbishop of Sens (1176–1193),
    81, 355–56, 391
Gui, archbishop of Vienne. See Calix-
    tus II
Gui of Châtel-Censoir, abbot of
    Molesme (1111–1132), 78, 234, 419
Gui, count of Bar, 122, 397
Gui II, count of Mâcon, 154, 271
Gui, count of Nevers (d. 1176), 34, 176,
    183 n. 34, 196, 348–49

Gui of Pierre-Pertuis, 198, 356
Gui IV, lord of Saulx, 115, 353
Gui of Thiers, count of Chalon, 107,
  126, 313
Gui, lord of Verdun-sur-le-Doubs, 74,
  177—79
Gui II, lord of Vignory (d. c. 1060), 126,
  381
Gui IV, lord of Vignory (d. c. 1126),
  188, 258, 381—82. *For wife, see*
  Beatrix of Burgundy
Gui the Rich, viscount of Dijon, 236,
  324
Guiard, nephew of Ulric of Aigremont,
  canon of Langres, 81, 282
Guichard IV, lord of Beaujeu, 186,
  196—97, 279, 294—95
Guigo of Chartreuse, biographer of
  Hugh of Grenoble, 66
Guindrecourt, 126
Gurgy-le-Château, 206

Halinard, abbot of St.-Bénigne
  (1031—1052), 52, 77, 425
Harduin of Tonnerre, bishop of Langres
  (1049—1065), 70, 80, 239, 371, 395
Heldric, abbot of Flavigny, St.-Germain,
  and Moûter-St.-Jean (d. 1009), 355,
  414, 427
Henry of Burgundy, bishop of Autun
  (1148—1170), 75, 81, 386
Henry III, lord of Brancion and Uxelles,
  167, 306—7
Henry, duke of Burgundy (d. 1002), 33,
  213, 257, 265—68, 270, 310—11, 427;
  role in monastic reform, 103—4, 107,
  126
Henry of Portugal, brother of Duke Odo
  I, 145, 258
Henry, count of Troyes, 130
Heribert, bishop of Auxerre (971—996),
  67—71, 104, 388
Herluin of Bec, 56
Herman of Tronsanges, 213
Hermits, 110—11, 121
Hervé of Toucy, provost of Sens,
  80—81, 390
Hervé IV of Donzy, count of Nevers,
  85, 176, 217, 329, 350
Honorius of Autun, 128
Hospitallers, 199, 216 n. 30, 251
Hugh I, count of Chalon and bishop of
  Auxerre (999—1039), 60, 70, 84, 216,
  250 n. 3, 309—12, 388; role in monas-
  tic reform, 106—10, 127
Hugh of Mâcon, abbot of Pontigny and
  bishop of Auxerre (1136—1151), 57,
  75, 389, 422
Hugh of Montaigu, abbot of St.-

Germain and bishop of Auxerre
  (1115—1136), 50, 75, 79—80, 389, 428
Hugh of Noyers, bishop of Auxerre
  (1183—1206), 81, 390—91
Hugh of Burgundy, archbishop of
  Besançon (d. 1100/1), 155, 273—74
Hugh, bishop of Grenoble, 66
Hugh of Verdun, bishop of Langres, 70,
  72—73, 394
Hugh I, bishop of Nevers (1016—1069),
  70, 73, 80, 400
Hugh II, bishop of Nevers (1074—1096),
  70, 80, 240, 400
Hugh, archbishop of Sens (1143—1168),
  80, 390
Hugh the Great, abbot of Cluny
  (1049—1109), 49—50, 58, 77, 80, 128,
  145—46, 257, 360, 410, 428
Hugh Capet, king of France (987—996),
  33, 388
Hugh, king of Italy (926—947), 97
Hugh III, lord of Beaumont, 236,
  320—22, 324
Hugh the Black, duke of Burgundy (10th
  century), 93, 320
Hugh the Great, duke of Burgundy
  (10th century), 68, 70, 94
Hugh I, duke of Burgundy (1075—1078),
  151, 179, 258, 275; entry into Cluny,
  50, 128—29, 154
Hugh II, duke of Burgundy
  (1102—1143), 117, 123, 129, 133,
  150-51, 199, 259, 293, 327, 348, 397
Hugh III, duke of Burgundy
  (1165—1192), 115, 151, 183, 190,
  198—99, 211, 220, 260—61
Hugh II, count of Chalon (d. 1078), 143,
  179, 258, 312, 327
Hugh of Maligny, 117, 227—28
Hugh of Pierre-Pertuis, 218
Hugh of Poitiers, 217, 340
Hugh, lord of Toucy, 123, 374
Hugh, lord of Vergy, 185, 261, 378
Hugh-Rainard of Tonnerre, bishop of
  Langres (1065—1084), 62 n. 51, 70,
  80, 84, 239, 371, 395
Humbald, bishop of Auxerre
  (1095—1114), 83, 106, 389, 427
Humbert, bishop of Autun
  (1140—1148), 81, 287, 387
Humbert, archbishop of Vienne, 156
Humbert, archdeacon of Mâcon, nephew
  of Joceran IV of Brancion, 74, 305
Humbert II, lord of Beaujeu, 183, 292
Humbert III "the Old," lord of Beaujeu,
  130, 293—94
Humbert IV "the Young" of Beaujeu,
  186, 293
Humbert, lord of Bourbon, 192, 312

Humbert of Mailly, 236
Humbert, count of Maurienne, 118, 275
Humbert of Senecé, 232

Igé, 95
Innocent II, pope (1130–1143), 171, 230
  n. 18
Investiture Controversy, 86–88
Israel of Uxelles, 161, 302
Ivo of Chartres, 65

Jarenton, abbot of St.-Bénigne
  (1076–1113), 77, 425
Jocelin of Arcy, 191
Joceran, bishop of Langres
  (1113–1125), 114, 120, 395
Joceran, bishop of Mâcon (1122–1143),
  156, 399
Joceran I, lord of Uxelles, 161–63,
  167–68, 300–302. *For wife, see*
  Rotrudis of Brancion
Joceran II, lord of Uxelles, 161, 302–3
Joceran III Grossus, lord of Uxelles,
  168, 303–4
Joceran IV Grossus, lord of Brancion
  and Uxelles, 74, 166, 305, 314
Joceran V Grossus, lord of Brancion,
  166–68, 306–7
Joceran, son of Israel of Uxelles, 161,
  302
John, bishop of Auxerre (996–999),
  70–72, 388
John, hermit, 120
John, viscount of Ligny, 49 n. 8, 222
  n. 54
Joigny, 130, 198 n. 35, 226, 347
Josbert Chapel, founder of Reigny, 121
Josbert of Vosne, 53
Joux, 197
Judith of Lorraine, countess of Bur-
  gundy, 158, 278
Jully, nunnery, 58, 122, 152, 207–8
Juvancourt, 206

Knights: as patrons of monastic reform,
  133–38, 148–49; rise of, 27–28,
  148–49, 250

Laignes, 243
Laizé, 213–14
Lambert, bishop of Langres
  (1016–1031), 70, 322, 381, 394
Lambert, count of Chalon (d. 978), 97,
  106, 307–9, 324, 388, 394
Land, as a form of gift, 174–76
Landric of Berzé, bishop of Mâcon
  (1074–1096), 70, 399
Landric of Brancion, canon of Mâcon,
  74

Landric, count of Nevers and Auxerre
  (d. 1028), 33, 216–17, 341–43, 372
Landric Grossus, lord of Uxelles, 164,
  168, 303–4
Langres: bishopric of, 31–32, 50, 68,
  70–71, 76, 80, 85, 122, 152, 187;
  bishops of, 393–97 (*see also* Bruno,
  Geoffrey, Harduin, Hugh of Verdun,
  Hugh-Rainard of Tonnerre, Joceran,
  Lambert, Manasses of Bar, Richard,
  Robert of Burgundy, Walter of Bur-
  gundy, Warner, Willenc of Aigremont,
  William of Sabran); cathedral chapter
  of, 50–52, 196, 236; county of, 151,
  351–53
Larrey, nunnery, 58, 331
Laudatio, 210–11. *See also* Witnesses
Law codes, Germanic, 37–38
Lay abbots, 72, 104
Leases, 220–21
Leo IX, pope (1049–1054), 72, 88–89
Leotold, count of Mâcon (941–962), 96,
  262–64, 267–68
Letbald of Brancion, bishop of Mâcon
  (993–1016), 70, 80, 100, 297, 398
Letbald I, lord of Brancion, 99, 297
Levécourt, 139, 176
Liège, 71
Loire valley, 71, 76
Lombardy, 200–201
Longchamp, 206
Longué, monastery, 37, 51, 115, 133,
  139, 151, 206; abbots of, 417–18 (*see
  also* Rudolph)
Lons-le-Saunier, 158–59
Lorraine, 46 n. 1, 67 n. 7, 71, 76, 81,
  158, 278, 305
Lothair, king of Italy, 97
Louis VI, king of France (1108–1137),
  129
Louis VII, king of France (1137–1180),
  129, 235, 275, 396
Louis the Blind, king of Provence
  (890–928), 97
Lournand, 167, 194
Lucius III, pope (1181–1185), 220
Lyon, 32, 91, 272

Mâcon: bishopric of, 31–32, 68, 70–71,
  76, 80, 91, 122, 192; bishops of,
  398–99 (*see also* Berard of Châtillon,
  Joceran, Landric of Berzé, Letbald of
  Brancion, Milo, Walter of Brancion);
  cathedral chapter of, 160, 183; counts
  of, 33, 126, 153, 168, 261–79 (*see also*
  Alberic II; Burgundy and Mâcon,
  counts of; Leotold); county of, 91,
  122, 201–2, 261–62; viscounts of,
  210

Magyars, 92
Maiolus, abbot of Cluny (948–994),
    96–97, 99, 104, 126, 236, 410
Maiolus Poudreux, canon of Mâcon, 80,
    99, 161, 167–68, 297, 302–3
Maizières, monastery, 37, 120, 151, 159,
    190, 194 n. 22; abbots of, 418
Manasses of Bar, bishop of Langres
    (1179–1193), 76, 81, 397
Manasses, bishop of Orléans, 81
Mansus, 173–74
Marcigny, nunnery, 39, 57–58, 154–55,
    199, 211, 217, 219–22; foundation of
    (1054), 51
Marigny, 204
Marmagne, 134–37
Marmoutier, monastery, 212 n. 14
Mathilda, countess of Nevers, 196–97,
    208, 260, 348–49
Matthew, canon of Langres, nephew of
    Archdeacon Warner, 79
Maurice, son of Geoffrey Greymantle,
    107, 309
Mediators, 214–15. See also Conflict
    settlement
Mileta of Aigremont, lady of Bourmont,
    147, 281–82, 316
Milites. See knights
Mills, as a gift, 185, 249
Milo, abbot of Bèze and bishop of
    Mâcon (981–993), 72, 398, 403
Milo, abbot of St.-Marien, 78
Milo, count of Bar, 122–23, 406
Milo, lord of Frôlois, 113
Milo of Montbard, 180, 336
Milo, lord of Noyers, 121
Milo of Thil, 193
Milo I, count of Tonnerre, 239, 369
Ministeriales, 28
Mirebeau, lords of, 191, 287, 289
Le Miroir, monastery, 157
Mohel, 176
Moisey, 202
Molesme, monastery, 34, 58, 75, 78, 84,
    123, 151, 180, 186, 200, 216, 234, 239;
    abbots of, 419–20 (see also Engelbert,
    Gui of Châtel-Censoir, Robert); advo-
    cates of, 126; burial at, 194; and
    Crusaders, 221–22; foundation of
    (1075), 117–18, 227–28
Molosmes, monastery, 243
Mont, 161, 164
Monasteries: burial at, 95, 174 n. 3,
    192–95, 219; entry into, 46–58; entry
    gifts, 52–54; foundation of, 116–24.
    See also Advocates; Gifts; Conversion,
    motives for; Patrons of monastic
    reform; Reform, meaning of; and
    names of individual monasteries

Montbard, lords of, 134, 334–38. See
    also Rainard
Montgerbert, 180
Montier-en-Der, monastery, 126
Montmelard, 210
Montmerle, 222
Montréal, lords of, 198 n. 35, 338–40
Mt.-St.-Jean, lords of, 138, 353, 378, 386
Montsaugeon, lords of, 74, 138, 191
Mores, monastery, 185, 218
Morimond, monastery, 34, 37, 159, 176,
    185, 187, 206, 279, 281; abbots of,
    421; foundation of (1115), 119–20;
    relations with local lords, 139–42, 147
Morment, house of Hospitallers, 216
    n. 30
Mortgages and pawns, 222–24, 244, 248
Morvan, 35, 193
Morville, 147
Motivations for noble generosity: crisis,
    238–40, 244; ecclesiastical relatives,
    234–38; economics, 231–33; politics,
    229–31; salvation, 225–29, 241–43,
    248
Moûtier-la-Celle, monastery, 185
Moûtier-St.-Jean, monastery, 191, 207

Narbonnia family of Toucy, 80
Narjod, lord of Toucy, 123, 199, 222,
    374
Nesle, 134
Nevers: bishopric of, 31–32, 68,
    70–71, 76, 80, 122; bishops of, 400-
    401 (see also Girard, Gui, Hugh I,
    Hugh II, Theobold); cathedral chapter
    of, 50, 213; counts of, 32–33, 67, 85,
    116, 126, 196, 198 n. 35, 216, 239–40,
    340–51 (see also Gui, Hervé IV of
    Donzy, Landric, Mathilda, Peter of
    Courtenay, Raynald, William I, Wil-
    liam II, William III, William IV);
    viscounts of, 32, 50, 70, 80, 84, 247,
    388, 400
Nobility: as church leaders, 65–67;
    composition of, 26–28; gifts from, see
    Gifts and Motivations for noble gen-
    erosity; patronage of monasteries over
    the generations, 150-69 (see also
    Patrons of monastic reform). See also
    Abbots, social origins of; Bishops,
    social origins of; Conversion, motives
    for; Donors, social origins of; Dynas-
    ties, ecclesiastical
Norman Anonymous, 128
Normandy, 71, 81
Notre-Dame of Auxerre, house of
    Premonstratensian canons, 113
Notre-Dame of Beaujeu, house of
    canons, 114–15, 197, 211, 232, 291

Notre-Dame of Beaune, house of
    canons, 204
Notre-Dame of Châtillon, house of
    canons, 49, 113–14, 130, 183, 207,
    331
Noyers, lords of, 175 n. 5, 198 n. 35,
    390. *See also* Clarembald
Nunneries, entry into, 47, 49, 60–61.
    See also names of individual nunneries

Oblates, 48–54, 62, 64, 136
Odilo, abbot of Cluny (994–1049), 40,
    77, 126, 175, 410
Odo I, duke of Burgundy (1078–1102),
    123, 151, 197, 258–59, 275, 332, 382,
    415
Odo II, duke of Burgundy (1143–1162),
    81, 129, 151, 259–60
Odo III, duke of Burgundy
    (1192–1218), 129, 151, 261, 379
Odo of Fulvy, 227
Odo of Issoudun, 196, 348
Odo Payen, 227
Oigny, house of canons, 112–13, 196
Oliver of Fresnes, 234
Orges, 206
Orsans, 241
Osmund, lord of Rougemont, 191
Otbert, abbot of Ste.-Marguerite, 59
    n. 42
Otto I, German emperor, 33, 236
Otto of Berzé, 213
Otto, count of Mâcon, 153–54, 192,
    269–71
Otto-William, count of Burgundy and
    Mâcon (981–1026), 33, 62 n. 51, 103,
    127, 152, 168, 213, 231, 236, 265–70,
    341; relations with Cluny, 84, 97–98,
    153, 155; role in reforming St.-
    Bénigne, 103, 153. *For children, see*
    Agnes, Otto, Raynald I; *for mother, see*
    Gerberge of Chalon
Ouroux, 234
Ovens, as a gift, 185

Paray-le-monial, monastery, 58, 93, 143,
    179; foundation of (973), 97, 106;
    reform of (999), 106–7
Paschal II, pope (1099–1118), 192
Pasture and forest rights, as a gift,
    186–88
Patrons of monastic reform, 125–49.
    See also Donors, social origins of
Pawns and mortgages, 222–24, 244, 248
Peace of God, 250
Peasants, as a gift, 186
Périgeux, 71
Peter of St.-Marcel, bishop of Chalon
    (1158–1178), 76, 81, 393

Peter the Venerable, abbot of Cluny
    (1122–1156), 51, 55, 56 n. 33, 77, 83
    n. 40, 85, 119, 130, 156, 158, 164,
    411, 431
Peter, abbot of La Ferté (1121–1126)
    and bishop of Tarentaise, 120, 414
Peter of Grancey, abbot of St.-Bénigne
    (1188–1204), 78, 397, 334, 426
Peter of Courtenay, count of Nevers,
    34, 185, 349–50
Philip I, king of France (1060–1108),
    199, 415
Picardy, 50 n. 11, 81
Planay, 134, 223
Poitou, counts of, 91, 142–43
Ponce, abbot of Cluny (1109–1122), 77,
    410
Pontigny, monastery, 34, 42, 49 n. 8,
    56–57, 75, 175–76, 184, 201, 206,
    215, 221–22; abbots of, 422–23 (*see
    also* Hugh of Mâcon); foundation of
    (1114), 119
Portugal, 145, 258
Poulangy, nunnery, 51 n. 15
Pouthières, monastery, 42, 103 n. 2, 138
Prebends, inheritance of, 79
Precarial grants, 98
Premonstratensian order, 113, 141
Provence, 73 n. 17, 200
Puits-d'Orbe, nunnery, 134, 337

Quarrels. *See* Conflict settlement
Quincy, monastery, 121, 190, 209 n. 2;
    abbots of, 423
Quincy-le-Vicomte, 207

Rainard, lord of Grancey, 199, 334
Rainard, lord of Montbard, 134, 336–37
Rainulph of Audenas, 232
Ramerupt, lord of, 61
Raoul Glaber, 48, 311
Raoul, king of France (923–936),
    97
Raymund of Burgundy, count of Galicia
    (d. 1107), 145–46, 155, 273–74
Raynald of Burgundy, abbot of Flavigny
    (1084–1090), 50, 258, 415
Raynald of Semur, abbot of Vézelay
    (1106–1125) and archbishop of Lyon,
    50, 361, 389, 431
Raynald, viscount of Beaune, 186, 231
Raynald I, count of Burgundy, 103,
    153–54, 269–70, 272
Raynald II, count of Mâcon (d. c. 1095),
    155, 273–274
Raynald III, count of Burgundy (d.
    1148), 156–58, 275–77
Raynald II, lord of Grancey, 121, 332
Raynald of Molesme, 227

Raynald, count of Nevers (d. 1040), 34, 175, 343–45
Raynald of Tonnerre (d. c. 1148), 217, 347
Rayner, lord of Choiseul, 118, 314–16
Rayner, lord of Salcy, 218
Reform, meaning of, 87–89, 100–110
Regina, countess of Mâcon, 155, 274
Reigny, monastery, 121, 191, 196, 206, 226 n. 7; abbots of, 424 (see also Stephen of Toucy)
Reims, Council of (1049), 72–73, 394, 400
Rennepont, 206
Reullée, 202
Riaucourt, knights of, 233
Richard, bishop of Langres (1031), 71, 394
Richard le Justicier, duke of Burgundy (10th century), 33, 96–97, 104, 320
Richard of La Douze, 59
Riel, 206
Robert of Burgundy, bishop of Autun (1140), 62, 75, 81, 386
Robert of Nevers, bishop of Auxerre (1076–1092), 70, 80, 240, 345–46, 388–89
Robert of Burgundy, bishop of Langres (1084–1111), 57, 62, 70, 81, 84, 120, 127, 151, 395, 404
Robert of Arbrissel, founder of Fontevraud, 57
Robert, founder and first abbot of Molesme (1075–1111) and Cîteaux (1098), 78, 117–18, 406, 419
Robert II, king of France (996–1031), 33–34, 71, 231, 257, 341, 343–44
Robert of Aisy, 243
Robert I, duke of Burgundy (1031–1075), 127–28, 179, 213, 257–58, 312, 388, 427
Robert II, count of Flanders, 146, 275
Robert of Vignory, 188, 382
Robert, nephew of Bernard of Clairvaux, 52
Robert Grossus, abbot of Cluny (1157), 305, 411
Robert Wicard I, count of Clefmont, 139, 141, 317
Robert Wicard II, lord of Clefmont, 139–41, 317–19
Rochefort, lords of. See Simon, lord of Rochefort, and Warner, abbot of Auberive and Clairvaux and bishop of Langres
Les Roches, monastery, 41, 63, 78, 210 n. 5
Roclenus, bishop of Chalon (1072–1079), 70, 392

Roger, lord of Vignory, 236, 379–81
Roland of Pommiers, 217
Romain-Môtier, monastery, 158
Rome, Council of (1073), 179–80, 182
Rotrudis of Brancion, lady of Uxelles, 161–63, 298, 300–302
Rouvres, lords of, 115
Rudolph, abbot of Longué, 51, 418
Rudolph III, king of Burgundy (d. 1032), 153
Ruffey, 223

St.-Amatre of Langres, 103 n. 2
St.-Andoche of Autun, nunnery, 58, 59 n. 52
St.-Bénigne of Dijon, monastery, 34, 52, 58, 77–78, 94, 110, 137, 145, 199–200, 213, 231, 236, 239; abbots of, 424–26 (see also Halinard, Jarenton, Peter of Grancey, William); advocates of, 127, 129; reform of (990), 103–4, 127; relations with the counts of Burgundy, 103–4, 127, 153, 155, 158; relations with the dukes of Burgundy, 150–52
St.-Benoît-sur-Loire, 94, 190
St.-Bertin, monastery (Flemish), 146
St.-Denis of Vergy, 196
St.-Étienne of Dijon, house of canons, 38 n. 22, 61, 79, 129, 137, 152, 156–57, 199, 220, 324; reform of (1032), 113, 236–37; reform of (1113), 114; relations with the lords of Til, 127
St.-Étienne of Nevers, monastery, 84, 131, 182, 185, 216, 218, 228, 240, 400
St.-Étienne of Vignory, 236
St.-Eusèbe of Auxerre, 103 n. 2
St.-Florent of Tilchâtel, 127
St.-Florentin, 192, 235
St.-Gengoux, 216
St.-Georges of Couches, cell, 93
St.-Germain of Auxerre, monastery, 34, 60 n. 44, 80, 175 n. 5, 184, 192, 195–96, 222 n. 54, 235; abbots of, 426-28 (see also Gervais, Heldric, Hugh of Montaigu); reform of (c. 985), 104; reform of (1100), 106
St.-Hippolyte, 168
St.-Jean-d'Angéley, monastery, 204
St.-Jean-le-Grand of Autun, nunnery, 58–59
St.-Julien of Auxerre, nunnery, 54 n. 23, 58, 355
St.-Marcel-lès-Chalon, monastery, 34, 53, 175, 177–79, 183, 198 n. 37, 233–34; reform of (10th century), 107, 110; relations with the counts of Chalon, 107, 110, 126–27

St.-Marien of Auxerre, house of
  Premonstratensian canons, 38 n. 21,
  78, 113, 195 n. 24, 196
St.-Martin of Autun, monastery, 34,
  92–93, 152
St.-Martin of Chablis, 130 n. 15, 221
St.-Martin of Langres, 117
St.-Michel of Tonnerre, monastery, 193,
  207, 239, 369
St.-Pierre-le-Moûtier, monastery, 42
St.-Pierre of Tonnerre, house of canons,
  116
St.-Procaire, 175
St.-Remi of Sens, monastery, 85
St.-Rigaud, monastery, 39, 111, 154 n.
  18, 235
St.-Seine, monastery, 117, 129, 137–38,
  152, 206 n. 55; abbots of, 428–29
St.-Symphorien of Autun, house of
  canons, 152
St.-Symphorien of Nevers, monastery,
  84
St.-Victor of Nevers, monastery, 84,
  239–40
St.-Vivant of Vergy, monastery, 42, 103,
  123, 204, 303
Ste.-Chapelle of Dijon, 115, 152
Ste.-Colombe, 207
Ste.-Colombe of Tonnerre, 239
Ste.-Marguerite, house of canons, 59.
  See also Otbert
Sales of property, 221–22
Salins, 33, 153, 158, 196, 278
Salo of Bouilly, 56
Sancerre, counts of, 130, 327
Sara of Seignelay, abbess of Crisenon,
  235, 356
Saulx, lords of, 34, 85, 115, 121,
  351–53. See also Eblo, Gui IV
Saus, 141
Savaric, lord of Vergy and count of
  Chalon, 119, 313, 327, 377
Savigny, monastery, 119
Savoy, 200, 293
Saxole, 179
Seignelay, lords of, 34, 81, 194, 198 n.
  35, 201, 235 n. 36, 355–57. See also
  Bochard
Seigney, 53
Seigny, 136
Semur-en-Auxois, house of canons, 214,
  416
Semur-en-Brionnais, lords of, 34,
  50–51, 83, 198 n. 35, 272, 310, 312,
  357–61, 389, 428. See also Hugh the
  Great, abbot of Cluny
Sens, 31 n. 15, 32; archbishops of, 62,
  71, 73, 80–81, 181, 390–91
Septfons, monastery, 41

Septfontaines, house of canons, 37, 113,
  141
Sercy, 164
Sermoise, 182
Servigny, 234
Sexfontaines, lords of, 141–42, 187,
  361–63. See also Simon I
Silvarouvres, 206
Simon of Nogent, canon of Langres, 74
Simon I, lord of Clefmont, 139, 317
Simon II, lord of Clefmont, 139–41, 317
Simon, lord of Rochefort, 84, 403, 409
Simon I, lord of Sexfontaines, 141, 363
Sombernon, lords of, 123, 131, 198 n.
  35, 221, 363–66. See also Walter,
  Warner
Spanish royal family, 143–46, 200
Stephen I, bishop of Autun
  (1112–1139), 81, 287, 386
Stephen II, bishop of Autun
  (1170–1189), 195, 387, 416
Stephen of Beaumont, abbot of Bèze,
  323, 404
Stephen Harding, abbot of Cîteaux
  (1108–1133), 120, 406
Stephen of Toucy, abbot of Reigny
  (1134–1162), 374, 424
Stephen, abbot of Les Roches, 78
Stephen of Beaujeu, 209
Stephen, count of Blois, 106
Stephen of Brive, 235, 356
Stephen I, count of Burgundy (d. 1102),
  155, 176, 273–75, 326
Stephen II, count of Burgundy (d. 1173),
  158–59, 198, 277–78. For wife, see
  Judith of Lorraine
Stephen III, count of Burgundy and
  Auxonne (d. c. 1237), 159, 278, 314
Stephen, lord of Pierre-Pertuis, 201

Taizé, 161, 167–68
Tart, nunnery, 58, 159, 190; custodia of,
  129; foundation of, 122–23
Templars, 130, 199, 251
Teresa of Spain, 145, 258
Tescelin Sorus, lord of Fontaines, father
  of Bernard of Clairvaux, 61, 237,
  279–81, 329, 334–38
Testa, lady of Brancion, 100, 298
Theobold, bishop of Nevers (1176–
  1188), 81, 401
Theobold, count of Chalon, 107, 211,
  216, 312, 359–60
Theobold, count of Champagne, 73,
  122, 329
Theoderic, count of Montbéliard, 146,
  275
Theuley, monastery, 37, 138, 151, 157,
  194, 215; foundation of, 191

Thomas of Marle, 55
Tilchâtel, lords of, 34, 38 n. 22, 85, 127,
    283, 357, 363, 366—69. *See also* Aimo
    I, Aldo III, William
Tilleul, 141
Tithes, as gifts, 182—83
Tonnerre, counts of, 34, 70, 84—85,
    122, 193, 208, 239, 369—72, 395. *See
    also* Milo I *and* Nevers, counts of
Toucy, lords of, 78, 123, 198 n. 35, 222,
    372—375, 424. *See also* Hugh *and*
    Narjod
Tournus, monastery, 34, 103 n. 2, 129,
    143, 158, 179; abbots of, 429—30
Toutenans, 204
Traînel, lords of, 78, 327, 378, 397
Trier, lords of, 157—58, 277
Troyes, 31 n. 15, 34, 185, 206; counts
    of, 34, 260
Truce of God, 250

Ulger, nephew of Bishop Humbald, pro-
    vost of Auxerre, 83
Ulric, nephew of Ulric I of Aigremont,
    canon of Langres, 81, 282
Ulric, nephew of Willenc of Aigremont,
    provost of Sts.-Géosmes, 81, 282, 396
Ulric I, lord of Aigremont, 120, 281,
    316, 329
Ulric III, lord of Bâgé, 179, 287
Urban II, pope (1088—1099), 180, 202
Urraca, queen of Spain, 145, 274
Uxelles: castle, 160; lords of, 160—68,
    300—307 (*see also* Bernard I, Bernard
    III Grossus, Bernard V Grossus,
    Henry III, Israel, Joceran I, Joceran II,
    Joceran III Grossus, Joceran IV
    Grossus, Joceran V Grossus, Landric
    Grossus, Maiolus Poudreux)

Varennes, 118
Vergy: lords of, 34, 185, 261, 323,
    375—79 (*see also* Arnulf Cornu, Hugh,
    Savaric); monasteries of, *see* St.-Denis
    of Vergy *and* St.-Vivant of Vergy
Vernolle, 133, 221
Vesoul, 103—4
Veuvey, 213
Vézelay, monastery, 34, 92, 103 n. 2,
    129, 201, 216—17; abbots of, 430—31
    (*see also* Raynald)
Vienne, 155—57. *See also* Calixtus II
    and Charles-Constantine
Vignory, lords of, 50, 151, 187—88, 198
    n. 35, 236, 317, 353, 379—84, 395.
    See also Gui II, Gui IV, Roger
Viking invasions, 87, 90, 92
Ville-sous-la-Ferté, 206
Villiers-Vineux, 235

Waldric of Couches, 210 n. 5, 386
Walter, bishop of Autun (978—1018),
    93, 386
Walter of Couches, bishop of Chalon
    (1080—1123), 70, 183, 392
Walter of Sercy, bishop of Chalon
    (1126—1158), 81, 392—93
Walter of Burgundy, bishop of Langres
    (1163—1179), 76, 81, 152, 397
Walter of Brancion, bishop of Mâcon
    (1031—1061), 57, 70, 80, 298, 398
Walter, canon of Chalon, nephew of
    Dean William, 79
Walter of Berzé, archdeacon of Mâcon,
    74
Walter of Brancion, dean of Mâcon, 81,
    298
Walter of Berzé, 233
Walter, lord of Sombernon, 131,
    365—66
Warner, archdeacon of Chalon, 79
Warner, archdeacon of Langres, 114
Warner, abbot of Auberive (1180—1185)
    and Clairvaux (1186—1193), bishop of
    Langres (1193—1200), 75, 84, 115,
    397, 403, 409
Warner of Dijon, abbot of St.-Étienne,
    236—37
Warner, lord of Sombernon, 123, 133,
    331, 365
Warulf II, lord of Brancion, 99, 297
Welfs, 104
Wigo, count of Albion, 154
Wigo of Berzé, 213
Willenc of Aigremont, bishop of Langres
    (1125—1136), 52 n. 17, 81, 120,
    281—82, 395—96
William of Seignelay, bishop of Auxerre
    (1207—1220) and Paris (1220—1223),
    49, 81, 335, 356
William of Toucy, bishop of Auxerre
    (1167—1181), 80, 195 n. 24, 390, 431
William of Sabran, elected to Langres
    (1138), 75, 396
William of Champagne, archbishop of
    Sens, 73
William, dean of Chalon, 79
William, canon of Chalon, nephew of
    Dean William, 79
William, abbot of St.-Bénigne
    (990—1031) and Bèze, 48—49, 77,
    103, 236, 403, 424—25
William I, duke of Aquitaine, 91, 142,
    261, 297
William II, duke of Aquitaine, 91, 143,
    262, 297
William V, duke of Aquitaine, 143, 270.
    For wife, see Agnes, daughter of Otto-
    William

William I "Tête-Hardi," count of Burgundy, 146, 154–55, 179, 258, 272–73
William I, count of Chalon, 119, 313–14
William II, count of Chalon, 190, 314
William II "the German," count of Mâcon, 155, 274
William III, count of Mâcon, 156, 164, 274
William IV, count of Mâcon (d. 1156), 156–58, 275–78
William V, count of Mâcon and Vienne, 159, 278–79
William I, count of Nevers, 106, 119, 228, 239–40, 345–46, 371

William II, count of Nevers, 121, 195, 217, 240, 346–47
William III, count of Nevers, 129, 195, 217, 347–48
William IV, count of Nevers, 185, 195, 215, 217, 348
William, viscount of St.-Florentin, 235
William, lord of Tilchâtel, 61, 368
Witnesses, of charters, 38–39
Women, role in spreading monastic reform, 136–37, 141–48. *See also* Nunneries

Library of Congress Cataloging-in-Publication Data

Bouchard, Constance Brittain
  Sword, miter, and cloister.

  Bibliography: p.
  1. Burgundy (France)—Church history. 2. Monasticism
and religious orders—France—Burgundy—History.
3. Burgundy (France)—Nobility. I. Title.
BR 847.B85B68 1987   274.4′403   86-29158
ISBN 0-8014-1974-3